Canadian Federalism
Myth or Reality
third edition

Methuen: Canadian Politics and Government

Canadian Federalism Myth or Reality

third edition

edited by

J. Peter Meekison

University of Alberta

Methuen

Toronto ● New York ● London ● Sydney

Canadian Cataloguing in Publication Data

Main entry under title:

Canadian federalism

ISBN 0-458-92400-8

1. Federal government—Canada—Addresses, essays, lectures. I. Meekison, J. Peter, 1937-

M42

JL27.C3 1977   321'.02'0971   C77-001210-8

Contents

Preface

In the six years since the second edition of this collection of essays was published, the Canadian federal system has undergone a significant transformation. During this time Canadians have seen the termination of the constitutional review process in June 1971; the strains developed between oil producing and consuming provinces created by the energy crisis; the establishment of the anti-inflation program; the resumption of constitutional discussions; an increase in federal-provincial conference activity on a wide range of subject matters; the uncertainty about the very future of Canada as a country resulting from the November 15, 1976 election in the Province of Quebec; and major modifications to the fiscal arrangements between the federal and provincial governments. During this same period scholars of Canadian federalism have directed their attention to new areas of inquiry such as the effects of regionalism within the federal system; attitudes towards federalism; and the influences of federalism on public policy formation. In addition, concerns about Quebec have gone beyond the perennial question—"What does Quebec want?"—to a more sombre question—"Will Quebec pursue separatism?"

The material included in this edition was selected and organized with the above considerations in mind. Part I focusses on an overview of the Canadian federal system, its problems, development and how it is perceived. Part II is devoted to material on the Canadian constitution, including its judicial interpretation, documents containing the most recent proposals for its reform, and an examination of how changing the Senate function might affect the federal system. Intergovernmental co-operation, an apparent reality in the modern federal state, is the subect of Part III. While intergovernmental co-operation has generally been considered in the context of federal-provincial relations, there is also a trend for greater interprovincial co-operation both on a national and regional scale. In Part IV the phenomenon of regionalism is examined. One gains an entirely different perspective on the problems of federalism when considering issues primarily from a regional point of view. While many studies on Canadian federalism have looked at problems of the constitution and approaches to Canadian federalism, few have examined specific policy areas to determine how public policy is shaped or influenced by the federal system. In Part V some of the complexities of policy making in a federal system are illustrated. Finally, Part VI contains pieces related to the current issue of Quebec separatism or independence.

Regardless of the quality of material which is selected for inclusion in any collection of readings, it is impossible to encompass the totality of knowledge, wisdom or opinion on a subject. Nevertheless, it is the editor's hope that the questions raised by these essays are sufficiently thought provoking to stimulate the students to delve more deeply into the subject. There are few federal countries in the world where the topic of federalism has been so widely debated by scholars, the communications media, political cartoonists and the public at large. If the November 15 election in Quebec demonstrates the fragility of the federal system, the ensuing wide-spread public discussion on national unity and constitutional change may result in a rejuvenation and strengthening of the Canadian federal system.

J. Peter Meekison

PART I
THE DIMENSIONS
OF CANADIAN FEDERALISM

1

Federal-Provincial Conflict in Canada*

Donald V. Smiley

Canada is elementally a federal country in that its major axes of social and political differentiation follow territorial lines.[1] Its essential components are relatively specialized regional economies at very different levels of prosperity and development and the concentration of most of the members of one of its two historic cultural communities in a single province. On this foundation of territorial particularisms, even the most integrative of its national organizations seldom go beyond the aggregation of provincial aspirations and interests.

This paper proceeds from the assumption that the structures and processes of government on the one hand and the ways in which public issues are raised and resolved on the other are inextricably related. The perspective is that of Daniel Elazar in his analysis of American federalism. "What kinds of issues are raised in American politics because the states (and their cities) exist as they do? and How are issues developed and resolved in the American political system because of the existence of the states (and their cities) in their present form?"[2] Similarly, Richard Simeon orients his recent study of federal-provincial relations in Canada around answers to these questions: ". . . does the federal system itself foster some kinds of conflict which would not arise were the system unitary; and, given disagreement among major groups, does the federal system provide mechanisms through which differences can be reconciled?"[3] In terms of this kind of perspective on federalism there is no analytic or other reason for regarding substance as the independent variable and process the dependent, or the reverse.

THE WEAKENING OF THE
CENTRALIZED FEDERAL ORDER

The current circumstances of federal-provincial conflict in Canada can be understood only against the background of the piecemeal though rapid disintegration of the relatively centralized regime which was established during and just at the end of the Second World War and was perpetuated through the late 1950s.[4] This regime had several elements. The federal government assumed the responsibility for appropriate

* From PUBLIUS, The Journal of Federalism, The Center for The Study of Federalism, Summer 1974, pp. 7-24. Reprinted by permission.

levels of employment and income through the use of generalized fiscal and monetary policies. In cooperation with the provinces Ottawa took the leadership in establishing and sustaining a national welfare state. The Canadian government participated in the reconstruction of the international economic order and in efforts toward the multilateral reduction of barriers to world trade. In its diplomacy, Canada turned its back on the quasi-isolationism of its policies in the interwar years and in the United Nations, N.A.T.O., the new Commonwealth and other forums pursued the goal of international peace and stability. These domestic and international initiatives were combined with federal leadership in the further development of the east-west structure of transportation and communication—viz. the St. Lawrence Seaway, a public television network, cooperation with the provinces in building the Trans-Canada Highway, the Trans-Canada Pipeline for natural gas, a national network of airports and two national airlines. Such responsibilities, taken together, ensured the dominance of Ottawa in the Canadian system of government.

During the period from the Second World War to about 1960 there were two dominant patterns of relations between the federal and provincial governments.

First, there was the periodic renegotiation of the five-year arrangements for sharing tax sources and revenues. This involved in the first instance elected and appointed treasury officials and inevitably at some point the heads of government.

Second, there were the continuing relations which were concerned with specific shared-cost programmes. These relationships were for the most part between officials involved with relatively specialized public functions and were characteristically regulated in terms of the common professional norms of these officials, as well as their mutual interests in enhancing the funds they had and in insulating their activities from treasury or other officials with more comprehensive concerns. In general terms, federal-provincial interactions related to fiscal sharing in the immediate post-war period tended to be sporadic, and in respect to other matters segmented and particularistic.

The story of Canadian federalism from the late 1950s onward is that of the relative weakening of the power of the national government and the strengthening of that of the provinces.[5] The redefinition of Quebec from the election of the Lesage government in 1960 was crucial in this process. However, several other factors worked in the same direction— the failure of national economic policies from the late 1950s onward to ensure adequate conditions of employment and growth; the shift in the balance of bureaucratic competence to the provinces; the defeat of the Liberal party in the general election of 1957 and the minority governments resulting from that election and those of 1962, 1963, 1965 and 1972; the changing balance of public expenditures toward functions mainly or exclusively within the constitutional jurisdiction of the provinces. These influences, taken together, have led to a situation in which the most crucial aspects of Canadian public policy are within the context of federal-provincial negotiation.

The substance of some of the most crucial conflicts between Ottawa and the provinces may be outlined briefly: first, there is the ongoing debate about tax sources and the revenues derived from these sources. There are the inevitable incompatibilities here between the interests of the "have" and the "have not" provinces and between the reluctance of all politicians to levy taxes and their enthusiasm for expending funds others have raised.

Second, Quebec and in widely varying degrees other provinces have rationalized their welfare policies and seek to reduce or eliminate federal influence in these matters. The federal authorities for their part assert broad responsibilities of a scope not yet precisely defined for the interpersonal and interregional distribution of individual incomes.

Third, conflicts about conditional grants have arisen. Most of the major shared-cost programmes commit Ottawa to half the expenditures for purposes defined as sharable made by provinces, local authorities and institutions of post-secondary education. In respect to three of the major programmes—hospital services, medical insurance and post-secondary education—costs are rising very rapidly and Ottawa is urgent about imposing limitations on its future commitments. The provinces understandably resist any such limitations and are increasingly restive about schemes which embody federal influence over both their expenditure priorities and programme standards.

Fourth, there are conflicts about control over new technological devices in the field of communications. Contrary to my colleague, Marshall McLuhan, the planet is not yet a "global village" and the developing technologies make possible the closer integration of relatively small areas as well as larger ones. The provinces have only recently become seriously involved in these matters and a particularly intense struggle is taking place with Ottawa in respect to control over cablevision.

Fifth, there are emergent conflicts about the limitation of foreign investment in Canada. Quebec and the Atlantic provinces are opposed to such limitations. Ontario and the three western provinces with socialist administrations appear to support more widespread restrictions than the incumbent federal government finds acceptable.

Sixth and last, federal-provincial and interprovincial conflict about the development and sale of natural resources has recently become perhaps the most crucial focus of Canadian public policy. This issue-area involves a very large number of disputed claims and fundamental choices between the respective jurisdiction of Ottawa and the provinces; environmental protection; the rights of Eskimos and Indians; the claims of public as against private ownership; continental economic integration; the geographical distribution of industrial activity; the balance in the national economy between manufacturing and resource development. In the nature of things, defensible resource policies must be oriented toward the long-range future in circumstances of extreme uncertainty about the technological and economic dimensions of that future as well as present reserves of natural resources.

Significantly, the early 1970s appear for the time being at least to put aside what seemed to be one of the most intractable issues of Canadian federalism. This was whether or not Quebec because of its cultural and linguistic particularity should have a broader range of autonomy than that wanted or needed by the other provinces. In broad terms, what has recently happened is that the larger, more prosperous and more influential of the provinces with English-speaking majorities have come to demand for themselves the same range of independent discretion that has been defined by Quebec as its own requirement for cultural survival.

THE MANAGEMENT OF
FEDERAL-PROVINCIAL CONFLICT

The remainder of this paper will analyze the institutional capabilities of the Canadian political system for giving authoritative resolution to federal-provincial conflict.

Judicial Review of the Constitution

There are a very large number of matters in contention where the Canadian constitution is judicially interpreted does not in any clear-cut way delineate the respective powers of the federal and provincial governments—the limits, if any, to the federal power to spend on matters within provincial legislative jurisdiction; the powers of the provinces to enact barriers against extraprovincial trade; the limits of the federal criminal law power in economic regulation; the powers of the federal Parliament to enact either partial or comprehensive controls over wages, prices and profits; federal and provincial powers in respect to such crucial aspects of modern communications as cablevision, etc., etc. Despite these ambiguities, the courts, and in particular the Supreme Court of Canada, have not had a decisive impact on Canadian federalism since the Judicial Committee of the Privy Council was displaced as the final appellate tribunal in Canadian constitutional cases in 1949. For whatever reasons, business corporations are less willing than before to sustain judicial challenges to the powers of one level of government or the other. Canadian courts are in the positivist tradition of constitutional interpretation and are thereby somewhat handicapped in making choices about public policy in the absence of taking into explicit account legislative history or expert evidence.[6] For more than a decade successive governments of Quebec have challenged the credentials of the Supreme Court of Canada as an independent arbiter in constitutional matters on the grounds that its membership, jurisdiction and procedures are determined exclusively by the federal authorities.[7] Most significantly, Ottawa and the provinces have shown a marked preference for intergovernmental negotiation over judicial decision in managing their conflicts with each other and appear to regard the submission of one of their disputes to the courts something like an ultimate weapon when one party or other has failed to come to an acceptable result through intergovernmental bargaining.

Federal-Provincial Conflict and Partisan Politics

Central-regional conflicts within a federal system might conceivably be resolved either through relations between national and state or provincial parties or through popular elections. It will be remembered that in his analysis of comparative federalism published in 1964 William H. Riker assigned intraparty relations a determining role in controlling whether the original federal bargain will develop in a centralized or peripheralized form.[8]

The partisan dimensions of Canadian federalism are complex and have only recently been investigated in a systematic way.[9] Several developments are in the direction of both separating the two major national parties from their provincial wings and thus "confederalizing" the party system and of making intraparty relations of diminishing importance in the resolution of federal-provincial conflicts. The following is a summary statement of the available evidence:

  —little is yet known about federal-provincial voting behaviour and the extent of the mutual electoral dependence of federal and provincial parties of the same designation varies among parties and provinces. It can, however, be said with some assurance that outside the four Atlantic provinces, a federal or provincial party which attains electoral success must win the support of a significant number of voters who cast their ballots for other parties or abstain in elections at the other level of government.
  —in terms of career-patterns involving elective office, a relatively small proportion of Members of Parliament or members of provincial legislatures have contested elections at the other level of government either successfully or otherwise. In federal-provincial relations politicians for the most part have neither experience or ambitions involving the other level.
  —increasingly, the federal Liberal and Progressive Conservative

parties are financially independent of their provincial wings. In the earlier periods of Confederation the national parties raised campaign funds mainly from private corporations centered in Montreal and Toronto and distributed portions of these funds to the parties' provincial wings. According to the most perceptive student of Canadian campaign finance, Khayyam Z. Paltiel, this was an important nationalizing force not only in the parties themselves but for the wider political system.[10] Although the federal Liberal and Progressive Conservative parties still rely heavily on the same kinds of corporate contributors as in the past, the provincial wings of these parties have found their own sources of funds independent of the national organizations, in many cases from corporations involved in the exploitation of natural resources under provincial jurisdiction. Further, there are influences at work toward the increasing support of electoral campaigns from the public purse either, as in Quebec and Nova Scotia, through direct cash subsidies to candidates of recognized parties or through free-time political broadcasts, franking privileges or the partisan employment of persons on the public payroll.[11] Such assistance is almost always available to parties for activities at only one or other of the levels of government rather than both.

—Canadian extra-parliamentary party organization has been little studied, but at the national level there has been the development of organizations oriented toward national politics almost exclusively. Under their respective national constitutions both the Liberal and Progressive Conservative parties are required to hold representative conventions at least once every two years to select leaders[12] and/or to discuss party organization and policy matters. These conventions are not dominated by provincial parties or leaders. Similarly, most of the provincial parties hold regular conventions outside the control of activists and officials oriented toward national politics.

What I have elsewhere designated as the "confederalizing" of the Canadian party system influences and is influenced by its asymmetry in which particular federal or provincial parties are oriented exclusively or almost exclusively toward electoral success at one level or the other rather than both. In the four Atlantic provinces, the classic Liberal-Conservative duality has endured and in this region the integration of federal and provincial parties is much closer than elsewhere in Canada. West of this region the Liberals are in power only in Quebec, although in that province the two wings of the party maintain a high degree of mutual independence, and the official opposition in only Ontario and Saskatchewan. The Conservatives have been in power in Ontario since

1943, although for about two-thirds of this time the Liberals have had a majority of Members of Parliament from the province. There are New Democratic Party governments in Manitoba, Saskatchewan and British Columbia. Social Credit is the official opposition in Alberta and British Columbia and the major opposition to the Liberals in federal politics in Quebec.

Despite the weakness of intraparty relations in federal-provincial integration it is of course conceivable that general elections might give authoritative resolution to conflicts between the two levels of government. Were this to happen, two requirements would have to be met:

First, some crucial aspect of federal-provincial contention would be so central to electoral competition that the voting results could reasonbly be regarded as a mandate for one side or other in such contention.

Second, in particular provinces the electorate would be consistent in giving its majority support in successive federal and provincial elections to parties whose policies in federal-provincial relations were compatible.

These conditions are seldom fulfilled. Most elections at both levels revolve about issues other than federal-provincial relations. But even when such issues are of extraordinary salience, as was the case in the 1968 federal election which returned the Liberals to power with a majority on Pierre Elliott Trudeau's formulation of Canadian federalism, it is not uncommon for provincial electorates in successive national and provincial elections to sustain disputants with contradictory policies in intergovernmental affairs.

The processes of partisan politics and federal-provincial conflict are of course related in that the major participants in this conflict are politicians who have achieved electoral success. However, as Simeon has argued, ". . . the party system does not serve as a channel for intergovernmental adjustment. Partisan factors are little help in explaining . . . federal-provincial conflict . . . . The [federal and provincial] party subsystems are largely separate and distinct, and again this fosters the pattern of government-to-government negotiation, more analogous to that between nation-states than between units in the same political system."[13]

Like nation-states, Canadian provinces have relatively durable and persisting interests whatever the partisan complexions of their respective leadership at any particular time. Similarly, the constraints on federal governments arise for the most part from responsibilities acquired by the constitutional division of powers as developed over time rather than from the shifting fortunes of provincial politics. Yet, as with nation-states, these persisting interests of governments do give political leaders a significant discretion in pursuing these interests in terms of their own ideologies and political and bureaucratic styles. Because of this, federal and provincial politicians are characteristically not indifferent to which party holds power at the other level. However, it not infrequently happens that these preferences cut across partisan allegiances. In many cases, it appears that provincial parties in power perceive that their own electoral fortunes are more dependent on appropriate policies on the part of the federal government, particularly in respect to fiscal matters, than its partisan complexion. Thus the records of such parties in committing their prestige and organizational resources to their counterparts in federal elections are highly variable. From the federal side, the electoral strength of the two major parties is much less dependent than in earlier periods on provincial politics.

Territorial Pluralisms Within the Central Government

Karl Loewenstein has made a useful distinction between interstate and intrastate federalism.[14] Interstate federalism involves the constitutional distribution of powers between the central and regional governments, intrastate federalism the channeling of territorial particularisms within the central government itself.

Intrastate influences in the operations of the government of Canada are weak.[15] The constitution does not provide the provincial governments as such with any role in the composition and functioning of national political institutions. Even more significantly, the workings of these institutions have been such as to deny important territorial pluralisms an influence in national affairs. The following circumstances can be noted briefly:

—the Canadian Senate has never been an effective outlet for interests which are specifically provincial or regional.[16]

—the cabinet has for the most part ceased to give decisive influence to territorially-based interests through members who have a base of provincial or regional support independent of the head of government. Canadian Prime Ministers still constitute their cabinets in terms of traditional practices of regional representation. However, ministers have come increasingly to be creatures of the Prime Minister rather than, as often happened in earlier periods of Confederation, leaders with commanding power in and in respect to their respective provinces or regions.

—the merit principle in the federal civil service has worked against a bureaucracy broadly representative of the various areas of Canada.

—the workings of the electoral system have often denied provinces and regions representation on the government side of the House of Commons proportionate to the popular vote they gave to government parties.[17] In recent Parliaments, the Liberals have been so disadvantaged in the Prairie Provinces, the Progressive Conservatives in Quebec.

The weakness of intrastate federalism in Canada has led important territorially based interests to find an almost exclusive outlet through the provincial governments. A comparison with the United States is useful here. In terms of obvious criteria the American system is more centralized. Federal financial assistance to the states is for more specific purposes than is the case with Canadian provinces and comes with more explicit conditions, and there is no tradition of unconditional subsidies. Under many circumstances the American national authorites deal directly with local governments bypassing the states; the Canadian provinces have been for the most part successful in frustrating such interactions. Judicial interpretation of congressional powers over interstate commerce gives the American government a range of control over economic matters denied its Canadian counterpart by reason of the narrow definition of Parliament's power over trade and commerce made by the Judicial Committee of the Privy Council. Congress has the legislative powers to implement treaties; the Parliament of Canada acquires no powers it would not otherwise have had by virtue of international obligations. Yet when we examine the operations of what seems in Canadian terms to be a relatively high centralized pattern of federal-state relations in the United States we find the pervasiveness of local, state and regional influences within the national government itself, circumstances occasioned by such interrelated factors as the decentralized nature of the party system, the separation of legislative and executive powers and the fragmentation of power in the executive branch. It is reasonable to conjecture that such a centralized federation on the federal-state dimension could be sustained only by the effective outlets given to territorial particularisms within the government of the United States. It is otherwise in Canada.

The weakness of intrastate federalism in Canada has crucial consequences for the ways in which interests which are specifically regional are articulated and aggregated and the resolution of such conflicts. Richard Simeon has pointed out that "*intergovernmental* interaction is likely to be more frequent the less the institutional arrangements at the national level accommodate regional interests."[18] The normal workings of British parliamentary institutions provide a number of devices for the authoritative resolution of conflicts between elements of particular governments—between the electorate and the House of Commons, between a Prime Minister and his cabinet and/or parliamentary colleagues, between a ministry and the House of Commons, between elected and appointed officials. Thus to the extent that regional interests are channeled through the national government, a permanent deadlock between them is almost impossible. In Canadian circumstances it is otherwise when such interests are opposed in federal-provincial relations.

Executive Federalism

Several alternative institutional procedures have been shown to have few capabilities for managing federal-provincial conflict in Canada—judicial review of the constitution, intraparty relations, general elections, intrastate federalism. Thus government-to-government relations, what might be called "executive federalism", play a central role both in shaping the claims which the provinces make on each other and on the national government and the resolution, if at all, of these conflicting aims.

During the period from about 1960 onward elected and appointed officials of the two orders of government in Canada have come to define their interests and their demands on each other in terms of increasingly comprehensive and rationalized objectives. In his study of federal-state relations in the United States Edward W. Weidner made a useful distinction between "principled, programmatic or organization goals" related for the most part to particular public services and "expediency or conservation goals" referring to "the preservation and extension of influence of individuals, agencies or units of government."[19] He concluded that in the American federal system programmatic rather than expediency goals were dominant. Thus, "Public policies, and consequent disagreement and conflict, are not the product of entire units of government. Particular individuals, more or less associated in groups and to be found both within a unit of government and without, are the central forces behind the molding of public policy."[20] Weidner's study was based predominantly on an investigation of federal grants-in-aid to state and local governments, and the American tradition is such that funds are disbursed for narrowly-defined programmes according to very specific conditions being met by the recipient agencies. In Canada as in the United States such arrangements characteristically give rise to complexes of interest composed of officials at both levels of government with common professional standards and with common concerns to insulate their specialized activities against external influences. As we shall see, integrative relations with such particularized focuses have become decreasingly important in the Canadian federal system.

The strategy of successive Quebec governments from the coming to power of the Lesage administration in June 1960 onward has been of decisive importance in the disposition of federal and provincial governments to press their interests in increasingly rationalized and comprehensive terms. This strategy is based on the premise that the safeguarding and extending of the province's autonomy is the essential requirement of the survival and integrity of the Francophone community[21] and Claude Morin's book-length account of federal-provincial relations between 1960 and 1971 is organized around what amounts to a zero-sum game in which Quebec's gains are measured in terms of such autonomy.[22] These new Quebec policies almost inevitably gave rise to counter-strategies on the part of Ottawa and, to widely varying degrees, the other provincial governments. Between February 1968 and June 1971 there was a series of federal-provincial conferences devoted to the comprehensive review of the Canadian constitution in the hope that constitutional reform might bring about some new accommodation between the country's two historic communities.[23] In April 1968 Pierre Elliott Trudeau became leader of the national Liberal party and two months later led this party to an electoral majority in the House of Commons on a platform embodying Mr. Trudeau's formulation of a new kind of relation between Anglophones and Francophones.[24]

The development from particularistic to more comprehensive goals has been inextricably related to the acceptance by the federal government and, to varying degrees, the provinces, of new and more rationalized administrative technologies expressed most characteristically in such procedures as cost-benefit analysis, 'Planning, Programming and Budgeting', systems analysis, the use of econometric models and economic forecasting. There have been significant reorganizations at the cabinet level. Quebec established a Department of Federal-Provincial Relations in 1961 and this portfolio under successive prime Ministers of the province has had a decisive effect in ordering Quebec's external relations.[25] In Ontario there has been established a Department of Treasury, Economics and Intergovernmental Affairs, a "Policy and Priorities Board" of cabinet set up and four "super-ministers" without specific operational responsibilities appointed.[26] Prime Minister Trudeau has rationalized the structure and operations of the federal cabinet by vastly extending the size and influence of the Prime Minister's Office and establishing powerful cabinet committees in various functional areas, including federal-provincial relations.[27] These new organizational technologies and their supportive justifications have two major elements, (1) deliberative processes of priority-setting, including inevitably the subsuming of narrower to broader objectives, (2) increasingly more sophisticated evaluation of the economy and effectiveness with which actual or postulated objectives are or might be attained.[28] Governments have thus come to formulate and pursue their interests in terms which are at the same time both more precise and more comprehensive than when their operations were less rationalized.

The new organizational strategies have important consequences for federal-provincial relations. To the extent that governments proceed in terms of comprehensive and precisely-formulated goals there are more incentives than otherwise for them to reduce the uncertainties of their external environments, including of course the actions of other governments in the federal system. Further, when governments act in this way agreement between them is inhibited by the emergence of very complex strategies and patterns of "pay offs". The kinds of circumstances which

Weidner described and which broadly speaking prevailed in Canada prior to 1960 were characterized by the compartmentalization of issue areas and the consequent minimization of spill-overs between particular matters of relations in respect to others. Contrary influences are now at work. Thus despite the vast amount of incantation both from Canadian scholars and Canadian officials about the need for federal-provincial coordination and the alleged association between such coordination and rationality, the increasing sophistication of these governments leads directly to conflict of a somewhat intractable kind.

The way in which Ottawa and the provinces define their respective interests and claims on each other has shaped and been shaped by the institutions and procedures by which such policies are formulated and implemented. As we have seen, federal-provincial interactions in fiscal matters in the immediate post-war period tended to be sporadic and in relation to other matters segmented and particularistic. The break in this pattern came with the election of the Lesage government in Quebec in 1960. This government embarked on an integrated strategy of safeguarding and extending the province's autonomy through its Department of Intergovernmental Affairs which has had a high degree of success in subsuming particular aspects of Quebec's relations with various federal agencies to this broad goal. To widely varying degrees, the federal administration and those of the other provinces have created similar departments or sub-departments and there are now a significant number of elected and appointed officials whose exclusive or major responsibilities are for federal-provincial relations as such. Inevitably, heads of government are more continuously involved in these relations than was the case prior to the 1960s. Inevitably also, these relations at or near the summit have the effect of subordinating particularistic objectives and agencies concerned with these objectives to more comprehensive policies. It might be pointed out and in contrast with the circumstances of the United States that the normal workings of British parliamentary institutions in their Canadian variants impose no institutional obstructions to such integration of policy within particular governments. Cabinet secrecy and solidarity, the cohesion of legislative parties and the deference of appointed to elected officials facilitate rather than frustrate global strategies. As we have seen, such rationalization has come to be associated with sophistication in the design and implementation of public policy.

During the past decade there has been a rapid development of meetings of federal and provincial officials at the ministerial level. The heads of government meet at least annually and have come increasingly to appoint committees headed by ministers or senior officials to investigate and report back on specific problems. Finance ministers meet in January at the time when most are in the process of making the final decisions about their respective budgets. Ministerial meetings of other ministers with specific responsibilities meet at least once each year—labour, health, welfare, Indian affairs, agriculture, etc. In the Speech from the Throne on January 4, 1973, the federal authorities announced a new kind of federal-provincial meeting, a conference between the federal government and those of the four western provinces to be held in the summer of that year.

Despite the rapid development of the institutions of federal-provincial relations few firm conventions have been evolved to regulate these relations. Who has the responsibility for convening a federal-provincial conference? Are conferences to be open or closed, and, if the latter, how firmly are the participants bound to confidentiality? Should a federal official always chair the conferences? Can the chairman's role be separated from that of the representative of a government with interests to defend? Should the communiques issued at the ends of conferences specify the areas of disagreement as well as agreement and, if so, should the policy positions of particular governments be attributed explicitly to them? To what extent, if at all, is an incoming government bound by its predecessor? Do regularized relations make necessary secretariats responsible to the various federal-provincial groupings as such? If so, how can effective staff services be made compatible with the apparent wishes of all participating governments to avoid these secretariats becoming centres of independent influence? These and other unresolved questions are compounded by the relatively rapid turnover of both elected and senior appointed officials. Observers of federal-provincial relations in the 1960s paid note to the "clubby" nature of these interactions and in part at least such personalization contributed to the authoritative resolution of conflict in the absence of developed conventions about procedures. More recently, eight of the ten provinces have had changes of government in the past five years and of the eleven Prime Ministers and Premiers Alexander Campbell of Prince Edward Island who came to power in 1966 is senior. There have been similar turnovers among senior appointed officials.

CONCLUSIONS

The most critical areas of Canadian public policy are now within the realm of federal-provincial decision. Yet the Canadian federal system has developed little institutional capacity for giving authoritative resolution to conflicts about these matters. The standard prescription is for more intergovernmental consultation and cooperation. Such prescriptions are based on the assumptions that (1) federal-provincial conflicts arise from a lack of information among disputants about the perceptions and priorities of other jurisdictions, (2) once governments are aware of each other, rational conduct will dispose them toward cooperation rather than conflict. There is here an almost total neglect of the circumstance that conflicts in federal-provincial relations in Canada arise for the most part from genuinely contradictory interests. As we have seen, what governments themselves and most informed observers of their activities define as administrative maturity has led directly to global rather than particularistic strategies and to federal-provincial conflicts of a more intractable kind than existed when issue-areas were more compartmentalized. Intergovernmental coordination would require Ottawa and the provinces to surrender some of their powers of independent decision. Neither level has shown much disposition to do this[29] and in the abstract it is impossible to judge whether this constitutes rational and responsible conduct.

The major deficiency of the existing system of federal-provincial relations is that it fails to deal adequately with what economists call the "interjurisdictional externalities"[30] that arise from provincial policies. So long as Canada retains a relatively integrated fiscal and monetary system and, despite provincial barriers, circumstances prevail in which there is relatively free movement of people, goods and money within its territorial boundaries, provincial policies will have important effects on citizens and governments elsewhere in the country. In the crucial matter of the actual and projected development of natural resources it has been argued in a recent study that ". . . in almost every case development occurred at the initiative of one of the various Provincial governments with little or no regard being paid to the national implications of development . . . . Exploitation was uniformly to the aggrandizement of the United States as the importer of the concerned water, energy, or petroleum resources . . . . The federal government's involvement was consistently unimposing in terms of ensuring optimum development from the Canadian point-of-view."[31] We very much need careful economic studies of the externalities of various provincial policies in such fields as health, welfare and educational services, transportation, fiscal policy and the simulation of economic development.

It is my conjecture, but scarcely more than conjecture, that the beneficiaries of the system in which the externalities of provincial policies are not effectively managed will increasingly be the residents and governments of the more prosperous provinces and the disadvantaged the governments and residents of the other provinces. The following examples are illustrative only:

> —all the provinces have programmes to narrow intraprovincial economic disparities. In the more prosperous jurisdictions the disadvantaged areas have locational and other advantages which may result in these developments taking place partially at the expense of other regions, particularly in Quebec and the Atlantic provinces.[32]

—all the major jurisdictions in Canada seek to encourage economic development through tax concessions and various forms of industrial incentives. Business corporations of course benefit from this competition[33] and in it the wealthier provinces and their constituent municipalities have advantages over governments less fortunately situated.

—the provinces in varying degrees are intent on rationalizing the structures of local and regional government.[34] Again the wealthier provinces and their constituent municipalities have a competitive advantage, and the comprehensive plans of Ontario for the area to the east and west of Toronto may well contribute to that metropolitan region's success in the historic competitive race with Montreal.

—in the deliberate use of fiscal policy toward full employment and growth and of industrial strategies to encourage provincial economic diversification the wealthier provinces have advantages over the others.

One might thus expect provincial policies to work in the direction of increasing regional economic disparities in Canada. Successive federal governments have accepted increasingly comprehensive responsibilities for narrowing such disparities. However, current provincial pressures are in the direction of denying Ottawa a decisive influence over the circumstances under which federal funds are expended for such purposes. In the long run if not the short one might expect a declining willingness of federal politicians to tax and of residents of the more prosperous provinces to be taxed outside the framework of national purposes as specified in some detail by the national government.

The second issue-area crucially affected by existing federal-provincial relations involves continental economic integration.[35] What we have here is the clash of pan-Canadian economic nationalism and the economic nationalisms of at least the larger provinces with the latter to widely varying degrees embarked on policies usually associated with sovereign states—provincial fiscal policies toward full employment and growth; various kinds of restrictions on the free movement of people, goods and capital between provinces; economic relations outside Canada apart from the supervision and control of the national government. The central government retains control over most of the infrastructure of transportation and communications and of course of tariff policies. Yet, on balance, these crucial elements of national economic integration have become of relatively less importance than counter-pressures toward continental integration by American corporations and the government of the United States. So far as federal policies to restrict direct foreign investment are concerned, the incumbent government has been very sensitive to provincial influences and is unlikely to impose such restrictions in the "have not" provinces. Further, to the extent that the government of the United States proceeds toward some sort of over-all bargain with Canada about economic matters, the Canadian government is institutionally handicapped by the federal-provincial division of powers related to economic policy.

NOTES

[1] On the sociology of federalism see W. S. Livingston, "A Note on the Nature of Federalism," LXVII *Political Science Quarterly*, No. 1 (March 1952), pp. 81-95.

[2] *American Federalism: A View from the States* (Crowell, New York, 1966), pp. 4-5.

[3] Richard Simeon, *Federal-Provincial Diplomacy: The Making of Recent Policy in Canada* (University of Toronto Press), 1972, p. 9.

[4] Donald V. Smiley, *Constitutional Adaptation and Canadian Federalism since 1945*, Documents of the Royal Commission on Bilingualism and Biculturalism (Queen's Printer 1970), Ottawa, Chapter II.

[5] Smiley, *op. cit.*, Chapter III.

[6] See generally B. L. Strayer, *Judicial Review of Legislation in Canada* University of Toronto Press, (Toronto: 1968).

[7] See generally Jacques Bicssard, *La Cour Suprème et La Constitution* Les Presses de l'Université de Montréal, (Montréal: 1968), and Peter H. Russell, *The Supreme Court of Canada as a Bilingual and Bicultural Institution*, Documents of the Royal Commission on Bilingualism and Biculturalism Queen's Printer, (Ottawa: 1969).

[8] W. H. Riker *Federalism: Origin, Operation, Significance* Little, Brown, (Boston: 1964), p. 136. "Whatever the general social conditions, if any, that sustain the federal bargain, there is one institutional condition that controls the nature of the bargain in all the instances here examined and in all others with which I am familiar. This is the structure of the party system, which may be regarded as the main variable intervening between the background social conditions and the specific nature of the federal bargain."

[9] See Donald V. Smiley, *Canada in Question: Federalism in the Seventies* McGraw-Hill Ryerson, (Toronto: 1972), Chapter 4, "The Politics of Canadian Federalism" and Simeon, *Federal-Provincial Diplomacy*, pp. 194-196.

[10] "Federalism and Party Finance: a Preliminary Sounding," in *Studies in Canadian Party Finance*, Committee on Election Expenses Queen's Printer, (Ottawa: 1966), pp. 1-21.

[11] For a description of these arrangements see Khayyam Z. Paltiel, *Political Party Financing in Canada* McGraw-Hill, (Toronto: 1970), p. 121 and pp. 124-132.

[12] For analysis of leadership conventions see J. Lele, G. C. Perlin and H. G. Thorburn, "The National Party Convention" in H. G. Thorburn, Editor, *Party Politics in Canada* Third Edition; Prentice-Hall of Canada, (Scarborough: 1972), pp. 106-119 and Donald V. Smiley, "The National Leadership Convention: A Preliminary Analysis," I *Canadian Journal of Political Science*, No. 4, Dec. 1968, pp. 373-397 and John C. Courtney, *The Selection of National Party Leaders in Canada* Macmillan of Canada, (Toronto: 1973).

[13] Simeon, *op. cit.*, p. 33.

[14] *Political Power and the Governmental Process* University of Chicago Press, Phoenix Edition, (Chicago: 1965), pp. 405-407.

[15] The analysis of this section is presented in more detail in my article "The Structural Problem of Canadian Federalism," *Canadian Public Administration* 14 (Fall 1971), pp. 326-343.

[16] Robert A. Mackay, *The Unreformed Senate of Canada,* Revised Edition Carleton Library Series, No. 6, McClelland and Stewart, (Toronto: 1963), pp. 112-123.

[17] For an analysis of the sectionalizing influences of the Canadian electoral system see Alan C. Cairns, "The Electoral System and the Party System in Canada, 1921-1965," I *Canadian Journal of Political Science,* No. 1 (March, 1968), pp. 55-80.

[18] Simeon, *op. cit.,* p. 303. Emphasis in text.

[19] "Decision-Making in a Federal System" in Aaron Wildavsky, Editor, *American Federalism in Perspective* Little, Brown, (Boston: 1967), pp. 235-236.

[20] *Ibid.,* p. 239.

[21] For one of the most lucid statements of the relation between provincial autonomy and cultural survival see the presentation of Premier Jean Lesage to the Federal-Provincial Conference of Nov. 26-29, 1963. *Proceedings* Queen's Printer, (Ottawa: 1964), particularly pp. 38-41.

[22] *Le Pouvoir Québecois . . . en négociation* Les Editions du Boréal Express, (Quebec/Montréal: 1972).

[23] For the best analysis of the constitutional review process available see Simeon, Chapter 5. See also Donald V. Smiley, *Canada in Question,* Chapter 2.

[24] For Trudeau's views on federalism see his book of essays *Federalism and the French Canadians* Macmillan of Canada, (Toronto: 1968).

[25] Claude Morin, "Le ministère des affaires intergouvernmentales," *Le Québec dans le Canada de demain, Le Devoir* (Montréal, Éditions du jour, 1967, Tome II), pp. 176-182.

[26] James D. Fleck, "Restructuring the Ontario Government," 17 *Canadian Public Administration,* Vol. 16, No. 1, (Spring 1973), pp. 55-68.

[27] Two recent books of essays deal with the structures and processes of decision-making in the federal government. See Thomas A. Hockin, Editor, *Apex of Power: The Prime Minister and Political Leadership in Canada* Prentice-Hall of Canada, (Scarborough: 1971), and G. Bruce Doern and Peter Aucoin, Editors, *The Structures of Policy-Making in Canada* Macmillan of Canada, (Toronto: 1971).

[28] For an excellent analysis of the intellectual assumptions of the new ways of decision-making see G. Bruce Doern, "Recent Changes in the Philosophy of Policy Making in Canada," *Canadian Journal of Political Science,* Vol. IV, No. 2 (June: 1971), pp. 243-264.

[29] For an account of the propensity of Canadian officials to support the general principle of federal-provincial cooperation but to have inhibitions about giving up their discretionary powers to such collaborative processes see *Report: Intergovernmental Liaison on Fiscal and Economic Matters,* Institute of Intergovernmental Relations, Queen's University Queen's Printer, (Ottawa: 1969), pp. 120-121.

[30] Wallace E. Oates, *Fiscal Federalism* Harcourt, Brace, Johanovich, (New York: 1972), pp. 46-49.

[31] R. St. J. Macdonald, Q.C., *et al.,* "Economic Development and Environmental Security," A Brief Submitted to the Nova Scotia representatives of the Canadian Council of Resource and Environment Ministers at Halifax on Sept. 26, 1972, *mimeo,* p. 14.

[32] T. N. Brewis, *Regional Economic Policies in Canada* Macmillan of Canada, (Toronto: 1969), pp. 213-214.

[33] For several case studies of provincial developmental schemes see Philip Mathias, *Forced Growth* James Lewis and Samuel, (Toronto: 1971).

[34] For a description and analysis of the Ontario efforts see C. R. Tindal, "Regional Development in Ontario," *Canadian Public Administration,* Vol. 16, 1, (Spring, 1973), pp. 110-123.

[35] The analysis suggested in this last paragraph is elaborated in detail in "The Federal Dimension of Canadian Economic Nationalism," *Dalhousie Law Journal,* September, 1974. See also Robert Gilpin, "American Direct Investment and Canada's Two Nationalisms," in Richard A. Preston, Editor, *The Influence of the United States on Canadian Development* Duke University Press, (Durham, N.C.: 1972), pp. 124-143.

2

The Five Faces of Federalism*

J. R. Mallory

Canadian federalism is different things at different times. It is also different things to different people. This is not the result of widespread error but of simple fact, for political institutions which accommodate diversity will reflect the dimensions which are vital to the actors who work them.

In the past century it is possible to see five different forms of Canadian federalism which may be described roughly as follows: the quasi-federalism (to use Dr. Wheare's description) which was most marked in the Macdonald era; federalism of the classic type characterized by the co-ordinate and autonomous relationship of the central and regional organs; emergency federalism, most obviously in being during the periods of extreme centralization in wartime; the co-operative federalism which reached its zenith in the period since 1945; and the "double-image" federalism which includes both the straightforward central-regional relationship between the central and provincial organs and a special relationship between French and English which to some extent transcends the other. While these various forms can be made to fit approximately into different historical periods, they overlap one another and do not in fact conform to a clear stage-by-stage development.

QUASI-FEDERALISM

In 1867, the new Dominion of Canada did not begin to operate as a full-blown federal structure. There were several obvious reasons for this. Canadians are always sensitive to the influence of the United States, and the American federal system was at that time in some disarray. The peril of state's rights and secession was manifest, and there were not a few of the Fathers of Confederation who noted with concern that states' rights afforded an opportunity for such democratic excesses as the spoilation of the vested rights of property. The new federal government in the first blush of its power in Ottawa was both a national coalition and a concentration of political talent which was bound to leave little political weight in the provinces. Furthermore, the opening of the West led to the cre-

---

* From P.-A. Crepeau & C. B. Macpherson (eds.), *The Future of Canadian Federalism* (Toronto, University of Toronto Press, 1965), pp. 3-15. Reprinted by permission.

ation or admission of new provinces whose early relationship with Ottawa was a colonial one.[1]

The influence of the forms of government on political action should never be underestimated. The "colonial" relationship with the provinces was a natural one—much more natural than the "co-ordinate and autonomous" relationship more appropriate to a federal system. Macdonald and his ministers had grown up politically in a system in which the governor still played a role as an imperial presence difficult to appreciate today. Most of them had been in politics long enough to remember when the governor still actively participated in policy discussion with his council, and before the cabinet had completely split off from the formal executive. For a wide range of matters that were beyond the reach of local self-government or were ones in which there was an imperial interest, they were accustomed to the idea that the governor possessed power as well as influence. In the British North America Act, the lieutenant-governor was just as much an agent of the federal government as the governor general was an agent of the British government.

It therefore seems more appropriate to think of the dominion-provincial relationship at that time as similar to the relationship of the imperial govenment with a colony enjoying limited self-government. This was most obviously true in provinces like Manitoba and British Columbia where the weakness of political parties and the lack of political and administrative experience meant that the provincial governments were in a state of tutelage. The difference between these provinces and the older provinces in this matter was a difference of degree.

Dr. Wheare, in discussing the nature of Canadian federalism, attaches some importance to the ambivalent role of the lieutenant-governor and concludes that the Canadian constitution is in form only quasi-federal.[2] During the first couple of decades after Confederation, when the federal government frequently resorted to disallowance and reservation to curb the growth of provincial powers of self-government, "quasi-federal" understates the case. The relationship was much more like that of mother-country and colony, and the institutions of control were essentially those of colonial rule. But there was the inescapable fact that the constitution was indeed federal, and the federal distribution of power nourished the strength of the provinces as the strains brought about by race, religion, economic exploitation, and the sheer impossibility of running such a disparate country further diffused power in the system.

Nevertheless, this quasi-imperial relationship was a long time dying. The long retention by the federal government of administrative control over the natural resources of the western provinces emphasized their colonial status. The rise of agrarian populism through the progressive movement was a revolt against the exploitation of the west by the banks, the railroads, and the tariff-protected industries of the east. When populism went too far, as it did under William Aberhart's Social Credit administration in Alberta, it was curbed by the old imperial remedies of reservation and disallowance.

CLASSICAL FEDERALISM

A federal constitution is in essence a division of jurisdiction between equally autonomous bodies. But no constitution can express, in precise detail, a distribution of authority so exact that no doubts can arise about which of the two legislative structures, central and regional, is within its powers in a particular regulatory statute. Some agency, external to both legislatures, must hold the balance between them. It was natural in Canada, as it was in the United States, that this role should be assumed by the courts, for both countries are part of a constitutional tradition that insulates the judicial process from the politics of the day. Furthermore, disputes of this kind—about the powers of constituted authorities—are justiciable.

This is not the place to consider this large and intricate subject, but only to make some general observations on its effect on the system and the boundaries within which it operates. There is one important difference between the role of the Supreme Court of the United States and the role of the Judicial Committee of the Privy Council, and that is in their approach to the problem of adjudication. Following the bold initiative of Chief Justice Marshall, the Supreme Court has approached its role in a spirit of constructive statecraft. "We must never forget," said Marshall in *McCulloch* v. *Maryland*, "that it is a constitution we are expounding."[3] Accordingly the Court has not hesitated to reverse itself in the light of changed circumstances, and to play the major role in adapting the constitution to the changing needs of succeeding generations.

A Canadian court might well have followed the same path. Much of the law is experience, and Canadian judges would no doubt have been more sensitive to the strains and the changing patterns of Canadian life than the Privy Council.[4] To the remoteness of the Privy Council and its reluctance to engage in judicial statecraft was added a further difficulty—the inability of English judges to understand the basic fact about federal constitutions, i.e., that a distribution of power written into the constitution is fixed and almost unalterable. In the United Kingdom it was a perfectly proper exercise of judicial self-restraint to take the view that, if the purpose of Parliament was frustrated by lack of foresight in drafting so that the courts found a section to be meaningless, it was not the business of the courts to interpose themselves and say, "This is what Parliament meant to accomplish by this Act, and we shall interpret it accordingly," but rather to interpret the words narrowly and as they found them. If this is not what Parliament wanted, then it has the right to amend the act itself. This is all very well in an unitary state, but in a federal system, a construction of the constitution which is too narrow, or wrong-headed, may do great harm, since constitutional amendment is extremely difficult.

There is no general agreement about the general effect of the interpretation of the Canadian constitution by the Judicial Committee of the Privy Council. It has been argued that the very wide meaning given to property and civil rights, together with the emasculation of the federal power of trade and commerce and the relegation of the "peace, order and good government" concept to a wartime emergency power, was clearly contrary to the intention of the Fathers of Confederation to create a strong central authority and to confine the provinces to local matters.[5] Whether this was the result of ignorance or high imperial policy is no longer of much importance. It is more than likely that the narrow construction placed on federal powers was the only reaction which could have been expected from common law judges in a period when the courts, in the United States as well as the United Kingdom, were responding sympathetically to the litigious pressure of powerful economic interests intent on resisting the growing role of the state in limiting economic liberty.[6] In any event, by the inter-war period the courts by using a "watertight compartment" theory of jurisdiction, had succeeded in interdicting effective action by the federal authorities to deal with the economic problems of the depression.

Whatever its consequences, what had evolved was federalism of the classic type, if I may borrow Principal Corry's phraseology, in which power is allocated to the central and provincial authorities so that each enjoys an exclusive jurisdiction, with disputes about the margins of power settled finally by the courts. This has certain advantages. It entrenches provincial rights, and at the same time it confines the provinces to their sphere. Disputes are settled by the impartial arbitration of the courts, as guardians of the constitution. It has its disadvantages. Since federal constitutions are notoriously hard to amend, the only dynamic element is the extent to which the courts are able to adjust the meaning of the constitution to face the facts of social change. That is what Dicey meant when he said that federations substitute litigation for legislation. But the courts are not the first to perceive the outlines of social change. And while the Supreme Court of the United States has shown considerable capacity to "follow the election returns," the Judicial Committee of the Privy Council was so deficient in both sense and sensibility that the allocation of power in the constitution, by the end of the 1930s, had achieved a remarkable incongruity between the resources, capacities, and responsibilities of the federal and provincial governments.

EMERGENCY FEDERALISM

But the Canadian constitution in one respect was totally lacking in the rigidity of its federal arrangements. This had not been by design, for there is nothing in either the Confederation Debates or the BNA Act itself which addresses itself to the distribution of power in an emergency. It was the courts themselves which made this dangerous opening in the system. Nobody before 1914 foresaw the effect of modern war on constitutional government or on the settled Victorian notions of propriety about the role of government in economic affairs. But when war came and Parliament abdicated to the executive the vast powers to make regulations for the peace, order, and good government of Canada, the federal government assumed a wide range of powers over matters of civil rights and property which in peacetime belonged to the sacrosanct powers of the provinces. And the courts gave their blessing to the proposition that the federal distribution of power was a peacetime luxury which must be foregone in wartime. Building on a dictum of Lord Watson in the *Local Prohibition Case,* they found that wartime was a situation which transcended the terms of sections 91 and 92 altogether and one which, in effect, made Canada a unitary state for the duration.

When the First World War was over the courts hurriedly began to erect a fence around this dangerous doctrine, to the exasperation of many Canadian lawyers during the depression years, and they stubbornly refused to seek a more flexible formula which would allow the central authorities power to deal with lesser emergencies. For the trouble with the emergency doctrine was that it went too far. It seemed to be all or nothing. And it went so far that it is not difficult to sense their reulctance to apply it. This is no doubt why Lord Haldane was led into the entertaining speculation in the *Snider Case* that the Judicial Committee had upheld federal jurisdiction in *Russell* v. *The Queen* only on the assumption that the country was confronted by such an epidemic of intemperance as to constitute a national disaster.

The emergency doctrine, in the form in which Lord Haldane left it, is one that we can well do without. For events have shown that it was of little value in conferring necessary jurisdiction on Parliament except in wartime and in the short period necessary to wind up wartime controls after the end of hostilities. From this difficulty we were extricated by the unexpected wisdom of Lord Simon who demonstrated, in the *Canada Temperance Federation Case,* that "emergency" is not just a rather frightening source of absolute federal power in wartime, but rather an aspect of things. Categories of the constitution are not absolutes which are mutually exclusive, as between the federal and provincial authorities. Each in its own way, and for its own purposes, may legislate about things which properly concern it. The facts have always been this way, but they have sometimes been neglected. For example, the courts early rejected the idea (in *Bank of Toronto* v. *Lambe*) that a province could not tax a bank just because it was a bank and therefore under federal jurisdiction.

In any event, the elaborate reasoning of the emergency doctrine may have been unnecessary since Parliament has exclusive power to legislate for defence, and it is obvious today that this is a concept that goes far beyond military arrangements for defence against an enemy. It is concerned with a very wide range of economic activity and, in these days of subversion on a massive scale, with internal order as well. It is noteworthy that the Essential Materials (Defence) Act (1950-51) was founded on a broad view of the defence power, and so was its successor, the Defence Production Act of 1951. In the federal constitutions of Australia and the United States the defence power has turned out to be the most powerful centripetal force in the constitution.[7]

One of the most striking developments of the past quarter of a century has been the decline in the role of the courts as arbiters of the balance of the federal constitution. "The courts are retiring, or being retired, from their posts as the supervisors of the balance," as Principal Corry notes in a perceptive analysis of modern Canadian federalism.[8] He attributes this change to an alteration in the interests and attitude of the business élites. The central role of the courts in the half-century before was brought about, as I have argued elsewhere,[9] by the persistent resistance of the business community to regulation by the state. Great aggregations of economic power have a strong vested interest in stability; they have come to accept the primacy of the federal government in regulating their affairs, and they find it better to exert influence at the summit of the political system rather than to fight every extension of state power in the courts. Since they cannot beat the welfare state, they have decided to join it.

CO-OPERATIVE FEDERALISM

At the same time there has been, as a result of a spectacular refinement of the techniques of economic and fiscal policy since the war, a quiet revolution in the structure of Canadian federalism. A whole new set of institutional arrangements has grown up under the name of "co-operative federalism." In spite of the separate and co-ordinate division between the authority of the provinces and the central government enunciated in the law of the constitution, the demands of modern government and the immense financial resources of the central authority have forced an incestuous relationship in which administrative co-operation has become an effective device for control and initiative from the centre. This system is the only effective answer to the size and complexity of modern economic institutions and everyone now has such a strong vested interest in this system that no one, Dr. Corry argues, can afford to rock the boat.

The essence of co-operative federalism in Canada is this: while the central and regional legislatures nominally retain their separate jurisdictions over different aspects of the same subject, there is close contact and discussion between ministers and civil servants of both levels of government so that even changes in legislation are the result of joint decisions. Since 1945, says Professor Smiley, the most obvious characteristic of Canadian federalism has been "a process of continuous and piecemeal adjustment between the two levels of government, which is still going on. To an overwhelming degree, these adjustments have come about through interaction between federal and provincial executives."[10] There are three principal areas of co-ordination. The first is through continuous consultation of officials on joint programs. In these consultations there appears to be a surprising degree of harmony, partly, no doubt, because there is a broad consensus among the economists about the goals of economic policy and partly because all officials are inclined to see problems in a practical and pragmatic way. The second area of co-operation is through the delegation by Parliament of regulatory functions to provincial agencies, a technique which gets around the bar against delegation of legislative authority from one level of government to another. The third "device of flexibility" is through federal spending on matters which fall within provincial and/or municipal jurisdiction.

The advantages of these arrangements are apparent. The "artificial" division of powers in the constitution, conceived before the dawn of the welfare state, can be ignored in achieving progress and uniformity comparable to that normally realizable only in a unitary state. The high administrative skills and deeper purse of the federal government result in better schemes. Finally, the obstruction to geographical mobility imposed by tying the citizen—like a medieval serf—to the area of land from which his pension, his hospitalization, and his other welfare benefits come, is removed.

The benefits of co-operative federalism are not achieved without serious costs. The joint-cost schemes involved the federal government in very heavy fixed commitments, though, since the Dominion-Provincial Conference at Quebec in April 1964, discussions have begun for ultimate federal withdrawal from some of them. A further disadvantage is that the financial and constitutional context of the arrangements has made it impossible to take into account differing provincial fiscal capacity so that, while rich provinces can participate readily, the poorer provinces must divert a substantial share of their resources to providing their share of the cost. Lastly, the main drift of these programs has been in the direction of health and welfare services.

The result has been seriously to limit provincial autonomy. Provincial priorities are distorted by the inability of a province to forego, for political reasons, a program which may inhibit financing its other obligations. The result has been to starve areas of provincial jurisdiction in which the federal government is not, for various reasons, interested. While a vast amount of time is spent in intergovernmental consultation, it nevertheless remains true that provinces find long-term budgeting virtually impossible, because they cannot foresee where the lightning of federal generosity will strike next.

A reaction against these cosy arrangements is now in train. Significantly it is led by Quebec, but Quebec is not alone in seeking to reverse the trend to centralize all economic and social policy in Ottawa. It is not improbable that the practical advantages of centralization, which English-speaking Canadians would probably accept, would have led—as it had done in the United States and Australia—to the growing obsolescence of federalism. But Canada is not the same kind of federal state as the United States or Australia, where the growing homogeneity of the population is likely to lead inevitably to national integration. The difference is what is now usually described as the French-Canadian fact.

DOUBLE-IMAGE FEDERALISM

The survival of French Canada as a fact has depended more on a sustaining national myth and on political power than it has on constitutional guarantees. For the Canadian constitution does not, except to a very limited extent, support the claims which French Canadians regard as necessary to their survival as a distinct group. In the matter of their rights in the Manitoba school question, or in their claim to retain French as a language of instruction in Ontario separate schools, they were either over-ridden by an unsympathetic majority or told by the courts that minority educational rights in the constitution were essentially questions of religion and not of language.

Indeed, one of the most striking things about French-Canadian rights and aspirations in the constitution is that the courts have played little or no role in protecting them. This is one of the striking differences between the American and Canadian constitutions. Where the American constitution extends its guarantees across the whole range of the social order, so that it is the Supreme Court which is presiding over the orderly assimilation of Negroes to full equality as citizens, the Canadian constitution provides no such protection. It confines itself essentially to the distribution of power between two levels of sovereign legislatures, and has little to say on any other rights than the rights of legislatures. In this respect it is indeed a constitution "similar in Principle to that of the United Kingdom." As de Tocqueville said of the British constitution, "elle n'existe point."

It is for this eminently practical reason that French Canadians have adopted as a national strategy the building up and guarding of the security of their fortress-province. The constitution has made such a strategy unavoidable, and the only possible defence against the aggressive nationalism of the dominant English-speaking majority. For even the most liberal of English-Canadians have seldom accepted the "French fact" as more than a transitory source of trouble and discomfort.

There has been among English-speaking Canadians an element of deep-seated Protestant suspicion of the Roman Catholic Church, a feeling that the French tongue is an anomaly in an English-speaking continent, a feeling that the French are both backward and reactionary and therefore an enemy to the forces of progress, and a touch of the North American radical belief that a good state could be built in the New World only by destroying the cultural roots of "foreigners" who must be assimilated in order to build a new Canada.

Against this persistent pressure the French-Canadian reaction was to husband their political strength, to limit as far as possible the impact of the twentieth century on the *habitant* whose backwardness and ignorance—it was thought—would be a solid political barrier against the secular and integrating forces of urban industrial society. Thus Duplessis pursued a policy of immobilism, staying aloof from federally sponsored welfare programs, leaving the educational system in a state of inanation on the grounds that it was bound to develop the kind of social leadership which would destroy him, and harrying those organizations, such as the trade unions, that seemed to be enemies of the traditional centres of community authority.

And yet in the end he could not stem the tide. At his death an irreversible political change began. The most striking change is the alteration in the pattern of power relations in the French-Canadian community. New élite groups of managers and technicians are challenging the traditional leaders. The intellectual of an earlier generation could accept the romantic myth of the mystical virtue of subsistence agriculture as the source of the political and moral strength of French Canada. The intellectual of today has no patience with a dream of bucolic *survivance*. The French-Canadian community has developed a new set of expectations from government, and looks to the power of the state to satisfy their new wants and to bring the economic development which will enlarge opportunities for all. For them, these things must be done by their own French-Canadian state of Quebec, and not by Ottawa. For this there are two reasons: the new élites wish to share in the management of the new society, and—as they say—Quebec has much ground to make up in order to pull level with the rest of Canada.

It is these new forces which have created the latest crisis in Canadian federalism. The growing centralization of the past fifty years created no great problems in Quebec as long as the province was seeking to contract out of the twentieth century. But with the French-Canadian community determined to use to the full the resources of the provincial government to achieve a national revival a whole range of problems has emerged in Canadian federalism which will require substantial readjustments in the system. The mechanics of this readjustment will not be easy, and the issues at stake are very large indeed.

The federal government must not lightly weaken its fiscal and monetary powers, for it alone has the capacity and the constitutional right to deal with problems of major economic policy—foreign trade, stability, economic growth. It alone can prevent us becoming, as Mr. Pearson said, "a country of developed and underdeveloped areas—Cadillac areas and cart areas."[11] So it must confront the provinces by clear-headed and hard-headed negotiations, but with a sympathetic and imaginative grasp of the difficulties which confront them. This is, in the last analysis, not a political problem at all, but one that can be solved by the ingenuity and sophistication of the economists.

There must be, at the same time, some recognition that Quebec is not a province like the others. Section 94 of the BNA Act already does so by providing for uniformity of laws relating to property and civil rights in all provinces except Quebec—a tacit recognition that the different needs of Quebec must in any event be accomplished within a conceptually different legal system. This is the contracting-out formula in reverse and should give some comfort to those who regard any special treatment of Quebec as both immoral and unconstitutional. For Quebec must always rate somewhat special treatment from the facts of countervailing power.

However, one of the lessons of constitutional government in its federal form is that the protection of interests by political means is a source of instability and uneasiness. The atmosphere is better if these basic interests become constitutional rights, so that conflicts about them become justiciable. It is difficult in these days not to admire the broad sweep of the American constitution which extends its protection not only to states but also to people. We should consider seriously a similar extension of our own constitution to include rights—including individual rights—to language and within reason to access to the courts and other community services in one's mother tongue whether it be French or English.

This will perhaps require a reconsideration of our present judicial structure to ensure adequate machinery for a constitution which protects not only the rights of government organs but also the rights of individuals and of minorities. It may be that a constitutional court, more fully representative than the present Supreme Court, should be created. A good case on practical grounds can also be made for limiting appeals in civil law questions, unless they raise important questions of public and constitutional law, from the courts of Quebec. Common lawyers cannot get their minds around the concepts of the civil law and, since the function of a court of appeal is to clarify the law, it seems obvious that where possible civil law should be dealt with by civilians.[12]

There is a major danger in the present situation, which is the calculated risk inherent in the public discussion of anything. French Canadians, excluded for so long from the power élite except at the price of becoming wholly English-speaking and operating in a wholly English-speaking environment, tend to attach enormous importance to symbols. The extent to which the debate about the refusal of Trans-Canada Air Lines [Air Canada] to adopt the Caravelle dominated Quebec politics, is a case in point. It is perhaps not surprising that Hon. René Lévesque got into the act, but he was not alone. Just as ministers of the Crown and newspaper editors adopt extreme positions about status symbols, those outside the fringes of power will show their frustration by reacting more violently.

Meanwhile, as they read in their newspapers of the latest outrageous speech or act from Quebec, English-speaking Canadians will become increasingly impatient and will in turn say things which moderate men will later regret. And as a consequence the fund of goodwill towards French Canada, founded on lack of interest and ignorance, will slowly be dissipated and the climate for negotiation slowly congeal. There is a too easy assumption about that which is needed to solve outstanding misunderstandings is a "dialogue." These exchanges are not a dialogue. Dialogue there must be. But first there should be some agreement on the subject matter.

It needs to be said that the crisis is real. One cannot turn one's back on two centuries of history. French Canadians have survived as a distinctive group by a series of overt and tacit acts. Canada is in fact a country based on the co-existence of these two cultures, and is the better for it. There has been a delayed revolution within the social structure of French Canada, and this social revolution has political implications. There will have to be some readjustment of the machinery of the constitution. We may even have to modify some of our out-of-date symbolism because symbolic gestures are important as an earnest sign of good faith. Just because the position of French Canada within confederation has never been clearly defined it is bound to be a source of unease in a group which is a permanent minority. There has been a comfortable and, on the whole, mutually satisfactory liaison between French and English for all these years, and we should not complain too much if one partner would now prefer more formal marriage lines.

Federalism, of all the forms of government, is the most difficult to work. The fact that we have been able to work it at all for nearly a century should be a matter of pride, and sustain our belief that it will continue to work. The fact that the Canadian federal system has materialized in so many forms is proof of its essential vitality, but the survival of any system depends on a consensus that it is worthwhile and worth paying for.

NOTES

[1] An excellent discussion of the theme that the relationship was essentially colonial is found in V. C. Fowke's *Canadian Agricultural Policy* (Toronto: University of Toronto Press, 1947).

[2] K. C. Wheare, *Federal Government*, 3rd Ed. (London: Oxford University Press, 1953), pp. 19-21.

[3] Wheat, 316, at p. 407 (1819).

[4] This has often been argued, but never more persuasively than by Alexander Smith in *The Commerce Power in Canada and the United States* (Toronto: Butterworth, 1963) where by reference to early cases he shows the Canadian courts appealing to history and experience in a way which would horrify "black-letter" lawyers.

[5] Thus Sir John A. Macdonald said, "The primary error at the formation of their constitution was that each state reserved to itself all sovereign rights, save the small portion delegated. We must reverse this process by strengthening the General Government and conferring on the Provincial bodies only such powers as may be required for local purposes." Sir Joseph Pope, ed., *Confederation Documents* (Toronto: Carswell, 1895) p. 14, n. 4.

[6] Cf. J. R. Mallory, *Social Credit and the Federal Power in Canada* (Toronto: University of Toronto Press, 1954), *passim*.

[7] Cf. Bora Laskin, *Canadian Constitutional Law*, 2nd ed. (Toronto: Carswell, 1960), pp. 242-43.

[8] J. A. Corry, "Constitutional Trends and Federalism," in Paul Fox (ed.), *Politics: Canada* (Toronto: McGraw-Hill, 1963), p. 36.

[9] Mallory, *op. cit.*

[10] D. V. Smiley, "The Rowell-Sirois Report, Provincial Autonomy, and Post-War Federalism", *Canadian Journal of Economics and Political Science*, Vol. XXVIII no. 1, (1968) p. 54.

[11] Canada, *House of Commons Debates* (unrevised) April 14, 1964, p. 2142.

[12] Anyone who doubts this should contemplate the effect of a century of House of Lords decisions on modern Scots law. Whatever the gains in apparent uniformity with English law they were more than offset by a blurring of concepts and a misunderstanding of the system.

3

A Different Perspective on Canadian Federalism*

Edwin R. Black
Alan C. Cairns

Traditional interpretations of Canadian federalism have stressed constitutionalism, legalism, the powerful influence of economic factors, and
the impact of distinctive geographic and ethnic communities. These interpretations are clearly inadequate. The constitutional approach, with
its structural emphasis, fails to explain political behaviour. While closer
to real life, the conventional economic wisdom has been too obsessed
with the centralist assumptions implicit in attempts to enlarge Ottawa's
historic role in managing the economy. Regional aspects of the traditional interpretations seem to be viewed either as self-evident facts
whose continued existence requires no further explanation or as inconvenient impediments to national unity which really ought to go away. It
seems essential, therefore, to investigate neglected elements of regionalism in order to explain contemporary developments. The deficiencies
thus far suggested have been compounded by two divergent ethnic traditions of scholarship. While English-speaking scholars stressed the
challenges of nation-building across vast distances, their French-speaking colleagues concentrated on problems associated with "la survivance".

The construction of more adequate explanations requires a fresh
perspective which recognizes these salient characteristics of the Canadian polity:

1. Almost regardless of the impact of the "French fact" on the state as a
   whole the maintenance of a federal form of government is required
   by the diversities of the English-speaking communities.
2. Since 1867 Canadians have been engaged in more than the construction of a new state; they have been building provinces and complex
   series of relationships between governments and societies as well.
3. Economic and social factors respond to political forces just as political
   forces respond to them.
4. The survival of a federal system depends upon the flexibility of its

* From *Canadian Public Administration*, Vol. IX no. 1 (March, 1966), pp. 27-45. This paper
was prepared initially for one of a series of radio lectures and for publication in Louis
Sabourin (ed.), *Le Système Politique du Canada: Institutions fédérales et québécoises* (Ottawa,
University of Ottawa Press, 1968). Reprinted by permission.

constitutional process in accommodating demands unforeseen at its birth.

A general preoccupation with discovering forces tending to create an impressive nation-state led many to ignore the creation and effects of social, political, and physical communication networks within the provinces, the growth of regional economies with international as well as national ties, and the burgeoning provincial bureaucratic and other elites which confidently manage state systems bigger in scope, competence, and importance than some foreign sovereignties. It is suggested that adding these perspectives to the more usual approaches will provide better explanations of Canadian politics than those to which we have been accustomed.

Federal systems are characterized by a division of lawmaking and administrative authority between a central government and several regional governments. Each type of government controls some significant aspects of public activity and is supreme within its own jurisdictional sphere. The difficulty of distinguishing boundary lines between governments has customarily required court arbitration the results of which were bound to displease at least one party and its supporters. For much of the past century the Judicial Committee of the British Privy Council had ultimate authority to determine the precise meaning of the powers distributed by the British North America Act. Thus arose the popular Canadian sport of lambasting British jurists who were usually accused of misinterpreting the clear meaning of sections 91 and 92, and particularly the relationship between the peace, order, and good government clause and the enumerated subjects following it. In essence, the British law lords were being asked to settle political questions arising from a changing, pluralist society whose governments were federally organized by a legal document. Much of the legal writing on Canadian federalism seems, however, to demand interpretation of the constitution according to technicalities encrusting the legal framework within and around which the actual system operates.

"Legal answers," Professor Livingston reminds us, "are of value only in the solution of legal problems. And federalism is concerned with many other problems than those of a legal nature."[1] Federalism is translated into governmental forms when a particular constellation of forces leads men to create institutions permitting diverse territorial groups to express themselves politically and to resist incorporation into the homogenizing framework of a unitary state. Logically, then, it is more important to analyse the federal nature of society than to analyse the legal framework it uses to achieve its diverse public goals.

The value of a socio-political approach is emphasized by the experience of Confederation's first three decades. John A. Macdonald and his colleagues had provided the federation with a highly centralized framework. That the new state was a most reluctant federation is shown by the division of functions and revenues and by the superior-inferior legal relationships contemplated between the central and the provincial governments. The concessions made to the pressures of geography, ethnic identities, and previous histories were restricted to as few as possible while the political institutions of the central government took on a strong majoritarian bias. In reflecting the principle of representation by population, the House of Commons was, and is, a highly majoritarian body. The Senate's organization displayed greater fidelity to regional considerations, but its general power and, in particular, its ability effectively to articulate the interests of the provinces was seriously inhibited from the outset. The chief executive officer of the provincial governments was a central government appointee, and the federation's Supreme Court owed its creation in 1875 to the central Parliament. The majoritarianism and centralization built into the legal structure of Canada can scarcely be denied.

It is highly significant that even though Macdonald, its chief architect, presided over this structure for a quarter of a century, it still proved incapable of resisting provincial assertions of local independence. One satisfactory explanation for this development may be found within the context of a new federal regime lacking even as much legitimacy as the former colonies had enjoyed. Confederation was the accomplishment of a small group of elites who neither sought nor obtained popular support for the new undertaking; this aspect of its origins effectively denied the new central government that widespread feeling of patriotic sentiment which it required to struggle successfully with recalcitrant provinces. The Fathers had gambled that the new policy would win legitimacy by its performance, particularly in terms of economic growth and rising standards of living throughout the country. That gamble failed. Within a few years of the union celebrations, economic depression set in and lasted almost three decades; only with the opening up of the prairies and the resultant wheat boom did that prosperity arrive which had been hoped for thirty years earlier. An inevitable consequence of this initial absence of legitimacy was the central government's inability to withstand strong pressures for enlarged areas of provincial self-assertion. From the '80's on, constitutional decisions began to favour the provinces, thus confirming the underlying realities of Canadian society. By 1896, when Laurier assumed office, the political system was established as thoroughly federal in nature—whatever might have been the intentions of the Fathers and their legal draughtsmen.

The course of Canadian federalism has displayed cyclical swings from centralization to decentralization and back again. One should beware, however, of equating centralizing periods with times of social integration. Centralization has been primarily a product of emergencies such as the years of birth, of war, and of depression when the very survival of the country was thought to be at stake. During the two world wars, Canada was largely run as a unitary state with the provinces subordinating their separate claims for a temporary period. But even war did not provide a completely effective solvent of internal differences. While English-speaking Canadians generally answered Ottawa's demands for complete support in the face of external crises, French Canadians were more hesitant; with their much longer identification with North America and the consequent weakening of their ties with Europe, the French-speaking people saw little justification for the demands put upon them by the majority. Both wars were marked by conscription crises which deepened the cleavages between the two main racial groups. The First World War decimated Conservative support in Quebec, with damaging effects on the party system as a whole, while the Second World War was skilfully exploited by Duplessis, whose reactionary regime helped isolate Quebec from the rest of Canada. If the war periods brought the English communities closer together, they did so at the expense of seriously weakening French Canadians' identification with the federal government. The unifying effects of the depression of the 1930's have also been miscalculated. While intellectuals of English expression were fond of arguing that the fluctuations of modern industrialism made federalism obsolete, federal governments at Ottawa were characterized by timid leaderships in considerable contrast to the demagogues elected to power in Quebec, Ontario, and Alberta who were volubly hostile to any accretion of power by the central administration. Thus, even when the facts of social crises seemed to indicate an imperative need for centralized political direction, Canadians have shown little disposition to scrap their regional political systems.

On the whole, Canadian experience gives little credence to the belief that federalism is a transitional stage on the road to a unitary state. While federalism has changed significantly in response to new demands, its basic features of two levels of government each wielding important powers seems to be durable. Indeed, at the present time, the question is not whether provincial governments can withstand centripetal pressures which would diminish their significance, but whether the federal system can successfully contain the powerful recentralizing pressure welling up from below without losing its essential character.

To survive and to thrive politically, a federation must be flexible enough to adapt to radical changes in circumstances over time. The presence of permissive political styles and of effective techniques for making short-run experimental adjustments in areas such as federal-provincial relations is especially helpful. But federations are dependent in their structures on legal distributions of authority, and constitutional adaptation is generally thought to require legal rather than political or customary procedures. Such legal procedures tend to be cumbersome, time-consuming, and rigid. During the '30's, structural changes were widely desired but neither of the major legal avenues of adaptation—formal amendment or judicial reinterpretation of the constitution—proved to be fruitful directions in which to seek desired reforms. The amending process was too difficult and too permanent, while the courts, dependent on the fortuitous arrival of appropriate cases, were much too unpredictable in their decisions. Lacking the expertise in assessing modern society with which political decision-makers are furnished, the courts exhibit great difficulty in giving shaded responses in complex problem areas, and in Canada they have been largely restricted to the black-and-white approach of ruling legislation either *intra vires* or *ultra vires*. In contrast with the American Supreme Court, which effectively kept the U.S. constitution abreast of societal shifts, the Canadian jurists were unwilling to consider political or sociological aspects of a case, and preferred to rule according to the technicalities of legal construction. The "constitutional impasse" referred to so frequently in the literature of the '30's reflects a despair of ever achieving structural changes in a federal system apparently tied to legal procedures. The courts specialized in delineating boundaries just at the time that public interest seemed to require blurring the boundaries. For these reasons, the courts and the formal amending process have been increasingly bypassed as mechanisms for resolving conflicts in the federal system.

All the more remarkable then, in the face of inadequate legal provisions for adaptation, is the occurrence of more important changes in Canadian federalism during the past quarter century than those of the preceding seventy years. The depression's revelations of the perils of an unregulated economy combined with the war years to foster an enhanced peacetime role for the state. Although the process is not completely clear, an increase in public economic control and much wider public provision of welfare services have been generally correlated in the western democracies with the type of dramatic speedup in industrialization and urbanization that Canada experienced during the 1940's. The exigencies of fighting the war had left the federal government to assume many of the normal provincial powers, but when the war ended Ottawa proved most reluctant to return these powers to the provinces. Immediately after 1945 federal politicians were seeking votes with fresh fervour, the electorate was demanding more extensive government services, egalitarian sentiments were growing, and the public was largely indifferent to constitutional niceties of federal-provincial dividing lines. No wonder, then, that postwar federal governments exploited their overall dominance in the taxation field in an effort to orient the federation more or less permanently in a centralist direction. Previous concern for provincial autonomy was probably reduced, and an enhanced rate for the federal government was legitimized by the ineffectiveness of provincial governments during the depression which stood in stark contrast with the federal government's much touted efficiency during the war years.

For the reconstruction period a series of highly centralist programs was drafted by senior civil servants at Ottawa. Presented as a package at the Reconstruction Conference, these policy proposals were vigorously rejected by provincial politicians, and the federal cabinet had to settle for achieving its objectives for postwar federalism on an *ad hoc* basis. Although the long-term direction of change was generally understood to be centralist, federal politicians were content to operate in the short run. They had, so they thought, developed a going concern. The anticipated postwar depression had not materialized. The country was prosperous. The prairie revolt of the '30's had subsided into agrarian reformism in Saskatchewan and conservative business administration in Alberta. Duplessis had amassed large electoral majorities in Quebec, but his antipathy to Ottawa was an irritant rather than a threat to the developing centralization. The Liberals at Ottawa seemed possessed of almost permanent tenure on the government side of the House of Commons, and to many observers the system seemed stable almost to the point of boredom. That these halcyon days are separated from the political excitement and uncertainty of the present by only ten years appears scarcely credible.

The federal structure had adjusted to the wartime crisis chiefly by monarchical *force majeure* with the emergency-powers legislation finding retroactive approval from the courts which evoked a defence-of-the-realm power said to be implicit in the constitution. Alternatives to the formal amending and judicial instruments of flexibility were found after the war in the new networks of bureaucratic and political collaboration which blurred jurisdictional lines between governments. A host of committees brought specialist civil servants together to develop and administer intergovernmental agreements and to discuss extensions of joint endeavours to solve problems outside any single jurisdiction. Periodic tax rental conferences provided a forum wherein federal and provincial ministers decided the allocation of the federation's total tax resources for the next five-year period. By these mechanisms[2] views were exchanged, tensions eased, and significant changes introduced into the federal system by short-term agreements capable of ready alteration should circumstances require it. In short, the practical workings of the federal system in the postwar decades came to be decided more and more by politicians and administrators who shared a common interest in making the system work rather than in determining its internal dividing lines. The result was an intertwining of the activities of ten (later eleven) governments through cooperative arrangements which made the British North America Act a less and less accurate guide for the determination of which government provided which service.

The many changes in the working constitution which developed in the post-war period are all the more remarkable when contrasted to the relatively slight impact on the system made by formal and visible changes to the founding document. The levelling of jurisdictional barriers resulted in a "fused federalism" characterized by involvement of the federal administration in virtually all of the provincial areas of "exclusive" jurisdiction: natural resources, social welfare, highway building, higher education, local government, and so on. The Sirois Commission had proclaimed earlier that the "mere importance of a service does not justify its assumption by the Dominion", but this opinion in no wise inhibited the federal government's diligence in discerning some kind of national interest in a great many provincial services in order to justify its intervention. The intervention was primarily accomplished through the mechanism of conditional grants. Close analysis of the conditional grants programs provides little compelling evidence that any consistent definition of the national interest was involved in their development.[3] On the contrary, they seem to have resulted from a series of complex bureaucratic and popular pressures and the desire of federal politicians to gain political capital by aiding popular causes directly. Most striking, however, of all the postwar changes was the virtual solution of the constitutional impasse of the '30's. The most important instruments in its solution besides conditional grants were the tax-rental agreements. These pacts while informal and legally unenforceable,[4] effected a massive shifting of provincial taxation powers to the federal government in return for huge transfer payments without strings attached. Both conditional and unconditional grants programs were accomplished by political agreements supported by a liberal use of the central government's spending power and did not require either constitutional reallocation of functions or formal transfer of fiscal rights from one level of government to another.

Critics of cooperative federalism in this period have seen it as largely a one-way street. While consultations did take place in some areas, the federal government launched conditional grant sorties into provincial fields quite often without even informing those provincial adminsitrations which were supposed to help finance the federal initiatives. The selective nature of federal financial inducements often distorted priorities which the provinces had set up for their own fields of constitutional authority, but there was no *quid pro quo*; the provinces whose policy-making autonomy was effectively diminished by Ottawa's manoeuvres were not compensated with any influence over the exclusive federal areas of policy-making. These tendencies led Professor J. A. Corry to observe in 1958 that the most a province could then hope for was "freedom for minor adventure, for embroidering its own particular patterns in harmony with the national design, for playing variant melodies within the general theme. . . . It is everywhere limited in the distance it can go by having become part of a larger, although not necessarily a better, scheme of things."[5] The determinants of this kind of federalism he located primarily in an interdependent economy requiring national regulation, the growth of large and powerful enterprises whose attention was focused on the federal government, and to a nationalizing of sentiment, especially among elites.

The pressures toward extension of federal government involvement came almost entirely from English Canada, a sign of potential trouble that was either unnoticed or ignored even when the federal prime minister was a French Canadian. "Pressures towards new federal initiatives are quite indiscriminate," Professor Smiley has observed, pointing out that English-speaking Canadians came to demand leadership and money from Ottawa for a great variety of matters they regarded as worthy national purposes. To this he adds:

> Anglo-Canadians have ordinarily not felt it necessary to demonstrate the administrative or other disabilities of exclusively provincial action or the constitutional appropriateness of their proposals; the case usually goes no further than a demonstration that the subject under discussion is of great importance and *ipso facto* Ottawa should do something about it.[6]

A number of English-speaking elite groups continued to behave as they had during the war—as if they lived in a unitary rather than a federal state. While their actions were influenced by lack of concern rather than any design to destroy federalism, the consequences were clear—a kind of centralization by indirection.

In 1955 Parliament was ramrodded by a cabinet that felt strong enough to seek the indefinite retention of over-riding powers almost the equal of those it had enjoyed during the war.[7] Today the pressures for decentralization have been so fired up by resurgent provincialism that many have questioned the very survival of the federal government as a decisive body. The factors lying behind this change are not easily deciphered because of its recency but some indication of the more important causes can be suggested. Popular commentators have been prone to attribute the change to the new Quebec, but such attribution is incomplete at best. French Canada has made a significant impact on the federalism of the '60's, but, even if Quebec had remained quiescent, it is likely that pressures for change emanating elsewhere in the system would have had an almost similar impact.

Relevant factors in the swing from centralization back to decentralization include:

1. A return to peace-time normalcy.
2. An important diminution in the legitimacy of the governing party at Ottawa, especially with respect to any proposed federal initiatives outside its constitutional sphere of jurisdiction.

3. A mid-century decline in the importance of the powers constitutionally assigned to Ottawa and a corresponding magnification in social importance of the provincial powers.
4. A relatively great increase in the competence and confidence of provincial administrations and a consequent growth in elites who identified their prospects with the fortunes and favours of the provincial governments.

The period of centralization from which the country is rapidly receding was in large part the aftermath of war, depression, and a degree of collectivism inspired by them. As the influence of these crises waned, so did the justification for federal political dominance. The provinces, in continually asserting their needs and rights to more tax money, have had the obvious justification that they and not Ottawa are constitutionally entrusted with authority over most of the expanding areas of government activity. In 1939, federal, provincial, and municipal governments shared almost equally in total government expenditures in Canada. Under wartime pressure the federal share rose to 87 per cent in 1944. By 1963 the federal share had dropped to 46 per cent, the provincial share had risen to 26 per cent, and the municipal was 28 per cent.[8] One recent analysis indicates that if there are no major changes in defence spending and no major reallocation of functions between governments, each level of government will be spending about one-third of the total by 1980—a return to the pre-war division.[9] Given provincial responsibility for municipalities, such a trend would put two-thirds of the total government expenditures in Canada under provincial jurisdiction.

Much of the federal government's current dominance in the taxation system has been justified by the size of defence expenditures and the need for Canada-wide economic stabilization and growth policies. But in recent years the use of fiscal policy to counter economic fluctuations appears to have declined in significance. The Conservative government's willingness to let the tax rental system expire in 1962 was a major indication of this change. Professor Hood has observed:

> Anti-recessionary fiscal policy is now less capable of providing support for monetary policy than at any time since the war. This feeling derives essentially from the fact that the provinces have so strategic a role in both tax and expenditure policy by virtue of the relative weights of their budgets and from the fact that much of the initiative for changes rests with them.[10]

Canadian defence expenditures are also declining dramatically from their peaks of ten and twenty years ago, and in this connection it might be suggested that defence expenditures today are unlikely to lead to the same degree of voter support for the federal government as equivalent expenditures on education, roads, and even sewers elicit for provincial and local governments.

The federal government's ability to offer uncompromising resistance to provincial pressures for decentralization has been seriously reduced. The capacity of the party system to contain the country's major centrifugal forces and to reconcile them was impaired by the social crises of war and depression, and it has never really recovered. The Diefenbaker revolution of 1957-58 was a climactic revelation of the traditional party system's failure to bring together and give effective expression to the new postwar mixture of disparate social forces demanding recognition. While restructuring is obviously taking place, informed opinion is virtually unanimous that no federal party effectively incorporates the interest and allegiance of the new bureaucratic and political elite in power in Quebec. A by-product of these changes in the party system has been the failure of a legislative majority to emerge in the House of Commons to legitimate the work of the last two governments. The continued lack of majority support has clearly sapped the nerve of the once-confident Liberal Party leaders and diminished the authority which formerly supported federal cabinet ministers in their forays into provincial fields. The atmosphere of uncertainty engendered by this situation inevitably pervades the psychological context of federal-provincial relations. Since the beginning of the '60's, federal political leaders have been unable to radiate a meaningful sense of Canadian purposes with which their citizens could identify. In decided contrast to this central government weakness has been the decisive leadership of the provincial premiers. Most provincial ministries are faced with ineffectual oppositions, and many have enjoyed exceptionally long tenure. While some of it can be described only impressionistically, the combination of federal weakness and provincial strength has undoubtedly strengthened the hands of the provinces in their negotiations with Ottawa.

One's assessments of the Canadian state as a whole should not be too much influenced by the preceding judgments about the relative weakness of governments at Ottawa in the '60's. For nearly a century Canadians have undergone the common experience of living together within the same political community, and in the process something of a common identity and habit of cooperation has emerged. The populace is bound together by numerous country-wide institutional arrangements, both formal and informal, in government, politics, economics, and socio-cultural matters. The importance of the political system as a whole in determining the life opportunities of Canadians from coast to coast and in providing the framework of law and regulation within which men work, struggle, and live has helped to create an identity which, if it be not strongly based on emotion, finds its roots in a curious combination of rational interest and customary self-identification. Rising standards of living and improved communications have widened the range of contact for many Canadians far beyond that of a century ago. Less and less people live out their lives within the confines of a single community or province; as their experience of other districts and other people expands, so do the standards change by which they assess the performance of particular political systems.

The process of state-building has given rise to a concept of Canadianism which seeks to minimize the disabilities which attend the accidental location of birthplace. This concept, which is a particular expression of egalitarianism, has facilitated satisfaction of some of the poorer provinces' claims, whether stimulated by a sense of historical injustice or by simple envy. Whatever the source of grievance, voters in the poor regions have been unwilling to accept the consequences of poverty in terms of public services. The interaction of inequalities in provincial revenue capacities with the widening frames of reference within which people judge their lot resulted in pressures for federal action to redress the perceived inequities. Funds were transferred from the wealthy to the less fortunate provinces with the federal administration performing the redistribution. Such recent attempts to reduce regional differences in public services, and consequently to minimize the price Canadians pay for their federal way of politics, are but modern manifestations of conventions and understandings which have been fashioned during the past century for promoting the welfare of the various provincial communities. That regional grievances are satisfied, at least partially, through the transfer of funds from the centre outwards rather than by the consolidation of functions at Ottawa reveals the persistent resistance to centralization. It is not for us to assess the degree to which that resistance is based on the hostility of provincial elites to any reduction in their roles, as distinguished from the tenacity of community identification.

The institutional protection of the provinces at the federal capital, originally a task of the politically enfeebled Senate, has been assumed by the cabinet whose members not only are responsible for their government departments but are spokesmen as well for the interests of their home provinces. Appointments to the Supreme Court, the Board of Broadcast Governors, the Board of Transport Commissioners, and numerous other central government institutions reflect to a greater or lesser extent the division of Canada into a number of regional societies and interests whose explicit recognition is essential to the legitimation of central government activities.

The distinctive regional interests and identifications underpinning the federal structure have long been thought to be temporary aberrations from the norm, and doomed to eventual disappearance. Many have agreed with Professor Alexander Brady who argued that the "socio-economic forces of modern industrialism tend to quicken the pace from federation to legislative union".[11] Professor Corry claimed that an independent economy with its nationally oriented big businesses would inexorably drive Canadian federalism in a centralist direction; American students like Karl Deutsch have argued similarly that regional emotional identifications become progressively weaker as transcending relationships are created by the forces of economic integration.[12] The thesis that federalism would disappear under the impact of modern economic development has been a popular one, but its application to Canada's experience encounters serious difficulties and must be reappraised.

The continuing power and influence of the provincial governments in Canadian federalism are intimately related to the importance of their considerable economic functions. The budgets of Ontario and Quebec together come close to equalling one-third of the federal budget, and the expenditures of all provincial governments exert a weighty influence on the country's economy as a whole. All but three of the provinces cover vast land areas whose lavish natural resources are exploited at the sole discretion of the provincial cabinets. The boom in most of the northern hinterlands is subject to their exclusive jurisdiction. Large numbers of frontier towns and communities are spread across Canada from Quebec westward, and their citizens are well aware that their immediate future is tied much more closely to the provincial capitals than to the federal. Such settlements have ever had their eyes focused on provincial legislatures because of their primary responsibility for most elementary and essential services—particularly those of local political organizations, health and sanitation, and communications (at first railways and now highways). The provincial orientation of frontier communities is given extra significance by the distribution of legislative representation which favours the rural districts to a greater extent in the provincial assemblies than in the House of Commons.

Even though the decline in the agricultural portion of the labour force is ironing out some of the differences in the provincial economies, they remain dissimilar in several important aspects. Canada's generally heavy dependence on foreign trade is reflected in the substantial connections which the regional economies have with international markets as well as with each other. The importance of these international links helps to explain the growing international role of the provincial governments, especially with regard to the expansion of their economies. Provincial missions to foreign capitals seeking trade, investment, and technical knowhow are becoming commonplace. Many of these regional enterprises are virtually independent of the country's finance capitals and are able to attract sizeable investment funds from abroad. The large funds which the Canada Pension Plan will make available to the provincial treasuries will augment even the smaller provinces' autonomy from the centre.

That socio-political structures need not be dictated by the alleged integrating effects of an evolving economic system seems to be quite clear. It is worthwhile noting the frontal assault being made on this primitive version of economic determinism in Quebec. From the French-

Canadian viewpoint, economic interdependence poses a serious challenge to a distinct culture and must therefore be countered by an even greater emphasis on the provincial government—the only one which French Canadians control. Political integration is not an inevitable consequence of urbanization, industrialization, and rising standards of living. The Canadian experience suggests that whatever integrating effect industrialism does exert is a function of the degree to which the internal economy is interlocking and approaches self-sufficiency. The Canadian economy falls far short of optimum conditions in this respect.

The disparate regional economies are complemented by the existence of distinguishable socio-political communities at the provincial level. The Canadian population is dispersed widely, and the provincial boundaries are still geographically meaningful except on the prairies. Despite improved communications, the country's great distances still require bureaucratic and political decentralization and seriously inhibit the ready dissolution of parochial identifications. While the psychological fibres may be weak in some of these provincial societies, they are sustained not only by their relative geographic isolation from each other but by networks of economic, cultural, and political self-interest. Their identities are reinforced by a large number of institutions organized along provincial lines. Many of these, such as political parties and associations of school teachers and school trustees, can be explained by the need of influencing the provincial political institutions. There are, however, many other organizations with few if any obviously public functions which organize within the same limits: churches, fraternal groups, ethnic associations, model railroaders, and other hobby and handicraft groups. There seems to be no obviously political need for organizing the Junior Red Cross League and the United Nations Associations along provincial lines, but that those associations are so structured is witness to the perceived naturalness of provincial boundaries for such purposes.

What this reveals is that since 1867 Canadians have been engaged not only in state-building but in province-building as well. The existence of separate provincial governments automatically elicits a more intense pattern of communications and associational activity within provincial boundaries than across them. Mechanisms set in motion by the creation of political institutions permit provinces such as Saskatchewan and Alberta which possessed little sociological legitimacy at their birth to acquire it with the passage of time and creation of a unique provincial history.

Probably the most important aspect of province-building concerns the growth of influential provincial elites in politics, administration, and resource-based industries. Recent writings on federalism have often remarked on the nationalization of elites as a factor in attenuating provincialism. Such nationalization is based on the high degree of geographical mobility of elites and the tendency of professionals to identify with their counterparts across the country. They belong to national organizations, read the same journals and attend frequent conferences tending to build up horizontal ties of loyalty. They belong to sub-cultures based on particular skill endowments and seem to have no geographical reference points. While these are important factors, they can be over-emphasized, for it is certain that not all elite groups possess an undiluted national orientation; in fact, elite groups exist which furnish potent incentives and supports for the expansion of provincial power against that of the federal government.

Members of the political elites, and particularly those involved in minor parties with only remote hopes of success in the federal field, may well see the province as the main arena for the pursuit of power. Capable people who are not at all interested in the preoccupations of federal policy-makers are often attracted by the type of activities in which provincial governments engage. The attractiveness of provincial politics for the public-spirited may be enhanced by statistical factors as well. Although the financial rewards are slighter and the duties less demanding the provincial legislatures make available more than twice the number of seats to be found in the House of Commons, and the chances of an able man winning a post in the provincial cabinet are infinitely better than they are at Ottawa.

For many of the new professional groups and some of the old engaged in public service the provincial administrations are almost the only source of employment. Professional educators, forest biologists, electrical power generation specialists, highway engineers, public safety inspectors and scientists, social workers, and large numbers of skilled program administrators find their lives intimately bound up with the size and prosperity of provincial governments. Professor Guindon's provocative interpretation of the new Quebec in terms of a bureaucratic revolution[13] seems especially to the point here. He indicates that the chief sources of dissatisfaction with confederation are found among intellectuals who, in French Canada, provide the legitimating ideas for political movements and among members of the postwar middle class located in the bureaucratic organizations that evolved to meet the problem of mass migration from country to city. In French Canada the bureaucrats are found overwhelmingly in the public and semi-public sectors, and their personal progress and prosperity have depended upon a rapid expansion in the scope and tempo of provincial government activity. Their demands for greatly expanded public support of their activities helped bring on a political crisis in federal-provincial relations that still exists.

The marked improvement in the competence and confidence of the public bureaucracies in almost every province has been a factor of peculiar influence in the course of federal-provincial relations during the past ten years. Civil service reforms, the elimination of patronage, entrance by competition, and security of tenure were introduced first at the federal level but began to spread at a slow pace to the provincial governments. Today the process is almost complete and it is no longer safe to assume that administrative competence resides only in federal hands. In many cases of public activity the real expertise is found only at the provincial level. In the fields of education, natural resource administration, municipal affairs, roads, law enforcement, and local economic promotion, the provincial civil servants will be found to be more numerous and generally more competent than the federal.

The improved quality of their civil services helps to invalidate the assumption, present at confederation and not yet dead, that the provinces should be entrusted with functions of only secondary importance. The traditional English-Canadian view of the federation as a pyramid of hierarchy becomes anachronistic with the location of superior administrative talent within the provincial rather than the federal functional departments. This redistribution of administrative competence has removed much of the paternalism from federal-provincial relations in specific areas, and we can expect provincial administrators and their political superiors to become even less likely to accept federal leadership as they grow more aware of their own capacities.

New political orientations within provincial cabinets are combining with this growing administrative competence to revolutionize the management of regional economic resources. During the 1950's it seems clear that provincial cabinets formulated their budgets with inadequate views of the future and were seldom prepared to make hard choices allocating different priorities to different services. That picture has changed. More and more cabinets plan their public policies within a broad context of long-range projections and expectations of economic development. Every example of *ad hoc* federal intervention in provincial fields becomes more difficult to tolerate because of the disruption in provincial planning; federal-provincial cooperation, requiring as it now does the fitting together of many governments' plans and expectations, grows more difficult to achieve. Saskatchewan's premier was the first to complain of such federal government disruptions, while the Quebec government, to take another case, has opposed conditional grants programs not only on principled grounds but because it wishes to establish its own policy priorities within a coherent development program free of any environmental disturbances caused by federal activity.

The Quebec government's official demands for a general withdrawal of the federal programs in provincial areas and for radical increases in the province's effective fiscal capacity are clearly of major importance for the federal system. Within four or five years the Lesage government demanded and secured more changes in federal-provincial relations than Premier Duplessis had brought about in twenty years. Quebec's silent revolution of the '60's involved a major political breakthrough by a new and influential class which Duplessis had treated with indifference despite its special degree of concern for the consequences of government decisions. The Lesage electoral victory permitted a virtual seizure of power by these once-scorned bureaucrats of the middle class, and a dramatic change in public attitudes toward the role of the state was set in motion.

Under the old regime there had been a widespread distrust of the state. Both Taschereau and Duplessis were hostile to what they regarded as paternalism, while French-Canadian Catholic thought displayed a general preference for private rather than public action to ameliorate social conditions. In any case, the grossly inadequate provincial administration could not possibly have played any role other than the negative one. Bureaucracy, in Weber's sense, simply did not exist, for neither Taschereau nor Duplessis appears to have tried to separate governmental from private affairs. The corruption, nepotism, and incompetence of the provincial government suffered neither electoral disapproval nor moral stigma except in a few relatively ignored journals of opinion.

By contrast, the present government gives state power a positive emphasis as the main collective instrument of modernization and as the main instrument for controlling an economy whose ownership and managerial positions are largely in "foreign" hands. Governmental power is now being used in Quebec with a vigour and élan which make most other provincial governments and the federal administration seem insipid by comparison. Since maximum exploitation of potential provincial powers requires expanded financial resources and the fullest possible arena for provincial legislative action, demands for more "tax room" and for federal withdrawal from provincial jurisdictions were both logical and inevitable.

Little general attention has been paid to province-building in Canada, or even to the related aspects of regional communication patterns, provincially oriented elites, and the development of overall planning approaches by a number of provincial cabinets. The natural desire of provincial elite groups to reduce planning uncertainties caused by outside interests such as the federal government contains implicit dangers of movements toward provincial autarchies. While speculation is hazardous, the possibility of accentuated economic regionalism must be scouted and guarded against if the federal system is to retain any significant control over its economic future.

While outside our immediate concerns, the recent emergence of the federal-provincial conference as an institution of unique influence in Ca-

nadian affairs must be noted. This institution must, in fact, be accounted
the only effective instrument available today for the authoritative resolution of some of the federation's most insistent political questions. Some
of the probable consequences of this development for the various
elected bodies can already be discerned. At the very least, it seems, even
further reductions may be expected in the effectiveness of Canadian parliaments as controllers of national and provincial policy-makers. What
more may come in connection can only be guessed at.

The capacity of political systems to maintain their legitimacy over a
long period of time is not easily addressed. As we have noted, the formal structure of Canadian federalism is reflected and reinforced in
scores of other associational patterns both public and private. Political
federalism is not the simple creature of existent, social, economic, and
geographical forces, but is itself a creative influence. Governments
within the system tend to create their own supports through a variety of
methods; among them are the charisma surrounding all distant authority, the identification of particular groups with the fortunes of particular
governments, the socializing of men to accept their political environment as the natural one, and the complex intertwining of modern government with society that endows any major proposal for change with
widespread and often unforeseen consequences for all parts of the structure. This reciprocal relationship between federalism and the society it
serves infuses both levels of government with durability and continuity
by sustaining the divided system of loyalties that a working federalism
requires. But the supports that governments build for themselves remain largely invisible. One level of government may appear to be much
the more soundly underpinned by public loyalty until, perhaps, some
dramatic event serves to thrust public sentiments for the "neglected"
government to the fore. Certainly there lay beneath the apparently
stable, centralized federalism of the postwar years a number of potent
factors leading to a divergence between the system's form and the demands being put upon it. As we have seen, these demands have overwhelmingly favoured a relaxation of central authority and an increase in
the provincial. So insistent has the pressure become that Canadian federalism is undergoing the greatest crisis since its inception.

Prediction of future developments is especially hazardous because
for the first time since the depression Canadians are discussing the basic
features of their federalism with passion and vigour. This renewed concern for fundamentals and its attempts to find guiding principles is one
of the most important manifestations of the changing climate. The
Laurendeau-Dunton Commission, the proposals for amending and delegation procedures, the swelling critique of conditional grants and the
consequent opting out provisions, the ending of tax rentals, and the frequent demands for a new constitution are all indicative of a revised con-

cern for the basic ground rules governing Canadian federalism. At the time of writing most of the basic issues appear to be open, but how long they will remain so is uncertain.

A new consensus on the purposes and structures of the Canadian state is clearly needed. The continued appropriateness of the federal form of government has been suggested by the analysis presented here. But if the state is to survive as a federation, it must embody a delicate balance between the forces of centralization and decentralization, a balance that obtains not only within the country as a whole but primarily from interregional disagreements about their relative importance. The centrifugal forces in Quebec and British Columbia cannot be offset by the centripetal forces in Ontario. That is a recipe for civil war.

To discuss Canada's federal system primarily in legal and economic terms is to misunderstand it from the beginning, and to discuss its problems in terms of ripping up the B.N.A. Act and beginning again from scratch is to hand over the decisions to the separatists both east and west. The present structure has exhibited a marvellous degree of flexibility, but if the assumption gains currency that this structure must be scrapped and a new constitution written in both form and substance, then the prospects will not be hopeful. Rewriting constitutional documents is neither a mere exercise in legal logic nor a simple process of transforming a few accounts from this side of the ledger to that. In rewriting such documents one embarks on the reshaping of the entire set of interdependent relationships between government and peoples which has evolved during a full century. If necessary, Canadians will undoubtedly undertake this complex task, but for them to attempt it lightheartedly and without a full understanding of the present system would be an act of political immaturity for which succeeding generations would long curse their ancestors.

NOTES

[1] W. S. Livingston, *Federalism and Constitutional Change* (Oxford, Clarendon Press, 1956), p. 1.

[2] J. H. Aitchison, "Interprovincial Cooperation in Canada", in J. H. Aitchison (ed.), *The Political Process in Canada* (Toronto, University of Toronto Press, 1963); a summary of federal-provincial taxation arrangements may be found in the Canadian Tax Foundation's *The National Finances, 1962-63*, Toronto, p. 117.

[3] D. V. Smiley, *Conditional Grants and Canadian Federalism*, Canadian Tax Paper no. 32 (Toronto, Canadian Tax Foundation, 1963).

[4] Bora Laskin, *Canadian Constitutional Law*, 2nd ed. (Toronto, Carswell, 1960), p. 659.

[5] J. A. Corry, "Constitutional Trends and Federalism", in A. R. M. Lower, F. R. Scott, *et al.*, *Evolving Canadian Federalism* (Durham, N. C., Duke University Press, 1958), p. 108.

[6] D. V. Smiley, "Two Themes of Canadian Federalism", *Canadian Journal of Economics and Political Science*, Vol. XXXI no. I (February, 1965), p. 86.

[7] For a discussion see John Meisel, *The Canadian General Election of 1957* (Toronto, University of Toronto Press, 1962), p. 7.

[8] Canadian Tax Foundation, *The Provincial Finances, 1965* (Toronto, 1965), p. 3.

[9] David Ivor, "General Expenditure Analysis", in Canadian Tax Foundation, *Report of Proceedings of the Fourteenth Annual Tax Conference* (Toronto, 1960), p. 103. For a similar analysis see Eric J. Hanson's discussion on municipal tax problems in the Canadian Tax Foundation's *Report of Proceedings of the Seventeenth Annual Tax Conference* (Toronto, 1963).

[10] William C. Hood, "Economic Policy in our Federal State", *Canadian Tax Journal,* Vol. XII no. 6 (November-December, 1964), p. 394.

[11] Alexander Brady, "Report of the Royal Commission on Dominion-Provincial Relations", *Canadian Historical Review* Vol. XXI no. 3 (September, 1940) p. 247.

[12] Karl Deutsch, *et al., Political Community and the North Atlantic Area* (Princeton, University Press, 1957), Chs. 2 and 3.

[13] Hubert Guindon, "Social Unrest, Social Class, and Quebec's Bureaucratic Revolution", *Queen's Quarterly,* Vol. LXXI no. 2 (Summer, 1964) pp. 150-62.

4

Public Opinion and Federal-Provincial Relations: A Case Study in Alberta*

David K. Elton

During 1968 and 1969, federal-provincial relations were brought directly into public view through the medium of open forum constitutional conferences. To the participants, the televising of the proceedings "underlined the importance of the discussions and facilitated public involvement in planning the future of our federal system."[1] While it was well and good for statesmen to speak of public involvement in federal-provincial negotiations and thereby justify the televising of the proceedings, the underlying assumption that the public at large is capable of, or wants to become involved in planning the future of our federal system needs to be examined.

The questions are legion, the responses few: of what import is federalism to the individual? Does it make any difference to the public that the division of powers in Canada allocates responsibility for education to the provincial government rather than the federal government? Would it make any difference to the citizens of a particular province whether or

---

* Reprinted by permission.

not their old age pensions or family allowance cheques came from the provincial government rather than Ottawa? Questions of this nature are often answered by the politician on behalf of the electorate, but unfortunately little empirical evidence is available concerning the understanding and attitudes of the electorate towards such problems.[2]

Various authors, who have taken it upon themselves to examine the effects and repercussions of Canada's federal system, have taken basically one of three positions: they have predicted the demise of Canada's federal system of government through an evolutionary process whose ultimate goal is a unitary form of government; they have predicted the demise of Canadian federalism through the balkanization of the country into its various regional entities; and/or they have predicted the maintenance of a federal constitutional form for Canada by extolling the virtues of this particular system of government and its ability to adapt to the forces of change within the Canadian polity. Each of these positions seems to be based upon certain assumptions concerning public opinion and federalism.

Those who predict the eventual demise of Canada's federal system and the creation of a unitary state feel that individual citizens are neither aware nor concerned about federalism. This position was taken by J. A. Corry some years ago when he suggested that "the truth is that the bulk of people are not really aware of what is at stake in federal-state issues."[3] More recently, a former advocate of federal systems, W. H. Riker, concluded his criticism of both the recent writings on the subject of federalism and the academics and lawyers who perpetuate the notion that federalism is a meaningful government structure by stating:

> . . . the ordinary citizen is quite indifferent to the idea of federalism. Indifference is a function I suspect of the realization that federalism is no more than a constitutional legal fiction which can be given whatever the content seems appropriate at the moment.[4]

During the 1960s another group of analysts in Quebec emerged who felt federalism was an outmoded form of government for Canada and that a balkanization of the country was necessary.[5] These individuals saw regional diversities as requiring a greater independence than that which a federal union affords. Unlike those who speak of the citizens' indifference towards formal government structures, proponents of this position feel that the residents of at least one of Canada's provinces, Quebec, are very jealous of the ability of their province to develop social and economic programs independent of the national government and as a result are not only hostile towards increasing federal power but would prefer to dissolve Confederation.[6]

Those who support the maintenance of Canadian federalism point out that regardless of the "French Fact," the diversities of the English-speaking communities demand regional political expression. Black and

Cairns base their argument upon the existence of developed regional, social, economic, and political loyalties.

> A general preoccupation with discovering forces tending to create an impressive nation-state led many to ignore the creation and effects of social, political, and physical communication networks within the provinces, the growth of regional economies with international as well as national ties, and the burgeoning provincial bureaucratic and other elites which confidently manage state systems bigger in scope, competence, and importance than some foreign sovereignties.[7]

The implications of this position are that Canada has both a social and structural federal system.

Another group of authors who support the argument that federalism is indeed a meaningful political structure, are those who find credence in the balance of power theory. These authors have argued that evidence of the meaningfulness of federalism is found in the alternate voting patterns of some Canadians which result in the election of regionally based parties at the provincial level, while at the same time electing a different party to power at the national level. This type of voting behaviour is taken as evidence of a "pragmatic perception of federal circumstances."[8]

To the political scientist, the constitutional lawyer, the politician, and leaders of groups who find their vested interests at stake, the level of government responsible for specific programs is of paramount importance as it affects their ability to study, influence, or participate in the decision-making process. That the opinions, attitudes, and evaluations of these élite groups and the population as a whole often differ significantly one from the other is often overlooked by the political activist.[9] One frequently finds leaders in politics, agriculture, business, and even academics, alluding to the desires of the populace as though they had the same understanding of the intricacies and/or appropriateness of specific government proposals and activities. This can and has, in the case of federal-provincial relations, resulted in contradictory statements being made by opposing sides, both of course alluding to the support of the masses.[10]

The contradictory nature of comments relating to public support or awareness of federalism suggests that there is a lack of empirical evidence upon which to base conclusions regarding this subject. This paper is an attempt to provide some empirical evidence upon which tentative conclusions can be drawn concerning public perceptions on federalism.

THE SURVEY AND ITS OBJECTIVES

During October and November of 1969 a survey of the Alberta electorate was undertaken. On the basis of a random probability sample, whose universe included approximately eighty percent of Alberta's eligible voters, 567 adults were interviewed.[11] During the course of this thirty-minute interview, questions dealing with the individual's concern, knowledge, and evaluation of federalism were asked. Specifically, the survey sought to answer the following questions pertaining to federal-provincial relations:

1. To what extent do Alberta residents understand the intricacies of the federal form of government (in particular the division of powers) under which he lives?
2. How important is it to Alberta citizens that a viable balance of power be maintained between the two levels of government?
3. How are the present activities of the federal and provincial governments evaluated?
4. Is there any relationship between perceptions of federalism and voting behaviour?

Awareness of Federalism

In order to measure public awareness of federalism it was necessary to define operationally the concept of federalism. While federalism entails much more than simply an understanding of the division of powers between provincial and national governments, it must be conceded that a basic knowledge of the division of powers is essential to the understanding of federalism. The Alberta study, therefore, set out to identify the citizens' level of awareness regarding the basic division of powers between their federal and provincial governments. Nineteen areas of government jurisdiction were examined and all respondents were asked to identify which government actually looked after the activity mentioned.[12]

As Table I indicates, there is little doubt in the minds of most Albertans as to which government is responsible for foreign affairs, banking, primary and secondary schools, city government, or family allowances, since nearly nine out of ten respondents correctly identified the government primarily responsible for these areas. Similarly, most respondents identified the government primarily responsible for old age pensions, people on welfare, Indians, hospitals and asylums, broadcasting, the building of roads, and unemployment insurance. In twelve of nineteen areas of jurisdiction nearly two out of three Albertans were aware of the government primarily responsible for the activity examined.[13]

In the six areas of government jurisdiction most often erroneously identified with a particular government, two important patterns emerge. First, the shared jurisdictions were correctly identified by fewer than one in three respondents. The response distribution in these three instances (income taxation, pollution control, and housing) suggests that few Albertans were aware of joint responsibilities in these matters

TABLE I

Knowledge of Government Jurisdiction:
Constitutional Division of Powers

Government Responsibilities	Percent correct answer		Percent most freq. wrong answer		Percent least freq. wrong answer		Number of respondents
	Percent	Gov't.	Percent	Gov't.	Percent	Gov't.	Number
Foreign affairs	95	fed	3	both	2	prov	554
Banking	93	fed	4	prov	3	both	564
Education	87	prov	8	fed	5	both	566
City government	86	prov	6	fed	6	both	555
Family Allowance	85	fed	10	prov	4	both	566
Inflation	84	fed	12	both	4	prov	561
Old Age Pensions	81	fed	13	both	5	prov	565
Indians	76	fed	13	both	11	prov	565
Hospitals/asylums	73	prov	14	both	13	fed	565
Broadcasting	70	fed	16	prov	14	both	564
Roads	67	prov	24	both	9	fed	566
Welfare	65	prov	18	both	17	fed	566
Unemployment Insurance	61	fed	31	prov	7	both	416
Property/civil rights	18	both	43	fed	39	prov	564
Medical Care	37	prov	40	fed	23	both	567
Income Tax	31	both	64	fed	5	prov	567
Natural Resources	29	prov	47	fed	24	both	566
Pollution	26	both	51	fed	22	prov	562
Housing	22	both	52	fed	26	prov	564

* The above percentages are calculated on the number of respondents who answered federal government, provincial government or both governments. The number of "don't know" responses to each question can be calculated by subtracting the number of respondents from 567 (e.g. in the case of foreign affairs thirteen people, or 2% of the sample indicated they did not have any idea which level of government was responsible for this activity).

even though both governments are not only actively involved in these areas, but also use extensive advertising programs to inform citizens about their involvement. A second tendency is the persistent overrating of the federal government's scope of responsibility. Although none of these areas of jurisdiction are the sole responsibility of the federal government, in all six cases the largest portion of the respondents felt that the federal government had jurisdictional responsibility. This finding suggests that the federal government's responsibilities are frequently exaggerated.[14]

In summary, although the electorate misperceived the jurisdictional responsibilities of the two governments in some instances, an overview of the findings presented in Table I indicates that most respondents were aware of the government primarily responsible for the areas of jurisdiction under consideration. When one takes into consideration the small number of responses that are clearly erroneous, given federal and provincial government activities and programs pertaining to the areas of jurisdiction examined, an even more convincing argument concerning the electorate's awareness can be made.[15]

A Conflicting Point of View

In 1968 a national survey research project was undertaken by the York University Institute of Behavioural Research which examined public knowledge of federal-provincial jurisdictions.[16] The study was initiated on behalf of the federal government's Task Force on government information, and a national sample of 6,800 Canadians fifteen years of age or older were interviewed by Canadian Facts Ltd. in November and December of 1968. The study asked respondents to identify seventeen areas of jurisdiction and, after analyzing the findings, concluded that "the general level of knowledge about government jurisdiction is quite low."[17]

Since the conclusion reached by the national study is contrary to the findings of this study, an analysis was made of the national study to determine specifically what differences existed between the two studies' data. Since the object of both studies was to examine the public's awareness of foreign affairs, people on welfare, primary and secondary education, unemployment insurance, and medicare, a comparison of the findings pertaining to these five jurisdictional areas was made. For comparative purposes, the Alberta portion (457 respondents) was extracted from the national sample and the responses categorized in the same manner that was followed in the Alberta electorate study. The results of this comparative data analysis indicated that the findings of the two studies were very similar.[18]

Why then do the two studies come to contradictory conclusions? The answer to this question lies primarily in the fact that the two studies focused upon basically different aspects of the division of powers even though several of the powers examined were identical.[19] The Alberta study was concerned with broad areas of jurisdiction which were considered to be of some importance to a cross section of the population and could be designated within the responsibility of either the provincial or federal government. The federal government information study, while choosing to examine some programs of broad application, focused primarily upon programs of limited scope and/or public exposure such as ARDA, and the retraining of unemployed persons, etc. In addition, the national study examined primarily areas of joint jurisdiction and, as has been noted earlier, people seem to be much less aware of joint or over-lapping jurisdictions.

An Evaluation of the Existing Division of Powers

Although the electorate is knowledgeable (by and large) about which level of government actually looks after broad areas of jurisdiction, their evaluation regarding which government should look after these same specific matters varies significantly from the *status quo* (see Table II). While there is relative unanimity regarding jurisdictional preferences dealing with foreign affairs (eighty-eight percent), banking (eighty-nine percent), and city government (eighty-one percent), there is a consider-able number of people who disagree as to which level of government should provide the remaining "necessary" services. Perhaps the most surprising evaluation is that of education, since only fifty-six percent felt that primary and secondary education should be looked after solely by the provincial government. A consensus as to who should administer family allowances and old age pensions is also lacking.

TABLE II
Jurisdictional Responsibilities Preferred*

Government Responsibilities	Federal Gov't. Percent	Provincial Gov't. Percent	Both Gov't. Percent	Doesn't Matter Percent
Foreign Affairs	88	3	6	2
Banking and Paper Money	89	4	5	1
Inflation	69	9	18	2
Old Age Pensions	68	18	9	5
Family Allowance	58	22	6	12
Indians	49	24	24	2
Broadcasting (radio/tv)	46	23	15	15
Unemployment Insurance	40	44	11	4
City Government	6	81	7	3
Hospitals and asylums	22	59	16	2
Building Roads	8	59	31	1
Primary and secondary educ.	25	56	17	2
Medical Care	25	55	16	3
People on Welfare	20	54	24	2
Property and Civil Rights	33	38	26	3
Natural Resources	33	37	28	1
Income Taxation	60	17	19	4
Housing	27	40	30	1
Air & Water Pollution	41	20	36	2

* In each case 567 respondents responded

While it has been suggested that it may be only myths that support the fragmentation of the political system, given the data in Table III, there seems to be little support for this somewhat pessimistic view of Canadian federalism. In evaluating government activities at least eighty-five percent of the respondents indicate a preference. Admittedly there will be disagreements as to which level of government should perform specific services. The citizen with a young family who has moved two or three times within Canada (e.g. Ontario to Alberta, Alberta to British Columbia), and has experienced their children's frustration in adapting to three separate educational programs may very well question whether education should be under provincial or federal control. On the other hand, those parents who have been actively involved in the development of education within a province may prefer local control of education. Whatever the motivational forces behind the citizen's preference for federal or provincial jurisdiction, the data indicate that relatively few respondents opt for joint government control or feel that it "doesn't matter" who looks after specific government activities.

Concern Over Federal-Provincial Powers

With the objective of obtaining data regarding the level of concern that people have regarding federal-provincial matters, respondents were asked: "Does it make any difference to you which level of government provides the necessary governmental services?" Sixty-two percent of the respondents indicated, "Yes it is important to me," twenty-eight percent said, "No it is not important," and ten percent didn't know whether or not it was important to them that different levels of government provided different services (see Table III).

Most respondents who indicated they were concerned about maintaining the division of powers felt that provincial governments were better able to appreciate local conditions and problems than was the federal government. The manager of a small business expressed this sentiment when he stated, "I'd sooner see things handled by the province as we're closer to them. There would be much less to go through. It's impossible to negotiate with the federal government." Other respondents in favor of maintaining the division of powers noted that a balance of power is necessary to ensure that neither government becomes too powerful. As one respondent put it, "The country is too big to have a central form of government. There needs to be more than one unit." Other respondents noted the efficiency of the provincial government's administration and expressed preference for provincially administered programs.

While most respondents concerned about maintaining the division of powers stressed the importance of provincial independence, ten percent indicated that there was a need for greater federal control. In most cases those concerned about federal powers were not fearful of the fed-

TABLE III

Importance of Maintaining a Division of Powers

Division of Powers*	Percentage of Category	Percentage of Total
Important (62 percent of sample)		
Proximity of provincial gov't	48	30
Maintenance of division of powers	14	9
Favor provincial government admin.	16	10
Federal government control advocated	10	6
Other responses	13	7
Not Important (28 percent of sample)		
Services provided regardless of government responsible	71	19
Governments are interdependent	8	2
Prefer federal government control	4	1
Other responses	17	5
Don't know (10 percent of sample) N = 567		

* The data displayed in this table were obtained through a series of three questions. The first question asked, "Does it make any difference which level of government provides the necessary governmental services?" Sixty two percent answered 'yes', 28 percent answered 'no'. Those respondents who said 'yes' or 'no' were then asked, "Why do you say that?" The responses above indicate the percentage of respondents who answered that question within the context of their first response.

eral government losing control over existing areas of federal jurisdiction, but rather felt that there was a need for increased federal government involvement in areas of provincial control. As one university student suggested, "I would like to see the federal government look after the major problems—things like education."

A sizeable minority, twenty-eight percent of the sample, was not convinced that the division of powers was really meaningful. For most of these respondents it was the services that mattered, not which government provided the services. As one housewife remarked "So long as they [necessary government services] are provided, I don't care which government provides them." Other responses given in explanation of disinterest in the maintenance of a division of powers included statements concerning the interdependence of the two governments. Some people simply did not think it was necessary to bother about which government looked after which specific service. There was also a small number of respondents (four percent) who seemed to prefer a unitary form of government as they reasoned that the federal government should have the authority to look after all important governmental matters. With the exception of this latter group, all other respondents were primarily concerned with utility; it was basically a question of which government could provide the necessary services most efficiently and effectively.

Involvement in Federal-Provincial Matters

One of the best exposures of federal-provincial relations to the Canadian public in recent years was the televised constitutional conferences during 1968 and 1969. The success of this endeavour in creating interest was reportedly high immediately after the conference, as one survey found that eighty percent of Canada's population either watched, listened to, or read about the conference.[20] The Alberta electorate, when asked whether or not they followed the proceedings of either constitutional conference (1968/1969), did not indicate such an awareness since only forty-six percent indicated that they followed the conference proceedings. This latter figure is probably a more accurate reflection of interest in the conference as it is not based upon simply an exposure factor, but rather on the individual's evaluation of the importance of this event.

The number of respondents who found the conference of considerable interest was even less, since only thirty-five percent of those who followed the conference indicated that they were very interested. Fifty-six percent admitted to a moderate interest in the proceedings, and ten percent indicated that, even though they followed the conference, they were not very interested in the proceedings.

AWARENESS, CONCERN AND INVOLVEMENT:
THE INTERRELATIONSHIPS

The relationship between awareness, concern and involvement is documented in previous political research and the Alberta study basically supports these earlier findings.[21] The data collected affirm: that people who are concerned about the maintenance of the division of powers are more likely to have been exposed to intergovernmental negotiations than those who did not indicate any concern, and that people who were found to be more knowledgeable about the division of powers were also more likely to have followed the constitutional conference proceedings. However, the degree of association between concern and awareness was not found to be very strong. People who were not concerned about the division of powers were just as likely to be aware of jurisdictional responsibilities as those who were concerned about maintaining a federal system.[22] As is the case with most research pertaining to the interrelationships between awareness, concern, and involvement, the Alberta study does not shed any light on whether awareness precedes concern, or even whether awareness precedes involvement.

Figure 1
Saliency of Federalism

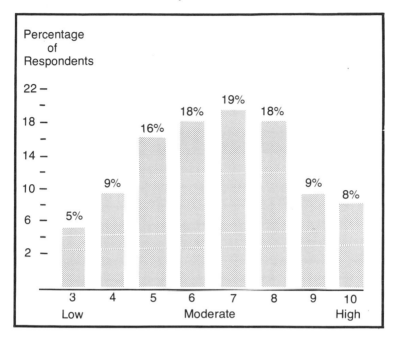

In order to examine the overall salience of federalism an index was created which ranked the respondents' saliency according to their awareness of federal and provincial government jurisdictions, the extent to which they were concerned about the maintenance of a division of powers between the two governments, and the extent to which they became involved in following the constitutional conferences.[23] As can be seen in Figure I, some respondents found federal-provincial matters to be relatively unimportant to them, since fourteen percent of the sample were basically unaware of the two governments' jurisdictional responsibilities, not concerned about the division of powers, nor did they follow the constitutional conference proceedings of 1968 or 1969. On the other hand, seventeen percent of the sample were found to be knowledgeable about the two governments' jurisdictional responsibilities, indicated that they were concerned about the maintenance of the division of powers, and followed either one or both of the constitutional conferences. Perhaps the most interesting aspect of this index is that sixty-nine percent of the respondents are to be found in the middle of the continuum. Thus, it is reasonable to conclude, given the above data, that federalism is not a highly salient issue for more than fifteen to thirty-five percent of the population. For most people, federal-provincial relations seem to be a factor within their political environment of which they are somewhat aware and moderately concerned.

Relatively few people, by their own admission, find the subject matter stimulating enough to become engrossed in even the following televised proceedings of federal-provincial constitutional conferences. This observation does not of course rule out the possibility that federal-provincial relations may be a motivating factor in the political behaviour of citizens, particularly those who find federalism to be a somewhat salient element of their political environment.

THE ALTERNATE VOTER AND FEDERALISM

During the late 1950s and early 1960s many authors argued that the widespread tendency of Canadians to support a different party at the provincial level than they did at the national level was based upon the desire to balance the power of the national government by voting against the party in power nationally, in provincial elections.[24] If there is any credibility to this position, it could be expected that people who alternate their party support would rate higher on the federalism saliency index than those who do not alternate parties.

An analysis of alternating party supporters (hereafter referred to as "party alternators") was therefore undertaken to determine three things: whether party alternators tend to come from any particular segment of the population; whether federalism is more or less salient among party alternators than it is among those who do not alternate parties (hereafter referred to as "party loyalists"), and whether party alternators are more provincially or federally oriented than party loyalists.[25]

An examination of the relationship between the standard demographic classifications (education, occupation, income, age, religion, and sex) and party identification patterns failed to provide any guidance in identifying those who alternate parties. Nor was it found that there were any significant differences between party alternators and party loyalists regarding the saliency of federal-provincial matters. The reasons given by party alternators for their mixed party loyalties were based upon leadership personalities, the administrative record of the provincial government (i.e., people felt that Mr. Manning and the Social Credit had provided Alberta with good government, therefore they voted Social Credit in provincial elections), the competitiveness of parties in provincial and federal campaigns, and local candidate appeal. Only 2 of the 567 interviewed utilized the balance of power notion to explain their voting behaviour. Thus, although the above findings do not conclusively rule out the possibility that one's perspective of Canadian federalism might be a contributing factor in influencing party identification, there is no substantial evidence to suggest that this might be the case. What these findings do suggest is that alternating voters support different parties provincially and nationally because they perceive the two campaigns to be basically independent one of the other. Alternate party supporters seem to evaluate both federal and provincial parties on the basis of their individual leaders, administrative record, competitiveness within their own electoral system and the appeal of their local candidates, rather than on the basis of the interrelationships between federal and provincial parties of differing or similar names.

CONCLUSION

In a recent publication *Constitutional Adaptation and Canadian Federalism*, Donald Smiley asked the following question: "Does contemporary co-operative federalism require widespread popular attitudes which are pragmatic and equivocal as to the appropriate level of government for carrying out particular public responsibilities?" Smiley partially answered the question by observing:

> It seems unlikely that the federation could survive if the prevailing attitudes came to the point of considering one or the other level more legitimate in respect to all public activities believed important.[26]

Inasmuch as the scope of this study was limited to Alberta, it is not possible to determine whether or not Canadians as a whole consider one level to be a more legitimate administrator of all important public activities. Certainly there is adequate evidence to infer that there is a balance between the forces of centralization and decentralization within the Alberta population. Since there is no substantial portion of the electorate that advocates total provincial or federal control over all important areas of government activities, there is reason to believe that for most Albertans there is an acceptance of the legitimacy of the Canadian federal system itself. Thus, although there is no evidence to suggest that federalism is a highly salient political factor for a substantial segment of the population, most Alberta citizens not only seem to possess a commitment to their nation and provinces, but also they seem to perceive the existing federal structure as both legitimate and functional.

NOTES

[1] *Constitutional Conference Proceedings,* First Meeting, 1968 (Ottawa: Queen's Printer, 1968), p. iv.

[2] For an overview of the data collected on public opinion and federalism see Mildred Schwartz, *Public Opinion and Canadian Identity* (Los Angeles: University of California Press, 1967), pp. 92-95. See also Fred Schindeler *et al., Attitudes Towards Federal Government Information* (Toronto: Institute of Behavioral Research, York University, 1968).

[3] J. A. Corry, "Constitutional Trends and Federalism," in J. P. Meekison (ed), *Canadian Federalism: Myth or Reality* (Toronto: Methuen Publications, 1968), p. 64.

[4] W. H. Riker, "Six Books in Search of a Subject or Does Federalism Exist and Does it Matter?", *Comparative Politics*, Vol. 2., No. 1 (October, 1969), pp. 135-146.

[5] René Lévesque, *An Option for Quebec* (Toronto: McClelland and Stewart, 1968), pp. 13-19; Daniel Johnson, *Egalité ou Independence* (Montreal: Les Edition Renaissance, 1965).

[6] *Ibid.*

[7] Edwin R. Black and Alan C. Cairns, "A Different Perspective on Canadian Federalism," in Meekison, *op. cit.*, p. 82.

[8] Steven Muller, "Federalism and the Party System in Canada," in Aaron Wildavsky (ed.), *American Federalism in Perspective* (Boston: Little, Brown and Company, 1967), p. 156.

[9] Heinz Eulau, *The Behavioral Persuasion in Politics* (New York: Random House, 1963), p. 19.

[10] For a striking example of this see the debate between the Honorable Pierre E. Trudeau and the late Premier of Quebec, Daniel Johnson, in *Constitutional Conference Proceedings*, February 507, 1968 (Ottawa: The Queen's Printer, 1968), pp. 63-67.

[11] During the 1967-69 period the meaningfulness of Canada's government structure was brought to the attention of Canadians very forcefully. For the first time in Canadian history the ordinary citizen was given an opportunity to become involved, if only vicariously, in a debate concerning the structure of Canadian government. That this study was undertaken during a period in time when federal-provincial relations had reached an apex of public exposure was not seen as a limitation, but rather it was considered a unique opportunity to study how the individual citizen perceived the government structure under which he lives. For a more thorough explanation of the methodology see David K. Elton, "Electoral Perceptions of Federalism: A Descriptive Analysis of the Alberta Electorate", unpublished Doctoral thesis, University of Alberta, 1973.

[12] Of the 19 areas of government jurisdiction which were examined in this study, eight areas were of federal government jurisdiction, another eight were of provincial government jurisdiction, while three of the areas examined were considered to be of joint jurisdiction. For each of the 19 subject areas chosen, all respondents were asked to identify which government actually looked after the activity mentioned. Any 1 or 4 responses was recorded: (1) federal government; (2) provincial government; (3) both governments; (4) respondents not sure (don't know). Those who responded "don't know" to any one of the 19 categories when the question was first read to them by the interviewer were then encouraged to choose one of the first three responses, as the interviewer was instructed to ask, "Which government do you thinks looks after this matter?" This procedure resulted in an exceptionally high response rate, since at least 98 percent of those interviewed indicated they thought they knew which government(s) were responsible for administering the 19 areas of jurisdiction tested.

Given the scope and number of conditional grant programs plus the spill-over effect of federal and provincial government programs, it is possible to argue that both governments are involved at least to some extent in each of the 19 areas of jurisdiction examined. Even in areas such as foreign affairs, banking, and education, it can be argued that both governments are actively involved in developing and/or maintaining specific programs. Thus, although it is not possible to divide the powers of government into "watertight compartments" that are solely the responsibility of either the federal or provincial government, it is possible to allocate to each government broad jurisdictional powers for specific programs on the basis of paramountcy.

[13] Admittedly, if the respondents were to guess in all 19 cases as to which of the three responses was correct, they would probably be correct in six or seven of the 19 cases. There is less than 5 chances in 100 that an individual would get more than 9 correct simply by guessing, and there is less than one chance in 100 that anyone would correctly identify 12 or more areas or jurisdiction by chance.

[14] This finding is substantiated by previous research. See Fred Schindeler *et al.*, *Attitudes Toward Federal Government Information* (Toronto: Institute for Behavioral Research, York University, 1969), pp. 20-25.

[15] Elton, *op. cit.*, pp. 133-136.

[16] Schindeler *et al., op. cit,*; See also *To Know and Be Known,* Report of the Task Force on Government Information, (Ottawa: Queen's Printer, 1969).

[17] Schindeler *et al.,* p. 17.

[18] Elton, *op. cit.,* pp. 141-144.

[19] Schindeler, *op. cit.,* pp. 18-23.

[20] Peter Regenstrief, "Survey finds support for bilingualism," *Edmonton Journal,* February 22, 1969.

[21] Lester Milbraith, *Political Participation* (Chicago: Rand McNally and Company, 1965), pp. 64-65.

[22] Elton, *op. cit.,* pp. 167-73.

[23] The index was constructed by allocating the following weight to each response category of the 3 variables:
   (1) Awareness: low (less than 10 areas of jurisdiction correctly identified) = 1; medium low (10 or 11 areas of jurisdiction correctly identified) = 2; medium high (12 or 13 areas of jurisdiction correctly identified) = 3; high (14 or more areas of jurisdiction correctly identified) = 4.
   (2) Concern: Not concerned = 1, don't know = 2, concerned = 3.
   (3) Involvement: Didn't follow either conference = 1, followed one conference = 2, followed both conferences = 3.

[24] See Steven Muller, "Federalism and the Party System in Canada," in Aaron Wildavsky (ed.), *American Federalism in Perspective* (Boston: Little, Brown and Company, 1967); F. H. Underhill, *In Search of Canadian Federalism* (Toronto: Macmillan Canada, 1961), p. 237; Dennis Wrong, "The Pattern of Party Voting in Canada," *Public Opinion Quarterly,* Vol. 21, No. 2, (1957), p. 255.

[25] One in three of the respondents interviewed in the Alberta study indicated that they supported a different party in the 1967 provincial election as compared to their voting behaviour in the 1968 federal election. Although there are 12 alternating party preference patterns possible, two party preference patterns tend to dominate the findings: 40 percent of the 1967 provincial Social Credit supporters voted Progressive Conservative in the 1968 federal election; 29 percent of the Social Credit supporters voted Liberal in the 1968 federal election.

[26] Donald V. Smiley, *Constitutional Adaptation and Canadian Federalism Since 1945* (Ottawa: Queen's Printer, 1970), p. 6.

5

Political Parties and Elite Accommodation: Interpretations of Canadian Federalism*

S. J. R. Noel

In Canada, as in all federations, there exists a complex reciprocal relationship between those political forms which are constitutionally defined and those which are not; and of the latter, political parties are certainly the most conspicuous and have long been regarded as the most important. The purpose of this paper is to show that the models, theories, or metaphors most commonly used to explain the role of political parties, and the political process generally, in the operation of the Canadian federal political system are in a number of important respects either defective or inadequate, and to suggest a possible alternative.

Three models in particular are chosen for discussion, either because they are widely found, explicitly or implicitly, in Canadian historical and political writing, or because they purport to provide a general theoretical framework which is applicable to the Canadian federal system.

1. THE BROKERAGE MODEL

The main function of Canadian political parties, according to this model, is to act as agents of political integration, combatting and neutralizing the notoriously fissiparous tendencies of Canadian society by providing for the representation within each party of every significant interest group. The underlying assumption is that the Canadian federation, being bound together by neither a transcending nationalism nor by the fact of being an inevitable economic or geographical unit, is far too fragile a creation to survive political conflict between parties which are basically dissimilar in composition or behaviour. Canada, the brokerage theorists point out, is a country divided by formidable social cleavages based upon language, ethnicity and culture, as well as by potentially disruptive regional economic differences. Its national political parties, therefore, must be 'omnibus' or 'department-store' parties, composed of similar coalitions of interests, which act as brokers (or 'interest aggregators'), reconciling the conflicting claims of different social groups. In the words of R. MacGregor Dawson:

---

*Reprinted by permission.

The parties are the outstanding agents for bringing about co-operation and compromise between conflicting groups and interests of all kinds in the nation; for as a rule it is only by a merging of forces that these can hope to become powerful enough to secure office.[1]

According to another textbook, party politicians

are always arranging deals between different sections of opinion, finding compromises that "split the difference", and thus concentrating votes behind the programme of their political party. As long as the sovereign electorate is of numerous diverse opinions, this is the only way majorities can be constructed and power gained to push through any political programme in a democracy.[2]

The authors were referring not only to Canadian but to American parties as well, which points to a second basic assumption underlying the brokerage model: that the Canadian Liberal and Conservative parties are analogous to the Democratic and Republican parties of the United States, and can therefore be understood in the same terms. In other words, there is a *North American type* of political party which functions in a similar way in both countries, and can be similarly analyzed.[3]

The difficulties in this interpretation (for there are certain differences between Canadian and American political parties which are too obvious to be ignored) are usually explained historically in terms of Canada's British connection:

Our North American environment (writes the historian F. H. Underhill) makes for fundamental resemblances between Canadian and American politics. Our cabinet system of parliamentary government makes for parties on the British model. And like most other Canadian institutions and habits, our Canadian parties show the constant interplay between North American environment and British inheritance.[4]

In other words, although in both countries the parties operate in essentially the same way because of the influence of their shared environment, there are also differences between them which result from the different constitutional frameworks within which they operate. The latter, however, affect mainly appearances and are not fundamental.

In the American system of presidential-congressional politics the brokerage functions of the parties are performed openly, and indeed amid considerable publicity. At the presidential level, the process through which an aspiring candidate bargains for the support in primary elections and in the nominating convention of the heterogeneous elements of his party is a matter of public knowledge and comment. In Congress, the legislative process likewise tends to emphasize the open interaction between parties and interest groups.[5]

The Canadian system, by contrast, is 'closed'; like the British, it operates behind a screen of constitutional conventions which normally shades its crucial areas of bargaining and decision-making from the public gaze. Moreover, the requirements of the unwritten part of the Canadian constitution, which defines the role of the Crown, cabinet and Parliament (and, through the convention of ministerial responsibility, of civil servants), also drastically limit our knowledge of how the political process actually works. It is significant that there are no studies of this aspect of Canadian politics comparable to the large American literature on governmental decision-making, interest group behaviour, and the analysis of roll-call voting in Congress.[6] This is not simply the result of an unfortunate oversight on the part of Canadian political scientists. The fact is that either the data upon which such studies might be based are for the most part not available in Canada (for example, almost nothing is known of the operation of cabinet committees, or of the interaction between interest group representatives and ministers and senior civil servants) or of little practical use (for example, an analysis of the voting record of M.P.'s in House of Commons divisions is hardly likely to illuminate the role of the parties as interest aggregators—however much it might show about the strength of party discipline). The one Canadian party institution which might appear at first sight to be amenable to the same sort of analysis as its American counterpart is the party leadership convention. Here, it might be argued, the attempts of leadership aspirants to build nation-wide coalitions in support of their candidates make these conventions very like the American parties' presidential nominating conventions. While superficially there is much to support such a view, (particularly in recent years when the television cameras have tended to turn the Canadian conventions into 'media-events', complete with American-style floor demonstrations by supporters of the various candidates), in reality there are fundamental differences between the two types. To mention only the most important, in the American convention voting is open and by state delegation; in Canada the *individual delegates* vote by secret ballot. This may mean only that our knowledge of the details of party brokerage and coalition-building is deficient in the Canadian case—or it may mean, as Donald Smiley concludes, that "the voting rules of the Canadian leadership convention preclude the deliberate creation of the kind of presidential coalition that is so central to American national politics."[7] The point is, however, that here too the Canadian system is relatively 'closed', and the type of analysis that is so enlightening in the study of American politics is therefore largely inapplicable.

There remain the Liberal and Conservative party platforms, which, it is commonly remarked, are typically constructed on the principle of 'something for everyone'. A study of the actual party platforms, however, does not show that this is the case, at least not in the American sense of being a list of promises designed to appeal specifically to different groups. Rather, the Liberal and Conservative platforms in the twentieth century have tended to be more like the election statements of the British Conservative Party; i.e., designed to appeal widely but not reflecting the outcome of some prior bargaining process.[8] They show, in fact, little more than that both parties are, or aspire to be, national parties; what they do now show is *how* they actually operate.

The brokerage theorist therefore is forced to make the assumption that Canadian parties function in the federal political system in much the same way as American, even though (because of certain constitutional 'peculiarities') they cannot be observed doing so! This, of course, may be the case. But it is not shown to be the case merely because the claims of conflicting and competing groups do in fact appear to be accommodated fairly successfully in the Canadian political system, for the means of accommodation may be drastically different. But even if they are not, even if the Canadian parties perform in the secrecy of their parliamentary caucuses a brokerage function similar to that performed more or less openly by the American parties, the brokerage model, as applied to Canada, remains no more than a dubiously useful analogy, for virtually all of its empirical underpinnings must be drawn from American experience.

2. THE SYSTEMS MODEL

A second model that has been employed in the analysis of Canadian parties and politics is the familiar systems model of David Easton.[9] This has the considerable merit of relating the political process to the functioning of political institutions, and is not difficult to apply plausibly, as long as it remains at a high level of abstraction. The usual inputs, outputs, conversion process, feed-back arrow, etc., can all be identified in a general way, and to this extent the model is pedagogically valuable. Beyond this, however, it provides few new insights into the way in which the Canadian federal system operates. To take an obvious example, it is undoubtedly useful for certain purposes to emphasize that the federal cabinet is a vital part of the 'conversion process', but it does not get around the fact that this vital part of the conversion process operates under an effective convention of secrecy. Even more serious is the difficulty in using an input-output model to explain the complexities of intergovernmental relations in a federal system where not only much of the conversion process but also much of the input side lies in a political *terra incognita*. There is perhaps no *intrinsic* reason why the subtleties and complexities of federal-provincial relations, including the relations of federal and provincial parties to one another and to the interest groups which operate within the respective jurisdictions, could not be illuminated by the application of a sufficiently sophisticated systems model, but it is as well to recognize that the *practical* difficulties are immense. Engelmann and Schwartz, in discussing in general terms the relatively simple questions of interest articulation and aggregation as inputs at the national level, and the interaction of interest groups and national parties, are forced to admit when it comes to applying their analysis to the hard world of political reality, that it would require the kind of empirical research bordering on military intelligence work to obtain a full picture of the extent to which interest groups seek access to parties on their way to the governmental structure.[10]

In summarizing their findings they conclude unhelpfully that "political parties may or may not be involved in carrying interest demands to the governmental structure."[11]

This of course does not mean that system analysis as a technique may not be useful in certain circumstances—only that the circumstances have to be carefully chosen. And in the case of Canada it would appear that the system itself does not produce as one of its outputs the data on the basis of which a satisfactorily rigorous and sophisticated systems model could be applied.

There is, however, a useful by-product of systems analysis in the Canadian context: it helps direct the attention of Canadian political scientists outward, away from their traditional concerns and towards those relatively unexplored intra- and extra-societal environments which interact with the formal and informal mechanisms of government. While the application of systems analysis has not notably advanced our understanding of that interaction, it remains to be seen whether other models might be applied, or new ones developed, which could be used to greater advantage. One as yet untried approach which appears to hold considerable promise—the European 'elite-accommodation' model—is discussed in Section 5.

3. THE FEDERAL 'BARGAIN'

To question the utility of the brokerage model as applied to Canada is not, it should be made clear, to deny the existence of a strong predisposition towards compromise and the peaceful resolution of conflict in the Canadian political culture (or cultures). In this respect, Canada is probably not very different from other democratic polities, whether their parties are of the brokerage type or not. In Austria, Sweden, Switzerland, the Netherlands, and Finland, to take but a few examples, the political process would certainly appear to be no less a process of compromise. The phrase 'brokerage politics', however, as normally used, implies something more than 'compromise'; it implies not merely the existence of a cultural norm but also the existence of a pattern of political behaviour, a *way* of doing this politically that can be distinguished from other ways. Hence to point out the importance of compromise in Canadian politics, or to suggest that "it is no accident that the three Prime Ministers with the longest terms in office—Macdonald, Laurier, and King— have all been conspicuous for their willingness to make concessions, their skill in avoiding awkward or hasty decisions, and their ability to bring together people of diverse interests and beliefs"[12] is to say hardly more than that Canadian politics are democratic and that some party leaders have been more successful than others. It tells us very little about the role of political parties or the way they perform that role.

The theory of the 'federal bargain', as advanced most recently and succinctly by W. H. Riker, contains a further model that merits examination in its application to Canada. Riker argues that federal systems result from a mutual desire of the member states or communities for greater security in the face of external threats, and for economic or territorial expansion. Once the bargain is struck it is maintained over time by a variety of factors, the most important of which is the party system:

> Whatever the general social conditions, if any, that sustain the federal bargain, there is one institutional condition that controls the nature of the bargain in all the instances here examined and in all other ways with which I am familiar. This is the structure of the party system, which may be regarded as the main variable intervening between the background social conditions and the specific nature of the federal bargain.[13]

In the United States the type of bargaining which takes place especially within the parties, tends to confirm the validity of the brokerage model. As Riker notes, "the life of a President . . . is one of constant bargaining—to get the votes to get nominated, to get the votes to get elected, to get the votes to get bills through Congress, to get the votes to get renominated, etc., etc."[14] In Canada, on the other hand, the type of bargaining which is most central to the federal system takes place not within or even between parties, but between the federal and provincial *governments*. And even when these governments are controlled by a single party (or more accurately, by federal and provincial parties bearing the same name) it would be highly misleading to suggest that the party therefore acts as a broker between federal and provincial interests. Rather, "even within the Liberal party, provincial prime ministers look to Liberal leaders in Ottawa, not for leadership, but for bargaining concessions of exactly the same sort that might be gained by Social Credit or Union Nationale provincial ministries."[15]

Riker, indeed, nowhere claims that brokerage-type national parties, or brokerage-type politics on the American model, are essential to the making or maintenance of a federal bargain. What he does claim is that the degree of centralization or decentralization in a federal system will vary "according to the degree to which the parties organized to operate the central government control the parties organized to operate the constituent governments".[16] It will also vary, he suggests, with the strength of popular identification with the federal state itself or with its constituent territorial units.

The first hypothesis has not been tested in the Canadian case by any empirical study designed specifically for this purpose, but the most extended recent treatment of the fluctuations in the level of centralization in the Canadian federation suggests that the internal structure of parties is not among the most important determinants.[17]

The second hypothesis, while also untested, nevertheless does appear to be confirmed by one of the most generally recognized features of the Canadian federation: the persistence within it of strong regional identities.

4. REGIONALISM AND 'NATIONAL' CONSENSUS

That Canada is a country without a strong sense of 'national identity' is a truism repeated *ad nauseum* in both old and new analyses of Canadian politics. While almost any statement of it would serve equally well, the following by John Meisel puts it succinctly and in contemporary terms:

> The most significant feature of Canada's value system, and the one with the most far-reaching consequences for the political process and the operation of the party system, concerns the almost total absence of a national fervor. Canada must, in many respects, be the least nationalistic country in the world. The French-speaking population has a highly developed sense of national cohesion when "national" refers to its own cultural group, but the country as a whole is almost totally lacking in a genuinely shared set of symbols, heroes, historical incidents, enemies, or even ambitions. Canada, in short, lacks a fully developed secular political culture, and the many divisions which are inevitable in a country of its extent and variety cannot be mediated within the context of a shared and similar complex of national values and emotions.[18]

The fact that even within English Canada there are a number of strong regional identities ('regional' being used here as a close synonym for 'provincial') is typically regarded as a major contributing cause of Canada's national weakness (or problem, crisis, etc.). Implicit in such a view is a comparison with the United States: what is missing north of the border is an over-riding sense of *pan-Canadian* identity. Hence the nation-building process has been thwarted and Canada remains essentially a hope unfulfilled.[19] The popular nation-building school of Canadian history, as is well-known, has tended to divide historical figures into nation-builders (good guys: Macdonald, Laurier) and provincialists (bad guys: Mowat, Duplessis).[20] Recently, however, it has been suggested that 'province-building' also might be considered a legitimate feature of Canadian federalism,[21] and the historians Ramsay Cook and J. M. S. Careless have called attention to the significance of "limited identities" in seeking to define the nature of the Canadian experience. Some of that experience, Careless remarks,

> is doubtless common to all as citizens in one political sovereignty, with many economic and social interconnections besides. But much of it surely lies in the "limited identities" of region, culture and class. . . . These represent entities of experience for Canadians no less than the trans-continental federal union; indeed, it is largely through them that Canadians interpret their nation-state as a whole.[22]

Cook suggests further that while "our over-heated nationalist intellectuals" find this situation lamentable, "it might just be" that Canadians in general find it "quite satisfactory".[23] In the case of English Canada it is neither class nor culture, but above all the province, which forms the basis of the strongest "limited identities". Careless advances a number of reasons for this, including metropolitanism (which in Canada gave the provinces strong urban centres of economic and political leadership), patterns of immigration and social class, and the values inherent in the political cultures:

> As for English Canada, the habitual emphasis on particularized social groupings rather than mass citizenship, on pragmatically nearer community interests instead of some generalized, idealized, national way of life, effectively ministers to strong identification with regions or provinces delineated by geography, economics, and history.[24]

The result, according to Careless, is (if we would but see it) to make of Canada a distinctive nation-state characterized by "pluralism, constraints, and compromises":

> A key word is articulation. What has been sought, and to some degree achieved, is not really unification or consolidation, but the articulation of regional patterns in one transcontinental state.[25]

Careless does not attempt to explain how, or through what institutions or mechanisms, the Canadian political system as a whole has managed to produce such an outcome, but his observation that federal leaders have tended to deal with provincial demands "pragmatically, rather than seek some broad, national counter-response"[26] is suggestive, and his general regional approach helps to cast the problem in fresh perspective.

The typical response of political scientists, when faced with the Canadian paradox of strong "limited identities" (or "weak national identity") existing within a federal system which for over a century nevertheless managed to maintain its existence by peaceful means, has been to turn to the concept of 'consensus' and particularly to view the national political parties as the promoters and vehicles of consensus. In other words, the political parties are seen not only as brokers between interests but also as being instrumental in creating a mass national consensus without which the Canadian federal system could not survive.

Consensus, however, is not a simple concept (as I. L. Horowitz has pointed out, it contains at least six ambiguities or "dimensions"),[27] but the usage which seems most generally favoured in writings on national identity is to treat it as a cultural term, meaning agreement on, or acceptance of, a generalized set of values, opinions, expectations and orientations towards national institutions and symbols. Unlike Britain, where a high degree of national consensus arises naturally out of a culturally homogeneous community, in Canada it must be artificially cultivated or "nurtured"—and this is a function of political parties. As John Meisel puts it:

> For the parliamentary system to function smoothly and, consequently, for the party system which has grown up in association with it to function effectively, a high level of cohesion and consensus is required. In a country lacking a strong national political culture and the institutions fostering it, political parties have a special role to play as agencies for the creation of national symbols, experience, memories, heroes, and villains, not to mention national favours, benefits and concessions. . . . An absolutely latent function of the party system in Canada is, therefore, the role it plays in the development and fostering of a national political culture; it must play a vital role, in fact, in generating support for the regime. So few other institutions do so and, in the event, few are as well suited for this task as the parties.[28]

Paul Fox posits as one of the chief factors explaining the growth of provincial powers the lack of consensus "in Canadian opinion coming to bear at Ottawa". On the role of the parties he comments:

> If parties are to fulfil the role that political science traditionally assigns to them, namely the function of being a unifying force by acting as a national broker to bring diverse and opposing interests together and by securing a consensus, then each of the parties must be agreed within itself on the fundamentals of its existence.[29]

Whether Canadian political parties do now, or have ever, fulfilled the role of creating a popularly shared national consensus, however, is a question to which the answer is far from clear. Presumably a consensus must be a consensus *on* something, and if this is the case it should be possible to establish empirically the strength and composition of such a consensus. The most thorough and systematic attempt to date to discover the content of the Canadian consensus, and to define the role of parties in promoting it, is to be found in Mildred Schwartz's exhaustive review of the data from twenty years of public opinion polling.[30]

After examining responses to a broad range of questions relating to national "problems" (external, internal and symbolic) the author concludes, as might be expected, that the level of consensus is low, and, moreover, that to "the proverbial average man, in this case a Canadian, the significant concerns are those which relate to his economic well-being. Neither the symbols nor the substance of national independence have troubled him unduly."[31] Thus, it would appear, while the study does not explicitly confirm Cook's view that Canadians by and large have found their "limited identities" quite satisfactory, it is perfectly consistent with it.

And although the study throughout places particular emphasis on the role of parties as instruments for the nurturing of consensus, the conclusion suggested by its data is that either Canadian parties do not seek to perform this task, or if they do, they perform it badly. Schwartz therefore concludes by questioning the basic assumption underlying the party-as-consensus-builder view:

To see in Canada specific categories of voters consistently differentiated by a large percentage margin could only be interpreted as indicating a lack of national consensus, at least on the issues surveyed. Yet Canada has existed in its present political form for almost one hundred years, and it is probably safe to assume that during most of that period consensus on similar issues has never been appreciably greater. We have explored the reasons why the major cleavages, the regional-economic and the regional-ethnic, have such a great impact on opinions and, correlatively, why political parties are restricted in their contributions to national integration. This investigation has suggested that countries such as Canada may provide alternatives to a general consensus.[32]

While it may be that Canadian survey research has simply never asked the right questions which would enable it to identify a national consensus, if this is not the case, and if therefore the search for an underlying national (i.e., mass) consensus in Canada is indeed a search for a chimera, several conclusions would appear to follow.

First, the lack of a national consensus has not necessarily been a hindrance to the survival and operation of the Canadian federal system; secondly, it has not been incompatible with the successful functioning of parliamentary democracy; and thirdly, Canadian political parties have not performed at least one of the roles (consensus nurturing) that political scientists have traditionally attributed to them. Indeed, it may well be that the importance of parties in the Canadian political system has been (and is) greatly exaggerated (partly, no doubt, because we still know so little about their operation that large, and perhaps false, assumptions about them are easily made and difficult to challenge).

It would, of course, be absurd to claim that political parties are of no importance in the political process. At the very least they remain the essential instruments for the recruitment of personnel for the elective offices of the system. But there are nevertheless numerous reasons for believing that they are less important in the operation of the *federal system*, or, assuming that their role was once greater, that their importance in this regard has diminished. In another terminology, though they perform the vital function of political recruitment, they are not similarly dominant in the performance of the functions of interest articulation and aggregation. Two developments would appear to be particularly responsible for this, one in the decision-making process of the federation and the other in the nature of provincial economies.

First, there has been a growing tendency over the past decade for decision-making in Canada to become a matter of federal-provincial consultation and negotiation, not only at the highest level of premiers and cabinet ministers but also down through various levels of the federal and provincial civil services. The effect has been to exclude parties from any significant role in the process.[33]

Secondly, the economies of most provinces, whether based on manufacturing or resource-exploitation, or a combination of both, are now extremely complex and dominated by large American corporations.

(It is remarkable how often discussions of the effects of American-owned industry in Canada overlook the fact that these industries exist *in provinces,* and often have their economic stakes heavily concentrated in one province only.) While these corporations no doubt provide substantial financial backing for the old national parties, I would suggest that they do so less in the manner of a business transaction (payment for services rendered or to be rendered) than in the manner of taking out an insurance policy: by their campaign contributions the corporations seek to insure themselves against the possibility of ideologically unacceptable or unsympathetic persons winning control of the federal government. That is to say, they are primarily concerned that the parties should continue to dominate the recruitment function, and less concerned with parties as interest articulators or aggregators. The old provincial economic structures on the other hand, were dominated by relatively simple regional interests (agriculture in its various forms, fishing, lumbering, locally-owned secondary manufacturing, etc.) whose demands, while often difficult to reconcile at the national level, were also relatively simple (concerning, for example, tariffs, market regulation, public works); hence the M.P.s of the national parties could to some extent represent and mediate between them.

In contrast, modern corporate interests operate within a sophisticated framework of governmental and self-imposed constraints, understandings, and "rules of the game"; they are affected by complicated international taxation, trading, and resource-sharing arrangements; and they engage in capital transactions which frequently involve special government concessions or guarantees. In their normal day-to-day and year-to-year operation they do not seek to promote their multifarious interests through the national political parties, for the parties as such are not for the most part directly involved in the relevant decision areas.[34] Instead, they adopt a 'non-partisan' stance, cultivate a 'responsible' image, and endeavour to place their executives on government regulatory and advisory bodies. Their associations employ professional representatives and spokesmen, and maintain regular channels of communication with federal officials and ministers. A 'lobby' campaign directed at party M.P.s is nowadays a sign that an interest group lacks influence where it really counts, or that the normal process of interest group representation has broken down. The parties are left to dispose of the dwindling 'small change' of local patronage, but this should not be confused with interest articulation and aggregation.

It therefore remains to be asked whether there are social or political mechanisms instead of or in addition to parties which have enabled the Canadian federal system to achieve at least the minimum level of harmony between its regional components necessary for its survival, and if there are, whether they are still capable of functioning effectively.

5. CONSOCIATIONAL DEMOCRACY AND ELITE ACCOMMODATION

It is only natural that Canada should most frequently be compared with the United States, and that models, metaphors and theories of the political system that are applicable to the one should be assumed to be applicable to the other. There are certain indisputable similarities: both are federations, both span the North American continent, both are affluent Western democracies, and both exist within the common economic framework of modern capitalism. These and other similarities, however, too often obscure the significance of those differences which do exist, or cause similarities which exist with other countries to be neglected. This is particularly true of European countries, even though it would appear to be the case that Canadians, with their attachment to regional identies, and their strong linguistic and cultural differences, have a good deal in common with at least some Europeans. This is not to say that Canada is more European than American. It is merely to suggest that there may be some advantages to be gained from occasionally viewing Canadian politics from a European perspective.

It used to be the case that European political studies were almost entirely historical or legalistic, but this is no longer so. Contemporary European writing on politics is distinguished by a new interest in empirical theory and model-building. The primary emphasis, moreover, is not on the 'developing' countries (as is the case with much contemporary American theory) but on the economically developed modern democracies of Western Europe. A number of these countries, like Canada, lack an overriding national identity or mass consensus and are characterized by strong limited identities, yet they nevertheless manage to function as stable and effective political entities. A theory which attempts to explain their successful operation is therefore of considerable interest to the student of Canadian politics. One such theory is the theory of "consociational democracy" developed by the Dutch political scientist Arend Lijphart.[35]

Lijphart's starting point is the inability of American empirical theory to deal adequately with the reality of politics in a number of West European democracies. In particular he argues, neither pluralist theory nor structural functionalism nor communications theory can deal with the politics of "fragmented but stable democracies" (such as the Netherlands, Austria, Belgium, and Switzerland) other than by treating them as 'deviant' cases.[36] In none of these societies is there a situation of "cross-cutting cleavages" or national consensus such as American theory holds to be necessary for the successful functioning of democratic government, yet each must be regarded as an effectively functioning democracy.

The explanation, Lijphart suggests, is to be found in the role played by political elites in these countries in deliberately overcoming the effects of cultural fragmentation. Hence, even in the absence of a national identity or consensus, if there are strong limited identities or subcultures it is possible for the political leaders of these units consciously to practice accommodation at the elite level in order to maintain the political system and make it operate effectively. For this to take place, however, it is necessary that within each subculture the political elite should possess the confidence of their respective societies. Lijphart's model of a consociational democracy may be portrayed diagramatically, as in Figure 1.[37]

Figure 1

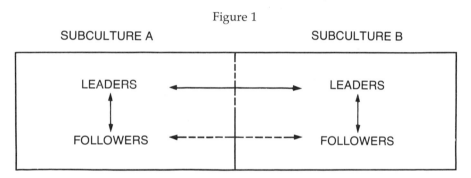

For the system to function successfully the elites (leaders) must have the following abilities or qualities:[38]

1. they must be able to accommodate the divergent interests and demands of the subcultures;
2. they must be able to transcend cleavages and join in a common effort;
3. they must be committed to the maintenance of the system; and
4. they must understand the perils of political fragmentation.

For the masses (followers) the requirements are only that they be committed to their own subcultures and that they trust and support their respective political elites. Lijphart maintains that the less contact between the masses of the subcultures the less friction there will be between them. "Hence, it may be desirable to keep transactions among antagonistic subcultures in a divided society—or, similarly, among different nationalities in a multinational state—to a minimum."[39]

In the perfect (i.e., most extreme) case of consociational democracy each of the units in the system would be perfectly encapsulated. There would therefore be no horizontal communication whatever at the mass level. Instead, there would be only vertical communication between mass and elite within each unit, and communication across subculture boundaries would be entirely a function of the political elite. However, in actual political systems, even when the subcultures are separated by a language barrier, there is always a certain amount of horizontal communication at the mass level (as well as a certain amount of communication between the elite of one subculture and the mass of the other). Consociationality, therefore, must be understood as a relative term. Moreover, even in societies with a fairly high degree of cultural homogeneity, such as Britain, there will be certain consociational features; e.g., the Welsh and Scottish representatives in the cabinet. In a consociational democracy such as the Netherlands, on the other hand, such features as subcultural representation in the Social and Economic Council are crucial to the maintenance and effective operation of the political system.

Theoretically, also, it is possible that a consociational democracy could function satisfactorily even if among the masses of the different subcultures there was absolutely no attachment to the national political system and no sense whatever of a national identity. In actual systems, however, some popular national sentiment is always present. What distinguishes a consociational political system from other types of political systems is the relative weakness of its mass national sentiments and the overcoming of this weakness through accommodation at the elite level. Thus, not only does Lijphart's model suggest parallels between Canada's experience and the experience of a number of other countries, it also offers a possible explanation of the way the Canadian political process operates. First, in broadest terms, it suggests that the lack of a pan-Canadian identity combined with strong regional subcultures is not necessarily a dysfunctional feature in terms of the successful operation of a federal political system, as long as within each subculture demands are effectively articulated through its political elite. Secondly, it suggests that in the relative absence of a national mass consensus, Canadian federalism has been maintained and made to work mainly through a process of accommodation at the elite level.

The fact that Canada is a federal system presents certain difficulties that Lijphart does not consider in the application of the model to European countries. The most important, perhaps, concerns the definition of the political elite. In Canada this could be defined, for example, as either the holders of the most important national political offices (federal cabinet ministers) or the holders of the most important federal and provincial political offices, or, more broadly still, it could be defined to include not only politicians but also senior civil servants and the members of the most important boards and commissions at either or both levels. Likewise, the definition of "subculture" could be applied only to English Canada and French Canada, or it could be applied to a number of regions with distinct identities: Newfoundland, the Maritimes, Quebec, Ontario, the Prairies, and British Columbia; or it could be applied to each of the ten provinces. These difficulties, however, are not insuperable. One possible method of operationalizing the concept of elite is demonstrated in Rodney Stiefbold's recent application of the consociational model to Austria.[40] Using a "reputational and positional method", Stiefbold distinguishes both between levels of elites, and between socio-economic and political elites. There is no reason why a similar classification could not be used in applying the model to Canada.

The significance of various elites (political, economic, bureaucratic, etc.) in Canadian society has been frequently noted. The landmark in the field of elite studies in Canada is of course John Porter's *Vertical Mosaic*, but Porter's main concern was apparently to show the extent to which elite recruitment in Canada is 'closed' (i.e., membership in the elites is not based on merit). Indeed, his entire work can be read as a sustained argument in favour of meritocracy, having as its unstated assumption the validity and paramountcy of meritocratic values, which are identified with democracy. Hence, factors which promote such goals as "equality of opportunity" and "social mobility" are regarded as good, and the obstacles to such goals are regarded as bad. It is this perspective which colours Porter's analysis of Canadian federalism. Cultural particularism and regionalism are treated by Porter as barriers to the achievement in Canada of a more perfectly democratic (i.e., meritocratic) society. He maintains that the federal system is based on "doubtful sociological assumptions"[41] and inhibits the development of "creative politics",[42] and deplores the absence in Canadian society of "a clearly articulated system of values, stemming from a charter myth or based on an indigenous ideology."[43] It is not surprising, therefore, that an approach so fundamentally unsympathetic to the regional factor in Canadian political life should attach little value or significance to the role of the political elite in maintaining Canada's existence and in enabling the political system to function even in the absence of "a charter myth" or mass consensus.

A better approach to the understanding of Canadian federalism is surely to start with the Canada that has existed and now exists, and to seek to explain the institutions and processes that have enabled so fragmented a country to achieve accommodation without integration. In other words, to begin with Careless's hypothesis that "the implicit aim of every regional community has been maximum autonomy for itself consonant with the maximum advantage to be gained from an overriding central regime."[44] Empirical studies (along the lines suggested by Lijphart's model of consociational democracy) into such subjects as elite-mass and inter-elite communication could well add a new dimension to our understanding of the Canadian political process. A possible adaptation of the model to Canadian circumstances is suggested in Figure 2.[45]

The implications of viewing the process of political communication and accommodation in the Canadian federal system in terms of such a model are several. First, it implies that, at the federal level at least, the

Figure 2
**Elite Accommodation Model of the
Canadian Federal System**

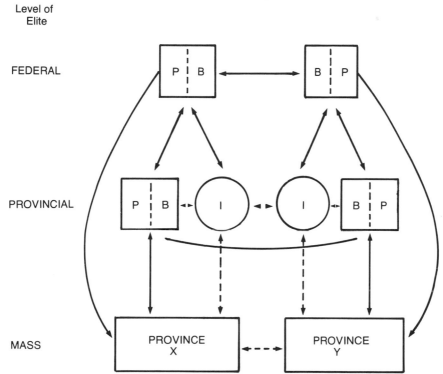

Level of
Elite

FEDERAL

PROVINCIAL

MASS

The Arrows Indicate the Direction and Strength of the
Flow of Communication

P = Political Elite

B = Bureaucratic Elite

I = Interest Group/Socio-Economic Elite

political and bureaucratic elites whose members are drawn from the provincial subcultures agree *in their federal roles* on the desirability of maintaining the system. Moreover, if the federal political elite is regarded as
consisting of federal cabinet ministers, there are ample historical cases,
from Joseph Howe onwards, of provincial politicians with no more attachment to the federal system than the mass of their constituents being
transformed in Ottawa into cabinet ministers intent on making the system work. The study of the contrasting provincial and federal political
careers of cabinet ministers would almost certainly prove a rewarding

exercise for the student of consociational democracy. (In the present cabinet, for example, a case that would merit attention is that of the Newfoundland representative and Minister of Transport, Donald Jamieson, who in 1948-49 was one of the leading figures in the campaign to keep Newfoundland *out* of Confederation.)[46]

Secondly, it implies that the mass of people in the provincial communities trust their political elites and continue to support them in spite of their absorbtion into the "Ottawa milieu".[47] On the other hand, it could be maintained that it is because their representatives are successful in reaching accommodation, and so enabling the system to produce certain desired material outputs, that the masses support them, (i.e., the masses are reasonably satisfied with the outputs of the system while remaining unattached to its symbols or substance).[48]

Thirdly, it implies that a key role in the working of the Canadian system must be accorded to provincial political and bureaucratic elites and interest groups. Given the division of powers in the Canadian constitution, it is inevitable that federal-provincial patterns of interaction and communication should be very complex, and that the articulation of demands should take place through a variety of channels. Provincial premiers are particularly important in articulating the demands of their respective communities to the federal government. This is not a process that takes place primarily within a political party, but is rather a transaction that takes place between different elite levels regardless of the party labels of the individual actors involved.[49] Specialized interest groups and corporate or socio-economic elites occupy a crucial role which places them in close communication with political and bureaucratic elites at both the federal and provincial levels.[50] Hence, it would appear to be necessary for a consociational system to survive in combination with federalism that the middle-level elites too be committed to the maintenance of the process of accommodation.

Fourthly, the model implies that in the system of responsible cabinet government, as it operates at both the federal and provincial levels, the political and bureaucratic elites are closely interlocked. This, however, is not to suggest that their functions are indistinguishable. It would appear to be the case in the Canadian system that the political elites at the federal and provincial levels are primarily responsible for the accommodation of broad cultural and regional interests, whereas the bureaucratic elites at both levels are increasingly important as the normal means through which the specific demands of interest groups are aggregated.

Finally, if some of the recent developments in Canadian politics are viewed in terms of the elite accommodation model a number of conclusions emerge. First, the decline of 'elitism' in Canada and a growing popular acceptance of the Jacksonian myth of popular or 'participatory' democracy may be detrimental to the maintenance of Canadian federalism if it leads to a situation in which the mass of the people are unwilling to accept the inter-elite accommodations made by their political leaders. If inter-elite accommodations must be popularly ratified they may be impossible to achieve. Secondly, 'national' policies aimed at promoting bilingualism and biculturalism may be misguided in the sense that they may increase friction between separate communities that previously paid little attention to one another. It may be that a system of consociational federalism works best when the "two solitudes" are preserved.[51] Thirdly, the emergence within any one subculture of new elites who, for nationalistic, economic, ideological, or any other reasons, are unwilling to provide "overarching cooperation at the elite level with the deliberate aim of counteracting disintegrative tendencies in the system",[52] will make the system inoperable, for there exists no mass concensus to which its defenders may appeal. Consociationality combined with federalism, however, creates the possibility of a conflict between federal and provincial elites within the same subculture, and so would appear to make the outcome more uncertain.

For the student of Canadian politics, the elite consensus model thus provides an alternative way of viewing the political process which has the advantage of requiring him to posit neither the chimerical notion of an 'underlying' national identity nor to regard the national parties as 'builders of consensus' and 'aggregators of interests' even though they are evidently not very active or are unsuccessful at such tasks. Though the model was originally applied by Lijphart to actual political systems only in the most general and theoretical way, the successful application of it by Stiefbold in his detailed and original analysis of Austrian politics indicates that it can be used as a framework for systematic empirical research. In the case of Canada, in view of the inadequacies of other theories, and the presence of factors that in Europe are conducive to consociational democracy and elite accommodation, there is reason to believe that the application of Lijphart's model would prove equally insightful.

NOTES

[1] *The Government of Canada*, 4th Ed., rev. by Norman Ward (Toronto: University of Toronto Press, 1963), p. 454.

[2] J. A. Corry and J. E. Hodgetts, *Democratic Government and Politics*, 3rd Ed. (Toronto: University of Toronto Press, 1959), p. 223.

[3] A book which appears to have had considerable influence on Canadian writers on politics in the 1940's and '50's is E. Pendleton Herring's *The Politics of Democracy* (New York: W. W. Norton, 1940).

[4] F. H. Underhill, *Canadian Political Parties* (Canadian Historical Association Booklet No. 8, 1964), p. 11.

[5] See V. O. Key, Jr., *Politics, Parties, and Pressure Groups*, 5th Ed. (New York: Crowell, 1964).

[6] For an attempt to apply the terminology of American legislative studies to the Canadian

House of Commons see Allan Kornberg, *Canadian Legislative Behavior* (New York: Holt, Rinehart and Winston, 1967), which is a study not of how M.P.'s behave but of their personal and political backgrounds and attitudes.

[7] D. V. Smiley, "The National Party Leadership Convention in Canada: A Preliminary Analysis", *CJPS*, Vol. 1 no. 4 (December, 1968), p. 380.

[8] See D. Owen Carrigan, *Canadian Party Platforms, 1867-1968* (Toronto, Copp Clark, 1968).

[9] See David Easton, *A Framework for Political Analysis* (Englewood Cliffs, N.J.: Prentice Hall, 1965).

[10] F. C. Engelmann and M. A. Schwartz, *Political Parties and the Canadian Social Structure* (Scarborough, Prentice-Hall, 1967), p. 107.

[11] *Ibid.*, p. 110.

[12] R. MacGregor Dawson, *Democratic Government in Canada*, rev. by W. F. Dawson (Toronto: University of Toronto Press, 1963), p. 125.

[13] W. H. Riker, *Federalism: Origin, Operation, Significance* (Boston and Toronto: Little, Brown, 1964), p. 136.

[14] *Ibid.*, p. 93.

[15] *Ibid.*, p. 118.

[16] *Ibid.*, p. 129.

[17] Paul W. Fox, "Regionalism and Confederation" in Mason Wade (ed.), *Regionalism in the Canadian Community, 1867-1967* (Toronto: University of Toronto Press, 1969), pp. 2-29.

[18] John Meisel, "Canadian Parties and Politics" in R. H. Leach (ed.), *Contemporary Canada* (Durham, N.C.: Duke University Press, 1968), p. 134-135.

[19] See e.g., S. M. Lipset, *The First New Nation* (New York: Basic Books, 1963).

[20] See e.g., Arthur R. M. Lower, *Colony to Nation*, 4th Ed. rev. (Toronto: Longmans, 1964).

[21] Edwin R. Black and Alan C. Cairns, "A Different Perspective on Canadian Federalism" in J. Peter Meekison (ed.), *Canadian Federalism: Myth or Reality* (Toronto, Methuen, 1968), pp. 81-97.

[22] J. M. S. Careless, "Limited Identities in Canada," *CHR*, Vol. I, no. 1 (March 1969), p. 3.

[23] Ramsay Cook, "Canadian Centennial Celebrations", *International Journal*, Vol. XXII no. 4 (1967), p. 663.

[24] *Ibid.*, p. 6.

[25] *Ibid.*, p. 9.

[26] *Ibid.*, p. 5.

[27] I. L. Horowitz, "Consensus, Conflict and Cooperation: A Sociological Inventory", *Social Forces* (December, 1962), pp. 178-82.

[28] John Meisel, "Recent Changes in Canadian Parties" in Hugh G. Thorburn (ed.), *Party Politics in Canada*, 2nd Ed. (Scarborough, Prentice-Hall, 1967), p. 34.

[29] *op. cit.*, p. 15.

[30] Mildred A. Schwartz, *Public Opinion and Canadian Identity* (Berkeley and Los Angeles, University of California Press, 1967).

[31] *Ibid.*, p. 231.

[32] *Ibid.*, p. 248.

[33] This point is discussed in John Meisel, *"Recent Changes in Canadian Parties"*, *loc. cit*, pp. 35-37.

[34] The degree of party involvement in particular decision areas is not easily determined. In general, however, I think there is a valid distinction to be made between the involvement of a party *as a party* and the involvement of, for example, a cabinet minister in *his ministerial role* even though he is of course also a party figure.

[35] See Arend Lijphart, "Consociational Democracy," *World Politics,* Vol. XXI no. 2 (January, 1969), pp. 207-25; *idem,* "Typologies of Democratic Systems," *Comparative Political Studies,* Vol. I, no. 1 (April 1968), pp. 3-44; *idem, The Politics of Accommodation: Pluralism and Democracy in the Netherlands* (Berkeley and Los Angeles: University of California Press, 1968).

[36] Arend Lijphart, "Typologies of Democratic Systems," *loc. cit.,* pp. 14-17.

[37] *Ibid.,* p. 26.

[38] *Ibid.,* pp. 22-23.

[39] Arend Lijphart, "Consociational Democracy," *loc. cit.,* pp. 220-21.

[40] Rodney P. Stiefbold, "Elite-Mass Opinion Structure and Communication Flow in a Consociational Democracy (Austria)," paper presented at the American Political Science Association, Washington, 1968.

[41] John Porter, *The Vertical Mosaic* (Toronto: University of Toronto Press,1965), p. 385.

[42] *Ibid.,* p. 383.

[43] *Ibid.,* p. 558.

[44] J. M. S. Careless, *op. cit.,* p. 9.

[45] To simplify the diagram only two provinces are included. Also, the model inevitably oversimplifies or omits certain patterns of communication. In particular, a more fully developed model might well include a pattern of direct communication between provincial political and bureaucratic elites—a pattern which in recent years appears to have developed considerably.

[46] See Richard Gwyn, *Smallwood: the Unlikely Revolutionary* (Toronto, McClelland Stewart, 1968), pp. 102-103.

[47] The relative ease with which new arrivals from the provinces develop 'national' perspectives upon assuming office in Ottawa suggests that political scientists concerned with 'socialization' might do well to include in their researches not only children but also federal politicians.

[48] This is certainly not unique. See the discussion of the German political culture in Gabriel A. Almond and Sidney Verba, *The Civic Culture* (Boston and Toronto: Little, Brown, 1965).

[49] See W. H. Riker, *op. cit.,* p. 118.

[50] And hence, it might be added, potentially in a position to play one government off against another.

[51] This view would appear to be supported by David Easton also. See *A Systems Analysis of Political Life* (New York: Wiley, 1965), pp. 250-51.

[52] Arend Lijphart, "Typologies of Democratic systems," *loc. cit.,* p. 21.

PART II
THE CONSTITUTION
AND CANADIAN FEDERALISM

6

The Living Canadian Constitution*

Alan C. Cairns

The dustbin of recent history is littered with discarded constitutions cast aside after brief and withering exposure to reality. Constitutions capable of responding and adapting to the perils of change have sufficient scarcity value to be treated with the deference appropriate to rare achievements. All the more curious, therefore, has been the detached, unappreciative Canadian attitude to one of the most durable and successful constitutions in the world.

A partial explanation is found in the nature of the British North America Act. It is a document of monumental dullness which enshrines no eternal principles and is devoid of inspirational content. It was not born in a revolutionary, populist context, and it acquired little symbolic aura in its subsequent history. The movement to Confederation was not a rejection of Europe, but was rather a pragmatic response to a series of economic, political, military and technological considerations. There was no need for the kind of political theorizing which accompanied the American experience of creating a new political entity, and which exercised a spell on subsequent generations. With the important exception of the federal system, Canada was endowed "with a Constitution similar in Principle to that of the United Kingdom." Constitutional monarchy and responsible government in a parliamentary setting were already part of the Canadian heritage and were approvingly translated to the larger sphere of action which the new Dominion created. No resounding assertions of human rights accompanied the creation of the new polity. The British tradition precluded any approach to their protection premised on comprehensive declarations of principle.

The absence of an overt ideological content in its terms, and the circumstances surrounding its creation, have prevented the BNA Act from being perceived as a repository of values by which Canadianism was to be measured. Further, the first thirty years of its existence were troubled by depression, threats of secession, and constant bickering over its terms. These scarcely constituted the circumstances for the Act to become the symbolic focus for the nascent political system. Consequently, a conscious ideological adherence and loyalty to the BNA Act and the

* From *Queen's Quarterly*, Vol. LXXVII no. 4 (Winter Issue, 1970), pp. 1-16. Reprinted by permission.

constitution of which it was a part never became overt integral components of the Canadian civil identity.

An additional factor in the Canadian lack of appreciation for the constitution is a confused understanding of the meaning of age and time for institutions.

With the passage of time the intentions of the Fathers unavoidably became an increasingly artificial concept with an ever attenuated contact with reality. Their visions were responses to the problems they faced in the light of prevalent conceptions of the role of government. Many of the conditions to which they addressed themselves faded away, to be replaced by conditions they could not predict. In such circumstances deference to their intentions became impossible, for they had none. Nevertheless, the BNA Act, which represents a consolidation of some of their intentions, remains an important constitutional document. This raises the question of how relevant for a contemporary evaluation of the Canadian constitution is the fact that the BNA Act is a century old.

At the most abstract level of institutional analysis, age has a double significance. Positively, a functioning institution of ancient origin acquires the special credibility that derives from its continuing utility for the attainment of one or more specified human goals. In the Darwinian process of institutional competition for survival it has emerged triumphant. Negatively, it is placed on the defensive by the fact that the contemporary circumstances to which it now applies are significantly different from the circumstances to which it was originally a response. Hence, it appears to be tinged with mortality. The graveyard, sooner or later, is its inevitable destination.

To continue the discussion on this level, however, is to grant to the question of age an undeserved importance and a spurious relevance. Institutions do not have a natural life span. They are, when wisely constructed and carefully tended, evolving human arrangements for avoiding the ravages of time by flexibly responding to the demands which confront them. Therefore to discuss the relevance of an institution in terms of its age, defined by the lapse of time since its first beginnings, is to misconceive what an institution is.

Canadian understanding of the constitution would have been much improved had it been consistently viewed in the significant American phrase as a "living constitution."[1] The wise admonition of Holmes reveals a perspective sadly lacking in Canada:

> The provisions of the Constitution are not mathematical formulas having their essence in their form; they are organic living institutions transplanted from English soil. Their significance is vital, not formal; it is to be gathered not simply by taking the words and a dictionary, but by considering their origin and the line of their growth . . . . When we are dealing with words that are also a constituent act, like the Constitution of the United States, we must realize that they have called into life a being of the development of which could not have been foreseen completely by the most gifted of its

begetters. It was enough for them to realize or to hope that they had created an organism; it has taken a century and has cost their successors much sweat and blood to prove that they created a nation. The case before us must be considered in the light of our whole experience and not merely in that of what was said a hundred years ago.[2]

It is the virtual absence of this understanding of a living constitution which has produced the mistaken belief that the constitution is a century old, that it has already outlived its alloted life span, and that *younger* means *better* and *older* means *worse*. Given this belief it is possible to advocate a new constitution simply because the BNA Act was drafted a century ago. The rather trite conclusion automatically follows that a constitution, or a constitutional document, so heavy with years must be out of date.

In the 1960s there has been a recurrence of the criticism of the constitution as obsolete which was so widespread in the Depression of the thirties. In that troubled decade, the constitution as judicially interpreted was roundly condemned by centralists for the barriers it placed in the way of decisive action by the federal government. The contemporary attack has different roots. One source is the spurt of nation building and constitution making which followed the demise of Western imperialism. In much of the Third World, constitution making became a normal political activity interrupted by secession movements, coups, assassinations, and civil war as the new states struggled to overcome appalling problems and to find a framework for modernization. Whatever the justification for their endemic efforts to resolve their constitutional difficulties, and there are many, only a masochist would find their experience worthy of emulation.

An additional source is the French-Canadian view of recent years that the existing constitution restricts the process of nation building in Quebec. Hence Marcel Faribault, the late Premier Daniel Johnson, Father Ares, Professor A. Dubuc, and numerous others have issued clarion calls for a new constitution to usher in the new age of emancipation which is part of the rhetoric of the Quebec nationalist intelligentsia. Their search for a new constitution is sustained by English-Canadian writers such as Peter O'Hearn, who finds the "battered hulk of the British North America Act and its train of amendments" unacceptable.[3] Other English-Canadian support is found in politicians who capitalize on any groundswell of opinion, or who naively assume that to be progressive requires a repudiation of the past, at least at the level of oratory. They sympathize with T. C. Douglas, whose own party is more trapped by the shibboleths of the nineteenth century than any other Canadian party, when he states: "The time has come for Canadians to free themselves from the dead hand of the past and forge a constitution that will enable Canada to keep its rendezvous with destiny. . . . I do not think that the dead hand of the past should be allowed to stay the onward march of progress. Human rights are sacred but constitutions are not."[4]

In an age when rapid obsolescence is viewed as the natural and inevitable end for every man-made product, such a thesis quickly finds attentive receptive hearers. Superficially it has compelling force, for clearly the conditions of 1867 have passed away. It logically follows that decisions made in the light of those conditions must become increasingly irrelevant with the passage of time.

Crucial to this widespread position is the belief that the constitution is by and large what the Fathers bequeathed to us a century ago. From this perspective the constitution emerged in 1867 in the form of the British North America Act and its accompanying understandings, the product of a small political élite, the Fathers of Confederation, and barring formal amendments, is now what it was then. The confusion is subtle. To view the constitution in terms of what the Fathers intended and immediately achieved fails to see that the constitution is a continuous creation. It accords too much deference to the constitution as it existed in 1867, and too little attention to the contribution of subsequent generations to its evolution.

The Canadian constitution is the body of understandings defining the basic institutions of government and the relationships between them, plus the relationships between governments in the federal system, and between the citizens and those governments. At any given point of time the content of the constitution is a series of living practices which has been worked out by successive generations. It is a product of continuous selection, rejection, and addition. It is always, in a practical sense, contemporary. It is a living instrument of government, wider in scope than the BNA Act, and not restricted to the 1867 intentions of the Fathers. It is an evolving institution which has responded to pressures and flexibly accommodated itself to a variety of needs and changing demands.

The distinction between the constitution as an institution and the key statute that went into its formation is cogently described by Llewellyn in his discussion of the American constitution:

> The discrepancy between theory and fact found in private law is exaggerated in the constitutional field, because under a code of rigid words no easy and gradual rewording of outmoded rules, in such manner as to hide the changes made in their content, is possible. The consequence is that with growing age all force in the actual words of a code withers and dies. What is left, and living, is not a code, but an institution. Many of the institution's roots trace back through time into the code. *Many do not.* But the living institution is neither the dead code nor its interpretation. It is not even by any parthenogenesis descended from its great-grandmother code alone. It is new, it is different, it is growing; and in its blood run so many other streams that resemblance to the code is seldom strong and always confined to single traits.[5]

Evidence on the living nature of the constitution is ubiquitous. The settlement of 1867 was only a beginning. It has been under constant transformation since that time. The major evidence is as follows:

1. The instruments of federal control—disallowance, reservation, and refusal of assent by the Lieutenant-Governor—have fallen into virtual desuetude. If not entirely dead, there is no likelihood that they will ever again be used in the coercive fashion of the early post-Confederation years.

2. The transformation of Empire into Commonwealth—from "Colony to Nation"—has reduced the ties to Great Britain until all that remains is an increasingly attenuated emotional link, a similarity in the institutions of parliamentary and monarchial government, and an embarrassing leftover in the continuing (entirely formal) role of the British parliament in the amending procedure.

3. As is well known, the division of powers in the BNA Act was importantly affected by the Judicial Committee of the Privy Council. While its decisions aroused much resentment and may or may not have been appropriate to Canadian needs, it cannot be denied that they made a fundamental contribution to the constitutional evolution Canadians actually experienced.

4. The division of powers was also transformed by the massive engine of the federal spending power and the conditional grants mechanism. Once again the evaluation may be favourable or unfavourable, but it is clear that the result was a marked change in the practical significance of Sections 91 and 92 of the BNA Act. Perhaps the spending power was used indiscriminately. Perhaps its use should have been (or should be) more tightly controlled, but that is not the issue here.

5. The proliferation of federal-provincial meetings of administrators and politicians, culminating in conferences of premiers and prime ministers has added, as many have pointed out, an important new mechanism of coordination for the federal system.

6. Since the onset of World War II the fiscal system has not been the chaos of clashing taxing jurisdictions which it was in the Depression. Further, as part of a succession of fiscal agreements, huge equalization grants have been paid to the less well-endowed provinces. The original compulsory federal subsidies have been rendered financially trivial by comparison.

7. The parliamentary system has been transformed by the development of the party system, the institution of party discipline, the emergence of third parties and their recognition, the institution of research staffs for the opposition parties, etc. Recently we have been told that before our very eyes the parliamentary system is being transformed into a presidential system without the requisite checks and balances. The truth of this latter statement is irrelevant for our purposes. What is

relevant is that the parliamentary half of the Canadian wedding of parliamentary government and federalism has not stood still.

8. Even prior to the passage of the Diefenbaker Bill of Rights, the Supreme Court, and particularly Mr. Justice Rand, began to develop a court-supported jurisprudence for the protection of civil liberties. Basing their decisions largely on the flimsy constitutional basis of the preamble to the BNA Act which stated that Canada was to have "a Constitution similar in Principle to that of the United Kingdom," the court enunciated an important series of civil liberties decisions.

9. Finally, there were the formal amendments to the Act which contributed to its evolution.

Even in the cryptic fashion expressed above, these changes have been of momentous significance in the evolution of the Canadian constitution.

The agents of these changes were largely the politicians and civil servants of both levels of government responding to the demands and opportunities which the possession of office imposed on them. To examine the above list is to have it confirmed that the constitution never has been, and is not now, only what the courts say it is. The evolution of the constitution has been largely guided by successive generations of political leaders and their influential bureaucratic advisers. Admittedly they did not have a clean slate to work with. Admittedly the result has been evolution rather than revolution. Admittedly certain key parts of the constitutional framework remain, in form at least, as they were originally established in 1867. It is also true that a different beginning would have produced a different outcome, but that is true of all human experiments. The point is not that what happened in 1867 did not matter, but that the decisions then made did not constitute a cake of custom which has held subsequent generations of Canadians in unwilling thralldom in a world they never made. The point is that the constitution has worked and grown in response to the shifting conditions thrown up by the passage of time. A constitution which had accommodated for a century the often competing demands of two ethnic groups, which had survived through depression and war, the transformation of a rural society into an urban society, the settlement of the West, and the technological revolution of recent years might have been appreciated in more prosaic times for its real practical virtues, rather than as was so often the case, being scorned for its absence of symbolic appeal, and criticized for a non-existent inflexibility. In the words of Eugene Forsey, "There is no point in change for its own sake, or just for the sake of having the very latest thing in constitutions. (What matters in a constitution is not how new it is but how good it is, how well it works.) The bigger the change, the heavier the onus upon those who propose it to prove that it is necessary, or even useful."[6]

It may be taken for granted that the Canadian constitution, like any other, prejudices some and fosters other public policy outputs. Any constitution, particularly a federal one, will regularly prevent some group of office holders from attaining some of their policy objectives. To criticize a constitution because it entails this consequence, however, is similar to criticizing the law of gravity. The more precise and relevant question is comparative, whether or not the existing constitution erects more barriers to desired governmental output than would its successor. The answer depends on the nature of the particular new constitution that is advocated. Until that information is available, it is entirely proper to note the flexibility of the existing constitution.

All of the changes noted above are obvious and well known. Why then has so little heed been paid to the message they contain about the flexibility of a living constitution? What explains the constant confusion implicit in the attacks on the constitution because of its age? First, there is sometimes failure to distinguish between the BNA Act and the constitution. Then the relative paucity of formal amendments, especially dealing with the division of powers, has produced a misleading impression of stability belied by our actual experience even in that area. Much of the change which has occurred has not been formally designated as constitutional, and it has not been accompanied by fanfare. It has simply represented the handiwork of busy men attempting to work an on-going system of government.

A good part of the explanation simply lies in a compartmentalization of the minds of the critics and analysts. While all the changes have been recognized and noted, they have frequently co-existed with the assumption that the constitution is a century old. The absence of the concept of a living constitution has aided in this compartmentalization. The confusion has been deliberately sewn by propagandists who have undertaken partisan attacks on the constitution because it stood in the way of their pet panacea. No century-old document (or constitution), they contend, should be allowed to stand in the way of the people. At the opposite pole, blindness on the part of some constitution-worshippers, who have been reluctant to believe that their god could be affected by anything so mundane as the passage of time, has had some influence.

Finally, the scholarship of historians and lawyers, and to a lesser extent of political scientists, has been obsessed with discovering the true meaning of 1867. Centralists and provincialists, compact theorists and their opponents, have all fought over the BNA Act in an attempt to discover its true meaning and often to further their partisan objectives. By so doing they have exaggerated the importance of the original agreement of 1867 and have downgraded the changes it underwent in its subsequent expression.

In view of the preceding, two frequent tendencies in the discussion and evaluation of the Canadian constitution have been based on dangerous misunderstandings. It is simply mistaken to attack the existing constitution because of the age of the BNA Act, one of the key documents which went into its making a century ago. Llewellyn describes a working constitution "as being in essence not a document, but a living constitution built (historically, genetically) in first instance *around* a particular document."[7] "With every passing decade," stated Carl Brent Swisher, "a constitution written long ago provides less and less guidance for its own interpretation amid patterns of social change and with sheer change in the dictionary meanings of familiar terminology."[8] It is equally fallacious to transform the constitutional settlement of 1867 into a measuring rod against which subsequent deviations can be assessed and their perpetrators chastised. Two American authors describe the "intentions of the framers" as a "filio-pietistic notion that can have little place in the adjudicative process of the latter half of the twentiety century. . . . A nation wholly different from that existing in 1787, facing problems obviously not within the contemplation of the Founding Fathers, can scarcely be governed—except in broadest generality—by the concepts and solutions of yesteryear."[9] The same point was lucidly expressed by Chief Justice Hughes of the United States Supreme Court: "It is no answer to say that this public need was not apprehended a century ago, or to insist that what the provision of the Constitution meant to the vision of that day it must mean to the vision of our time. If by the statement that what the Constitution meant at the time of its adoption it means today, it is intended to say that the great clauses of the Constitution must be confined to the interpretation which the framers, with the condition and outlook of their time, would have placed upon them, the statement carries its own refutation."[10] To attack the constitution on grounds of age is to fail to see its living nature. It is the same failure which produces the description of post-1867 changes as deviations.

This latter approach was very widespread in discussions of judicial review, particularly in criticisms of the Privy Council. Since lawyers constitute the professional group which has arrogated specialized expertise to itself in this matter they have an important responsibility for the misconceptions which heavily influence our constitutional discussion. I do not forget that one category of legal criticism of the Judicial Committee was based on the alleged failure of British judges to treat the BNA Act as a living instrument of government. It is true that to this group Lord Sankey, with his "living tree" analogy, was the closest thing to a judicial hero that is found in the law periodicals. However, the other major group of criticisms was specifically based on the unacceptable conduct of the Judicial Committee in departing either from the intentions of the Fathers, or the clear meaning of the BNA Act in which those intentions were presumably embodied. Further, the "living tree" school of Canadian criticism typically also reproached the Privy Council for leading Canada down the provincial path away from the limited, centralized federalism so wisely chosen in the sixties of the nineteenth century. This was partly because those critics willing to overtly discuss the constitution in terms of current need were usually centralists. Consequently, they could not resist appealing to the Fathers and their original creation as the touchstone of constitutional wisdom.

In general, the basic language of both constitutional case law and its Canadian critics stressed fidelity to an ancient document. O'Connor, the author of the classic fundamentalist statement that judges should apply the Act in terms of the meanings deliberately embodied in it by its creators, strongly attacked the Judicial Committee for "most serious and persistent deviation . . . from the actual text of the Act." He was highly critical of Lord Watson's "assumption of the guardianship of the autonomy of the provinces. His proper function was merely that of an interpreter of the meaning of the words of a statute."[11] This position reflected the British tradition which instructs judges to apply statutes literally. Thus, jurisprudence in Canada, both in the language of courts and that of their critics, has not devised adequate criteria to guide judges in the employment of the discretion they unavoidably possess. This has been unfortunate, for it has meant that much constitutional advocacy has been, literally, meaningless. It has also contributed to the misunderstanding of what a constitution is.

The critics of the Privy Council frequently asserted that its failure rested on an unwillingness to use the variety of historical evidence available to throw light on the intentions of the Fathers, and thus clarify obscurities in the BNA Act. This approach was always fraught with difficulties, but with the passage of time its desirability became increasingly questionable. This was recognized by Professor Strayer in a recent publication. He noted the "very limited" evidence available on the formation of the Act and, more important, questioned its utility in principle. "Conditions have so drastically changed since 1867," he pointed out, "that the particular context in which the Act was passed may have little bearing on the context in which it is now expected to operate."

This position represents a marked change from the obsessive concern with the intentions of the Fathers in the decades prior to the abolition of appeals to the Privy Council. Yet Strayer is still caught in a historical quagmire of his own making. The obligation to appeal to the past is irresistible. His argument continues: "The more crucial question now is: What would the framers have intended had conditions been in 1867 as they are today? Even if the courts could now be induced to make use of external evidence as to the conditions of that time such evidence would be of limited value in answering this hypothetical question."[12]

Unfortunately, we are not told what evidence would be helpful. Given the impossibility of deciding how to undertake this pseudo-historical quest, one wonders why it should be undertaken at all. The assertion of Learned Hand is as valid for Canada as for the United

States: "It is impossible to fabricate how the 'Framers' would have answered the problems that arise in a modern society had they been reared in the civilization that has produced those problems. We should indeed have to be sorcerers to conjure up how they would have responded."[13]

In the evolution of a constitution, it is evident that the passage of time does and should reduce the weight to be given to the views and desires of the Fathers or of influential moulders of the constitution at other points of time. As time transforms the conditions to which the constitution must be responsive, the search is not for what was originally intended, but for what can be creatively extracted from a constitutional heritage of which the BNA Act is only a part. The search for the contemporary meaning of the constitution does not consist in minute examination of what was said or intended or achieved a century ago. Such an approach would deny to constitutional unfolding the benefits which a century of experience has given us. This generation, its predecessors and successors, partially have and certainly should view the constitution for what it is, a developing responsive tradition neither to be lightly departed from nor to be casually obeyed.

The arrangements of 1867 were never a sacrosanct body of holy writ. Approaches which so regarded them constituted a disservice to the Canadian polity and rested on a misunderstanding of the nature of a constitution. They inhibited change and thus reduced the flexibility essential for survival. Equally important, they blinded their possessors to the changes which did occur. Realistically, all working constitutions are living constitutions springing from, but not bound and gagged by, history. Inadequate recognition of this truth is a significant cause of the constitutional morass in which we now find ourselves. Cryptically we might say that the constitution has not failed us, so much as we, by our inadequate understanding of its living nature, have failed it. In a living constitution all generations are simultaneously Fathers and Sons, by necessity even if not by choice. King, Bennett, Diefenbaker, and their provincial counterparts were in their own way Fathers as were Macdonald and Cartier. Like Macdonald and Cartier they were also sons in that they built on the achievements of their predecessors. There can be no quarrel with the fact that each succeeding generation of Canadians has decided what parts of the constitution they received were viable and worthy of continued life, and which were not. However, we can quarrel with those who, either blinded by a deification of the past, resist new departures because the Fathers intended otherwise, or propose a new constitution on the mistaken grounds that the existing one, because of its time or origin, is necessarily an inflexible, incompetent instrument for new conditions. The first approach makes us prisoners of the past. The second approach deprives us of the benefits which a rich tradition provides.

To view a constitution as a living constitution has important consequences. It is to recognize that the processes of constitutional change are manifold and unpredictable. The process of formal amendment and judicial review are neither the only nor the most important vehicles for change. The constitution is constantly interpreted and modified by the men who work it. No new division of powers can prevent the intermingling of the activities of both levels of government in modern conditions. Predictable, clear-cut procedures for change can be obtained in the area of formal amendment, but nowhere else. The Supreme Court can be revamped in various ways, but "the history of judge-made law invites no other view than this: that the parties to the original federal 'bargain' can never be certain that the words in which they have clothed their intentions can ever be more than a rough guide to political activity, or that the range of permissible activity at any time after will bear any exact relation to their intentions."[14]

The terribly difficult problem, frequently overlooked because of obsession with the written text and the more blatant methods of change by amendment and judicial review, is how to devise conventions and understandings by which the other less obvious methods of change can be brought within a framework of constitutionalism. The main weakness, for example, of the compact theory as a set of criteria for constitutional change did not lie in its hotly contested validity, but in the restricted scope of its intended operation. Even if whole-hearted agreement to its terms had existed, this would have represented no more than a control of the amending procedure, one of the least important methods of constitutional change in Canadian history.

This problem is, of course, recognized by influential Quebec spokesmen. The late Premier Daniel Johnson, for example, stated in 1967:

> Canada today is faced with a whole series of problems which the Fathers of Confederation . . . could not conceivably have foreseen . . . . Therefore, when a new problem arises in Canada, we are more and more likely to base each government's responsibilities for it, not on constitutional principles, but on considerations of the moment which, in turn, derive from a variety of factors such as relative capacity to act, financial resources or merely the political power wielded by a given area of government. Hence even though there is a written document called the British North America Act from which we may expect some light to be cast on such traditional fields as education and municipal institutions, the allocation of new tasks among governments has not been guided by this document but by decisions mainly based on exigencies of the day. . . . Our present Constitution, perhaps admirable during the age of steam trains, no longer suits Canada's needs in this era of interplanetary rockets.[15]

At the 1966 Federal-Provincial Conference on taxation, Johnson stated:

> Having reached what it considers a turning point in its history, Quebec expects some specific things from the present constitutional system. First, it wants proof that the division of powers written in the constitution is not

mere window-dressing and that, accordingly, it can count on the fiscal and financial resources it requires in order to discharge its obligations properly. . . . Quebec also wants assurance that it can exercise, fully and without interference from any quarter, all its power under the present constitution. It wants the Government of Canada to withdraw from fields which are not federal or in which the provinces have priority.[16]

Essentially the same point was made by Professor Dubuc who asserted that a century of change had rendered the BNA Act "too far removed from the basic structure and values of . . . [contemporary] . . . society to remain the touchstone for the division of powers," with the consequence that the "most important conflicts are settled on the political level and become confrontations of power; these are the conditions of political chaos."[17]

The general cogency of these critiques can be accepted. The question, however, is what can be done about them. To Johnson and Dubuc the obvious answer is a new constitution whose division of powers reflects the worked-out results of a contemporary agreement, responding to today's conditions, as to what the responsibilities of each level of government should be. Assuming for the moment that agreement could in fact be reached on a new constitution, the contribution that this would make to the solution of the problem which troubles Dubuc and Johnson is debatable. Obviously, if Quebec were to be granted greatly enhanced jurisdictional authority, the seriousness of the problem from Quebec's viewpoint would be greatly diminished. The problem would still exist, but its scope would be less extensive. If, however, as seems more likely, a new division of powers did not deviate markedly from the existing division, we would be little better off. It is not entirely clear that an ancient division of powers is more likely to produce "decisions mainly based on exigencies of the day" than is a division freshly minted at a constitutional conference. To some extent the problem arises from the impossibility of devising a comprehensive catalogue of powers into which all proposed legislation can be easily fitted. The operations of modern governments are too complex, the future is too unpredictable, and words are too full of imprecision and ambiguity for such an achievement. Further, the very political processes which Johnson and Dubuc decry for the uncertainties they generate can be seen as the instruments to produce the concordance between the division of powers and contemporary requirements which they seek. If such processes did not exist, we would really be in a bad way. The difficult problem, as suggested earlier, is to find ways by which they can be brought within a framework of constitutionalism.

The assault on the existing constitution has led to a process of constitutional review out of which a new, or at least a drastically modified, constitution is supposed to emerge. Unfortunately, the justification for this review does not reside in any self-evident likelihood that a new and better constitution can be created. The existing constitution was caught in a barrage of criticism based on its age, which is largely a fraudulent consideration, and a confused battery of French-Canadian demands to break with the past and stake out for themselves a status in Canadian federalism superior to what was apparently possible under the constitution as they perceived it.

From the evidence which is available, there is little possibility that a new constitution will emerge. Most of the political leaders engaged in constitutional review are dutifully going through the motions with little hope or desire that any major changes will transpire. If their pessimism is correct, Canadians will be left with the existing constitution whose limited sanctity has been further eroded by the criticism to which it has been subjected in the process of review. Its claim to our continued allegiance may come to rest on the flimsy basis that it is the only constitution Canadians have.

The perspective on the constitution adopted in this essay is a reminder that a constitution is not merely a piece of paper. It is a set of relationships between governments and between governments and peoples which has become embedded in the evolving habits and values of successive generations of Canadians. Tinkering with constitutional documents in an era of *laissez faire* might have left the mass of the citizenry unaffected. However, when governments increasingly involve themselves in the nooks and crannies of our lives, dramatic constitutional change presents a less attractive and less plausible face. It is only necessary to observe the difficulties of successfully introducing major policies, such as medicare or tax reform, to question the feasibility of attempting to change a large part of the very constitutional framework from which governments derive their authority and by means of which citizens deal with government.

A new constitution can be no more than a point of departure. The day after it is proclaimed its evolution away from the agreement just reached will commence. The new settlement will inevitably be subject to the informal processes of change and growth which helped "undermine" the BNA Act. The security and control of the future which can be obtained from a written document are only relative. Further, if a new constitution is created, the shortrun result of its implementation inevitably will be an increase in uncertainty and insecurity until the text is fleshed out by the actions of men struggling to make it work. This, of course, is in addition to the uncertainties automatically generated by the simple fact of change from the old constitution to the new. Given these corollaries of a new constitution, we might consider whether constitutions are not like wine—much better when well aged. Perhaps, however, 1867 was not a good year for constitutions.

NOTES

[1] For an excellent American discussion of the living constitution, see K. N. Llewellyn, "The Constitution as an Institution", *Columbia Law Review* (1934), p. 34.

[2] Cited in Archibald MacLeish and E. F. Pritchard, Jr., (eds.), *Law and Politics: Occasional Papers of Felix Frankfurter* (New York, Capricorn Books, 1962), p. 71. The eloquence of Holmes can be supplemented by Marshall's famous description of "a constitution intended to endure for ages to come, and consequently, to be adapted to the various crises of human affairs".

[3] Peter Joseph Thomas O'Hearn, *Peace, Order and Good Government* (Toronto, Macmillan of Canada, 1964), p. 6.

[4] *Globe and Mail* (Toronto, April 13, 1966), p. 7.

[5] Llewellyn, *op. cit.* p. 6 *n.*

[6] "Constitutional Monarchy and the Provinces", *Ontario Advisory Committee on Confederation: Background Papers and Reports* (Toronto, Queen's Printer, 1967), p. 180. Ronald I. Cheffins, *The Constitutional Process in Canada* (Toronto, McGraw-Hill, 1969) provides a well-argued defence of the existing constitution. See especially Chapter 1 and pp. 150-51, 167.

[7] Llewellyn, *op. cit.,* p. 3.

[8] *The Supreme Court in Modern Role*, rev. ed. (New York, New York University Press, 1965), p. 192.

[9] Arthur S. Miller and Ronald F. Howell, "The Myth of Neutrality in Constitutional Adjudication", *University of Chicago Law Review,* 27 (1960), p. 683.

[10] Cited in Paul Abraham Freund, *The Supreme Court of the United States* (Cleveland and New York, Peter Smith, 1965), p. 20.

[11] *Report Pursuant to Resolution of the Senate to the Honourable the Speaker by the Parliamentary Counsel Relating to the Enactment of the British North America Act, 1867, any lack of consonance between its terms and judicial construction of them and cognate matters* (Ottawa, King's Printer, 1939), 11, Annex 1, p. 47.

[12] Barry L. Strayer, *Judicial Review of Legislation in Canada* (Toronto, University of Toronto Press, 1968), p. 156.

[13] Learned Hand, *The Bill of Rights* (Cambridge, Mass., Harvard University Press, 1958), pp. 34-35.

[14] Rufus Davis, "The 'Federal Principle' Reconsidered", in Aaron B. Wildavsky (ed.), *American Federalism in Perspective* (Boston, Little, Brown, 1967), p. 14.

[15] *The Confederation of Tomorrow Conference: Proceedings* (Toronto, Queen's Printer, 1968), Appendix B, p. 8.

[16] *The Federal-Provincial Conference, Quebec—Federal-Provincial Tax Structure Committee* (Ottawa, Queen's Printer, 1966), pp. 56-57.

[17] Alfred Dubuc, "The Decline of Confederation and the New Nationalism", in Peter Russell, (ed.), *Nationalism in Canada* (Toronto, McGraw-Hill for the University League for Social Reform, 1966), p. 131.

7

Judicial Review and the Division of Powers in Canada*

Martha Fletcher

One of the most obvious consequences of judicial review is that political questions often come to the courts clothed as legal, constitutional questions. The most notable political questions in federal systems are usually those involving the constitutional division of powers between the two levels of government. The constitutional framework within which the Canadian federation operates and from which judicial adjustment within it proceeds is the British North America Act, 1867 (B.N.A. Act). There the powers of government are divided between the Dominion[1] and the provinces, with section 91 of the Act containing the scope of central government power, and section 92 containing that of the provinces. Yet, because even the most carefully drawn language is subject to multiple interpretations, and because the context in which the arrangements operate changes over time, the division of powers presents to those who govern a continuing problem of adjustment. It is in these areas of adjustment that the choices made by the courts are of political importance, since they may determine which governments may carry out which activities and whether, indeed, some activities may be carried out at all. Thus, judicial review has considerable significance for the way in which the political process responds to the demands placed upon it.

As the court of final appeal for Canada until 1949, it was the responsibility of the Judicial Committee of the Privy Council, sitting in London, to adjudicate conflicts over the division of powers in the Act. Composed of some of the most eminent jurists of the United Kingdom and, later, of the Empire and Commonwealth, the Judicial Committee is technically not a court but rather an advisory body to the Crown, though its "advice" is invariably taken. During much of the time it ruled on Canadian cases it was criticized for its remoteness from the political system and the facts of Canadian life. It was felt by many that an indigenous court would have made different, more "realistic" decisions. The demand for a final court of appeals within Canada ultimately led to the abolition of appeals to the Judicial Committee in 1949 with the Supreme Court of Canada assuming the role of final constitutional arbiter.

Two problems arose in the interpretation of the Dominion and provincial powers conferred by the Constitution under sections 91 and 92.

---

* Reprinted by permission.

One was the changing definition of what matters are of national concern. The second was the sharp difference of opinion between the courts (particularly the Judicial Committee of the Privy Council) and Canadian political leaders and legal scholars concerning both what had been meant in 1867 by the specified functions contained in these sections and how they should be applied to current problems. Further, because the B.N.A. Act has the legal status of merely another statute of the British Parliament, the judges took the view that they were not to go outside the contents of the Act in determining its meaning.

Within sections 91 and 92, four of the constitutional powers which have often been the legal clothing for political disputes concerning the division of powers between Dominion and province are the powers of the Dominion parliament to legislate for the peace, order, and good government of Canada and to regulate trade and commerce; and the powers of the provinces to control property and civil rights in the provinces and to legislate on all matters of merely a local or private nature in the province. Though the litigation involving these powers does not by any means comprise the totality of decisions concerning the federal division of powers, it can serve as an example of the impact of the judicial review on the framework of the federal system, for the interpretation of the boundaries of these powers has been perhaps one of the conspicuous areas in which the courts have played the role of arbiter in the federal system.[2]

THE LOCATION OF THE RESIDUARY POWER

The residuary power—the general grant of legislative authority to the Dominion on all matters not assigned specifically—is a useful example for the study of the impact of judicial review on the working of the federal system. This is true both because the residuary power can be used to legitimate expansion of governmental authority if the court is sympathetic to that expansion and because its expansion or contraction is a sign of the courts' view towards the "proper" division of powers in the federation. Thus it is important both as a source for legitimization of a changing balance of power in the federation and as a sign of the judicial attitude towards such an alteration.

The residuary power in the British North America Act is normally considered to reside in the Dominion authority granted in the opening paragraph of section 91:

> It shall be lawful [for Parliament] to make laws for the peace, order, and good government of Canada, in relation to all matters not coming within the Classes of Subjects by this Act assigned exclusively to the Legislatures of the Provinces; and for greater certainty, but not so as to restrict the Generality of the foregoing Terms of this Section, it is hereby declared that (notwithstanding anything in this Act) the exclusive Legislative Authority

of the Parliament of Canada extends to all Matters coming within the
Classes of Subjects hereinafter enumerated . . . .

The meaning of this grant has been, however, a subject of considerable
litigation for nearly a century, and its interpretation in relation to the totality of legislative powers granted in sections 91 and 92 of the B.N.A.
Act has varied over time, with the result that other sections at times
have taken precedence over it.

From the standpoint of legal interpretation, the meaning of the
peace, order, and good government clause can be understood only in
the context of the two sections which comprise the division of legislative
powers between the Dominion and provincial legislatures, and one
must begin with an analysis of the grammar of the two sections. In the
Parsons case, the Board identified the following grammatical construction as the correct one, and this opinion has been shared by many later
writers on the Canadian constitution.[3]

The opening clause of section 91—"It shall be lawful [for Parlia-
ment] to make laws for the peace, order, and good government of Canada, in relation to all matters not coming within the Classes of Subjects
of this Act assigned exclusively to the Legislatures of the Provinces;"—
states that the Dominion is to have authority over *all matters* not specifically enumerated in section 92. The next clause—"and for greater certainty, but not so as to restrict the Generality of the foregoing Terms of
this Section,"—emphasizes that this general grant of power is not
restricted by the enumerated heads that follow. The words in parenthe-
ses—"notwithstanding anything in this Act"—serve to make explicit
that the power of the Dominion to make laws for peace, order, and good
government takes precedence over the enumeration in section 92. The
final words of the sentence—"the exclusive Legislative Authority of the
Parliament of Canada *extends* [emphasis supplied] to all Matters coming
within the Classes of Subjects . . . enumerated"—implies that the general grant is the sole authority given to the Dominion and that the authority exercisable under the enumerations comes from the one general
grant of power rather than from a separate source to which the general
power is merely supplementary (as subsequent decisions were to maintain).

The final paragraph of section 91, coming after the enumerations,
says that "any matter coming within any of the Classes of Subjects in
this Section shall not be deemed to come within the *class of matters* [em-
phasis supplied] of a local or private nature comprised in the enumeration of the Classes of Subjects by this Act assigned exclusively to the
Legislatures of the Provinces." The significant point in the understanding of this paragraph's place in the Act is to note that the word "class" in
the phrase "class of matters" is singular. When read in conjunction with
section 92, grammatically, the phrase can only refer to section 92, head

16—"generally all matters of a merely local or private nature in the province."

In summary, it is argued here that the peace, order and good government clause was intended to give to the Dominion all subjects of legislation not covered in the provincial list of powers in section 92. The enumerations in section 91 neither add to nor subtract from the Dominion's residuary power over all subjects other than those in the section 92 list, since they are examples of the sorts of powers contemplated in the general grant rather than powers in their own right. The closing paragraph of section 91 was intended to make clear that the mere fact that a matter was of a local or private nature did not remove it from Dominion jurisdiction when it also came within the enumerations of that section. Thus, none of the enumerated heads in sections 91 could, by definition, be considered a provincial matter under any circumstances.

The interpretation of the application of the power to legislate for peace, order, and good government by the Dominion in specific situations has, however, been considerably different from the grammatical reading presented above. In an early landmark case, *Russell* v. *The Queen* (discussed below), the Committee based its decision on a similarly broad interpretation of the Dominion's residuary power. But this view was soon considerably altered by the decisions which followed.

The decisive point in the interpretation of the powers of the Dominion conferred by section 91 came with the *Local Prohibition*[4] case in 1896, in which Lord Watson presented what was to become the prevailing Judicial Committee interpretation of section 91. Watson's decision set out that the power of the Dominion to legislate for the peace, order, and good government of Canada was merely supplementary to the primary power of the Dominion given in the enumerations in section 91. Moreover, the power granted in the section 91 enumerations was not absolute. The closing words of section 91 did not contemplate that the authority of the Dominion under all matters enumerated in section 91 was absolute in its application to local and private matters coming within those subjects, but was merely an authority to legislate on local and private matters when such legislation was necessarily incidental to the exercise of the power over the Dominion as a whole. "It appears to their Lordships that [the closing words of section 91 were] not meant to derogate from the legislative authority given to the provincial legislatures . . . save to the extent of enabling the Parliament of Canada to deal with matters local or private in those cases where such legislation is necessarily incidental to the exercise of the powers conferred upon it by the enumerated heads of clause 91."[5] And, the Board declared, Sir Montague Smith was in error in the *Parsons* case when he declared that the closing words of section 91 applied only to head 16 of section 92. "It appears . . . that the language of the exception in section 91 was meant to include and correctly describe all the matters enumerated in the sixteen heads of section 92."[6] Thus was ruled that the Dominion could not consider its powers listed in the enumerations as paramount over any of the powers given the provinces in section 92. The opening words of section 91 that "(notwithstanding anything in this Act) the exclusive Legislative Authority of the Parliament of Canada extends to all Matters coming within the Classes of Subjects hereinafter enumerated . . ." were ignored rather than explained. The power of the Dominion to legislate for the peace, order, and good government of Canada was ruled to be a supplementary power which gave the Dominion authority to legislate "on such matters as are unquestionably of Canadian interest and importance" but it could not in so legislating "trench upon provincial legislation with respect to any of the classes of subjects enumerated in section 92".[7]

What this view of the peace, order, and good government power would mean became clear in the *Insurance Reference,* where Lord Haldane made more explicit what Lord Watson had begun. "It must be taken to be now settled," Haldane said, "that the general authority to make laws for the peace, order, and good government of Canada . . . does not, unless the subject matter of the legislation falls within some one of the enumerated heads which follow, enable the Dominion Parliament to trench on the subject matter entrusted to the provincial legislatures by the enumerations in section 92."[8] Thus only if the matter is not mentioned in section 92 can the Dominion legislate outside the enumeration of section 91 concerning a province. As Frank Scott put it, "the examples swallowed up the rule".[9] The idea of a general power to legislate for peace, order, and good government which would take precedence over provincial claims in section 92 when matters falling under the section became of national importance was rejected. The general power of legislation disappeared into the enumerated heads of section 91 and reappeared as a provincial power in head 16 of section 92.

As the Dominion power to legislate for peace, order, and good government lost its original significance the Judicial Committee developed a new role for the phrase, while attempting to demonstrate that this interpretation was consistent with previous decisions. The most notable of the cases which the Board had either to refute or re-interpret if the new use of peace, order, and good government was to stand was *Russell* v. *The Queen,*[10] decided in 1882. Here the court had ruled that the pith and substance—what the act was actually intended to do—determined whether it was to be viewed from the Dominion or Provincial aspect and the section into which it would fall.

The act in question, the Canadian Temperance Act of 1878, provided, according to its preamble, uniform legislation on the subject of temperance throughout the Dominion: "the objects and scope of the law are general—to promote temperance by means of a uniform law throughout the Dominion". On this ground the Dominion felt the measure properly fell under "peace, order, and good government" and not under the class of subjects "property and civil rights". The fact that the act was applied individually to each particular place could not alter its character as general legislation.[11] The Board agreed with this view of the Act, saying that "their Lordships cannot think that the Temperance Act in question properly belongs to the class of subjects property and civil rights". Instead, they said that it was very similar to laws placing restrictions on the sale of poisons and drugs, emphasizing that while such items are property, their character is such that their sale and custody can be regulated by the Dominion on the grounds that their use is dangerous to public safety. This sort of regulation, they insisted, does not deal with those items as they are viewed under section 92, head 13. "What Parliament is dealing with is not a matter in relation to property and its right, but one relating to public order and safety," their Lordships maintained. It is the aspect of public order and safety with which the Dominion is concerned, and its overriding interest is not negated by the fact that property is incidentally interfered with. The purpose of the Act is not to interfere with property but to protect public safety, and the section of the B.N.A. Act under which it falls depends on what the Act in question is basically intended to do.[12] As for the local option section of the law, the Board again insisted that the basic intent of the Act was decisive, and this intent was that there should be uniform legislation in all provinces respecting the traffic in intoxicating liquors. "Parliament does not treat the promotion of temperance as desirable in one province more than another. . . . The objects and scope are still general. . . ."[13]

With the redefinition of the Dominion's general power, however, the decision of the Board in the *Russell* case and the meaning of the opening words of section 91 took on new connotations. In the *Board of Commerce* case in 1922[14] Lord Haldane suggested that the decision in the *Russell* case was made to deal with an abnormal, *i.e.*, emergency, situation. Otherwise, the general Dominion powers could not have been called into play. It was in *Fort Francis Pulp and Paper Co.* v. *Manitoba Free Press*[15] two years later that this emergency doctrine was clearly and systematically stated. Here measures taken under the War Powers Act of 1914 were held *intra vires* Dominion authority not under the general powers of peace, order, and good government conferred in section 91, but under an emergency power "discovered" by the Committee. In the event of an emergency, national survival may depend upon the use of exceptional means. It would be suicidal to say that the Dominion could not provide for its own survival, said the Board. Therefore, the interests of the individual might have to be subordinated to those of the community and the Dominion permitted to act under power to legislate for the peace, order, and good government of Canada.

Their application of this heretofore unknown doctrine, however, resulted in some rather unusual legal reasoning. In 1925, basing its opinion on the two earlier Haldane decisions (see above), the Board declared the Industrial Disputes Investigation Act of 1907 *ultra vires* the Dominion on the ground that its subject matter was not among the enumerated subjects of section 91, and its powers trenched upon section 92, head 13, concerning property and civil rights in the provinces.[16] In specifically rejecting the decision in *Russell* v. *The Queen* that an act could be held *intra vires* simply on the grounds that it was to the general advantage of Canada, the court hypothesized in the following terms as to the true grounds upon which the *Russell* case had been decided:

> Their Lordships think that the decision in *Russell* v. *The Queen* can only be supported today, not on the footing of having laid down an interpretation such as has sometimes been invoked of the general words at the beginning of section 91, but on the assumption of the Board, apparently made at the time of deciding the case of *Russell* v. *The Queen,* that the evil of intemperance at the time amounted in Canada to one so great and general that at least for the period it was a menace to the national life of Canada so serious and pressing that the National Parliament was called upon to intervene to protect the nation from disaster. An epidemic of pestilence might conceivably have been regarded as analogous.[17]

To this rather incredible statement by their Lordships came the following Canadian reply:

> I [said Mr. Justice Anglin of the Supreme Court of Canada] cannot find anything in the judgment delivered by Sir Montague E. Smith in the *Russell* case suggestive of such a view having been entertained by the Judicial Committee. On the contrary, the whole tenor of the judgment seems to me inconsistent with its having proceeded on that basis. I should indeed be surprised if a body so well informed as their Lordships had countenanced such an aspersion on the fair name of Canada even though some hard-driven advocate had ventured to insinuate it in argument.[18]

The peace, order, and good government power, then, was to apply in only two very limited cases.[19] First, in normal times, it was limited to only those items which did not fall into either the enumerations of section 91 or 92 (and these instances were rare indeed).[20] Secondly, it would override the provincial powers in section 91 in times of extreme emergency, with the question of whether the situation was a sufficient emergency to justify the use of the power in this fashion to be determined by the courts.

In 1929, however, a less restricted view of the B.N.A. Act was taken by Lord Sankey, when, in ruling on whether women could be called to the Senate, he said: "The British North America Act planted in Canada a living tree capable of growth and expansion within its natural limits. . . . Their Lordships do not conceive it to be the duty of this board . . . to cut down the provisions of the Act by a narrow and technical construction, but rather to give it a large and liberal intrepretation. . . ."[21]

The Sankey "living tree" concept also seemed to carry over in the *Radio* case, decided in 1932, which interpreted the power of the Dominion to implement the International Radiotelegraphy Convention of 1927.

Taking notice of the fact that those involved in radiotelegraphy "must so to speak be kept in order by legislation and the only legislation that can deal with them all at once is Dominion legislation", the Board stated that control of the field was *intra vires* the Dominion under the general power of Parliament to legislate for the peace, order, and good government of Canada, rather than being divided between Dominion and province, provision by provision, according to the heading in section 91 and 92 under which each fell.[22]

In 1937, however, court decisions on the scope of the Dominion general power reverted to the extreme of the *Snider* opinion (1925) with the decisions of the Judicial Committee concerning the Bennett "New Deal" legislation. These enactments were perhaps some of the most crucial ones, both economically and politically, to come before the Board during the years in which it ruled on the B.N.A. Act. This legislation was introduced in an attempt to cope with the problems of the great Depression and dealt with a wide variety of subjects.[23] Three of these acts—the Weekly Rest and Industrial Undertakings Act, the Minimum Wages Act, and the Limitation of Hours of Work Act—were defended before the courts both as coming under the Dominion power to implement treaties (since they were enacted in compliance with agreements of the International Labour Organization) and also under the general power of the Dominion to legislate for the peace, order, and good government of Canada.[24] The Board, however, ruled that neither of these grounds was sufficient to bring the legislation under the power of the central government.

To the argument that treaty legislation as a category was a Dominion affair both under section 132 and under the peace, order, and good government clause, their Lordships said: "While the ship of state now sails on larger ventures and into foreign water she still retains the watertight compartments which are an essential part of her original structure."[25] Rejecting the use of the general power as it had been applied in the *Radio* case, they stated that the true ground of the *Radio* decision was that the legislation fell under the general clause only because it could not be fitted under any of the enumerations in sections 91 and 92.[26]

Finally, to the plea that an emergency situation existed and therefore the acts were valid under power to legislate for the peace, order, and good government of Canada, their Lordships replied that in their view no such overriding emergency existed and ruled the Dominion acts *ultra vires*. In their view,

> It is only necessary to call attention to the phrases in the various cases, "abornmal circumstances," "exceptional conditions," "standard of necessity" (*Board of Commerce* case [1922] 1 A.C. 191), "some extraordinary peril to the national life of Canada," "highly exceptional," "epidemic of pestilence," (*Snider* case [1925] A.C. 396), to show how far the present case is from the conditions which may override the normal distribution of powers in sections 91 and 92.[27]

The Employment and Social Insurance Act was also ruled *ultra vires* the Dominion on the ground that the general powers of the Dominion did not apply here any more than in the previous case and that the Act trenched on section 92, head 13, property and civil rights.[28] With these cases, the height of the emergency doctrine was reached, as bitter Canadians noted that the only emergencies which the Pricy Council had recognized were World War I and the "public drunkenness" sufficient to a national emergency read into the *Russell* case.

In 1946, however, the Privy Council shows signs of retreat from the position taken in the "New Deal" cases. In another test of the temperance legislation which had been in question in *Russell* v. *The Queen*, the Board was asked specifically to rule on the meaning of that case. There Viscount Simon expressly repudiated the reasoning of *Toronto Electric Commissioners* v. *Snider* which had postulated the emergency doctrine in its fullest form. To quote him,

> . . . the British North America Act nowhere gives power to the Dominion Parliament to legislate in matters which are properly to be regarded as exclusively within the competence of the provincial legislatures merely because of the existence of an emergency. Secondly, they can find nothing in the judgment of the Board in 1882 which suggests that it proceeded on the ground of emergency; there was certainly no evidence before the Board that one existed. The act of 1878 was a permanent, not a temporary Act and no objection was raised to it on that account. . . . [T]he true test must be found in the real subject matter of the legislation: if it is such that it goes beyond local or provincial concern or interests and must from its inherent nature be the concern of the Dominion as a whole . . . then it will fall within the competence of the Dominion Parliament as a matter affecting the peace, order, and good government of Canada, though it may in another aspect touch on matters specially reserved to the provincial legislatures. . . . It is the nature of the legislation itself, and not the existence of emergency, that must determine whether it is valid or not.[29]

While liquor legislation was considered to be a matter of such general interest to the Dominion as a whole as to fall under the peace, order, and good government clause, the regulation of hours of work of employees of hotels run by the Canadian Pacific Railway was considered, as late as 1950, to be "substantially" a matter of property and civil rights in the provinces rather than of general interest to Canada.[30]

In 1951 the Judicial Committee again utilized the reasoning of the *Labour Conventions* cases, ruling that legislation controlling the manufacture and importation of margarine in the interest of protecting and encouraging the dairy industry throughout Canada could not be justified by appealing to the sufficient interest rule so recently stated in the *Canadian Temperance Federation* case. Without countering the reasoning in that case, Lord Morton quoted the contrary view found in the *Labour Conventions* opinion as controlling in this instance and made no further comment.[31] Thus the final decisions of the Judicial Committee left the matter of the scope of the peace, order, and good government clause in considerable doubt, and the Supreme Court of Canada (which became the court of final appeal in 1949) was presented with a considerable variety of precedents to follow in interpreting the clause.

The Supreme Court was presented with an opportunity to decide on the scope of the general power soon after the Court became Canada's final constitutional authority. The case was a reference on the validity of the Wartime Leasehold Regulations which were adopted during World War II and carried over into the post-war era.[32] The precedent which the Court used in unanimously upholding the validity of Dominion rent controls came directly from the "emergency" doctrine of *Fort Francis Pulp and Paper Co.* v. *Manitoba Free Press.*[33] In deciding that the Act was valid, the Justices emphasized both the "abnormal" and "emergency" situation arising out of the war and its aftermath and the explicitly temporary nature of the legislation. Noting that in normal times the subject of rent control lay exclusively with the provinces through their power over property and civil rights, the Court emphasized that "the rights of the provinces are not . . . permanently suppressed, and their jurisdiction temporarily suspended . . . flows afresh when the field is finally abandoned".[34] In a spirit unlike that which animated the Judicial Committee in the "New Deal" cases, however, the existence of the emergency in this instance was attested to both by "common sense" (an expression of Mr. Justice Taschereau) and by the view expressed by Kerwin and others that its existence as asserted by the Dominion could only be disregarded in the light of "very clear evidence" or "clear and unmistakable evidence that the Government was in error".[35] Nowhere in the decision was the reasoning of the more recent *Canadian Temperance Federation* case considered worthy of more than passing mention, with Taschereau explicitly denying its applicability.

The second case in which the Supreme Court ruled on the scope of this power in the post-Privy Council era was *Johannesson* v. *West St. Paul*,[36] which harks back strongly to the reasoning and tone of the *Aeronautics* and *Radio* references of the early 1930's. Quoting the *Aeronautics Reference*, Mr. Justice Rinfret echoed the view of a unanimous court in declaring aerial navigation to be a "class of subject which has attained such dimension as to affect the body politic of the Dominion".[37] Thus municipal legislation controlling the erection of airports was invalid as encroaching on the power of the Dominion to legislate for peace, order, and good government. Once the determination is made that the subject falls under the Dominion general clause, the Court said, the powers of the provinces over property and civil rights and matters of merely a local or private nature in the province have no standing, even if the Dominion has not exercised its jurisdiction over the matter. In his opinion Mr. Justice Locke quoted approvingly the words of Lord Sankey in the *Aeronautics Reference*:

While the courts should be jealous in upholding the charter of the Provinces as enacted in section 92, it must be borne in mind that the real object of the Act was to give the central government those high functions and almost sovereign powers by which uniformity of legislation might be secured on all questions which were of common concern to all the provinces as members of a constituent whole.[38]

It took nearly fifteen years for two more cases on the general residuary power to arise before the Supreme Court, and these, like the other two cases from the post-Judicial Committee period, upheld the power of the federal government to act for the "peace, order, and good government of Canada". In the first of these two—a case involving the power of the federal government to expropriate land in Ontario near Ottawa to create a green belt surrounding the national capital—Mr. Justice Cartwright, speaking for a unanimous court, rested the decision firmly on the more generous construction of the *Radio Reference, Johannesson* v. *West St. Paul,* and the *Canadian Temperance Federation* case. Noting that the subject matter of the National Capital Act (the creation of a national capital with the appropriate setting) was not mentioned in either section 91 or 92, and citing both *Johannesson* and the *Radio Reference* as precedents, he concluded that ". . . such legislation [*i.e.,* legislation not mentioned in ss. 91 and 92] falls within the general words at the opening of section 91. . . ."[39]

The second ground for the decision, however, followed the slightly different tack of the *Temperance Federation* case. There the reasoning was in the tradition of *Russell's* case, holding that the relevant test was whether the subject matter of the legislation did or did not go beyond local or provincial concern. Again the Court's answer was unequivocal: "I find it difficult to suggest a subject matter of legislation which more clearly goes beyond local or provincial interests and is the concern of Canada as a whole than the development, conservation and improvement of the National Capital Region. . . ."[40] And, to the objection that the Act trenched on civil rights in the provinces, the Court answered in the same vein: "Once it has been determined that the matter in relation to which the Act is passed is one which falls within the power of Parliament, it is no objection to its validity that its operation will affect civil rights in the provinces".[41] There is hardly a more unequivocal statement in support of the Dominion's general power in the entire history of Canadian constitutional interpretation.

In three more instances in the past decade, each involving a major question of public policy, the court has used the residuary power to confirm Dominion authority. In the *Off-Shore Mineral Rights Reference,* decided in late 1967, a unanimous court held that the control and exploration of minerals in the lands under Canada's territorial seas was the sole responsibility of the Federal government, not the provincial government (in this case British Columbia). Basing the judgment squarely on a wide view of Dominion authority, the Court, having found that the lands in question did not fall within the historical boundaries of the provinces and therefore were federal territory, concluded that control of mineral rights must be "regarded as a matter affecting Canada generally and covered by the expression "the peace, order, and good government of Canada."[42] Since the lands did not fall within the boundaries of the province they could not, logically, fall within the subjects of section 92. Moreover, the court ruled, "The mineral resources of the lands underlying the territorial sea are of concern to Canada as a whole and go beyond local or provincial concern or interests".[43] Thus even if the lands had been within the boundaries of the province, their resources would have been of sufficient concern to the nation as a whole to take them out of the ambit of "matters of a merely local or private nature in the province."

Again in 1975 a unanimous Court upheld the Official Languages Act asserting, ". . . I am in no doubt that it was open to the Parliament of Canada to enact the *Official Languages Act* (limited as it is to the purposes of the Parliament and Government of Canada and to the institutions of that Parliament and Government) as being a law for the peace, order and good government of Canada in relation to [a matter] not coming within the Classes of Subjects . . . assigned exclusively to the Legislatures of the Provinces."[44]

The *Anti-Inflation Act Reference*, decided in July 1976, conformed to the post-Judicial Committee pattern in that federal legislation was again upheld, but the reasoning of the majority returned to the emergency doctrine as the source of support. The legislation in question dealt broadly with subject matters long conceded, at least during peacetime, to be matters of property and civil rights, including wages, prices and profit margins in the private sector of the economy. Here the Court held that Parliament's power to deal with national emergencies through temporary legislation was not limited to war and post-war circumstances and that inflation was at that time the source of such an emergency. But in doing so a majority of five to four explicitly denied that such legislation could be upheld by a "national dimensions" test. "It is not difficult to envisage many different circumstances which could give rise to national concern," Mr. Justice Ritchie observed, "but . . . I take it to be established that unless such concern is made manifest by circumstances amounting to an emergency Parliament is not endowed under the cloak of the 'peace, order and good government clause' with the authority to legislate in relation to matters reserved to the Provinces under s. 92 of the British North America Act."[45]

With these six decisions, then, the Supreme Court of Canada has demonstrated that both strands of interpretation of the meaning of "peace, order and good government"—the national dimensions doctrine and the emergency doctrine—are still accepted as tests of an act's validity. The Court has, however, been willing to apply each doctrine to a wider variety of circumstances than was the Judicial Committee. The consistency with which they have done so in the past quarter century suggests that the Dominion may again be able to rely with some measure of confidence on "peace, order and good government" as a support for action.

THE SCOPE OF "TRADE AND COMMERCE", SECTION 91(2)

The facts of the peace, order, and good government clause and of the enumerated heads of section 91 were, certainly, closely interrelated. With the interpretation of the closing words of section 91 to mean that the Dominion enumerations could extend only to necessarily incidental control of matters of a local or private nature (this phrase being defined as including the totality of section 92) and the eclipse of the *non obstante* clause, the authority of the Dominion under those enumerations was clearly circumscribed in comparison with what it had previously been.

The trade and commerce power of section 91, head 2, which on its face would seem to have the widest scope of any Dominion enumeration, however, received a still more restrictive interpretation than the other enumerated powers in section 91. Thus it was doubly restricted: first by the generally restrictive interpretation of the relation of section 91 to section 92, and also by a narrow reading of the meaning of the words "the regulation of trade and commerce" themselves. The potential usefulness of this heading to centralists as a device for moving the control of the nation's economy from the provinces to the Dominion as Canada entered her industrial phase can hardly be exaggerated. (This is especially notable when the application of the commerce clause in the United States is compared to the role of its somewhat more forcefully stated counterpart in Canada.) As one observer has noted, there is considerable irony in the fact that the United States has done so much with so little while Canada has done so little with so much.[46] The expansion or contraction of this power has, of course, fundamentally influenced the way in which the federation has approached the crucial issues growing out of the development of a national economy.

The narrowing of the potential scope of the trade and commerce power began the first time the clause was considered by the Judicial Committee in *Citizens Insurance Company* v. *Parsons* in 1881.[47] There the Board rejected the contention of the appellants that the words "trade and commerce" were meant to be "the most generous words which can be used, and include every kind of business which can possibly be carried on". Their Lordships asserted that the Act could not have contemplated such a wide meaning, or several other classes of subjects enumerated in section 91, such as banking, bills of exchange and promissory notes, and weights and measures would not also have been mentioned.[48] Instead, their Lordships speculated that the true intent of the words of head 2 correspond to those used in the Act of Union between England and Scotland which allowed differing controls and rules of trade in those two kingdoms.[49] "Trade and commerce" in the meaning of the B.N.A. Act, their Lordships said, "would include political arrangements in regard to trade requiring the sanction of Parliament, regulation of trade in matters of inter-provincial concern, and it may be that they would include general regulation of trade affecting the whole Dominion". The Board ruled, however, that the phrase did *not* support legislation regulating contracts of a *particular* business or trade carried on in a single province.

When the Supreme Court of Canada had considered the matter, Mr. Justice Taschereau had also maintained that the power of the Dominion parliament to incorporate companies was derived from the trade and commerce power, but Sir Montague Smith suggested that this power was more correctly derived from the general power of the Dominion to legislate on all matters not expressly given to the provinces.[50] The *Parsons* case, then, set several precedents. First, the words trade and commerce were not to be taken in their common meaning, for such an interpretation "would all but destroy the autonom of the provinces". Secondly, the Dominion could not regulate the contracts of particular business in a single province. Finally, the tentative definition of the power was that it encompassed political arrangements for trade, interprovincial trade, and perhaps general trade affecting the whole Dominion.

Some of the ramifications of the *Parsons* case became evident in the *Local Prohibition* case. Citing *Parsons* as precedent, the Board confirmed that the Dominion power over trade and commerce did not extend to intraprovincial trade itself. Here the Judicial Committee, however, went beyond that holding and also limiting the power of the Dominion to regulate local trade and commerce even as a part of a general regulation of these activities.[51]

While their Lordships noted that "the provisions of the Act of 1878 [involved in the *Russell* case] were in all material respects the same with those which are now embodied in the Canada Temperance Act of 1886 [being tested in this case]",[52] they ruled that it could not also be sustained under the trade and commerce power but only under peace, order, and good government. The reason for this holding, Lord Watson explained, was the distinction between regulation and prohibition:

> A power to regulate, naturally, if not necessarily, assumes, unless it is enlarged by the context, the conservation of the thing which is to be made the subject of regulation. In that view, their Lordships are unable to regard the prohibitive enactments of the Canadian statute of 1886 as regulations of trade and commerce.[53]

Thus the general power to regulate trade and commerce could not include prohibition as a means of regulation.

Again, in the *Insurance Reference*, the Judicial Committee restricted the scope of the commerce powers, declaring that not only were contracts of particular businesses operating in a single province beyond the scope of the power (as held in *Parsons*) and regulation by prohibition invalid, but the regulation of particular *trades* whether local or interprovincial by a licensing system was also beyond the competence of the Dominion.[54] This limiting trend reached its logical conclusion in 1922, when in the *Board of Commerce* case Lord Haldane concluded that interference with particular trades and businesses (such as insurance) in any way, was not consistent with a power limited to general regulation of trade (that is, general commercial intercourse), *not trades*.[55]

A more sweeping, if not more serious, limitation on the ambit of section 91(2) came in a series of cases which culminated in *Toronto Electric Commissioners* v. *Snider*. As early as 1912 the Judicial Committee implied that the limitations placed on the peace, order, and good government clause which restricted its application to only those situations where it supplemented a power enumerated in section 91 were also to apply to the trade and commerce clause.[56] It was not until ten years later in the *Board of Commerce* case, however, that this view was expressed explicitly. There Lord Haldane suggested that the trade and commerce power could *only* apply when used in conjunction with another Dominion power, particularly the general power over peace, order, and good government.[57] Thus the trade and commerce clause was not even to have the status of an ordinary enumerated head, but, because of the generality of its terms, the Board ruled that it had to be buttressed by a more explicit, additional authority as well.

In *Toronto Electric Commissioners* v. *Sniders*, Lord Haldane stated the point succinctly, saying:

> It is, in their Lordships' opinion, now clear that, excepting so far as the power can be invoked in aid of capacity conferred independently under other words in s. 91, the power to regulate trade and commerce cannot be relied on as enabling the Dominion Parliament to regulate civil rights in the Provinces [in this case the settlement of industrial disputes.][58]

Far from being the most far-reaching of the enumerated Dominion powers, trade and commerce was seen as nothing more than a weak relation.

It was not long, however, until the Judicial Committee beat a retreat from the extravagance of this opinion. In a 1931 opinion Lord Atkin spoke for the Board, saying:

> Their Lordships merely propose to disassociate themselves from the construction suggested . . . in the judgment in the *Board of Commerce* case under which it was contended that the power to regulate trade and commerce could be invoked only in furtherance of a general power which Par-

liament possessed independently of it. . . . The words of the statute must receive their proper construction where they stand as giving an independent authority to Parliament over the particular subject-matter. . . .[59]

And again, in the *Aeronautics Reference*, heard the following year, the Board intimated that the trade and commerce power might have been a ground for upholding Dominion regulation of aeronautics, had not the treaty power given in section 132 been sufficient ground in itself.[60] The argument that the authority of the trade and commerce clause was supplementary became a dead issue with the *Trade Mark* case (1937), in which Ontario questioned the Dominion's power to establish a national trade mark. In answering the question affirmatively, the Board made it clear that this was an appropriate exercise of the trade and commerce power unaided by any other power of the Dominion. In its view, "There could hardly be a more appropriate form of the exercise of this power than the creation and regulation of a uniform law of trade marks".[61]

But though the extravagance of the "supplementary" view of the trade and commerce power had been discarded, the restrictions of narrow reading of the words and the understanding that none of the enumerations of section 91 could reach farther than a necessarily incidental interference with the provincial matters in section 92 remained. A crucial test of the extent to which these views still applied came with the reference of the Dominion's Natural Products Marketing Act to the courts (also in 1937).[62] The Act was part of the Bennett Government's "New Deal" legislation through which the Dominion sought to cope with the marketing problems of the Depression by claiming sweeping federal authority to regulate time and place of selling and, when necessary, prohibit marketing of any product. This the Board declared wholly *ultra vires* the Dominion on the ground that aspects of the scheme which controlled interprovincial and international trade were so intermixed with control of purely local transactions that the whole scheme was invalid as an infringement of section 92(13). Said the Board, ". . . the regulation of trade and commerce does not permit the regulation of individual forms of trade or commerce confined to the Province".[63]

It was nearly fifteen years before the Judicial Committee was again called upon to comment on the meaning of the trade and commerce power. In 1951 Section 5A of the Dairy Industry Act was referred to the courts for an opinion as to whether it was valid for the Dominion, in an effort to support and develop the dairy industry, to prohibit the manufacture and sale of margarine throughout Canada. Again, noting that the Act prohibited these activities even when carried on solely within the boundaries of a single province, the Board (appealing to the considerable precedent for the view) ruled that such a measure was an invalid encroachment on property and civil rights in the province. In their final word on the subject before appeals were ended, the Board summed up the Judicial Committee view:

> . . . [T]he present case is typical of the many cases in which the Board had felt bound to put some limit on the scope of the wide words used in head 2 of section 91 in order to preserve from serious curtailment, if not from virtual extinction, the degree of autonomy which, as appears from the scheme of the Act as a whole, the provinces were intended to possess.[64]

The end of appeals to the Judicial Committee of the Privy Council left the Supreme Court with a considerable bulk of precedent for a narrow construction of the meaning of section 91, head 2. In 1957, with its first opportunity to rule as the final court in a case involving the commerce power, however, it took a more venturesome tack. The matter in question was the validity of the Ontario Farm Products Act, which was designed to regulate the sale of farm products throughout Ontario.[65] Seven of the eight justices sitting in the case pronounced it *intra vires* the province, but the case was seized as an opportunity to comment on the meaning of trade and commerce as stated in section 91 and the problem of setting the limits of geographical areas of jurisdiction in an integrated economic system. Questioning the validity of considering trade and commerce a part of the power of the provinces over property and civil rights, as it had so often been in the past, Mr. Justice Rand commented: "The production of goods as an economic activity does not take place by virtue of positive law or civil right, it is assumed as part of the residual free activity of men upon or around which law is imposed. It has an identity of its own recognized by section 91(2)."[66] Trade, the Court said, was not static but "dynamic, the creation and flow of goods from production to consumption . . . as an individualized action". Thus, the boundaries of the province and the bounds of provincial authority over trade were not to be considered coextensive. In matters of trade and commerce within the province but with effects beyond the province, the Dominion power under section 91(2) was held paramount. But, though the use of the provincial boundary as the mark of the division of jurisdictions has now been at least temporarily discredited, it is not clear what formula or test of jurisdiction will take its place.

Murphy v. *Canadian Pacific Railway,* decided in the next year, however, offered a more clear-cut test of the Court's view of the commerce power.

There Mr. Justice Locke, writing for himself and for Justices Taschereau, Fauteux and Abbott, specifically upheld the Canadian Wheat Board Act. He ruled that the Act was a valid regulation of trade and commerce and added: "the fact that . . . it [necessarily] interferes with property and civil rights in the province . . . is immaterial".[67] To the argument that the Dominion did not have the power to regulate the activities of a particular trade (as held in the *Insurance Reference*), the Justices replied that the Act did not regulate just one trade but several, and since their activities were directed to the export of grain from the province, the provincial governments were powerless to control them.

These two decisions held for a decade without amplification, but in the period 1968-1976 the court was called upon five times for decisions on the limits of 91(2). In the first of these the validity of provincial marketing regulation was again the question. The appellant, the Carnation Company, bought and processed milk in Quebec but sold the bulk of the product outside Quebec. The regulation of the price at which it bought from milk producers was regulation of inter-provincial trade, the company asserted. The Court, however, held the regulations valid. The test, it said, was not whether or not the regulations *affected* inter-provincial trade but whether they were made "in relation to" the regulation of trade and commerce. "In the present case the orders under question were not directed at the regulation of trade. They did not purport directly to control or restrict such trade."[68]

The same test was used in 1971 when, in a reference brought to the Court by Manitoba, that province's legislation on the marketing of eggs was struck down on the grounds that the legislation was intended to regulate inter-provincial trade directly. "It is designed to restrict or limit the flow of trade between provinces as such. Because of that it constitutes an invasion of the exclusive legislative authority of the Parliament of Canada over the matter of the regulation of trade and commerce."[69]

In a second 1971 case, a federal gasoline marketing scheme, designed to foster the development of the petroleum industry by giving it a secure market, prohibited importers of gasoline from selling it west of the Ottawa Valley line. In upholding the legislation, the Supreme Court rejected the contention that regulation of the sale of any product at the retail level, even an imported one, was solely a matter of provincial jurisdiction. Harking back to *Murphy*, the Court considered that "the true character of the enactment appears to be an incident in the administration of an extra-provincial marketing scheme . . ." and as such not an unwarranted invasion of provincial jurisdiction.[70]

In its two most recent decisions on trade and commerce, the Court has returned to earlier themes in invalidating both federal and provincial legislation. In the first case, the Court ruled invalid Manitoba regulations requiring meat processors in the province to purchase all their hogs from the Manitoba Hog Producers Marketing Board, in effect prohibiting the direct importation of live hogs from other provinces. The Court declared that the regulations directly controlled extra-provincial trade operations in their essential aspects and were therefore beyond the competence of the province. To the claim that such regulation was necessarily incidental to the efficient operation of the intra-provincial marketing scheme, the Court, citing the 1937 Natural Products Marketing

Act decision, said: "If the federal Parliament cannot regulate local trade [as in the 1934 Act] because it would be more efficient to regulate it together with the extra-provincial trade, *a fortiori* a provincial legislature cannot regulate inter-provincial trade in a given product because this appears desirable for the effective control of intra-provincial trade."[71] And in January, 1976, the Court, for the first time in a quarter-century, struck down a federal act, section 7(e) of the Trade Marks Act, which prohibited certain unfair business practices, declaring the subject a matter of property and civil rights in the province rather than a valid regulation of trade and commerce.[72]

While it is clear that the Supreme Court has taken a wider and more pragmatic view of trade and commerce than precedent might suggest, it is also clear that the conceptual boundaries of local and inter-provincial trade have not been replaced with a "flow of commerce" principle. But the emphasis on the purpose or intent of marketing legislation and a willingness to view extra-jurisdictional effects as "necessarily incidental" in some cases has meant that the status of trade and commerce is no longer that which the Judicial Committee assigned. While in no way approaching the U.S. model of broad federal jurisdiction, these trends suggest that governments in Canada now have more flexibility in their attempts to cope with economic problems.

SUMMARY AND CONCLUSION

The impact of judicial review on the legal framework within which Dominion and provinces operate, then, has been substantial. The peace, order, and good government clause was transformed from a general residuary power to legislate on all matters not specifically excepted by section 92 to a supplementary power operating (1) only on those matters not covered by either of the enumerated lists, (2) as a supplement to powers possessed independently in section 91 and (3) in time of emergency, when it could temporarily override the normal jurisdiction to save the nation from catastrophe. From the early 1930's until 1949, decisions by the Judicial Committee wavered back and forth between this restrictive interpretation and the broader scope given the clause prior to 1896.

The interpretation of the trade and commerce power followed a similar pattern. The scope of the power was limited first by a narrow reading of the meaning of the words, then by an interpretation of its relation to section 92 which settled that it could not extend into the realm of the powers given the provinces in section 92 and, finally, by an interpretation which declared it to be operable *only* as a supplement to another federal power. Again, as in the case of the residuary power, the courts retreated from the extremities of their position in the early 1930's only to return to them in the later years of that decade.

After the Supreme Court became the final arbiter of the federal balance in 1949, it began to throw its weight behind broader definitions of the scope of federal action under these powers. Several times in the past quarter-century, the Court has shown itself willing to repudiate sharply the more restrictive and abstract elements in the earlier interpretation of the trade and commerce clause. In its more recent cases, however, it has avoided conclusively abandoning these precedents. Similarly, in the case of the residuary power, the Court has found it possible in each instance to uphold Dominion legislation enacted under Parliament's authority to provide for the "peace, order and good government" of Canada. Yet, although the Supreme Court, unlike the Judicial Committee, has been willing to uphold most legislative initiatives, it too has failed either to choose conclusively between the various strands of interpretation or to explain how they can be harmonized. Thus, while providing approval for government action in recent years, the courts have still failed to provide the clarity and certainty as to the meaning of the law which is one of the prime functions of the judiciary. Attempts to delimit the boundaries of legislative authority remain something of a guessing game.

The result of the judicial interpretations of the boundaries of legal authority between Dominion and province with regard to the crucial powers in question here, however, has been primarily to enlarge the provincial area of power and to restrict that of the Dominion. Thus the legal framework has operated as a centrifugal force in the federation, dividing jurisdiction and thwarting attempts to centralize control in important areas of economic and social concerns. There can be little doubt that for much of its history the Judicial Committee brought a "states' rights" bias to its interpretive task. The decisions based on this normative position could not fail to have significant repercussions on the policy-making process in Canada, and thus important consequences for political life. Perhaps the Committee's invalidation of the "New Deal" legislation is the outstanding example of their Lordships' determination to give the provinces their rights—whether they wanted them or not. In this, as in several other areas, judicial decisions made it more difficult for Canada's governments to cope with their problems than it might otherwise have been.[73]

One of the most important functions of a court which adjudicates constitutional questions in a federal system is to provide flexibility in the allocation of responsibilities between governments, so that the system may adjust, over time, to changing economic, social and political realities. The absence of a settled amendment procedure has made this function particularly important in Canada. The initial rigidity of constitutional interpretation and the unpredictable fluctuations in interpretation which followed have no doubt played their part in discrediting the judicial review process. Among the consequences of this loss of faith are an increase in the use of informal mechanisms of adjustment and, perhaps, a decline in the legitimacy of the courts as arbiters of the federal balance.[74] Two recent examples are illustrative. In the aftermath of the Manitoba Egg case, the agriculture ministers of the affected provinces met to work out a mutually acceptable solution to the marketing problems, stating at the outset "that the Supreme Court decision would not be the basis of their final settlement."[75] Similarly, in the continuing debate over the allocation of jurisdictions over communications, it has been common ground among the governments that "we want a political settlement," not a judicial one.[76] In an article written before he became Chief Justice of the Supreme Court of Canada, Bora Laskin summed up the situation:

> It is as if a stalemate has been reached in the legal relations of Canada and the Provinces, but with no legal, no judicial means of resolving current conflicts. In fact, there are such means. But what has been evident for many years is that the mood of our political leaders is less and less for acquiescence in a judicial order of constitutional change through reinterpretation of the division of legislative powers.[77]

If, as Professors Corry and Laskin suggest, the courts are no longer a major mechanism for constitutional adjustment, certainly at least part of the explanation of this apparent lack of faith of governments and other potential litigants in the results of judicial decision-making lies in the record of past performance.[78]

NOTES

[1] Though in recent years the term "federal government" has been the proper designation for the government in Ottawa, the term "Dominion" has been used in this study. Since it is less ambiguous than "federal" and was the term used by the courts in referring to the central authority in nearly all of the cases discussed here, it was felt that greater clarity would result from its use.

[2] For a discussion of the ways in which constitutional cases came before the courts see J. A. C. Grant, "Judicial Review in Canada: Procedural Aspects", *Canadian Bar Review*, Vol. XLII (1964), pp. 195-224.

[3] *Citizens Insurance Co.* v. *Parsons* (1881), 7 A.C. 96 at 107-108. For others who agree with this grammatical interpretation see Bora Laskin, *Canadian Constitutional Law*, 2nd ed. (Toronto, Carswell, 1960), pp. 65-66; W. R. Kennedy, "The Interpretation of the B.N.A. Act", *Cambridge Law Journal*, Vol. VIII, 1943, pp. 146-59; Fredrick P. Varcoe, *The Distribution of Legislative Power in Canada* (Toronto, Carswell, 1954) pp. 18-22.

[4] *Attorney-General for Ontario* v. *Attorney-General for Canada*, [1896] A.C. 348.

[5] *Ibid.*, p. 359.

[6] *Ibid.*, p. 359.

[7] *Ibid.*, p. 360.

[8] *Attorney-General for Canada* v. *Attorney-General for Alberta* [1916], A.C. 588 at 595.

[9] F. R. Scott, "The Development of Canadian Federalism", *Papers and Proceedings, Canadian Political Science Association*, Vol. III (May, 1931), p. 247.

[10] (1882), 7 A.C. 829.

[11] *Ibid.*, p. 829.

[12] *Ibid.*, pp. 837-39.

[13] *Ibid.*, p. 841.

[14] *In Re The Board of Commerce Act, 1919* [1922], A.C. 191.

[15] (1923), A.C. 695.

[16] *Toronto Electric Commissioners* v. *Snider* [1925], A.C. 396.

[17] *Ibid.*, p. 412.

[18] *The King* v. *Eastern Elevator Company* [1925], S.C.R. 434 at 438.

[19] Laskin, *op. cit.*, p. 267.

[20] One of the few examples is the incorporation of companies with Dominion objects. *Great West Saddlery Co.* v. *The King* [1921], 2 A.C. 91.

[21] *Edwards* v. *Attorney-General of Canada* [1930], A.C. 136.

[22] *In Re the Regulation and Control of Radio Communication in Canada* [1932], A.C. 304 at 312.

[23] For a general discussion on the new deal see J. R. H. Wilbur (ed.), *The Bennett New Deal: Fraud or Portent?* (Toronto, Copp Clark, 1968).

[24] *Attorney-General for Canada* v. *Attorney-General for Ontario* (Labour Conventions Case) [1937], A.C. 327.

[25] *Ibid.*, p. 354.

[26] *Ibid.*, p. 351. That this interpretation is a patent misreading of the *Radio* decision is shown by quoting from the decision itself: "As their Lordships' views are based on what may be called the pre-eminent claims of section 91, it is unnecessary to discuss the question which was raised . . . whether, if there had been no pre-eminent claims as such, broadcasting could have been held to fall either within 'property and civil rights,' or within 'matters of a merely local or private nature' ". *Radio Reference* (1932) A.C. 302 at 312.

[27] *Ibid.*, p. 353.

[28] *Attorney-General for Canada* v. *Attorney-General for Ontario* (Employment and Social Insurance Act Reference) [1937], A.C. 355.

[29] *Attorney-General for Ontario* v. *Canadian Temperance Federation* [1946], A.C. 196 at 205-206.

[30] *Canadian Pacific Railway* v. *Attorney-General for British Columbia* [1950], A.C. 123 at 142.

[31] *Canadian Federation of Agriculture* v. *Attorney-General for Quebec* [1951], A.C. 179 at 198.

[32] *Reference Re the Validity of the Wartime Leasehold Regulations* [1950], S.C.R. 124.

[33] [1923], A.C. 695.

[34] *Wartime Leasehold Reference* [1950], S.C.R. 124 at 140.

[35] *Ibid.*, p. 135.

[36] [1952], 1 S.C.R. 292.

[37] *Ibid.*, p. 303, quoting the *Aeronautics Reference* [1932], A.C. 54 at 77.

[38] *Ibid.*, pp. 327-28, quoting the *Aeronautics Reference*, p. 70.

[39] *Munro* v. *National Capital Commission* [1966], S.C.R. 663 at 670.

[40] *Ibid.*, p. 671.

[41] *Ibid.*

[42] *Reference Re Ownership of Off-shore Mineral Rights*, 65 D.L.R. (2nd) 353 at 376.

[43] *Ibid.*

[44] *Jones* v. *Attorney-General for Canada* 16 C.C.C. (2d) 297 at 303.

⁴⁵ *Reference Re Anti-Inflation Act*, Opinion of Mr. Justice Ritchie, p. 2. This decision is as yet unreported. The page number here referred to is found in the typed reasons for judgement issued by the Court on July 12, 1976.

⁴⁶ Alexander Smith, *The Commerce Power in Canada and the United States* (Toronto, Butterworth, 1963), p. 4.

⁴⁷ (1881), 7 A.C. 96.

⁴⁸ *Ibid.*, p. 100.

⁴⁹ *Ibid.*, p. 112.

⁵⁰ *Ibid.*, p. 116.

⁵¹ In *Russell* v. *The Queen* the Board had emphasized that, while the prohibitory liquor legislation there in question was primarily to be upheld under the peace, order, and good government power, this "must not be understood as intimating any dissent from the opinion . . . that the Act, as a general regulation of the traffic in intoxicating liquors throughout the Dominion, fell within the class of subject 'the regulation of trade and commerce' . . . and was, on that ground a valid exercise of the legislative power of the Parliament of Canada.

⁵² [1896], A.C. 348 at 362.

⁵³ [1896], A.C. 348 at 363.

⁵⁴ *Attorney-General for Canada* v. *Attorney-General for Alberta* [1916], A.C. 588.

⁵⁵ *In Re The Board of Commerce Act, 1919* [1922], A.C. 191.

⁵⁶ *Montreal* v. *Montreal Street Railway* [1912], A.C. 333 at 344. See also *John Deere Plow Co.* v. *Wharton* [1915], A.C. 330.

⁵⁷ [1922], A.C. 191 at 197-98.

⁵⁸ [1925], A.C. 396 at 410.

⁵⁹ *Proprietary Articles Trade Association* v. *Attorney-General for Canada* [1931], A.C. 310 at 326.

⁶⁰ [1932], A.C. 54 at 73.

⁶¹ *Attorney-General for Ontario* v. *Attorney-General for Canada* [1937], A.C. 405 at 417.

⁶² *Attorney-General for British Columbia* v. *Attorney-General for Canada* [1937], A.C. 377.

⁶³ *Ibid.*, p. 387.

⁶⁴ *Canadian Federation of Agriculture* v. *Attorney-General for Quebec* [1951], A.C. 179 at 194.

⁶⁵ *Re The (Ontario) Farm Products Marketing Act* [1957], S.C.R. 198.

⁶⁶ *Ibid.*, p. 211.

⁶⁷ [1958], S.C.R. 626 at 632.

⁶⁸ *Carnation Company Ltd.* v. *Quebec Agricultural Marketing Board* [1968], S.C.R. 252.

⁶⁹ *Attorney-General for Manitoba* v. *Manitoba Egg and Poultry Association* [1971], S.C.R. 689 at 703.

⁷⁰ *Caloil Inc.* v. *Attorney-General for Canada* [1971] S.C.R. 543 at 551.

⁷¹ *Burns Foods Ltd.* v. *Attorney-General for Manitoba* [1974], 40 D.L.R. (3d) 731 at 737.

⁷² P. W. Hogg, "Comments," *Canadian Bar Review* Vol. LIV (June, 1976) pp. 365-368.

⁷³ Some scholars have argued that such decentralization was both desirable and necessary for the survival of the Canadian federal system. For the most insightful expression of this view see Alan Cairns, "The Judicial Committee and Its Critics," *Canadian Journal of Political Science*, Vol. IV (Sept., 1971) pp. 320-325.

⁷⁴ See J. A. Corry, "Constitutional Trends and Federalism," in A. R. M. Lower, F. R. Scott, *et al.*, *Evolving Canadian Federalism* (Durham, Duke University Press, 1958) pp. 117-18.

⁷⁵ Paul Weiler, *In the Last Resort: A Critical Survey of the Supreme Court of Canada* (Toronto: Carswell/Methuen, 1974) p. 164.

[76] Gérard Pelletier, then federal minister of communications, quoted in the *Toronto Star*, November 28, 1973.

[77] Bora Laskin, "Reflections on the Canadian Constitution After the First Century," *Canadian Bar Review*, Vol. XLV no. 3 (September, 1967), pp. 395-96.

[78] Other factors than the trends in interpretation have obviously also played a part in the decline in the role of the Court as arbiter of the federal balance. As Richard Jones points out, one such factor is the doubt that Supreme Court justices, selected solely by the central government, can act as unbiased arbiters in conflicts between the two levels of government. See Richard Jones, *Community in Crisis: French-Canadian Nationalism in Perspective* (Toronto, McClelland and Stewart, 1967), p. 103. Others, such as Paul Weiler, suggest that inherent limitations in the judicial role make judicial decisions necessarily less satisfactory in resolving questions of public policy than political solutions arrived at through negotiations among elected governments. See Weiler, p. 179.

8

The Methodology of the Constitutional Review*

Canadian Intergovernment Conference Secretariat

The approach adopted by the First Ministers regarding the work methods which would effect the examination of the constitution was marked by the same pragmatism which characterized the other aspects of the constitutional review. Generally, the Conference appears to have assumed that the procedures and organization which would be necessary for the proper development of the constitutional discussions should be examined and dealt with as requirements developed. While certain procedural questions were to require attention in the early stages of the review, little attempt was made to develop procedural guidelines in anticipation of events.

In retrospect, however, it is now possible to identify a number of elements regarding the general methodology of the review which evolved or were applied as the revision progressed. These have since become part of the review's procedural features. The following paragraphs seek to describe and analyse some of these elements.

*From *The Constitutional Review, 1968-1971, Secretary's Report*, Canadian Intergovernmental Conference Secretariat, (Ottawa: Information Canada, 1974), pp. 223-244. Reprinted by permission of the Minister of Supply and Services, Canada.

CONCEPTUAL APPROACHES TO THE REVIEW

A Political Process

From the outset the First Ministers recognized that the revision of the constitution would be a political process to be carried out under the direct supervision of the heads of the federal and provincial governments. A clear expression of this approach is given in the conclusions of the Constitutional Conference of September 1970:

> The First Ministers considered the nature of the review, and it was agreed that it must continue as basically a political process, involving consultations between governments. At the same time, an essential part of the review was seen to be the preparatory and background work carried out by the existing committees of ministers, officials and consultants and by the Secretariat.

This approach was to have implications in various areas of the review and, in particular, on the decision-making process. At the ministerial committee level, it became clear as discussions progressed that delegates often saw their role as being limited to a further exploration of the various government positions, few attempts being made to arrive at decisions which could be recommended to the First Ministers. The same consideration applied more forcefully, although quite justifiably, at the level of officials. Similarly, the acceptance of the political implications of their actions was to lead governments away from their initial use of general statements which it had been agreed would not commit their authors. Gradually, these statements came to be replaced by theme papers often representing approved positions which evidenced all the political sensitivities involved. In the same sense, the desire for a certain candor in the discussions was to be one of the reasons for the use of closed sessions of the Constitutional Conference.

Total Versus Partial Review

At the first meeting of the Constitutional Conference in February 1968, the First Ministers had listed seven subjects to be examined "without limiting" the process of constitutional review. After a year of organization and background work, the Conference was to further clarify its intent for a total review:

> . . . to complete a comprehensive review of the Constitution of Canada, to assess its adequacy for present and future requirements, and to determine the extent to which constitutional change is desirable either through amendment of the existing Constitution or through promulgation of an entirely new Constitution.

There were however some initial differences of view preceding this decision for a total review by the First Ministers. It was proposed, for example, at the first meeting of the Continuing Committee of Officials

(C.C.O.) in May 1968, that the Committee might proceed by limiting its examination to obvious possible amendments of the existing constitution, while another view held that constitutional revision should essentially be carried out through a study of the distribution of powers. In the end the process of review was to begin in the C.C.O. with the submission of general propositions covering the full range of both written and unwritten aspects of the constitution. Although this initial approach could not be continued indefinitely, the propositions formed a background against which the First Ministers could start examining more specific questions; the use of propositions had also confirmed that the discussions to follow would seek to cover all aspects of the constitution. The latter approach continued to be used until February 1971, when the First Ministers decided they would attempt to achieve a limited number of constitutional agreements in the immediate future.

The "Propositions Approach" and Theme Papers

As noted above, the first year of the constitutional review was marked by the use of what came to be called subsequently the "proposition approach." This arose from a federal proposal made at the first meeting of the Continuing Committee for developing a systematic approach which would provide the means of examining not only the seven questions listed at the February 1968 Constitutional Conference, but all aspects of the Canadian constitutional structure. It was proposed that this could be effected by having all governments submit "propositions" setting forth basic concepts that it was felt should be examined during the review together with supporting material in explanation thereof. These propositions however were not meant to express, at that stage, firm statements of position.

This proposal was accepted, and a considerable number of propositions were submitted for examination by the C.C.O. Although contributions varied greatly, the combination of propositions submitted produced a comprehensive framework for discussion. These discussions were reported to the Constitutional Conference in February 1969. The proposition approach was not continued after that date because of the decision to request the C.C.O. to deal immediately with the taxing and spending powers. However, it is recognized that the procedure had been helpful in initiating discussions on most aspects of the constitution and in encouraging an expression of views from all governments, even those which had previously shown only a limited interest in the general constitutional question.

Following the Constitutional Conference in February 1969, the Continuing Committee began to concentrate on a preliminary examination of specific subject areas. This in turn led to an emphasis on papers of greater length and substance than could be achieved in short propositional statements. These theme papers often reflected the policy positions of the submitting governments and their examination by officials or ministers was in fact part of the negotiation process through which agreements could be sought. In some cases, such as the federal papers on the spending and taxing powers, much of the initiative in guiding the thrust of the discussions thus fell to the federal government.

This procedure continued until the Constitutional Conference of February 1971 when it was decided to concentrate on reaching agreement on those subjects on which final agreement might be possible at that time. This last stage, which led eventually to the draft charter examined at the Victoria Conference in June 1971, was to be characterized by the preparation and study of draft constitutional provisions instead of more general working papers.

Approach to the Question of the Distribution of Powers

One of the issues on which substantial differences of view continued throughout the review process was the question of how to tackle the discussions regarding the distribution of federal and provincial legislative powers in the constitution. There were two aspects to the general issue. The first concerned the timing of the discussions within the revision process; the second involved the method for tackling this subject once it had been agreed to proceed with it.

On the question of timing, although the distribution of powers had been included as one of the seven questions identified by the February 1968 Conference it was the view of the federal government that it would be desirable to begin with the rights of individuals (the charter of fundamental rights) and the central institutions of government with relevance to the federal system before proceeding to an examination of the federal and provincial legislative powers. For its part, Quebec took the position that the constitutional revision should essentially be carried out through a study of the distribution of powers and it was anxious therefore that detailed discussions in this area be initiated from the outset. In the end it was agreed to examine propositions on all subjects, including the distribution of powers. This was to be followed, after the Constitutional Conference of February 1969, by more extended discussions on selected topics.

As for the procedure for tackling the actual examination of legislative powers, there developed a divergence of opinions between delegations as to whether this should proceed on a "subject-by-subject" basis or in accordance with a previous "overview" of the totality of the federal and provincial legislative powers (the "grid approach"). An overview of its own total position on this subject had been presented by Quebec during the first months of the revision but subsequent discussions had been initiated by the federal government on the basis of analysing one function at a time. In this way, for example, the spending and the taxing powers had been brought forward for detailed and independent examination, supported by a mandate from the Constitutional Conference. There were considerable discussions amongst delegations in the Continuing Committee (with New Brunswick taking a leading role) on the merits of the two approaches. In the end, since many governments were not prepared to present a "grid", the federal pattern of analysing one function at a time continued unchanged.

CHAIRMANSHIP OF COMMITTEES

The chairmanship of meetings at all levels during the constitutional review was assumed in all cases by the senior federal representative. In the case of meetings of First Ministers, the Prime Minister of Canada assumed the role and title of "Chairman of the Constitutional Conference" with a responsibility for the Conference as a whole which was independent from his function as senior federal spokesman. Part of these chairmanship functions included consulting with the Secretary of the Constitutional Conference regarding general Conference procedures and organization. A similar Chairman-Secretary relationship existed at all levels of meetings.

The exercise of the dual role of chairman and of senior federal spokesman necessitated the occasional underlining of this distinction by the individual chairman when acting in one capacity or the other. Nevertheless, the identification of the capacity in which the chairman intervened was not always clear.

It might be noted that although the principle of a federal chairmanship of the Conference and its committees continued to be applied throughout the review, this was not without some reservations being expressed in this regard. During the first meeting of the Continuing Committee in May 1968 certain provinces questioned the compatibility of the two roles which the federal spokesman would have to play within the Committee. Alternatives proposed at that time included a rotational chairmanship or the appointment of an outside person. The question was raised again during the examination of the mechanisms of intergovernmental relations at subsequent meetings of the C.C.O. with Ontario expressing the view that federal-provincial meetings, with the exception of the First Ministers, should be free to choose their chairmen from amongst the respective delegations.

Delegates and Observers

The choice and number of delegates to the Constitutional Conference and its committees were left to the discretion of each government. They were usually chosen from each government's own personnel. However, persons outside the federal or provincial Public Services were occasionally recruited to form part of delegations; this was especially true of the sub-committees which had a requirement for specialized expertise.

As a rule the senior representatives of each government on the Continuing Committee of Officials tended to remain unchanged, while the remainder of the respective delegations varied in accordance with the nature of the subject being examined at a particular time. The composition of specialized committees such as the ministerial committees or the sub-committees was usually characterized by personnel associated with the committee's subject matter, whereas both the C.C.O. and the Constitutional Conference usually represented a wider and more mixed array of professional backgrounds. In the more technical sub-committees, several governments could choose to be represented by a single person.

In the case of ministerial meetings, including those of First Ministers, the distinction between "delegates" and "advisers" was introduced in order to distinguish between ministers and officials within each delegation. A complete list of delegates for all meetings of the constitutional review is attached as Appendix C.

The attendance of observers at Constitutional Conferences was limited to open Conferences. The general principle followed was that only official delegates and advisers forming part of the respective delegations would be allowed to attend closed Conferences. It would appear that the rationale for the invitation of observers to be present at open meetings was based more on the proprieties of protocol rather than on any right to participate, and the seating of observers was usually set apart from that of the delegations themselves. The status of official observer, however, was not without significance for persons so selected since this meant a right to receive any non-confidential documentation produced for the Conference, invitations to social events and a listing in the official attendance records.

The selection of observers was left to the discretion of each delegation, but the privilege was not always exercised. Equally it is not possible to ascertain which of those who were invited chose not to attend. It would appear that in the main the intention was to recognize persons whose position in Parliament or the Legislatures marked them as having a special interest in the review. In the case of the provinces whose practices were not uniform, their own selection was often based on information they might have regarding the expected federal observers. The limitation on numbers imposed by the available seating arrangements for a particular meeting applied to all governments.

Some delegations considered it appropriate to recognize the interest of opposition leaders in the constitutional question by inviting them to attend as observers. In the case of the federal government, the position of the former Prime Ministers of Canada and of the two Speakers was also recognized as appropriate. Other observers included M.P.s, Senators, M.L.A.s, municipal and academic officials, government members and officials from the Yukon and Northwest Territories. (See Appendix C regarding attendance at the Constitutional Conferences.)*

With respect to the representation of municipal governments, it was agreed that decisions in this regard would be the responsibility of each provincial government. These could decide, if they so wished, to include municipal representatives as full participants in their delegations for either open or closed meetings; alternatively, they could designate them as observers only for open meetings. As to the two Territorial governments, they were not accorded independent representation by the federal government but were distinguished as territorial observers forming part of the federal delegation, not in the general observer group.

In those cases where the open Conference proceedings had to be adjourned for the purpose of holding a private meeting of First Ministers or in order to continue in closed session, observers present were excluded. The latter possibility led the federal Leader of the Opposition to refuse the Prime Minister's invitation to attend the opening session of the June 1971 Victoria Conference.

CONFIDENTIALITY OF DISCUSSIONS

Private Versus Public Meetings

All constitutional meetings at both the ministerial and officials' level were held in camera. The four exceptions were the Constitutional Conferences of February 1968, February 1969, December 1969 and the opening session of the June 1971 Victoria Conference when Conference proceedings were public.

As with the Confederation of Tomorrow Conference in November 1967, the first two meetings of the Constitutional Conference in 1968 and 1969 were televised. However, it soon became apparent that some advantage could be gained by resorting to closed meetings where, in addition to simpler administrative arrangements, it would be possible to pursue more direct and candid discussions with less public pressure. Time would also be saved by dispensing with opening statements which were a feature of open meetings. It was therefore decided during the second meeting of the Constitutional Conference in February 1969 to accelerate discussions by holding "informal working sessions with the Continuing Committee of Officials," although in fact there was no significant increase in the participation of officials. These "working sessions" were to become identified with the closed meetings of the Con-

*Editor's Note: see pp. 405-491 of the Secretary's Report.

ferences and became the rule (although not always with unanimous agreement) for all subsequent meetings of First Ministers except for the Conference in December 1969 and the short opening proceedings of the Victoria Conference.

It should be noted that during both closed and open Conferences there were occasions when the First Ministers thought it desirable to meet privately in executive session without any officials present, although the Conference Secretary sometimes attended. This further degree of privacy was to prove very effective in accelerating Conference decisions.

PUBLICATION OF CONFERENCE DOCUMENTS

Although some Conference documentation was produced for immediate release to the public, such as the conclusions and the edited verbatim reports of public Conferences, the greater part of the documents produced during the review were intended to be restricted, at least initially, to the use of the participants. In the latter case, inter-governmental consultation was usually considered appropriate in instances where it was thought desirable that a particular document should be made available to the public. Examples of documents which were issued during the course of the review in this way include individual government "propositions," government position and working papers, reports of committees and of the Secretariat and the agendas for the meetings of First Ministers. In spite of advance agreements it was sometimes difficult, however, to ensure complete adherence to a single release date.

In the case of closed Conferences, it was agreed that no delegation would release Conference documents or statements before or during the proceedings, although sometimes papers were released afterwards. As for Conference agendas, these were, subject to agreement, released either immediately before the Conference or following the agenda's formal adoption at the opening session. The agendas and conclusions for meetings of First Ministers were also occasionally tabled in the House of Commons by the federal government.

In general, the constitutional revision documents which became available to the public served to provide information on the positions of individual governments rather than a continuing analysis and assessment of the progress of the review. While a number of released documents did have the latter purpose in mind, such as the Secretary's briefing paper on discussions within the Continuing Committee, the majority were designed to seek public support for individual positions being debated within the formal committee structure. Nonetheless, information on formal delegation positions provided a measure of public participation which was not without effect. This was to be illustrated by the public reaction to the constitutional Charter in Quebec, following the Victoria Conference.

Two instances of unofficial disclosures of important Conference documentation were recorded during the review. The first occurred in September 1968 and concerned a number of Quebec "propositions" on the constitution which had been submitted previously to the C.C.O. by the Quebec delegation, and which subsequently appeared in a Toronto newspaper with an Ottawa dateline. Both the Quebec and the federal governments were of the view that the leak had not come from their midst. The incident was closed, with Quebec publishing shortly thereafter the full set of the propositions it had submitted in order to remove any inaccurate impressions which the unofficial and more limited publication might have created. A second instance occurred in January 1969 when a draft of a Secretariat briefing paper to be presented to the February 1969 Constitutional Conference fell into the hands of the press. Again, there was no success in ascertaining the source of the leak, but the final version of the document was subsequently released in accordance with plans which had been made prior to the leak.

BILATERAL DISCUSSIONS AND PRIVATE MEETINGS OF FIRST MINISTERS

Bilateral Discussions

Private discussions between the federal government and individual provinces regarding the process and subject matter of the constitutional review were an important part of the consultative machinery used during the review. Four series of such bilateral discussions, each of which was undertaken by the federal Minister of Justice, can be identified.

The first series took place in January 1968, as part of the preparations for the first Constitutional Conference, when Mr. Trudeau, then the federal Minister of Justice, visited each Premier for the purpose of a preliminary exchange of views regarding the Conference agenda and the proposed federal charter of human rights. The same practice was to be followed prior to the second Constitutional Conference in February 1969, with Mr. Turner having informal discussions in each province regarding the federal bill on official languages and the general federal programme on the constitution. In addition to exposing the federal positions and views, these discussions were to contribute to the development of a common understanding of some of the constitutional issues and facilitate in some measure the multilateral discussions that were to follow.

A third and fourth series of bilateral consultations were held by Mr. Turner with each Premier following the Constitutional Conferences of September 1970 and February 1971 regarding the "package" of constitutional provisions which were to be incorporated eventually in the Victoria Charter. Exploratory talks on the possibility of an agreement on a limited number of constitutional reforms were held in January 1971, following the decision which had been taken at the previous Constitutional Conference to carry out consultations between individual governments and to examine the question of an amending formula. Mr. Turner visited each provincial capital again in April 1971 in order to discuss a number of draft constitutional texts which had been prepared by the federal Department of Justice following the First Ministers' decision in February 1971 to patriate a constitution incorporating new constitutional provisions. Both of these instances marked a definite shift of accent from the multilateral to the bilateral process, and were part of the private consultation and bargaining which would lead to the Victoria Charter.

In addition to the above, the occasional meetings of individual Premiers with the Prime Minister in Ottawa for the purpose of general discussions provided other occasions for bilateral consultations on the constitutional review. It must also be assumed that numerous additional personal contacts must have taken place on a continuing basis between officials and ministers of the eleven governments.

Private Meetings of First Ministers

These took place during the formal proceedings of certain Constitutional Conferences as well as during private dinners given by the Prime Minister.

Conference proceedings were sometimes adjourned so that the First Ministers might continue their discussions in private executive sessions from which both their officials and other ministers were excluded. These private meetings provided an opportunity for more free and direct exchanges and usually resulted in decisions regarding the programme of work or in agreement on subjects under review. This technique became an essential part of the general Conference procedures for achieving forward movement. This was particularly true of the five-hour executive session held on the last day of the Victoria Conference during which agreement was reached on a number of points which had eluded the plenary Conference, as well as on the procedure and deadline for the consideration of the proposed Charter by each government following the meeting (federal and provincial Attorneys General were invited to attend for a specific purpose during a part of this private session).

The Prime Minister's private dinners restricted to Premiers only (or on occasion a representative)—a feature of most Constitutional Conferences—were other opportunities for free and informal discussions during which agreements could be consolidated and Conference proceedings sketched out. Although little is known about what took place during these gatherings, the following day's Conference discussions sometimes reflected these consultations. During one such instance, the Prime Minister's supper on the eve of the February 1971 Conference, the First Ministers were able to develop considerable consensus regarding the possibility of patriating the constitution and adopting a new amending formula. The importance of these discussions was specially underlined in this instance when, on the following day, the Conference was adjourned so that the two Premiers who had not attended the supper might be briefed on what had taken place. Similarly, the Prime Minister's dinner on the eve of the Victoria Conference was to provide an opportunity for reaching an initial understanding on the general procedure to be followed during the subsequent Conference discussions.

PROCEDURE FOR EFFECTING CONFERENCE AGREEMENTS

Use of the "Consensus"

There was no formal mechanism for determining when agreement had been reached during the course of the constitutional review. It had been generally agreed during the first Conference in February 1968 that the use of formal motions and votes would be undesirable. During this same Conference, the Prime Minister of Canada had also expressed serious reservations with respect to the suggestion that part of the Consensus on Language Rights might be stated in terms of a "majority" agreement only.

The mechanism for determining whether an agreement had been reached or a recommendation could be made usually called for the chairman of the meeting to formulate the nature of the agreement or recommendation that appeared to be emerging from a particular discussion, and to submit his assessment to the delegates for their own confirmation. Whatever modifications delegates might then feel were necessary as well as alternate proposals were similarly presented through the chairman. Any agreement was subsequently recorded in the Secretariat summary record of proceedings and in other reports where applicable. All questions were subject to final consideration by the First Ministers.

A modification to this procedure was introduced during the Victoria Conference when it was decided that a delegation which had a reservation concerning any constitutional provision in the draft Charter, but which did not wish its position to prevent an overall Conference agreement, could express its "reluctant agreement" to the provision and have the nature of its reservation noted by the Secretariat. Such reservations would only hold in the event that overall agreement on the Charter could not be reached during the Conference.

Initial Absence of Plan for Implementation of Possible Constitutional Agreements

Until the Constitutional Conference of September 1970, where it was agreed "that the examination of the question of amending procedures should now be given attention" and following which the amending formula as well as the mechanisms for patriation were to be discussed, there was little consideration given at either the Continuing Committee or Conference levels to the procedure which would be required for the implementation of any agreements that could be reached during the constitutional review. Similarly, although individual governments might have had their own timetables for the comprehensive review of all constitutional questions, the Conference as a whole was able to proceed without any initial comprehensive "game plan" other than the seven questions which had been referred for study in February 1968.

The decision to consider an amendment formula and the patriation of the constitution following the September 1970 Conference was, in contrast to the previous period, to initiate a period of review during which objectives in terms of substance and of time could be contemplated. The February 1971 Conference was to identify the major questions which First Ministers hoped to resolve at the Victoria meeting in June as well as outline the steps which could be used to patriate the constitution following an agreement in June. This scenario was followed as planned until interrupted by the Quebec government's rejection of the Victoria Charter following the June Conference.

Procedure Leading to Victoria Charter

The procedure for the discussions which were to lead to the submission of a draft charter of specific constitutional provisions at the Victoria Conference was characterized by a number of bilateral discussions at the ministerial level between the federal and each of the provincial governments. Although the question of the amending formula was discussed at both the 13th and 14th meetings of the Continuing Committee of Officials in accordance with the First Ministers' request in September 1970 that the Committee should "carry out detailed investigation of the ways of amending the Constitution," the September 1970 Conference had also agreed that individual governments could submit their views directly to the federal Minister of Justice who would decide if any real progress was possible. On the basis of the provincial submissions, Mr. Turner visited each Premier in January 1971 to discuss the amending formula, patriation and other possible constitutional reforms and it was apparently on the basis of these bilateral consultations that the next meeting of First Ministers in February 1971 was able to formulate the "elements" which it was felt should be included in the proposed new constitutional provisions. This departure from discussions within the regular committee structure was recognized by the February 1971 Conference when it decided that "the next steps would include further bilateral discussions leading up to the next meeting of First Ministers, and in addition as required, the on-going coordinating work of the Continuing Committee of Officials." There were, however, to be no further meetings of the C.C.O., although an "ad hoc meeting of senior officials" was convened at the end of March. An additional series of bilateral consultations between Mr. Turner and each province took place in April; these in turn were followed by a meeting of Attorneys General in Ottawa at the end of May and by the subsequent submission of a draft constitutional charter in Victoria in June.

THE ROLE OF DOCUMENTS

Secretariat Summary Records

A confidential summary record for the use of participants only was prepared by the Secretariat following each meeting during the constitutional review, with the exception of the two technical Sub-Committees on Sales Taxes and Death Duties. This applied to meetings of officials or ministers, as well as to all meetings of First Ministers including those for which a verbatim record was subsequently made available (no summary record was produced for the February 1968 Conference since the Secretariat had not yet been established). Each summary record summarized the main points raised by each delegation and any conclusions reached on the various subjects discussed during the meeting. They were prepared by the Secretariat on the basis of detailed notes taken during the meeting and by using the verbatim record where available. The record was then circulated to delegations with the indication that any comment regarding the Secretariat interpretation of the discussions would be circulated separately as an addendum to the summary record.

In addition to providing a summary of discussions, these documents were used as a basis for further discussions and as a record of conclusions reached. They were the main instrument through which the variety of views and positions could be digested and organized so as to ensure continued forward progress in the intergovernmental discussions. There were few instances of serious disagreement with the Secretariat's interpretation of discussions, its role as an objective and independent reporter of the various positions being accepted.

Discussion Papers and Reports

Documents on the substance of the review submitted by individual delegations were classified by the Secretariat as "position papers" or "working papers" depending on whether they represented a governmental position or more informal notes for discussion. Briefing papers on discussions which had taken place and background information regarding subjects under review were also prepared by the Secretariat and circulated as Secretariat "working papers" or "background papers." The "reports" to the Conference from committees of ministers or officials were usually prepared in draft form by the Secretariat for submission by the respective committees. The Secretariat also occasionally submitted its own reports to the First Ministers regarding the constitutional review activities. Notes on these various types of documents follow.

"Position papers" reflecting the formal views of a delegation on a particular constitutional question were, in general, mostly limited to the formal statements made by governments during meetings of the Constitutional Conference. They also included some policy papers such as the federal document on "Federalism for the Future." These papers permitted an identification of governmental policies and a point of departure from which discussions and negotiations could take place. The "working papers," however, were a more popular and fruitful instrument for discussions since they did not reflect firm positions and could be used to invite a common approach to the study of constitutional issues. Their first general use occurred with the submission and study of propositions on the constitution within the Continuing Committee. Subsequently they were to be used for the presentation of views on those questions that were to be examined in detail, for instance the taxing and spending powers. This technique was followed at both the official and ministerial levels as the main vehicle for expressing respective governmental views.

Working papers prepared by the Secretariat were meant to provide a summary of the discussions that had taken place within the C.C.O. or a ministerial committee for the use of the First Ministers (in which cases they were also designated as "briefing papers") or to otherwise assist the consideration of individual questions. The latter category included Secretariat comments on the programme of work and on procedures and organization for the review. Background information on subjects under review, such as extracts from other constitutions, was made available by the Secretariat in the form of "background papers" prepared on request or on its own initiative. This type of document was also used to provide delegates with checklists and summaries concerning the overall review process.

The "reports" issuing from one committee level to another within the constitutional review structure were the formal instruments for communicating the state of progress that had been achieved at any one level. They were also used to communicate the results of studies on particular subjects that had been requested by the First Ministers. In nearly all cases these were prepared in draft form by the Secretariat for review and approval by the issuing committee. The nature and usefulness of these documents were usually a reflection of the progress that had been made within the respective committee discussions. Thus while some reports, such as that of the Committee of Ministers on the Senate, were largely perfunctory, others were able to facilitate a further discussion of the issues. In no case, however, were these documents deemed to be substitutes for the individual private briefings which each delegation was expected to provide for its government.

It might be noted that only one report on the general constitutional discussions was made by the Continuing Committee to the Constitutional Conference, in February 1969, although the Committee continued to report on requests made by the First Ministers for the examination of specific questions. Summaries of the general discussions in the C.C.O. were presented to the First Ministers in the form of Secretariat "briefing papers."

Conference Conclusions

A statement of "conclusions" was issued following each of the seven Constitutional Conferences, those for the first Conference only taking the form of a "consensus" and of "proposals" adopted by the Conference. These conclusions served to record the progress made and the decisions taken by the First Ministers as well as to indicate the general direction the review process would be expected to take between formal Conferences. Both questions of procedure and decisions on substance were covered.

As the majority of the constitutional discussions were in camera, these conclusions constituted a continuing source of public information regarding the developing status of the review. For the participants in the review, both officials and ministers, they served as the authoritative register of the First Ministers' directions regarding their own work and as general guidance for the on-going conduct of the review.

The task of preparing an initial draft of the conclusions for each Conference was given to the Secretariat early in the review in recognition of the independent and neutral approach this body could take to formulate the expressed views of all governments. The procedure was for the Secretariat to circulate a draft during the Conference so that comments from individual delegations could be received and collated for incorporation into a second draft which was then circulated for the final review and approval of the First Ministers. The discussion of the draft conclusions often provided the necessary catalyst for the finalization of agreements that had remained until then either uncertain or undefined. They also called for concentrated exercises of negotiation in which the federal government was often able to use its central position for resolving remaining issues and for influencing the direction of the future discussions.

Verbatim Records

It was agreed at the first meeting of the Continuing Committee in May 1968 that no tape recording or other type of verbatim record of the Committee's proceedings would be made. This decision was to also apply to the sub-committees of officials and to the ministerial committees throughout the review.

As for the meetings of First Ministers, a verbatim record had been taken and subsequently published in an edited form for the first open Conference in February 1968; this practice continued to be followed for the two subsequent open Conferences in February and December 1969. In the case of the closed meetings no verbatim record was taken for the Conference of June 1969. However, for the September 1970 Conference it was decided that such a document would be helpful to the Secretariat for purposes of preparing the usual summary record. This precedent was followed for the following two Conferences in February and June 1971. In addition, as interest had been expressed regarding the usefulness of the document for delegations themselves, it was agreed that one copy of the unedited and unofficial verbatim record would be made available to each of the eleven First Ministers for the internal and confidential use of their respective delegations only. This arrangement left the Secretariat summary record as the only official record of the proceedings for each Conference.

THE ROLE OF THE CONTINUING COMMITTEE OF OFFICIALS

The actual work of the C.C.O. has already been described. The approach which was adopted by this Committee in its task was set out as follows in its first report to the Conference in February 1969:

> It was clear to all participants from the outset that the Continuing Committee could not and should not presume to take decisions. The Committee felt that it should seek to assist the Constitutional Conference by attempting to identify and define problems, by seeking to clarify issues, and by helping to focus attention on the questions requiring the consideration of First Ministers.

During the course of the review, the C.C.O.'s role as an instrument for the clarification of issues for the attention of First Ministers was applied to most subjects examined by the Conference, a position which in turn was to provide heads of government with a permanent group of advisers regarding the overall revision process. This unique position of the Continuing Committee as the First Ministers' main continuous source of advice was recognized early in the review in the proposals at the end of the first Conference; it was later consolidated by the Committee's submission in February 1969 of a report on the procedures which the First Ministers could adopt to ensure a comprehensive review of the constitution, including the seven questions that had been listed by the Conference in 1968. The C.C.O.'s role in this respect continued throughout the revision process until February 1971, when it was decided to emphasize bilateral negotiations as part of the procedures which were to lead to a draft constitutional charter.

The Continuing Committee's position was also notable in that it was often the first forum in which detailed discussions could take place and initial expertise developed. When certain issues were subsequently referred to ministerial committees, the C.C.O. continued to retain a "watching brief" over developments for the purpose of providing advice to the First Ministers. This latter function in turn accorded with the First Minister's own expectation that they would be able to use members of the C.C.O. both formally through the Committee's reports, and privately in briefings from their own representatives as a continuing central point of information concerning all aspects of the constitutional discussions.

Continuing Committee members also usually acted as the focal point for each government's contact with the Secretary of the Conference. This made possible an additional source of general information which served to facilitate each delegation's own participation in the review process.

THE ROLE OF THE SECRETARIAT

The Secretariat of the Constitutional Conference was the main instrument available to the Conference for the organization of the constitutional discussions. The principal role of the Secretariat was to provide the mechanisms through which an orderly and integrated discussion of issues at all levels could take place. A detailed description and analysis of the Secretariat's functions in this respect is given in the following chapter.

9

1976 Correspondence on the Constitution*

Prime Minister Trudeau to All Premiers,
March 31, 1976

I had been hoping to be in touch with you well before this to advise you about progress in the exercise we started last April, with our discussion at 7 Rideau Gate, for "patriation" of the B.N.A. Act. Since then, all of you, with the exception of Premier Bennett, have received Mr. Gordon Robertson who has discussed the project with you on my behalf. Those discussions took place between May and mid-July of 1975. Premier Barrett was unable to arrange a meeting prior to the election in British Columbia but Mr. Robertson will be meeting Premier Bennett in early April. Discussions with Quebec have taken a good deal of time and it was not until March 5th that I had the opportunity of reviewing the question with the Premier of Quebec. I thought it essential to know his attitude before proceeding to further action.

You will recall that we started with agreement in principle on the desirability of "patriating" the B.N.A. Act and, at the same time, establishing as law the amending procedure that had been agreed to in Victoria in 1971. We also agreed that we would not, in the present "patriation" exercise, consider substantive changes to the B.N.A. Act itself since any entry on that course would, as the discussions from 1968 to 1971 had shown, make early action impossible. Mr. Bourassa indicated, however, that it would be difficult for his government to agree to this, unless the action also included "constitutional guarantees" for the French language and culture. We agreed that our general acceptance of the plan, in principle, would be subject to more precise exploration and definition, and this was the purpose of the discussions Mr. Robertson had with you on my behalf. I should first report on what developed in the course of those discussions, although the Premiers Mr. Robertson saw later will be generally aware of the way in which our original proposal grew.

It quickly became apparent in Mr. Robertson's discussions that the action for "patriation" and establishment of the amending procedure would be more meaningful for, and more acceptable to, a number of provinces if certain other alterations in our constitutional situation could be established at the same time. Most of these alterations, with the exception of Mr. Bourassa's "constitutional guarantees", were among

---

* Reprinted by permission.

the things that had been included in the Victoria Charter. They included the provision for consultation with the provinces about appointments to the Supreme Court of Canada and the special handling of cases arising from the civil law of Quebec. They included also the provision concerning the reduction of regional disparities. Certain of the western provinces wanted to have the amending procedure itself modified so that the requirement with regard to consent from the four western provinces would be the same as that for the four eastern provinces. This would mean deletion of the population provision respecting the western provinces that was inserted at Victoria.

The main problem was the definition of the "constitutional guarantees" to which Mr. Bourassa had referred at the outset. Mr. Robertson found that the Premiers he spoke to after the initial discussions with Mr. Bourassa in May had no objection in principle to "constitutional guarantees", although all made it clear that they would want to consider them in detail once they had been worked out with Quebec and reduced to writing.

I will not go into all the difficulties that are presented by the concept of "constitutional guarantees"; they are many and complex. Discussions with Mr. Bourassa's representatives finally led to a formulation that was included in a document sent to him in November, 1975. I am enclosing a copy of the full document herewith. I would draw your attention especially to Parts IV and VI. The formulation of the principal "constitutional guarantee" is Part IV (Article 38). It is buttressed by Part VI (Article 40) and also by the provisions concerning language in Part III.

As I have mentioned, the "constitutional guarantee" was a concept raised by Mr. Bourassa and stated by him to be essential. Articles 38 and 40 attempt to cover points made by his representatives. Mr. Bourassa knows that my colleagues and I share some concern about the Articles, and he understands that it will fall to him to explain them to his fellow Premiers, in the light of the facts relating to the position of the French language and culture in Canada.

I should emphasize that the document, while it is styled a "Draft Proclamation", was put in this form simply to show with maximum clarity what the result would be if all the proposals, as they had emerged in the course of Mr. Robertson's consultations, were found acceptable by all governments. It should not be regarded as a specific proposal or draft to which anyone is committed at this stage, since there has not been agreement to the totality of it by anyone. It is rather in the nature of a report on the various ideas, including Mr. Bourassa's "constitutional guarantee", as they developed in the course of the informal discussions from April to November, 1975.

As I stated earlier, most of the "Draft Proclamation" consists of provisions of the Victoria Charter which various Premiers have asked to have included in any action we take. In some cases there are adjustments of the Victoria provisions in order to take into account altered circumstances since 1971 and to benefit by some hindsight. The new parts of this "report" are the Parts IV and VI to which I have already referred. For ease of reference the main elements are:

(a) A Preamble. This is entirely new and is simply an idea of the way a total presentation might look.
(b) Part I is the amending formula contained in the Victoria Charter made applicable to those parts of the Constitution not now amendable in Canada. Thus Articles 49, 50, 51, 52, 56 and 57 of Part IX of the Victoria Charter are included, while Articles 53, 54 and 55, which were designed to replace Articles 91(1) and 92(1) of the British North America Act, are not. The amending formula has not been modified to take account of the views expressed by certain Western Premiers concerning the population qualification for agreement by the Western provinces. I suggest that this might be a matter that, in the first instance, the four Western Premiers might attempt to solve among themselves.
(c) Part II, which is Part IV of the Victoria Charter concerning the Supreme Court, with a final Article (included in another Part of the Victoria Charter) to protect the status of Judges already appointed.
(d) Part III, which is a modified version of Part II of the Victoria Charter concerning language rights. It would entrench the constitutional status of the English and French languages federally. It would not affect the provinces, but it would permit a province, under Article 35, to entrench its own provision if it so wished.
(e) Part IV, which is the "guarantee" designed to protect the French language and culture against adverse action by the Parliament and Government of Canada.
(f) Part V, which is essentially Part VII of the Victoria Charter on Regional Disparities. The presentation has been slightly altered but there is no change in substance whatever.
(g) Part VI, which is a new Article designed to indicate the spirit in which Governments may enter into agreements. In two of the three areas specifically mentioned, major agreements with Quebec have been concluded over the past two years (family allowances and consultation on immigration).

Mr. Bourassa advised me in our conversation on March 5th that the things he considers to be necessary might well go beyond what we, in the federal government, have understood to be involved in the present exercise. In part they might relate to the distribution of powers. I advised him that the Government of Canada, for its part, feels that it can go no further as part of this exercise than the constitutional guarantees that are embodied in the document and that indeed even they might find difficulty of acceptance in their present form. To go further would involve entry upon the distribution of powers, with the consequences to which I have referred. We must, then, consider three alternatives that are open to us in these circumstances.

Let us begin with the simplest alternative. The Government of Canada remains firmly of the view that we should, as a minimum, achieve "patriation" of the B.N.A. Act. It is not prepared to contemplate the continuation of the anomalous situation in which the British Parliament retains the power to legislate with respect to essential parts of the constitution of Canada. Such "patriation" could be achieved by means of an Address of the two Houses of the Canadian Parliament to the Queen, requesting appropriate legislation by the British Parliament to end its capacity to legislate in any way with respect to Canada. Whereas unanimity of the federal government and the provinces would be desirable even for so limited a measure, we are satisfied that such action by the Parliament of Canada does not require the consent of the provinces and would be entirely proper since it would not affect in any way the distribution of powers. In other words, the termination of the British capacity to legislate for Canada would not in any way alter the position as between Parliament and the provincial legislatures whether in respect of jurisdictions flowing from Sections 91 and 92 or otherwise.

However, simple "patriation" would not equip us with an amending procedure for those parts of our constitution that do not come under either Section 91(1) or Section 92(1) of the B.N.A. Act. To meet this deficiency, one could provide in the Address to the Queen that amendment of those parts of the constitution not now amendable in Canada could be made on unanimous consent of Parliament and the legislatures until a permanent formula is found and established. In theory this approach would introduce a rigidity which does not now exist, since at present it is the federal Parliament alone which goes to Westminster, and the degree of consultation of or consent by the provinces is a matter only of convention about which there can be differences of view. In practice, of course, the federal government has in the past sought the unanimous consent of the provinces before seeking amendments that have affected the distribution of powers.

A second and perhaps preferable alternative would be to include in the action a provision that could lead to the establishment of a permanent and more flexible amending procedure. That could be done by detailing such a procedure in our Joint Address and having it included in the British legislation as an enabling provision that would come into effect when and only when it had received the formal approval of the legislatures of all the provinces. The obvious amending procedure to set forth would be the one agreed to at Victoria in application to those parts of our constitution not now amendable in Canada (Part I of the attached

"Draft Proclamation"). This could be with or without modification respecting the four western provinces. (On this last point, the federal government would be quite prepared to accept the proposed modification and it is my understanding that the other provinces would equally agree if the western provinces can arrive at agreement.)

If we took the above step, we would achieve forthwith half of our objective of last April—"patriation"—and we would establish a process by which the other half—the amending procedure—would become effective as and when the provincial legislatures individually signify their agreement. Over a period of time, which I hope would not be long, we would establish the total capacity to amend our constitution under what is clearly the best and most acceptable procedure that has been worked out in nearly fifty years of effort, since the original federal-provincial conference on this subject in 1927. Until full agreement and implementation had been achieved, any constitutional changes that might be needed, and which did not come under Section 91(1) or Section 92(1) or which could not otherwise be effected in Canada could be made subject to unanimous consent. This would impose an interim rigidity for such very rare requirements for amendment, but, as I have said, the practice has, in any event, been to secure unanimous consent before making amendments that have affected the distribution of powers.

A third and more extensive possibility still, would be to include, in the "patriation" action, the entirety of the "Draft Proclamation" I am enclosing. In other words the British Parliament, in terminating its capacity to legislate for Canada, could provide that all of the substance of Parts I to VI would come into effect in Canada and would have full legal force when, and only when, the entirety of those Parts had been approved by the legislatures of all the provinces. At that point, we would have, not only "patriation" and the amending procedure, but also the other provisions that have developed out of the discussions thus far. Here again, of course, until all the Provinces had approved the entire Draft Proclamation, any constitutional change which did not come under Section 91(1) or Section 92(1) would be subject to unanimous consent.

As you can see, there are several possibilities as to the course of action now to take. So far as the federal government is concerned, our much preferred course would be to act in unison with all the provinces. "Patriation" is such a historic milestone that it would be ideal if all Premiers would associate themselves with it.

But if unanimity does not appear possible, the federal government will have to decide whether it will recommend to Parliament that a Joint Address be passed seeking "patriation" of the B.N.A. Act. A question for decision then will be what to add to that action. We are inclined to think that it should, at the minimum, be the amending procedure agreed to at Victoria by all the provinces, with or without modification respecting the western provinces, and subject to the condition about coming into force only when approved by the legislatures of all the provinces as explained above.

The implications of the different possibilities are complex, and you will undoubtedly want to consider them with care. To facilitate consideration, Mr. Robertson would be glad to come to see you, at a convenient time, for such discussions as you might wish to have. When opportunity offers at an early meeting, we might also discuss the matter together.

I would welcome your comments. Mr. Robertson will be in touch with your office to see if you would wish to have a meeting with him and, if so, what time would suit.

Prior to my meeting with Mr. Bourassa, I did not feel that I was in a position to place any documents before Parliament, but I now feel it proper to do so. I would like to table copies of this letter, as well as of the "Draft Proclamation" that is enclosed. If you have any objection, could you please advise me forthwith. If I do not hear to the contrary, I shall plan to table on April 9th. Should you wish to do the same in your legislature, I would of course, have no objection.

DRAFT
FORM FOR A PROCLAMATION OF THE
GOVERNOR GENERAL, NOVEMBER 10th, 1975

Whereas it is fitting that it should be possible to amend the Constitution of Canada in all respects by action of the appropriate instrumentalities of government in Canada acting separately or in concert as may best suit the matter in question;

And whereas it is desirable to make more specific provision respecting the constitutional status of the English and French languages in Canada and to ensure that changes in the Constitution, interpretation of its provisions or action by the Parliament or Government of Canada should not endanger the continuation and full development of the French language and the culture based thereon;

And whereas it is desirable that the Parliament and Government of Canada and the Legislatures and Governments of the Provinces act effectively to promote equality of opportunity and an acceptable level of public services among the different regions of Canada;

Therefore it is desirable to establish among other things:

(a) A method for the amendment in Canada of those parts of the Constitution of general interest and concern that cannot now be amended in Canada in which the consent will be required of the Legislatures of Provinces representative of both the official language groups of Canada as well as of the Legislatures of Provinces in all of the geographical regions of Canada;

(b) means by which Provinces can participate in the selection of persons to be appointed to the Supreme Court of Canada; and

(c) principles to guide the Parliament of Canada in the exercise of powers allotted to it under the Constitution of Canada and to guide the Government of Canada in the exercise of powers conferred upon it by the Constitution of Canada and by laws enacted by the Parliament of Canada;

Now therefore We .... do proclaim as follows:

PART I

Amendments to the Constitution

Art. 1   Amendments to the Constitution of Canada may from time to time be made by Proclamation issued by the Governor General under the Great Seal of Canada when so authorized by resolutions of the Senate and House of Commons and of the Legislative Assemblies of at least a majority of the Provinces that includes:

(1) every Province that at any time before the issue of such Proclamation had, according to any previous general census, a population of at least twenty-five per cent of the population of Canada;

(2) at least two of the Atlantic Provinces;

(3) at least two of the Western Provinces that have, according to the then latest general census, combined populations of at least fifty per cent of the population of all the Western Provinces.

Art. 2   Amendments to the Constitution of Canada in relation to any provision that applies to one or more, but not all, of the Provinces may from time to time be made by Proclamation issued by the Governor General under the Great Seal of Canada when so authorized by resolutions of the Senate and House of Commons and of the Legislative Assembly of each Province to which an amendment applies.

Art. 3   An amendment may be made by Proclamation under Articles 1 or 2 without a resolution of the Senate authorizing the issue of the Proclamation if within ninety days of the passage of a resolution by the House of Commons authorizing its issue the Senate has not passed such a resolution and at any time after the expiration of the ninety days the House of Commons again passes the resolution, but any period when Parliament is prorogued or dissolved shall not be counted in computing the ninety days.

Art. 4   The following rules apply to the procedures for amendment described in Articles 1 and 2:

(1) either of these procedures may be initiated by the Senate or the House of Commons or the Legislative Assembly of a Province;
(2) a resolution made for the purposes of this Part may be revoked at any time before the issue of a Proclamation authorized by it.

Art. 5   The procedures prescribed in Articles 1 and 2 may not be used to make an amendment when there is another provision for making such amendment in the Constitution of Canada, but the procedure in Article 1 may nonetheless be used to amend any provision for amending the Constitution, including this Article, or in making a general consolidation and revision of the Constitution.

Art. 6   In this Part "Atlantic Provinces" means the Provinces of Nova Scotia, New Brunswick, Prince Edward Island and Newfoundland, and "Western Provinces" means the Provinces of Manitoba, British Columbia, Saskatchewan and Alberta.

Art. 7   The enactments set out in the Schedule shall continue as law in Canada and as such shall, together with this Proclamation and any Proclamation subsequently issued under this Part, collectively be known as the Constitution of Canada, and amendments thereto shall henceforth be made only according to the authority contained therein.

PART II

Supreme Court of Canada

Art. 8   There shall be a general court of appeal for Canada to be known as the Supreme Court of Canada.

Art. 9   The Supreme Court of Canada shall consist of a chief justice to be called the Chief Justice of Canada, and eight other judges, who shall, subject to this Part, be appointed by the Governor General in Council by letters patent under the Great Seal of Canada.

Art. 10   Any person may be appointed a judge of the Supreme Court of Canada who, after having been admitted to the Bar of any Province, has, for a total period of at least ten years, been a judge of any court in Canada or a barrister or advocate at the Bar of any Province.

Art. 11   At least three of the judges of the Supreme Court of Canada shall be appointed from among persons who, after having been admitted to the Bar of the Province of Quebec, have, for a total period of at least ten years, been judges of any court of that Province or of a court established by the Parliament of Canada or barristers or advocates at that Bar.

Art. 12   Where a vacancy arises in the Supreme Court of Canada and the Attorney General of Canada is considering a person for appointment to fill the vacancy, he shall inform the Attorney General of the appropriate Province.

Art. 13   When an appointment is one falling within Article 11 or the Attorney General of Canada has determined that the appointment shall be made from among persons who have been admitted to the Bar of a specific Province, he shall make all reasonable efforts to reach agreement with the Attorney General of the appropriate Province, before a person is appointed to the Court.

Art. 14   No person shall be appointed to the Supreme Court of Canada unless the Attorney General of Canada and the Attorney General of the appropriate Province agree to the appointment, or such person has been recommended for appointment to the Court by a nominating council described in Article 16, or has been selected by the Attorney General of Canada under Article 16.

Art. 15   Where after the lapse of ninety days from the day a vacancy arises in the Supreme Court of Canada, the Attorney General of Canada and the Attorney General of a Province have not reached agreement on a person to be appointed to fill the vacancy, the Attorney General of Canada may inform the Attorney General of the appropriate Province in writing that he proposes to convene a nominating council to recommend an appointment.

Art. 16   Within thirty days of the day when the Attorney General of Canada has written the Attorney General of the Province that he proposes to convene a nominating council, the Attorney General of the Province may inform the Attorney General of Canada in writing that he selects either of the following types of nominating councils:

(1) a nominating council consisting of the following members: the Attorney General of Canada or his nominee and the Attorneys General of the Provinces or their nominees;
(2) a nominating council consisting of the following members: the Attorney General of Canada or his nominee, the Attorney General of the appropriate Province or his nominee and a Chairman to be selected by the two Attorneys General, and if within six months from the expiration of the thirty days they cannot agree on a Chairman, then the Chief Justice of the appropriate Province, or if he is unable to act, the next senior Judge of his court, shall name a Chairman;

and if the Attorney General of the Province fails to make a selection within the thirty days above referred to, the Attorney General of Canada may select the person to be appointed.

Art. 17   When a nominating council has been created, the Attorney General of Canada shall submit the names of not less than three qualified persons to it about whom he has sought the agreement of the Attorney General of the appropriate Province to the appointment, and the nominating council shall recommend therefrom a person for appointment to the Supreme Court of Canada; a majority of the members of a council constitutes a quorum, and a recommendation of a majority of the members at a meeting constitutes a recommendation of the council.

Art. 18   For the purpose of Articles 12 to 17 "appropriate Province" means, in the case of a person being considered for appointment to the Supreme Court of Canada in compliance with Article 11, the Province of Quebec, and in the case of any other person being so considered, the Province to the Bar of which such a person was admitted, and if a person was admitted to the Bar of more than one Province, the Province with the Bar of which the person has, in the opinion of the Attorney General of Canada, the closest connection.

Art. 19   Articles 12 to 18 do not apply to the appointment of the Chief Justice of Canada when such appointment is made from among the judges of the Supreme Court of Canada.

Art. 20   The judges of the Supreme Court of Canada hold office during good behaviour until attaining the age of seventy years, but are removable by the Governor General on address of the Senate and House of Commons.

Art. 21   The Supreme Court of Canada has jurisdiction to hear and determine appeals on any constitutional question from any judgment of any court in Canada and from any decision on any constitutional question by any such court in determining any question referred to it, but except as regards appeals from the highest court of final resort in a Province, the Supreme Court of Canada may prescribe such exceptions and conditions to the exercise of such jurisdiction as may be authorized by the Parliament of Canada.

Art. 22   Subject to this Part, the Supreme Court of Canada shall have such further appellate jurisdiction as the Parliament of Canada may prescribe.

Art. 23   The Parliament of Canada may make laws conferring original jurisdiction on the Supreme Court of Canada in respect of such matters in relation of the laws of Canada as may be prescribed by the Parliament of Canada, and authorizing the reference of questions of law or fact to the court and requiring the court to hear and determine the questions.

Art. 24   Subject to this Part, the judgment of the Supreme Court of Canada in all cases is final and conclusive.

Art. 25   Where a case before the Supreme Court of Canada involves questions of law relating to the civil law of the Province of Quebec, and involves no other question of law, it shall be heard by a panel of five judges, or with the consent of the parties, four judges, at least three of whom have the qualifications described in Article 11, and if for any reason three judges of the court who have such qualifications are not available, the court may name such *ad hoc* judges as may be necessary to hear the case from among the judges who have such qualifications serving on a superior court of record established by the law of Canada or of a superior court of appeal of the Province of Quebec.

Art. 26   Nothing in this Part shall be construed as restricting the power existing at the commencement of this Proclamation of a Provincial Legislature to provide for or limit appeals pursuant to its power to legislate in relation to the administration of justice in the Province.

Art. 27   The salaries, allowances and pension of the judges of the Supreme Court of Canada shall be fixed and provided by the Parliament of Canada.

Art. 28   Subject to this Part, the Parliament of Canada may make laws to provide for the organization and maintenance of the Supreme Court of Canada, including the establishment of a quorum for particular purposes.

Art. 29   The court existing on the day of the coming into force of this Proclamation under the name of the Supreme Court of Canada shall continue as the Supreme Court of Canada, and the judges thereof shall continue in office as though appointed under this Part except that they shall hold office during good behaviour until attaining the age of seventy-five years, and until otherwise provided pursuant to the provisions of this Part, all laws pertaining to the court in force on that day shall continue, subject to the provisions of this Proclamation.

PART III

Language Rights

Art. 30   English and French are the official languages of Canada, but no provision in this Part shall derogate from any right, privilege, or obligation existing under any other provision of the Constitution.

Art. 31   A person has the right to use English and French in the debates of the Parliament of Canada.

Art. 32   The statutes and the records and journals of the Parliament of Canada shall be printed and published in English and French; and both versions of such statutes are authoritative.

Art. 33   A person has the right to use English and French in giving evidence before, or in any pleading or process in the Supreme Court of Canada and any courts established by the Parliament of Canada, and to require that all documents and judgments issuing from such courts be in English or French.

Art. 34   An individual has the right to the use of the official language of his choice in communication between him and the head or central office of every department and agency of the Government of Canada.

Art. 35   A provincial Legislative Assembly may, by resolution, declare that provisions similar to those of any part of Articles 32, 33 and 34 shall apply to the Legislative Assembly, and to any of the provincial courts and offices of the provincial departments and agencies according to the terms of the resolution, and thereafter such parts apply to the Legislative Assembly, courts and offices specified according to the terms of the resolution; and any right conferred under this Article may be abrogated or diminished only in accordance with the procedure prescribed in Article 2.

Art. 36   A person has the right to the use of the official language of his choice in communications between him and every principal office of the departments and agencies of the Government of Canada that are located in an area where a substantial proportion of the population has the official language of his choice as its mother tongue, but the Parliament of Canada may define the limits of such areas and what constitutes a substantial proportion of the population for the purposes of this Article.

Art. 37   In addition to the rights provided by this Part, the Parliament of Canada may, within its legislative jurisdiction, provide for more extensive use of English and French.

PART IV

Protection of the French Language and Culture

Art. 38   The Parliament of Canada, in the exercise of powers allotted to it under the Constitution of Canada, and the Government of Canada, in the exercise of powers conferred upon it by the Constitution of Canada and by laws enacted by the Parliament of Canada, shall be guided by, among other considerations for the welfare and advantage of the people of Canada, the knowledge that a fundamental purpose underlying the federation of Canada is to ensure the preservation and the full development of the French language and culture based on it and neither the Parliament nor the Government of Canada, in the exercise of the respective powers, shall act in a manner that will adversely affect the preservation and development of the French language and the culture based on it.

PART V

Regional Disparities

Art. 39   Without altering the distribution of powers and without compelling the Parliament of Canada or the Legislatures of the Provinces to exercise their legislative powers, the Parliament of Canada and the Legislatures of the Provinces, together with the Government of Canada and the Governments of the Provinces, are committed to:

(a) the promotion of equality of opportunity and well-being for all individuals in Canada;
(b) the assurance, as nearly as possible, that essential public services of reasonable quality are available to all individuals in Canada; and
(c) the promotion of economic development to reduce disparities in the social and economic opportunities for all individuals in Canada wherever they may live.

PART VI

Federal-Provincial Agreements

Art. 40(1)   In order to ensure a greater harmony of action by governments, and especially in order to reduce the possibility of action that could adversely affect the preservation and development in Canada of the French language and the culture based on it, the Government of Canada and the Governments of the Provinces or any one or more of the Provinces may, within the limits of the powers otherwise accorded to each of them respectively by law, enter into agreements with one another concerning the manner of exercise of such powers, particularly in the fields of immigration, communications and social policy.

(2)   Nothing in this Article shall be held to limit or restrict any authority conferred either before or after the coming into force of this Proclamation upon the Government of Canada or the Government of a Province to enter into agreements within the limits of the powers otherwise accorded to it by law.

Premier Lougheed to Prime Minister Trudeau,
October 14, 1976

Further to my letter of September 2, 1976 and my telex of October 4, 1976, I wish to inform you of the outcome of the deliberations by the ten Canadian Premiers on the issues raised by you in your letter of March 31, 1976 relative to patriation of the Constitution from Westminster to Canada.

Your letter of March 31, 1976 outlined three possible options and served as a framework for our deliberations. The provinces agreed in May 1976 to proceed with an examination of all three options. You will recall that your option 3 includes patriation, an amending formula and a number of other substantive changes to the British North America Act which were contained in the draft proclamation appended to your letter of March 31, 1976. You will also recall that when the premiers had private discussions on this matter at your residence during the evening of June 14, 1976, you indicated that you would be prepared to accept any proposal which had been unanimously agreed to by the provinces.

At the same time, you indicated that you hoped we could consider the matter over the summer and report to you early in the fall as to the outcome of our deliberations and discussions.

As Chairman of the Annual Conference of Premiers, I would like to now deal with the matters as they were outlined in your letter of March 31, 1976.

Patriation

All provinces agreed with the objective of patriation. They also agreed that patriation should not be undertaken without a consensus being developed on an expansion of the role of the provinces and/or jurisdiction in the following areas: culture, communications, Supreme Court of Canada, spending power, Senate representation and regional disparities. Later in the letter I will endeavour to give you some idea of our discussions on the above matters.

Amending Formula

Considerable time was spent on this important subject and the unanimous agreement of the provinces was not secured on a specific formula. Eight provinces agreed to the amending formula as drafted in Victoria in 1971 and as proposed by you in your draft proclamation. British Columbia wishes to have the Victoria Formula modified to reflect its view that British Columbia should be treated as a distinct entity with its own separate veto. In this sense it would be in the same position as Ontario and Quebec. Alberta held the view that a constitutional amending formula should not permit an amendment that would take away rights, proprietary interests and jurisdiction from any province without the concurrence of that province. In this regard, Alberta was referring to matters arising under Section 92, 93 and 109 of the British North America Act.

Matters Unanimously Agreed To

A number of matters were dealt with and unanimously agreed to. Specific texts were considered and given approval, subject to revision by draftsmen.

(a) A greater degree of provincial involvement in immigration.

(b) A confirmation of the language rights of English and French generally along the lines discussed in Victoria in 1971.

(c) A strengthening of jurisdiction of provincial governments of taxation in the areas of primary production from lands, mines, minerals and forests.

(d) A provision that the declaratory powers of the federal government to declare a particular work for the general advantage of Canada would only be exercised when the province affected concurred.

(e) That a conference composed of the eleven First Ministers of Canada should be held at least once a year as a constitutional requirement.

(f) That the creation of new provinces should be subject to any amending formula consensus.

As already mentioned under the remarks on patriation, the provinces were of the view that while patriation was desirable it should be accompanied by the expansion of provincial jurisdiction and involvement in certain areas. The Premiers believed that discussions on these matters should be held with the federal government because they involve the federal government to a significant degree.

(a) Culture—You will recall that culture was referred to in Parts IV and VI of the draft proclamation. The interprovincial discussions on culture focussed on the addition of a new concurrent power to be included in the Constitution. This power would refer to arts, literature and cultural heritage and would be subject to provincial paramountcy. On this matter, there was a high degree of consensus on the principle and considerable progress was made with respect to a solution. There was also, however, firm opinion from one province that the provinces and the federal government should have concurrent jurisdictional powers in the area.

(b) Communications—In the draft proclamation, communications were referred to in Part VI. Discussions on this subject related to greater provincial control in communications, particularly in the area of cable television.

(c) Supreme Court of Canada—In general, discussions on this topic developed from those articles found in Part II of the draft proclamation. The provinces unanimously agreed to a greater role for the provinces in the appointment of Supreme Court judges than provided for in the draft proclamation. In addition, a number of other modifications were suggested to the provisions found in the draft proclamation.

(d) Spending Power—Discussion on this matter focused on the necessity and desirability of having a consensus mechanism which must be applied before the federal government could exercise its spending power in areas of provincial jurisdiction.

(e) Senate Representation—Discussion on this subject related to British Columbia's proposal that Senate representation for that province be increased.

(f) Regional Disparities and Equalization—In the draft proclamation, Regional Disparities was referred in to Part V. The discussions on this topic focussed on the expansion and strengthening of this section to include a reference to equalization. There was unanimous agreement on the clause contained in the draft proclamation and a high degree of consensus on incorporating clauses in the Constitution providing for equalization.

Other matters were discussed, but it was felt by the Premiers that their deliberations had been of a preliminary and exploratory nature. As such, in any future meeting it is possible that individual provinces may present additional suggestions for consideration.

The Premiers were of the view that significant progress on this complex matter had occurred. It was felt that further progress would require discussions between the provinces and the federal government. It was concluded by the Premiers that the next step should be for you to meet with the Premiers and develop the discussions reflected in this letter. The Premiers felt that it would now be appropriate for them to accept your invitation for further discussions in the near future, at a mutually agreeable time.

Given the importance of this subject and the referencd to it in your Throne Speech of October 12, 1976, the other Premiers may wish to join with me in tabling this letter before our respective provincial legislatures or otherwise making this letter public on October 20, 1976. If you have any objection could you please advise me forthwith.

Prime Minister Trudeau to Premier Lougheed,
January 19, 1977

I was glad to have the occasion, presented by my dinner with you and the Premiers of the other provinces on December 13th, to discuss briefly your letter of October 14th reporting on the discussions of the Premiers in August and October, 1976, on "patriation" of the constitution. I told you then—and this seemed to be agreeable to the other Premiers—that I would be replying to your letter, further to the interim reply I sent on October 18th, to round out this particular part of our constitutional discussions.

It seems to me that the results of the meetings of Premiers, as reflected in your letter, are, in a sense, either too much or too little. They are too much in relation to the limited exercise we embarked upon in April, 1975. That, as reflected in my letter of April 19th, 1975, was intended to accomplish "patriation" of our constitution from Britain with the amending clause agreed on at Victoria. We—the provinces and the federal government—decided deliberately to avoid the complexities of constitutional reform which had been so clearly demonstrated in the conferences, meetings and discussions from 1968 to 1971. While the very limited scope of our exercise grew somewhat in the course of discussions in 1975 and early 1976, the proposals embodied in your letter carry the exercise into new areas and even raise some aspects of the distribution of powers. This is precisely the sort of thing we had, in April 1975, sought to avoid.

If the proposals in your letter are too much in relation to the immediate exercise, they are too little in relation to constitutional reform. We got into many other aspects of the constitution in 1968-1971 and, if we are now to embark on changes in the distribution of powers and other fundamental matters, I think our review and our changes should be much more extensive than those covered in your letter of October 14th. I have made it clear on many occasions that the federal government is prepared to re-embark on a fundamental review of our constitution. We would be quite prepared to have such a process begin at a very early date if that is the general wish. The exercise since April 1975 has been based on experience, over the many years of effort in this area, which seemed to demonstrate the wisdom of trying to proceed by stages: first to "patriate" with an amending procedure that most think satisfactory; then to decide upon the changes in a document that would be totally Canadian and totally amendable by procedures to be executed entirely in Canada. The federal government is prepared to proceed by either route:

action by stages, such as we have been concentrating on, or action all at once by fundamental constitutional revision.

Having said that the proposals in your letter are, in our judgment, either too much or too little, the federal government is prepared to see if agreement can be achieved on the basis of your letter, but with modifications, so that "patriation" can be effected as soon as possible. The most significant modification we would suggest is that we should not, if we are to adhere to this limited exercise, enter in any way into the distribution of powers. The federal government is quite ready to go into that problem but it is both complex and difficult. To do it partially, in the way your letter suggests, without a coherent total plan would, in our view, be a serious mistake. We have, therefore, tried to see what might reasonably be done to meet the concerns to which your letter refers, while leaving all matters of constitutional powers for comprehensive study and action at the second stage, after "patriation." So that there can be no possibility of misunderstanding I repeat that, if the provinces now feel that this is not the right course, the federal government is ready to embark on the other route of total constitutional review. If we adopt that course, it will be essential for all of us to be willing to meet the challenge that this task will pose in as open-minded a way as possible consistent with our responsibilities, unburdened by commitments to any preconceived outcome, and constrained only by the dictates of our sense of what will best serve the interests of Canadians in all parts of Canada. In this spirit, I am convinced, lies the greatest promise of a constitution that will be Canadian in the best sense, that is to say an institutional framework for our future that will be effective and workable, yet justly and sensitively balanced as between its constituent elements. Having made these points, I return to the possibility of action in stages, with a first stage built upon the proposals in your letter.

If "patriation" can be agreed upon using the discussions of the last two years as the basis, we will need to implement it by means of a Proclamation by the Governor General and legislation by the British Parliament to terminate its powers to legislate with regard to Canada. A draft of such a Proclamation was sent to you and the other Premiers with my letter of March 31st, 1976. It has seemed to us that it might advance matters if the proposals of the federal government, in reply to your letter of October 14th, were communicated in the form of a revised Proclamation. Such a document is enclosed herewith as part of a draft of a resolution that might be placed before Parliament. The limitations on what it contains relate in large part to the comments I have already made and that it would be unwise, in this limited exercise, to touch the distribution of powers. Apart from that broad comment, possibly it would be helpful if I were to make the following brief explanations concerning the different parts of the document.

PART I—AMENDMENTS TO THE CONSTITUTION

This sets forth the Victoria amending formula. While the formula may not be perfect, there is general agreement that it is the best that has been devised in nearly fifty years of effort. It was agreed to by all eleven governments in 1971 and by eight of the ten provinces at your meeting in Toronto last October. We are never likely to get a higher degree of consensus on any formula. Accordingly, while the federal government is not entirely satisfied about one or two aspects of the formula, it seems to us that the wise course would be to accept it and get ahead with "patriation" on the basis of it. If we ever get anything that has a higher level of consensus, it can be established by use of the Victoria formula.

PART II—SENATE REPRESENTATION

This is entirely new and represents a response to the view that the western part of Canada is much under-represented in the Senate at the present time. While Senate representation has never been directly related to population in Canada, but rather to regions, it is clear that the west is indeed under-represented when one considers the way in which its importance in confederation has grown since the present Senate membership was set in 1915. Various formulae can be devised for increased representation from the western provinces. Part II represents a suggestion that the federal government would support.

When we come to fundamental review of the constitution, we will want to consider many things relating to the Senate. The federal government will have a number of proposals to make. For purposes of the present exercise, however, we would be prepared to have early decision on modification of western representation since that seems clearly to be unsatisfactory and capable of correction at this stage.

PART III—LANGUAGE RIGHTS

Your letter includes, as one of the matters "unanimously agreed to" by the provinces in the 1976 meetings, "a confirmation of the language rights of English and French generally along the lines discussed in Victoria in 1971". The Victoria provisions included certain obligations that specific provinces then agreed they were prepared to accept with regard to the official language that is in a minority position within its boundaries. We are not at all certain whether the wording of your letter indicates that those provinces are now prepared to accept the same or similar obligations. The federal government is prepared to do so. Articles 14 to 20 in the enclosed draft are along the lines of Victoria but, in view of the uncertainty to which I refer, they are in this text made applicable to the Parliament and government of Canada only, with a provision like that contained in the Victoria Charter (Article 19 here) whereby a province can adopt similar provisions and give them constitutional status if it so wishes. If provinces would be prepared, as at Victoria, to have obligations inserted in the various articles with respect to themselves that would, of course, strengthen the provisions. I hope that is the sort of possibility to which your letter refers.

Article 21 was not a part of the Victoria proposals. It is a modification of Article 38 in the draft I sent you on March 31st, 1976. I understand that a number of the Premiers were concerned at the indefiniteness of the reference to "culture" and "development" in the earlier Article. Article 21 is limited to language and preservation of it. It applies to federal powers only. The provinces could be included in such a provision or the possibility could be contemplated by a modification of Article 19. Such a thing might give the degree of assurance to linguistic minorities in some provinces that we feel Article 21 will give to the linguistic minority nationally.

PART IV—REGIONAL DISPARITIES

Your letter says the meetings of the Premiers produced "unanimous agreement on the clause contained in the draft proclamation." It also says there was "a high degree of consensus on incorporating clauses in the constitution providing for equalization". Article 22 reproduces the article that met with unanimous agreement. Part (b) of it was, as you know, designed as a constitutional commitment to the objective of equalization as now developed.

PART V—FEDERAL-PROVINCIAL CONSULTATION

Article 23 would provide the "constitutional requirement" to which your letter refers that a conference of First Ministers "be held at least once a year."

Article 24 would provide for consultation at such a conference before a new province was established. The federal government is of the view that to require the use of the amending procedure to establish a new province, as your letter suggests, might prove a source of rigidity. The admission of new provinces would not, of course, affect in any way the specific requirements in the proposed amending formula for the degree of consent required among the existing provinces for any future constitutional change. Nor would what is proposed affect the existing provision that the boundaries of a province cannot be altered without the consent of its Legislature.

Article 25 would require consultation before any use of the declaratory power of the federal Parliament. A requirement for provincial consent, as your letter suggests, would be tantamount to changing the division of legislative powers. As I have already said, we feel that any entry upon the distribution of powers is too fundamental a matter for the present exercise. Such a change could be considered following "patriation" as a part of a total review.

Article 26 is a substantial and structured constitutional obligation to consultation in the areas referred to. Your letter referred to a desire for "a greater degree of provincial involvement in immigration", which is now a concurrent power with federal paramountcy under Section 95 of the B.N.A. Act. Your letter also refers to "a new concurrent power" in relation to culture and to "greater provincial control in communications." These comments all appear to suggest changes in the distribution of powers. As I have said, the federal government considers such changes to be proper material for consideration at the second stage of our constitutional reform if we are to proceed by stages. For this stage, we would suggest that an obligation to consult along the lines of that in Article 26 would provide a new measure of assurance that provincial interests would be taken into account to the greatest possible degree before the federal government or Parliament acted within federal constitutional powers in these areas. This would not, of course, preclude any changes in the relevant powers that might be agreed upon in the second stage. They could be brought into effect under the amending procedure.

PART VI—MISCELLANEOUS

Article 37 would remedy a deficiency in our constitution as it now stands: the lack of an official French-language text with full force and effect. It would be critically important that such a text should be approved by a means acceptable to all and therefore the approval mechanism has for the time being been left blank. One possibility is that a small group of eminent jurists might be appointed to review the French-language versions to ensure complete accuracy before they become law.

Draft British Legislation

This is along the lines discussed in the meetings preparatory to the Victoria Conference. It would provide the legal base for the Proclamation and would terminate the power of the British Parliament to legislate with respect to Canada.

The only parts of your letter to which I have not referred are those relating to the Supreme Court of Canada, the "jurisdiction of provincial governments of taxation in the areas of primary production" and the exercise of the federal spending power. With regard to the last two, both get into the distribution of powers. As I have already indicated, the federal government considers that this is a matter for extensive and full discussion after "patriation" if we are following the course of action by stages.

So far as the Supreme Court of Canada is concerned, the Victoria Charter contained a number of specific articles dealing with the procedure to be followed in making appointments to the Court. They would have given the provinces a limited but explicit role in the appointment process. In your letter you indicated that, at the October meeting, the provincial Premiers agreed that the provinces should have a greater role in this process than was accorded to them by the Victoria provisions, although your letter does not detail what that greater role should be. You said that "a number of other modifications were suggested" to the Victoria provisions.

The federal government, for its part, has also had some second thoughts about the articles agreed to at Victoria. We reached the conclusion that they appear to have sufficiently adverse implications for the Supreme Court, as a vital institution of our federation, that they ought not simply to be reintroduced as part of this current proposal without at least a very careful reexamination of those implications by all of our governments. We also concluded that it would be possible to achieve a better regional distribution of the judges, as well as more effective consultation, through a constitutional provision that would require selection of the judges on a geographical basis. This would ensure that a regional distribution is invariably present on the Court. It would, of course, retain and guarantee constitutionally the presence on the Court of at least three judges experienced in the civil law of Quebec. We would welcome the views of the Premiers on a new provision of this kind, combined with a constitutional obligation to consult with the Attorney General of the province or provinces concerned before an appointment was made.

I am sending copies of this letter to your fellow Premiers so they may be aware of these proposals that the federal government is making in response to your letter and the meetings of August and October, 1976. As I have said, we would be happy to see "patriation" effected forthwith on the basis of the draft proclamation and legislation I am enclosing, to which could be added provisions about the Supreme Court if there is agreement on them. If it seems likely that that result could be achieved after a further conference to discuss modifications that any of the Premiers might think desirable, I would be happy to join in such a conference at a mutually convenient date.

It is quite possible, however, that the areas of disagreement may be various and perhaps substantial. If so, I cannot help wondering whether it would not be better to return to our original plan of April 1975—nothing but "patriation" with the Victoria amending formula—leaving everything else for discussion and action at the next stage, after "patriation". You will have noted that Premiers Schreyer and Campbell in their letters to me of October 21st and November 10th made clear that they do not consider that "patriation" need be conditional upon a consensus with regard to the matters referred to in your letter.

I should appreciate your comments on the proposals in this letter and particularly your suggestion as to what the next stage ought to be in order to complete the "patriation" exercise that we have now been working on for nearly two years. I am asking the Premiers of the other provinces for their comments and suggestions in the same way. I do hope that we can achieve "patriation" with the Victoria amending formula, without much more delay and bring to an end this remnant of our colonial condition of a century ago.

As our correspondence in October was made public forthwith, I would think that the same ought to be done with this letter and the brief covering letters I am sending to the premiers of the other provinces. I would propose, therefore, to make them public on Friday next, January 21st, and to table the letters in the House of Commons when it resumes its session on January 24th, 1977.

DRAFT RESOLUTION RESPECTING THE CONSTITUTION OF CANADA

WHEREAS it is in accord with the status of Canada as an independent state that the Canadian people should be able through their chosen representatives to provide for themselves the means by which to alter their own Constitution in all respects.

And whereas hitherto certain amendments to the Constitution of Canada have been made by the Parliament of the United Kingdom at the request and with the consent of Canada;

And whereas it is desirable that it should be possible to amend the Constitution of Canada in all respects by action of the appropriate instrumentalities of government in Canada;

And whereas the Proclamation hereinafter referred to embodies provisions with respect to the Constitution of Canada and the means whereby it may hereafter be amended;

Be it therefore resolved that we, the Senate and House of Commons approve the promulgation of a Proclamation by the Governor General, to have the force of law as well in Canada as in the United Kingdom, in the following terms:

Proclamation respecting the Constitution of Canada

PART I

Amendments to the Constitution

Art. 1 Amendments to the Constitution of Canada may be made from time to time by proclamation issued by the Governor General under the Great Seal of Canada when so authorized by resolution of the Senate and House of Commons and of the Legislative Assemblies of at least a majority of the provinces that includes:

(1) every province that at any time before the issue of such Proclamation had, according to any previous general census a population of at least twenty-five percent of the population of Canada;

(2) two or more of the Atlantic provinces; and

(3) two or more of the Western provinces that have, according to the then latest general census, combined populations of at least fifty percent of the population of all the Western provinces.

Art. 2 Notwithstanding paragraph (3) of Article 1, when the Legislative Assemblies of each of the Western provinces have, either before or after the coming into force of this Part, by resolution so authorized, that paragraph shall read as follows:

"(3) two or more of the Western provinces."

Art. 3 Amendments to the Constitution of Canada in relation to any provision that applies to one or more, but not all, of the provinces may be made from time to time by proclamation issued by the Governor General under the Great Seal of Canada when so authorized by resolutions of the Senate and House of Commons and of the Legislative Assembly of each province to which such amendments apply.

Art. 4 An amendment may be made by proclamation under Article 1 or Article 3 without a resolution of the Senate authorizing the issue of the proclamation if within ninety days of the passage by the House of Commons of a resolution authorizing its issue the Senate has not passed such a resolution and at any time after the expiration of those ninety days the House of Commons again passes the resolution, but any period when Parliament is prorogued or dissolved shall not be counted in computing those ninety days.

Art. 5 The following rules apply to the procedures for amendment described in Articles 1 and 3:

(1) either of such procedures may be initiated by the Senate or House of Commons or the Legislative Assembly of a province; and

(2) a resolution made for the purposes of this Part may be revoked at any time before the issue of a proclamation authorized by it.

Art. 6 The Parliament of Canada may exclusively make laws from time to time amending the Constitution of Canada, in relation to the executive government of Canada or the Senate or House of Commons.

Art. 7 In each province the legislature may exclusively make laws in relation to the amendment from time to time of the constitution of the province.

Art. 8 Notwithstanding Articles 6 and 7, amendments to the Constitution of Canada in relation to the following matters may be made only in accordance with the procedure described in Article 1:

(1) the offices of the Queen, the Governor General or the Lieutenant Governor of a province;
(2) the requirements of the Constitution of Canada respecting yearly sessions of the Parliament of Canada or the Legislature of a province;
3) the maximum period fixed by the Constitution of Canada for the duration of the House of Commons or the Legislative Assembly of a province;
(4) the powers of the Senate;
(5) the number of members by which a province is entitled to be represented in the Senate, and the residence qualifications of Senators;
(6) the right of a province to a number of members in the House of Commons not less than the number of Senators representing the province;
(7) the principles of proportionate representation of the provinces in the House of Commons prescribed by the Constitution of Canada; and
(8) the requirements respecting the use of the English or French language.

Art. 9 The procedure described in Article 1 may not be used to make an amendment where there is another provision for making such amendment in the Constitution of Canada, but that procedure may none the less be used to amend any provision for amending the Constitution, including this Article, or in making a general consolidation and revision of the Constitution.

Art. 10 In this Part, "Atlantic Provinces" means the provinces of Nova Scotia, New Brunswick, Prince Edward Island and Newfoundland, and "Western Provinces" means the provinces of Manitoba, British Columbia, Saskatchewan and Alberta.

Art. 11 Class 1 of section 91 and class 1 of section 92 of the *British North America Act, 1867*, as amended by the *British North America (No. 2) Act, 1949* are repealed on the coming into force of this Part.

PART II

Senate Representation

Art. 12 Notwithstanding anything in the Constitution of Canada or in Article 8,

(a) the number of Senators provided for under section 21 of the British North America Act, 1867, as amended, is increased from one hundred and four to one hundred and sixteen;

(b) the maximum number of Senators is increased from one hundred and twelve to one hundred and twenty-four;

(c) the portion of the first sentence following paragraph 2 of section 22 of the British North America Act, 1867, as amended, shall read as follows:

> "3. The Atlantic Provinces of Nova Scotia, New Brunswick, Prince Edward Island and Newfoundland;
>
> 4. The Western Provinces of Manitoba, British Columbia, Saskatchewan and Alberta;

which Four Divisions shall (subject to the Provisions of this Act) be represented in the Senate as follows: Ontario by twenty-four Senators; Quebec by twenty-four Senators; the Atlantic Provinces by thirty Senators, ten thereof representing Nova Scotia, ten thereof representing New Brunswick, four thereof representing Prince Edward Island and six thereof representing Newfoundland; the Western Provinces by thirty-six Senators, seven thereof representing Manitoba, twelve thereof representing British Columbia, seven thereof representing Saskatchewan, and ten thereof representing Alberta; and the Yukon Territory and the Northwest Territories shall be entitled to be represented in the Senate by one member each."

Art. 13 For the purposes of this Part, the term "Province" in section 23 of the British North America Act, 1867 includes the Yukon Territory and the Northwest Territories.

PART III

Language Rights

Art. 14 English and French are the official languages of Canada having the status and protection set forth in this Part, but no provision in this Part shall derogate from any right, privilege, or obligation existing under any other provision of the Constitution.

Art. 15 A person has the right to use English or French in the debates of the Parliament of Canada.

Art. 16 The statutes and the records and journals of the Parliament of Canada shall be printed and published in English and French; and both versions of such statutes are equally authoritative.

Art. 17 A person has the right to use English or French in giving evidence before, or in any pleading or process in the Supreme Court of Canada or any court established by the Parliament of Canada, and to require that any document or judgment issuing from any such court be in English or French.

Art. 18 A member of the public has the right to the use of the official language of his choice in communications between him and the head or central office of every department and agency of the Government of Canada.

Art. 19 A provincial Legislative Assembly may, by resolution, declare that provisions similar to those of any part of Articles 15, 16, 17 and 18 shall apply to the Legislative Assembly, and to any of the provincial courts and offices of the provincial departments and agencies according to the terms of the resolution, and thereafter such parts apply to the Legislative Assembly, courts and offices specified according to the terms of such resolution; and any right conferred under this Article may be abrogated or diminished only in accordance with the procedure described in Article 1 of this Proclamation.

Art. 20 A member of the public has the right to the use of the official language of his choice in communications between him and every principal office of a department or agency of the Government of Canada that is located in an area where a substantial proportion of the population has the official language of his choice as its mother tongue, but the Parliament of Canada may define the limits of such areas and what constitutes a substantial proportion of the population for the purposes of this Article.

Art. 21 The Parliament of Canada, in the exercise of powers assigned to it by the Constitution of Canada, and the Government of Canada, in the exercise of powers conferred on it by the Constitution of Canada or by any law enacted by Parliament, shall be guided, among other considerations for the welfare and advantage of the people of Canada, by the knowledge that a fundamental purpose underlying the Canadian federation is to ensure that the diverse cultures of its people may continue to be respected within that federation and by its institutions, and by the appreciation, as a consequence, of the importance of the two official languages of Canada as the languages of cultural expression used by those for whom the official languages of Canada are mother tongues; accordingly, neither the Parliament of Canada nor the Government of Canada, in exercising the respective powers so assigned to or conferred on them, shall act in a manner that will adversely affect the preservation of either of the two official languages of Canada.

PART IV

Regional Disparities

Art. 22 Without altering the distribution of powers and without compelling the Parliament of Canada or the Legislatures of the Provinces to exercise their legislative powers, the Parliament of Canada and Legislatures of the Provinces, together with the Government of Canada and the Governments of the Provinces, are committed to:

(a) the promotion of equality of opportunity and well-being for all individuals in Canada;
(b) the assurance, as nearly as possible, that essential public services of reasonable quality are available to all individuals in Canada; and
(c) the promotion of economic development to reduce disparities in the social and economic opportunities for all individuals in Canada wherever they may live.

PART V

Federal-Provincial Consultation

Art. 23 A conference composed of the Prime Minister of Canada and the First Ministers of the Provinces shall be called by the Prime Minister of Canada at least once a year unless, in any year, a majority of those composing the conference decide that it shall not be held.

Art. 24 Before the Parliament of Canada may establish any new province in territories forming part of Canada, the question of the establishment of such province shall be placed on the agenda of a conference composed of the Prime Minister of Canada and the First Ministers of the Provinces for discussion by them.

Art. 25 Before the Parliament of Canada may exercise its authority under section 92(10) (c) of the British North America Act, 1867 to declare any work or undertaking within a province to be for the general advantage of Canada or for the advantage of two or more provinces, the Government of Canada shall consult with the Government of the Province or Provinces in which the work or undertaking is located.

Art. 26 The Government of Canada, in order to ensure the fullest and most complete consultation practicable with the Government of any Province of Canada with respect to federal activities affecting, or likely to affect, the survival and development of the language used by any group of persons residing in that Province, or with respect to federal activities in support of or related to cultural activity, broadcasting or broadcasting services, or immigration, shall, if the Government of that Province so requests, establish with that Government a joint commission to heighten co-operation between them in relation to those federal activities, subject to a protocol of agreement defining the functions, attributes, composition and duration of that commission.

PART VI

Miscellaneous

Art. 27 The Governor General of Canada may by Proclamation under the Great Seal of Canada proclaim a French-language text of the Constitution of Canada, or any part thereof, when so authorized by

---

and thereafter that text shall be as authoritative as, and shall have the same force and effect as, the English-language text to which it corresponds, but shall not be held to operate as new law.

Art. 28 All laws in effect in Canada immediately before the coming into force of this Part, including those enactments set out in Article 29, shall continue as law in Canada except to the extent altered by this Proclamation, subject to be repealed, abolished or altered by the Parliament of Canada, or by the Legislatures of the respective Provinces, according to the authority of each under the Constitution of Canada.

Art. 29 Without limiting the meaning of that expression, the "Constitution of Canada" includes the following enactments and any orders thereunder, together with this Proclamation and any amendments thereto made by proclamation issued thereunder:
  The British North America Acts, 1867 to 1975;
  The Manitoba Act, 1870;
  The Parliament of Canada Act, 1875;
  Canada (Ontario Boundary) Act, 1889 52-53 Vict., c. 28 (U.K.);
  The Canadian Speaker (Appointment of Deputy) Act, 1895, Session 2, 59 Vict., c. 3 (U.K.);
  Alberta Act, 1905, 4-5 Edw. VII, c. 3;
  Saskatchewan Act, 1905, 4-5 Edw. VII, c. 42;
  Statute of Westminster, 1931, 22 Geo. V, c. 4 insofar as it applies to Canada.

Art. 30 This Proclamation shall come into force on the day it is promulgated by the Governor General.

And be it further resolved
    That a humble Address be presented to Her Majesty the Queen in the following words:

To the Queen's Most Excellent Majesty:

Most Gracious Sovereign:

We Your Majesty's most dutiful and loyal subjects, the [Senate] [and Commons] of Canada in Parliament assembled, humbly approach Your Majesty praying that You may graciously be pleased to cause a measure to be laid before the Parliament of the United Kingdom to be expressed as follows:

WHEREAS it is in accord with the status of Canada as an independent state that the Canadian people should be able through their chosen representatives to provide for themselves the means by which to alter their own Constitution in all respects.

And whereas hitherto certain amendments to the Constitution of Canada have been made by the Parliament of the United Kingdom at the request and with the consent of Canada;

And whereas a proclamation entitled the "Proclamation respecting the Constitution of Canada" that was approved by the Senate and House of Commons of Canada on the _____ day of _____, 19___ to be proclaimed by the Governor General of Canada embodies provisions with respect to the Constitution of Canada and the means whereby it may be amended;

And whereas Canada has requested, and consented to, the enactment of an Act of the Parliament of the United Kingdom to make appropriate provision in connection with the matters aforesaid and the Senate and House of Commons have submitted an Address to Her Majesty praying that a measure be laid before the Parliament of the United Kingdom for that purpose:

Be if therefore enacted by the Queen's Most Excellent Majesty . . . etc.:

1. When promulgated by the Governor General of Canada, the Proclamation shall, as well in the United Kingdom as in Canada, be recognized as having by virtue of the Proclamation the force of law.

2. No Act of Parliament of the United Kingdom passed after the promulgation of the Proclamation shall extend, or be deemed to extend, to Canada or to any province or territory of Canada as part of its law.

3. As from the promulgation of the Proclamation the enactments mentioned in the Schedule to this Act are, to the extent specified in column 3 of the Schedule, hereby repealed as enactments of the Parliament of the United Kingdom, but without prejudice to any operation which any of those enactments or any law, order, rule, regulation or other instrument made thereunder may continue to have by virtue of the Proclamation.

4. This Act may be cited as the Canada Act, 1977.

SCHEDULE

Enactments Ceasing to Have Effect as Acts of the U.K. Parliament

Chapter	Short Title	Extent of Repeal
22 & 23 Geo. V. c. 4	The Statute of Westminster, 1931	Sections 2 to 5, in their application to Canada. Section 7. In section 10(3) the words "and Newfoundland."

Such other statutes as the British wish to repeal for their purposes. For example: the British North America Acts, 1867-1964.

10

The Constitutional Position of Natural Resources*

Merv Leitch

I was very pleased to receive your invitation to speak on the constitutional analysis of resource ownership. It is a timely topic. Today in Canada one of the most important and controversial issues is who will make the decisions as to when, how and by whom the nation's natural resources will be developed and who is to have control over the funds generated by that development. The energy crisis has really precipitated these issues and as petroleum and natural gas are two of the key sources of energy I will direct my remarks primarily to the control, development, production, use and marketing of petroleum and natural gas, but what I have to say will be equally applicable to other natural resources.

When one says, "What are the constitutional aspects of resource ownership?", one is really asking what laws can the federal government make with respect to natural resources and what laws can the provincial

* Notes for an Address given to the Canadian Council of Resource and Environment Ministers in Victoria, British Columbia on November 21st, 1974. Reprinted by permission.

governments make? The cornerstone of the Canadian constitution is The British North America Act and, to answer questions about jurisdiction over natural resources, one has to turn to an examination of that Act.

Before doing so it might be helpful if I made some general remarks about constitutions and constitutional law. In the hope that I can make understandable a difficult and complex subject I'll of necessity have to oversimplify but will endeavour to do so with as little damage as possible to accuracy.

I think a workable definition of a "constitution" is: that body of rules establishing governments and outlining what they can and cannot do. Using that test it is accurate to say that Great Britain, for example, does not have a constitution because there is nothing, save for the Queen's assent, which restricts the power of the British Parliament. It is free to enact any law it chooses and once it receives Royal assent it becomes part of the law of the nation.

The United States is an example of a different constitutional system. It does have a constitution which imposes limits on the power of government. There the courts frequently hold that legislation is unconstitutional in the sense that no government has the power to pass it and the only way a United States government could get that power would be by an amendment to the constitution.

There is also in the United States the additional question of whether the federal government or the state government has the jurisdiction to pass a particular law.

Canada's constitution is similar to the British in that, with a very few exceptions, there is no restriction on what laws governments may pass, the sole question is, "Has the federal government or the provincial government the necessary jurisdiction to support the law?" That question is answered as I've earlier indicated by an examination of the terms of The British North America Act and its related statutes.

As a concluding general observation about constitutional law I would like to stress that it is probably the most difficult of all laws to interpret because constitutions usually contain statements of principle and are written in broad terms. They are filled with general words such as "peace," "order," and "good government," "property" and "civil rights." The federal government has the authority to make laws for the peace, order, and good government of Canada. If those words were taken in their widest sense one would have to say that the jurisdiction to make all laws fell within the federal sphere because it's hard to think of any law that wouldn't be for the peace, order, and good government of the nation. Equally it's hard to think of a law that doesn't in some way deal with property or civil rights which is within the jurisdiction of the provinces. Books can and have been written about the different judicial philosophies of interpreting constitutions and it has been strenuously argued by many that the courts in Canada and the United States have, by interpretation, produced constitutions for those two nations fundamentally different from what their respective founders intended. It's argued that at the time of union in the United States the intention was to have strong state governments and a relatively weak federal government. As you all know that has not been the result. In Canada many historians contend that the Fathers of Confederation contemplated a strong federal government and provincial governments with substantially lesser powers. However, the broad scope given to the property and civil rights provision in The B.N.A. Act and the relatively narrow field assigned by the courts to the federal trade and commerce and similar powers has led to a nation where provincial governments in the legislative sense play as dominant a role as the federal government. In short, because of the nature of constitutions and the history of their interpretation, lawyers when giving opinions on constitutional law must include more than the usual number of "ifs", "ands", and "buts".

Now to turn to the specific question of legislative jurisdiction over natural resources. It might be helpful to begin by quoting section 109 of The British North America Act which reads:

> All Lands, Mines, Minerals, and Royalties belonging to the several Provinces of Canada, Nova Scotia and New Brunswick at the Union and all Sums then due or payable for such Lands, Mines, Minerals or Royalties shall belong to the several Provinces of Ontario, Quebec, Nova Scotia, and New Brunswick in which the same are situate or arise, subject to any Trusts existing in respect thereof, and to any Interest other than that of the Province in the same.

That is the section by which the Fathers of Confederation confirmed that the provinces would own the natural resources.

The Judicial Committee of the Privy Council which for many years was the final court of appeal for Canada commented on the purpose of that section in the case of *A.G. Ontario* v. *Mercer* (1882) 8 A.C. 767 at 779:

> The general subject of the whole section is of a high political nature. It is the attribution of royal territorial rights *for purposes of revenue and government to the provinces* in which they are situate or arise.

In essence its purpose was to provide a revenue source for the provincial governments.

The other provinces, at the time of or after entering confederation were placed in the same position with respect to natural resources as the founding provinces of Nova Scotia, New Brunswick, Ontario and Quebec. Indeed with the Western Provinces the argument that natural resources were intended to be a revenue source is even stronger. For example, natural resources were transferred to Alberta in 1930, well after there were producing oil and gas wells in Alberta.

In my view the key to the answer to nearly all questions of jurisdiction over natural resources lies in the ownership given to the provinces by The British North America Act. I want to stress that there is a very fundamental distinction between legislative control over those natural resources owned by the provinces and those owned privately. In Alberta approximately 85 percent of the conventional petroleum and natural gas is owned by the province and about 15 percent is owned privately. The Oil Sands are owned nearly 100 percent by the provincial government. Thus, from a practical point of view, so far as Alberta is concerned, and I think this is true of virtually all provinces and virtually all natural resources, we can ignore the question of which government has what legislative capacity over privately owned natural resources.

The essence of my point is that a provincial government under the constitution has vastly greater control over the natural resources it owns than it does over natural resources it doesn't own.

It is important to call to your attention section 92(5) of The British North America Act which reads:

92. In each province the Legislature may exclusively make laws in relation to matters coming within the classes of subjects next hereinafter enumerated, that is to say:
(5) The management and sale of the public lands belonging to the province and of the timber and wood thereon.

Thus not only does The British North America Act specifically provide that the provinces own the natural resources but also specifically provides for legislative capacity over them. However, in my view, apart from section 92(5), a provincial government may in the exercise of the Royal prerogative deal with property owned by it without first passing legislation.

So the provinces own their natural resources, the next question is, "What can a province do with them?" The answer certainly is no less and conceivably more than any other owner can do with his property. An owner of property can do anything he likes with it until some government, exercising a legislative capacity given to it by The B.N.A. Act, says there are certain things he can't do.

Perhaps it will help to make clear to you the importance of this concept of provincial ownership of natural resources if I refer to some judicial decisions. The first is the case of *Smylie* v. *The Queen* (1900) 27 O.A.R. 172, a decision of the Court of Appeal of the Province of Ontario. In that case the government of Ontario had issued permits entitling people to cut timber on Crown lands. They inserted in the permit a clause requiring that the timber be manufactured into sawn lumber in Canada. It was admitted on all sides that this condition would curtail the existing practice of exporting Ontario timber out of the country and it was contended that this condition was *ultra vires* of the province because it infringed on the federal power over the regulation of trade and commerce under 91(2) of the B.N.A. Act. It's important to keep in mind that had the province of Ontario passed such a law with respect to timber cut on privately owned lands undoubtedly the law would have been held to be beyond the powers of the provincial government. However, they were dealing with rules governing the timber cut from Crown lands. The principles enunciated in that case are so important that I think it would be informative to quote them to you at some length. The trial judge said at 31 O.R. 202 at p. 221:

> . . . if the regulations in question be sustained the export of logs cut under such licences will be entirely stopped . . . I am asked to draw from these circumstances the conclusion that the Acts and regulations of which the suppliants are now complaining are a contravention of that part of The British North America Act which reserves to the Dominion Legislature the exclusive right of making laws for the 'regulation of trade and commerce,' and to hold that the Provincial Legislature, under the guise of a regulation for the management of its timber, has in reality attempted to interfere with the regulation of trade and commerce.
>
> In my opinion, the Act and regulations complained of are clearly within the powers of the Provincial Legislature and are not in any way an interference with the regulation of trade and commerce, within the meaning of the 91st section of The British North America Act.
>
> In the first place it is to be borne in mind that the Provincial Legislatures in passing this Act, are dealing with property belonging to the province, over which they have the fullest power of control. They are entitled to sell it or to refuse to sell it; and if they sell they have the right in my opinion, to impose upon the purchaser such conditions as they deem proper with regard to the destination of the timber after it is cut, including the state in which it shall be exported, just as they have the right in selling cattle from the farm at their Agricultural College to stipulate that the purchaser shall not export them alive. The condition that the timber shall be sawn into lumber before exportation in the one case no doubt reduces the quantity of logs exported just as the supposed stipulation in the other case reduces the quantity of live cattle exported. But in each case the matter is one purely of internal regulation and management by the province of its own property for the benefit of its own inhabitants.

The Justices of the Court of Appeal expressed similar views. Mr. Justice Osler said at p. 189:

> The great sources of provincial revenue consist of mineral and pine and spruce lands and to hold that such legislation as is here in question is legislation affecting trade and commerce, would be to restrict and interfere with the rights of the Province to dispose of its own property, whether it be timber or minerals, or whatever it may be, in such a way as best to advance the general interests of the Province by encouraging manufacturers, promoting settlement, establishing saw mills, pulp mills, or smelting mills, or in other ways improving the economic conditions of the country.

Mr. Justice McClennan said at p. 187, 8:

> It was also contended that the Act imposing the manufacturing condition is ultra vires of the Legislature of the Province, as an interference with trade and commerce, by in effect prohibiting the exportation of logs to foreign countries. The argument on which I think Mr. Scott principally relied was the great extent of the trade in logs and lumber derived from the

public lands of the Province. I do not perceive, however, that the question can be affected or determined by that consideration. The question is simply whether the Province can sell its timber, which it is free to sell, or not to sell at all, subject to a stipulation that it shall be manufactured within any prescribed area. I am at a loss to see how such a stipulation can be regarded as an interference with trade and commerce within the meaning of The British North America Act.

In commenting on that case, LaForest, in his major text, *Natural Resources and Public Property Under the Canadian Constitution*, says at p. 168:

> Smylie v. R. illustrates that the provinces' power to control their public property gives them a most effective weapon for controlling their economic destiny. Thus, laws such as the one in question in that case have had the effect of developing the pulp and paper industry in Canada in preventing the export of the material in its raw state for manufacture in the United States. It has also given the provinces some control in areas that otherwise would have been totally within federal competence.

While the Smylie case was a decision of a Provincial Court of Appeal there are decisions in both the Supreme Court of Canada and the Privy Council indicating that the principles stated by the court in the Smylie case would be followed by those courts. For example, in a case which arose in British Columbia *Brooks-Bidlake and Whittall Limited* v. *A.G. B.C.* [1923] A.C. 450, the Privy Council was required to rule on the validity of a condition in a lease granted by the government of British Columbia in respect of timber rights to the effect that no Chinese or Japanese were to be employed. The question was whether this was a valid provision in view of section 91(25) of the B.N.A. Act which grants jurisdiction to the federal government over aliens. The Privy Council upheld the validity of the stipulation in the timber licence and very neatly drew the distinction between provincial action applicable only to the provinces own property when it said at p. 457:

> In *Union Colliery Co.* v. *Pryden* (1): this Board held that a section in a statute of British Columbia which prohibited the employment of Chinamen in coal mines underground was beyond the powers of the Provincial Legislature; but this was on the ground that the enactment was not really applicable to coal mines only—still less to coal mines belonging to the Province— but was in truth devised to prevent Chinamen from earning their living in the Province.

What is the effect of the provisions I've referred to in the B.N.A. Act and the cases I've referred to? In my view they clearly establish that a province can with respect to natural resources it owns:

A. decide whether to develop them,
B. decide by whom, when and how they're going to be developed,
C. determine the degree of processing that's to take place within the province,

D. dispose of them upon conditions that they only be used in a certain way, or in a certain place, or by certain people,
E. determine the price at which they or the products resulting from their processing will be sold.

Because the right to do the things enumerated above depends on the province owning its natural resources it is important for provinces to examine the terms and conditions under which they are authorizing the development of their natural resources. For example, in Alberta up until recently, the ownership of the bulk and perhaps all of the oil and natural gas was transferred at the wellhead from the province to the producing company. Once that occurred, the province to a very large extent lost its control over those natural resources and had little more control over them than it did over oil or natural gas produced from private lands. Following the federal government's imposition of a price freeze on oil within Canada and an export tax on oil going to the United States, Alberta passed legislation which provides that the royalty share of the oil (roughly a third of the total production from Crown lands) remains, even after production, the property of the provincial government and it is now sold through the Petroleum Marketing Commission.

A discussion about control over natural resources is, of course, not complete by merely examining the rights of the provinces as owners; one must go further and consider the ways in which the federal government might in the exercise of its jurisdiction under the B.N.A. Act restrict the exercise of those ownership rights.

There are several actions which the federal government has taken which materially affect the province's proprietary rights in its natural resources.

For example, it has imposed an export tax on oil going to the United States. If that tax is valid for oil, there is no reason why it isn't valid with respect to timber leaving British Columbia, iron, copper and other minerals leaving Quebec and Ontario; and indeed any natural resource. No one really questions the federal government's general capacity to impose export taxes on goods leaving Canada but whether it can validly do so with property owned by the province at the time it leaves the country is to my mind an open question. I say it's an open question because section 125 of the B.N.A. Act reads:

"No lands or property belonging to Canada or any province shall be liable to taxation."

What would happen if the province of Alberta arrived at the border with a barrel of its royalty oil which it owned in the ground and has owned through production and processing to the point where it is ready for delivery and the federal government says you can't take it out of Canada without paying an export tax? I only know of one case which bears on the question and interestingly enough it's a case in British

Columbia and involves a case of Johnny Walker Scotch. There the province bought the liquor in Scotland and on bringing it in to British Columbia argued that it didn't have to pay the federal customs and excise taxes because of the provisions of section 125. The court held otherwise but I suggest there are some very fundamental distinctions between that case and the case of a barrel of Alberta-owned oil arriving at the United States border. There is no doubt the federal government could say, "You can't take it out at all." It could also say, "You must take it out in a specific way, i.e. by pipeline or truck," but the question is whether section 125 prevents it from saying, "You can only take it out after you've paid the tax." One difference between the Johnny Walker case and the barrel of oil is that in the former the British Columbia government was really acting as merchants; they were buying property, bringing it into the province and then reselling it. In addition they were dealing with property acquired by purchase and not by the terms of the B.N.A. Act or under subsequent statutes transferring natural resources to the province. Thus there appears to be a sufficient factual distinction between the only case that has come before the courts and the export tax on oil, to say that the validity of that tax is open to serious question.

The federal government also proposes by certain provisions of The Petroleum Administration Bill now before the House of Commons to fix the price at which a provincially owned resource can be sold outside of that province. I think it arguable that that legislation is beyond the federal government's capacity because it is an attempt to do indirectly what it cannot do directly, i.e. tax provincially owned property.

However, supposing the federal government does have the jurisdiction to fix the price at which a province's natural resources are to be sold outside of the province, what counter action can the province take?

The province could decline to produce or if it produces decline to sell at the fixed price.

Such action would no doubt lead some militants in the federal administration to contemplate all retaliatory measures that may be available under the constitution. They might consider using the provision of section 92(10)(c) of the B.N.A. Act which provides that the federal government may declare any "works" situated within a province to be for the general advantage of Canada or for the advantage of two or more of the provinces. This appears to be a very sweeping power limited only by the meaning of the word "works" and the "general advantage" of Canada or two or more of its provinces. Conceivably, under that provision, the federal government might (it did during the war years do something similar with uranium) attempt to declare the producing facility of any mineral a work for the general advantage of Canada and thereby assume total control over it.

Another step I'm sure some would consider, is expropriation of the provincially owned mineral resource. The power of the federal government to expropriate property owned by the provincial government has been upheld in the case of *A.G. Que. v. Nipissing Central Railway* [1926] A.C. 715 and *A.G. B.C. v. C.P.R.* [1906] A.C. 204 but only in connection with a valid exercise of federal legislative power, that is the federal government has no power to expropriate simply because it would like to become the owner.

A third option open to the federal government would be to disallow provincial legislation in those cases where changes in existing legislation might be necessary to impose conditions on the production and sale of natural resources.

I'm sure everyone appreciates that the exercise of any one or more of these extraordinary powers would put such severe strains upon the Canadian Federation as to make their use unthinkable.

There is another federal action whereby the central government is seeking to limit the province's capacity to deal with its natural resources and that is the provision in the current federal budget prohibiting companies from deducting, in calculating their income tax, certain royalties paid to provincial governments. In connection with that proposal one has to keep in mind that legislation which on its face appears to be within the power of either the federal or provincial governments will be struck down if it is in fact an attempt to do indirectly that which a government under the B.N.A. Act is not able to do directly. The question is whether the federal government is under the guise of its taxing power really indirectly imposing a tax upon provincial property.

The applicable principle was stated by Lord Phillimore in *Caron* v. *The King*, [1924] A.C. quoting from an earlier decision when he said at page 1006:

> No provincial legislature could use its special powers as an indirect means of destroying powers given by the Parliament of Canada . . . (and) by a parity of reason the Parliament of Canada could not exercise its powers of taxation so as to destroy the capacity of officials lawfully appointed by the province.

In a similar vein Laskin said in Canadian Constitutional Law referring to *Forbes* v. *A.G. Man.* [1936] S.C.R. 40, and *Abbott* v. *City of St. John* (1908), 40 S.C.R. 597:

> The respective taxing powers of Dominion and provinces may not be used by either of them to sterilize powers conferred by the other upon its functionaries or substantially to impair their status.

I've spoken at length about the legal position of the provinces and the federal government in relation to controlling the development, processing and sale of provincially owned natural resources but in concluding my talk I do not want to leave the impression that I'm arguing for a provincial position whereby the provinces keep for themselves all of the revenues generated by resource development. In this connection I think it is worth pointing out that Alberta, by selling the oil that comes from its lands, at a price of approximately $6.50 per barrel rather than the going price of about $11.50 per barrel, is contributing to the Canadian consumer who uses Alberta oil and to the federal government through the export tax, more money each year than the entire Alberta budget.

In short, in the past Alberta took the view that the critical and potentially divisive issues relating to natural resources ought to be resolved by consultation and not confrontation. The First Ministers' Conference of March 1974 demonstrated a presence, strength and vitality of the national concept in a way which I believe may be unparalleled in Canadian history. The Petroleum Administration Bill and the recent federal budget, have raised an apprehension on our part that the federal government is determined to displace that statesmanship and co-operation with the unilateral imposition of the federal will upon the provinces. To have done so in an area dramatically affecting a province's economic future is in my view most regrettable.

11

Resources, the Constitution and Canadian Federalism*

Premier Allen Blakeney

I would like today to give you one western view on resources, and offer some comments on the importance of resource questions to the future health of Canada as a federal state.

Let me begin by saying I do not subscribe to the proposition that easterners, whether born in or out of wedlock, should freeze in the dark. Most of us in Western Canada would agree—and have agreed—that the national interest demands, *first,* that Canada should have first claim to our depleting energy resources, and *second,* that the jolt of sharply increasing energy costs should be cushioned over a reasonable period of time. I believe Canada is the only nation in the world that has retained

---

* Notes for Remarks by Premier Blakeney, the Canadian Club (Toronto), January 4, 1977. Reprinted by permission.

an artificially low price for oil with the cost being borne by the oil producers and the royalty owners.

As I have said, we in the West have agreed. But let me point out that we are acutely aware that this action taken in the national interest in accepting less than the world price for our gas and oil is costing the West a great deal of money. Furthermore, we ask a very pointed question, which is this: If we are going to share nationally the benefits of provincial resources, why just *western* resources?

Because, historically in Canada, resources and their benefits have been unreservedly provincial. Until recent years no one has even suggested that it should be any other way. When the power potential at Niagara Falls was harnessed at the turn of the century, the total benefit of cheap power went to Ontario. And that involved an international river—certainly reason enough for the Government of Canada to step in.

At that time, prairie people were paying four or five times as much for electricity as were Ontario people. And these higher costs were true up to the 1950s. But there was no national policy of equalizing energy costs then.

Or take the vast mineral wealth of the Sudbury Basin. Certainly all the direct taxes from those minerals have gone and are going to the Government of Ontario. The fact that Ontario chose to keep its royalties low and to look for its rewards in the multiplier effects of the economic activity generated makes no difference. That choice was Ontario's, and the national interest went unnoted. No one suggested that Canadians should get nickel from Sudbury at less than the world price—or iron ore from Steep Rock, or asbestos from Black Lake, or copper from Val D'Or, or cobalt from Gowganda. The price to Canadians was the price the mineral would bring on the world market. If the world price went up, so did the Canadian price.

But this policy no longer applies. Until just a couple of months ago, the price of wheat for Canadians was substantially below world prices. When wheat was selling on world markets at more than $5 a bushel, Canadian millers were buying it for $3. And where is most of our wheat grown? In the West.

We have a new feed grains policy in Canada, put in place by Ottawa. Under that policy, the Western farmer gets substantially less than the world price for his barley if he sells it to feed lots in Ontario or Quebec, rather than selling it to the Canadian Wheat Board for export. Another two-price system which works to the disadvantage of the West.

Oil, of course, is a spectacular example. Even today, after Saturday's increase in the domestic price of oil to $9.75 a barrel, Western oil is still underpriced by $3.50 or more. For Saskatchewan alone, with our very modest production, this means we are subsidizing Central and

Eastern Canadian oil consumers by at least $175 million this year. On a per capita basis, if Ontario were providing the same subsidy, the cost to Ontario would be $1 billion $487 million dollars. And that does not contemplate an increase in the world oil price—an increase that is almost certain to come.

At the same time, energy in another form—electric power—still commands the full export price, no export tax, no sharing, despite the obvious need for cheaper power in the Atlantic provinces. We in the West have little surplus power to export.

I think of gold. While the world price of oil was going up by four times, the price of gold was going up by perhaps five times. The gold industry has been a perennial recipient of federal government subsidies. The federal government stepped in to take a huge slice of the increased value of oil. So far as I am aware, except for corporate taxes, the entire increased value of gold in (say) Ontario went to the producing companies and the Province of Ontario.

Now it is sometimes being suggested that we should have a two-price system for uranium, with Canadian power utilities paying less than the world price to fuel their reactors. Let me point out that there is not one nuclear power plant in Manitoba, Alberta, Saskatchewan or British Columbia. Who would benefit from a lower uranium price? Primarily Ontario, with some eventual benefit to Quebec and New Brunswick.

Please note that I am not saying that there is no legitimate national interest to be served in these matters. But, we in the West find it passing strange that the national interest emerges only when we are talking about Western *resources* or Eastern *benefits*. If oil, why not iron ore and steel products? If natural gas, why not copper? If uranium—and we in Saskatchewan may well be Canada's biggest uranium producer in a few years—if uranium, why not nickel?

And, to add insult to injury, we in the West are now being told by the Federal Minister of Transport that the national interest demands a rail transportation policy in which the user pays the full cost. What user will pay the most under that kind of system? Land-locked Saskatchewan. Air transport is subsidized. The Seaway runs monumental deficits. Our ports are all subsidized. Truck transport is subsidized by many provincial highway systems in Canada. But in rail transport—the one upon which we depend, we are told that the user must pay.

But enough. I do not wish to give a full list of reasons for dissatisfaction but rather to set the context in which the current resource controversies are being viewed in Western Canada.

A few short years ago, we in Saskatchewan thought we knew with some exactitude what rights were conferred on the provinces with respect to natural resources by the British North America Act. We thought—and all the constitutional authorities supported us—that provincial jurisdiction over its lands and resources was clear and exclusive, including:

—the rights of ownership;
—the power to regulate production;
—the power to levy royalties of whatever magnitude.

The actions we took to increase provincial revenues from oil and potash were not different in kind, and only somewhat different in degree, from the actions of previous provincial governments in Saskatchewan and across Canada. We knew it would be argued that the royalties were too high—but that's not a jurisdictional argument. There could be no argument—we thought—on our right to levy those royalties and taxes.

Our position was—and is—that clear windfall increases in the value of oil and other depleting resources should flow in the main to the province and not to the resource companies. Our royalty and tax systems were designed to capture a large share of the windfall increase in value.

Those systems have been challenged by the resource companies— and that was no great surprise. They are in business for profit, and they naturally don't like paying sharply increased royalties and taxes.

So, that did not surprise us.

But we have also been challenged very aggressively—and this did surprise us—by the federal government. First, by Mr. Turner when he was Finance Minister in 1974. His May budget of that year decreed that royalties paid to a province could no longer be claimed by a resource company as a deduction before calculating federal corporate income tax. Not private royalties, mind you. The resource company could still deduct royalties paid to the C.P.R., a major owner of mineral rights in Western Canada or indeed royalties paid to a foreign state, but not royalties paid to the government of Saskatchewan. That was a direct challenge to the right of the provinces to control and receive the benefits from the resources they own.

More recently, the federal government has joined with the resource companies in a series of legal attacks on the constitutional basis of our resource policies. Not all of these have to do with resource *taxation* as such. Some involved regulation of production. Before the NDP came to office in Saskatchewan, the potash industry was in deep trouble. Too many mines had come into production too quickly, and the price of potash fell below the costs of production. To save the industry from itself, my predecessor in office, Premier Ross Thatcher set up a production limiting or a pro-rationing scheme and a floor price so that all the mines would have a share of the market. All of the potash companies approved of the scheme—all, that is, except one. Central Canada Potash Company, owned fifty-one percent by Noranda, had a captive market for its full output. When we came to office we said Central Canada should not be exempted from production controls—and they filed suit, challenging the constitutional validity of production pro-rationing.

At this point, the federal government took a step which I believe to be unique in Canadian history. The Attorney General of Canada joined Noranda as a co-plaintiff—not as an intervener to argue a constitutional point of law—that's common enough—but as a co-plaintiff entitled to call witnesses and submit evidence at trial in the action in which Central Canada was claiming damages against the Government of Saskatchewan. The Attorney General of Canada denied the authority of our government to regulate production of a provincially-owned resource.

Bill 42—the law establishing our royalty surcharge on oil—is under legal attack by Canadian Industrial Oil and Gas Limited—CIGOL, and more recently by Imperial Oil. That law was upheld at trial and on appeal in Saskatchewan courts—over the objection of the Attorney General of Canada. Again the federal government intervened on the side of the company. And when the case was argued before the Supreme Court in November the Attorney General of Canada again argued against Saskatchewan. Standing unreservedly in support of Saskatchewan were Alberta, Manitoba and Quebec. There was Federal intervention against Saskatchewan in yet another potash taxation case heard recently by the Supreme Court.

Now, I think I am not being unusually sensitive when I judge these actions collectively as an aggressive attempt by the federal government to limit and abridge the clear constitutional rights of the provinces in dealing with resources. What Saskatchewan has done in oil and potash is not different in kind from the actions which provinces have taken for decades. Yet the attack by the federal government has been relentless and markedly different from previous practice.

Let me now try to draw a fine distinction. I am a confirmed federalist. I believe in and support whole-heartedly the unity of Canada as a federal state. I therefore believe that in the key areas of sovereignty and national management of the economy, the federal power is paramount.

But we are a federal state with a division of powers. Generally, those powers are divided in three ways: exclusive federal powers; exclusive provincial powers; and shared powers—as, for example, in agriculture. The federal interest is paramount in the exclusive federal sphere. The federal interest is paramount where power is shared. No argument. But I believe it to be equally true that in the exclusively provincial sphere—the provincial interest is paramount. True, the federal government has overriding emergency powers, but that is not relevant to my argument.

Federalism as we understand it in Canada—or at least as I understand it—means that in a case where provincial interest is paramount under our constitution it stands just as high and unassailable as does the federal power in a reverse circumstance. If it is to be overridden, it must be by an Act of Parliament which clearly establishes the emergent conditions which validate federal action, for example, the Anti-Inflation program.

I have become convinced that the present political leadership in Ottawa does not share this view. I have become convinced that their unrelenting attack on our resource policies is prompted—not by a belief that we are acting beyond our powers—as these have been understood for one hundred years—but rather by a desire to extend the central powers of the federal government at the expense of provincial powers.

They have a model to follow here. The required mix is an aggressive central government and an active, centralist Supreme Court. In the United States, over the decades, this mix has vastly diminished the powers of the states and firmly entrenched the federal government in a position of supremacy. So complete has been the transformation that one rarely hears these days about "states' rights." The result has been big federal government with a vengeance, with all the inflexibility and remoteness from the ordinary citizen which this involves.

Happily, in my view, Canada has not in the past chosen to follow that model. Our courts have not considered their role to be one of making policy through judicial interpretation. Professor Ronald Cheffins, in his book, *The Constitutional Process in Canada*, came to this conclusion in 1969 about Canada's courts:

> . . . the judges have never been willing to bluntly and openly substitute their view of policy for that of the legislators. The subordinate role assumed by the courts in their relationship to Canada's legislatures constitutes one of the most fundamental differences between Canada's constitutional system and that of the United States.

I say, *vive la difference!*

But that was 1969. Since then, a new Chief Justice of the Supreme Court has been appointed. Three other new justices have joined him on the bench. Will this Supreme Court take a more activist, centralist role than its predecessors in creating policy through judicial decisions?

It is, perhaps, too soon to tell. But we shall soon know. The CIGOL case, to which I referred earlier, has been argued before the Court. We are awaiting the judgment. At issue is the right of the province to levy its oil royalties. Both trial and appellate courts in Sastkachewan followed the traditional subordinate role referred to by Professor Cheffins. They upheld the validity of Saskatchewan's legislation. The question now is, what will the Supreme Court do?

Saskatchewan faces other court cases whose outcome is critical to our resource policy and financial future. All will be decided in the Supreme Court. Should we lose on all major issues, we may be directed to return to the resource companies some $500 million in taxes already collected.

Whether this will give satisfaction to the federal government, I do not know. What I do know is that all federal actions in the courts to date have been in support of the resource companies and against the Province of Saskatchewan.

Because Saskatchewan has been particularly active in attempting to use our resources as a base for economic development and a source of public revenue—by regulation and taxation—we find ourselves in the vanguard of this fight. But all of the provinces recognize they are involved. Their future—like ours—is on the line. As Alberta, Manitoba, and Quebec recognized in the CIGOL case.

Arrayed against us are the big resource companies and the federal government. An adverse decision will be a decision against all the provinces, a telling blow against their fiscal capability. An adverse decision will be a victory for centralist power and a defeat for federalism.

I am not saying that such a decision would be the end of the world for Saskatchewan. We have announced our firm intention to take all steps open to us to retain the royalties we have collected. We believe, of course, that what we have done was, and is, within the province's powers. But if the Supreme Court disagrees, we will do all we can to validate our authority to levy royalties, both past and future.

What disturbs me most is the impact that a new and centralist interpretation of provincial rights to resources could have on the delicate balance of Confederation at this critical period in our history. Whatever you or I may think about the election of René Lévesque and the Parti Québecois, we must face it as a fact. We may rationalize the result by saying the PQ has no mandate to separate; that it was a negative vote against Bourassa, not a positive vote for separation—or in a dozen other ways. The bald fact is that the people of Quebec have elected a party to power which has as one of its central purposes the establishment of an independent Quebec.

Now, I for one believe Mr. Lévesque when he says his mandate is only to form a provincial government within Confederation. And that he will proceed to the next step deliberately, and only on the basis of an affirmative referendum. But I also believe that Mr. Lévesque has set this next step of separation as a personal goal for himself.

And certainly this new fact in Canada puts the bright glare of the spotlight on our federal system and how well it works. We can be sure that every failure will be vigorously noted by Mr. Lévesque and his ministers. Indeed, he and Mr. Parizeau have already begun this process. When the federal and provincial finance ministers failed to agree on a new fiscal arrangements formula in early December, the Quebec finance minister called it added proof that Confederation does not work, and Mr. Lévesque's comments following the first ministers' conference were in the same vein.

I don't believe that many people inside or outside Quebec will feel that failure to reach full agreement on how to divide tax revenues represents a failure of Confederation. But a dramatic change whereby the federal government can remove effective provincial control over natural resources is a very different thing.

What could be more damaging to our future as a united Canada at this point in time than a change in interpretation of the constitution which limits, erodes or circumscribes provincial jurisdiction over resources?

I don't very often quote the editorial columns of the Winnipeg *Tribune*. It has not, over the years, reflected my views. Nor does it now. But I pass this on as one fairly widespread point of view in Western Canada. The *Tribune* says, and I quote:

> Much of the semblance of disunity that bedevils Canada today—and not just in Quebec—is due to the serious imbalance between the federal and provincial sectors. The only way this can be disposed of is by a renegotiation of Confederation to produce a new contract which will recognize this is not one monolithic country with weak and dependent provincial divisions, but a federal state organized to give greater opportunity for development to the different regions with their different interests.

I would not go so far. I think our existing constitution has most of the elements required to provide that opportunity. A part of the problem does lie in the division of powers. But on the whole, the provinces and the federal government have been remarkably adaptable in exercising their respective powers and fulfilling their responsibilities within the Constitutional framework.

Let me now say a few things which are fairly obvious but still can usefully be repeated.

We are engaged in a struggle to keep Canada intact.

Many people in Quebec favour independence for Quebec.

They have a government which proclaims separatism—independence as its goal.

There are likely to be elections and referendums when independence is the issue.

I heard the Prime Minister express the hope that the separatist idea would be to use his word "clobbered."

I hope he's right. You hope he's right.

But the best way—perhaps the only way to beat one idea is with a better idea.

If the battle is for the minds and hearts of the people of Quebec and the rival idea is separatism, what is the better idea?

Is it to increase the centralizing power of Ottawa in new fields:

—resource taxation,
—closed circuit communications,
—post-secondary education,

to name three areas where the federal government now appears to be moving in on the provinces. Is that a better idea?

No leader in provincial politics in Quebec for the last 10 years, Liberal, Union Nationale, or P.Q. has been willing to champion a stronger federal government. Nor have the policies of the present federal government made this course more acceptable in Quebec. All evidence suggests that quite the opposite is the truth.

A federal government with more power, a provincial government with less, has no champions in Quebec.

In the fight against separatism that is not the better idea.

If the Canadian option is to have a chance to win the allegiance of Quebec voters it must allow for a provincial government in Quebec which has the power and the means to meet—not fewer—but more of the economic and cultural aspirations of the people of Quebec.

There's an old political axiom that you can't beat somebody with nobody.

And when it comes to defeating—clobbering—the separatist idea in Quebec, the idea of an even stronger federal government with a weaker Quebec provincial government is a nobody—a non-starter in that race.

The times require of all governments—but particularly the federal government—a new sensitivity to the issues that divide us and a new determination to resolve those issues in a spirit which will meet provincial and regional economic and cultural aspirations within one Canada.

As a start, I recommend to the federal government that it re-examine its position toward provincial rights in some key areas:
—resources and resource taxation, which I've touched on today,
—cultural affairs, and
—communications.

To fail to do so will not only serve to strain the bonds of Confederation among the nine predominantly English-speaking provinces, at a time when such strains could be immensely dangerous. It will also make the battle against the separatist idea in Quebec very much tougher by offering to the people of Quebec only an unattractive, unresponsive, centralist alternative. In the fight to keep Canada intact to give such hostages to fortune would be unnecessary if not foolhardy.

The alternatives must not be Mr. Trudeau's centralism or separation. Those have never been the alternatives of this nation. The regional and cultural pressures which threaten Canada in 1977 have always been with us. Our ancestors dealt with them, wisely and skillfully, in 1867.

We would do well today to look back to the Fathers of Confederation who framed this country just because the centralist ideas built into the Act of Union of 1840 were not working. The framers of our Constitution understood that Canada was unique in the world, and that for the country to survive all regions would have to compromise a little. And they understood too that these compromises could not be forced. It was clear in 1867, as it is today, that Canada can only survive with the consent of each region and each major cultural group. This consent means now, as it did then, a willingness to share fairly in the burdens as well as the many advantages of this great nation.

No new ideas are necessary to win the hearts and minds of the people of Quebec, or of the West. The old idea, which has lasted for over a hundred years, will do, if we can dedicate ourselves to it with fresh sincerity and strength of purpose.

12

Second Chambers: German Experience and Canadian Needs*

R. M. Burns

A variety of issues was raised in the extensive discussions which took place in the period of the Canadian constitutional review from 1967 to 1971. But if we put aside the many individual questions we come to the central issue of a struggle of political forces. This revolved around the search of provincial leaders for additional power and the efforts of the federal representatives to preserve their established position of political dominance, a product of the years of depression, war, and reconstruction.

A continuing issue and one on which agreement seemed most likely to be available was the development of a process whereby the Constitu-

Acknowledgement must be gratefully made to the many people in the Federal Republic of Germany who helped with the preparation of this article. In particular mention must be made of Dr. Michael Bothe of the Max Planck Institute of International Law and Comparative Public Law in Heidelberg, who, with his colleagues, was always most generous with his help. Senator Eugene Forsey also read the manuscript and aided with his usual volatile comments. The study was supported by a travel grant from Canada Council.

* From *Canadian Public Administration*, Vol. 18, No. 4 (Winter, 1975), pp. 541-568. Reprinted by permission.

tion could be amended in Canada. This never turned out to be an attainable goal failing the ability of federal and provincial leaders to reach complete agreement on the limits of the amending procedures. Again this involved a competition for political authority. What still remains to be found is a practical means of providing a mechanism for translating the changing political relationships into a workable reality.

One approach to this objective which has received a good deal of attention from time to time and which seems to many to be central to the issue is the form and powers of the Senate. Many ideas have been advanced in an attempt either to remove the second chamber entirely or, alternatively, to provide it with a more meaningful role in our governmental system. Both the Government of Canada, in *The Constitution and the People of Canada,* and the Special Joint Committee of the Senate and the House of Commons had proposals for a provincial participation in Senatorial appointments and for limiting Senatorial legislative powers to a suspensive veto which could be over-ridden by the House of Commons. The question whether or not the parliamentary system operates better under a unicameral or a bicameral system is a secondary concern here. But it does seem of some significance to Canada whether or not our parliamentary federal system demands the existence of a second chamber for the representation of provincial interests.

But the measures for adjustment have really only been half measures and have done little to meet the central issues. They would do little to advance the cause of considered legislation, to raise the standards of Senate representation, or to provide a more effective provincial voice. There is, in fact, good reason to suspect that we might fall between the two stools we have set out for ourselves, achieving neither a more effective nor a more representative institution. Certainly we would not obtain what seems to us the most essential object of our pursuit— provincial political responsibility for its growing influences on national affairs.

In all the approaches there has been an air of unreality. It has been as if there was a fear both of what existed and of what the future might hold. Although various aspects of discussion on the Senate occupy a good deal of space in the index to the *Report* of the Special Joint Committee there is always an inadequate concern with the positive part a reformed second chamber might play in the actual processes of government in a federal state.

The kind of second chamber that we should have will depend very largely on what we think it should do. In the federal form its two theoretical functions have been to provide a responsible voice for the regional governments in the conduct of national affairs, and to provide an instrument for the review of public policies before they become law. While the Senate in Canada operates more usefully than it is generally given credit for, not even its best friends are likely to argue that it performs either of these functions very effectively. In the first place, through the method of appointment by the central government in power, senators, even though regionally based, are politically part of the central authority and provide little provincial representation in parliamentary actions in national affairs. Their part here has been largely taken over by the ubiquitous federal-provincial conference. In the second place, the very nature of the appointment makes it difficult for the senators to oppose legislation which the popularly elected House of Commons has approved despite the legally unrestricted nature of Senate authority.

The operation of second chambers in a parliamentary system is notably difficult. The concentration of power in the executive and the emphasis on responsibility through the elected members of Parliament makes the exercise of authority by an appointed member, such as the Canadian senator, very difficult. Even where the second chamber is on an elective basis, as in Australia, it is hard for it to exercise responsibility independently of government authority and party interests. That being so, it is necessary to ask what we can reasonably expect from such a body and how these expectations might be realized. No doubt some will argue that this is an unnecessary and fruitless task, that no second chamber is necessary, the protection of provincial rights being a proper function of the governments concerned, while the right of veto or suspension of Commons legislation is an archaic and undemocratic idea.

On the other hand there are some very good reasons why a regional voice in the governance of national activities may be desirable. True, the federal-provincial conference provides some opportunity, but any extension of its consultative powers would be regarded by many as an infringement of the system of parliamentary government. In any event, the representation of regional views would be better supplied at an earlier stage when particular policies and legislation are first being considered. Even though evidence of the positive value of review by the Senate in Canada is limited, this is a fault not of the role itself but of the constitutional form in which the capacity to resist politically popular measures in the elected House is limited. Given a more adequate body this function could contribute to the efficiency of government, particularly as the melding of national and regional responsibilities becomes more pronounced.

What then do we require in a second chamber under a federal parliamentary system? What seems to be called for is one in which there is a strong responsible element of provincial representation and at the same time sufficient popular prestige to provide not only the voice of regional interest but the constraints of a chamber of sober second thought. The solution most generally proposed is based on the prescription of partial responsibility of the provinces for the appointment of senators, along with the restriction of legislative review functions, perhaps to the extent that it would become merely a glorified personnel selection body for judges, ambassadors, and other government functionaries. All in all this seems directed to the worst of all possible worlds for not only would we have a second chamber of questionable utility, we would not have solved the basic problem, that of provincial representation of meaning. As Eugene Forsey has already suggested, among other things, it is difficult either to expect provincial satisfaction or a higher level of provincial representation under such a hesitant approach.

The strength of any representative institution must be in its possession of a political base. No matter how it is consulted, no matter how worthy are its members, unless it has a recognized role in the political system which enables it to provide an alternative source of political judgment, it will serve no real purpose.

For this reason, if no others, the suggestion of an appointed Senate with limited powers does not meet the question at issue. True, a second chamber appointed from the best the community has to offer might improve the quality of advice. But it would not matter very much whether its members were chosen by the prime minister, as is now the case, by the provincial governments, or by some sort of electoral college (as I once suggested myself). Lacking a political base, it would be no more effective as representing the provinces or in controlling the government and the Commons than it is now.

I am by no means convinced that this would be a better country if the provinces were given a greater voice in the conduct of our affairs. There is little doubt in my mind that many of the affairs of modern government are responsive only to the opportunities for the decisiveness of central control. Fragmentation is an increasingly doubtful answer to many of these problems. Somehow I doubt that our difficulties lie in the nature of our institutional organization as much as in the current lack of national consciousness and in a reversion to narrow provincialism—power without responsibility. Perhaps this is but a counsel of despair, but, regardless of my persuasions, there are mounting pressures which indicate that some greater degree of determinable provincial responsibility in national affairs may be necessary if this country is to survive.

Centralization, whether economically desirable or not, is not likely to be acceptable as a remedy under present circumstances. Having said this, where should we turn for ideas? Comparison of federal systems in a search for transferable institutions and organizations is not always a rewarding pursuit and may be full of pitfalls. Dr. Watts has pointed out that "it may be argued with some cogency that because Canadian problems are unique, the experience of other federations has little relevance to them. But although any reference to experience in other federations will certainly have to allow for the special features of the Canadian situation, useful lessons may be learnt from their attempts to cope with similar problems."[1]

In his very useful examination of second chambers, Watts came to the tenative conclusion that the Bundesrat, the second chamber in the Federal Republic of Germany, might provide us with some useful clues. Peyton Lyon had earlier come to a similar, rather tentative conclusion.[2] Mackay makes no direct mention of the German system; Kunz, although noticing it, does not analyse it seriously and concludes, without a very serious look, that it would 'probably block the operation of the system.'[3] What is perhaps surprising is that so little attention seems to have been given in our constitutional review to a process which, for all its complications, provides a basis for state political responsibility in national government and seems not only to work but to provide a basis for national unity which we have not seen for some years now in Canada.

I have no intention of arguing that the German system is readily adaptable to the Canadian scene. A good many differences of politics, history, economics, language, temperament, and geography would have to be taken into account, and in the end we might find the distinctions too great and the ultimate effects too different to permit any practical adaptation. However, this is hardly sufficient reason to neglect the possibilities. I would not expect to convince anyone to change the constitution on the basis of what I have found, but I have seen enough to convince me that in any further examination of the nature and role of a Canadian second chamber more attention should be paid the Bundesrat of West Germany. I have only scratched the surface; the lack of an adequate knowledge of the German language has been a great handicap, and only through the linguistic abilities and courtesy of many people in West Germany have I been able to progress as far as I have.

The German system provides a most effective way for the development of a provincial responsibility in national affairs. The direct representation of provincial governments in the Senate would establish a political influence that could not be easily disregarded. At the same time the political knowledge and experience of the members would add greatly to the ability to review legislative proposals.

It may be that granting provincial governments even suspensive powers over national legislation is carrying matters too far. The success of the process would depend on the way the provincial representatives approached their new responsibilities. If, however, it is felt that such powers are too extensive, the authority of the second chamber could be restricted to matters where provincial interests were determined to be directly involved. Admittedly this could create some difficult problems of definition, but the question is not insurmountable if German experience is our guide.

What we really come to is the question whether or not we want or need a second chamber to aid in the coordination of national and provincial interests. If we do believe one to be a necessary part of our federal system of government, it does not seem unreasonable to suggest that some application of the Bundesrat concept is worthy of study. As Mackay wisely remarked, 'Reform to be acceptable can come about only by agreement among various competing political interests; it cannot be drafted in a study.'[4] But the fact that we cannot write the final prescription should not prevent us from attempting the diagnosis.

Before we try to adapt the Bundesrat to Canadian conditions we should get to know what it is and how it came to be. It has an historical background over a period which closely parallels the life of this country. Before Bismarck took matters in hand between 1866 and 1871 Germany was a loose confederation of local provinces. Under his leadership Prussian domination was secured but the supremacy of dynastic rulers was confirmed. The German Empire from 1871 to 1918 was a monarchy supported by an elected chancellor, a popular chamber (the Reichstag), and a federal council or second chamber representative of the twenty-five nation states. While in theory a government based on popular support, the executive under Bismarck was to a large extent independent of the Reichstag. In fact during much of this period it was an autocracy under the kaiser and the chancellor, leaving the popularly elected parliament very little real power. However, the states through the Prussian-dominated Council retained considerable authority, and the loose nature of the confederacy was maintained at least in principle.

Following the collapse of the Empire at the end of the first world war a new constitution, much more centralized in form, was proclaimed. In it the Reichstag was the dominant power with Prussia still the predominant force. The Reichsrat, or state council, had limited powers and could neither initiate nor finally over-rule legislation in the parliament. While technically Germany became a democratic republic the system soon proved unequal to its task under stress, and with the advent of Hitler the power of the states was effectively abolished and for all practical purposes the country operated in a unitary form. Despite the experience under the Weimar Republic and under Hitler in particular, strong prejudices in favour of centralized authority remained in many parts of Germany after the second world war, Bavaria being the principal exception. Had it not been for the influence of the Allied Occupying Powers, particularly the United States, a much more centralized form of government would likely have developed. As it was, the political reconstruction of Germany was undertaken from the bottom up, from local units to the national government. Throughout the process the emphasis of the Allied influence was on decentralization, and it was in considerable measure responsible for the return of political authority to the Laender, not to the extent that existed prior to the first world war, but far more than in the Weimar Republic and the Nazi era.

In some important respects the influence of the United States representative in the Western Military Governors, General Clay, is to be seen. He was able to convince his British colleagues of the desirability of limiting the powers of the national government within a strong federal system. The French and the Benelux representatives who were also consulted would have preferred a looser form, for they were not anxious to see a new and united Germany, but all were in agreement on a clear division of authority with specific delineation of central power. Eventually in the autumn of 1948 the Parliamentary Council, representative of the state parliaments, was convened in Bonn. After some months of negotiation the Basic Law was approved and was proclaimed on 23 May 1949, having in the meantime been altered to meet some of the objectives of the military governors who saw a persistent leaning towards central authority.

The Basic Law is in effect the constitution of the Federal Republic of Germany. It is much too long to be dealt with here in any detail. It should be sufficient for our understanding to note that it provides for a division of powers between the federal government and the Laender by providing exclusive authority for the federal government in certain specified matters, such as foreign affairs, defence, currency and coinage, customs, post office, railways, etc., while the residual powers are left with the Laender. There is a very important exception in the extensive concurrent list where the federal government not only has priority but the power (subject, of course, to jurisdiction of the Constitutional Court) to regulate by federal legislation if 1/ a matter cannot be effectively regulated by the legislation on individual Laender, 2/ the regulation of a matter by law might prejudice the interests of other Laender or of the people as a whole, or 3/ the maintenance of legal or economic unity, especially the maintenance of uniformity of living conditions beyond the territory of one Land, necessitates such regulation.[5] One may be forgiven for wondering how the military governors were so persuaded, for the effect of this allocation of powers was to put much more authority in central hands than would appear to have been the original intention.

Germany is a federal republic under a titular president who is elected by a Federal Convention consisting of the members of the Bundestag and an equal number of representatives of the Laender. The government itself consists of the federal chancellor and the federal ministers who are nominees of the chancellor and appointed by the president. It is an interesting feature of the German Executive that while the chancellor is elected by the Bundestag he is not responsible to it in the way the first minister is in our parliamentary system. Under normal circumstances the Bundestag can voice its lack of confidence in the chancellor only by electing a successor by a majority of its members and requesting the president to dismiss the incumbent; this is not readily done and has never been successfully undertaken. The ministers are not directly responsible to the Bundestag and within the general policy guidelines determined by the chancellor are able to conduct the affairs of their departments entirely on their own responsibility, within, of course, the ability to get the two Houses to pass the necessary laws.

On the basis of what we have seen so far the political power of the Laender would seem to be of no great weight. The authority for most important areas of public responsibility is at the discretion of the federal government and the freedom of the Laender to advance regional interests would appear on paper to be correspondingly restricted. This would be so except for certain compensating factors which can, in the proper circumstances, effectively change the balance.

Perhaps the most influential is the nature, composition, and operation of the second chamber, the Bundesrat or Council of States. It is a unique institution in federal systems, although one does find some general similarities in certain Swiss cantons. It is so unusual that some observers have questioned whether it can be considered a second chamber, or whether more properly it is part of the executive government itself. Regardless of the classification, its operations are certainly more powerful than those of most federal second chambers, with the obvious exception of the Senate of the United States.

The Bundesrat is neither elected nor appointed. It is the representative not of a people or group but of the executive governments of the ten Laender of the federal republic, that is, it not only represents the Land governments but is actually made up of them, with the minister-president (premier) leading the group and exercising the vote of the Land en bloc. Voting power is graded by population with a maximum of five and a minimum of three, depending on the size of the Land. Berlin has four non-voting members who do, however, exercise this right in committee. What makes the executive nature of this form of representation even more specific is the fact that the Landtage (the state parliaments) can have no direct influence on the decisions taken with reference to the vote in the Bundesrat. The Land representatives are not petitioners to the federal parliament; they are an integral part of it. Lyon has suggested that this form is similar to a standing dominion-provincial conference, but this analogy is not entirely convincing because it is the Bundesrat's power to affect directly, not merely to influence, federal government policies and actions which is the essential ingredient.[6]

The mere fact of direct representation of the Land government in the Bundesrat is not the governing source of Land impact in national policies. Rather it is in the power of suspension or absolute veto supported by a working political structure. Under the provision of the Basic Law, bills may be introduced in the Bundestag by any of the three governing agencies, the federal government, the Bundestag, or the Bundesrat. The basis of Bundesrat authority is not contained in this power to introduce legislation. Actually it is not frequently used. Where the power really lies is in the direct and indirect influences over the passage of legislation. In the case of bills where the Basic Law indicates a Land interest (in cases of dispute settled by the Constitutional Court) this takes the form of a complete right of veto. In other legislation the power is limited to temporary suspension, but through a complex system of arbitration by a committee of the two houses, not unlike that in the U.S. Congress, a good deal of practical weight is still carried.

The degree to which the Bundesrat role in legislation is recognized by the Constitution is set out in Article 76 of the Basic Law. While most bills are introduced by the federal government, they must first be submitted to the Bundesrat before going to the Bundestag, the elected chamber. The Bundesrat is required to voice its position on the proposed legislation within six weeks (in certain cases of emergency in three weeks). If such a statement is not then received the bill goes forward to the Bundestag and the statement is transmitted when it is forthcoming. If the Bundesrat introduces a bill in the first instance it must be forwarded to the Bundestag by the federal government with a statement of the views of the executive.

While the arbitration procedure can be invoked by the federal government or the Bundestag in cases of 'laws of consent' (i.e. where the Bundesrat can exercise a veto), this is not usual. If the Bundesrat exercises the right of veto the process generally stops and the bill dies. It is in the cases where the Bundesrat exercises only the suspensive power that the process is most useful. In such cases the Bundesrat is generally able to reach a compromise agreement with the Bundestag through the joint arbitration procedure. In the twenty years from 1949 to 1969, of 267 bills that went to the Arbitration Committee 243 appeals were originated by the Bundesrat, and of these 228 were finally proclaimed.

While the Bundesrat in the last analysis cannot veto 'simple laws' (that is, those not directly affecting the Laender), it can exercise a great deal of influence even after the arbitration process has been concluded. By entering a protest against a bill which has been adopted by the Bundestag it can force an over-riding vote of that body which requires the same majority in the Bundestag as that by which the protest was adopted in the Bundesrat. Thus, if a protest was adopted by two-thirds of the Bundesrat, the Bundestag must have a two-thirds majority to pass the measure over the protest.

A further authority over the actions of the federal government lies with the Bundesrat. Most decrees and statutory instruments made ancillary to legislative authority under Article 80 of the Basic Law, require Bundesrat but not Bundestag approval. This applies to all legislation and no distinction is made between 'simple' and 'consent' laws. In the complexities of modern legislation such a control is of increasing importance.

From one point of view the powers exercised by the Bundesrat over both legislation and statutory instruments make it a committee of review of public policy. Despite the fact that the exclusive responsibilities of the Laender are limited, under the constitution, the power to veto or delay, or amend, federal legislation makes it a central element in the government of Germany. Certainly its actual powers are much greater than those of the Canadian Senate, although somewhat more confined than those of the Senate of the United States.

This raises a pertinent question. The system gives a great deal of power to the representatives of the Laender in the national government. Are they, as regional politicians with the special interests attached to that role, qualified to fulfill the responsibilities they have acquired? If the process relied solely on the political representatives acting as a second chamber there would probably be very good reason for concern. Two main factors operate to influence this, one administrative in nature, the other political. Without them the whole process would come into question.

In the first place many of the decisions taken in the Bundesrat are the product of extensive committee work which is generally preceded by consultation among the interested federal departments and their opposite numbers in the Laender. The actual proceedings in the Bundesrat are not those of parliamentary debate but rather a formal confirmation of decisions arrived at in detailed discussion in the standing committees in such areas as foreign affairs, finance, economics, agriculture, etc., and in certain cases by special committees which are dissolved when they have served their purpose. The preliminary work having been carried out, much of the detail is decided in the committees, in most cases by permanent officials either of the offices maintained by all the Laender in Bonn, or by special delegations which join the committees to contribute expert knowledge. The value of these contributions can only be appreciated when we consider it in conjunction with the administrative responsibilities of the Laender.

The other element that enters into the process is political. In the German political scene there is an increasing tendency toward the polarization of political support around the two main parties, the right centre CDU-CSU and the left centre SPD. At present in the Bundestag the SPD holds power in coalition with the liberal FDP, but the coalitions are loose and capable of shifting. Between 1966 and 1969 the federal government was in fact under control of the 'great coalition' of the two principal parties. But what is of interest and importance is the fact that the party organization in the Laender is much the same as on the national scene and various coalitions have at times been required. Thus while the attitudes in the Bundesrat may be to a considerable extent determined by Land interests, they are also often strongly influenced by political relationships. These tend to moderate each other. In some circumstances the ruling party/parties in the Bundestag can rely on the political loyalty of their members in the Bundesrat but in other cases the issue will rest on other considerations. The experience so far has been that the Bundesrat has been very careful to avoid confrontations in major political issues, appreciating that its opportunity for effective influence is greater if it does not encourage party conflict. The policies of the different Land delegations in the Bundesrat tend to vary widely on different issues, groupings take place sometimes around political affiliations but perhaps even more often around competing financial needs, the rich versus the poor. The situation is not unlike that with which we are familiar here. One factor of considerable significance is that there is a relatively limited degree of cultural identity among Laender in which original boundaries were artificial, Bavaria and the city states of Bremen and Hamburg being the notable exceptions.

A further consolidating factor which must have a good deal of influence on attitudes is the extent to which political results in Land elections are valued on the national scene. This, of course, operates on two fronts. First, the political repercussions of success or failure in a Land election provide a measure of the public popularity for the national party. Secondly, the change in balance of party power in the Bundesrat can have important effects on the ability of the governing party both in the federal government and in the Bundestag to secure approval of its legislative programme.

But the position which the Laender hold in the national legislative structure through the Bundesrat would certainly be less acceptable were it not for another very important factor. Under Article 83 of the Basic Law the Laender are charged with the responsibility of administering federal laws as a matter 'of their own concern' unless the Basic Law provides otherwise. For this they receive no direct reimbursement, the responsibility being considered in the financial settlement. Direct administration of federal laws by the federal government is limited to relatively few basic services such as the foreign service, railroads, postal service, defence, etc. In certain cases, such as social insurance, special corporate bodies under federal jurisdiction may be formed. But generally the bulk of federal laws are administered by the Laender, including the income and corporation taxes. The federal government under the Basic Law has very substantial powers of supervision and with the consent of the Bundesrat may issue 'pertinent general administrative rules.' However, this is seldom necessary, and there is little experience with federal interference in Laender administrative activities. A slightly different situation exists with regard to certain specific functions, such as civil defence, highway traffic (autobahn) administration, air-traffic administration, and atomic energy. In these cases the Laender act as agents for the federal government and the powers of supervision are more direct; as Article 85(4) states: 'Federal supervision shall extend to conformity with law and appropriateness of execution. The federal government may, for the purpose, require the submission of reports and documents and send commissioners to all authorities. In such cases costs of administration are reimbursed by the federal government to the Laender.'

A further complication was introduced in 1969 by amendment to the Basic Law. Under Article 91A federal participation in certain responsibilities of the Laender is provided for as 'joint tasks' similar to our conditional grant programmes. These are limited to responsibilities that are important for the improvement of living conditions and include expansion and construction of institutions of higher learning, improvement of regional economic structures, and improvement of agrarian structures and coast preservation. Such federal enactments are 'laws of consent' and require Bundesrat approval. While the administrative responsibility for these joint tasks remains with the Laender, there seems to be a growing possibility of more federal activity in the administrative process than is the case under the established procedure.

Despite these exceptions the extent of Land authority in the administration of federal laws is extensive and on the whole complete. If the lack of pressures for federal supervision is any guide, the system works reasonably well and with considerable saving over-all in public administration costs. One might expect that the level of administrative capacity would vary rather widely from Land to Land, but this does not appear to be the case and the general view is that there is sufficient interchange between the Laender to provide a reasonably consistent standard of efficiency. It does not seem in line with the German character to continue to accept the situation if it were otherwise.

The advantage of a reduction in the size of bureaucracies has a good deal of appeal in these days. This, however, is not the principal value of the West German system. The value lies in the contribution made toward the Bundesrat's legislative capacity. The fact that the Land governments have administrative power over much of the day-to-day activity in the public sector gives the representatives in the Bundesrat an authority and prestige they could enjoy in no other way. This is given additional weight by the fact that the influence is largely exercised in the first instance by experts in the committee system. The division of powers and their actual distribution has become heavily weighted on the side of the central authority. If it were not for the advantage that administrative responsibility gives to the Laender it is hard to visualize the Bundesrat being able to exercise any consistent influence, at least in the area of the simple laws, even to some extent in the laws of consent. The trend toward centralization which has been evident for some time would inevitably have been stimulated but for this important constraint.

Such success as has been achieved in the integration of national and regional interests would not have been possible if the components of government had operated in isolation. As a practical response to the needs of the situation an extensive network of intergovernmental coordination has been developed between the federal government, the Bundestag, and the Bundesrat, as well as between the federal government and the individual Laender and between the Laender themselves.

At the formal political level there has been a considerable effort at developing a basis of mutual understanding and while disagreements and confrontations obviously take place, the system is designed to avoid this happening by default. The result is that they generally occur only when the issues are of sufficient importance to justify them. Somewhat unusual arrangements are made for a 'dialogue' between the various government components. There is provision for the attendance of the chancellor and other members of the federal government in the Bundestag, and under Article 43 of the Basic Law the Bundestag and its committees may demand the presence of any member of the federal government before them. Under the same article members of the Bundesrat or of the federal government or their agents have access to all meetings of the Bundestag or its committees and have the right to be heard at any time. Provision is made for seating members of the federal government regardless of whether they are actually members of parliament, and members of the Bundesrat, on the dais of the plenary chamber of the Bundestag. Similarly, under Article 53, the members of the federal government have the right, and on demand of the Bundersat, the duty, to attend meetings of the Bundesrat and its committees and must be heard at any time. On its part the Bundesrat must be kept currently informed by the federal government of the conduct of its affairs. Seating in the Bundesrat chamber is provided for representatives of the federal government, but no reciprocal arrangements exist for attendance of Bundestag members. All these formal provisions may not be of the same political significance, but they do indicate an intent of integration of legislative work which is important to the process. The practical approach to co-ordination is through the committees in which much of the legislative work is prepared.

What cannot be taken lightly is the close-knit influences of party affiliation, particularly as the polarization of the political scene into a two-party relationship proceeds. The political relationship is by no means inviolate, for, as we have already noted, economic issues frequently take precedence, but it does provide a strong tie which is enhanced by the movement of politicians between federal and state affairs and that of civil servants in and out of the political field. This polarization, which began to be of significance when the SPD took power under Brandt, may be of increasing importance involving as it does growth in the political nature of the senior civil service, a phenomenon now not unknown in some Canadian provincial governments. The effects this may have in the Bundestag/Bundesrat/government relationship could be of some importance and may not always operate to the advantage of a harmonious system.

Much of the co-ordination of Bund-Land affairs is inherent in the terms of the Basic Law. Here the provisions for interlocking of interests are clearly visible. Aside from the broad area of concurrent powers, the financial provisions are such that a close relationship of the two levels of government is inevitable. This is most noticeable in the taxing provisions, for here the important revenues are shared under the Basic Law (personal income tax 43 per cent federal, 43 per cent Land, and 14 per cent local; corporation income tax 50 per cent federal and 50 per cent Land). The turnover tax, while not divided by the Basic Law but by federal legislation, is also shared (70 per cent federal, 30 per cent Land) as are other taxes. While the proceeds of these taxes are distributed, the legal responsibility for them is divided in a different way. Federal paramountcy in the legislation of taxation is more or less complete, although any such legislation must have the approval of the Bundesrat. The interests of the states are maintained because the administration of tax laws is a matter for the Laender.

The German acceptance of the indivisibility of fiscal responsibility is thus recognized and the acknowledgement of this mutual interest is evident both in the law and its operation. The need for new financial measures was one basic reason for the 'great coalition' of 1966 and an outstanding example of this and of the recognition of the need for intergovernmental co-ordination in such matters was the Economic Stability and Growth Law of 1967. The recognition of the problem eventually led to the amendment of Article 109 of the Basic Law providing for close linkage of federal and Land instruments in budget matters. The article states: 'the Federation and the Laender are autonomous and independent of each other in their fiscal administration. They shall take due account in their fiscal administration of the requirements of over-all economic equilibrium.' Provision is made for extensive federal legislation (with Bundesrat consent) providing for the regulation of public borrowing and for the control of budgetary inflation through the freezing of budgetary surpluses of both the Land and federal governments.

The degree of co-operation obtained is seen in the two bodies set up under the Economic Stability and Growth Law. The Trade Cycle Council advises on matters of business cycle control, including the level of spending and borrowing and the freezing of reserve funds. The Financial Planning Council concerns itself with medium-range financial planning for both the federal and Land governments. The councils are both made up of two representatives from the federal government and one from each Land and four from local governments. The idea perhaps owes something to the Australian Loan Council but has been considerably extended and does not appear to have been as centralizing, largely due to the role of the Bundesrat, which has been of great value in making this approach viable by providing not only a legal veto but an ongoing interest on the part of the Laender in fiscal policy and its administration. Perhaps its results have not yet been proven in the longer term, but the attempt is at least being made. The advantages of central direction have been realized, but at the same time a sense of regional responsibility for national economic well-being has been confirmed.

While perhaps the most formal organizations, the Councils are not the sole means of practical intergovernmental communication. Prior to 1969 there was a ministry for affairs of the Laender. The minister's principal responsibility was to maintain liaison with the Bundesrat and the Land governments. Like the office of the Secretary of State for the Provinces in early Canadian history it failed because of the vagueness of its purpose and its lack of executive authority. Much of what it had been intended to do was taken over more directly by federal and Land departments and that is where the larger part of intergovernmental political and administrative contacts remains today, between the permanent officials and ministers of the two levels. Informal arrangements of course will always exist. They take place from time to time between the chancellor and the ministers-presidents of the Laender, but these have tended to be symbolic and social rather than productive. More important are the meetings of the ministers-presidents to discuss matters of mutual interest, and in these cases federal ministers are usually present as observers by invitation. It is to be noted that matters are usually those of administrative concern, and those which involve the Bundesrat prerogatives are seldom discussed.

The permanent offices maintained by each of the Laender in Bonn are important elements in the federal-Laender machinery of co-operation. They are generally the continuing points of contact, political as well as official, for much of the integration process in federal-Land affairs constantly in progress. As might be expected there is extensive consultation between the various Land governments. Given their extensive administrative responsibilities, frequent meetings and both formal and informal agreements have become the way of business. By 1962 it was reported that there were eleven such permanent ministerial committees in existence, and the number of conferences and meetings of various kinds probably exceeds by a good margin even the federal-provincial record in Canada. Certainly there is no comparison with the limited interprovincial relationship that has existed here.

While our concern is only indirectly with the financial relationships, some weight must be given to them in evaluating the background of intergovernmental interests. We have already noted the extent and nature of tax-sharing and the growth of joint tasks. Direct federal-Land equalization is not a significant factor, although horizontal equalization from the richer to the poorer Laender is governed by Federal law. This provides an additional direct link of interest between the states and the national government. While sometimes a cause of friction, it does not appear to be any more so than are the vertical transfers used in most federal countries, including Canada.

The success of the German federal system is grounded in a number of diverse factors which in one way or another tend over-all to be supportive rather than divisive. Perhaps this would not be possible without the climate of rapid and continuous economic growth characteristic of the years since 1949 when the republic came into being. On the other hand perhaps the economic growth would not have been so successful had not a climate of compatible stability been provided. Many countries suffered in the second world war and had to face the struggle of recovery. Few, if any, progressed to the level of prosperity of Germany.

There have been a great number of reasons why the German experiment in state participation in national government has succeeded. In the first place the ground was favourable, for it seems true that most of post-war Germany sought the security of authority in a central government. Even Bavaria, while unenthusiastic, never actively opposed. A further influence was to be found, and to an extent still exists, in the lack of historical bases for the regional divisions. A few had such a base, but most were artificial boundaries created by the Allied Military Government and are only now beginning to develop local attachments. Nor can the purely political factors be neglected. Germany began the post-war period with a multiplicity of parties. In 1949 ten different parties had membership in the Bundestag. Due to the search for stability and some appropriate election laws which eliminated parties inimical to the state and those securing less than 5 per cent of popular support, today only three are represented and a two-party system seems to be a possibility. The situation now is not unlike that of the United Kingdom: two major parties, one of the right centre and one of the left centre, with a Liberal party on the fringe but often close to holding the balance of power. The important influence of the party system on German federalism is not in its divisions but in the similarities of the pattern through the Laender where the same party alignments predominate. This political homogeneity has on the whole proved a valuable and cohesive element in the federal-Land relationships.

Many factors have entered into the development of the working relationship of the federal and Land governments. But the most important has probably been in the way the division of powers and responsibilities has been arranged. Under the Basic Law the central government has been able to assume the greater part of public responsibility for law making, but the Laender have retained an important influence. This has been possible through the powers of the Bundesrat as an integral part of the national government system, being a unit of the parliament with strong powers over much of federal activity. The administrative responsibility of the Laender for many federal laws not only provides a practical power but gives political weight both through direct contact with the people and through the expert experience which adds to the legislative judgment of the Bundesrat. German federalism has integrated policy making at the centre with administrative responsibility in the regions. The Bundesrat has been able through its dual role to convert controversial policy issues into resolvable issues of administrative procedure. This is sometimes considered as reinforcing the traditional conservatism of second chambers, and to the extent that bureaucratic influence tends to be conservative the charge is likely valid. But there is no evidence that Germany has suffered from the results; all the evidence is that its governments have been able to respond as well as, if not better than, most to the challenge of change.

It is through these means that the atmosphere of Land responsibility in national affairs has been developed, a factor too often lacking in federal systems. This responsibility can be seen clearly reflected in a number of areas, but particularly in those of fiscal and economic policy where the attempts at rational co-ordination, while perhaps not fully successful at least have been moves in the right direction. If the German approach to modern federalism has had success, as much as anything it can be attributed to the melding of those elusive ingredients, authority with responsibility.

At the beginning we expressed some reservations on the comparative values of federal experience. Certainly the factors in the growth of the Federal Republic of Germany have been very different from those of our own experience. Nevertheless, there are sufficient elements of similarity to make us wonder why we have not given more consideration to the recipe. Regardless of how one may feel about the kind of federal form that would best suit our purposes, there can be no doubt that the present situation is not satisfactory. This is not necessarily so much the fault of our constitution as of ourselves. But, given the growth of provincial power in the demands on the public sector, whether we like it or not some way must be developed of more effectively recognizing the regional role. But recognition divorced from responsibility could destroy this country. The whole purpose of this article is to suggest that the federal system of West Germany may have useful ideas which we could explore with some hope of profit.

There are a great many questions that would have to be answered before any adaptation of the German system could be applied to Canadian needs. Given the current divisive nature of our political life perhaps the most important would be whether or not a second chamber composed of representatives of partisan provincial governments would be able to use its power in a manner to benefit the nation as a whole. Mackay has asked whether a senate composed even in part of provincial representatives might not become too strong and influential for the nation's good. His concern applies even more to a second chamber directly representative of provincial governments. The answer will not be found in any brief survey. Such questions will only be met by a continuing study of historical precedents and political actions over the longer term. The role of any such second chamber should not be merely to protect the provinces against the misuse of power by the national government. It must be a positive and responsible influence in the operation of provincial interests in a national federal state. The real issue is not the protection of the provinces but the strengthening of the nation itself. In this the direct responsibility of provincial governments for their actions is an essential ingredient.

We have already acknowledged that the present place of the Senate in our parliamentary system does little to satisfy the need for regional representation in the federal system. The Senate, as an appointed second chamber, has constitutional power but no political base of significance. It has in a sense become a politically oriented advisory committee and even when it functions effectively (as it does in many particular situations) its credibility is seldom widely recognized. The fact that it has not been able to perform the part intended for it by the drafters of our constitution has not been very important except at certain periods in our national existence. One of those periods is certainly with us now as we struggle in a mass of conflicting ambitions and indecisions as to what we should and can do.

The developing Canadian political scene is one of great uncertainty. No one can study the course of events in recent years without sensing an urgent need, not just for a greater appreciation of regional interests in national policies, but for a greater acceptance of political responsibility on the part of provincial governments in the broader role they apparently want to play. Since the mid-fifties (and at earlier periods in our history) we have seen a growing interest on the part of provincial governments, particularly in the larger and wealthier provinces, in exerting greater influence over federal policies on the grounds that their interests are directly involved. We now see ourselves in the destructive situation where provincial elections are called largely as a pressure measure to influence national policies. The increase in intergovernmental involvement is undeniable. Federal policies certainly influence provincial interests, just as provincial policies affect those of the nation. If it were not for other factors one could easily conclude, as Laski once did, that the divided responsibilities of federalism are ill-suited to the needs of the modern world. But no one is seriously suggesting that there is a practical political alternative to federation in legislative union, at least at this time. Therefore it makes a certain amount of sense to try to see how we can combine the provincial interest in national affairs with some responsibility for them, and at the same time permit the federal government the necessary measure of influence and control where the national interests make them necessary and desirable.

Before we attempt to apply the German experience to Canadian needs we should be clear as to just what we expect the Senate to be. Are we seeking a body which is an integral part of our parliamentary system and whose basic function is that of a second chamber to deal with the business of Parliament? Kunz argues that any other approach is a misconception of the nature of the Canadian governmental system, which is that of responsible cabinet government. He appears to believe that the provision for provincial representation would 'unduly complicate, disturb and probably block the operation of the system.'[7]

There would be much to be said for this view except for one rather important fact: Canada is a federal state, and one of the primary reasons for a second chamber in such a setting is to represent the viewpoints of the regions in the determination of national policies which concern them. There may be other ways in which a second chamber in a federal parliamentary system can operate to control the government (for it is the government it must control, not the Commons), but one possible way is to have the provinces directly represented in the decision-making apparatus.

There are two main functions that must be fulfilled. If a second chamber is given the power to represent the regional view through direct representation it must also be given the power to act as a body of review. It is difficult to see the dual responsibility being carried out by the half measures of provincial appointment as proposed by both the government of Canada and the Special Joint Committee, regardless entirely of the fact of the removal of much of the legislative power and the demotion to some sort of formal advisory committee.

The solution to the problem then, if there is one, really lies in the ability to devise a way in which the provincial interest in national policies can be joined with the responsibilities of sober second thoughts. One answer may be in the system adopted in the Federal Republic of Germany through the direct representation of the state governments in the second chamber charged with a two-part responsibility for the review of legislation, an absolute power of veto in matters of direct Land concern, and a suspensive power over legislation of a fully national character. Thus it not only performs its function as a representative of regional interests but carries on the traditional review role of the second chamber in a parliamentary system.

Whether or not the German federal system can provide the answer in Canada will not be easily determined or readily accepted. Perhaps we have lost the basic understanding of our nationhood and lack a sufficient incentive to regain it. The attitude toward central responsibility in Germany today is not unlike that of Canada in the early post-war years. Then we had the goal of a new world in which petty ambitions took a lesser place to the ultimate goal. The politicians of today are largely unacquainted with the pressures of crisis and the national responsibilities that go with them and have turned inwards to their own more limited concerns. Many people will no doubt reject the idea that the German people have anything to teach us either of parliamentary government or democracy; they will believe that it is only the German acceptance of order and discipline that has made the system work. It may be so, but if discipline and order are all that are standing in our way in regaining a sense of national identity we might usefully consider whether this is too great a price to pay or whether it is really a price at all.

But failing some world catastrophe of the order of the 1930s or 1940s, the situation is not likely to change in any radical way. The government of Canada after yielding a good deal of ground over the past decade or so shows no sign of being interested in many more concessions. On their part provincial political leaders urged on by public demand, political opportunity and the pressures from their municipalities, are not likely to experience a change of heart. But the rapidly increasing complexities of modern political economy make the continuation of the present struggle a luxury the country could do without. Our attempts at co-ordination in the fields of fiscal and economic policy have been singularly slow and unsuccessful. We have made little progress since the ideas of co-operative federalism first began to be discussed. Perhaps we must accept the fact that in a federal state national policies must be adapted as far as possible to the varying interests and attitudes which made the fragmented form a necessity in the first place. It is not efficient but may be inevitable. The adaptation may best be made by providing a formal role and responsibility for the provinces in the central system.

The adaptation of the German federal structure to Canadian requirements would not be a simple task of reorganizing the structure and powers of the second chamber. The system, as we have tried to emphasize, depends on much more than that. It would involve basic re-examination of the division of powers and responsibilities, a fundamental restructuring of our administrative system, a probable period of shifting in our political affiliations and, most of all, a rethinking of political and public attitudes toward the nature of the Canadian state. In the German experience there is an observable tendency toward centralization, a product of public preference and history as well as the form of the federal system. In Canada, while the trend does change from time to time, the movement is in the opposite direction, with federal and provincial governments competing in an adversary relationship while the business of government suffers and the taxpayer pays.

While there are valid reasons why the German system cannot be applied as a package in Canada, we might profit from trying to synthesize its basic ingredients in order to utilize them in a system of our own. Our stated objective is the melding of legal authority with political accountability and the German approach, in which the state governments are directly represented in the second chamber and have important powers over legislation, could be a workable approach. It would not be easily adaptable to Canadian conditions, particularly in view of our different traditions of parliamentary responsibility, the geographical difficulties, the historical biases, and the cultural and linguistic barriers. Clearly it would not be possible to make wholesale and arbitrary changes, however rational they might appear. But this should not prevent our seeing the objectives and the means by which they might be reached. The application of systems analysis procedures to constitution making may be unusual, but it could be worth a try.

It seems reasonably evident from the examination of the record of the constitutional review that no one, not even the provinces, took the question of the second chamber very seriously. Only one meeting of this subcommittee of the constitutional conference took place, and its results were described as a useful exchange of views which would require further examination. The Special Joint Committee did somewhat better, but even it seemed hesitant about a fundamental examination of the objectives of a second chamber or about the recommendation of anything likely to be of useful effect.

Our goal of provincial responsibility for actions that affect national policies may not be fully achievable. It may not be practicable for the premier of a province to head the delegation to the second chamber in view of the different parliamentary traditions. But it does not seem beyond reason that provincial representatives should be more than appointed members without continuing the direct responsibility to the government that appointed them. If their political responsibility is to be a reality there must be some sort of formal relationship between the provincial representatives in the second chamber and the government that appointed them. Their accountability must be seen and publicly recognized.

Before we attempt to define what might be done it will be useful to look at the areas of activity where change may be required. Obviously the fewer changes we have to make in our traditional and accepted system of government the greater are the prospects of acceptance. Failing some form of social upheaval, we must acknowledge that any effective change will have to be by easy stages and involve only such fundamental departures from the established way as are absolutely necessary. The barriers to change in the constitution itself and in the administrative bureaucracy will be formidable enough without any unnecessary challenges. The essential ingredient of the change required in the approach we are considering is that of political power, both legal and administrative. The question then is: how can this change be made in such a way that it would eventually accomplish what we seek but would also have some chance of political and public acceptability?

If our objective is the development of a parliamentary system for the nation in which the provincial governments have a working element of authority and responsibility, we must be prepared to make some important alterations in our scheme of the distribution of powers. This does not necessarily mean a great number of radical changes in the present locus of authority nor a devolution from the national to the provincial level; it may be that in certain areas federal power would have to be increased rather than moderated. We need only recall that in the German federal system legal power through direct allocation and concurrent authority is heavily concentrated in the centre. But what it does require is a clearer definition of federal and provincial responsibilities under the different circumstances which may prevail.

It would be an idle exercise to attempt to define here the desirable allocation of responsibility under any revised constitutional system. The Joint Parliamentary Committee has examined this in great detail. Probably the attainable answer would be different only in degree from that with which we have been long familiar. The essential element if we are to use a system where provincial authority is directly related to the degree of provincial interest is that this authority can be defined and stated as far as is possible. What we would have to decide upon would be a division of authority into three main parts: first, those of the central government; second, those which under all circumstances would be those of the provincial governments; and third, those powers of a concurrent nature where the power might be in either jurisdiction depending on precedence and the particular circumstances of the case.

The most difficult decisions would arise in the third case for we would be faced with two variables; the determined constitutional responsibility and the immediate designation of the particular case. But if we are to adopt the basic element of the German system which distinguishes the provincial power in the federal parliament by the degree of regional interest, it is necessary for the distinction to be made. In the final analysis for this purpose it is not which jurisdiction has the authority to legislate, although this, of course, has to be defined, but to what extent the exercise of these concurrent powers impinges on provincial interests. This would determine the rights of the second chamber as representative of the provincial power whether they are merely suspensive, where the provincial interest is non-existent or marginal, or absolute where that interest is direct and acknowledged. A difficult problem indeed!

No doubt, as in German experience, the area of disagreement would be substantially limited by the processes of political negotiation. But there would remain, probably more in the Canadian case than in the German, very substantial areas where some agency of arbitration would be necessary. In Germany this is a function of the Constitutional Court but it does not seem likely that the Supreme Court could carry out the function in Canada. A deliberately appointed Court of Arbitration, designed solely for the settlement of such disputes, would likely be required, at least until a body of decisions had been developed. This is not an ideal solution by any criteria, but few political decisions are ideal, and given the nature of the division of authority it is essential that there be a substantial degree of flexibility, and, in the circumstances of the changes being examined here, machinery for achieving such flexibility is essential.

We have less experience in the adjustment of expenditure responsibilities in Canada than we have in the raising of revenues. Due to our experience with the tax agreements there do not appear to be any insurmountable difficulties in developing a revenue system which will meet the needs of both levels of government. The problem of an acceptable division need be no more difficult under the proposed system than it is under our present one. In fact, given acceptance of the concept of provincial responsibility related to authority, some more workable plan might be achieved more quickly than in the present quarrelsome atmosphere. Administrative problems there will always be, but if the system is politically acceptable these should be handled without too much trouble.

In our examination of the German federal system we placed a good deal of emphasis on the part of the Laender's administrative responsibility in legitimizing their role in the federal governmental system. The responsibility for federal laws provided a basis both for knowledge and responsibility that would otherwise have been absent. Whether there is the additional advantage of economy and efficiency is an open question. In these times of apparently unchecked expansion of the public services any possibility of such a return will not be lightly held. If there is a reduction in public service costs that is a bonus. The principal value of provincial administrative responsibility for the regional administration of many federal laws would not lie in the monetary savings but in the integration of interests of the two levels. It is in fact difficult to see how the system would succeed without some form of delegation of this kind.

Again, there are a great many obstacles to be met, and experience indicates that the mechanical problems of this transfer would likely be the least formidable. The greatest difficulty would be in the area of political and bureaucratic possession. Few federal ministers are likely to favour the surrender of their administrative powers and all the political advantages that go with the control of a large organization. Bureaucrats are likely to see very little personal advantage in the transfer of responsibility to another jurisdiction with the breakup of the established patterns of communication and command with which they have become intimately connected. The situation was much easier in the German case because the collapse of the Third Reich made it possible to start from a completely new base. But if the constitutional base could be agreed upon the difficulties should not be insurmountable although it seems clear that such changes would have to be approached with caution.

If our analysis is valid there are three main steps required to provide Canada with a second chamber that would become an operational unit of our federal system: 1. the Senate must be reconstructed as a body representative of the governments of the provinces; 2. the constitutional division of powers must be revised in such a manner as to distinguish between matters of purely national concern, matters of purely provincial concern, and matters of national authority which are of significant influence on the provinces; and 3. administrative responsibility must be decentralized in certain areas of national authority in a way that will provide the provincial governments with the ability to make informed contributions to the development and enforcement of national policies.

Even if we were able to develop acceptance of the idea in principle, the problem of how to proceed to implement the proposed changes remains. Ideally, as in the German case, it should be something of a package deal for all the elements are strongly related. But as we found in the constitutional review of 1968-71, it is easier to construct a new constitution than to reconstruct one that is over a hundred years old.

The temptation to approach the whole process by tinkering with the administrative responsibilities first is very strong. Not only does this provide a gradual approach but it avoids the constitutional difficulties with which we are only too familiar. But to do this, desirable as it would be on economic, administrative, and even political grounds, will do very little to accomplish a reformed federalism. Administrative efficiency might be as easily achieved through decentralized administration under federal control.

Much as we may appreciate the merits of gradualness, there does not seem any alternative available except to grasp the nettle firmly and start with the basic question, the reorganization of the second chamber in a manner more truly representative of the regional nature of this country. While this might be accomplished with the help of measures giving provinces some power of appointment over the second-chamber membership, there is little reason to believe that this would result in the increase in provincial responsibility which we regard as the essential ingredient. Today provincial governments attempt to influence national policies by indirect political means without any responsibility for their actions. Only if such responsibility and authority are directly linked will provincial governments properly realize their role in a reformed federation.

The first steps then must be the constitutional change that would alter the present Senate into a second chamber directly representative of provincial governments. The greatest measure of responsibility would undoubtedly be achieved if we followed the German federal system in which the premier of each province would lead a delegation of ministers in the second chamber. Given the heavy reliance on committee work by appointed officials that characterizes the operations of the Bundesrat, plenary sittings can be limited in number and duration, and it might be quite feasible for provincial premiers to serve in this manner. But if this is not practicable a particular cabinet minister could be so designated and could provide the necessary authority and leadership. This might be regarded as an open invitation to establish permanent ministers in residence in Ottawa, but while permanent offices would no doubt be desirable, a permanent minister might too easily lose contact with his colleagues and become an integral part of the Ottawa scene, something the system is designed to avoid.

This first move, however, is of no great value unless the role and purpose of the reformed second chamber is defined. Unless this is done any action to give provincial governments power over national legislation would have dangerous implications. A second chamber of that sort, with the practically unlimited powers of the present Senate, could become seriously disruptive of national policies without providing any acceptable alternatives. Its proper purpose can only be realized if its powers are related to the responsibility it is intended to assume.

In such a reconstructed Senate it would be necessary to redefine the powers and responsibilities of the federal and provincial governments in a way that would make the exercise of the new authority of the second chamber consistent with our perceived needs. Following the German system, we would have to be able to distinguish those legislative powers which can attract a second-chamber veto from those in which the power is merely one of suspension and delay. The problem is not easily settled, for many issues of national importance have regional impact. But, given the will and the experience, should we consider ourselves less capable of gradually developing a solution than has been possible in the German case?

We have placed a good deal of emphasis on the relationship of political and administrative responsibility in the effectiveness of the provincial governments' role in a reformed second chamber. There would be many advantages in having this administrative responsibility established before the constitutional changes were undertaken. It is likely, however, that the incentive of formal change would be required before any extensive transfer would be accepted. There are, however, some obvious areas where earlier moves might be indicated. Perhaps a transfer of federal responsibility to the provinces in such fields as agriculture, fisheries, and environmental protection would provide a guide to future conduct. It is even possible that a transfer of power over natural resources to the government of Canada might work to the public good of the future. Certainly the situation could not be much more ineffective than it now is.

This is all very tentative. We make no pretence of having been able to provide a blueprint for a new institution of Canadian federalism. Exchanging ideas in political organization is useful. Exchanging forms and processes in a different context can be something else again. The many differences between the two countries make the process of adaptation a difficult and uncertain task. Aside from the greater national solidarity of post-war Germany, with fewer divisive influences of geography, language, and culture, there is the predominating fact that the Federal Republic of Germany rose from the ashes of political chaos, and under the sponsorship of the Allied powers it was possible to develop a new system with only limited constraints from the past. We do not downgrade the amazing accomplishments of Adenauer and his colleagues and successors in suggesting that the circumstances were very special and contributed much to the achievement of a modern miracle in political, economic, and social organization.

The same conditions do not exist in Canada. In making the sort of changes we have discussed we would be undertaking some fundamental alterations in an established system which is in fact working, though not as well as we might wish. It is not merely a matter of changing the representation in the Senate. To provide the provinces with some voice in the appointments would be relatively simple (if they could be persuaded to agree among themselves) but it is also likely to be ineffective. What has been put forward here is a suggestion for consideration of a fundamental restructing of the Canadian federal system. This restructuring would provide for a more extensive recognition of the provincial interest in the conduct of national affairs as they affect provincial affairs, but, at the same time, would attach a formal political responsibility which might well contribute to a stronger and less divided nation. There would be wide-ranging effects, and great care would have to be taken to see that in protecting provincial interests the true national interests were not impaired. (Protecting provincial interests and determining the balance of power would be no easy task, especially in reconciling the demands of larger and smaller provinces.) Political alignments would be subject to changing influences. Established bureaucratic procedures and interests would undergo substantial change. It is not a problem that will be solved in a short paper or by the study of one individual.

Regardless of the difficulties it is a possible solution to the present state of conflict which needs detailed examination. It may not work. The provinces may be too difficult to satisfy. The federal government may not want to give up any of its traditional authority. The fragmentation of Canadian provincial politics may make agreement too elusive. But unless we are prepared to examine all avenues of approach the dangers for national survival are very real. The important fact cannot be emphasized too often. It is not the reform of the Senate itself that matters, but rather the contribution of the provinces as responsible partners to the Canadian nation.

NOTES

[1] R. L. Watts, *Second Chambers in Federal Political Systems, The Confederation Challenge*, Toronto, Ontario Advisory Committee on Confederation, 1970, p. 318.

[2] Peyton Lyon, 'A new idea for Senate reform,' *Canadian Commentator*, July-August, 1962.

[3] F. A. Kunz, *The Modern Senate of Canada*, Toronto: University of Toronto Press, 1965, p. 370.

[4] R. A. Mackay, *The Unreformed Senate of Canada*, revised ed.; Toronto: McClelland and Stewart, 1963, p. 177.

[5] Basic Law, Article 72(2) (Official English Translation, 1973).

[6] Ibid., p. 24.

[7] Kunz, *The Modern Senate of Canada*, p. 370.

PART III
INTERGOVERNMENTAL
RELATIONS

13

The Machinery of
Federal-Provincial Relations*

Edgar Gallant

Let me say at the outset—before it becomes obvious—that I have come
to the field of federal-provincial relations only recently. I came to it from
work in other fields including that of international trade relations where
I have had the opportunity to observe intergovernmental consultation in
international organizations.

We are all aware of the growing importance of consultation between
the federal and provincial governments in Canada, in this age of "cooperative federalism," and I should like to begin with an indication of this
growth. Some of you no doubt remember an address given by Dr. K. W.
Taylor at the Ninth Annual Conference of this Institute in 1957 on the
subject of "Coordination in Administration."[1] The list of federal-provincial committees which he appended to his paper contained 64 items. At
the Federal-Provincial Conference of Prime Ministers and Premiers last
July, a calendar of federal-provincial conferences and meetings for 1965
was distributed. There are 125 items in this list. To judge by these comparisons, the number of conferences and committees doubled over a
period of eight years!

This rapid growth, it could be observed, is not out of line with the
striking development of international machinery for intergovernmental
consultation. Since the Second World War we have witnessed the birth
of several new international organizations, and new ones seem to
appear every now and then. If independent countries have found it in
their interest, in this age of growing interdependence, to set up such
elaborate machinery for intergovernmental liaison, should it not be expected that different levels of government within a federal country
would provide machinery for even closer consultation?

Before I attempt to analyse the federal-provincial machinery we
now have, it might be useful to reflect briefly on the need for consultation as it has developed in the past and as it is now evolving.

THE NEED FOR CONSULTATION

In theory there would appear to be two types of federal state: one in
which all fields of responsibility are precisely defined and properly allo-

* From *Canadian Public Administration*, Vol. VII, No. 4, December, 1965, pp. 515-26.
Reprinted by permission.

cated, requiring little machinery for intergovernmental consultation; and one in which many fields of responsibility are shared by two levels of government, requiring much more elaborate machinery for coordination. The Canadian constitution did provide for a fair amount of abutting or overlapping jurisdictions—for example, in the fields of agriculture and immigration. Nevertheless, I would suggest that the Fathers of Confederation intended to establish the first type of federal state. Over the years, however, as Canada evolved into a modern and increasingly complex industrial economy, and as the role of government underwent drastic changes, our federal system evolved into the second type.

In the early days of confederation there was not much need for federal-provincial consultations. At the beginning, relations between the federal government and the provinces were of a formal legal character, with the Secretary of State and the Lieutenant-Governors being the channels of communication. Subsequently there were periods when federal-provincial relations played an important role at the political level, and other periods when they subsided. Since then, increased use of financial power has expanded fields of influence and concern of the federal and the provincial governments. Through the use of such devices as shared-cost programs, and grants and loans to institutions under provincial jurisdiction, the federal government has considerably expanded its field of influence, though not its field of jurisdiction. Parallel to this growing role of both levels of government, and as a consequence of it, there has been an increasing crowding of the tax fields. Obviously, given such a large scale of government activity, together with this high degree of interaction between levels of government, effective intergovernmental consultation has become a basic requirement.

It is in matters relating to the overall management of the economic affairs of the country that this requirement is becoming, in my opinion, particularly pronounced. Like other modern industrial countries, Canada seems to be paying increasing attention to the use of government economic policies for the achievement of basic social and economic objectives. While, broadly speaking, the citizens of a country will tend to look to their national governments for leadership in reaching such goals, we have to recognize that in Canada all levels of government are active in matters having definite implications for the economy as a whole. Let me try to illustrate this with a few obvious examples.

Consider first the objective of economic growth. It goes without saying that the behaviour of the public sector as a whole has a definite impact on the growth of the national economy. This applies not just to the sheer magnitude of government activity—and total government expenditure amounted to 31 per cent of the G.N.P. in 1964—but also to the priorities given to the different functions of government, the timing of public expenditure, and the means by which the funds are raised. In all of these decisions, governments may stimulate or retard growth.

When one considers that the provincial-municipal governments spent $8.1 billion in 1964, compared to $6.5 billion spent at the federal level (excluding intergovernmental transfers), and that provincial-municipal expenditures have grown by over 200 per cent in the last ten years compared to 56 per cent for federal expenditures, it becomes more than obvious that the management of government financial transactions to maximize economic growth is a matter of concern for all levels of government in Canada. We can also illustrate this point by passing from the aggregate activity to individual government measures, particularly those specific programs relating to economic growth, in which both levels of government are active. Think, for instance, of the many programs relating to the provision of trained manpower—the technical and vocational training programs, the financing of institutes of technical training and higher learning, the rehabilitation of disabled persons, and so on. Think, also, of the programs for development of primary resources—the dual roles in agriculture and fisheries, ARDA, PFRA, roads to resources, etc. One could mention also many undertakings involving both levels of jurisdiction in such important fields as energy, transportation, communication, and industrial development.

Now let us consider some further illustrations by referring to economic stabilization. Generally speaking, governments can alleviate the effects of short-term fluctuations in the economy by building automatic stabilizers into the fiscal system or by making discretionary fiscal changes. An important automatic stabilizer is, of course, the personal income tax with its basic exemptions and progressive rates. We are all aware of the recent developments in the sharing of this revenue source, and the growing importance of the provincial shares. On the expenditure side of the budget, we have an example of automatic stabilizers in unemployment insurance and other programs of assistance to the unemployed—the one involving the federal government, and the others involving the provincial and federal governments.

Turning to the ability of federal and provincial governments to implement discretionary stabilization policies, as opposed to automatic ones, an examination of the 1964 National Accounts shows that provincial and municipal governments spent over $5.6 billion on goods and services in that year while the federal government spent about $3.0 billion. One could also note that expenditures of a capital nature, which are generally more susceptible to changes in timing, are estimated to be about five times as great at the provincial-municipal level as at the federal level. Clearly, there is more potential for implementing discretionary stabilization policies through the timing of purchases in the provincial-municipal sphere than in the federal.

I have mentioned a few examples to establish the point that the two levels of government are both intimately involved in many matters which bear heavily on economic policy. This is just one, although a very important one, of several areas of joint federal-provincial concern, but it serves to illustrate, I think, the increasing need for consultation which our machinery will have to meet.

THE MACHINERY FOR
FEDERAL-PROVINCIAL RELATIONS

I now move back to the machinery. I mentioned previously that there are now some 125 committees and conferences. These do not, of course, encompass all federal-provincial consultations. There are many informal or *ad hoc* meetings to deal with particular problems. Also, and this is perhaps even more significant, individual contacts between officials and between ministers, by letter, telephone, or visits, appear to be increasing. Therefore, when one speaks of the machinery for federal-provincial relations, one has in mind much more than just the formally constituted bodies with a more or less continuing role in facilitating federal-provincial consultations and coordination. In this paper, however, I intend to analyse mainly this ensemble of federal-provincial committees.

The first point that strikes me about this machinery is a notable difference between it and that which exists for intergovernmental liaison at the international level. At the international level, we have, as I said earlier, a vast structure of international organizations and specialized agencies, conferences and committees, covering a very broad range, if not all areas of governmental activity. In addition, we have a large network of diplomatic sessions which, it should be noted, was established well before the rapid growth of specialized agencies and specialized missions.

In our federal-provincial relations, our machinery has evolved in a reverse order. We have first developed numerous committees and conferences at a specialist level. We have not had a comparable network of intelligence concerned with the total picture of intergovernmental relations. While Canada has over 400 professionals engaged in international relations, we still have very few engaged full-time in a professional way in federal-provincial relations, and our machinery makes relatively little provision to ensure continuous liaison with respect to the over-view of matters which concern both the federal and provincial governments.

The central body of our federal-provincial machinery is the Plenary Conference of Premiers and Prime Ministers. It seems to me to have been concerned more with specific policy issues than with the continuous over-view of federal-provincial matters. It began meeting sporadically in the early years of Confederation, but only in recent years has it taken on the role of a more continuing body for federal-provincial consultations. It now meets at least annually.

The rest of the machinery reflects the concentration on special program areas that I mentioned. As would be expected, this machinery
tended to develop first where the constitution provides specifically for
concurrent roles, notably in the agricultural sector. Then, as the country
matured and the activities of government increased, we witnessed a
growing interdependence between the programs of the federal and provincial spheres. Associated with this was the growth of shared-cost programs and the appearance of new consultative machinery to facilitate
coordination in the areas where federal and provincial activities were
coming together. This machinery sometimes developed at the ministerial level, and sometimes it involved deputy ministers or other officials. Several different committees, at different levels, have evolved
within particular fields to meet specific needs.

This process has taken us to the point where in 1965 there are some
125 committees and conferences meeting on federal-provincial matters.
They have taken so many different forms that a simple, concise description of the machinery becomes difficult. However, I think it will contribute to our understanding of the subject if I attempt a brief description.
Before I do, I should make the point that federal-provincial machinery
by no means included every body which exists to facilitate coordination
of government activity in Canada. There is also a substantial body of
interprovincial machinery committees and conferences which bring provincial representatives together to deal with matters of purely provincial
concern. And there are the intragovernmental machinery devices which
operate within one government for the purpose of dealing with federal-
provincial matters. They include cabinet committees, interdepartmental
committees of officials, and specialist federal-provincial relations divisions. The latter exist in the federal government, and in some if not all of
the provinces. They aid in developing the positions which are taken at
conferences, and in facilitating communication between conferences.

Taking all of these together, we have a large package of committees;
and there are those who still disparage the committee as a device. They
belong to the school of thought which defines a committee as "a collection of people who individually believe that something must be done
and who collectively decide that nothing can be done," or which says of
a committee's labours, "Never have so many spent so much time to
accomplish so little."

THE FEDERAL-PROVINCIAL
CONFERENCES AND COMMITTEES

When one is faced with the task of describing a collection of many entities, one seeks first a convenient system for classifying them. I see several different possible classifications for these committees and conferences: the broad structure, the participants, the subject matter, and the

broad purpose or type of consultation. I think it could be illuminating to give a little attention to each of these possibilities.

1. The Broad Structure

Under the heading of what I call, for lack of a better word, the broad structure, I would identify seven groupings.

a. Federal-provincial committees as such.

These, I think, are what we would normally think of first when considering the subject of federal-provincial machinery. I consider them to be federal-provincial bodies in the truest sense of the word. They are composed of ministers or officials from the federal and provincial governments, who come together as official representatives of their governments to work on matters of mutual concern. Note first that they are definitely committees of government. Note next that they are made up by the participation of individual governments, each in its own right. The federal government by virtue of its central position usually provides the chairman and secretarial services. I would place most of the committees—approximately 100, including sub-committees—in this category, and I would offer, as examples, the Plenary Conference of Prime Ministers and Premiers, the Conference of the Ministers of Welfare, the Continuing Committee on Economic and Fiscal Matters, and the meeting of Federal and Provincial Directors of Vocational Education.

I should note, also, that committees may be national in scope, involving all provinces, such as the examples I have given, or they may be regional in nature, with representation from only a few provinces plus the federal government. Of the 100 noted above, about 30 could be considered to be regional in nature. The Atlantic Fisheries Committee is one example.

These federal-provincial committees are established with varying degrees of formality. Some annual meetings are called as a matter of tradition, some are handled more casually, being called together as circumstances dictate.

b. Federal advisory councils.

A compilation of federal-provincial committees and conferences has to include certain councils which are appointed under federal statute or order-in-council to act as advisory bodies to federal ministers. As such, they would not appear to belong in a classification of federal-provincial bodies. However, their composition, with representation from all provincial governments, is such, that they do, in effect, function as federal-provincial committees to a large extent. The process is roughly as follows. The council deliberates on a matter with the benefit of the provincial points of view. When it decides to recommend something to its ministers, this means that its provincial members are in agreement or go along with the decision and will be ready to advocate acceptance in their provinces. If the minister accepts the advice of his council and gains the approval of the federal government, he can then make a proposal to the provinces with reasonable prospects for ready acceptance. In effect, then, this body has been instrumental in facilitating the development of federal-provincial policy.

Examples of these advisory councils include the Dominion Council of Health, the National Advisory Council on Rehabilitation of Disabled Persons, the Technical and Vocational Training Council, and the National Council of Welfare.

These councils all have members not only from the governments, but from outside organizations, as well. The wide representation means they tend to become quite large, and they look as if they could be somewhat cumbersome to handle. It is interesting to speculate on the reasons for their formation. Are they needed primarily as a source of ideas, or as a public relations device to satisfy all interest groups by giving them a voice? Or are they meant to serve primarily as a device for federal-provincial consultation, but with these other elements thrown in for good measure? Whatever the answer, it seems clear that their federal-provincial role has been substantial.

c. Quasi-independent associations.

There are certain bodies which are made up wholly, or almost wholly, of ministers or civil servants, and which are supported by government, but which are not federal-provincial committees in the usual sense of the term. They are constituted as associations and function to some extent as professional organizations or special interest groups. Their stimulus comes more from within themselves than from the governments, and the participants function more as association members than as representatives from governments. And yet, because they do bring together people in a particular field from all governments, they serve to some extent as a vehicle for federal-provincial consultation and coordination.

Examples of bodies I would place in this category include the Canadian Council of Resource Ministers, which has its own letters patent and its own staff, the Canadian Association of Administrators of Labour Legislation, and the Association of Canadian Fire Marshals.

d. Interprovincial conferences.

A relatively new but in my view very significant development in intergovernmental liaison in Canada is the growth of the interprovincial machinery for consultation. One compilation, which may be incomplete, indicates that there are now about 60 formally constituted interprovincial bodies, some of which could be defined as quasi-independent or independent associations. They convene for the purpose of discussing matters of interest primarily to the provinces, or perhaps for agreeing on a joint approach to the federal government, and the provinces usually take turns acting as host to them. These conferences and committees at ministerial and official levels have a definite impact on federal-provincial relations. Indeed, they can be regarded as essential for the effective functioning of the country. I mention them here in this classification of federal-provincial devices because some do in fact assume a considerable federal-provincial role.

The Provincial Ministers of Mines Conference is an interesting example. One of the things the provincial ministers do at these conferences is to agree on the substance of a brief to be submitted to the federal government. However, the federal minister or his representatives are present as observers so that, when the provincial ministers make their formal presentation a few months later, the federal minister has had time to consider their conclusions and is in a position to discuss them.

Other examples in this category include the Conference of Provincial Premiers, which was held in Winnipeg last year, the Trade and Industry Council, and the Conference of Provincial Deputy Ministers of Public Works. (I think I should like to be invited as an "observer" to the Motion Picture Censor's Association Conference—at least I should if they compare cuttings.)

e. Subcommittees.

Perhaps I can complicate the picture somewhat now by noting that there are also subcommittees. Committees seem to have two tendencies which are sometimes thought to be unfortunate: they tend to live forever, and they tend to produce offspring. The former possibily suggests something angelic about their nature; the latter, however, might be taken to invite a description of their activities which is really too uncharitable to be used here.

There are about 30 committees in my list which I would call subcommittees because they seem to have a direct reporting relationship to some other committee. They are usually at a technical level, with terms of reference requiring them to give attention to a specific problem area. The Dominion Council of Health has several such committees reporting to it, for example. Sometimes a description of the organization becomes difficult. For example, I would describe the Committee on Technical and Vocational Training as a federal-provincial committee since it works to achieve coordination of technical and vocational training programmes at an administrative level. However, it is considered to be subordinate to the Technical and Vocational Training Council, a federal advisory body.

f. Provincial advisory committees.

At the risk of extending this list excessively, I should note that in individual provinces there are some provincial committees with federal representation created to advise on matters relating to federal-provincial programs. They may be formed and chaired by provincial authorities but can be initiated on the basis of a federal proposal. Examples are the Coordinating Committees on Indian Affairs and the ARDA Joint Advisory Committees.

g. Non-government associations.

There are some organizations which are quite independent of government, unlike the quasi-independent associations noted earlier, but which play an important role in federal-provincial relations nevertheless. Some associations have a substantial number of members representing governments across the country and are interested in subjects relating directly to some area of government activity. When the membership comes together to discuss its area of interest, it is inevitable that ideas will be born, thinking influenced, and policy eventually affected. The Canadian Good Roads Association is a notable example of this type of organization. Perhaps I might be so bold as to suggest that the Institute of Public Administration is another.

I have attempted so far to describe the federal-provincial machinery under a classification I have called "the broad structure." This became complicated enough, but I am now going to compound the problem by introducing a number of other possible classifications. I shall deal with them more briefly, however.

2. The Participants

The first of these I call "the participants." One could classify the federal-provincial meetings by the people who attend them. When I group them by hierarchical levels, I come up with the following count (excluding non-government associations):

Level	No. of 1965 Conferences and Committees
Prime Ministers and Premiers	2
Ministers	13
Deputy Ministers	14
Directors	27
Professional and Technical	65

I should explain that this was a rough classification involving arbitrary judgments about the level of meetings, and that the picture is frequently not clearly defined. Deputy Ministers may attend meetings which are primarily technical in nature, and so on.

I might also note that when Dr. K. W. Taylor did this exercise in 1957 he counted 5 conferences at the Ministers level, 13 at the Deputy Ministers level, 18 at the Directors level, and 28 professional or technical meetings. He, also, was modest about the absolute validity of his figures.[2]

This classification does not match up in any way with the broad structural classes previously defined. To take the ministerial conferences only, some of them could be defined as federal-provincial committees as such, while some are interprovincial, and at least one, the Resource Ministers Council, I have described as a quasi-independent association. Ministers may also meet at non-government organizations such as the Canadian Good Roads Association. Technically, it would be possible for provincial ministers to appear on some of the federal advisory councils, since the composition of some councils includes representation from some organizations to which provincial ministers belong.

3. The Subject Matter

Another obvious classification which may be used is based on the subject matter discussed by the committee. In the lists of conferences and meetings I have referred to, the committees are grouped under headings of Agriculture, Finance, Health and Welfare, and so on. As one would expect, the largest number of committees occurs in those fields where the activities of both levels of government overlap the most. For example, in the 1965 calendar of meetings the two areas with the most committees listed are Health and Welfare with 21 and Agriculture with 16.

It is of interest to note that there is a wide variety in the character of the committees which have developed for each class of subject matter. Some sectors have ministerial conferences, others do not. Some have advisory councils, others do not. Some have extensive network of technical sub-committees, while others do not.

4. The Broad Purpose or Type of Consultations

One might also attempt to group the committees according to broad categories of purpose. Some, such as the Plenary Federal-Provincial Conference, have very broad terms of reference. Others obviously have a restricted field of activity, as, for example, the National Potato Breeding Committee. Some have elaborately spelled-out terms of reference, perhaps as a part of a formal constitution, requiring them to work toward uniformity of legislation across Canada in their field, or toward objectives of comparable significance. Others have no terms of reference other than to provide an opportunity for an exchange of views on matters of mutual interest. Some are created to advise a minister, others to advise other committees, and so on.

One might define a range of the different kind of purposes which have to be served by intergovernmental consultation in Canada. I should like to suggest the following spectrum of purposes:

a. *Public relations.*

I use the term "public relations" here, even though the public is not involved, to designate the process of getting to know one's counterparts in other governments, to the extent that a sense of *rapport* and conviviality is established. This presumably helps to oil the channels for smoother intergovernmental consultations in future.

b. *Professionalization.*

There are some areas of specialized activity which lie almost entirely within the governments, and the specialists involved tend to want to express themselves as a professional group. A federal-provincial meeting sometimes serves as the vehicle for such expression. This type of gathering does much to advance an area of specialization through the exchange of ideas, and it also permits the development of a brotherly feeling of togetherness.

c. *Advancement of knowledge.*

The exchange of information is a frequent purpose behind the function of a committee. Also, some federal-provincial technical committees are created specifically to inquire into a problem area to learn more about it or to encourage research for this purpose. I believe these committees have convincingly demonstrated the truth in the old adage that eleven heads are better than one.

d. *Harmonization.*

I use this word to describe the process by which purposes are explained, suspicions are assuaged, and conflicts are removed.

e. *Coordination.*

This is a step farther than harmonization. It implies a conscious effort to work together toward some mutually acceptable goal. In our more sceptical moments, we might describe it as the process by which activities which would otherwise be completely unintelligible become merely muddled.

f. Persuasion.

This type of consultation is getting closer to the policy level. Governments may use a committee to attempt to influence the actions of others in directions deemed to be desirable.

g. Negotiation and decision making.

At this end of the spectrum is the consultation which results in a decision being reached either through agreement or through compromise. This may sound impressive. Sometimes, however, the decision may be to refer the matter to another committee.

The wide diversity in the committees' terms of reference and the problem in some cases of determining what the terms of reference are, if there are any, would make it a difficult exercise to attempt to assign present committees to these categories. For that matter, many of the committees probably work at some or even most of these objectives at some time or another. However, one might speculate that a more consistent committee structure could be established if it were formed on the basis of an accepted definition of purposes.

CONCLUDING OBSERVATIONS

I hope that the approach I have taken of outlining a number of possible classifications of the federal-provincial committees will have left a reasonable overall impression of the formally established machinery which exists. By way of conclusion I would like to make a few observations on the relationship between the *need* for consultation between the provinces and the federal government—about which I spoke earlier—and the *machinery that exists* for this consultation. Is the present machinery adequate to meet present and future needs, and how might it be improved?

I think one could say, first of all, that machinery exists in most of the individual program areas where both levels of governments are active. I will go even further and say that in most if not in each of these individual program areas consultation seems to have been reasonably effective. Certainly if these consultations have had anything to do with the rapid growth in shared-cost programs, I am impressed with their success.

I would say secondly, however, that we have to take a close look at our provision for coordination of this machinery. When a complexity of devices exists to permit consultation on a multitude of intergovernmental activities, we run the risk, unless there is adequate provision for coordination, of having a situation in which the right hand does not know what the left hand is doing. More than once I have seen this happen in international organizations. It is not inconceivable to me that it could happen in federal-provincial relations and that the position taken by the representative of one government at one federal-provincial meeting may not be wholly consistent with the position taken by another representative of the same government on a related question at another meeting.

Another and related observation that could be made on the relationship between the need and the machinery for consultation has to do with the basic economic objectives I have referred to earlier in this paper. The various federal, provincial and joint programmes may be proceeding satisfactorily, taken individually, but how do we assess their combined effect on the economy, or determine which area should receive emphasis relative to another at a particular time? Similarly, what machinery exists to facilitate consultation and coordination with regard to other areas of fiscal and economic management? I note that the federal and provincial ministers of finance and provincial treasurers held a pre-budget meeting for the first time last December. If this new ministerial committee holds annual meetings, as I hope it will, it could well develop into a body which meets this need, at least in part.

Finally, I would like to raise a question concerning the direction in which the process of federal-provincial relations is evolving. At the start we relied largely on the connections built up within the political parties representing Canadians in the House of Commons and in the provincial legislative assemblies. This machinery proved to be not entirely adequate: it was not always reliable, it was often not available when needed, and governments could not hold it responsible. Over the years we developed a considerable number of committees and other devices for consultation. The majority of these provide for contacts among specialists in a wide range of specific areas of government activity. We appear to see now the need for more frequent contacts among those who see the over-all picture of federal-provincial relations. The establishment of units responsible for federal-provincial relations in a broad way in some provinces and within the federal government indicates that our governments are responding to this need. The question which I would like to raise is this: where does this evolutionary process lead us? How far are we going to go in providing machinery for improving intelligence and coordination in Canadian federal-provincial relations?

NOTES

[1] *Proceedings of the Sixth Annual Conference of the Institute of Public Administration of Canada,* Toronto, 1954, p. 253.

[2] *Ibid.,* p. 255.

14

Canadian Conference Activity 1975: Alberta Participation*

R. D. Olling

Attempts have been made on a number of occasions to document and describe the evolving system of intergovernmental contact as it exists in Canada. Beginning with the K. W. Taylor's address to the Ninth Annual Conference of the Institute of Public Administration in 1957[1] and continuing in the works of Edgar Gallant,[2] Donald Smiley,[3] Richard Simeon,[4] and Gerard Veilleux[5] considerable effort has been devoted to explaining when governments meet and what kind of conventions and procedures govern such gatherings. The constitutional review process of 1968-71, itself, examined the system of intergovernmental contact with the view of improving both coordination and consultation between the federal government and the ten provinces.

More recently, however, attention has shifted to the apparent proliferation of meetings and conferences. Indeed, while it remains a common theme of public comment that intergovernmental relations should be more constant and intimate in order to remove the disagreements that tend to be a feature of Canadian national life, one senior public servant has wryly observed that "a Canadian Parkinson could probably demonstrate that the number of federal-provincial disputes in any one year varies in direct proportion to the number of federal-provincial meetings multiplied by the cube of the number of federal-provincial coordinating agencies in the respective governments."[6] Though somewhat of an overstatement, such an observation nevertheless serves to focus upon the very nature of intergovernmental conference activity.

How often do governments make use of the formal intergovernmental meeting and conference in the Canadian federal system? What are the characteristics of such gatherings? No definitive answer can be provided to these questions without an exhaustive, department-by-department inventory of conference activity involving both the federal and all provincial governments. As yet, no such inventory has been completed. Consequently, it would appear appropriate to add to our knowledge through use of existing data as they relate to individual governments.

The following is a description of conference activity during the year 1975 in which the *Province of Alberta* was a participant. Based upon infor-

---

* Reprinted by permission.

mation supplied by the province's Department of Federal and Inter-governmental Affairs, this documentation profiles the interaction between one provincial government, the federal government, and other provincial governments.

FEDERAL-PROVINCIAL ACTIVITY

During the 1975 calendar year, 337 federal-provincial meetings and conferences were held in which an Alberta delegation was in attendance.

For descriptive purposes these gatherings may be divided into three basic categories: *bilateral* (i.e., meetings between representatives of the Province of Alberta and the federal government); *regional* (i.e., the meeting of representatives from all "western" or "prairie" provinces in conjunction with the federal government); and *multilateral* (i.e., meetings of representatives of the Province of Alberta, all other provinces, and the federal government). On the basis of this classification, seventy-nine bilateral, eighteen regional, and 240 multilateral meetings and conferences may be found to have taken place in 1975.

With regard to the level of government representation at these meetings, five standard ranks are often identified in governmental service. These include: *first ministerial* (involving Premiers and First Ministers); *ministerial* (involving ministers of the Crown); *deputy ministerial;* *assistant deputy ministerial;* and *officials* (involving "directors," "senior officers", and all other officials ranked below assistant deputy minister). Alberta conference activity ranges through four first ministerial, seventy-six ministerial, seventy-three deputy ministerial, forty assistant deputy ministerial, and 144 officials' gatherings.

Multilateral meetings at the level of First Minister include an Energy Conference in April 1975, and a private, informal meeting concerning implementation of the anti-inflation program held in October 1975 at the residence of the Prime Minister. Two bilateral meetings, one involving Premier Lougheed and Prime Minister Trudeau, and another involving Premier Davis of Ontario, were held to discuss energy related issues.

Below the first ministerial level exists a vast and complex network of ministerial and administrative meetings dealing with more specifically defined, functional areas of government activity. Summarized in Tables II and III, these meetings have been divided into eighteen separate categories of subject-matter in which federal and provincial interaction has become necessary. These include the areas of health and welfare, finance, manpower and labour, industrial development, and native affairs.

Ministerial conferences vary considerably in both organization and intent. Annual meetings, for example, were convened in numerous

TABLE I

Frequency of Federal-Provincial Meetings and Conferences According to Category and Level of Representation—Alberta Participation, 1975

	Bilateral	Regional	Multilateral	Total
First Ministerial	2	—	2	4
Ministerial	18	3	55	76
Deputy Ministerial	7	4	62	73
Asst. Deputy Ministerial	7	4	29	40
Officials	45	7	92	144
TOTAL	79	18	240	337

TABLE II

Frequency of Federal-Provincial Meetings and Conferences According to Category and Area of Government Activity—Alberta Participation, 1975

	Bilateral	Regional	Multilateral	Total
General Government	5	—	5	10
Finances	—	—	18	18
Agriculture	1	—	17	18
Transportation	5	5	2	12
Education	—	—	3	3
Energy and Resources	9	—	12	21
Environment	9	6	11	26
Manpower-Labour	5	—	15	20
Statistics	1	—	35	36
Welfare	—	—	21	21
Health	1	1	29	31
Industry and Trade	10	2	15	27
Urban Affairs	21	1	16	38
Justice and Laws	1	1	17	19
Consumer Affairs	1	—	8	9
Communications	1	1	3	5
Native Affairs	7	—	3	10
Miscellaneous	2	1	10	13
TOTAL	79	18	240	337

TABLE III

**Frequency of Federal-Provincial
Meetings and Conferences
According to Level of Representation and Area
of Government Activity—Alberta Participation, 1975**

	First Ministerial	Ministerial	DM	ADM	Officials	Total
General Government	—	1	6	—	3	10
Finances	1	3	7	1	6	18
Agriculture	—	7	5	4	2	18
Transportation	—	5	2	—	5	12
Education	—	1	1	—	1	3
Energy and Resources	3	6	8	2	2	21
Environment	—	3	5	4	14	26
Manpower-Labour	—	6	5	—	9	20
Statistics	—	2	1	3	30	36
Welfare	—	4	5	8	4	21
Health	—	2	10	4	15	31
Industry and Trade	—	3	6	6	12	27
Urban Affairs	—	7	1	4	26	38
Justice and Laws	—	13	2	2	2	19
Consumer Affairs	—	2	3	1	3	9
Communications	—	3	—	—	2	5
Native Affairs	—	5	—	1	4	10
Miscellaneous	—	3	5	1	4	13
TOTAL	4	76	73	40	144	337

areas of government jurisdiction throughout 1975. In the case of the Annual Meeting of Ministers of Finance and Provincial Treasurers, an agenda calling for discussion of Canada's general economic and financial climate was altered so as to allow the beginning of negotiations with respect to a new fiscal arrangements act and the conclusion of talks related to provincial participation in the federal government's anti-inflation program. Agriculture ministers sought to utilize the occasion of their yearly meeting in order to publicize various programs available for their clientele group and to educate the public on projected forecasts for the upcoming crop year. The Canadian Council of Resource and Environment Ministers (C.C.R.E.M.) met with the purpose of coordinating federal and provincial research activities in the fields of environment protection and water and land management. This latter body remains somewhat unique in that it is served by its own secretariat on a permanent basis.[7]

Ad hoc meetings and conferences also have taken place, from time to time, between almost all members of the Alberta cabinet and their federal and provincial counterparts. Usually convened on the initiative of the federal government, such gatherings provide a basis for the discussion of extraordinary issues in which both levels of government identify an interest. Thus, many specific ministerial meetings were held in order to search for agreement on both long and short-term policy questions touching upon federal-provincial relations. These resulted from a recognition of the fact that both a particular problem and its apparent solution may transcend several governmental jurisdictions and, consequently, require a sharing of expertise and resources. Meetings of the Alberta Tri-Partite Committee on Native Affairs, the Federal-Provincial Committee on Western Transportation (F/P COWT), and the Federal-Provincial Conference of Ministers Responsible for Human Rights illustrate several instances in which intergovernmental consultation and coordination was carried out in such ministerial forums.

Whereas ministerial meetings often deal with more general policy questions, the specialization of tasks characterize formal governmental interaction at the administrative level. For example, many administrative meetings perform work in preparation for, and upon the instructions of ministerial conferences. Thus it fell to the 57th meeting of the Continuing Committee of Officials on Fiscal and Economic Matters to prepare for the proposed December meeting of Ministers of Finance and Provincial Treasurers. Similar groupings of deputy ministers, serving all eighteen areas of government activity, fulfill clearly identifiable support functions. The development of alternate policy options, formulation of agendas and communiques, and discussion in detail of proposed federal-provincial agreements emerge as the most prominent of these activities.

Assistant deputy ministers are regularly called upon to participate in various federal-provincial "task forces" and "working groups". Notable in this regard is the Federal-Provincial Working Party on Income Maintenance. Formed in 1973, this body convenes at least four times per year with the purpose of studying and discussing proposals for a new Social Services Act. Other research-oriented groups in the areas of transportation and urban affairs met with similar frequency during 1975.

Federal-Provincial contact of an on-going nature is finally provided in the multitude of meetings and conferences taking place as part of "normal" government business between "directors", "senior officers", and those more generally termed "officials". As reflected in the large number of meetings in the areas of health, manpower-labour and industry, such interaction at the officials level often focusses upon programs involving federal conditional grants. The Canada-Alberta General Development Committee, for example, is called into session on a monthly basis in order to deal with the implementation, supervision and assessment of programs offered by the federal government's Department of Regional Economic Expansion. At other times, it is the purpose of officials' meetings to facilitate the communication of information of a technical nature. At least two-thirds of these meetings presently involve annual or biannual discussions of technological and scientific advancements with regard to specialized aspects of health care, disease control, environmental protection, water and wildlife management, and statistical tabulation.[8] The relatively large number of federal-provincial contacts in the area of statistics further reflects the continuing efforts of governments to devise and implement an orderly system of metric conversion across Canada.

INTERPROVINCIAL ACTIVITY

Though an increasingly important area of governmental involvement in the 1970s,[9] interprovincial meetings and conferences have not reached the proportions of federal-provincial conferences. Table IV shows only sixty instances of formal governmental interaction between Alberta and its provincial counterparts in 1975.

Viewed by category, these sixty interprovincial meetings and conferences consisted of six bilateral, ten regional, and forty-four multilateral contacts. In this instance, regional contacts involve meetings between representatives of the Province of Alberta and the other "western" or "prairie" provinces.

Extended to level of representation, Alberta conference activity ranges through one first ministerial, twenty-two ministerial, nine deputy ministerial, three assistant deputy ministerial, and twenty-five officials gatherings.

The Annual Premiers Conference remains the capstone of these interprovincial contacts. Assembling for the 16th occasion during August, 1975 in St. John's, Newfoundland, this body provided a forum for discussion of matters such as: the state of the economy, foreign ownership of land, the Foreign Investment Review Act, and the domestic pricing of petroleum products. Of particular importance at this session was a reso-

TABLE IV

Frequency of Interprovincial Meetings and Conferences According to Category and Level of Representation—Alberta Participation, 1975

	Bilateral	Regional	Multilateral	Total
First Ministerial	—	—	1	1
Ministerial	2	5	15	22
Deputy Ministerial	1	—	8	9
Asst. Dep. Ministerial	—	—	3	3
Officials	3	5	17	25
TOTAL	6	10	44	60

TABLE V

Frequency of Interprovincial Meetings and Conferences According to Category and Area of Government Activity—Alberta Participation, 1975

	Bilateral	Regional	Multilateral	Total
General Government	3	—	1	4
Finances	—	—	—	—
Agriculture	—	2	—	2
Transportation	—	3	5	8
Education	—	1	8	9
Energy and Resources	2	—	5	7
Environment	—	—	1	1
Manpower-Labour	—	—	4	4
Statistics	—	—	2	2
Welfare	—	—	—	—
Health	—	1	3	4
Industry and Trade	—	2	2	4
Urban Affairs	—	—	4	4
Justice and Laws	1	—	2	3
Consumer Affairs	—	—	—	—
Communications	—	1	3	4
Native Affairs	—	—	—	—
Miscellaneous	—	—	4	4
TOTAL	6	10	44	60

TABLE VI

Frequency of Interprovincial Meetings and Conferences According to Level of Representation and Area of Government Activity—Alberta Participation, 1975

	First Ministerial	Ministerial	DM	ADM	Officials	Total
General Government	1	—	1	—	2	4
Finances	—	—	—	—	—	—
Agriculture	—	—	—	—	2	2
Transportation	—	5	1	—	2	8
Education	—	6	1	—	2	9
Energy and Resources	—	3	3	—	1	7
Environment	—	1	—	—	—	1
Manpower-Labour	—	—	1	1	2	4
Statistics	—	—	—	—	2	2
Welfare	—	—	—	—	—	—
Health	—	2	—	2	—	4
Industry and Trade	—	—	—	—	4	4
Urban Affairs	—	2	2	—	—	4
Justice and Laws	—	2	—	—	1	3
Consumer Affairs	—	—	—	—	—	—
Communications	—	—	—	—	4	4
Native Affairs	—	—	—	—	—	—
Miscellaneous	—	1	—	—	3	4
TOTAL	1	22	9	3	25	60

lution criticizing the federal government's decision to establish "unilaterally" expenditure limits on Medicare programs. In addition the Premiers agreed to study the question of patriation of the Constitution and to prepare a report for their next meeting.

Unlike previous years, no first ministerial contacts of a regional nature may be found among the western provinces.[10] However, rather than indicating a general decline in the Western Premiers Conference as an instrument of regional consultation and coordination, this situation, instead, was more a result of certain organizational difficulties encountered because of a general election and change of government within the Province of British Columbia. In spite of such problems, Tables V and VI reveal continued regional interaction in those areas of government activity traditionally considered of economic and political interest to the western provinces. Agriculture, transportation and industrial development emerge as issues in which representatives of Alberta assumed positions of particular prominence.

Outside of the western region, it is the areas of energy and resources, communications, and education which provide evidence of significant concentrations of interprovincial meetings and conferences involving all ten provincial governments. The high number of intergovernmental contacts in the areas of energy and communications is a reflection of governing provincial concern. Under the auspices of the Council of Ministers of Education of Canada (C.M.E.C.) regular dialogue is conducted with the object of coordinating educational activities at the interprovincial, federal-provincial, and international levels.[11] Presently sub-committees of C.M.E.C. convene on a continuing basis in order to facilitate the exchange of information concerning such matters as school curriculums, student bursaries, the standardization of school credits, the financing of post-secondary education and the promotion of French language teaching. Similar to the Canadian Council of Resource and Environment Ministers, this body is served by a small support staff responsible to a committee of ministers and an advisory committee of deputy ministers of Education.

CONCLUSION

The foregoing survey of conference activity involving the Province of Alberta indicates to a very great extent the importance of extra-constitutional processes in the Canadian federal system. In a period when it is again fashionable for both academics and political leaders to talk of the necessity of constitutional change, the continuing use of federal instrumentalities cannot be overlooked. Indeed, it is possible to state that the successful functioning of any federal system, in which the division of power and responsibility is subject to on-going change, imprecise definition or political stress, is likely to depend upon the ability of political representatives to maintain a working consensus.

The development of a highly complex system of intergovernmental contact reveals a distinctly Canadian response to this problem of system maintenance. Fostering intergovernmental co-operation, consultation and co-ordination, federal-provincial and interprovincial meetings and conferences now constitute an integral part of Canadian federalism with respect to policy development. These meetings provide a forum where ideas can be expressed and exchanged, where positions can be presented and problems recognized and perhaps resolved.

Most notable among recent trends in federal-provincial relations has been the increase in intergovernmental contacts at all levels and in all categories. Whereas only 182 federal-provincial contacts were recorded by Alberta's Department of Federal and Intergovernmental Affairs during the 1974 calendar year,[12] 337 meetings and conferences characterized a similar period in 1975. Less growth may be found in interprovincial meetings, their total rising from fifty-four in 1974[13] to sixty meetings in 1975.

Several factors may be suggested as leading to a sudden growth in federal-provincial contacts. Without doubt, this pattern is a reflection of the expanding range of problems confronting federal and provincial governments. While it is possible in some areas of government activity to draw clear and distinct lines between federal and provincial responsibilities, in many other areas such attempts have proven neither practical nor desirable. Independent action at one level of government often has an important influence and impact on other. Thus if federal and provincial policies in areas of mutual concern (e.g. energy pricing and supply, health, welfare, or the economy) are to be in harmony, more institutionalized interaction becomes necessary.

The question of whether the rapid growth in intergovernmental meetings and conferences ultimately results in more or less tension and conflict within the Canadian federal system will only be resolved through the study of particular meetings, their participants, their results and outcomes over a specific time period.

NOTES

[1] K. W. Taylor, "Coordination in Administration," in J. E. Hodgetts and D. C. Corbett (eds.), *Canadian Public Administration: A Book of Readings* (Toronto: MacMillan, 1960), pp. 145-164.

[2] Edgar Gallant, "The Machinery of Federal-Provincial Relations," Chapter 13 in this book.

[3] Donald V. Smiley, *Canada in Question: Federalism in the Seventies* (Toronto: McGraw-Hill Ryerson, 1972).

[4] Richard Simeon, *Federal-Provincial Diplomacy: The Making of Recent Policy in Canada* (Toronto: University of Toronto Press, 1972).

[5] Gerard Veilleux, *Les Relations Intergouvernementales au Canada, 1867-1967: Les Mechanisms de Cooperation* (Montréal: Les Presses de l'Universite du Quebec, 1971).

[6] Gordon Robertson, "The Changing Role of the Privy Council Office," in *Canadian Public Administration,* Volume XIV, 1971, pp. 496-497.

[7] Administrative, recording, translation and secretarial services are provided for many other conferences on a priority basis by the Canadian Intergovernmental Conference Secretariat (C.I.C.S.).

[8] Often it is federal advisory committees which provide the vehicle for intergovernmental discussions in these areas of government activity.

[9] For a development of this theme, see Richard H. Leach, "Interprovincial Co-operation," in David Bellamy, Jon Pammett, and Donald C. Rowat (eds.), *The Provincial Political Systems: Comparative Essays* (Toronto: Methuen, 1976), pp. 381-394.

[10] A description of the Western Premiers Conference is provided in M. Westmacott and P. Dore, "Intergovernmental Co-Operation in Western Canada." Chapter 22 in this book.

[11] For a full discussion of the Council of Ministers of Education of Canada, see *Review of Educational Policies in Canada: Foreword and Introduction,* a study prepared by the C.M.E.C. and the Government of Canada for the Organization for Economic Cooperation and Development (O.E.C.D.).

[12] For a description of Alberta's federal-provincial conference activity during 1974 see The Province of Alberta, Department of Federal and Intergovernmental Affairs, *Second Annual Report, 1974-75* (Edmonton: Queen's Printer, 1975), pp. 6-10.

[13] For a description of Alberta's interprovincial conference activity during 1974 see *ibid.,* pp. 10-13.

15

Western Provincial Co-operation*

Premier Allan Blakeney

It is a great pleasure to be back in Nova Scotia once again. And it is both an honour—and a challenge—to address this particular group on the topic of economic development.

As one who feels a strong affinity for both the Atlantic region and the West, I am particularly pleased to have this opportunity to share with you some observations on the situation in western Canada, and how the western provinces have organized to deal co-operatively in the area of economic development.

Let me begin with some background.

* Notes for remarks by Premier Allan Blakeney Annual Conference of The Altantic Provinces Economic Council, Halifax, October 25, 1976. Reprinted by permission.

The four western provinces are not a monolithic bloc; indeed, they are very different in many ways.

At the present time, the governments of the four provinces represent three different political parties. It is interesting to note that such party political variety has been the norm in the West, rather than the exception, for the past three decades.

The economies of the four provinces are very different. Under the Federal-provincial tax sharing formula—the equalization formula—Alberta and British Columbia are "have" provinces, while Saskatchewan and Manitoba are "have nots". Per capita personal incomes show corresponding variations.

The populations of the four western provinces are markedly different, both in number and in ethnic composition.

Finally, the four western provinces have different historical roots. Their settlement patterns were different. So were the dates and circumstances of their respective entries into Confederation.

And yet, despite these differences, most of us regard the four western provinces as a distinct region, with shared perceptions, with mutual concerns, and, in many respects, with common objectives. And the governments of those four provinces have worked together—as have the Atlantic provinces—to promote regional interests.

I think that at the core of western regional identity are a few basic elements.

1. All four western provinces have economies that are built upon the exploitation of natural resources, which were to be the basis of our regional wealth—we are all resource rich and industry poor.
2. We are all heavily dependent for our well-being on transportation—especially rail transportation. Indeed B.C. came into Confederation because the Canadian Pacific Railway was promised and Saskatchewan and Alberta came into Confederation because the C.P.R. was built.
3. Stemming from the first two—and perhaps most important of all—people in the four western provinces tend to have a common perception of Canada and what Confederation is all about.

As we see it Canada does not now and never did make economic sense. It was created to achieve political and social objectives—not because of economic realities, but despite economic realities.

The bargain as we see it was that tariffs set by the federal government would protect Canadian industry—mostly in central Canada—against international competition. At the same time transportation policies pursued by the federal government would allow people in the hinterland—east and west—to get their products to market outside the region and to get the manufactured goods they needed into the region.

Clearly that is an over-simplification. But it sets out in a rough way the perception of western Canadians of the Confederation bargain.

That is why Westerners feel aggrieved by recent efforts to change the rules, that is

—to change the rules on who should benefit from resources, which were supposed to be our source of wealth
—to change the rules on tariffs and transportation.

We in the West are hearing Federal spokesmen say that those who benefit from transportation should pay for it in full—"the user pay" principle, I believe it's called.

We will be more receptive to this so-called principle when we see the Federal plans to make sure that those who benefit from tariffs pay their cost in full.

You will have noted already, I suspect, a number of common elements in the cement of Western regionalism and that of Atlantic co-operation.

The West, like the Atlantic provinces, because of its dependence on natural resources, is subject to chronic instability of prices and markets and wild fluctuations in local economic circumstances. And to combat this Western provinces have relentlessly pursued industry to diversify our economies, or ways to bring stability to our primary industries, or both. Economic policy in the West is in an important way the pursuit of stability.

Like the Atlantic region, the West is dependent on an efficient transportation system to move its goods to distant markets, and it suffers, as do you, from the anomalies and inequities that are so much a part of our freight rate structures.

And, like the Atlantic region, the western provinces tend to share a common sense of grievance against central Canada. You may call it Upper Canada. We may call it the East, but in both cases we have an uneasy feeling that our region is regarded as an "appendage" to the Canadian Confederation.

There is not too much that is new or interesting in all this. What may be of interest is what we have tried to do about it.

In the West, as in the Atlantic provinces, the shared interests and concerns of the four Western governments have resulted in institutions and procedures for regional co-operation that have become increasingly elaborate and sophisticated over time.

Perhaps I should begin my account of these developments in 1965, with the first meeting of the Prairie Economic Council. That Council consisted of the Premiers of the three Prairie provinces. It was established with four major objectives in mind:

1. to set out goals for general regional progress;
2. to co-ordinate economic development policies on a regional basis;
3. to cut down areas of unnecessary conflict;
4. to discuss ways to resolve problems of mutual concern.

The Prairie Economic Council existed from 1965 to 1972. The Council was never rigid in form. Rather, its structure was permitted to change through the years as circumstances dictated.

Its attention was focussed primarily on specific technical questions rather than broader issues of regional development strategy.

Then came WEOC—the Western Economic Opportunities Conference.

While most of you here are likely to recall the background, I perhaps could give you a very brief sketch.

There had been a federal election in 1972, and the Liberals had been reduced to a minority position. Perhaps the most conspicuous result of the election was the virtual absence of Liberal M.P.'s from anywhere west of Ontario—none in Alberta, one in Saskatchewan and a scattered few from Manitoba and B.C. The message was getting through. For whatever reasons—in Western Canada the natives were restless.

So the Speech from the Throne in January of 1973 announced that there was to be a Western Economic Opportunities Conference that July—full dress—with the Prime Minister and other Cabinet Ministers in attendance—to discuss the grievances of the West.

As we saw it, this was an opportunity that the West could not pass by.

The first effect was to force the Western provinces to forge a more effective instrument to prepare for WEOC. Thus, the Prairie Economic Council was expanded to include British Columbia and was renamed the Western Economic Council—later, the Western Premiers' Conference.

Also, it was obvious that the WEOC challenge would require the four provincial governments to broaden our horizons, to set out a more coherent framework for economic development than we had done up to then. The onus was squarely on the Western provinces to decide and set out, in the clearest possible terms, the directions in which we wanted Western Canada to go in the future.

We took this Conference very seriously. We worked hard and we worked together to put our case as persuasively as possible. The four Premiers and the four governments struggled—and it was a struggle—to reach common positions to put to the federal government. That was a valuable exercise, though not always an easy one. It made us face realities. It encouraged us to cut down areas of competition and conflict amongst ourselves in the interests of the region as a whole. It forced us to consider our specific grievances within a broader framework for development of the region.

Surprisingly perhaps, we found that the conflicts that arose—and that had to be resolved—did not follow political party lines. Such differences as existed tended to be geographically based, particularly between "the Prairies", on the one hand, and British Columbia on the other. But these were faced squarely and dealt with.

Perhaps we were assisted in our task by the fact that none of the western provincial governments was of the same political stripe as the federal government.

After months of preparation, WEOC arrived. The whole conference was televised. And under the bright glare of those TV lights—and more than a little political pressure—the federal government listened as we presented our case. The provinces hammered three themes:

1. Canada needs a conscious national policy for regional development;
2. Canada's national transportation system should be used as a deliberate tool for the regional development; and
3. Canada needs national policies to bring greater stability for producers of primary products.

Looking back, I am forced to conclude that, to date, not many concrete results can be attributed to the Conference itself. While there have been some important specific projects, I would have to say that WEOC failed to bring us much closer to the goal then enunciated by the Prime Minister—a new "National Policy".

But to assess the impact of WEOC only in terms of its concrete results would be a mistake. WEOC provided an unparalleled opportunity for the systematic analysis and articulation of fundamental issues facing Western Canada. It played an important part in shaping the debate on Western development and in creating a better understanding of our problems—both within the four provinces and elsewhere in Canada.

And, as a result of our close collaboration in preparing for the Conference, personal rapport developed among the Premiers, Ministers and officials of the four western governments. Many of these personal relationships endure today, and a habit of close consultation and co-operation among the four western provinces has developed.

It would be difficult to argue that WEOC succeeded in changing the direction of federal policies, but its impact on western provincial co-operation was substantial.

Today, that co-operation is highlighted in the annual meetings of the Western Premiers' Conference.

The agenda of our most recent meeting, held in Medicine Hat last April, indicates the scope of topics covered: federal transportation policy; federal-provincial fiscal arrangements and shared-cost programs;

patriation of the Constitution; agricultural stabilization; and co-ordination of western economic strategy.

Our discussions, as a rule, are friendly and informal. Over time, we have developed a common understanding of both the opportunities and constraints of joint action: we concentrate on those areas in which we agree, or where agreement seems possible, and deemphasize areas of conflict.

Below the level of the Premiers, and often operating on their instructions, a number of ministerial task forces and officials' committees operate either on a more or less continuous basis or as a particular need arises.

One example is the Committee of Western Industry Ministers, which was formed in February 1974, on instructions from the Premiers, to examine the potential for mutual co-operation in industrial development and trade. The Committee has achieved a number of concrete results in its short history:

(a) it prepared a joint position paper to the federal government on trade policy as part of the current GATT negotiations in Geneva;
(b) the four provinces sent a joint trade mission to Latin America;
(c) the Ministers organized a study of the purchasing policies of the federal government and of the four western provincial governments;
(d) some progress has been made toward complementary industrial specialization in the West—seeing that we don't compete in a wasteful way with each other to attract industry.

Also, in 1974, at the direction of the Premiers, a Fertilizer Prices Review Panel was established, and had considerable success in securing adequate supplies of fertilizer at reasonable prices.

WESTAC—The Western Transportation Advisory Council—brings together representation from the four western governments and a wide range of private interests—farmers, grain companies, shippers, railway unions—to discuss the many transportation problems in Western Canada.

At their last Conference, the Western Premiers established an interprovincial task force on constitutional trends. That body, involving Ministers and officials from the four western governments, is undertaking an examination of federal intrusions into areas of provincial jurisdiction, and will report back to the Premiers next year.

All these Conferences, Committees and task forces are supplemented by close and frequent consultations among Ministers and officials—in the areas of agriculture, transportation, education and manpower training, communications, and Indian land claims.

This activity has produced a number of concrete results—a jointly-financed veterinary college; a jointly-financed farm machinery testing institute (PAMI); regional arrangements for the training of specialists like dental nurses; and the harmonization of policy and development strategy in a number of key areas (e.g. steel).

All our problems, of course, are not yet solved.

We have not yet succeeded in persuading the federal government that transportation is an important tool for regional economic development; that it should be operated as a public utility; that the railway roadbeds should be owned and maintained by the public, as are highways and airports; that the highly selective—I might almost say capricious—application of the "user pay" concept is totally inappropriate in a country like Canada.

In agriculture we are making some progress in trying to bring greater stability to that traditional boom and bust industry.

The federal grain income stabilization plan is a useful start.

We would like to see a similar start in levelling out the incomes of beef producers. Perhaps the best way to tackle this is with a program to which the producer, the federal government and the respective provincial governments all contribute. We have not been able to solve the problem on a regional basis.

On these and other issues, a start has been made; the habit of regional co-operation has been fostered; the necessary mechanisms have been established. But our job is a long way from finished.

That is the story of what we are trying to do as four western provincial governments.

Let me try to draw some conclusions from all of this—conclusions that, in my view, have relevance to the Atlantic provinces as well as to Western Canada.

First, we in the West and you in the Atlantic region must face and accept the fact that political power in Canada is now and for the forseeable future concentrated in Ontario and Quebec. Neither the Atlantic region nor the West can expect the federal government—whatever its party stripe—to take the initiative in introducing the basic structural reforms that are needed to encourage more balanced regional development. Within the limits of our abilities and our jurisdictions, we must solve our problems. And to do so effectively, our provincial governments must work together to achieve common objectives for our regions.

Secondly, we would do well to organize to deal more effectively with the federal government in those areas—increasingly numerous—where federal and provincial jurisdictions interface and overlap. With the possible exception of Ontario and Quebec, no province alone has the money or the people to challenge a determined federal government in an effective way. If we can develop the necessary instruments to pool our resources—both within regions, and where appropriate, on a national scale—we will operate more effectively in our dealings with Ottawa.

Thirdly, there is probably no better time than now for concerted action. Strong Federal governments—particularly strong Federal governments with a solid Ontario-Quebec base become less sensitive to your and our concerns. Governments which are under pressure are more receptive to a well co-ordinated approach with a short list of objectives.

It is not my role to offer advice. But a concerted approach for action in a small number of areas, e.g. rail and ferry transportation, electrical energy generation and transmission, based upon an agreed four province position hammered out in advance might well bear fruit.

Finally, I believe we are on the threshold of a new era in Canadian Confederation—an era marked by greater awareness of provincial and regional needs and sensitivities; greater respect to the diversity of culture and heritage which characterized the various parts of our great land; perhaps, in the not-too-distant future, a new balance between the centre and the periphery, the federal authority and the provinces.

We in Saskatchewan seek this. We do not wish a weakened federal government—far from it. But we wish strong provincial governments made strong when necessary by financial muscle coming from the Federal government.

That is our concept of the Canada we strive for. There are new ways and new opportunities to move towards that goal. One of those is close regional co-operation.

You in the Atlantic provinces, we in the West, should seize the opportunity—for the benefit of our regions and for the good of Canada. That is our task. That is our challenge.

16

Established Program Financing: A Proposal Regarding the Major Shared-Cost Programs in the Fields of Health and Post-Secondary Education*

Prime Minister Pierre Elliott Trudeau

THE NEED FOR CONTINUED FEDERAL-PROVINCIAL COOPERATION

1. During the last several months the Government of Canada has been reviewing the nature and terms of its participation in the major shared-cost programs in the fields of health and post-secondary education. Out of this review has emerged one salient conclusion: that past achievements in these fields are the result of, and future progress depends upon, joint federal and provincial efforts. Canada can be proud of the high quality of health services and post-secondary education facilities which are available across the country. The raising of standards to their present high level is due of course in large part to the dedication of the professional and other people working in these fields. But it has also been made possible because the Government of Canada and the provinces have worked together. We need to preserve what has been achieved and to build upon it, to ensure that all Canadians are provided with adequate services at a price that both individuals and the country as a whole can afford. Any intergovernmental arrangements for the future which seek to achieve this goal must be based upon a pooling of the financial, professional and organizational resources of both orders of government.

THE OBJECTIVES BEHIND THE ESTABLISHED PROGRAM FINANCING PROPOSAL

2. It is in this spirit that the Established Program Financing Proposal, which is described later in this paper, is put forward. The objectives which have guided the Government in drawing up the Proposal are as follows:

---

* Statement tabled by the Prime Minister of Canada, the Right Honourable Pierre Elliott Trudeau, on the occasion of the Conference of Federal and Provincial First Ministers, held at Ottawa, June 14/15, 1976. Reprinted by permission.

(a) to maintain across Canada the standards of service to the public under these major programs, and to facilitate their improvement;

(b) to put the programs on a more stable footing, so that both levels of government are better able to plan their expenditures;

(c) to give the provinces flexibility in the use of their own funds which they have been spending in these fields;

(d) to bring about greater equality among the provinces with regard to the amount of federal funds they receive under the programs;

(e) to provide for continuing joint policy discussions relating to the health and post-secondary education fields.

THE PRESENT ARRANGEMENTS

3. The existing programs are provided for under three statutes: the Hospital Insurance and Diagnostic Services Act, the Medical Care Act, and Part VI of the Federal-Provincial Fiscal Arrangements Act. They were begun at different times: the hospital insurance legislation took effect from 1958, the Medicare legislation from 1968, and the main provisions of the present post-secondary education legislation from 1967. In the current fiscal year federal payments to the provinces under these programs amount to over five billion dollars, including the value of the post-secondary tax transfer to all provinces and the special tax abatement to Quebec for hospital insurance. The programs account for between 40 and 45 per cent of all federal cash payments to the provinces.

4. The nature of the federal participation in these three programs varies, reflecting the differing circumstances of their introduction and the federal-provincial thinking at the time. They do have, however, important elements in common:

(a) They are all large, in cost and in their effect upon society in general;

(b) They have been in place for a number of years, and public demand for the services in question continues at a high and fairly predictable level;

(c) The cost-sharing formula has basically been a fifty-fifty sharing of eligible program costs between the federal and provincial governments.

5. While it is difficult to guess what other arrangements might have been developed in various parts of the country had the federal government not taken the initiative to introduce these major programs on a Canada-wide basis, most would agree that their introduction, and their subsequent operation by the provinces, have brought great benefits to all Canadians. The quality of our health programs, in particular, has attracted world interest in the arrangements we have made, and officials

from other countries such as the United States and Australia have carried out extensive studies to see what can be learned from the Canadian experience. The financial arrangements for post-secondary education have contributed substantially to the development of Canadian universities and colleges, thus helping to make advanced education accessible to a large number of Canadian students.

PROBLEMS WITH THE PRESENT ARRANGEMENTS

6. These problems have varied somewhat from one program to another, but generally have included the following:

(a) Some provinces have complained that federal grants distort their own priorities in favour of the program fields in which the federal government stands ready to pay half of program costs;
(b) It has been difficult for provincial governments to keep program costs down in the fields for which federal grants are available, given the relative inflexibility for provinces in administering the programs, and that half of any cost increases are covered by another government;
(c) There has been uncertainty for the federal government from year to year about the dollar level of its originally open-ended financial commitment, as total program costs have risen;
(d) Because of the difficulty in controlling costs, and federal uncertainty about the future extent of its financial commitment, the federal government has had to impose for two of the programs a ceiling on the rate of increase in its contribution;
(e) This had led to uncertainty on the part of the provinces about the extent of continued federal participation or "partnership" in the programs in question;
(f) Disparities have arisen among the provinces in federal per capita contributions, notably in the field of post-secondary education, as some provinces were able to or chose to benefit more than others from the available federal funds;
(g) There have been auditing and administrative difficulties and added costs associated with determining eligible expenditures.

THE REVIEW UNDERTAKEN WITHIN
THE FEDERAL GOVERNMENT

7. An attempt was made to deal with a number of these problems in proposals which were made by the Government to the provinces early in 1973 for new financing arrangements with regard to health and post-secondary education. These proposals were not accepted by the provinces, largely because in their view the fiscal compensation being offered

was inadequate to meet rising program costs. The review undertaken during the last several months has been, in part, a continuation of the process begun in 1973. In another sense, however, a fresh start was made which sought to take into account new developments. These developments include the growing need for spending restraint which affects all levels of government. They also include the evolving nature of our federal system, reflecting the increasing interdependence of federal and provincial areas of jurisdiction. A good illustration of this interdependence is the area of income security and social services, where there has been exceptionally close federal-provincial co-operation in the past few years.

8. The review has also taken into account the various proposals that have been made to the federal government from time to time by provincial governments, whether for a continued major federal presence in the fields of health and post-secondary education or for partial or complete federal withdrawal. The Government has likewise been mindful of the representations made by interested groups across the country, representations which have urged strongly a continuation of federal participation in policy development or financing, or both.

9. Most of the provisions of the Federal-Provincial Fiscal Arrangements Act expire on March 31, 1977. With them expires the authority for federal payments to the provinces of a major share of post-secondary education operating costs. Also in 1977 the authority for financial arrangements with Quebec under the Established Programs (Interim Arrangements) Act comes to an end. A bit further down the road, but not far in terms of the need for governments to plan together, the present federal-provincial hospital insurance agreements will be terminated on July 15, 1980; and meanwhile there has been a wide expression of interest in conducting a thoroughgoing review of health legislation. This is, therefore, a good time to take stock of the basic principles which should underlie federal-provincial cooperation in these fields.

THE PROPOSAL FOR NEW ARRANGEMENTS

10. Consequently, the Government of Canada wishes to propose a set of new principles which should, in its view, form the basis for continued federal participation in the three major shared-cost programs in health and post-secondary education. These principles underlie the Established Program Financing Proposal. If governments working together can find an acceptable way to apply these principles, a remedy will have been found for most if not all of the problems referred to earlier. The Government believes that the application of these principles will provide an opportunity for continued development in the interest of all

Canadians of programs that have already achieved a high degree of success.

11. There are five principles which the Government believes should apply to these programs. The five are:

(1) The federal government should continue to pay a substantial share of program costs;
(2) Federal payments should be calculated independently of provincial program expenditures;
(3) There should be greater equality in per capita terms among the provinces with regard to the amount of federal funds they receive under the programs;
(4) The arrangements for these major programs should be placed on a more permanent footing;
(5) There should be provision for continuing federal participation with the provinces in the consideration and development of policies of national significance in the fields of health and post-secondary education.

12. The first principle is that the federal government should continue to pay a substantial share of program costs. Canadians from many parts of the country look to the federal government to use its spending power under the Constitution to help the provincial governments in less wealthy parts of Canada to maintain a reasonable standard of services generally. In the same way Canadians will continue to look to the Government of Canada for financial help in the maintenance of reasonable standards in the fields of health and post-secondary education. By international standards, Canadian expenditures on health and post-secondary education rank high. While it is difficult to predict precisely how these expenditures will or should develop in the coming years, the federal government believes that it should be prepared to maintain its contributions at a level which rises at a rate not greatly different from the rate of increase in the Gross National Product. If the provinces were to do likewise, these programs would be assured in the future of a proportion of the national wealth no less than they receive now.

13. The second principle is that federal payments should be calculated independently of provincial program expenditures. The implementation of this principle would mean that there would be no distortion of provincial priorities, and that other problems which have arisen because of the fifty-fifty cost-sharing formula would tend to disappear. These problems, which include financial uncertainty for both orders of government, were referred to earlier.

14. The implementation of the third principle, greater equality in what provinces receive, would reduce or eliminate disparities which have

arisen under the existing formulas, notably in post-secondary education. This would work generally to the advantage of the poorer provinces.

15. The implementation of the fourth principle, by placing the programs on a more permanent footing, would introduce additional stability into the arrangements that would facilitate financial planning by governments.

16. The fifth principle calls for continuing federal involvement. The Government of Canada has a deep interest in and concern for the two fields of health and post-secondary education. In the health field this interest and concern find their expression in, for example, the fundamental objectives which underlie the existing Medicare legislation and which would be embodied in future federal health legislation. These objectives are: comprehensiveness of coverage with regard to services, universality of coverage with regard to people, portability of benefits, accessibility to services uninhibited by excessive user charges, and non-profit administration by a public agency. In post-secondary education, the federal government is also concerned with matters such as accessibility, and with the great importance of the field for the development of our national life, our economy and technology, and so on. Provincial and federal government interests and concerns coincide in many of these areas, and the maintenance of high standards across the country requires the combined and coordinated efforts of both levels of government.

IMPLEMENTING THE PRINCIPLES

17. If the five principles are a sound basis for the future of the three programs, how should they be implemented? The first principle calls for the federal government to pay a substantial part of program costs. It recognizes that there is as much certainty of a continued demand for federal help in these program fields as there is for equalization. And, when funds are made available by Parliament under the spending power, there is need to ensure that the funds are spent wisely. The federal government does not administer these programs because they are in fields which are basically under provincial jurisdiction. It does nevertheless have to concern itself with what is done with the funds that Parliament makes available. It is with these factors in mind that proposals are made in this paper for the provinces and the federal government to work together.

18. The first principle also raises the question of how the federal government should pay its share of increasing program costs. Should it be in cash? Or, should it be in the form of a transfer of "tax room" to the

provinces, that is to say, should the Government of Canada reduce its taxes so that the provincial government could increase theirs by an equivalent amount, and so achieve an increase in their tax revenues? The Government has come to the conclusion that a substantial part of its contributions should continue to be in the form of cash; on the other hand, it accepts that a substantial portion of the contributions could be transferred in the form of tax room. This important question is dealt with more extensively later on.

19. The second principle is that federal payments should be calculated independently of provincial program expenditures, and the third principle is greater equality in per capita terms in what provinces receive from federal contributions. Both of these principles can be implemented by a system of equal per capita grants for all provinces. Provinces would agree to spend these federal funds in the fields in question, giving public acknowledgement of their source, but would not have to make matching expenditures of any kind from their own resources.

20. In the case of Medicare, the federal payments which provinces receive are already equal in per capita terms, but there is some divergence from equality in hospital insurance and an even greater divergence in the case of post-secondary education. In the latter two cases, the cost-sharing formula has allowed provinces which were able to or chose to spend more of their own funds to receive, generally, matching federal payments and consequently more than other provinces that spent less. Under the arrangements which are now proposed all provinces would receive equal per capita grants in each of the health and post-secondary education fields, and this would involve bringing some provinces down to, and other provinces up to, the national average. This uniformity at the national average could be achieved over a transitional period of, say, five years, which would ease the burden of adjustment on those provinces which receive above-average per capita contributions.

21. The fourth principle is that the arrangements be established on a more or less permanent footing, to reduce the uncertainty that has attended in the past the question of continued federal involvement and the dimensions of federal financial contributions. The relevant federal legislation would not provide for any specific termination date. There would, however, be a provision for three years' notice to terminate the arrangements. Such notice would not be given lightly, because the intention is to underline the relative permanence and stability of the new arrangements. The Government contemplates inserting a provision in the relevant legislation that notice would be given only if authorized by a Resolution of the House of Commons. In this way, the question of giving notice would be aired for debate in Parliament and the country.

Notice would not in any event be given before April 1, 1979, two years after the date on which it is envisaged the new Established Program Financing arrangements would come into effect, so that the arrangements would be in place for a minimum initial period of five years. The formula by which federal payments would grow each year would be established in advance, so that both levels of government would be in a better position to plan their finances ahead of time.

22. The fifth principle concerns continued federal and provincial partnership. Combining and coordinating federal and provincial efforts require appropriate arrangements for intergovernmental consultation at the ministerial level, so that governments may together consider and develop policies of national significance in the fields of health and post-secondary education. In the health field we already have an established forum at the ministerial level. For post-secondary education there have been occasional contacts, but we need to establish a more permanent forum.

23. So far as legislation is concerned, federal health legislation would continue, embodying the kind of fundamental objectives already contained in the Medical Care Act, but it would be modified as necessary to accord with the several principles of the Established Program Financing Proposal. A full examination of federal and provincial health legislation should be carried out in the context of a joint federal-provincial review, of a kind which has been proposed by the Minister of National Health and Welfare. For post-secondary education, suitable legislative provision would be made for the continuation of federal financial contributions.

THE SHAPE OF FUTURE FINANCIAL ARRANGEMENTS

24. The application of the principles leads then, in concept, to a continuation of federal contributions to health and post-secondary education, beginning at about the present levels and rising in future years quite independently of provincial expenditures, but at a rate not greatly different from the rate of increase in GNP. Individual provinces should, after a transitional period, receive equal amounts in per capita terms. These new arrangements could be implemented in the case of post-secondary education when the current legislation expires in March 1977. The arrangements could be implemented in the health field in 1981/82, by which time the period of notice under the hospital insurance agreements will have come to an end. In the meantime, the approach can also be used as a basis for forecasting the minimum size and nature of the federal contribution to the health field as it would be in 1981/82 and in subsequent years.

25. Before individual provincial "entitlements" for future years can be forecast, it will be necessary to decide upon a "base year" from which the total federal contributions to the health field and to post-secondary education would rise year by year. The definition of the base year presents a number of technical difficulties which will need to be considered by the two orders of government over coming months. Similarly, the more precise definition of the escalation factor which would govern the growth of future contributions will also be a question for federal-provincial consideration.

THE QUESTION OF A TRANSFER OF "TAX ROOM"

26. A number of provinces have expressed an interest in the federal government transferring tax room in full or part payment of federal contributions under the programs. The Government of Canada can see some advantages to such a transfer. When governments are responsible directly for raising the revenues which they spend, the principle of fiscal responsibility is served and necessary economies stand more chance of being implemented. A certain amount of tax room has already been transferred in respect of post-secondary education. This was done in 1967 in the form of several percentage points of the personal income tax (now equal to 4.357 points as the result of tax reform), and one point of corporate income tax. However, in the case of that transfer the increasing value of the tax room has been offset against provinces' entitlements.

27. While the Government of Canada is willing to contemplate a further transfer of tax room, it is of the view that a transfer which would defray the total amount of current provincial entitlements under the three programs would have several important and unacceptable drawbacks:

(a) Because such a transfer would eliminate all federal cash contributions for the programs themselves, this basis for preserving the standard of services to all Canadians would be largely eroded;

(b) The move to equal per capita payments which is contemplated under the Established Program Financing Proposal would, as noted earlier, tend to favour the poorer provinces. This result would gradually be nullified and eventually reversed in moving from a tax transfer which covered only a small part of the federal contribution to one which covered it all. The disparity between provinces which would be associated with a tax transfer covering the whole contribution would be unacceptable to the federal government and to the provinces adversely affected.

(c) The disparity mentioned above could be removed if the federal government were to equalize the tax transfer up to the yield of the richest provinces, rather than to the national average yield which is the current basis for the equalization program. Such an approach would call on the federal government to pay out larger sums of money from a tax base which would itself have been reduced by the tax transfer. Bearing in mind its responsibilities to all Canadians, the Government of Canada does not believe it would be justified in making an addition of this nature to the very large unconditional funds which are now flowing under the existing equalization arrangements to the majority of the provinces.

28. The Government has concluded, after weighing all the factors, that a substantial part of the future federal contributions toward health and post-secondary education taken together should be covered by a transfer of tax room, and that this tax room should include the tax points already transferred in respect of post-secondary education. What is proposed is that provinces' entitlements would be divided into two parts, one of cash and the other of tax room equalized to the national average, and that the two parts should increase independently of one another. The cash part would grow in accordance with an escalation factor as mentioned earlier, and would rise more or less in line with the growth in GNP. The tax part would grow with the increasing yield from the tax room. The additional tax transfer now proposed would include a combination of taxes, the yield of which is rising faster than the GNP. Taken together, the cash payments and the tax room could well increase at a rate somewhat greater than GNP, and this should be of considerable assistance in meeting the increased costs which provinces are predicting in the three program areas.

29. The amount of tax room transferred would be identical for all provinces, to ensure uniform federal taxation across the country (with the exception of the interim arrangements already in place in Quebec). The amount would be calculated with reference to the province or provinces with the highest per capita yield from the taxes in question. For some provinces, the value of the cash payments plus the equalized tax transfer would not in the early years of the new arrangements amount to as much as if the whole of their entitlement had been paid in cash. Therefore, transitional payments would be made to make up the difference. Consequently, all provinces would be assured that in the early years of the new arrangements their total receipts would increase at least at a rate that was more or less in line with GNP; and after a few years, as the yield from the tax room increased, all provinces' receipts would rise at an even faster rate.

30. To the extent that the additional tax room may include personal income tax "points", no additional tax points would be transferred to Quebec, because that province alone is already collecting under interim

arrangements taxes on twenty-four percentage points of personal income tax in lieu of federal cash grants for certain programs. Sixteen of these twenty-four points are attributable to the hospital insurance program, one of the three programs with which we are now concerned. However, Quebec would receive an outright as distinct from an interim transfer of as many of those twenty-four points as would be transferred to other provinces in the form of additional tax room; for those points and for the tax room transferred in 1967 in respect of post-secondary education, Quebec would receive the full and increasing yield. For the remainder of the twenty-four points, the full yield is being and will be deducted from Quebec's entitlement under various programs. Consequently, it seems clear that Quebec would not stand to lose financially in working with the federal government towards a greater uniformity in the application of the federal personal income tax across Canada.

THE PROPOSED FEDERAL-PROVINCIAL HEALTH REVIEW

31. As mentioned earlier, there is wide interest in a joint federal-provincial review of health legislation and programs. The Government of Canada is strongly in favour of such a review, the purpose of which would be to lay the groundwork for improved and more economical delivery of services, and to place greater emphasis on sickness prevention, such as by encouraging people to assume more responsibility for maintaining and improving their own health. During the review, the basis for federal participation in the longer term could be worked out to conform, so far as the major two existing programs are concerned, with the principles already outlined. The precise dimensions of federal financial contributions could be established, as well as the need for any supplementary programs that have more specific purposes than the large Medicare and hospital insurance programs.

32. Evidently, the discussions among health Ministers will have to take account of the rights which provinces have under the unexpired hospital insurance agreements to federal contributions based on existing legislation. It will be clear from what has already been said that it is the intention to continue federal contributions after the expiry of the hospital insurance agreements in July 1980. Indeed, the Government of Canada is now prepared to guarantee that the total payments under the two major health programs would in 1981/82 and thereafter represent a proportion of the GNP reasonably in line with recent experience. It would be further contemplated that the payments to provinces in 1981/82 would begin on an equal per capita basis.

33. As for the program conditions that should continue to be attached to the federal payments, it is the Government's belief that conditions reflecting fundamental objectives of the kind contained in the Medical

Care Act would be appropriate for both of the major health programs, thus giving the provinces much greater flexibility in the administration of their programs.

POST-SECONDARY EDUCATION

34. So far as post-secondary education is concerned, the federal government has a common interest with the provinces in achieving certain broad objectives. Indeed, it is in recognition and support of this common interest that the federal government believes it should continue to make contributions to post-secondary education costs. The establishment of a continuing federal-provincial forum at the ministerial level would, in the Government's view, provide an essential vehicle for realizing common objectives in this field. The broad subject areas of interest to both levels of government which the Government of Canada thinks should be kept under review in such a forum include, among others, the question of accessibility to post-secondary education; the extent to which it is practicable and desirable to rationalize on a national basis the use of existing post-secondary education resources; bilingualism in education; and the introduction into appropriate academic disciplines of a greater knowledge and understanding of Canada.

THE ESTABLISHED PROGRAM FINANCING PROPOSAL: SUMMARY

35. The Government of Canada is proposing that it continue its involvement in the three major programs of assistance to health and post-secondary education, on the basis of financial contributions a substantial part of which could be in the form of tax room and the rest in cash. These contributions would escalate at a rate, taking cash payments and the tax transfer together, that would at least equal and eventually exceed the rate of increase in GNP. The cash payments would, after a transitional period, be in the form of equal per capita grants for all provinces. While the federal funds paid in respect of health and post-secondary education would need to be spent in each of these fields respectively, with public acknowledgement of their source, there would be no requirement for matching expenditures by the provinces. The arrangements would be permanent, subject only to three years' notice, and this notice would not be given before the first two years of the new arrangements had elapsed. There would be a forum at the ministerial level for each of the health and post-secondary education fields to facilitate federal-provincial pursuit of common objectives.

36. Assuming the basic principles and elements involved in the Proposal are broadly acceptable to the provincial governments as a basis for

further discussion, it is suggested that Ministers concerned with finance, health and post-secondary education should meet together or separately as appropriate to attempt to reach agreement on the important details which would remain to be settled. With regard to the health programs, the Government of Canada proposes that all governments agree to proceed with a review along the lines that were discussed in a preliminary way at the April 27/28 Conference of Federal and Provincial Ministers of Health. The government would give in more precise terms a minimum guarantee of the extent of its per capita financial contributions in 1981/82 under the two major health programs. Also it is hoped that by October 1, 1976 the provinces will have made known their position regarding the federal offer of extended cost-sharing under existing health legislation. So far as the federal government is concerned, the Minister of Finance will have a co-ordinating responsibility with regard to the financial aspects of the various ministerial negotiations, because of the need to integrate the discussions into federal-provincial negotiations about other fiscal matters such as equalization. It is contemplated that there will be a further meeting of First Ministers in the fall to review progress.

37. It is the Government's belief that the adoption of new arrangements along the lines proposed could bring about a fruitful new phase in the life of these important programs, resulting in more efficient and improved services for the Canadian public. At the same time, a number of sources of federal-provincial friction would be removed. Because of the relative permanence and stability of the arrangements, there would be greater opportunity for both levels of government to plan their various expenditures. Provinces would have greater flexibility in the use of their own funds. Intergovernmental administrative and auditing arrangements could be much simplified. The Government believes that the Established Program Financing Proposal will provide the basis for useful discussions between governments, and hopes that it will constitute an important step forward in federal-provincial co-operation to the advantage of the people of Canada.

17

Cooperative Federalism: An Evaluation*

Donald V. Smiley

Cooperative federalism is in essence a series of pragmatic and piecemeal responses by the federal and provincial governments to the circumstances of their mutual interdependence. We will try in this article to evaluate this evolving system of relations in answer to three kinds of general questions.

First, what are the general preconditions of success in cooperative federalism?

Second, what are the relative possibilities of cooperative federalism and explicit constitutional reform in meeting the demands for change in the Canadian federal system?

Third, what are the possibilities of the ongoing procedures of cooperative federalism in meeting the demands of English and French Canadians and of securing the survival of the Canadian federal union?

A. CIRCUMSTANCES OF SUCCESS
1. Public Policy Effectiveness

There can be little disagreement with the general proposition that if liberal-democratic institutions are to survive they must somehow find ways of dealing with the very great number of varied and often contradictory demands made upon them, and that only by demonstrating such effectiveness can enough support be generated among the politically influential elements of democratic communities to ensure the long-run continuance of these institutions. In federal systems the individual jurisdictions must not only learn to respond effectively to demands upon them but must also evolve adequate means of central-regional articulation to cope with the circumstances of the interdependence of the two levels. Such articulation can take two forms, coordination and consultation.

Coordination is the process by which a complex of public activities is ordered according to some set of goals or priorities. Coordination relates both to the ranking itself and the subsequent actions to implement these decisions.

* From Donald V. Smiley, *Constitutional Adaptation and Canadian Federalism Since 1945.* Volume 4 of the Documents of the Royal Commission on Bilingualism and Biculturalism (Ottawa, Queen's Printer, 1970), pp. 111-28. Reprinted by permission.

Consultation is the process by which officials and public agencies, with some significant degree of both independent discretion and mutual interdependence, communicate to each other their respective perceptions of situations and their judgments of the appropriate way of dealing with these situations. Coordination will be facilitated by effective procedures of consultation but does not always result from them.

Coordination and consultation in respect to public policy are of course easier to achieve when only one jurisdiction is involved and when, in principle at least, activities can be ordered through one hierarchical structure of authority than when, as in a federal system, the participants have legal and political safeguards for their independent positions. Within a hierarchical system authorized channels of communication are usually provided, although other patterns grow up through deliberate design or otherwise. Hierarchy also provides formal procedures by which solutions may be imposed in the absence of agreement and, as J. A. Corry pointed out many years ago, the very existence of these procedures may inhibit "bickering."[1] The relations between the federal and provincial governments cannot of course proceed within a pattern of hierarchical authority. On the surface, it would seem that the processes of joint decision-making which characterize cooperative federalism must lead almost inevitably to delays and frustrations in the framing and implementation of public policy.

Despite the inherent difficulties in working the institutions of cooperative federalism, it is significant that in the past two years a very large volume of public policy has resulted from the collaborative procedures. Agreements of fundamental importance have been reached in respect to contracting-out public contributory pension plans and important aspects of economic direction and control. Important changes appear to be coming in the fields of medical insurance and public assistance. The agreement to set up the Tax Structure Committee was a major achievement in this direction and one can be reasonably optimistic that this committee will have some measure of success in attaining the ambitious objectives set out in its terms of reference. I am not here stating that these actual and anticipated policies resulting from the processes of cooperative federalism were the appropriate responses of the governments concerned to the demands upon them. Rather, I would argue that the record indicates that these procedures of joint decision-making have not in the recent past imposed insuperable barriers to the formulation and implementation of public policies of fundamental importance.

Consultative procedures leading to federal-provincial policy coordination are extraordinarily subtle and one cannot predict with any assurance the form which the most effective of these procedures will take. What seems reasonably certain, however, is that the establishment of administrative machinery, even though ingenious, will not of itself bring about constructive relations. The following general points can be made:

1. Consultation leading to effective coordination will be facilitated when the participants can speak authoritatively for their respective governments. This does not mean that the officials involved have received explicit "instructions" from their governments on every matter under discussion; such a formal requirement would inhibit effective consultation. What is necessary is that the participants perceive each other as persons closely in touch with the perspectives of their respective administrations and with some degree of influence in determining these perspectives. There is also the requirement, that is probably not completely fulfilled in any of the governments, that effective procedures of cabinet and treasury control be maintained so that programme agencies and programme goals are subordinated to more comprehensive goals. As we saw in Chapter VII, a complex pattern of functional relations has developed between counterpart agencies of the two levels and in some circumstances those involved in these relations may resist attempts to subsume their activities under less particularistic goals. Although the effective articulation of federal and provincial objectives involves these functional interactions being sustained and in some cases strengthened, effective relations concerning more comprehensive kinds of public policies require greater measures of overhead control than have been developed in some jurisdictions.

2. Consultation and coordination will be facilitated when the participants come to share as much of a common frame of reference as is compatible with their continuing loyalty to their respective governments. Federal-provincial collaboration in respect to a very large number of specific programmes and projects has been possible largely because those involved were members of the same professions or subprofessions. Such membership characteristically means not only the common possession of specialized knowledge and techniques but also commitment to certain public-policy preferences. When matters of more fundamental political and economic choice are at issue it is unreasonable to expect that federal-provincial agreement can be reached in terms of such professional criteria, although agreement on matters of economic policy is more likely than otherwise if the elected and appointed officials involved are relatively sophisticated in the ways of contemporary economic analysis. However, a prolonged period of constructive relationships between the elected and appointed officials of the federal and provincial governments can be expected to result in a kind of community being developed, a community with its own characteristic perspectives and procedures and with its own subtle ways of distributing status and influence among its members. This development will of course be encouraged if the membership in such a group becomes relatively stable

and if there is some movement of personnel among the governments involved. It is obvious that the growth of community is dependent upon the politicians of the federal and provincial governments continuing to support such kinds of collaborative behaviour.

3. Consultation and minimum levels of coordination will be facilitated if the participants are more committed to the substantive results of particular policies than to enhancing the influence of their respective governments. Cooperative federalism requires a high degree of pragmatism, even opportunism, among those officials involved in federal-provincial relations as to what functions each level should perform. Thus any assumption by federal officials that decisions by the central government are somehow inherently "better" or more legitimate than those of the provinces is clearly incompatible with effective federal-provincial collaboration. Conversely, if some or all of the provinces carry out a persistent policy of attempting to extend their range of discretion at the expense of the federal authorities, the prerequisites of cooperative federalism are challenged in the most fundamental way. Any effective system of federal-provincial relations must of course deal with circumstances in which there are conflicts between the interests of the governments involved. It is only realistic to recognize that these differences characteristically arise from the divergent responsibilities these jurisdictions have assumed rather than from the perversity of the authorities of one level or the other. However, no government can be a constructive collaborator in the enterprise if its overriding objective is to decrease its dependence on the others regardless of the consequences of such actions for the substantive results of public policy.

4. Effective consultation leading to at least limited measures of coordination will be facilitated if the participating governments are predisposed to include the objectives of the others within their own priorities. Let us take a simple example. Assume federal-provincial discussions about a proposed measure where the result would be to increase municipal borrowing for capital purposes. Assume further that the primary objectives of the federal authorities relate to the income and employment aspects of these expenditures and that the first aim of the provinces is to safeguard the financial solvency of the municipalities. If each government presses its primary aim to the exclusion of the concerns of the other it is likely that these will prove incompatible, to a greater or lesser degree. But let us make more optimistic assumptions that either before or as a result of intergovernmental consultations (a) the provinces recognize both that the increase in aggregate demand expected to result from the measure is desirable and that the federal authorities have a legitimate interest in ensuring full employment, (b) the federal government shows a genuine interest in the continuing financial stability of the municipalities and a sympathetic appreciation of provincial concern for this objective. Under such circumstances effective con-

sultation can lead to a solution which includes both federal and provincial aims, a solution agreed upon against a background of mutual respect among the governments concerned for the constitutional responsibilities of each other.

5. Consultation will be facilitated when for the most part it takes place within a framework of confidentiality and when both formally and informally the governments come to share with each other information about situations and their appreciation of these situations which are not available to the public. It does not seem necessary to argue that the processes of federal-provincial collaboration and consultation about fundamentals cannot be successful unless to some considerable degree they can take place without publicity until agreements are reached. The sharing of information and views among the officials must be continuous and it is impossible to defend the situation which existed in the past where the federal authorities were prepared to share these more freely with friendly foreign governments than with provincial administrations. In the present context of federal-provincial relations, however, the federal government appears more sensitive to provincial responsibilities which may have significant implications for federal policies than at least some of the provinces.

In general, the relative success of cooperative federalism in recent years in harmonizing to some tolerable degree the objectives of the federal and provincial governments has depended much more on the attitudes of the officials involved and on the restraints they have placed on their own behaviour than on the development of more institutionalized procedures of intergovernmental collaboration. The existing structures are extraordinarily complex and work as well as they do largely because of the individuals involved, including both elected and appointed officials, have come to know and respect each other in their increasingly frequent contacts. Whether or not this somewhat personalized fabric of cooperation could survive the dislocation of a rapid displacement of the present personnel is a matter of conjecture.

2. Political Competition and Articulation

The preceding chapters of this study have analyzed cooperative federalism exclusively as it relates to interactions between the federal and provincial executives. It would, however, be unrealistic in such an evaluation to ignore completely the political context within which these relations take place, to ignore the fact that the overriding decisions in federal-provincial relations are made by successful politicians who must periodically fight campaigns for re-election and who must continually defend their public conduct both in their respective legislatures and outside. There are two difficulties of a broadly political nature in the contemporary variant of cooperative federalism.

First, federal-provincial relations have dealt increasingly with policy matters of the most fundamental kind, matters which a democratic community has a disposition to settle by the processes of free and open debate and political competition. Yet the success of the governments concerned in reaching tolerable settlements requires a considerable degree of insulation from publicity and from certain varieties of partisan political pressures.

Second, the interdependence of federal and provincial officials in their policy-making and policy-executing roles exercises strong influences towards collaborative behaviour. There are, however, fewer such influences on elected officials in their partisan political capacities.

The situation involving the so-called Fulton-Favreau formula illustrates one of the kinds of political difficulties which cooperative federalism may face. From the time that federal-provincial discussions on an amending procedure were reactivated by the Minister of Justice in 1961, until the publication of the draft formula upon which all the governments had agreed in the summer of 1964, there was little public debate on the issue even among specialists in constitutional matters and it was impossible for those outside government to know, except in a general way, what was going on.[2] Between the time the draft formula was agreed upon and the spring of 1965 the projected amendment was approved by the legislatures of all the provinces except Quebec without causing the incumbent provincial administrations significant political difficulties. By this time, however, considerable opposition to the Fulton-Favreau formula had been aroused—opposition from members of the Progressive Conservative and New Democratic parties in the House of Commons, from the Union Nationale and several influential private groups in Quebec and both from French- and English-speaking specialists in constitutional matters. The federal and Quebec governments thus faced a difficult situation. They had been precluded from cultivating public support for the new procedure because of the relative and confidential nature of the discussions preceding the agreement. The matter at hand was a complex one and the draft formula was the result of a complicated compromise among the governments involved. Yet many of its critics put their arguments in terms of broad and easily understandable considerations quite unrelated to the acceptability of their proposals to the 11 governments. Despite these difficulties, the failure of either or both of the administrations to press the issue to legislative approval would place on them the onus for delaying the enactment of a Canadian amending procedure which had been under discussion for nearly 40 years. Such a failure might also complicate their relations with administrations which had secured the assent of their legislatures. It is likely that similar situations will arise in the future. Fundamental policy discussions will be carried on in confidence between the federal and provincial governments and will culminate in an agreement which becomes the subject of vigorous debate largely precluded until that time. Neither the members of the opposition parties nor the other members of politically influential publics have apparently fully accepted as legitimate the fact that high policy may be made by federal-provincial agreement. Because of this, policies devised by these procedures may be subjected to more severe criticism than if they were made by a single jurisdiction, and criticism somewhat harder for their supporters to answer.

The relationships between federal and provincial political parties and the impact of these relations on the stands on public issues that these parties take are extraordinarily complex and have never been systematically examined.[3] In some cases the electoral success of a federal or provincial party is significantly aided or frustrated by actions of the party of the same name at the other level; in other circumstances there may be little interdependence. Partisan political interactions between members of Parliament and members of the same parties in the provincial legislatures are conditioned by this kind of factor, by financial and other relationships between federal and provincial party organizations, by antagonism and friendships growing out of previous political experience and by other influences. In most cases, however, it would appear that successful federal and provincial parties have resources of funds, organizations and popular support independent of party fortunes at the other level. It seems that usually only very weak parties are effectively subordinated to their electorally more successful federal or provincial counterparts. In circumstances where the federal government and that of a province bear the same party label there is thus no assurance that their relations will be harmonious, and Canadian political history has many contrary examples. On the other hand, where federal and provincial parties in power are of different complexions, there are no overriding partisan political inhibitions imposed on collaboration in policy matters. In general, however, the influences on the federal and provincial administrations to collaborate because of their mutual interdependence in policy matters have little counterpart in the partisan political custom.

3. The Legitimation of Cooperative Federalism

If cooperative federalism is in the long run to survive, the politically influential publics in Canada must be persuaded that this is a legitimate way of making crucial public decisions. Such persuasion will be extraordinarily difficult in the face of alternative proposals for reforming our federal institutions, proposals which are on the surface simpler and more conceptually consistent. These difficulties inherent in the complexities of the existing procedures and institutions are compounded by the incompatibility between cooperative federalism and at least three influential systems of ideas about how government in Canada should be carried on.

First, cooperative federalism is difficult to defend in terms of British parliamentary traditions. The underlying assumption of this tradition is that the legislature is sovereign—in the United Kingdom over all matters and in federal countries over all those matters conferred on it by the constitution. This assumption is challenged when the actual locus of decision-making is transferred from the cabinet, which is collectively responsible to the elected chamber, to intergovernmental bodies. Cooperative federalism has been called "government by diplomacy" by one student of the Canadian constitution. Contemporary democratic theory and practice, both where British parliamentary traditions prevail and elsewhere, have found it extraordinarily difficult to deal with situations involving the external relations of governments.

Second, cooperative federalism in its symbolic aspects gives Quebec no special status in the Canadian federal system. Daniel Johnson has said of this system:

> Au lieu d'une véritable constitution, nous avons un régime mouvant, qui est constamment en mutation et qui est le produit des accords formels ou tacites entre Ottawa et la majorité des provinces. *L'autorité suprême du pays . . . c'est une institution qui n'est même pas mentionnée dans l'Acte de l'Amérique britannique du Nord.* C'est le forum des conférences fédérales-provinciales. Et là, le Québec n'a pas plus de droits que Terre-Neuve.[4]

The Honourable Jean-Luc Pepin in the most systematic defence of cooperative federalism that has ever been made[5] has argued that this alternative recognizes both "cette réalité socio-politique du binationalisme" and "un statut particulier" for Quebec in the Canadian federal system. However, in the formal aspects of federal-provincial relations and in the strict adherence to the rule that the various contracting-out options are available to all the provinces, the symbol, if not the substance, of the equality of the provinces is upheld.

Third, cooperative federalism to be successful requires a degree of secrecy in decision-making which is believed by many to be incompatible with the requirements of democracy. Members of the working press have become increasingly restive with the confidential nature of these processes and many have suggested that conferences of prime ministers and premiers be held in public. The necessity for secrecy until the results of federal-provincial negotiations are concluded can be expected to inhibit the legitimation of cooperative federalism.

B. COOPERATIVE FEDERALISM AND CONSTITUTIONAL CHANGE

Those who wish changes in the Canadian federal system can be divided into two groups—those who press for such reforms to come through the processes of federal-provincial collaboration and those bent on explicit alterations in the text of the existing constitution. The debate between them is not easily joined. Persons who are convinced that a substantial rewriting of the constitution is necessary often appear to place a high value on clarity and explicitness in our governmental arrangements and on the symbolic significance of a constitution as embodying the fundamental moral and political principles on which the regime is founded. By these tests, cooperative federalism is of course deficient. On the other hand, supporters of a new constitution have not, so far as I am able to discover, made a careful study of the traditions and institutions of Canadian federalism as they have evolved in the past five years, or of the possibilities that some or most of the objectives they seek could be attained through the processes of federal-provincial interaction. But proponents of cooperative federalism have not investigated in any detail the incidence of formal constitutional arrangements on these institutions or the constraints that these arrangements impose on the attainment of particular substantive objectives.

Our evaluation of the relative appropriateness of the two broad alternatives as procedures of constitutional evolution will proceed in terms of answers to three questions.

First, if we assume that changes will require the agreement of the federal government and those of most if not all of the provinces, is it more likely that agreement will be secured for explicit constitutional change or for adaptation through federal collaboration on particular public policy matters?

Second, can the relations between the federal and provincial governments be more appropriately regulated through interactions between federal and provincial executives than through other procedures?

Third, is it appropriate to amend the constitution to provide explicitly for the institutions and procedures of federal-provincial relations?

1. The Necessity for Federal-Provincial Agreement

So far as I am able to discover, those who wish the Canadian constitution to be rewritten have never seriously considered whether or not it is likely that politically influential elements in the country could be brought to agreement on this matter. This applies to supporters in Quebec of the associated states solution, to Peter J. T. O'Hearn[6] and to Marcel Faribault and Robert M. Fowler[7] who have presented detailed draft constitutions and to those persons who have called for a new constitution without suggesting what they believe its nature should be. It appears unlikely that the required measure of agreement could be secured in the near future. The political relations between the "two founding races" are in a critical and fluid state. The institutions and procedures of federal-provincial relations are evolving rapidly. I would therefore agree with one scholar who remarked "to try to redraft the Canadian constitution now would be the same as trying to write a peace treaty while a war was still on." It is possible, however, to foresee limited changes in the constitution. One could imagine agreement to drop its obsolete sections and improve its literary qualities. Perhaps progress could be made toward a constitutional bill of rights binding on all governments and not subject to unilateral amendment by any. It may be possible to find agreement on more adequate protection for French-speaking and English-speaking cultural minorities. On the other hand, any attempt to rewrite the constitution to change in a fundamental way the division of legislative powers between Parliament and the provinces would require simultaneous federal-provincial agreement on a very wide range of basic political issues. It seems to me unlikely that such an agreement will emerge in the immediate future.

The processes of cooperative federalism allow politicians and civil servants to search for agreement where it can be found. I argued in the last chapter that the current circumstances of federal-provincial interdependence make necessary effective measures of intergovernmental collaboration in respect to fairly fundamental policy alternatives. On the other hand, a federal-provincial conference, unlike a constitutional convention, deals with specific proposals for action and does not have to strive for agreement on matters of abstract definition or on how to deal with hypothetical situations which may arise in the future. In the crucial area of the direction and control of the Canadian economy Jacques Parizeau has advanced a persuasive argument which is applicable to an even broader range of problems facing the Canadian federal system:

> [can we] conclude . . . that changes in the constitution are likely to help the organization of adequate and co-ordinated economic policies? Personally, I doubt this very much. On the contrary, the constitution as it stands now has helped to narrow the areas of conflict. To attempt, in present circumstances, a full revision or redrafting of the constitution means really that the whole front will be ablaze; any rational solution to urgent problems of economic policies might have to be postponed for a long time. It would seem much more fruitful to find first an empirical equilibrium between the governments and then draft it into a legal text.[8]

2. "Executive" Federalism and other Alternatives for Regulating Federal-Provincial Relations

There are two alternatives to cooperative federalism in regulating the relations between the federal and provincial governments. The first is that the judiciary should assume a more active role in delineating the respective powers, privileges and responsibilities of the two levels. This appears to be unrealistic in the light of recent experience in Canada and in other developed federations. Judicial interpretation of the constitution is almost inevitably sporadic and the predilection of the courts is to emphasize the exclusive jurisdiction of central and regional governments rather than the articulation of their activities. Furthermore, in Canada at least, many of the more important problems of federal-provincial relations, particularly as these concern fiscal matters and the direction and control of the economy, do not seem appropriate for judicial determination. The second alternative is to vest in some group or groups other than the courts the tasks of making some of the most important decisions in Canadian federalism. Such a group or groups would require some degree of independence of both levels of government. The Rowell-Sirois Report recommended "the establishment of a permanent and independent Commission to advise the federal government on the payment of National Adjustment Grants to the provinces and to reappraise each five years the criteria according to which such subsidies were paid." This recommendation received little support at the time it was made and has since been regarded as one of the commission's less constructive suggestions. In his recent book proposing a new Canadian constitution Peter J. T. O'Hearn suggests a "Federal Council" which, according to his draft constitution:

> shall consist of Delegates of the Government in Canada. Each Provincial Government shall appoint one Delegate and the Government of Canada shall appoint Delegates not exceeding in number the Provincial Delegates. The Chairman shall be elected from the Delegates of the Government of Canada and the Council shall meet at the Call of the Chairman or any Five Delegates. The Council may make a binding Allocation between the Government of Canada, on the one Hand, and the Governments of the Provinces, on the other Hand, for any Period not exceeding Ten years, of the Powers to tax and borrow, and may determine the limits of Rates or Amounts that shall apply to the Allocation; but to do so a Majority of the Delegates of the Provincial Governments representing a Majority of the Population of Canada, according to the latest general Census, must concur.[9]

It is significant that O'Hearn's proposal would permit such a "binding Allocation" of taxation and borrowing powers to be imposed on any or all of the provinces without their consent provided that the federal government and the requisite number of other provinces agreed. This condition alone would appear to make the proposal unrealistic. In general, the past history and present circumstances of Canadian federalism make it very unlikely that the federal government and the provinces will choose to have their relations regulated in fundamental ways either by the courts or by independent executive agencies explicitly charged with these responsibilities; nor, in my opinion would they gain any important advantages by doing so.

3. The Constitutional Recognition of Cooperative Federalism

Is it appropriate to redraft the constitution to provide for the institutions and procedures of cooperative federalism? The draft constitution suggested by Marcel Faribault and Robert M. Fowler provides for three federal-provincial agencies—an economic development bank, a fiscal commission and an economic and social council.[10] Under the proposed constitution each of these bodies would be composed of four members appointed by the federal government and two each appointed by Quebec, Ontario, the four western provinces and the Atlantic provinces. The economic and social council would be an information-gathering agency to transmit to all jurisdictions materials on "the general trend of the Canadian economy, its medium and long-term prospects, its productivity, and the rate of growth, as well as on the comparative growth of the several Canadian provinces, the improvement of the standard of living in their several regions and the general betterment of social relations in Canada." The economic development bank was to aid in the development of depressed regions, to remedy serious and unforeseen economic disturbances in particular provinces and to "aid in the execution" of important interprovincial projects. The major task assigned to the fiscal commission was to advise the governments concerned on their taxing and spending policies. The "statutes, regulations and by-laws" of the latter two groups were to be determined, according to the draft constitution, by "protocol between the federal government and the provinces by a three-fourth majority of the latter."

Faribault and Fowler nowhere demonstrate that the institutions and procedures they suggest would be preferable to the ones which are now in process of evolution. There is no evidence given, for example, that the proposed social and economic council would proceed more effectively than the present Economic Council of Canada in its rapidly developing pattern of relations with counterpart agencies in the provinces. Would the "fiscal commission" be more adequate in the devising or implementing of rational taxation and spending policies than the institutions which are now developing? Would the proposed federal-provincial bodies work under the direction of the increasingly frequent meetings of premiers and prime ministers? Such matters appear to have been ignored. Serious proposals for reform in federal-provincial relations must of necessity be based on a careful assessment of the adequacy of existing patterns of interaction. There is no evidence that Faribault and Fowler have done this.

It would seem prudent to try to rewrite the Canadian constitution only after the limits of adjustment possible through the procedures and institutions of cooperative federalism have clearly been reached. As we shall see in the last pages of this study there was some evidence early in 1966 that these limits were being approached.

C. COOPERATIVE FEDERALISM:
THE LIMITS OF ADJUSTMENT

In its legal-constitutional, political and administrative dimensions Canadian federalism has since 1867 demonstrated great resources of adaptability. The major procedures of adaptation in the postwar period have become the processes of federal-provincial executive interaction rather than constitutional amendment or changing patterns of judicial review. In the past 10 years through these interactions the dominance of the federal government established during the Second World War has been attenuated by the effective reassertion of provincial vigour and purpose. Is there then the danger that the influence of the federal government in part or all of the country will be so weakened by piecemeal attrition that Canadian federalism in any recognizable form will cease to exist? For the reasons presented in the concluding pages of this study, I believe this danger to be "clear and present."

The first kind of danger to the Canadian federal system in cooperative federalism is that provincial pressures for autonomy will so weaken the federal government that it will be unable to discharge its responsibilities for the integration and development of the Canadian economy, for economic stabilization and growth and for interregional and interpersonal equalization. There are strong forces towards the enhanced power of the provinces. The proportion of total public expenditures made by the provinces and local authorities is likely to continue to increase, barring rapid increases in defence spending. The new and more specific kinds of social and economic policies which now seem to be necessary make less feasible than before certain kinds of federal control over these matters. The provinces are likely to continue to attract able and purposeful people to their public services. In the House of Commons elected in November 1965, the under-representation of certain provinces in the government party and cabinet may work to make the governments of these provinces the most effective outlet for their distinctive sentiments and interests. Despite these influences, there are strong countervailing forces at work to restrain the further weakening of federal power, at least in the governments of the provinces other than Quebec if not the general public in English Canada. Several premiers have expressed their anxiety about this trend very explicitly and the government of Ontario has been particularly sensitive to these considerations. None of the other provinces has shown any desire to take advantage of the contracting-out option and none has been willing to cooperate with Quebec on a permanent basis to weaken federal influence. It appears too that all of these provinces are actively seeking increased federal financial assistance for particular functions, specifically for higher education and health services. It seems likely that the support of other provincial administrations for federal power will increase as the pressures of the

Quebec government for autonomy are pressed more aggressively and as the implications of the *statut particulier* alternative become more apparent.

The second kind of danger, and the one I believe more immediate, is that cooperative federalism will result in a situation in which the political and constitutional relationships between the people of Quebec and those of the other provinces will be so tenuous and so fragmentary—and so much mediated through the government of Quebec rather than being carried on within the institutions of the federal government—that a constitutional revolution destroying Canadian federalism will have been effected. The Lesage administration when it came to power and for some time afterward asserted the traditional Quebec position that it was demanding for itself only what under the constitution belonged equally to all the provinces; Mr. Lesage's defence of the Fulton-Favreau formula was largely on the grounds that any procedure for amendment acceptable to Quebec must provide for unanimous provincial consent in respect to changes in the most fundamental aspects of the constitution. The existing constitutional system, however, makes possible a very considerable amount of *de facto* differentiation between the position of Quebec and that of the other provinces. The Lesage government exploited these possibilities in a sophisticated and successful way. In its last months in power the official position of the Lesage administration apparently reversed the traditional position of the equality of all the provinces and embraced the doctrine of the *statut particulier*. The Honorable Paul Gérin-Lajoie at his convocation address to Carleton University in April 1965, gave advance notice to the new position by questioning in somewhat hypothetical terms the traditional viewpoint that in a constitutional sense Quebec was a province "comme les autres."[11] In his speech to the Ste-Foy Chamber of Commerce on December 14, 1965, Premier Lesage committed his government to the *statut particulier* alternative in the most explicit way.[12]

The claims for a special status for Quebec made by the Lesage government in its last year in office were more than a *post hoc* justification of the contracting-out arrangements which had already been implemented. These arrangements, so far as Quebec was concerned, confined the federal authorities, with several important exceptions, to matters within federal legislative jurisdiction. The attainment of such an objective did not satisfy the requirements of the Lesage government for a wider range of provincial autonomy or for an enhanced provincial influence over federal policy-making. In his Labour Day address in 1965, the Premier asserted that as his administration came to formulate more far-reaching and explicit plans in respect to manpower and employment it would press for modifications of federal activities in these fields, particularly those of the National Employment Service.[13] The new social security policy, whose outlines were announced by the Honourable René Lévesque in November 1965, included a system of family allowances based on very difficult principles than the federal scheme[14] and the same kind of considerations would logically have justified an attempt to replace the federal Old Age Security programme with a provincial one. As Quebec plans for regional development became more explicitly formulated it became reasonable to expect more aggressive efforts to bring federal developmental policies through the Department of Industry, ARDA and other agencies into harmony with provincial requirements. The assertion of the "personnalité internationale" of Quebec was leading to increasingly insistent demands that, without federal supervision or control, the province should be able to enter into direct relations with foreign nations in regard to matters within provincial legislative jurisdiction. The objectives of the Lesage government in the projected steel complex, the newly-created public sector of the mining industry, new plans for rationalizing agriculture and so on could be expected to result in new pressures to influence federal policies closely connected with these objectives. In December 1965, Mr. Lesage announced the creation of a committee under the chairmanship of Jacques Parizeau to study and report by the end of 1966 on the activities of certain classes of financial institutions and appropriate provincial legislation which might be enacted to regulate them. Eric Kierans is reported to have informed the federal-provincial conference the same month that Quebec would find contracting-out applied to new federal programmes unacceptable and would demand fiscal equivalents without undertaking any commitments about the service or facility in question.[15] Thus the pressures of the Lesage government in respect to specific fields of policy-making were working steadily towards a situation in which Quebec had a significantly larger scope of *de facto* autonomy than that possessed by the other provinces.

The creation of a special status for Quebec has implications of the most fundamental kind for the workings of the institutions of the federal government. If the present trends continue, Parliament will deal increasingly with matters for which Quebec has assumed exclusive responsibility within that province. Increasingly, important federal agencies which deal with matters of crucial concern elsewhere in Canada will have only a tangential relationship to the people and government of Quebec. Increasingly, federal elections will revolve about matters which have a direct relevance only outside Quebec. Such a situation will likely create new tensions between Quebec and the rest of Canada, and it seems unlikely that English Canada will accede simultaneously to pressures for both a special status for Quebec and a more influential role for French-speaking citizens from Quebec in the institutions of the federal government.

One might argue that here are changes which might be made in the structure and workings of federal institutions to accommodate the situation of a *statut particulier*. Paul Sauriol, editorialist with *Le Devoir*, envisaged a group of reforms in which the normal traditions of parliamentary government would prevail concerning matters within the exclusive jurisdiction of the federal authorities, while in "les domaines mixtes" the responsibilities would be assumed either by a reconstituted Senate or some federal-provincial body to which each level would delegate its powers in these affairs.[16] It seems unlikely, however, that such a solution could harmonize the differing conceptions of Quebec and the rest of the country on the appropriate role of the federal government.

The establishment of a *statut particulier* for Quebec within the Canadian constitutional system has important implications for the organizational relations between English- and French-speaking Canadians outside the governmental sphere. The theory and practice of the constitutional *statut particulier* mean that the most important political relations between the two cultural communities are conducted by their respective leaders "at the summit." This pattern of political relations would have to sustain and be sustained by corresponding kinds of interactions among private and quasi-public associations, those primarily concerned with public policy matters. In general terms, a special status for Quebec makes less possible the establishment of effective bicultural organizations on a country-wide basis than does a situation in which all the provinces assume broadly the same responsibilities. During a period when the division of functions between the two levels of government is a matter of controversy, organizations including important elements from the two cultural communities are subjected to severe internal strains when French Canadians from Quebec wish their province to have the exclusive powers to deal with affairs which other Canadians see as appropriate objectives of federal action. As particular aspects of the *statut particulier* are implemented, associations dealing with such vital concerns of public policy as higher education, welfare and health services, the exploitation and conservation of natural resources, municipal government, manpower and collective bargaining and so on can be expected to organize themselves into autonomous of semi-autonomous Quebec and non-Quebec elements. It is possible and even probable that the organizations will carry on some kind of formal relationships but these relations will be almost of necessity of a "fraternal" variety, precisely because their major focuses of attention are on different governments. It is to be expected also that these associations will be almost exclusively unicultural in both form and spirit. English-speaking Canadians from Quebec and French-speaking Canadians outside Quebec will find these associations inadequate vehicles for expressing their particular sentiments and interests.

The situation as it is evolving thus contains these elements.

First, so far as the provinces other than Quebec are concerned, the pressures towards autonomy which began in the late 1950s seem for the time being to have run their course. Among these administrations there is apprehension about the further weakening of federal power.

Second, the province of Quebec continues to press her demands both for a wider range of autonomy and for an enhanced degree of influence in matters within the legislative jurisdiction of the federal authorities.

Third, as the *de facto* differentiation between the position of Quebec and that of the other provinces increases, deep incompatibilities are revealed between federalism and the normal workings of federal parliamentary institutions, and between the *statut particulier* situation and the increased influence of French-speaking Canadians in the institutions of the federal government.

Can the continuing procedures of federal-provincial interaction enable the Canadian constitutional system to adapt to the new and contradictory demands now being made upon it? This seems unlikely. The directions in which the system is now being taken involve a constitutional revolution. There is nothing in the Confederation settlement as it was planned in 1864-67 or as it subsequently evolved which provides for a *statut particulier* in the form and dimensions clearly contemplated by the two successive governments of Quebec. It seems improbable that change of such a fundamental nature can be effected through piecemeal federal-provincial negotiation. Because Quebec has now charted its course in such explicit terms it is likely that in the future the federal government and the other provincial governments will evaluate Quebec demands within the framework of broader considerations than they have done in the recent past. The institutions and procedures of cooperative federalism have shown some capacity to deal with questions of ever-increasing generality. Federal-provincial relations in the period after the Second World War were dominated by considerations relating to specific programmes and facilities. More recently progress has been made concerning broader functions of government. The Tax Structure Committee has been charged with questions related to the most fundamental aspects of federal and provincial policies and more particularly with attempting to find agreement on broad expenditure-priorities. There may be continued success in these directions. It seems improbable, however, that federal and provincial executives could by agreement effect a revolution that would change the constitutional ties between Quebec and the rest of Canada to a quasi-diplomatic rather than a federal variety.

In spite of the analysis given above, I believe that it would be imprudent to take a deterministic view of the current crisis in the Canadian federal system.

On the one hand, it is unreasonable to take comfort in the "pendulum theory of federal and provincial powers," which asserts that there are somehow inherent forces at work which will as in the past prevent the attenuation of the powers of one level or the other to the extent that federalism is destroyed. There are of course conceivable circumstances which would lead to the effective reassertion of federal power so far as the government and people of Quebec are concerned. The partial or complete mobilization of the country in response to a deteriorating international situation would bring this about. It is possible to imagine a situation where politically influential groups throughout Canada come to believe that decentralization of power was costing too much in terms of economic stability and growth. Some new federal political leadership might emerge which would successfully commit the country to a bold and popular programme of reform, even in the face of the opposition of the government of Quebec and perhaps the governments of some other provinces. It is impossible to predict the likelihood of these circumstances occurring. It is unreasonable, however, to believe that any or all of them are inevitable.

On the other hand, it seems that Canadian federalism has not yet passed the point of no return. It is possible that the Quebec leadership will press its demands towards the *statut particulier* less aggressively than a reading of recent official pronouncements would lead one to believe. Fortunately, viable political arrangements do not need to conform to standards of logical consistency. It is possible that Canadians may be able to agree on a set of devices which allow each of the contradictory demands on the Canadian constitutional system to be met in part. Perhaps some new distribution of revenues, revenue sources and functional responsibilities can be effected which would provide both for the dominance of the federal government in economic matters and exclusive provincial responsibility, without the existing extent of federal involvement, in matters of provincial concern. Such a development would help to ensure the historic role of the federal government in economic matters and would also mitigate the difficulties inherent in a special status for Quebec within the Canadian federal system. Perhaps too the demands of the government of Quebec concerning particular matters will be discussed in the future within a framework which considers the cumulative impact of these demands on the survival of Canadian federalism. It is this last alternative rather than the piecemeal adjustments of cooperative federalism which gives best hope for the immediate future.

NOTES

[1] J. A. Corry, *Difficulties of Divided Jurisdiction: A Study Prepared for the Royal Commission on Dominion-Provincial Relations* (Ottawa: King's Printer, 1939), p. 10.

[2] Mr. Fulton did, however, submit the draft proposals to a selected group of university law teachers for their comments.

[3] For one of the few systematic attempts in this direction see Edwin R. Black, "Federal Strains within a Canadian Party", *Dalhousie Review*, Vol. XLV (1965), pp. 307-23.

[4] Daniel Johnson, *Egalité ou indépendance* (Montréal: Les éditions renaissance, 1965), p. 73.

[5] Hon. Jean-Luc Pepin, "Le fédéralisme coopératif" in Conférence annuelle de l'Institut canadien des affaires publiques, *Le Canada face à l'avenir* (Montréal, 1964), pp. 113-24.

[6] Peter J. T. O'Hearn, *Peace, Order and Good Government* (Toronto: MacMillan, 1964).

[7] Marcel Faribault and Robert M. Fowler, *Ten to One: The Confederation Wager* (Toronto: McClelland and Stewart, 1965).

[8] Jacques Parizeau, "Prospects for Economic Policy in a Federal Canada" in P.A. Crépeau and C.B. Macpherson (eds.), *The Future of Canadian Federalism* (Toronto: University of Toronto Press, 1965) p. 57.

[9] *Ibid.*, p. 45.

[10] *Ibid.*, pp. 145-48.

[11] Hon. Paul Gérin-Lajoie, "Convocation Address to Carleton University, April, 1965" (Quebec, Department of Education, Information Service, mimeo.). "Up to the present, Quebec has asked nothing for itself which it would be unwilling to recognize for the other provinces. But one may wonder if this is the correct attitude to take!" (p. 5) and "What objection or difficulty would there be if Canada were to adopt a constitutional regime which would take account of the existence of two 'nations' or 'societies' within one Canada?" p. 7.

[12] Reprinted in *Le Devoir*, 23 et 24 décembre, 1965.

[13] *Ibid.*, 3 septembre, 1965.

[14] *Ibid.*, 20 novembre, 1965.

[15] *Ibid.*, 14 décembre, 1965.

[16] Editorial, *ibid.*, 17 décembre, 1965.

PART IV
REGIONALISM AND
CANADIAN FEDERALISM

18

Regional Interests and Policy in a Federal Structure*

J. E. Hodgetts

Almost overnight, regionalism in Canada has become the current fashion and a subject for much intellectual speculation as well as administrative experimentation. This symposium** is but one of many testimonials to the growing interest in the subject. In 1964, the Committee on Statistics of the Canadian Political Science Association considered the problem. Early in 1965, Queen's University sponsored a conference on areas of economic stress that was the forerunner to a much larger conference on regionalism convened by the Province of Ontario. The Institute of Public Administration of Canada selected regionalism as the theme for its autumn conference. Recent reports of a royal commission in New Brunswick and of a legislative committee in Ontario are implicitly concerned with regionalism in so far as they propose basic remodelling of the local government services in their respective provinces. The Resources Ministers Council is grappling with the concept, as are also the federal departments of Industry and of Agriculture. On the international plane, the St. Lawrence Seaway and the Columbia River development have projected more grandiose conceptions of regionalism. In short, regionalism, with concomitant regional administrative structures, is being advanced as an answer to the new problems of interdependence that cut across traditional political boundary lines, whether they be municipal, provincial, or national.

The title chosen for this symposium suggests that regional interests are, indeed, a reality within the Canadian federal structure and that policy must accommodate itself not only to the familiar strains of dominion-provincial tensions but to the newer cross-currents of regionalism. The detailed implications of regionalism cannot be considered here, but resort to the analytical tools of the new school of systems analysts may help to develop certain general conclusions.

In essence, the systems analyst would picture the Canadian political system as a box surrounded by the environment. "Inputs" from the

* From *Canadian Journal of Economics and Political Science*, Vol. XXXII no. 1 (February, 1966), pp. 3-14. Reprinted by permission.

** This paper is a revision of a contribution made to a Symposium on "Regional Interests and Policy in a Federal Structure" sponsored jointly by the Association of Canadian Law Teachers and the Canadian Political Science Association, University of British Columbia, June, 1965.

environment are typically divided into demands and supports. Within the box marked "Canadian political system" the demand inputs are subjected to a conversion process that produces "outputs" which lead back to the environment; presumably the outputs must satisfy the demands or create new ones if they are to generate support for the system.[1]

Thus systems theory as envisaged by Gabriel Almond, one of its leading proponents, circulates through three phases—input, conversion, output. "The inputs and outputs which involve the political system with other social systems are transactions between the system and its environment; the conversion processes are internal to the political system."[2] Stability of the political system is found when (again according to Almond) "The demands can be handled by the political system; the strains which they impose are bearable without any basic change in structure or culture. The outputs are responsive to the demands in expected or legitimate ways; and the supports are responsive to the outputs again in expected or legitimate ways."[3]

In the light of this analysis regional interests would be treated as demand inputs, policy as an output, and the federal structure, in its widest sense, as the system that makes its transactions with the environment and in which the mysterious alchemy of the conversion process takes place.

What might be termed the classical model of the Canadian federal political system incorporates at least three sets of assumptions which may be stated in terms of the input-output model of the system analysts. The first assumption, on the input side, relates to the way in which the dispersed interests of free and rational individuals are pooled into a reservoir of will power to be channelled into the political system as the driving force for public policy outputs. The prerequisites are free speech, free association, the ballot, and a consensus that accepts the temporary ascendency of majority opinion. The transaction is accomplished preferably by two parties competing in the task of mobilizing nation-wide majorities. Parliament is the lens for bringing these demand inputs to a focus, sifting out the "demand overloads," and converting the remainder into public policy.

The classical model assumes, further, a separation between the agencies that are responsible for reconstituting, in the form of public policy, the scattered wills of the people and the agencies responsible for implementation of policy. That is to say, on the output side of the system, the executors of policy are viewed as separate from and subordinate and instrumental to the substantive policy-formers.

Finally, the addition of a federal framework complicates but does not necessarily disturb the tidiness of the traditional model. The classical conception of federalism assumed that the provinces occupied relatively clearly defined areas of local self-determination separated from an equally clearly defined set of jurisdictions assigned by the British North America Act to the central government. Thus, the democratic processes of policy formation could operate in virtually autonomous compartments whose edges touched but did not interpenetrate enough to cause confusion or require much collaboration.

The facts of Canadian life one hundred years ago may have approximated the conditions postulated by this classical model in which provincial political subsystems worked in relative isolation within a national system having rigidly defined jurisdiction. Today, however, it is clear not only that the circumstances with which public policy must come to grips have altered drastically but also that the assumptions implicit in the classical model have been eroded or warped by the many factors that have contributed to the shift from independence to interdependence of all the units embraced within the Canadian political system. There are now more elements attracted out of the orbit of other systems such as the family, the church, or the economy and, because they are assumed to have political relevance, they must swell the demand inputs of the political system. At the same time, these more numerous and more heterogeneous elements have to be rallied to the support of the system.

These transforming forces necessitate substantial revision of the classical model of the Canadian political system. Advanced students in political science courses are alerted to the necessity for adopting a more sophisticated analysis; practising politicians, on the other hand, are still often reluctant to admit that the conversion processes over which they preside have shifted their power centres, even though the old constitutional forms may have persisted.

Thus, the first assumption of a simplistic chain of demand reaching from the electorate to sovereign policy-making Parliament must be adjusted to make allowance for the growth of a mass electorate, the uneven expansion of individual constituencies, and the consequent growing heterogeneity of the interests and demands forcing themselves on elected representatives. Moreover, there are numerous indications that parties are losing their power to mobilize majorities drawn from all sections, thereby diminishing the integrating and articulating functions required of them by our political system. Parliament, itself, as the point of focus and conversion for the demands on the input side shows signs of the confusion which exists in its supporting party and electoral adjuncts. No matter how it extends the number of sitting days, Parliament as a corporate institution (rather than a mere reflector of party strengths in the nation) finds itself wedded to inefficient procedures, poorly organized, and inadequately staffed with the permanent expert help it needs nowadays to provide the information and knowledge required to grapple with complex public business. In short, the policy-making initiative has long since shifted to the executive.

Deriving from this shift and related to the growing complexity of public affairs, the classical view of a dichotomy between politics and administration—policy-making and execution—has disappeared to be replaced by administrative policy-making and adjudication. And, as the power centres change within the political system, our traditional channels leading from electorate to Parliament are no longer adequate to transfer the demand inputs to the relevant conversion machinery in the political system. New channels, new methods of aggregating, consolidating, and sifting demands have to be invented. By the same token, additional devices for measuring the effectiveness of the outputs in meeting demands and thereby generating supports for the system are needed. The old "feedback" devices (to borrow yet another term from the systems analysts)—the elected representative and the local party organization—require supplementation. Similarly, the role of the judiciary in ensuring fair play and thereby fortifying the support inputs for the system is pre-empted, in part, by the bureaucracy.

The classical conception of federalism has also undergone drastic revisions now submerged under the vague title "co-operative federalism."[4] On the one hand, the notion of self-determining, self-contained, viable administrative jurisdictions for each of the several provinces and the central government has been undermined by nation-wide transportation and communication links; "provincial" economies have been displaced by economic interdependence and complementarity; the forward thrust of the federal government into monetary and fiscal policies gives a new prominence to the centre and constrains the activities open to the provinces; governments at all levels by intruding into economic life as regulators or operators and by the rapid accretion of their welfare functions have been compelled to deploy their assigned powers to the fullest extent. It is not surprising that these efforts should end up on collision courses—that friction is generated, and that both duplication and jurisdictional no-man's lands should appear. The positive but sporadic and piecemeal efforts to ameliorate these jurisdictional and functional imbalances give rise to the new approach characterized as co-operative federalism. At the moment, however, the term more aptly describes the frame of mind with which governments face new problems and needs rather than a stable set of mechanisms for collaboration.

For two decades following publication of the report of the Rowell-Sirois Commission the conclusion, derived from the convergence of pressures reinforcing the trend toward interdependence, was that the central government would have to play the main role on the Canadian stage. Mobilization of society and the economy for all-out war pushed the provinces temporarily into the background and confirmed the pre-eminent role of the Dominion. During the war and for some time after the Canadian political system performed virtually as a single system. Now the pendulum has swung decisively in the other direction. The nationalistic modernizing revolution in Quebec is only the most dramatic expression of a fresh provincial self-assertiveness that derives in part from a buoyant economy and from mounting expenditures on such programs as education, welfare, health, highways, and resources that fall within provincial jurisdiction. But these advances of the affluent society cannot readily or sensibly be undertaken by reverting to the old pattern of a congeries of loosely connected subsystems. Now more than ever before it would seem imperative that we view the Canadian federation as a single political *system*. If co-operative federalism is to become more than a pious platitude of the politicians, the forces of interdependence and the interpenetration of the functions performed at all three levels by the traditional units of government compel us to adopt this new perspective on an old principle.

At first blush it might be assumed that the proliferation of regional structures will inevitably produce further irritants for the Canadian federal structure and that we will be driven even farther away from the ideal model of a single Canadian system. On the other hand, it may well be that the new stress on regionalism is a measure of the growing recognition that one cannot work the Canadian political system as a series of discrete compartments contained by traditional political boundaries. No more can one expect the long-standing departmental portfolios, whether provincial or federal, will provide the right mix of function or of appropriate jurisdictional reach for dealing with the new combination of skills and authority required by regionalism. Nor, finally, can we expect that the conventional channels for mobilizing the interests of the nation will adequately serve the new regional structures and the policy to be developed by them.

These generalized observations require elaboration and clarification. First, the meanings attached to the terms regionalism and regional interest ought to be stated. Regionalism, as used here, should not be confused with sectionalism, for as two American authorities claim: "Sectionalism—as a spirit, as a movement and as a political rallying point—tends to emphasize rivalry, provincialism, isolation, and self-sufficiency."[5] They go on to say that "the new regionalism . . . emphasizes the recognition of diversity of land and culture, the idea of integration and balance: integration of region with the whole nation, and balance of region with region."[6]

The spatial concept of a region supplemented by a homogeneity of culture or other features has enjoyed a paramount place amongst the analytical concepts applied to American politics and government. Thus David Lilienthal can remark that

The growth and development of our national policies is not the result of conflicts between states; it represents an attempted reconciliation between the interests of the various natural regions. . . .

Modern regionalism, by contrast, rests squarely upon the supremacy of the *national* interest. It admits that there are problems and resources common to areas larger than any single state—a river basin, for example. It recognizes that certain points of view develop in some portions of the country and are not shared by the nation as a whole. It affirms and insists, however, that the solution of regional problems and the development of regional resources are matters of concern to the whole country.[7]

REGIONAL INTERESTS AND POLICY

It would appear, then, that Americans have long become accustomed to thinking of a region as something more than a state but something less than the whole nation. Parenthetically, one may observe that even within the US counterpart of our Canadian Political Science Association the standard regions are enshrined in the subunits of the national Association, i.e., the Pacific Northwest, the Southern, the Western, etc., Political Science Associations.

In Canada, on the other hand, we are far less clear about the existence of regions with identifiable interests separate from the interests historically contained in and expressed through provincial units. In the First Annual Review of the Economic Council, under a Table labelled "Level and Growth of Personal Income per capita by region," we find the "regions" entitled Atlantic (with a footnote to say Newfoundland is excluded), Quebec, Ontario, Prairies, and British Columbia. This nomenclature, which is quite typical, reveals how quickly we exhaust the regional concept when applied across the nation: once the Maritimes and the Prairies have been mentioned we immediately fall back on the standard political, provincial boundaries. As for that region called the Canadian North, experienced observers are the first to proclaim its heterogeneity and the consequent impropriety of viewing it as a single entity. At the federal level positive administrative recognition of this restricted regional concept is to be found only in such agencies as the Atlantic Development Board, the Prairie Farm Rehabilitation Administration and the Northern Affairs Branch in the Department of Northern Affairs and National Resources.

Thus, if we are defining our region in national terms and thinking of it as an identifiable area having sufficiently common interests that they can be articulated and aggregated and urged on the federal government as part of the demand inputs of our political system, we really have nothing to compare with the American situation. The explanation for this difference may lie in the lack of party discipline in the US Congress and the popular nation-wide election of the Chief Executive. The fluidity of party lines in Congress permits bloc voting across party lines to take place without undermining the parties or the completely separate office of the presidency. In Canada, the rigour of party discipline imposed on MP's virtually eliminates the possibility of bloc voting in the name of the Prairies, the Maritimes, or any other region of transprovincial dimensions. We have no "corn belt" or "cotton bloc" voting. Indeed, the only way a regional interest can be assembled is through the political party processes *within* each province, by which means a Social Credit ramp from Alberta or a New Democratic party bloc from Saskatchewan may consolidate a minority voice in the House of Commons—but, once again, it should be noted, we are compelled to equate so-called regional interests with the separate provincial interests.

The popular election of the President under a system in which the majority winner takes all of the electoral vote in each state has made it possible to identify regional groupings of states that either hold the balance of power or have a species of veto power in the determination of the presidential winner. In Canada, while we now recognize that a national election tends to turn on the prime minister and the opposition leaders and thus becomes more like a US presidential election, in place of the concentration of support by identifiable blocs of states, the process is splintered into individual constituency contests that prevent us from identifying a genuine regional influence on the final outcome.

If the concept of region viewed from the national perspective in Canada lacks the substance and political influence that may be claimed for it in the United States, at the provincial level it is clearly emerging as a significant working concept. The increasing emphasis placed on region within the provinces derives from two complementary pressures. First, it has long been apparent to students of local government that the traditional political units are proving increasingly unsatisfactory in meeting the costly demands of urbanization, industrialization, and secularization. The problem is that functions have spilled out over the political boundaries, while authority to perform the functions remains legally chained to the traditional units of local administration. And, as functional responsibilities grow in number and expand in scope, the financial, technical, and manpower resources required for adequate performance need to be pooled across political boundaries. Over the last decade or so these deficiencies have become more marked under the impact of rapid social and technological change. The solution, reiterated in one official report after another, is amalgamation to form larger units or, at a minimum, a merger to perform specific functions.

Further support for the stress on region comes from a more recent acknowledgement by the provinces that there are actually elements missing from their existing organizational apparatus; there is a growing awareness that new functional needs and programs cannot be handled either by the long-standing departmental machinery of the province or even by the merging of present units of local government. One can think here, specifically, of the conservation authorities in Ontario or the more ambitious regional development associations in the same province.[8] The increasing respectability of government planning and the urgent demands for conserving and purifying our soil, water, and air all add to the pressures for a regional approach to these problems. The recently created Saskatchewan Water Resources Commission is an excellent example of a new agency for investigation, planning, co-ordination, and regulation of the development and use of water and related land resources—a multi-purpose assignment with which no single existing department could cope.[9] And, it should be added, not only are provincial and local authorities responding to these pressures, the federal government, too, is making its contributions through such legislation as the recent Agricultural Rehabilitation and Development Act which has fostered regional projects like the one for the Gaspé and has relied on two other regionally based federal agencies—the Prairie Farm Rehabilitation Administration and the Maritime Marshland Rehabilitation Administration—for its "operational arm."[10] The new Department of Industry, under Part II of its authorizing statute, visualizes yet another range of designated development areas.

The proliferation of new agencies, the amalgamation of old agencies, and the recombining of divisions pulled out of existing agencies would appear to provide ample testimony for the thesis that "regional interests" now constitute a significant element in the demand inputs to which the Canadian political system is clearly responding. This conclusion is nevertheless suspect on two counts. First, as already indicated we must discount the influence of regionalism of the American type that rallies interests and demands other than those that have always been expressed through traditional provincial political units. Second, one can go further by asserting that regionalism, at any level one wishes to take it, does not generate spontaneous demands that thrust themselves on the political system and are instrumental in influencing the policy outputs of the system. The region, in this particular stage of development at any rate, is not so much the creator of policy as the creature of policy.

Rephrasing this contention in terms of systems analysis, it can be argued that regionalism is not part of the demand inputs entering the system, but is a creation of the political system itself. David Easton, one of the founding fathers of the systems approach, has anticipated this possibility by coining the expression "withinput"[11] to apply to the not-uncommon situation where events and conditions within the political system may be as significant as any environmental inputs in shaping the ultimate outputs.

Obviously, there has to be a region if we are to think of a regional interest which, in turn, we visualize as shaping or influencing the control of public policy. What is argued here is that in most instances the region is, so to speak, the natural outcome of the adoption of a particular program or policy. The execution of the policy entails the creation of administrative units that must be set up on a regional basis in order to provide the most appropriate combination of functions and resources. In short, the policy, by defining the function or program, explicitly or implicitly creates a concept of the region required for the particular purposes envisaged.

One or two illustrations may serve to buttress what may appear to be a perverse attempt to put the cart before the horse. In the case of "the areas of slow economic growth" to which the Department of Industry was authorized to direct its services, it is clear that the regions might properly be called "bureaucratic constructs." The Minister explained, in 1964, how the initial designation of the areas was based on thirty-five national employment service areas "to bring about quick results and meet an emergency situation." He went on to say that his department was "presently engaged with the departments of finance and labour in making a detailed and exhaustive review of criteria for designating areas . . . which will enable us to single out those areas where special efforts will be required over the years if they are to participate more fully in the general prosperity of the country."[12] In this operation we find little evidence of pre-existing regional interests urging their demands on government; rather, we see the areas "designated" initially on the most convenient, available criteria and ultimately on the basis of more sophisticated statistical data processed within the public service itself.

The regional development program in the Province of Ontario affords a less extreme but perhaps more typical example. While stressing the element of partnership between "province, local municipal governments, and public-spirited local groups and individuals," the official pronouncement goes on to state quite frankly: "In initiating and financially supporting regional development through legislation, the Government of Ontario in the 10 Development Associations has officially recognized both the real need of, and the great potential benefits, which stem from this Provincial-Municipal partnership." It would not be unfair to claim that the Government of Ontario, and more precisely the Regional Development Division of the Department of Economics and Development, has, in effect, said to the municipalities: "Look, whether you know it or not, you have certain common regional interests in such matters as promoting tourism, industry, research and conservation and community planning; we, as a Department can deal with you best if you organize in regional groups; we are prepared to go half way in financing such organizations; and we confidently expect 'regional interests' will soon cluster around the organizations to which we shall be happy to respond in formulating subsequent policies." Again, we may conclude that the political system and not the environment has initiated the input in order to facilitate the conversion process and so trigger a policy output.

In my view this is the normal flow of events as they bear on the alleged forces of regionalism. Parenthetically, it is worth noting that this particular sequence has not been uncommon in the development of pressure group relations with the political system. The government has found it more convenient to respond to an organized pressure rather than attempt to negotiate with individuals or isolated groups. Thus, in 1906 the Department of Agriculture sponsored the meeting of the Canadian National Live Stock Association, and in 1914 helped finance the Sheep Breeders Association. H. H. Hannam, once president of the Canadian Federation of Agriculture, claimed that the Federation was brought into being because the first Bank of Canada Act called upon "organized agriculture" (then non-existent) to nominate members to the Bank's board of directors. And, just as advisory committees have been popular devices for giving official recognition to organized functional groups in the political system, so too, we almost invariably find provisions for setting up advisory adjuncts to the newer regional organizations.[13]

A final example, drawn from the Province of Quebec, illustrates one further aspect of the positive contribution of the political system to regionalism. The significant reorganization of the educational system of that province has apparently followed the path already described; that is, the political system has produced a global educational program and the ministry has designed the administrative apparatus which they think will permit the most effective implementation of the general goals. Decentralization was necessary and areas had to be designed for administrative purposes. One of the marked features of this development has been the extent to which political and permanent officials alike have had to carry the appeal to the regions in order to enlist their interest and participation. Some senior civil servants—and not merely those in educational administration, for much missionary work has had to be undertaken in other fields as well—have been perturbed by their inevitable public identification with a particular policy. This had its parallel in the Province of Saskatchewan two decades ago and perhaps Quebec civil servants, witnessing the recent exodus from that part of the West after a change in government, may fear that history will repeat itself in their province. In any event, reverting once more to systems analysis, we find this particular experience in Quebec illustrates not only how the political system can generate its own demands but can at the same time take positive action to create its own supports by manipulating the regional environment in the way just described. The reliance on advisory committees, in conjunction with such programs, shows that in the absence of spontaneous regional interests to create demands and provide supports, the government itself has had to create the organizational framework in which such demands and supports might be expected to germinate. These examples of a pervasive and universal development also buttress an earlier contention; our traditional techniques for aggregating demands and supports—the geographic constituency, the political party, and Parliament itself—have had to be supplemented and possibly even by-passed by these more direct and deliberately constructed tools.

It would be tempting to extend this paper to take into account more specific bureaucratic responses to the forces of regionalism. One might, for example, describe in detail the particular organizational pattern developed by each federal department and agency to resolve the problem of administering a federal domain where three-quarters of the work force has to be employed outside the headquarters area. On the whole, however, such a detailed story would simply reinforce the main conclusions of this paper, namely, that there are few genuinely spontaneous regional interests in Canada that have an independent impact on policy; and where they do exist our political system working through disciplined parliamentary parties, only permits them to be aggregated and articulated within conventional political boundaries. Thus the growing recognition of regions is basically an artifice of administrators who, working within the political system, play a creative role in constructing regions appropriate to the functions entrusted to them; in some cases, this positive initiatory role may even compel public servants to desert their neutrality in order to generate support from a sometimes indifferent environment which has to be alerted to the task of formulating its own interests around the regional construct. Finally, it may perhaps be argued that, once over the present formative stage, the genuine need for a regional approach to policy-formation and implementation will in itself begin to create self-generating demand and support inputs which will no longer be bureaucratically inspired.

It remains to be seen whether parties can retain their role as aggregators of demands based on new regional interests that are not necessarily tied to the traditional provincial units or whether, along with the proliferation of advisory committees, we will need to design new mechanisms for this purpose. The larger question of Parliament's capacity to convert such regional demands into acceptable policy outputs also constitutes a major challenge to our ingenuity. Meanwhile, at the present intermediate stage of growth, governmental agencies are all energetically throwing themselves into the breach and we are already faced with such a maze of special regions that we may be unable to co-ordinate disparate regional entities. If this development persists we must abandon any hopes we have of gearing our institutions and policies to the conception of a single Canadian political system.

NOTES

[1] The clearest, most succinct, and up-to-date description of political systems analysis is in Gabriel A. Almond's "A Development Approach to Political Systems," *World Politics*, Vol. XVII, no. 2 (January, 1965) pp. 183-214.

[2] *Ibid.*, p. 189.

[3] *Ibid.*, p. 193.

[4] The precepts of classical federalism and the forces that have contributed to the growth of so-called "co-operative federalism" are perceptively developed in J. A. Corry, "Constitutional Trends and Federalism" in A. R. M. Lower, F. R. Scott, *et al., Evolving Canadian Federalism* (Durham, N.C: Duke University Press, 1958), pp. 92-125.

[5] Richard Carlton Snider and H. Hubert Wilson (eds.), *Roots of Political Behaviour: Introduction to Government and Politics* (New York: American Book Company, 1949), pp. 452-53.

[6] *Ibid.*, p. 453.

[7] Quoted in *Ibid.*, pp. 463-64, from David E. Lilienthal, *TVA: Democracy on the March* (New York: Harper, 1953,).

[8] The guiding philosophy for the development associations is that: "Local development serves the local citizen best when it takes into account regional development and harmonizes with it. Today more than ever before, the township, the village, the town, city, county and district are economic partners. What each does affects the other. We live in regional economic neighbourhoods and this is not a theory; it is a fact." See brochure of Ontario Department of Economics and Development, Regional Development Division, *Regional Development*.

[9] *Statutes of Saskatchewan*, chap. 32 (1964). The Commission brings together the permanent heads of the three agencies which each carry responsibility for a part of the task, together with three other cabinet appointees, the provincial premier is the minister responsible for the Commission—thereby suggesting its essentially co-ordinative role.

[10] *Statutes of Canada*, 9-10 Eliz. II, chap 30 (1961). See Department of Agriculture, *Annual Report for 1962-63*, p. 56.

[11] *A Framework for Political Analysis* (Englewood Cliffs: Prentice Hall, 1965), p. 114.

[12] *Debates*, House of Commons (Canada, 1964), p. 7395.

[13] For example, the appropriate Minister is authorized to appoint advisory committees under the Agricultural Rehabilitation and Development Act and the Department of Industry Act and the Saskatchewan Water Resources Commission Act.

19

Regionalism and Canadian Political Institutions

Richard Simeon

"Region," "regional," and "regionalism" are three of the most common terms in Canadian political discourse, whether academic, governmental or journalistic. Yet the meanings and significance of these terms remain confused. I will try to clarify some of these usages and then go on to argue that the regionalized character of Canadian politics—part of our conventional wisdom—is not only a function of the territorial character of our underlying ethnic, economic and cultural diversity, but also, perhaps more important, a result of the operation of three major institutional characteristics of Canadian Government: the federal system, the electoral system and British-style cabinet government. These serve systematically to reinforce and make salient the territorial dimensions of political life, and to dampen, minimize or curtail non-regional—or national—cleavages. We institutionalize the regional dimension. This effect is supplemented by a kind of self-fulfilling prophecy in the work that many Canadian political scientists do. To some extent, we usually find what we are looking for: thinking regionalism to be important, that's what we study, and lo, that is what we find.

Before pursuing this argument, let us look a little more closely at the meaning of regionalism itself. Virtually all students of Canadian politics have emphasized such things as the regional character of Canadian life and politics generally, the highly regionalized economic structure, the differences in national and ethnic origins of the populations of the various provinces, the strong correlation of region with voting preference, the regional character of party strength, the visibility of conflict between regions—whether central Canada versus the extremes or east versus west, the regional elements in representation in the federal cabinet, and so on. Canadian politics is indeed regional politics.

But we need to be a good deal more systematic both in how we conceive of the phenomenon "regionalism" and in how we describe its dimensions and effects. We must first recognize that in no sense is it an

Author's note: This paper was originally presented to an honours seminar at the University of Saskatchewan in Saskatoon, in January, 1975. I thank the Department of Economics and Political Science for giving me the opportunity to develop these ideas. In large measure they represent an elaboration and restatement of some points which were less explicit in my *Federal-Provincial Diplomacy* (Toronto: University of Toronto Press, 1972).

explanatory variable: by itself it doesn't explain anything; nothing happens because of regionalism. If we find differences of any sort among regions, it remains for us to find out *why* they exist; regionalism is not an answer. In this sense, regions are simply containers, whose contents may or may not differ. And how we draw the boundaries around them depends entirely on what our purposes are: it is an *a priori* question, determined by theoretical needs or political purposes. We can have regions within provinces, or regions made up of groups of provinces, or regions cutting across provincial lines. That we have come to identify regionalism in Canada as being almost synonymous with *province* is a nice example of the institutional effect I mentioned. We do so because the provinces are the significant political units.

We also need to distinguish between regionalism used in several different senses. First, there is a distinction between regionalism in the sense that regions or provinces differ among themselves along such dimensions as demographic make-up, economic and social structure, party systems, patterns of policy outputs, and the like; and regionalism in the sense that national politics is about the interplay between the interests of different provincial governments, or between their interests and those of the federal government. The first perspective takes us in the direction of comparative politics, conceiving of Canada as a collection of ten loosely integrated political systems in which our prime concern is to describe and explain the differences among them. Much more of this kind of work needs to be done. The other focus takes us in the direction of the study of federalism itself, looking at the means by which provincial interests are expressed, at conflicts and negotiations between the two levels of government, at the role of national political institutions (like parties) in expressing and accommodating the interests of different regions, and so on. There is an important difference between politics *within* a province, the participation of provincial populations in national parties and institutions, and the role of *provincial governments* in making national policy.

We also need to make a distinction between regional differences in what may be called political culture, and regional differences in substantive political goals and interests. To say there are differences in the political cultures of the provinces—that their citizens tend to think in quite different terms about their role as political actors, or about the legitimacy of political leaders—is not to say that we can predict there will be conflict or division between their governments. Areas with very similar cultures can have very different substantive interests, and therefore engage in high levels of conflict. Conversely, areas with very different cultures may have similar interests. Indeed, the cultural difference might minimize conflict: for example, if Maritimers had the activist political orientations of British Columbians, we could predict that conflict between the

Maritime provinces and central Canada or the federal government would be much more intense, since the Maritimers would be much less willing to accept their deprived lot. Thus we need to be careful not to equate one kind of regional difference with another. There may be such relationships, but they should be investigated, not assumed.

In addition, it is important to distinguish between three levels of analysis when looking at differences among the provinces or regions. There are differences in basic social and economic structure—proportions of people in different kinds of occupations, differences in ethnic, linguistic or demographic makeup, different kinds of industry, different levels of wealth, and the like. These basic differences may or may not give rise to variations at the next level, that is to different political goals, attitudes and interests. Potential cleavages may or may not become politicized; they may or may not be defined in regional terms. For example, a poor New Brunswick logger may explain his poverty by saying he is disadvantaged because he is a New Brunswicker, or because he speaks French, or because loggers everywhere always get a poor deal. Which attitude or perception he and others like him develop will have very important consequences for whether or not political conflict comes to take the form of conflicts between regions or takes some other form. The third level is that of political action or behaviour. Different attitudes again may or may not be translated into different political activity; some will be acted upon, others will not. Some divisions in the electorate become reflected in voting behaviour, party platforms and parliamentary debate; others are ignored.

Which potential divisions become translated into attitudes, how people come to explain and define the issues and which viewpoints find political expression is a vital question. The answer depends very much on the role played by political leaders and institutions. Which lines of division do they stress, which do they ignore? Given a problem or grievance, how do the leaders define it? And what vehicles or opportunities do leaders provide for people to act on their feelings? A person might feel passionately about an issue, but if no party mentions it, or if both give the same response, then he cannot make his opinion politically effective. Thus the translation into politics of latent political cleavages, resulting from differences in the socio-economic base, depends very greatly on the role of political leaders, who have considerable autonomy in deciding which to highlight and which to downplay, and on the role of institutions in placing hurdles in the way of politicizing some divisions and facilitating the politicization of others. As E. E. Schattscheider has said, "All forms of political organization have a bias in favour of the exploitation of some kinds of conflict and the suppression of others. . . . Some issues are organized into politics while others are organized out."[1]

Many studies have shown that there are indeed some clear differences among the Canadian provinces along a number of different dimensions. At the level of attitudes, work by David Elkins and myself [2] suggests that there are some systematic variations in basic orientations towards politics from province to province, and that these are not merely because of differing socio-economic characteristics: there do appear to be regional climates of opinion or cultures, which appear to be the product of long-standing political traditions, historical experience, and the like. The results of surveys designed to measure the extent to which people identify more strongly with the provincial community than with the national community are very unclear, but we do know that in some provinces large proportions of the population identify strongly with the provincial community. At the level of political behaviour, province, along with religion and language, is one of the most important determinants of voting. Party strength varies greatly from province to province. Gallup polls suggest that on some issues, the province of residence seems to be more important in shaping opinion than other causes. So the case for a view of Canada as a highly regionalized society is well-established.

But there are problems. First, many of these dimensions are not well mapped. Only a few of the important elements of significant cultural differences have been explored. Very little has been done to map interprovincial variations on opinions about substantive policy issues.

Second, we very often tend to overestimate the degree of homogeneity within provinces, and to underestimate the similarities across provinces. To say Quebec wants this or the west wants that is to assume that their populations are somehow unanimous. They may be, but my guess is that they would be only on a small number of issues, and we know that even in Quebec, internal divisions are deep and powerful. This perception of provincial unity occurs partly because of a natural tendency to stereotype, and unconsciously to translate differences in proportions into absolute ones. When we think of Saskatchewan, we—at least in Ontario—think of a province full of farmers; when we think of Ontario we assume everyone is an auto worker and lives in Toronto; in British Columbia everyone is a logger; in the Maritimes, everyone is poor. This tendency is often reinforced by the way we present our data. The regional breakdown is presented first, and other possible breakdowns are neglected. But there is a very big difference between saying what proportion of all Maritimers are poor and saying what proportion of all poor people are Maritimers. One's policy responses to the problem of poverty will be very much influenced by which proportion one has in mind. In fact, we know that, while there are some fairly strong associations between region of residence and other variables, especially language and (to a lesser extent) occupation, there are few lines of difference or potential cleavage which perfectly co-incide with or reinforce the provincial difference. And few provinces are perfectly homogeneous in basic social and economic characteristics, or in attitudes and behaviour.

I do not want to argue that differences between regions are insignif-icant or that they are politically unimportant. My argument is that the differences are not as great as often assumed, that there is more crosscutting of region with other cleavages than is usually assumed, and most important, that the *reason* we have formed these perceptions, and the reason that Canadian political life does indeed revolve largely around regional considerations is not to be fully explained by the dif-ferences themselves. They are to be explained also by the interaction of the underlying differences with the effects of the institutional struc-ture.

Thus, some of the kinds of regional differences in attitude we have discussed are not so much the cause of regionalized politics, but are themselves the result of a regionalized political structure. The political framework leads politicians, commentators and academics to assert the regional or provincial perspective, in turn encouraging voters to see the world in this way. The New Brunswick logger is thus more likely to see the cause of his grievance as being the evils of central Canada than he is to see it as being the result of the wrongs of the economic system.

To be politically important, as it undoubtedly is, regionalism there-fore needs to be more than simply the correlation of certain economic, social or other characteristics with provincial boundaries. It must also in-clude some degree of self-consciousness, some widespread sense of the provincial community as the most relevant political unit or category, some sense that when people say *we* they are referring not to people of the same religion, or class, or educational groups, or occupation, nor to *we* in the sense of an undifferentiated whole national community, but rather to *we* the residents of this province. When an Albertan says "We should reap the benefits of our oil," the community he has in mind could plausibly mean Albertans, Westerners, all Canadians or even some non-geographic group such as oil workers. Which it is, and how such identities are formed is crucial. Now that process of self-definition does depend partly on the sharing of certain characteristics. But not en-tirely. Residents of any country may share loyalties but differ on many other grounds. Conversely social characteristics can be shared with resi-dents of other communities without their being strong shared feelings of identity. In large measure, these identities come from a common tradi-tion and history, mediated through such mechanisms as schooling (which, of course, is a provincial matter in Canada). They also require some form of institutional focus, some organizing mechanisms which will define the boundaries and provide the means of making decisions.

Without such a focus, it seems likely that all but the most strongly entrenched identities will begin to wane, and that new identities will start to form. Moreover, the existence of a set of boundaries and institutions sets in motion a series of political interactions which may themselves lead to the development of a particular sense of community, to the emergence of political differences, and to the development of new loyalties. Perhaps an example in Canada is what happened after Alberta and Saskatchewan were split and made provinces in 1905: a single undifferentiated area rapidly developed into two quite distinct political systems.

This suggests that institutions are not simply the outgrowth or products of the environment and that they are not just dependent variables in the political system. They can also be seen as independent forces, which have some effects of their own: once established they themselves come to shape and influence the environment. To take the most obvious example: clearly we have a federal system in Canada in large part because of the regional diversity of Canada; but, once established, does federalism in the long run operate so as to diminish these differences or rather to highlight and perpetuate them? I think the latter. There must be some congruence between institutions and the underlying social system, but it is equally evident that the effect is two-way. We might note here that some of the most important institutional characteristics of Canadian government did not, so to speak, evolve out of pressures from the society below, but were imported and imposed from the top. This is the case with cabinet government, with our electoral system and—dramatically at one point in our history—with some of the decisions about the operation of the federal system handed down by the Judicial Committee of the Privy Council. Moreover, a given social and economic structure may be equally congruent with a variety of institutional forms. Thus, the nature of Canadian society seems to ensure that, one way or another, Canadian politics is going to be heavily concerned with the problems of accommodating the interests of groups in different regions. But one can imagine a variety of political forms in which that accommodation might take place. For example, the central government itself might be so structured as to respond to regional interests: federal departments could be structured not along functional lines, but on regional lines, as is the Department of Regional Economic Expansion (DREE), or regions could have direct representation in a national legislature, as in the United States Senate or the German Bundesrat.

Let us look at some of the possible effects of the major institutions of Canadian politics in this light. First, they appear to affect the kinds of identities which Canadians develop. Second, they influence the kinds of cleavages which are given formal, organized expression, and which, on the other hand, remain weakly articulated and thus condition the basis and intensity of social conflict. Third, they shape the way policy issues are perceived, the manner in which they are debated and decided, and the nature of the outcome.

We need not spend long on the first institutional dimension, the electoral system, since it has been discussed by Alan Cairns and others.[3] The point is simply that while it is true that voting is highly correlated with region, the electoral system appears to operate so as to exaggerate greatly this regional effect. An inspection of party representation in Parliament by region gives a quite different image than an inspection of votes by region. Cairns suggests that the electoral system under-represents those whose support is more evenly distributed nationally. It also leads parties to pursue regionalized strategies, so that we find national party leaders arguing strenuously for national unity, and, at the same time, stressing regional differences. This was nicely illustrated by the Liberal strategy in 1972. Moreover, the freezing-out of regions like the west from adequate representation in the governing party exacerbates regional tensions. Party strategies might be very different if each province were a single constituency with proportional representation, or if we had a few large constituencies not coterminous with provincial boundaries, or if we had pure proportional representation and one national constituency. The assumption here is that one very important effect of institutional factors is to provide political leaders with different incentives—to make some courses of action more attractive, and to make others less so. Political strategies will be based both on perceptions of policy attitudes in the public and on the constraints and opportunities imposed by the institutional framework. Another way of looking at institutional characteristics like the electoral system is as S. M. Lipset and Stein Rokkan do, namely, as raising or lowering the hurdles facing potential groups in getting organized and gaining representation.[4] I think Cairns is right here—our electoral system does raise the hurdles for parties like the NDP and lower them for parties like Social Credit. One other institutional characteristic concerned with elections might be mentioned. In the United States, local, state and federal elections are typically all held on the same day. While straight-ticket voting does seem to have declined in recent years, it still suggests a tendency for state and national politics to be linked together and to move in similar directions. It also encourages state and national candidates to advocate roughly complementary policies. The separation of the three levels in Canada means that each election is a new event, with new issues, parties and leaders. It helps maintain the largely non-partisan character of local elections and to stress the separation between national and provincial parties and politics generally.

The second major institutional characteristic is the organization of the national government, influenced especially by the importation of the

British cabinet system. The logic of cabinet government, and the conco-mitant strict party discipline, sharply reduce the ability of the federal government to reflect within itself Canada's regional diversity. To the extent that the institutions were able to do so, the pressure to use pro-vincial governments to propound the views of important provincial groups would decline. Cabinet solidarity places severe limits on the abil-ity of a minister to act as a regional spokesman. Party discipline does the same for MPs and inhibits cross-party regional alliances. For both, the system of incentives in Ottawa leads them to concern themselves with national matters, to stress issues in federal jurisdiction, and to stress their loyalty to the party—all in contradistinction to a view of themselves as spokesmen of a region, or of a province or provincial government. The organization of the departments both reflects and reinforces this tendency. With partial exceptions, like DREE, departments are structured along functional or economic lines rather than along regional lines. The increased size and complexity of the federal government in recent years may, in fact, have lessened the ability or desire of ministers to act as regional spokesmen—certainly Otto Lang plays his role of a Minister from Saskatchewan very differently from Jimmy Gardiner.

Two objections might be made to this analysis. First, it could be, and has been, argued that the institutions of the central government are in fact highly responsive to regional interests. Thus we have the well-known and long established principle of regional representation in the cabinet. But I do not think that this can automatically be translated into actual regional influence, or sensitivity to regional interests among cabi-net ministers. An obvious case of regional representation recently is the role of the cabinet membership from Quebec, but even here it is clearly not representative of a very large body of opinion in that province.

Part of the difficulty is in defining just what is the "interest" of a region. It could be defined as the interests of the provincial government, but as we shall see, a government's interests may be quite distinct in some respects from those of its population and very different from those of a federal minister from the province. Or a province's "interest" might be that of the most influential groups within the province, but that leaves out other groups who may have potential alliances with groups in other provinces. Or, it can be an interest somehow of the whole of the citizens of a province. It seems to me to be very important not to reify the idea of province or region too much: they don't have interests—groups and organizations do. Beyond general, and perhaps mainly sym-bolic, feelings—such as "western alienation"—it seems to me that there are probably few issues on which provincial populations as a whole can be said to espouse different interests. Again, there is a tendency to exag-gerate. For example, many people seem to associate concern with foreign ownership with Ontario, since there has been a traditional concern for protection of manufacturing there, and to see westerners as hostile to such demands. But I do not think that survey evidence supports that view. I would very much like to see an analysis of Gallup poll issue questions classified by subject area and time period: my guess is that on only a few types of issues would the primary division be regional. Thus it is difficult to think of cabinet ministers as primarily representing regional interests.

It might also be said that Ottawa has become more sensitive to regional interests in recent years. Witness the protestations of concern for the West after the 1972 election (but witness also the quick receding of this interest). Or witness the establishment of the regional desks in the Privy Council office and the Prime Minister's office (the latter, which appear to have faded away, were in themselves a recognition of MP's inability to act as effective regional spokesmen). It is true that the Trudeau government has responded not just to Quebec's demands for autonomy, but also to those of other provinces, by arguing that they can find a home in Ottawa too. But it is a recent development, and the recent regional sensitivity of Ottawa is in large part a product of the provinces' own greater power and assertiveness. Some of this regional sensitivity also seems mainly symbolic, for example, the headquarters of the Canada Development Corporation was to have been established in Vancouver. But in fact only a token operation was established there—the main office and most of the President's time is spent in Toronto.

A more powerful objection to this analysis is to say that this view of Ottawa is insensitive to regional interests, however defined, demonstrates the existence of a major institutional thrust towards the decline of regional distinctiveness, rather than to a stressing of regional divisions. But if the Ottawa government was explicitly organized around the representation of regional interests, then they would be incorporated into *national* policy making at the centre. Ottawa—not federal-provincial conferences—would become the prime arena for accommodation. The participants in that accommodation process would be much less tied to particular regional and—more important—provincial government interests than they are now. Regional considerations would therefore be domesticated or diluted; policy coalitions based on other factors would be more important on many issues. As it is, local interests are pushed to express themselves through the provincial governments, bargaining as co-equals with Ottawa. Lipset once argued that the persistence of third parties is partly due to the awkwardness of British style cabinet government in a diverse social setting; the same argument can be made for assertive provinces. In this sense, the consequence is that the structure of national institutions tends to separate federal and provincial political systems.

The third and most important institutional factor is, of course, federalism itself, though again I should note that it is not so much the institutional factor itself, but the way it interacts with other social forces that shapes the way the system operates at any given time.

Federalism can be analyzed from two perspectives. We can ask, does it institutionalize and perpetuate the salience of regional communities and interests; or we can ask does it serve as an institutional means whereby territorially-based cleavages can be regulated or accommodated. As we all know, it does the latter by allowing local majorities to pursue their own goals in some areas, without the possibility of being vetoed or frustrated by other groups, and by providing a set of mechanisms for negotiating differences when interests do overlap. Without disagreeing with this, I wish to concentrate on the first perspective. Federalism is not only a *response* to regionalism, but also ensures that it will continue. It does so in several ways. As mentioned before, it provides an institutional focus for loyalty and identity. There is a *political* cleavage laid over the other cleavages in the society and it tends to force other cleavages into the same mould. That is, those cleavages which reinforce the territorial division will be highlighted; cleavages which do not do so will either be defined in such a way that they do conform to the pattern, or they will tend to be ignored. There are two reasons for this. At the societal, or mass level, conflicts will tend to be encapsulated at the provincial level. Because provincial governments make the decisions, groups will have to turn to them, will have to respond to provincial policies and to the demands of other groups with which they are in competition at that level. Communication with similar groups in other provinces will therefore be inhibited, and indeed be strategically wasteful. For example, labour law in Canada is largely a matter of provincial jurisdiction. The labour movement itself therefore must take on a federated character and provincial labour federations must be primarily concerned with fighting their own local battles. If labour laws were primarily a national concern, the national labour groups would presumably be more powerful, and there would be a strong incentive for labour groups and associated political leaders to promote labour unity across provincial boundaries. The same analysis might be made for other groups and interests in other fields. The point is that the federal structure fragments these social forces, and inhibits their mobilization on a national basis. It thus perpetuates the regional difference.

At the elite level, federalism has similar effects by conferring leadership on a set of leaders in provincial governments who have vested interest in maintaining and strengthening the salience of the regional dimension. The provincial governments do more than just respond to demands from their populations. First, they respond to some groups more than others; and, more important, they have, as complex organizations in their own right, certain bureaucratic needs, especially the need to gain power, to enhance their status, and to maintain their political support. So, of course, has the federal government. This is the truth behind the common observation that somehow the interests of the public get lost in federal-provincial discussions. Thus to maintain support, a provincial government is motivated to accentuate the degree of internal unity, and to exaggerate the extent of difference with Ottawa, and to divert political conflict onto an external enemy. They are likely to stress issues in such a way that their internal divisions are minimized, and to stress most those issues on which there is least internal disagreement. They are also less likely to be concerned with the substance of issues, and more likely to be concerned with those aspects of an issue with the greatest importance for them as governments. They are less concerned with what is done than with questions like who does it and who gets the credit. One does not need to assume that provincial leaders are foolish or evil, or that each will pursue the same policies. One simply has to recognize the importance of certain well-known characteristics of organizational behaviour. In this sense the interests of a provincial government are quite different conceptually from the interests of the residents of the province. And it is governments which have most prominence in the policy-making process.

Another institutional characteristic reinforces this process: the cabinet system centralizes power within each government. This inhibits the development of the common American pattern of a complex set of relationships between bureaucrats at the professional and technical levels (at which shared professional and policy norms might outweigh governmental rivalries), and instead channels conflict to the senior level where the political and organizational concerns are likely to be strongest.

The consequences of this pattern are well-known: a complex pattern of bargaining between governments, in which there is at one and the same time a high level of interdependence, and a strong measure of built-in conflict and disagreement. It ensures that the significance of territory will constantly be emphasized, and that policy making will focus primarily on the territorial dimension. Thus, discussion of poverty tends to be transmuted into the problem of regional disparities; transportation debate focusses on such problems as where a service facility will be located and on the Crow's Nest Pass rates, rather than on how other social groups are served. Discussion of major social programs such as the Canada Pension Plan, or medicare, or university financing, turn on who will operate them, who will pay, and so on, rather than on such questions as how best to serve the social need. The acrimonious debate on energy policy is largely about which government should control the industry and reap the benefits. French-English relations are defined as a Quebec-Ottawa problem about the division of powers. Competing problems, and competing definitions of the issues are not easily expressed. The governmental preoccupation with the federal-provincial game reduces their ability to respond to other interests. In recent years, each level of government—though this applies to some provinces more than others—appears to be continually probing the other's areas of primary responsibility. While the "feds" are more active in urban affairs and worrying about a bigger federal role in education, the provinces are acting on cable television, manpower and others. There are enough constitutional grey areas that some constitutional peg can always be found on which to hang a new policy initiative. The motives, of course, are complex—each government is responding to its own substantive policy interests and to the perceived needs of its constituents. Thus, it is not all a matter of intergovernmental jockeying for status and prestige. But nor should the importance of such motives be ignored. Moreover, the arcane constitutional and fiscal language of federal-provincial diplomacy, and the secrecy of negotiations may also have the effect of freezing out general public awareness of and participation in policy making. For all these reasons, we get the impression from watching the Canadian policy process that the territorial dimension is central; I suspect it is much less so for most citizens.

It is impossible to weigh the impact of the constitutional characteristics I have discussed against other social and political forces making for regional differences and regional cleavages. Nor did these institutions create regionalism: but they do perpetuate it, and give it particular forms. Wars, depressions and other major events may well change the balance between governments, and alter the focus on region; so might the longer-term effects of such nationalizing agencies as the CBC. But it is interesting to note that these nationalizing forces have been long predicted, and regionalism has probably actually increased in recent years. The institutions we have discussed provide powerful resources by which governments and others interested in stressing regional dimensions of politics can resist these forces, or even redefine them in such a way as to fit them into the regional mould. Thus Canada is a major exception to the developmental model of Rokkan, for whom modernization implies a progressive diminution of territorial and cultural divisions, and their replacement by functional and national ones.

The argument I have made is not terribly new: much of it, we know has been made by Cairns, Lipset and others. It also bears some resemblance to John Porter's discussion of federalism, and to those of the other writers of the "creative politics" school. Like them, I think federalism has inhibited the development of national, class-based politics (though it is by no means the only factor). They, however, stress the role of institutions less than the role of ideology (brokerage politics and national unity), and its link with powerful conservative economic interests. In Porter's view, institutions are subordinate to ideology, and provincial leaders are subordinate to powerful interest groups. While not wishing to diminish the importance of ideology, I give institutions a more prominent role than he does. I do not share the hostility to federalism of some of these writers. Creative politics does not necessarily need to be carried out on a national stage. My main point here, though, is empirical. We have concentrated too much on the causal linkages from society to institutions. I hope I have shown that the arrow runs the other way too.

NOTES

[1] Richard Simeon and David Elkins, "Regional Political Cultures in Canada," *Canadian Journal of Political Science* VII (Sept. 1974), 394-437.

[2] E. E. Schattscheider, *The Semi-Sovereign People* (New York: Holt, Rinehart and Winston, 1966), p. 71.

[3] Alan C. Cairns, "The Electoral System and the Party System in Canada 1921-1965," *Canadian Journal of Political Science*, I (March, 1968), 55-80.

[4] S. M. Lipset and Stein Rokkan, *Party Systems and Voter Alignments* (New York: The Free Press, 1967), pp. 26-33.

20

Whither Canadian Federalism? The Challenge of Regional Diversity and Maturity*

David M. Cameron

It would be an exaggeration to suggest that federalism in Canada is at a crossroads. Such an analogy implies a dramatic choice, a deliberate decision to turn this way or that. However, Canadian federalism has not been the product of grand decisions born of crises. It has evolved, surely if slowly, by adjustment, interpretation, manipulation, and accommodation. This is not to say we have been totally without crises. War,

* Paper presented to the 28th Annual Conference of the Institute of Public Administration of Canada, September 7-10, 1976, Halifax. Reprinted by permission.

depression, and once—at least so we were told—apprehended insurrection, have all left their marks on the structure and style of our federation.

It is not, however, the intention of this paper to review the evolutionary course of Canada's federal history. That has been done more than once elsewhere.[1] If students of Canadian federalism hold different views on the lessons to be learned from our past, that in itself is testimony to the richness of our heritage.

The purpose of this paper is to explore the implications of a distinctly modern phenomenon: the maturation of the provinces, the constituent units in the Canadian federation. Coupled with diversities both old and new, regional maturity constitutes a profound challenge to both the reality and the myths of contemporary federalism. This is a challenge which is no less real for its lack of immediate drama.

In exploring the challenge of regional diversity and maturity, I shall attempt to do four things. First, it is essential that we give some consideration to the nature of federalism itself, not to define an abstract model against which to compare Canadian experience, but to clarify the essential principles of this form of government in order to assess its relevance and limits for the contemporary challenge. Second, I shall discuss—necessarily briefly—some of the factors which together constitute and explain the challenge of regional maturity and diversity. Third, I shall outline the dominant responses that have emerged to date and try to account for their inadequacies in charting the future course of Canadian federalism. Finally, I shall consider the properties of a more satisfactory concept of federalism for Canada. The first task, then, is to consider the essential nature of federalism and the peculiar myths which have surrounded its evolution in Canada.

FEDERALISM AND ITS MYTHS IN CANADA

Federalism is a form of government simple in concept but exceedingly varied and complex in reality. Federalism implies, quite simply, the territorial division of the power to govern.[2] It is essentially in the nature of this division, the means adopted to ensure its stability, and the direction of its almost inevitable transformation over time that the distinguishing characteristics of individual federations are to be found.

There is probably no single myth which has so dominated interpretations of Canadian federalism—at least in English-speaking circles—as has the proposition that the "Fathers of Confederation" intended to create a highly centralized federation and that they did, in fact, negotiate the basis of a centralized constitution. The evidence that is normally cited to support this proposition is not questioned here. The intent if not the wording, of the "peace, order, and good government" clause, the central appointment of provincial lieutenant-governors, the power of the central government to reserve and veto provincial legislation, and the virtual absence of an independent revenue base for the provinces (perhaps the most centralizing feature of all) certainly add up to the inescapable conclusion that the British North America Act did indeed diminish provincial governments to little more than the status of glorified municipal councils.

What is inadequate in this proposition is its failure to take account of the limited acceptance of a centralized federation (let alone a "legislative union") even in the 1860s. Newfoundland was never a serious participant in the discussions, and Prince Edward Island withdrew before the agreement was concluded. Only three colonies were united under this constitution, and the two maritime provinces were included only after the most draconian manoeuvrings which, as an example of manipulative statecraft, would have struck envy in the heart of Niccolo Machiavelli. The electors of Nova Scotia certainly left no doubts about their sentiments when—too late as it turned out—they overwhelmingly repudiated the "botheration scheme."

The British North America Act may indeed represent a centralized federal constitution, but the principles upon which it was based were developed in the province of Canada and reflected the aspirations of its spokesmen and the conditions necessary to break the political deadlock into which the two former colonies had fallen as a result of their ill-fated union. Is it surprising, then, that this central Canadian design, which obtained so little popularity in the maritimes when it was first enacted, should have suffered substantial modification as the federation expanded to encompass not four but ten provinces?

Yet the dominant view of English-speaking students of Canadian federalism—and until recently virtually the only view—has continued to emphasize the centralist biases of the original settlement. Here a second myth becomes particularly useful: that the courts—and particularly the Judicial Committee of the Privy Council—have been responsible for "turning the constitution on its head." Canadians may place great store in the wisdom and authority of judges, but it would be simply incredible to suggest that Canadians blithely accepted so thoroughgoing and fundamental a transformation of their constitution from a committee of British lords. The courts have played a significant role in the authoritative interpretation of the British North America Act, but we must look beyond the courts to the nature and evolution of Canada's political communities to understand the reasons why we have had to evolve a more decentralized federal constitution than that prepared by the Fathers of Confederation.

There is a less judicial, and less judicious, myth which sees in the evolution of Canadian federalism an almost mechanical process often referred to as a pendulum swing from centralization to decentralization and back. Despite the unattractiveness of comparing a federation to a grandfather clock, this proposition is probably harmless enough—although distinctly unimaginative—when employed as a literary device in describing our past. The weakness in the pendulum myth is its implied assertion that events must somehow continue to push back and forth without actually taking us anywhere.

A brief glimpse at Canadian history suggests that there have been essentially only three periods of centralization in the operation of our federation. The first, inseparable from the leadership of John A. Macdonald, was a remarkably short-lived period of nation-building. These were the years in which great works, and especially railroads, captured the spirit of a bold, mercantilist nation with transcontinental aspirations. The central government, armed with the awesome powers of the constitution, assumed as natural its dominance over the "local" legislatures of the provinces. It was also a period in which—following the seductive influences of the initial federation—the political leadership of the provinces had been truncated by the exodus to Ottawa.

Great works tend eventually to be completed, however, and a new generation of provincial leaders emerged, joining a few like Mowat in Ontario who had made the return voyage. The experiment in centralized government failed, and Canadians rather quickly went back to more parochial concerns. No more certain demonstration of the end of this era could be found than the 1896 election of a national government pledged to respect provincial autonomy!

Aside from this initial phase of nation-building, the remaining periods of centralization are irresistably associated with depression and war. In other words, power has gravitated to Ottawa when external conflict or economic collapse have impelled the federation to pool its collective resources in an all-out struggle for security.

An alternative and more convincing interpretation of this dimension of Canadian history would suggest that apart from periods of crisis, the federation has been moving consistently toward greater and greater decentralization. Rather than a pendulum swing, there has been a pervasive trend in which the balance of power has been shifting from the nation to the provinces. The trend has been interrupted by economic and military crises, only to re-emerge with each return to "normalcy."

One myth, which this pervasive trend toward a more decentralized federation might have been expected to bring forth, has been remarkably absent from our political tradition. This would be a myth accounting for the persistent strength of regionalism or provincialism. However, as Black and Cairns observed in their pioneering, revisionist treatment of Canadian federalism in 1966:

Regional aspects of the traditional interpretations of Canadian federalism seem to be viewed either as self-evident facts whose continued existence requires no further explanation, or as inconvenient impediments to national unity which really ought to go away.[3]

Black and Cairns quite properly find a partial explanation for this neglect of regionalism in "two divergent ethnic traditions of scholarship."

> While English-speaking scholars stressed the challenges of nation-building across distances, their French-speaking colleagues concentrated on problems of "la survivance".[4]

English-speaking scholars who have not neglected regionalism have generally attacked it. J. E. Hodgetts, for example, has argued that regions in Canada are essentially "bureaucratic constructs."

> Regionalism, at any level one wishes to take it, does not generate spontaneous demands that thrust themselves on the political system and are instrumental in influencing the policy outputs of the system. The region . . . is not so much the creator of policy as the creature of policy.[5]

In the conclusion to this same article, Professor Hodgetts clarifies his own nation-building preferences.

> If this development persists we must abandon any hopes we have of gearing our institutions and policies to the conception of a single Canadian political system.[6]

Alan Cairns has suggested an alternative explanation for what he, like Hodgetts, considers to be the artificiality of regionalism in Canada (which, significantly, he refers to as "sectionalism"). The villain in the piece this time is the single-member, plurality electoral system.

> The electoral system favours minor parties with concentrated sectional support, and discourages those with diffuse national support. The electoral system has consistently exaggerated the significance of cleavages demarcated by sectional/provincial boundaries and thus tended to transform contests between parties into contests between sections/provinces.[7]

Cairns joins Hodgetts in attacking regionalism (sectionalism) as a constraint on nationalism. His preference for an electoral system based on proportional representation derives in part from his belief that it "encourages the parties to develop a national orientation."[8] Closely related to this assertion is the second premise from which Cairns indicts regionalism and the electoral system.

> Sectional politics is potentially far more disruptive to the polity than class politics. This is essentially because sectional politics has an inherent tendency to call into question the very nature of the political system and its legitimacy. Classes, unlike sections, cannot secede from the political system, and are consequently more prone to accept its legitimacy.[9]

In this argument, Cairns joins forces with John Porter. Porter's argument rests on the assertion that political change and innovation (what he calls "creative politics") depend upon a contest for power between left and right, between progressive and conservative values.

Canada, says Porter, "must be one of the few major industrial societies in which the right and left polarization has become deflected into disputes over regionalism and national unity."[10] Significantly, Porter assigns much of the blame for this "deflection" to "the hallowed nonsense that goes into the theory of Canadian federalism,"[11] a federalism that "as such has meaning only for politicians and senior civil servants who work with the complex machinery that they have set up, as well as for the scholars who provide a continuing commentary on it, but it has very little meaning for the bulk of the population."[12]

The fact that regionalism is as important as nationalism in sustaining a viable federation seems hardly to be recognized in the traditions of Canadian scholarship.[13] This is all the more surprising when it is realized that it is the very strength and persistence of regionalism which underlies the trend toward decentralization in Canada's federation. What essentially has been missing is the simultaneous consideration of the growing diversity and maturity of Canada's provinces as political communities or, because they exist within the framework of a federated nation-state, as regions.

REGIONAL DIVERSITY AND MATURITY

A region is a self-conscious political community—a polity. A region is distinct from a nation only in that the former exists within the geographic boundaries of the latter. In other words, regionalism and nationalism are essentially similar phenomena, distinguished only to clarify the territorial extent over which they apply.

Federalism presumes the existence of both nationalism and regionalism. It is the coexistence of centripetal and centrifugal forces, of pressures for centralization and decentralization, of desires for unity and diversity, of attachments to the nation and the region which are the very foundations of federalism as a principle of political organization. Federalism is a mechanism through which these countervailing forces can be both balanced and preserved. If either is missing, federalism cannot survive. Without attachments to the nation, the central government will lack political legitimacy and the power to govern will fall to the constituent states. Without attachments to the region, the reverse will occur.

The essential task of a federal constitution is thus to define an acceptable balance between nationalism and regionalism. If a constitution fails to do so—if it allocates power disproportionately to the central or regional governments—one of two things must happen: either the constitution will collapse, or it will be changed to conform to the exigencies of the political communities within which it operates.

It is not altogether unreasonable that the initial years in the life of a federation should be devoted to policies and myths of nation-building.

After all, this is the element which must be added to balance the existing attachments to state or province (region). But there is more to federating than nation-building. As Black and Cairns have so properly pointed out, province-building (strengthening the capacity of provincial political systems to govern in the interests of regional communities) is as fundamental to federalism as nation-building.[14] Moreover, province-building has been remarkably successful in Canada.

It is not possible to give anything approaching an exhaustive account of several centuries of province-building in Canada. Indeed, much of the data required for such an account remain to be collected. Fortunately, if belatedly, Canadian scholars are now beginning to turn their attention to aspects of this extremely important dimension of Canadian society and politics.[15] It will suffice for the purposes of this paper to make note of several of the more salient determinants and elements of this process.

Patterns of Economic Development

There is some irony in the fact that while economic development was perhaps the major domestic benefit expected to accrue from federation, it has been the later patterns of this very development which beginning in the 1920s, have underpinned the decentralization of the federation. This argument has nowhere been put as concisely as in the 1940 Report of the Royal Commission on Dominion-Provincial Relations, from which the following lengthy extract is taken.

> The age of steel and steam within which Canadian economic development had hitherto taken place had to make way for the age of alloys, hydro-electric power and the internal combustion engine. The new techniques, the development of which had been forced by the War, opened up vast new Canadian resources for development and heavy investments were made for their effective exploitation. The impact of these developments brought rapid changes in the pattern of the Canadian economy. The national integration (achieved through wheat), which tied the country together by East-West bonds of trade and opportunity was weakened as Central Canada and British Columbia felt the direct and competing tug of export demand on their regional resources. New economic frontiers, the exploitation of which was of primary interest to Ontario and Quebec, developed on the Pre-Cambrian Shield,—where water power, base metals and pulp and paper came into their own—began to usurp the place of the old national frontier in the West. In the successful development of these new frontiers, the importance of a national economic integration for some regions declined and the material basis which had bolstered political unity in the past was measurably weakened.
>
> In the past, the Dominion has been able to prosecute with vigour certain national policies which promoted national integration because of the common interest of all regions in the result. As these national policies lost some of their unifying power, the common agreement necessary for reso-

lute political action by the Dominion became more difficult to secure. Still more important, with the opening of the West finally and fully accomplished, it seemed that many of the national economic policies had been carried to completion. No obvious and pressing challenge to action presented itself in the federal sphere in this period. To many it seemed that the time had come when the Federal government might rest from its arduous labours and muse over how it had justified the faith of the Fathers.[16]

The patterns—and their consequences—which the Rowell-Sirois Commission so clearly detected in the 1920s and 1930s have continued since the Second World War. Oil, natural gas, and potash have provided the foundations for prosperity and autonomy in Alberta and Saskatchewan. Not all regions have shared in this diversified prosperity. For the maritime provinces, the earlier prosperity derived from wood, wind, and water turned to a stagnation resting upon fishing, farming and forestry.

Interpreting the Constitution

Without exaggerating their role, the courts must nevertheless be given some credit for aiding—or at least legitimizing—the decentralization of Canada's constitution. Although its full meaning will probably remain clouded by uncertainty, the "peace, order, and good government" clause has at least been stripped of the gargantuan proportions assumed by many to derive from its literal interpretation.[17] We need not exaggerate in the contrary direction to conclude that the courts have at times found in "property and civil rights" the constitutional basis upon which to legitimize an expanding provincial jurisdiction.[18] The symbolic value of judicial interpretations should also not be underestimated. Thus, while the role of the monarch's representatives was destined to diminish for other reasons, the ruling that "a Lieutenant-Governor, when appointed, is as much the representative of Her Majesty for all purposes of provincial government as the Governor-General himself is for all purposes of Dominion government,"[19] secured for provincial executives an important constitutional independence.

Changes in custom and statute have added their own powerful contributions to decentralization. The termination of the right to hold seats simultaneously in the national and a provincial legislature probably aided the development of stronger provincial parties and independent political leadership at the provincial level.[20] Custom has diminished the significance of the central government's veto power over provincial legislation to the point where all of Canada's first ministers have agreed with its removal from the constitution.[21] While the courts have played a modest role in clarifying its precise boundaries, new forms of direct taxation—particularly on sales and income—developed by provincial governments have generated a revenue base for the provinces which effectively negates the centralizing effects of the original division of taxing powers.

The Elements of Regional Maturity

We have previously alluded to at least two of the elements which help to account for the growing maturity of Canada's provinces as regional societies and polities: natural resource endowments and their exploitation largely under provincial jurisdiction,[22] and constitutional interpretation which in expanding provincial authority has been both cause and consequence of regional maturity. A wide variety of other factors could also be mentioned, including the patterns of immigration which have done so much to foster diverse provincial populations,[23] the process of urbanization which has created a series of metropolitan centres each bearing a special provincial character,[24] and, as Thomas Hockin notes in his most recent book, the parliamentary system of government itself which in its executive dominance of the legislature has given provincial governments considerable visibility, certainly more so than in the case of American states.[25]

One further factor is worthy of special note. It is of considerable importance that most of the essential institutions through which a society is formed, maintained, and given expression have been subject to provincial regulation or creatures of provincial sponsorship. It is here, of course, that provincial jurisdiction over education takes on particular significance. For the original colonies the rudiments of these essential social institutions had been set in place before Confederation, and it was natural that the resultant diversities should have been recognized and protected by provincial retention of jurisdiction over education, health, welfare, municipal institutions, and "all matters of a merely local or private nature."[26] At the same time we should not underestimate the significance of such jurisdiction even in the newest provinces. As Black and Cairns have observed:

> Mechanisms set in motion by the creation of political institutions permit provinces such as Saskatchewan and Alberta which possessed little sociological legitimacy at their birth to acquire it with the passage of time and creation of a unique provincial history.[27]

Finally, as Mildred Schwartz suggested:

> Provinces are the arenas for mobilizing and expressing contending interests. Through their jurisdictions, the lives of citizens are regularly touched in ways distinct from any other level of government.[28]

Evidence of Regional Maturity

It is much to be applauded that several scholars have recently turned their attention to questions relating to regionalism in Canada. The data now emerging are still very sparse and far from adequate but they point consistently to the conclusion that Canadians have evolved deeply rooted attachments to their provincial societies and derive from those societies some of their most important political values and attitudes. What very little evidence we have which measures attitudes over time suggests that these provincial attachments may well be stronger now than in the past. As an example of the latter evidence, the Gallup poll revealed in 1946 that fifty percent of their respondents felt that "Canada would be worse off if all provincial governments were abolished and the whole country governed from Ottawa." Twenty-five percent felt Canada would be better off. By 1960, however, the proportion indicating opposition to the abolition of provinces had increased to sixty-two percent while that supporting their abolition had dropped to seventeen percent.[29]

Most of the available empirical evidence contains no comparisons over time. It does, however, point to strong regional differences in the attitudes of Canadians. Regarding Canadians' support for the national and regional governments, Richard Simeon concludes that while "the real distribution of loyalties is unclear . . . it is certain that there is much variation among provinces."[30] Even in a study of regional cultures using national post-election surveys (and the limitations imposed by that partial contradiction) Richard Simeon and David J. Elkins concluded that "there are strong differences among the citizens of Canadian provinces . . . in some basic orientations to politics."[31]

By far the most thorough analysis of Canadian regionalism to date is that of Mildred Schwartz in her *Politics and Territory*.[32] Asking a sample of Canadians "which government is more important in affecting how you and your family get on?" Schwartz received a four to three "vote" in favour of the provincial government.[33] Interestingly, respondents in British Columbia were by a considerable margin the most provincially oriented, and only in Ontario did a larger proportion indicate that the national government was more important.[34]

Canadians, concluded Schwartz, are extremely ethnocentric in terms of where they consider it desirable to live. "Not only did residents select their own region with great frequency but they looked on no other with comparable favour."[35] "That ethnocentrism should be so pervasive with respect to preferred region suggests an emotional strength of attachment to a home territory that historical migration trends do not penetrate."[36] Summing up her analysis, Schwartz indicated that:

> The dominant responses found set each region apart . . . with sufficient clarity to permit speaking of regional political orientations. We see these as contributing to a milieu in which the recognition of common interests and concerns can emerge into a group consciousness, one with potential for political mobilization.[37]

Finally, and returning us to the realm of federalism, Schwartz asserts that "whatever perspective we take, there are two discernable realms of interest in Canadian life, the national and the local-provincial."[38]

The central argument of this paper is that Canadians hold strong attachments to their provinces as regions and that along with other—and particularly economic—factors these attachments have become interwoven with provincial institutions to produce mature societies and political systems at the provincial level. If this is so, then we ought to expect a parallel strengthening of provincial governments. Again the empirical evidence is scanty, but some hint of what has been going on can be derived from the fact that while the number of employees of the national government increased by nineteen percent between 1959 and 1971, that of provincial governments increased by eighty-one percent. If one includes local government employment, which properly falls within the provincial ambit, total provincial-local employment increased by 104.2 percent in these twelve years.[39]

Increases in provincial employment have not been only quantitative. Because of the intergovernmental diplomacy associated with contemporary executive federalism,[40] a special importance attaches to provincial administrative competence. As Richard Simeon has pointed out, "following the Second World War the weight of technical expertise seems to have been overwhelmingly in Ottawa. The balance has shifted."[41] "What appears to be most important is a growth in the activism, competence, and, most important, self-confidence of provincial administrations . . . ."[42] Of course the increased quality of provincial administration and policy advice has not occurred equally in all ten provinces.[43] Some appear to be most notable for the degree to which they have remained the same.

Levels of spending also provide some indication of the increased importance of provincial governments. Thus, between 1955 and 1965, federal expenditures on goods and services declined from 8.5 percent of G.N.P. to 5.1 percent. Provincial and local expenditures, on the other hand, increased from 6.0 percent to 7.9 percent.[44]

Donald Smiley provides perhaps the most succinct summary of this post-war process of provincial maturation.

> The most urgent of public priorities thus came to be within provincial rather than federal jurisdiction. This was reflected not only in the new fiscal balance but in the increasing disposition of Canadians to look to their provinces and local governments rather than to Ottawa for meeting emergent social and economic needs.[45]

The Special Role of Quebec

It would be unthinkable to discuss provincial diversity and maturity in Canada without mentioning the special role of Quebec. At the same time, it is not my intention to undertake an analysis of the unique properties of province-building in Quebec. Indeed, as I shall argue shortly, the preoccupation of many English-speaking Canadians with the challenges and implications of Quebec regionalism has not only blinded them to parallel, if less dramatic, developments elsewhere, but has generated unnecessary stresses on Canadian federalism.

The point I wish to emphasize here is that Quebec has played two profoundly important roles in shaping the contemporary pattern of the Canadian federation. First, during the sequential crises of war, depression, and war which blighted the first half of this century, it was Quebec—virtually alone—which resisted the process of centralization and thus maintained the form—if not always the substance—of provincial independence. Quebec's insistence on respecting the principles of federalism provided all provinces with a model toward which they were able to move in the post-war era. Second, Quebec was one of the leaders—and, given its special significance in national politics, a crucial leader—in the strengthening of provincial administrations especially in the 1960s. Perhaps no single situation better demonstrated the extent and consequences of this leadership than Quebec's role in the 1963-65 pension negotiations. Relating the impact of Prime Minister Lesage's unveiling of Quebec's own pension plan at the March 31—April 2, 1964 federal-provincial conference, one official is quoted by Richard Simeon as stating, "It made an absolutely enormous impression."[46] Another official concluded that "the federal plan as it then stood was dead. It was obvious at that point if there ever was to be a pension plan, it would be Canada joining the Quebec plan."[47]

Questioning the Constitution

If English-speaking Canadians have long held to the myth that the Fathers of Confederation provided us with a highly centralized constitution, that myth—along with many others—may have been laid to rest with the 1968-71 exercise in constitutional review. The significant upshot of that process, however, is that it made of the British North America Act a "lame duck" constitution. Having agreed that the Act was no longer adequate to guide the Canadian federation, and having been unable to set anything in its place, Canada's first ministers succeeded in nothing so much as heaping abuse on the very constitution which must continue for the foreseeable future to shape the operation and evolution of our federation.[48] The effect this will have is difficult to estimate. It may be that the whole issue of constitutional reform, which appears never to have excited great interest among Canadians, will simply fade from memory. It could also be that the fact of failure will live on to haunt and restrain future advocates of less holistic, but perhaps more important, constitutional changes.

Whatever the longer term effects, it is difficult to avoid the conclusion that the failure of the constitutional review has retarded the necessary process of adjusting the federal structure to accommodate the regional diversity and maturity which is now so prominent a feature of Canadian political life.

What answers do we have to the challenge of regional diversity and maturity? I propose to review but three, not because these exhaust the capacity of Canadians to generate constitutional propositions but because they appear to capture the essential choices from which a new concept of Canadian federalism might be derived.

RESPONSES TO REGIONAL DIVERSITY AND MATURITY

It is my contention that where responses to the challenge of regional diversity and maturity have gone beyond tinkering with the existing structure of Canadian federalism, they have tended to derive from one of three concepts of the essential character of a successful federal arrangement for Canada. Each of these concepts is, in its own way, uniquely Canadian; yet each suffers from an overemphasis upon, or a misreading of, the contradictory pressures and constraints of nationalism and regionalism.

Quebec Nationalism

I am not here concerned with the internal sociological and political dynamics of Quebec. That Quebec should constitute the most distinctive and self-conscious of Canada's provinces is hardly surprising. That this distinctiveness and self-consciousness should yield vigorous demands on the rest of the federation, and particularly its national government, is neither surprising nor, in itself, destructive of Canadian federalism.

Whether we apply the term regionalism or nationalism to the political assertiveness of Quebec is, up to a point, a matter of semantics. These are essentially two words for the same phenomenon, and the scholar has no right to expect political protagonists to confine their arguments within his own definitions of the meaning of words. For analytical purposes, it is more convenient to associate nationalism with nations and regionalism with regions than to have to deal with regional nationalism.

Be that as it may, there have developed in Canada a set of responses to Quebec's regionalism which seek to dissolve this distinction. The essential proposition is that Quebec should be considered a nation, but that somehow this can be rendered compatible with the continued existence of something called Canada. Of course, if all provinces were elevated to similar status as nations, nothing but words would have been changed. The change comes in discovering a new nation, something called English Canada. Accepting Quebec as a French-Canadian nation, and creating a new concept of an English-Canadian nation, a variety of schemes can then be posited in which "Canada" becomes an association or federation of these nations.

It is difficult to imagine a more nonsensical proposition. Canada is a nation consisting of ten provinces. These provinces have developed degrees of diversity and maturity which have impelled the federation toward greater decentralization. To fly in the face of this reality by positing an English-speaking "nation" comprising, one assumes, all provinces save Quebec is sheer fantasy. To contemplate a situation in which simply because they share one of the world's major languages and certain traditions as former British colonies, Newfoundlanders and British Columbians would consent to the dissolution of their provinces into a unitary state called English Canada is to ascribe to language and history a political potency that is everywhere contradicted.[49] If it is envisaged that "English Canada" would be other than a unitary state, it would have to be a federation. What then becomes of Canada? Is it to be a federation of a federation and a unitary state? No, Canada is a federation or it is nothing.[50]

The human intellect can at least cope with the possibility that the regional interests of Quebec are so fundamentally at odds with those of other regions in Canada that her continued participation in a Canadian federation should be reconsidered. But if such incompatibility exists, the solution lies in dissolving the federation,[51] not in conjuring up a new political entity called English Canada whose existence derives entirely from the analytical necessities of a federation of two nations.

Canadian Nationalism

It can be argued that Canadian nationalism is a necessary corollary of the existence of a Canadian nation. Up to a point this may be true, so long as the concept of nationalism is capable of containing values other than ethnocentric chauvinism.[52] The search for a Canadian identity or national culture is as revealing of Canada because we must search for it as for what might constitute such an identity or culture if we succeeded in "finding" it.

There is another side to Canadian nationalism, however, which seeks to use the instruments of the national-state to erect a national identity. This is, in one sense, simply a new attempt at nation-building, concentrating this time on culture rather than territorial frontiers. Cultural nationalism has developed two dominant strains in Canada which are sometimes combined but almost always with the primary emphasis on one or the other. The first strain may be referred to as cultural dualism, and the second as cultural protectionism.

Cultural dualism, otherwise known as bilingualism and biculturalism, consists essentially in seeking to establish across Canada the institutions and facilities considered important in fostering active French- and English-speaking communities. Such a notion is to be distinguished from the concept of "official bilingualism" which carries with it the rather compelling objective of ensuring that both French- and English-speaking Canadians are represented in and served by the central and other governments in their own language.

Cultural protectionism, otherwise known as cultural nationalism, consists in erecting regulatory barriers and domestic subsidies designed to reduce the quantity of foreign "culture" and increase the quantity of Canadian "culture" to which Canadians are exposed. To date it appears that most proponents of such protectionism are concerned less with the content of this cultural expression than with the certainty that it was produced by Canadians.

My objections to these variants of Canadian nationalism are twofold. First, and not directly related to the central concern of this paper, they both lead all too easily to the coercion of Canadians into forms of cultural expression and consumption which they manifestly do not want. The second objection is of direct relevance to Canadian federalism. Both forms of cultural nationalism require penetration by the central (national) government into the most basic area of provincial jurisdiction and the most fundamental component of province-building. The federal-provincial conflict over control of communications would be nothing as compared with consequences of a thoroughgoing commitment by the central government to control the content of cultural expression. Furthermore, there is an inescapable association between cultural nationalism and the regional interests of central Canada. It is overwhelmingly Quebec and Ontario which provide the respective cultural roots of the two streams of nationalist rhetoric. It took us many decades to modify the centralizing elements of a constitution derived from central Canadian interests. Is it now to be proposed that we sacrifice our diverse provincial interests on the altar of cultural nationalism?

Constitutional Fragmentation

The third response has been the wholehearted acceptance of regional diversity and maturity even to the point of discounting the existence or value of a national polity.

I have argued in this paper that what sparse evidence we have is supportive of the proposition that Canada's provinces have developed into diverse and mature political regions. This evidence is in no sense indicative of the demise of a nation. Of course, if no nation exists—a proposition for which virtually no empirical evidence has been produced—then the consequence is obvious. As with the separatist tenden cies inherent in the more strident forms of Quebec regionalism, it is patently within the competence of Canadians anywhere to decide that the costs of maintaining a Canadian federation exceed the benefits. If we determine that the good life would be more fully attained in ten republics or principalities that is for us to decide and our political leaders to accept. This is simply to say that federalism did not arrive in Canada by an act of God (despite the decision to exploit a biblical reference to His dominion). Our federation was erected by men, and it can be discarded by men, regardless of whether the preferred substitute is a unitary state or independence for the provinces.

All the same, we shall have to be one thing or another. Thus, when Edwin R. Black suggests a federal constitution which "might permit Quebec (or any other province) to negotiate her way right out of the Canadian Confederation,"[53] he has crossed the dividing line between a federal union and an association of convenience. True federalism requires the coexistence of nation and region within the same country, of a national and regional government under the same constitution.

In no way would I deny the right of any province to leave the federation, although whether that right would be granted by the other members of the federation—including the national government—is quite another matter. But to include in a constitution an acceptable procedure for withdrawal is to have so little confidence in its propriety that a federation would exist in name only.

Black is quite correct in asserting that all provinces enjoy a degree of special status.[54] In the same vein, J. Stefan Dupré, one of the most astute students of Canadian government, coined the phrase "multifaceted federalism" to describe a dimension of our constitution which has been present from the very beginning.[55] If the system is to remain federal, however, there must be limits to the variations that exist in centre-regional relations, just as there must be limits to the concentration of the power to govern at either level.

The challenge to Canadian federalism is to arrive at a new balance between nation and region, one that recognizes and respects the reality of regional diversity and maturity. If Canadians do not possess the tolerance and respect for diversity which alone can render federalism viable, then none of us can claim the right to impose our intolerance and disrespect on others. But surely before we depart in rude antagonisms it behooves us to look once again at the possibilities of federalism and the principles that might guide the adaptation of that concept to the Canadian situation.

PRINCIPLES OF NEW FEDERALISM

Canada possesses a constitution which has survived a quite remarkable decentralization of power to the provinces. At the same time, the principles or myths through which we understand and operate our constitution have not kept pace with the growing maturity of our provincial regions. It may well be, therefore, that what we need is not so much principles of a new federalism, as new principles for a transformed federation.

One thing we certainly do not require is another full-fledged constitutional review. We have already weakened our constitution with one such exercise; to try again could prove fatal to the federation itself. What we require at this stage in our constitutional evolution is less a new constitution than a new set of principles which can guide the operation of the constitution we already have.

I do not propose to offer anything approaching an exhaustive set of principles for the Canadian federation of the future. Rather, I shall conclude this examination of the question, whither Canadian federalism, by posing only six principles. If these were to become significant additions to the political philosophy of Canadian federalism, I believe we would have turned an important corner in meeting the challenge of regional diversity and maturity.

RECOGNITION OF PROVINCES AS POLITICAL COMMUNITIES

This principle has both a positive and a negative connotation. On the positive side it implies an acceptance of the reality of regional attachments in Canada and the formulation of popular concepts of federalism which can accommodate this reality. On the negative side, it implies a rejection of alternative conceptions of provinces, particularly as economies and as territorial abstractions representing at best useful categories for the aggregation of performance indicators. In short, we need to bring our myths about federalism into line with the strength of regionalism, and the central role played by provinces in defining our federal existence.

RESPECT FOR THE POWER OF PROVINCIAL GOVERNMENTS TO GOVERN

It is time that the preoccupation with efficiency in the delivery of public services was tempered with a greater concern for the responsibilities necessary to govern. Federalism can never be a system of government dedicated to maximizing efficiency, and we should recognize that the strength of our provinces may be as important to our welfare as the strength of abstract indicators within our provinces.

RECOGNITION OF THE DIFFERENCE BETWEEN DECENTRALIZATION AND DECONCENTRATION

The major theme of this paper has been that Canadian federalism has witnessed a persistent trend toward the decentralization of power from

Ottawa to the provinces. Lately, however, there has developed a disturbing tendency on the part of the national government to counter this trend by deconcentrating its own operations into the provinces, and often in areas of provincial jurisdiction. If we are to retain respect not only for federalism but also for representative and responsible government, then we must recognize that there is a profound difference between a regional (provincial) government and a regional office of a central department. We do not have provinces merely because it is more efficient to deliver services on a localized basis; we have provinces because we wish to govern ourselves in part as provincial communities.

GREATER COMMITMENT TO
INTERPROVINCIAL COLLABORATION

One of the more powerful means of strengthening provincial governments would be a greater commitment of resources—by the provinces themselves—to mechanisms of interprovincial collaboration and cooperation. This may deprive some provincial leaders of a very handy central scapegoat to blame for their own unwillingness or inability to respond to public demands, but it could also provide a useful alternative to the presumption that only a central government can respond to problems or demands which extend beyond the boundaries of a single province.

CONSTRAINTS ON THE SPENDING POWER
OF PARLIAMENT

Whether by constitutional amendment or custom, it is time that the admitted prerogative of the crown in right of Canada to make gifts to beneficiaries of its choice was rendered compatible with the principles of federalism. Up to a point, the almost unrestricted spending power of Parliament has provided a valuable measure of flexibility in what might have been a rather rigid constitution. On the other hand, the excessive use of this power threatens in some cases to make a mockery of that constitution. We have evolved a carefully constructed division of legislative power between the national and provincial governments; it is time their respective spending powers were rendered compatible with this division.

PROVINCIAL RESTRAINT IN
ACCEDING TO CENTRAL OFFERS

The spending power of Parliament has been such a powerful tool in the circumvention of the constitution in large part because the provinces have shown such remarkable alacrity in accepting cost-sharing arrangements. It is not a healthy federal system which permits one government to impose its will upon another using resources extracted from a common citizenry. At the same time it would strengthen one's confidence in the future of federalism if provincial governments would more often refuse to accept this coercion. There is a price to be paid for federalism, and provincial governments might well ponder whose interests they are really serving when they so readily exchange their capacity to govern for tax revenues raised by another government.

It would be folly to predict the future course of Canadian federalism. If it is correct to draw from the past the conclusion that this federation must face the challenge of regional diversity and maturity, then it is appropriate to consider the principles upon which a suitable response might be based. In the final analysis, the specific principles we ultimately choose to promote may be less important than our willingness to invest the energy necessary to engage in debate at the level of principles.

NOTES

[1] For a general discussion of the nature and development of Canadian federalism from two very distinct but compelling perspectives, see Donald V. Smiley ed., *The Rowell-Sirois Report, Book I* (Toronto: McClelland and Stewart, 1963), and David Kwavnick ed., *The Tremblay Report,* (Toronto: McClelland and Stewart, 1973). Both are in the Carleton Library Series.

[2] A very useful treatment of federalism as the areal, or territorial division of power may be found in Arthur Maass, ed., *Area and Power: A Theory of Local Government* (Glencoe, Ill.: The Free Press, 1959), chapter 1.

[3] Edwin R. Black and Alan C. Cairns, "A Different Perspective on Canadian Federalism," in J. Peter Meekison, ed., *Canadian Federalism: Myth or Reality* 2nd. ed.; (Toronto: Methuen, 1971), p. 83.

[4] *Ibid.,* p. 83.

[5] J. E. Hodgetts, "Regional Interests and Policy in a Federal Structure," in J. Peter Meekison ed., *Canadian Federalism: Myth or Reality,* p. 346.

[6] *Ibid.,* p. 347.

[7] Alan C. Cairns, "The Electoral System and the Party System in Canada: 1921-1965." *Canadian Journal of Political Science,* Vol. 1, no. 1 (March, 1968), p. 62.

[8] *Ibid.,* p. 80.

[9] *Ibid.,* p. 75.

[10] John Porter, *The Vertical Mosaic* (Toronto: University of Toronto Press, 1965), p. 369.

[11] *Ibid.,* p. 382.

[12] *Ibid.,* p. 384.

[13] Porter, at least, is consistent in this respect. However, he is consistent only because he implicitly denies the value of federalism along with regionalism.

[14] Black and Cairns, "A Different Perspective on Canadian Federalism."

[15] Black and Cairns offer a refreshing and provocative discussion of regionalism in terms of province building. Mildred A. Schwartz, in *Politics and Territory: The Sociology of Regional Persistence in Canada* (Montreal and London: McGill-Queen's University Press, 1974), provides a solid theoretical base for the analysis of regionalism and some solid attitudinal data on Canadian regionalism. Thomas A. Hockin, in *Government in Canada* (Toronto: McGraw-

Hill Ryerson, 1976), has written the first general text on Canadian government which gives a proper place to the role and strength of the provinces.

[16] Donald V. Smiley, ed., *The Rowell-Sirois Report: Book I,* pp. 138-39.

[17] Although the number of cases in which arguments grounded in this clause have been fewer than the purported strength of the clause might suggest, some of these cases have been among the most significant interpretations of the constitution. See, for example, *Russell* v. *The Queen* (1882), *Attorney-General for Ontario* v. *Attorney-General for Canada* (1896), *Toronto Electric Commissioners* v. *Snider* (1925). *Attorney-General for Canada* v. *Attorney-General for Ontario* (1937), and *Johannesson* v. *West St. Paul* (1952). The very recent judgment of the Supreme Court of Canada regarding national and provincial wage and price control legislation will undoubtedly become a significant decision as well.

[18] While the courts may well have read more into this clause than was originally intended, I think it is an exaggeration to suggest, as Donald Smiley does, that this clause became the virtual residual clause of the constitution. See Donald V. Smiley, *Canada in Question: Federalism in the Seventies* (Toronto: McGraw-Hill Ryerson, 1976), p. 19.

[19] *Maritime Bank* v. *Receiver-General* (1892). Cited in J. Murray Beck ed., *The Shaping of Canadian Federalism: Central Authority or Provincial Right?* (Toronto: Copp Clark, 1971), p. 96.

[20] For a very useful discussion of political parties and federalism, see Donald V. Smiley, *Canada in Question,* chapter 4.

[21] See *Ibid.,* pp. 46-7 for a summary of the contents of the "Victoria Charter."

[22] Black and Cairns make a telling observation regarding the provincial orientation of frontier resource communities. See "A Different Perspective on Canadian Federalism," p. 38.

[23] Thomas A. Hockin, *Government in Canada,* p. 35.

[24] See *Ibid.,* p. 35 and Mildred A. Schwartz, *Politics and Territory,* pp. 318-19.

[25] Hockin, *Ibid.,* pp. 46-7.

[26] British North America Act, 1867, s.92, 16.

[27] Black and Cairns, "A Different Perspective on Canadian Federalism," p. 95.

[28] Schwartz, *Politics and Territory,* p. 324.

[29] Mildred A. Schwartz, *Public Opinion and Canadian Identity* (Toronto: Fitzhenry and Whiteside, 1967), p. 93.

[30] Richard Simeon, *Federal-Provincial Diplomacy: The Making of Recent Policy in Canada* (Toronto: University of Toronto Press, 1972), p. 205.

[31] Richard Simeon and David J. Elkins, "Regional Political Cultures in Canada," *Canadian Journal of Political Science,* vol. 7, no. 3, September, 1974, p. 432.

[32] See above, note 15.

[33] Schwartz, *Politics and Territory,* p. 217. Canadians were much more likely to name the national government, however, when asked which government handles the most important problems.

[34] Ontario's pronounced orientation toward the national government is also noted by Richard Simeon in *Federal-Provincial Diplomacy,* pp. 206-7.

[35] Schwartz, *Politics and Territory,* p. 90.

[36] *Ibid.,* p. 95.

[37] *Ibid.,* p. 241.

[38] *Ibid.,* p. 283.

[39] J. E. Hodgetts and O. P. Dwivedi, *Provincial Governments as Employers* (Montreal and London: McGill-Queen's University Press, 1974), p. 7.

[40] See Donald V. Smiley, *Canada in Question,* chapter 3.

[41] Simeon, *Federal-Provincial Diplomacy,* p. 214.

[42] *Ibid.*, p. 224.

[43] See *Ibid.*, p. 217.

[44] Smiley, *Canada in Question*, pp. 120-1.

[45] *Ibid.*, p. 121.

[56] Simeon, *Federal-Provincial Diplomacy*, p. 56.

[47] *Ibid.*, p. 56.

[48] For analyses of the constitutional review and its results see Donald V. Smiley, *Canada in Question*, chapter 2, and R. I. Cheffins and R. N. Tucker, *The Constitutional Process in Canada*, (2nd ed.; Toronto: McGraw-Hill Ryerson, 1976), chapter 7.

[49] One need only ponder the facts that the French-Canadian "nation" excludes contiguous French Canadians in Ontario and New Brunswick, while the English-Canadian "nation" would presumably exclude over 200 million Americans who share the same language and a similar colonial past.

[50] Donald Smiley offers a solid denunciation of this "two nations" concept in *Canada in Question*, pp. 224-5.

[51] It is conceivable, but hardly probable that the other nine provinces might design a new federation in the absence of Quebec. The improbability derives both from the gulf—only partly geographical—which would separate the Atlantic provinces from the remainder, and from the magnetic attraction that would be exerted by that other English-speaking, North American federation.

[52] Ramsay Cook draws an interesting and useful distinction between a nation-state and a nationalist state. See *The Maple Leaf Forever* (Toronto: Macmillan, 1971), chapter 1.

[53] Edwin R. Black, *Divided Loyalties: Canadian Concepts of Federalism* (Montreal and London: McGill-Queen's University Press, 1975), p. 234.

[54] *Ibid.*, pp. 232-4.

[55] See J. Stefan Dupré, "Contracting Out: A Funny Thing Happened on the Way to the Centennial," *Report, 1964 Conference*, Toronto: Canadian Tax Foundation, 1965, p. 218. See also Dupré, et al., *Federalism and Policy Development* (Toronto: University of Toronto Press, 1973), p. 237.

21

Some Comments on
Prairie Economic Alienation*

Kenneth H. Norrie

I

Prairie economic alienation has once again emerged as a major issue on the Canadian political scene. Dissatisfaction with federal economic policies has been a constant theme of politicians since the earliest days of settlement, but the recent resource taxation dispute has created yet another area of conflict as well as rekindled many of the old ones. As a result, anti-Ottawa speeches make good political platforms on the Prairies, and the last Alberta election had it as a key issue. In the most extreme cases the dissatisfaction has spawned groups who are studying the economic implications of political independence, or who already openly advocate it.[1]

It thus seems like an opportune time to assess the western case. Surprisingly, given the duration and intensity of the dispute, there has been little attention given to the Prairie position as a whole. Most often the grievances are presented and responded to, on a point by point basis. What emerges is a confusing array of issues, some perhaps valid but others often misdirected or only partially thought through. Given this, any hope of proper empirical work being done or a political consensus being reached is slight, and the debate seems fated to drag on and on.

This paper attempts to provide an overview of some of the main areas of Prairie economic discontent. We begin with specific criteria by which to assess the areas of contention. A claim of economic discrimination will be judged legitimate if it is directed at economic distortions clearly initiated by the federal government or other national institutions, and if removal of the distortion would unambiguously benefit the region. Based on these criteria two conclusions are reached. The first, outlined in the next section, is that many of the Prairie grievances must be interpreted as dissatisfaction with a market economy rather than with discriminatory policies of the federal government. The importance of this distinction for policy purposes, not to mention ideological consis-

* From Canadian Public Policy—Analyse De Politiques, II:2 Spring 1976 pp. 211-224. Reprinted by permission.

** I gratefully acknowledge comments by Bruce Wilkinson, Tom Powrie, Dave Gillen and Bill Rogerson.

tency[2] is obvious. The second observation, discussed in section III, is that many of the apparently more legitimate arguments are incompletely analyzed. Achievement of one goal may in fact prejudice the attainment of others, or involve an income redistribution within the Prairies that is not necessarily desirable. In such cases, it is argued, the more general impacts of any specific policy proposal must be carefully considered.

II

Prairie economic discontent is generally focussed on such things as tariffs, freight rates, the commercial banks, monetary policy, the regional distribution of manufacturing industries and (now) resource taxation. Upon inspection however, these issues can be seen as a mixture of dissatisfaction with the inevitable fate of a small region in a market economy, and unhappiness with distortions in such a system initiated or at least tolerated by the federal government. Failure to make this distinction is the basis of the confused nature of much of the debate, for only in the latter case can the term regional economic discrimination be legitimately applied.

A good example of the first type of grievance is the widespread complaint about the lack of secondary industry on the Prairies. It is commonly felt this is a direct result of federal government policies, past and present. For example (Western Premiers, 1973a).

> . . . the pattern of settlement and development has been influenced by economic, financial and tax policies of the federal government, which early assisted the concentration of the nation's business and industrial activity in central Canada. These policies which have led to this concentration of financial and industrial resources and population have worked against the allocation of financial and production resources to bring balance to the economies of all regions of Canada.

This belief is not restricted to politicians alone. A recent study by a University of Calgary economist (Blackman, 1974) sketches a hypothetical economic structure of an independent Alberta as a means of measuring the 'costs' of Confederation. The 'independent' Alberta of 1981 is substantially more industrialized than its provincial counterpart. The reasoning is that only Alberta's current position within the Canadian free trade area is preventing industrialization. Thus, it is assumed that if independent the region would necessarily have an industrial economy like that of a typical OECD country.

The correct response to these assertions, of course, is that the industrial structure of the West derives from its geographical isolation, relative lateness of settlement and small and diffused population base. Profit maximizing industries locate where the sum of materials acquisition, production and distribution costs is minimized. For most types of secondary industries only the latter costs differ substantially over alternative locations. Since distribution costs are minimized by locating close to the major markets for the production there is a tendency for industry to agglomerate around already established population centres.

The geographically peripheral areas of the country are just not feasible sites to naturally attract most types of secondary industry. Their advantage lies rather with the further processing of locally available resources where there is a large weight loss, with the provision of certain kinds of inputs into resource industries and with production of some consumer goods for the local market. Hinterland regions do not become industrial centres in a market economy, and the distribution of manufacturing industries across Canada is a simple reflection of this fact.

The confusion about the regional location of industry stems in part from a continuing belief that the Canadian tariffs in some inexplicable way ' . . . favour Eastern industry.'[3] If one means by this that the very existence of tariffs leads to regional disparities in industrialization then it is true only to the extent that the tariff has induced more manufacturers to locate in Ontario and Quebec than might have in the absence of the tariff. But the claim is not true if by it is meant that the West has less industry because of the Canadian protective system. A duty on goods coming into Canada may change relative prices sufficiently that Canadian production of a commodity of the domestic market is preferable to importing it. But where in Canada that firm locates is still a matter of simple location economics, and here the above points hold. In fact, if anything the Prairies, especially Manitoba, have more industry absolutely than they would have with no Canadian tariffs.

The only other possible interpretation of this argument is a belief that foreign tariffs are preventing the establishment of world scale industries in Canada of a type that would find the Prairies the best location. Examples most often cited are petro-chemical products of various types and livestock and lumber products (Western Premiers, 1973b). But this is only legitimately related to the Canadian tariff if it can be shown either that foreign duties were initially imposed in response to the Canadian ones which seems unlikely, or that they could be affected by reciprocally lowering ours. In the latter case pressing for sectoral free trade arrangements along the lines of the Auto Pact makes sense from the Prairie point of view, as do suggestions that we bargain for lower foreign tariffs in these areas in exchange for lowering Canadian ones in industries where the country has an obvious large comparative disadvantage. But it is important to realize that the real targets in these cases are foreign tariff structures and all the interest groups behind them rather than the Canadian tariff structure *per se*.

Another example of a misdirected complaint is the often voiced puzzlement that Prairie residents must bear transportation costs on both exports and imports. A general increase in freight rates would mean lower raw materials prices at the production site rather than higher prices at the market. Yet consumer goods imported into the region would also increase in price by the amount of the extra shipping and handling charges. This has understandably generated considerable discussion in the past, and has been cited by some as an example of discriminatory freight rate setting.

In fact, this asymmetry in the incidence of transportation charges results from being a peripheral economy. Most Prairie products are sold into world markets in close competition with other countries. Thus the demand curve is highly elastic, meaning the producers face a given world price which they must meet if any output is to be sold. As such, the local price is determined by this world price less transportation and handling charges. On the other hand, Prairie demand for imported manufactured products is relatively price inelastic because of the natural absence of competing suppliers locally. Thus the freight charges are shifted forward rather than backward as in the case of exports. Hinterland regions generally absorb the major portion of transport costs both ways even in situations where the rates reflect the true marginal costs of supplying the service.[4] The basic problem lies in being small rather than being the target of discriminatory action by the carriers or the central government.

Two additional examples will suffice on this general point. It has been asserted that the commercial banks transfer savings out of hinterland regions to Central Canada. They allegedly receive more savings deposits than they reinject locally in the form of loans. The result is a net transfer of investible funds from the West to the East and a concomitant reduction in western development potential. Thus (Western Premiers, 1973a:5).

> The chartered banks' stimulation of development in Central Canada appears to have been done at the expense of the other regions of Canada. By mobilizing Western Canada saving and transferring them to Central Canada, the banks, in effect, have reduced the development potential of the West.

Again, to the extent the claim is empirically valid it is precisely what one would expect a profit maximizing institution to do. The net transfer of funds is simply a reflection of the fact that funds are being reallocated from an area of relatively low returns to another where the risk-adjusted returns are higher.

It could be argued that the Canadian banks demand too high a risk premium in their lending: i.e., that the extra rate of return they need as compensation for taking on a riskier loan is in some sense excessive. If the variance in rates of returns differed markedly across regions then it might well be that specific areas of the country are less well served by the banking system than others. The problem here however is to define exactly what is meant by a 'too high' risk premium, and to determine the factors underlying it.

One sometimes hears the view that the banks often practice non-price discrimination in the allocation of funds, to the detriment of the West. Eastern borrowers have closer personal contacts with high level banking officials, and thus are more likely to obtain loans and on more favourable terms. But this is perfectly consistent with profit maximizing behaviour. Part of the costs of providing loans is obtaining information on the credit worthiness of the borrower. If he happens to be well known to the bank the cost of obtaining this information is minimized.

Even if the banks were locally controlled and headquartered it might still pay them to be net lenders to the most rapidly developing areas of the country. The result of this financial intermediation is a more efficient utilization of scarce resources, at least in a private rate of return sense. The problem the slower growth areas within the West face is not a discriminatory commercial banking system, for that is inconsistent with long run maximization of banking profits, but rather an inability to compete in the private market for investible funds.

A final example in this section is the allegedly regionally discriminatory features of restrictive monetary policy. As interest rates rise, it is argued, smaller firms without adequate supplies of internal funding will be most directly affected by the credit squeeze. Since smaller firms are proportionately much more important in the Prairies a move to restrictive monetary policy dampens the Western economy more even though the inflationary pressures are most likely emanating from the more industrialized areas.

This argument assumes first that smaller firms are more sensitive to the cost of capital, which is only true if larger firms ignore the opportunity costs of internal funds, or if there are non-interest rate costs to financing externally. But even if true, this is how monetary policy is expected to operate. Interest rates are prices in the same sense that wheat or steel prices are. A rise in price allocates an increasingly scarce resource to its most efficient uses. Borrowers whose expected rates of return were close to the previous cost of funds are the ones who should be priced out if aggregate demand is too high. The result is a rationing of funds to those able to use them most productively.

In each of the above examples it can be seen that the real dissatisfaction is with the market economy rather than with discriminatory acts by the federal government or eastern-based companies. Western policy proposals in these areas are actually demands for intervention in the market. Industry could be more equally spread across the country by employing various forms of subsidies, tax breaks, preferential federal government purchasing policies and the like to compensate firms for the extra cost of sub-optimal locations. Provincially owned and operated banks could concentrate on local borrowing needs and ignore the opportunity costs of these loans. Existing commercial banks can, and are often forced to discriminate between large and small borrowers in a period of tighter credit conditions. But it is obvious that these types of proposals are actually demands to counteract decisions made by the market rather than to offset rationally discriminatory behaviour by private institutions or the federal government.

A demand for market intervention could be justified on the grounds that there are social returns to regional industrialization over and above the private ones. But in this case the social returns would have to be based on a special concept of a region within a national economy. The view must be that regional or provincial boundaries have significance in and of themselves, beyond administrative convenience. The federal government would then take this constraint into account when formulating its economic policies. This attitude, implicit in much of the discussions, must be made explicit at the outset and defended on political and historical grounds if any of the subsequent points are to have any meaning. It is ironic that this is the same kind of view that Westerners have long been critical of Québecois or Maritimers for holding.

III

Other examples of western economic discontent can be interpreted as unhappiness with market distortions introduced or tolerated by federal government policies which allegedly have regionally discriminatory effects. Under this heading fall such things as tariffs, freight rates not set on a competitive basis, feed grain transportation subsidies and resource taxation. These issues, if legitimate, can properly be called regional economic discontent since the source of the disputes lies with explicit federal government policies, and recourse lies in lobbying to have them removed. Two things need to be demonstrated, however, before the Prairie governments demand specific types of corrective legislation. It needs first to be shown that the claims are theoretically valid and empirically significant. Then the overall implications of removing the distortions must be carefully analyzed. It can be shown that in some cases the costs to the Prairies of certain policy proposals may be as large as any perceived gain, or else would involve an intraregional income redistribution in a generally regressive direction.

The regional impact of the cash cost of the tariffs on manufactured consumer goods is a case where the theoretical underpinnings of the arguments are unclear. The Prairie provinces argue that while consumers in all parts of the country pay the cost of the tariff in the form of higher prices for protected goods, the inequitable distribution of industry means that the benefits accrue disproportionately to Central Canada. The cash cost of the tariff is allocated regionally according to shares of national income and the benefits by the distribution of protected industry. The difference between the latter and the former, positive for

Quebec and Ontario and negative for the other regions, is the interregional income redistribution occasioned by the tariff on consumer goods. For the Prairies the estimate is put at approximately 200 million dollars for 1970 (Western Premiers, 1937b; Powrie, 1967).

It is important to ask, however, in what sense this can truly be called a regional burden. What is at issue here is not whether the Prairie consumer faces a real income loss because of the tariff, and is therefore justified in opposing it. Clearly he does, and clearly he should oppose it. But so should consumers in the rest of the country. The question is whether Prairie residents or, for that matter, those in British Columbia, the Maritimes or even areas in Quebec or Ontario outside the industrial heartland) bear a *special* burden. The best way to analyze this is to determine exactly what the 200 million dollar net transfer represents. The evidence is that in the Canadian case the tariff allows the continued existence of a large number of small, inefficient firms (English, 1964; Eastman & Stykolt, 1967). Thus the net benefit of the tariff to central Canada is largely the added expenditure on labour in protected industries. There are more jobs in manufacturing in Canada than there would be in the absence of the tariff, with most of them concentrated in Ontario and Quebec. The regional impact essentially is that Prairie residents pay a share of this excess wage bill but receive a disproportionately small percentage of the jobs.

Since there are no formal barriers to labour mobility within the country there is nothing preventing workers of all areas from migrating to the industrial centres to take these jobs. The 200 million dollars is a true regional burden only if labour is immobile regionally. This may be true, but if so it is important to ascertain the factors behind the immobility. If it is a matter of job information, relocation costs and the like, then the usual dictum of using the most direct policy tool for the problem at hand prevails. The correct response in this case, for example, is for better manpower programs.

The immobility may result in fact from special attachments to the area for a variety of historical, cultural and political reasons. In this event the reduction in real income without the concomitant creation of employment opportunities locally can be interpreted as the cost of choosing to live where one wants. People who remain in the Prairies must be judged willing to incur certain costs in return for unspecified non-monetary benefits in lifestyle. The only other possible reaction is to invoke the special concept of a region and the unique rights of regional inhabitants as discussed above. In this case it is assumed that the federal government has the responsibility of providing everyone with equal access to remunerative employment irrespective of where they choose to live.

A regional burden could possibly be demonstrated from the specific structure of the Canadian tariff system. Duties tend to be high on manufactured products and low or non-existent on certain types of primary products, especially those being sold in export markets. Thus the effective rate of protection for some primary industries is negative, meaning that actual value added is below that it would be in a free trade situation. Assuming that lower net returns are reflected in lower prices paid for the right to exploit the resources, the burden falls ultimately on the owners of the resource. In the case of farm land this is the farmer himself,[5] while for natural resources the provincial governments or private owners receive lower bids for exploration and development rights. Since these factors are immobile by definition, the argument advanced above for labour does not apply. If the Prairies were disproportionately dependent on primary industries, as seems likely, some kind of regional argument might be defensible.

Even here though one must be careful. It is easy to overstate the extent to which tariffs reduce value added in these sectors.[6] Duties on agricultural implements were removed in 1944 for example, and there is a system of rebates for duty paid on inputs to a product which is eventually exported. In addition, there are or have been numerous non-tariff barriers to entry in the primary products sectors such as the ban on DES-fed beef or the National Oil Policy restrictions on imports of cheaper off-shore crude into Ontario. If these restrictions were expressed in tariff equivalents the low effective rates would be increased substantially.

A second example of the distortions argument is the claim of discriminatory pricing by the railways. The National Transportation Act of 1967 relies largely on intermodal competition to regulate freight rates. Western spokesmen argue that this is only an effective policy for the East where water and truck transport are serious competitors to the railroads, or on the west coast where ocean shipping is important. On the Prairies however, the railways have a near monopoly of most types of freight movements. As such they act as a discriminating monopolist, setting freight rates on a value of service rather than a cost of service basis.[7] The predictable results of this 'charging what the traffic will bear' policy are relatively high rates on products with low price elasticities of demand and lower rates on products that are highly price sensitive.

The demand for imported processed products on the Prairies is likely relatively price inelastic given the absence of local industry. Hence a discriminatory monopolist could charge more than costs[8] for transporting manufactured products into the region, thus increasing prices and reducing the real incomes of western residents. Prairie politicians accordingly have asked that the current rate structure be replaced by one which more closely reflects the actual costs incurred by the railways providing the service.

If one grants that it is the responsibility of the federal government to prevent monopolistic pricing in any part of the economy, and if it can be shown that the discriminatory pricing values of the railroads impose a significant burden on the Prairie economies, the freight rate issue can be classed as a legitimate regional grievance. But this is a case where not all the implications of the policy proposal have been carefully thought out. It is true that lower freight rates on incoming products would lower prices and would thus seem to increase real incomes. But it is quite possible also that less total income would be generated in the region, leaving the overall impact uncertain. For example, artificially high rates on incoming goods are a positive inducement to Prairie industrialization. Consumer goods or processed inputs intended for Prairie consumption are more likely to be produced locally if they enjoy this natural protection. Lower rates would just extend the range of competitiveness of eastern producers. How empirically significant this point is depends on the position and elasticity of the supply curve of locally based industries. The present industrial structure indicates that there has been little positive impact from the current high prices, so the impact of any reduction would most likely be minimal. But the contradiction in the Prairie position is still there.

In addition, what is often overlooked in lobbying for a cost of service basis for freight rate pricing is that the current rates on outward bound shipments of raw or semi-processed goods would probably go up. These products are sold into world markets where the demand for a specific country's output is highly price elastic. In such cases there is little scope for the carrier to arbitrarily increase rates beyond costs, and there may even be some incentive to provide services at lower rates. If these rates were raised the result would be lower incomes to the primary industries. Selling into a competitive market means the producer must bear the brunt of the transportaion and handling charges. Rates on Prairie exports lower than the true cost of providing the service act as a direct subsidy to the producer. The local prices for sulfur, coal, timber, potash and the like would have to be lower if the products were to remain competitive in external markets. Lower prices mean lower net incomes in all industries, and for marginal ones such as lumbering may mean the difference between survival and shutting down.

This effect is most evident on grain rates. The Crow's Nest Pass rates of 1897 were reaffirmed and extended in 1925 and have been in place ever since. In this case the evidence is clear that current rates do not even cover variable costs of operation (McDougall, 1966; Rogerson, 1975: 77-92). A cost of service freight rate structure would definitely mean substantial income losses for Prairie grain growers. This has not gone unnoticed in the Prairies of course, and explains the very vocal opposition to any suggestions that the statutory rates be altered. The usual justification is that these rates were to exist in perpetuity in exchange for concessions granted to the railway companies. But on this

334 / Regionalism and Canadian Federalism

point it must be noted that the 1897 agreement was between the federal government and the CPR, with the subsidy of $11,000 per mile for a railroad into the mining areas of BC being paid out of federal coffers. Prairie grain growers benefited from the deal, but there were no direct concessions made by them to close it. It is actually the federal government that has the right to insist the railways live up to the agreement or to allow its abrogation.

A second transportation issue concerns Prairie industrialization. It is often argued that the current structure of rail rates is a 'major barrier to economic development and diversification' (Western Premiers, 1973c). Since this claim is quite vague it is useful to consider under what types of situations a move to cost of service freight rate pricing would have beneficial effects on Prairie industrialization. For locally based industries serving the Prairies the impact of the proposed schedule would be detrimental, as discussed above. Lower rates on incoming products would further enhance the competitiveness of eastern or externally located firms. The argument might be taken to imply that under the current structure rates on products processed on the Prairies for export are too high. But by the logic of the freight rate discussion overall, this could only be true for products where the external price elasticity of demand was low. Only in these cases would the railways find it profitable to add on freight charges above costs. One is hard put to think of any Prairie export of processed products that would have this kind of demand curve. The more likely case, given the relative unimportance of Prairie suppliers, is a highly elastic price response in external markets. The proposed new rate structure would if anything mean higher rates on these types of products, making it even more difficult to compete.[9]

The other interpretation of the industrialization argument is that the current rail rates on raw material exports are too low. An increase in these charges, assuming a highly elastic demand curve for the products, would mean lower primary product prices on the Prairies. Lower input costs might in turn induce shifts in the location of forward linked industries. Meatpacking, processing of timber, sulfur, potash and the like might be drawn more to the extraction site and less to the market.

This seems to be the only sense in which the bias against industrialization argument makes theoretical sense. Just how empirically significant it is is another matter of course. One would have to know what kind of local raw materials price advantages would be needed to induce such a location shift. But even if successful the region as a whole is trading an increase in industrialization for lower prices and hence incomes to producers of these raw materials. In the successful cases local raw materials prices could never rise above the level that is just sufficient to retain the West's locational advantage. In other cases there would be a fall in local net returns as a result of higher transport costs without any impact on industrial location. Prairie governments should thus be very careful about demanding specific changes in the freight rate structure. It must first be determined which industries, if any, might respond to lower local prices by switching from a market to a site location. But even then these benefits must be weighed against the income distributional implications of such a move.

Meatpacking is a good example of this general point. The technology of the industry is such that about seven pounds of grain are used per pound of finished beef or five pounds of grain per one pound of pork (Gainer, 1974). If transportation costs per pound on grain and meat products were identical there would be a significant incentive for feed-lots and meatpackers to locate near the supply of western feed grains. But the current freight rate structure operates to more than offset this advantage. In the first place the rail rate for dressed meat products is three to four times that for an equivalent weight of feed grains, even at non-statutory rates for the latter. But the differential is even further broadened by the fact that feed grains move to the Lakehead under the normal statutory grain rates and from the Lakehead to eastern Canada under the special provisions of the Feed Grains Assistance policy. Thus any weight saving that would be gained by locating meatpacking on the Prairies is at least offset by the much cheaper costs of hauling grain. The net result is the Prairies lose what seems to be a natural secondary industry.

While this argument appears to be generally persuasive two points are in order. In the first place, it is not clear that a significantly higher rate on dressed meat products over grain is necessarily discriminatory. Given specialized equipment such as refrigerated cars plus the need for more careful and rapid handling a higher rate is perhaps justifiable on purely cost of service grounds. Whether this is actually true, and if so what the true size of the cost differential is, can only be resolved by carefully examining the relevant cost data—which the railroads steadfastly refuse to provide access to unfortunately.

That the two statutory grain rates reduce the West's comparative advantage is clear. But it is important in this case to recognize the implications of the changes being proposed. If Eastern Canada can quite easily turn to imported beef or feed grains then its elasticity of demand for western feed grains will be quite high. In such an event the removal of the transportation subsidy will mean significantly lower feed grain prices on the Prairies. This might be just the advantage western meat-packers need to compete in eastern markets, but the brunt of this will be borne by established grain growers. It is not at all obvious this is the kind of income redistribution one would necessarily condone. Prairie farmers would likely offset some of these costs by putting more emphasis on livestock production, but not without incurring adjustment costs.

In any event the expected return to this diversification will still be lower than the present product mix at current prices.

Another result of value of service pricing is the existence of discriminatory agreed charges between the railways and certain shippers. Larger eastern producers are able to extract more favourable shipping terms than smaller western ones. The result is that it can cost more to ship the same product from Edmonton to Toronto than vice versa. While this would seem on the surface to discourage industrial diversification in the West it is important to realize that this apparently incongruous situation is most likely a symptom of the relative attractiveness of eastern versus western industrial locations rather than a cause of it. For most products it is difficult to imagine how a change in rate structure could radically reorient location decisions. Agreed charges are thus not likely actively retarding western industralization. Indeed, to the extent that the shipper can negotiate special rates for products which would be produced externally anyway Prairie residents benefit from lower prices on these items.

The dispute over crude oil taxation is an example of a situation where proper historical perspective is needed. In general the arguments of the western[10] provinces are valid. Economic rents properly belong to the owners of the resources when ownership is public rather than private, and as such clearly should accrue in the first instance to the provincial governments. This fact, plus the long standing tradition of one level of government not taxing another, means that the export tax on crude oil and the domestic price freeze are clearly regional burdens. There is a direct subsidy from the producing provinces to the federal government and to Canadian consumers of western oil to the extent of the difference between world and Canadian oil prices. The punitive features of this policy are even more apparent given that the federal government has not imposed similiar measures on other types of products.

This position is generally convincing, and seems to be one of the few areas where the distortionary impact of a federal policy is truly one way only. But there are historical grounds for arguing that the federal government's actions were defensible on a short term basis, and that the transitional period to the higher prices is not inequitable. The imposition of the export tax in the fall of 1973 and its rapid rise to the current level of effect redistributed income largely from oil companies rather than Alberta. Just before the OPEC price rises the province had initiated a new royalty policy based on taxing reserves rather than some kind of sliding scale for price increases on existing wells. The effective average royalty rate was slightly over 20 percent, meaning that more than three-quarters of the price increases would have gone to oil companies. Assuming that all of the price increase for existing wells was economic rent, the federal export tax was a much more efficient way to collect this windfall gain.

The federal government and Canadian consumers gained rather than the preponderantly foreign owned oil industry.[11] As an interim measure, until Alberta and Saskatchewan could devise more efficient royalty schedules, the tax was defensible.

The reason for arguing that it is not necessarily discriminatory for Alberta to bear the brunt of a transition period is that historically the western based oil and gas industry received very preferential treatment from federal policies. The National Oil Policy guaranteed a market for western oil in spite of significantly higher costs (Debanné, 1974). For many years consumers in Ontario were paying more for crude oil than what off-shore imports could have been brought in for, and were forbidden by the National Energy Board to switch suppliers. While it admittedly does not take long for a subsidy of $5.20 per barrel to more than offset years of paying 25-35¢ more, even with the miracles of compound interest, there is still the fact that Ontario partly justified its paying for higher oil on the grounds of a secure supply.

The other way in which the industry received favourable treatment was in the area of corporate income tax. Eric Kierans has long argued that the tax laws disproportionately favoured resource extractive industries. More specifically, the fact that the industry was allowed to write off for tax purposes any money they spent securing exploration or development rights meant that Alberta received more revenue from these auctions than she would have under a more neutral tax scheme. It is ironic that the present dispute stems from an attempt by the federal government not to tax the oil industry disproportionately high, but rather to tax it more along the lines of all other sectors.

IV

The intent of this paper has been to demonstrate that the explicit economic discrimination faced by the Prairies is somewhat less than is commonly imagined. A claim of regional economic discrimination was judged legitimate if it was directed at distortions clearly initiated by the federal government or by other institutions and tolerated by Ottawa, and if removal of the distortions would unambiguously benefit the West. Upon examination, only the western position of federal government taxation of resources met these criteria. All the other major areas of contention missed on one of the counts.

In some instances, Prairie industrilization being perhaps the best example, the problem lies in being small and isolated rather than with discriminatory treatment. The present economic structure of the region is adequately explained by standard location theory concepts. It is incorrect to suggest that the federal government or other institutions have industrialized the East at the expense of the West. It must be recognized rather that any significant decentralization of industry in Canada can only be achieved by committing real resources to that end, and that this means a subsidy for persons residing in the recipient regions at the expense of other Canadians.

Even in instances where a specific federal economic policy is the source of contention the validity of the discrimination claim is unclear. The cash cost of the tariff on consumer goods can only be given regional significance under very special assumptions. The entire freight rate question is one where the region has conflicting interests rather than a single common one. The western diagnosis of monopoly freight rate power is basically correct, and some of the costs have been correctly identified. But the proposal to rectify these, a move to a complete cost of service pricing principle—the so-called Equitable Pricing Principle, involves new costs not explicitly recognized. The issue comes down to the familiar welfare economics quandary of not being able to evaluate unambiguously a policy that makes some groups within the region better off while making others worse off. This must be a political decision ultimately.

NOTES

[1] For example, the Independent Alberta Association was formed to ". . . educate the public about the true costs of Confederation to the province." (*Edmonton Journal, 1975*)

[2] The Independent Alberta Association is composed largely of individuals who profess total attachment to a pure market economy. Thus copies of Ayn Rand's books were circulated at the founding meeting, and the 'Vive l'Alberta Libre' buttons one sees occasionally are distributed by the Alberta Libertarian Party.

[3] Blackman (1975). This article was in response to a comment by the present author (Norrie, 1975).

[4] This point is restricted to the asymmetrical incidence of transportation charges that are competitively determined. It does not refer to the levels of the rates actually charged and whether they reflect the true costs of providing the service. Thus there may be discrimination in this latter sense even if not in the former. This point is discussed at some length in the next section.

[5] This was discussed by W. M. Mackintosh (1939) some 35 years ago. Since the tariffs were in place before there was much settlement or development in the Prairies, any negative impact they had on the flow of agricultural income should have been exactly reflected in lower capitalized values for land. Thus the only real losers were the original owners of the land—the CPR Hudson's Bay Company and the federal government itself—who received less from the sale of the land than they would have in the absence of the tariffs. In fact, given that the general trend of tariffs, especially those on farm inputs, has been gradually downwards there have been unanticipated capital gains to landowners.

[6] Wilkinson and Norrie (1975) calculate effective rates of protection for all industries using the 1966 input table. For the primary sector the simple effective rate was positive for five of the eleven industries, and the largest negative rate was −1.80%.

[7] Note that this is a different issue than the one raised in the first section. There it was

shown that the Prairies would naturally pay transport costs both ways, even if transportation were a perfectly competitive industry. But since the industry is clearly not competitive, and there is great potential for discriminatory pricing by the railroads, it may be that the costs incurred by Prairie residents are in excess of what they would naturally bear. It is this latter issue that is discussed here.

[8] The National Transportation Act allows rates to be up to 250% of variable cost. See Gillen, Beaton and Jones (1975).

[9] In one of the few studies directed at this question, Gainer and Drugge (1973) found that for the petrochemical industry rail rates on eastbound manufactured petrochemicals from Edmonton are usually lower than comparable rates on Eastern produced petrochemicals westbound, or on comparable American hauls.

[10] This issue is one of those where the interests of Manitoba differ from those of Saskatchewan and Alberta (the other notable one being tariffs where Manitoba has a disproportionate amount of protected industry, and hence is cooler to the idea of a general reduction in these duties). Since Manitoba's oil and gas production is insignificant she more naturally lines up with Ontario on the issues of the export tax, a domestic price freeze and the like.

[11] The distribution of benefits from an increase in the price of crude oil under the old royalty structure is analyzed by Wilkinson and Roseman (1973).

REFERENCES

Blackman, W. (1974) 'The Cost of Confederation: Part I.' A study commissioned by the Independent Alberta Association.

Blackman, W. (1975) 'The Cost of Confederation,' *Edmonton Journal*, January 28.

Debanné, J. (1974) 'Oil and Canadian Policy' in E. Erickson and L. Waverman (eds), *The Energy Question, Volume II*, (Toronto: University of Toronto Press)

Eastman, H. C. and S. Stykolt (1967) *The Tariff and Competition in Canada* (Toronto: University of Toronto Press)

Edmonton Journal (1975) 'Frustration Fires Alberta Separatist John Rudolph,' February 6.

English, H. E. (1964) *Industrial Structure in Canada's International Competitive Position* (Montreal: The Private Planning Association)

Gainer, W. D. and S. E. Drugge (1973) 'Economic Analysis of the Effects of Transport Rates on Products of the Industrial Chemical and Meat Packing Industry with Special Reference to Edmonton.' A study commissioned by the Canadian Transport Commission.

Gainer, W. D. (1974) 'Economic Factors in the Conflict Between Alberta and Ottawa.' Mimeograph, University of Alberta.

Gillen, D. W., J. Beaton and M. R. Jones (1975) 'Pricing Policies, Freight Rates and the West.' Mimeograph, University of Alberta.

Mackintosh, W. A. (1939) *The Economic Background of Dominion Provincial Relations.* (Ottawa: King's Printer Appendix III of the Royal Commission on Dominion Provincial Relations)

McDougall, J. L. (1966) 'The Relative Level of Crow's Nest Grain Rates in 1899 and 1965.' *Canadian Journal of Economics and Political Science*, XXXII February, pp. 46-54.

Norrie, K. H. (1975) 'The Real Costs of Confederation.' *Edmonton Journal*, January 4.

Powrie, T. L. (1967) 'Regional Effects of the Canadian Tariff.' Unpublished paper, Department of Economics, University of Alberta.

Rogerson, B. (1975) 'Canadian Freight Transportation.' A background paper prepared for Arnold Malone, M.P.

Western Premiers (1973a) 'Capital Financing and Regional Financial Institutions.' Joint Submission of the Western Premiers to the Western Economic Opportunities Conference, July 24-26.

Western Premiers (1973b) 'Economic and Industrial Development Opportunites.' Joint Submission of the Western Premiers to the Western Economic Opportunities Conference, July 24-26.

Western Premiers (1973c) 'Transportation.' Joint Submission of the Western Premiers to the Western Economic Opportunities Conference, July 24-26.

Wilkinson, B. W. and K. H. Norrie (1975) *Effective Protection and the Rate of Return to Capital,* forthcoming Special Study for the Economic Council of Canada.

Wilkinson, B. W. and F. Roseman (1973) 'Who benefits? The Alberta Energy Price Increase,' *Canadian Forum,* June-July, pp. 48-52.

22

Intergovernmental Cooperation in Western Canada: The Western Economic Opportunities Conference*

M. Westmacott and P. Dore

INTRODUCTION

In 1959, Richard Leach observed that there was a tendency on the part of academics, politicians and bureaucrats to view all intergovernmental relations in Canada as "federal-provincial."[1] Such analyses in his view neglected an increasingly important aspect of intergovernmental relations within a federal state—interprovincial cooperation. While cooperation between the provinces in Canada was "ad hoc" and "informal" when compared to interstate relations in the United States, Leach concluded that ". . . the Canadian provinces . . . are exploring new possibilities of cooperative action and in so doing may gradually alter the nature of Canadian federalism."[2]

The nature and character of the Canadian federal system has changed significantly since 1960. From 1945 to 1960, cooperative federalism was characterized as a period of "programme collaboration."[3] Federal-provincial and inter-provincial interaction on a non-technical level was rare and there were only infrequent attempts on the part of the two levels of government to relate specific programmes to broader federal-

---

* Reprinted by permission.

provincial issues and objectives. However, since 1960, the federal-provincial conference has become the forum for the development of national policies and for the establishment of long-term goals and priorities for the nation. During this same period, the provinces have become more aggressive in their demands for consultation prior to the enactment of federal legislation in areas of provincial jurisdiction and in areas of federal jurisdiction that have a direct impact on the provinces. This change in posture on the part of the provinces has necessitated the creation of specialized agencies and secretariats to facilitate regularized consultation between the two levels of government as well as the establishment of more frequent and more regularized channels for inter-provincial communication. More recently, an additional dimension of inter-provincial cooperation has emerged with the attempts on the part of the Maritime and the four Western provinces to develop common policy positions on issues of concern to the region.

INTER-PROVINCIAL COOPERATION

Since 1960, inter-provincial cooperation has become more structured. Provincial premiers and ministers in policy areas such as education, health and welfare, natural resources and communications meet on an annual basis. Initially the premiers' meetings were designed to facilitate the exchange of information and to promote cooperative efforts on the part of the provincial governments in areas of provincial jurisdiction.[4] Discussions at the early meetings were devoted to topics such as the financing of education and hospitals, the coordination of retail sales tax, and the development of uniform regulations for off-shore mineral rights. There were no substantive debates on issues of national concern and it was repeatedly emphasized that the meetings would not be used to "gang up" on Ottawa.[5]

Since 1966, the tenor of the Premiers' Conference has changed dramatically. Increasingly, the topics under discussion are "national" issues of concern to both the provinces and the federal government. For example, recent conferences have been devoted to discussions of pollution, off-shore mineral rights, energy policy, and the role of the provinces in the development of economic policy. In addition, the conference has become a vehicle for communicating provincial views to the federal government. At the meeting in Halifax in 1972, resolutions were adopted and forwarded to the federal government for the first time since the inception of the Premiers' Conference.[6]

There is a growing body of literature devoted to inter-provincial cooperation in the Maritimes.[7] Virtually no attempt has been made, however, to explore the increasing degree of cooperation among the four Western provinces. While the existence of administrative agreements between the four provinces has been documented, there has been no discussion in the literature of the attempts on the part of the premiers to use the Prairie Economic Council and the Western Premiers' Conference as forums for the development of regional policy positions.[8] It is the objective of this essay to examine and to assess the increasing degree of inter-provincial consultation among the four Western provinces. In particular, the paper will explore the objectives, the accomplishments and the limitations of intergovernmental consultation as it has evolved in Western Canada in recent years.

WESTERN CANADIAN ALIENATION— A RECURRING PHENOMENON

Although the term "Western Canadian Alienation" is difficult to define precisely, its origins are well known. A feeling of political and economic isolation has been a recurring theme in the political history of Western Canada and it is this feeling which has been characterized in recent times by the press and by politicians as an important dimension of the phenomenon. The nature of both the economic and the political grievances of the region has been documented throughout the literature dealing with Western Canadian politics.[9]

Since the late nineteenth century, national economic policies have had a detrimental effect on the regional economy. In particular, freight rates and tariffs have protected Central Canadian financial and industrial interests and have inhibited the diversification of the Western Canadian economy.[10] W. L. Morton has observed that Western Canadians become aware of their political impotence, at the national level, at an early stage in the political development of the region. Western Canadian politicians have continued to believe that they are unable to articulate their opinions effectively at the federal level, on issues that are of vital concern to the region. The emergence of the Progressive Party in the 1920s and the C.C.F. and Social Credit parties in the 1930s symbolized, in Morton's words, ". . . a revolt against the concept of Canadian political practise."[11] Neither Parliament nor the two traditional parties were perceived as adequate forums for the articulation and accommodation of Western views. Increasingly, the governmental party in each province became the predominant instrumentality for the expression of Western Canadian views.[12]

One of the more recent and comprehensive statements delineating the nature of Western Canadian grievances was presented by Premier Harry E. Strom of Alberta to the Constitutional Conference of February 1969.[13] Rather than using the cultural terms which define the alienation of Quebec, Strom perceived western alienation in both economic and political terms. After citing the traditional economic grievances, he criticized the failure of the federal government to consult with the provinces and to accommodate Western Canadian views in the formation of national policies. Since 1969, feelings of alienation have been further aggravated by the extensive efforts of the federal government to deal with the relatively urgent economic problems of the Atlantic provinces and with the constitutional demands presented by various Quebec governments. Increasingly, Westerners have come to view themselves as a neglected group who are penalized by the federal government in order that other areas of the country may be benefited.

There have been several political manifestations of this alienation. First, the inability of the Liberal Party to elect a significant number of representatives from the Prairie Provinces, in both the 1972 and 1974 federal elections, appears to be a reflection of Western Canadian disenchantment with federal policy. The Liberal Party continues to be perceived as the party of Central Canada and therefore insensitive to the needs of the West. Furthermore, several pressure groups have commissioned studies to examine the implications of secession. In 1969 the Saskatchewan Wheat Pool approved a resolution calling for "the consideration of secession if the federal government does not give due consideration to the problems of Western Canada."[14] In October of 1974, the Independent Alberta Association concluded that there would be distinct economic benefits to the secession of Alberta from Confederation.[15] Moreover, in a second study, the Association concluded that Alberta has the legal right to secede.[16] These developments are but variations on a theme that has pervaded Western Canadian history.

In contrast, since 1969, the political leaders in Western Canada have directed their efforts towards increased intergovernmental cooperation. While the goals have not been precisely defined, there would appear to be two overriding objectives—the development and diversification of the Western Canadian economy and a strengthening of the West's position in Confederation.[17]

ORIGINS AND DEVELOPMENT

Intergovernmental cooperation among the four Western Canadian provinces can be directly traced to the establishment of the Prairie Economic Council in October 1965.[18] Initially the Council met on a yearly basis to facilitate the exchange of information among the three Prairie Provinces. Among the topics for discussion were the abolition of provincial preferences on public purchases and contracts, the utilization of the Port of Churchill and the elimination of discriminatory practices affecting interprovincial trucking. No attempt was made to develop common policy positions nor to convey a "Western Canadian" viewpoint to the federal government. After reviewing the nature of the discussions at the initial meetings of the Council, D. V. Smiley concluded that ". . . co-operation on the part of the prairies will be less oriented towards presenting a common regional policy front to the federal government than has been the case with the Atlantic Region."[19]

Since 1968, the Prairie Economic Council and later the Western Premiers' Conference have become the forums for the development of regional policy positions on issues such as industrial development, regional economic expansion, and agricultural and transportation policy. Increasingly, provincial politicians have accepted the proposition that Western Canada's bargaining position can be significantly strengthened in any discussions with Ottawa if the four Western provinces develop regional policy positions.[20]

What factors contributed to the growing degree of intergovernmental cooperation in Western Canada? In retrospect, the inadequacy of existing instrumentalities within the federal system would appear to be the most important. In the past, Western Canadian politicians relied very heavily on three major channels of communication to convey their views to the federal government—political tactics on the part of Members of Parliament in the House of Commons, the presentation of briefs to Royal Commissions and representations to federal regulatory boards and agencies.[21]

Each one of these instrumentalities proved to be inadequate. Since 1963, the overwhelming majority of Members of Parliament from Western Canada have been members of the opposition parties. The failure to elect Liberal members effectively deprived Western Canada from representation in the Cabinet and in the government caucus. In addition, Western Canadian MPs are federal politicians and are therefore limited in their ability to articulate a regional or a provincial point of view by factors such as party discipline.[22] On many occasions in the 1960s, expressions of discontent on the part of Western Members were viewed by the government as being a partisan ploy and not a genuine expression of regional discontent. Representations to federal boards and to Royal Commissions proved to be only marginally successful.[23] Increasingly, the federal-provincial conference came to be viewed as the most effective mode of articulating Western Canadian grievances to the federal government.[24]

Prior to 1968, there had been virtually no attempt on the part of the four Western provinces to present a "Western Canadian" position at federal-provincial conferences with the expectation that such a posture would ultimately strengthen the West's bargaining position.[25] Differences in political affiliation and provincial economies as well as personality conflicts inhibited the development of a "Western Canadian" position. This, of course, permitted the federal government to employ the familiar tactic of "divide and conquer." Many provincial politicians and officials were coming to the view that the federal government would be more inclined to accommodate their demands when faced with a "Western Canadian" position on various policy questions.

The first evidence that a new strategy was evolving in Western Canada's relations with Ottawa was at the meeting of the Prairie Economic Council in the summer of 1968.[26] At that meeting, the three premiers laid the groundwork for a "Western Canadian" position on transportation policy. It is not surprising that this was one of the first policy areas where there was significant intergovernmental consultation among the three provinces. Transportation policy has consistently occupied the attention of Western politicians since Western Canada was settled. Prior to 1968, there were no consultations among the three Prairie Provinces and there were no regularized and in depth discussions between the provinces and the federal government. Those consultations that did occur were unstructured and very general in nature.[27] Emerging from the meeting of the Prairie Economic Council was an agreement that the issue of transportation policy would be raised at the Constitutional Conference of December 1969 and that the three governments would work towards the development of a "Western Canadian" position.

The Lethbridge Conference, convened in 1970 to discuss the political, social, and economic consequences of prairie union, had an important impact on officials and politicians from the three prairie provinces. While political union was rejected, there was an acceptance of the need for greater cooperation between the provinces.[28] Messrs. Blakeney and Lougheed, who were leaders of the opposition within their respective provinces, attended the conference and proposed the establishment of specialized intergovernmental machinery to facilitate greater consultation. Mr. Blakeney specified the format of such cooperation when he advocated a "Canada West Council."

> The Council would have to have representation from the three Prairie Provinces and with an independent secretariat. Its terms of reference might well be . . . the identification of areas requiring inter-provincial cooperation and the recommending of mechanisms for achieving this cooperation. . . .[29]

Mr. Lougheed suggested that the Prairie Economic Council be revised to become

> . . . an effective interprovincial agency—provided with a strong secretariat and with staff charged with examining proposed national policies and assessing them in terms of their prairie implication. The legislatures should provide substantial funds and full support.[30]

Between 1969 and 1972, new governments were elected in each of the four Western provinces.[31] In retrospect, the change in political leadership facilitated greater intergovernmental cooperation among the four governments. Each of the premiers indicated a greater willingness than his predecessor to set aside partisan and personality differences in the hope that a regional policy could be developed. In short, they recognized the potential benefits of such intergovernmental activity and since 1969, intergovernmental consultations have become increasingly more structured and more regularized. The federal government's decision to convene the Western Economic Opportunities Conference gave official recognition to what many commentators had been observing in Western Canada for several years.

WESTERN ECONOMIC OPPORTUNITIES CONFERENCE

A. Origin

The repudiation of the Liberal Party by Western Canadians in the 1972 federal election prompted the Trudeau Government to reassess its relations with Western Canada. Consequently, in January 1973, the federal government proposed that a federal-provincial conference be convened to discuss matters of particular concern to the West.[32] This decision established an important precedent. This would be the first occasion when the federal government would meet with a particular group of provinces to discuss issues of concern to the region. As a result of consultations between Ottawa and the four Western provinces, an agenda emerged that included provisions for discussions in five policy areas— transportation, industrial and commercial development, regional economic expansion, agriculture, and financial institutions. The four Western provinces and the federal government agreed to produce background papers in each policy area and it was understood that these documents would form the basis for discussion and debate.

B. The Provincial Response

Despite their enthusiastic response to the federal proposal, the four Western premiers indicated to federal officials that they expected the Conference to produce concrete policy proposals that would alleviate Western grievances. Consequently, in March 1973, the three prairie premiers met in Winnipeg to discuss strategy for the forthcoming Conference.[33] Premier David Barrett was invited to participate in the discussions. This was the first indication that British Columbia was prepared to cooperate with the three prairie provinces in the development of regional policies. Prior to this, Premier W. A. C. Bennett had resisted the overtures of the prairie provinces to engage in inter-provincial discussions. During the course of the meeting, the premiers agreed to establish a new structure, the Western Premiers' Conference, to facilitate greater intergovernmental cooperation. In addition, they instructed their officials to explore the possibility of developing a regional policy position on each of the agenda items. Between March and June of 1973 there were a series of meetings involving politicians and officials from the four Western provinces.[34] The particularity of provincial economics, the existence of problems peculiar to one province, differing political affiliations and personality conflicts tended to impede the development of regional policies. Despite these rather formidable obstacles, intensive discussions at the official level and good will and pragmatism at the political level ultimately produced regional policy positions.[35] A new strategy of dealing with Ottawa was beginning to develop and by June of 1973, four policy papers were forwarded to Ottawa that had the endorsement of each of the four provinces.[36] The publication of the papers marked the first occasion on which the federal government entered into discussions with a regional grouping of provinces that were united behind a common position on a broad range of issues. This development prompted the federal government to reassess its strategy with regard to the Conference.

C. The Federal Reaction

Initially, the federal government regarded the Western Economic Opportunities Conference as little more than an opportunity to discuss, in general terms, some of the longstanding grievances of the four Western provinces. The comments by the Honourable Otto Lang typify the federal government's attitude. He observed that the Conference would be

> . . . an opportunity to look at the aspirations of the west . . . . [Growth] is important in this region to sustain and maintain our population and our activity . . . . [Therefore] ways and means of developing the economy . . . must be examined with this kind of objective in mind.[37]

As the Conference drew nearer, the federal government became increasingly critical of Western Canada's insistence that it deal with specific policy proposals. On June 16, 1973, Otto Lang accused the premiers of employing "a tunnel vision approach" in their preparations for the Conference.[38] Such a strategy in his view could ultimately sabotage the Conference. In rebuttal, the four Western Premiers sent a joint telegram to Prime Minister Trudeau inquiring if Mr. Lang's remarks represented the federal government's attitude toward the Conference.[39] The next day, the Prime Minister assured the Opposition that the government was indeed prepared to bring specific proposals to the Conference. However, when pressed for details as to the nature of these proposals, Mr. Trudeau merely replied that they had been set forth in the Speech From the Throne.[40]

Unfortunately, the communications between Ottawa and the Western provinces failed to define the parameters of the conference with any greater precision than had been originally agreed to in January 1973. By early July it was clear that the four Western provinces would arrive at the Conference with the expectation that concrete and detailed policy proposals would be discussed. However, the federal government refused to commit itself to such a course of action. The release of the four federal position papers, containing general policy statements, gave no further indication of a willingness on the part of the federal government to negotiate specific changes in federal policies at the Conference.[41]

D. The Conference Proceedings[42]

After the initial complimentary remarks, the proceedings of the Western Economic Opportunities Conference were delayed by a procedural dispute over the presentation of position papers. The Prime Minister expressed a desire to proceed with the federal papers in the "usual fashion"; however, this course of action was opposed by three of the Premiers. Finally a compromise, suggested by Premier Schreyer, was reached whereby each side would alternate in presenting the first paper on each agenda item. This incident gave some indication of the intensity with which each side approached the conference.

As the Conference progressed, the federal government outlined in very broad and general terms the impact of federal policies on the development of Western Canada. The four premiers countered these arguments with their well-prepared and detailed proposals. The premiers emphasized their desire for comprehensive remedies to the various grievances of Western Canada and for a better understanding of the West's role in Confederation. In contrast, Prime Minister Trudeau strongly defended the federal position papers on each agenda item and he consistently refused to engage in discussions that committed the federal government to legislate specific changes in national policies.

Personalities played an important part in the proceedings. Premier Lougheed of Alberta emerged as the strongest and the most persuasive of the four western spokesmen while Premier Schreyer's was the most conciliatory voice at the Conference. In conclusion, the provincial Premiers and their advisors were prepared to discuss and to negotiate specific policy proposals. On the other hand, the federal government, through the Prime Minister and his cabinet colleagues, responded with a disjointed and piecemeal set of proposals.

The concluding remarks of the various participants give some indication of their assessment of the Conference. Mr. Trudeau punctuated his final address with non-committal phrases such as "the federal government and the provinces should intensify discussions and reciprocate consultation on major areas of current concern."[43] The most used adjectival phrase by the federal delegates was "desirable and feasible." The tone of their comments was one of cautious optimism. In contrast, all four premiers were disappointed with the Conference and pessimistic over the federal proposals for western development. Premier Lougheed stated that he was disturbed by the continued failure of the federal government to understand the West despite the concerted efforts of the provincial governments. Premier Schreyer was concerned with the unwillingness of the federal government to consider a comprehensive regional development policy. It was Premier Blakeney, however, who was most critical of the Conference proceedings. In his view, there had been no significant progress in the critical areas of transportation and industrial development.[44]

E. Post Conference Developments and Conclusions

It is difficult to assess with precision the accomplishments and the shortcomings of intergovernmental collaboration as it has evolved in Western Canada during the past few years. In general terms, it would appear that the new strategy of dealing with Ottawa has produced some tangible results for Western Canada. In recent times, Ottawa has indicated a greater sensitivity to the grievances and demands of the West than it has in the past. The federal government's decision to convene the Western Economic Opportunities Conference is perhaps indicative of Ottawa's interest. Furthermore, there is even some indication that the federal government is prepared to discuss revisions in national economic and transportation policies that could be of direct benefit to the West.[45]

The creation of federal-provincial structures at both the political and the official level to facilitate more structured consultations between the two levels of government in policy areas such as transportation, agriculture and industrial development must be regarded as a major accomplishment.[46] These instrumentalities were not available a few years ago. Therefore, one of the direct consequences of increased intergovernmental consultation among the four Western Provinces has been more consistent contact between Ottawa and Western Canada. It is important to note, however, that these consultations in no way commit the federal government to enact legislation that will accommodate Western Canadian demands to any greater extent than they have in the past.

There are indications that the four Western provinces are working towards the development of a regional economic policy.[47] Greater interprovincial cooperation would eliminate competition for new industry and would ultimately expand the industrial base of the region. In addition, it could facilitate the formulation of more comprehensive economic policies that could offset the detrimental impact of national economic policies on Western Canada.

What are some of the factors that will impede greater intergovernmental cooperation in Western Canada? Differing political affiliations, the existence of problems peculiar to one province and inequities in the distribution of resources could impede the development of regional policies. Regional and provincial interests are not necessarily coterminus. Recent federal-provincial discussions on energy are a case in point. The policy positions of the four Western provinces revealed a substantial divergence of opinion with regard to the development of a national energy policy. Even though Alberta and Saskatchewan share similar objectives, the means that each government was prepared to employ to achieve those goals differed considerably.

The four Western provinces will continue to work towards the development of regional policies in an ever increasing number of policy areas. However, each provincial premier will continue to act in the best interests of his own province when the occasion demands. There has been no hesitancy on the part of the provincial premiers to indicate to their respective electorates the positive and tangible benefits that can evolve from increased intergovernmental cooperation. However, they have failed to specify some of the inevitable consequences that flow from such activity. Limitations in the exercise of political power and in the initiation of the policy are perhaps the most striking. These factors will continue to impede intergovernmental cooperation in Western Canada.

NOTES

[1] Richard Leach, "Interprovincial Cooperation: Neglected Aspect of Canadian Federalism," *Canadian Public Administration,* Volume II (June 1959), p. 84.

[2] *Ibid.,* pp. 94-95.

[3] For a discussion of the evolution of Canadian federalism since 1945, see D. V. Smiley, *Constitutional Adaptation and Canadian Federalism Since 1945* (Ottawa: Queen's Printer, 1970); D. V. Smiley, "Public Administration and Canadian Federalism," *Canadian Federalism: Myth or Reality?,* ed. J. P. Meekison (Toronto: Methuen, 1968).

[4] See J. H. Aitchison, "Inter-Provincial Cooperation in Canada," *The Political Process in Canada,* ed. J. H. Aitchison (Toronto: University of Toronto Press, 1963), p. 155. In addition see Government of Canada, *Report on Intergovernmental Liaison,* pp. 139-144; and R. M. Burns, "The Machinery of Federal-Provincial Relations: II," *Canadian Federalism: Myth or Reality?,* ed. J. P. Meekison (Toronto: Methuen, 1968), pp. 300-301, for a discussion of the Premiers' Conference.

[5] D. V. Smiley, *Constitutional Adaptation and Canadian Federalism,* pp. 101-103.

[6] See J. N. Benson, "Interprovincial Cooperation" in D. C. Rowat (ed.), *Provincial Government and Politics Comparative Essays* (Ottawa, Carleton University 1973), pp. 93-94 and Joe Martin, *The Role and Place of Ontario in the Canadian Confederation* (Toronto: Ontario Economic Council, 1974), pp. 57-60.

[7] With regard to inter-provincial cooperation in the Maritimes, see Guy Henson, *Interprovincial Relations in the Maritime Provinces* (Fredericton: Maritime Union Study, 1970); R. H. Leach, *Inter-Provincial Relations in the Maritime Provinces* (Fredericton: Maritime

Union Study, 1970); *Council of Maritime Premiers First Annual Report* (Halifax, 1973); A. B. Campbell, G. A. Regan, and R. B. Hatfield, "The Move Toward Maritime Integration and the role of the Council of Maritime Premiers," *Canadian Public Administration,* Volume 15, Number 4 (1972), pp. 591-610.

8 While Richard Leach in his article, "Inter-provincial Cooperation," notes the existence of administrative agreements between the four Western provinces and the extent of informal contacts between officials, there is no discussion of the attempts on the part of the provincial premiers to use the Prairie Economic Council as a vehicle for developing regional policy positions.

9 For example, see W. L. Morton, *The Progressive Party in Canada* (Toronto: University of Toronto Press, 1950); S. M. Lipset, *Agrarian Socialism* (Berkeley: University of California Press, 1955); Paul F. Sharp, *The Agrarian Revolt in Western Canada* (Minneapolis: University of Minnesota Press, 1948); and C. B. Macpherson, *Democracy in Alberta* (Toronto: University of Toronto Press, 1953).

10 For an incisive criticism of the national policies by an economist, see John H. Dales, "Some Historical and Theoretical Comment on Canada's National Policies," in *Queen's Quarterly,* Volume LXXI, Number 3 (Autumn, 1964), pp. 297-316.

11 W. L. Morton, *op. cit.,* p. 288.

12 C. B. Macpherson, *op. cit.,* p. 21.

13 Honourable H. E. Strom, *Opening Statement to the Constitutional Conference, February 1969, Proceedings* (Ottawa: Queen's Printer, 1969).

14 *Winnipeg Free Press,* January 31, 1970.

15 W. Blackman, *The Cost of Confederation, Part I: Economic Activity* (Calgary: University of Calgary, October 1974).

16 *Globe and Mail,* April 3, 1975.

17 Both objectives are predominant throughout many of the statements on Western Canadian grievances by various spokesmen. See, for example, the address delivered by Premier Lougheed to the Empire and Men's Canadian Clubs on May 7, 1973.

18 For a discussion of the role and performance of the Prairie Economic Council see, D. V. Smiley, *op. cit.,* pp. 102-103.

19 *Ibid.,* p. 103.

20 The nature of the discussions that took place at the meetings of the Prairie Economic Council since 1968 were revealed in interviews with officials of the three prairie governments in the summer of 1971.

21 For a discussion of the channels of communication utilized by the three prairie provinces in the field of transportation, see M. W. Westmacott, "The National Transportation Act and Western Canada: A Case Study in Cooperative Federalism" (Unpublished Ph.D. dissertation, University of Alberta, 1972).

22 For a discussion of the role perceptions of Western MP's see D. Hoffman and N. Ward, *Bilingualism and Biculturalism in the Canadian House of Commons* (Ottawa: Queen's Printer, 1970) Chapter IV.

23 This is particularly true in the fields of energy and transportation policy.

24 This information was revealed in interviews with the officials of the Governments of Manitoba, Saskatchewan and Alberta in the summer of 1971.

25 A review of the proceedings of federal-provincial conferences since 1945 indicates that there was very little consultation among the four Western provinces prior to federal-provincial conferences.

26 The nature of the discussions that took place at the meeting of the Prairie Economic Council in 1968 were revealed by officials of the Governments of Alberta and Saskatchewan in the summer of 1971.

27 M. Westmacott, "The National Transportation Act and Western Canada: A Case Study in Cooperative Federalism," *Canadian Public Administration,* Volume 16, Number 3 (1973) p. 463.

[28] For details of the conference see, D. K. Elton (ed.), *One Prairie Province? Conference Proceedings and Selected Papers* (Lethbridge: *Lethbridge Herald,* 1970).

[29] *Ibid.,* p. 404.

[30] *Ibid.,* p. 399.

[31] Peter Lougheed became Premier of Alberta on September 10, 1971. David Barrett became Premier of British Columbia on August 30, 1972. Edward Schreyer became Premier of Manitoba on July 15, 1969 while Allan Blakeney became Premier of Saskatchewan on June 30, 1971.

[32] Canada, Parliament, *Parliamentary Debates* (House of Commons), 1st Session, 29th Parliament, Volume I (1973), p. 6.

[33] In their communique of March 31, 1973, the Premiers proclaimed a united stand on the most contentious areas of freight rates, agriculture and regional development. *Winnipeg Free Press,* April 2, 1973.

[34] The Premiers met on two occasions: in Winnipeg on March 30; and in Victoria on June 18, 1975.

[35] Details of the discussions among the four provinces prior to the Western Economic Opportunities Conference were obtained in interviews with officials of the Government of Alberta in December 1973 in Edmonton, Alberta.

[36] The papers dealt with each of the following areas: Transportation, Agriculture, Economic and Industrial Development Opportunities; and Capital Financing and Regional Financial Institutions.

[37] Canada, Parliament, *Parliamentary Debates* (House of Commons), 1st Session, 29th Parliament, Volume I (1973), p. 308.

[38] *Vancouver Sun,* June 16, 1973.

[39] *Ibid.,* June 18, 1973.

[40] Canada, Parliament, *op. cit.,* Volume V, p. 4884.

[41] The titles of the Federal papers were: Regional Development Opportunities; Industrial and Trade Development; Mineral Resource Development; and Capital Financing and Financial Institutions.

[42] For the unrevised and unofficial transcript of the proceedings see the Verbatim Record which is available from the Privy Council Office.

[43] Proceedings, p. 665.

[44] Proceedings, pp. 680-681.

[45] At the present time, the federal government is reviewing federal transportation policy. In addition, there have been discussions between the four Western provinces and the federal government on questions related to tariffs.

[46] Since the Western Economic Opportunities Conference, inter-governmental committees at both the official and the political level have been established in policy areas such as transportation and industrial and commercial policy. For details of the developments since the Western Economic Opportunities Conference see Canada West Foundation, *Follow-up to the Western Economic Opportunities Conference* (May 1974).

[47] For example, the Minister of Industry and Commerce for Saskatchewan acknowledged that "[a]11 four Western Ministers of Industry have been asked by their respective Premiers to meet from time to time and formulate industrial development strategy for Western Canada." Letter from the Honourable Kim Thorson to the writers, April 16, 1975.

23

The Council of Maritime Premiers
Report and Evaluation After Five Years*

A. A. Lomas

I

Just over five years ago, the Premiers of the three Maritime Provinces
signed the Agreement, confirmed by appropriate Statutes of the three
Legislatures, establishing the Council of Maritime Premiers. The origins
of this action date back to the time of Confederation and, it might be
argued, long before to the time when the region formed part of a single
administrative unit of New France. Throughout this period, whether in
the longer or the shorter view, there has been a persistent paradox
regarding the comparative advantages and disadvantages of closer or
more distant relationships among the component parts of what is now
referred to as the Maritime Region.

Geography, climate, resources, ethnic origins, economic interests,
and traditions have always exerted a diversity of "push-pull" influences
which, until recently, diverted any concerted effort by Maritimers to
investigate and experiment with co-operative measures.

It was to provide such a concerted and coherent review that the
Maritime Premiers undertook, in March 1968, "to sponsor a special
Study on Maritime Union including the possibilities for economic and
other forms of regional co-ordination and co-operation." The late Dr.
J. J. Deutsch agreed to organize the study. The Study commissioned a
wide range of sub-studies on many aspects of Maritime life, received
many public briefs, engendered a major debate by press and public and
in the fall of 1970, presented its report and recommendations to the Premiers.

The Study proposed "full political union as a definite goal" and,
after summarizing both its reasons for this conclusion and the problems
associated with it, recommended, as the machinery necessary to attain
the objective of Maritime Union, three "essential elements:

The Council of Maritime Premiers
The Maritime Provinces Commission
The Joint Legislative Assembly."

---

* Report delivered at the Twenty-eighth Annual Conference of the Institute of Public Administration of Canada, September 7-10, 1976. Reprinted by permission.

Each of these was viewed as an integral part "of a program of formal co-operation and joint action which evolves progressively to full political union, which should be accepted as a definite objective from the outset."

It is vital to this review to recall the warning of the Study that,

unless full political union can be accomplished within a reasonable time [ten years was suggested, with a first check-point of progress after five years] it is unlikely that co-operative efforts will continue to be effective or constructive for very long. It will be necessary to try to avoid 'the worst of all worlds' which would result from the mere piling-up of bureaucracies, costs, complications and uncertainties on top of already serious disabilities.

The six months following presentation of the Study was a period of intense and complex activity, as two new governments organized themselves to deal with their respective provincial mandates, while, at the same time, all three governments endeavoured to reach a consensus with regard to the basic recommendations of the Union Study. The consensus which finally emerged was to set aside, at least as an immediate goal, the objective of Maritime Union. Having done so, the interim steps of a Maritime Legislative Assembly, a Maritime Commission and a Council of Maritime Premiers *appeared* to be no longer necessary. However, with full recognition of the warnings of the Union Study about fiddling with variations of voluntary co-operation, the Premiers, in May 1971, nevertheless signed the Agreement which established their Council as just such an experiment. This agreement, in a somewhat indirect fashion through its preamble, established the objectives of the Premiers to be:

—to promote unity of purpose among their respective governments
—to take steps to improve communication between their respective provinces
—to establish the framework for joint undertakings.

The Premiers almost immediately assigned to themselves, in their new Council role, a number of functions:

a) discussion of matters of importance to the three provinces,
b) initiation of studies on economic, social and cultural programs and policies which affect or concern the three Maritime Provinces,
c) co-ordination of public policies which affect or concern the Maritime Provinces,
d) approval of joint submissions of the Maritime Provinces to the Government of Canada or any agencies thereof,
e) initiation and sustaining joint programs of the three provinces,

f) power to constitute a Maritime Provinces Commission, to define its duties and functions, and to appoint the members thereof.

The Agreement was later confirmed by the three legislatures in identical Act(s) "To Establish the Council of Maritime Premiers," which added the highly significant clause that the Agreement may "authorize the Council to do or cause to be done, on behalf of the parties [the governments of the three provinces] any or all such things as the parties thereto are otherwise empowered to do and deem necessary or ancilliary to the attainment of the objectives set forth in the preamble to this Act . . . ."

At the time of signing their Agreement, the Premiers, again acting as Council, adopted a seven-point program of joint action on a number of matters of mutual interest and concern to the three provinces:

1. To establish a Maritime Provinces Higher Education Commission.
2. To establish a Maritime Provinces Industrial Research Council.
3. To co-ordinate policy and programs in the field of environmental affairs.
4. To standardize regulations for the trucking industry with respect to truck weights, licensing and a common bill of lading, and to initiate reciprocal arrangements for motor vehicle licensing.
5. To develop a single centre for police training in the Maritime Provinces which will be associated with Holland College in Charlottetown, Prince Edward Island.
6. To establish a central organization for mapping and surveying programs for the region.
7. To develop a regional data bank and statistical service.

II

During the next fifteen months, Council met five times, adding substantially to the number and nature of the matters to which it was giving consideration such as the proposed Maritime Provinces Commission, offshore resources, a uniform Maritime Building Code, common concerns about fisheries and overall economic development, joint positions for a first Ministers' meeting, Maritime tendering and procurement practices, the establishment of the Maritime Resource Management Service at Amherst, Management training facilities, the establishment of the Land Registration and Information Service, preliminary steps toward the proposed Maritime Provinces Higher Education Commission, Agreement on the Atlantic Police Academy, telecommunications policies, a common Maritime information service, uniformity and harmonization in a number of areas of legislation, and a whole set of per-

sonnel policies, practices and procedures for the Council as the employer of a growing staff.

Fifteen months after the Council's formal establishment, the 24th
Annual Meeting of IPAC (Fredericton, September 1972) had the opportunity of hearing the three Premiers provide their first review on the
broad topic of "The Move Toward Maritime Integration and The Role of
the Council of Maritime Premiers." Premier Campbell of Prince Edward
Island, spoke about the unique experience of the Council in setting up
permanent means of regional co-operation:

> We have had to experiment with various methods of consulting with one
> another, of establishing consultative bodies at various levels among our
> three governments, of involving members of government and of the civil
> service in the ongoing activities of the Council, of working out procedures
> for our three legislative assemblies, and in attempting to keep the public
> well informed on our activities. We have by no means finally resolved
> these various questions, but I believe we have made substantial progress.

Premier Campbell stressed the practical work of the Council's first
few months:

> In my view we have already met in a substantial way the Council's imme-
> diate objectives: (1) we have developed a basic legislative and administra-
> tive framework to carry out joint or regional operations; (2) we have
> launched projects which should demonstrate that the regional approach
> can bring about improvements in the quality and efficiency of provincial
> services; (3) we have demonstrated that cooperation among our three
> provinces is possible and that such a course of action is beneficial to all
> Maritimers; and (4) we have demonstrated that coordination effectively
> strengthens the position of the Maritimes in discussions with the federal
> authorities or with outside interests.

At the same meeting, Nova Scotia's Premier Regan noted the ironic
nature of criticism addressed to the Council:

> It is a curious fact of political life that if three premiers were to meet to dis-
> cuss a matter of little importance, they would probably be applauded for
> working together or, at minimum, for creating good will. Of course, in
> such a situation, few of any important concerns or interests are threat-
> ened. However, should three premiers meet to explore some concrete and
> substantive issues; then the critics are legion . . . . The basis of this curious
> state is quite obvious—so long as nothing is done, no-one is threatened;
> once one attempts serious discussion on any matter, some part of the
> existing fabric is challenged and it quite naturally reacts.

Premier Regan went on to identify the dilemma facing each Premier
in seeking to reconcile his obligations to his own province with his role
in the Council. Like Premier Campbell he noted the historic and social
variations from province to province:

> It must be recognized that many priorities, pressures, personalities, and
> preoccupations exist in each province with great variety. What is currently
> desirable and possible for one government or province may not be pos-

sible—at that time—for another . . . . We have made progress because the integrative efforts to date have not seriously challenged the political process in each province; a considerable amount of general goodwill exists to allow integration a chance to prove itself and some economic benefits can be demonstrated. Sustaining integrative activity will depend greatly upon the success of each step.

Premier Hatfield, in his remarks at the same meeting identified some of those very practical and pragmatic issues which are today facing those who are connected with the Council—whether as Premiers, Provincial Ministers or Officials, or CMP staff. He noted first that the traditional forums of voluntary interprovincial co-operation, while useful and, hopefully, to be continued, were *not* the new forums of co-operation envisaged within the context of the Council of Maritime Premiers:

> I am assuming that we are not going to revert to what I have called the traditional form of inter-provincial co-operation. Indeed, I am convinced that the direction in which we have launched ourselves is the only realistic one for the Maritime region.

Premier Hatfield made the following statement about the Council in the light of his analysis of the problems of regional cooperation:

> These factors raise two basic questions: how to ensure regional political leadership and continuing responsible political direction; and how to provide for the development of regional approaches to policy formulation and planning. . . . For these reasons, I rather think that although the Council of Premiers is an absolute necessity at the present time, it will have to be augmented by other structures to bring about alterations to the manner in which government has functioned traditionally.

III

Five years after the signing of the Agreement (the first check-point envisaged by the Union Study) and three years since that initial statement to IPAC by the Premiers, it seems reasonable to attempt a further assessment of the endeavour. This can be done from the viewpoint either of the optimist who sees the bottle as half-full or of the pessimist who sees it as half-empty.

On the optimistic, or half-full side, much has been accomplished—both in terms of the original objectives of unity of purpose, improved communications and joint undertakings, as well as in other more recent areas and activities. On the half-empty side, it must be understood that some of the problems foreseen in the Union Study and later identified by the Premiers have indeed proven all too true.

Of the original "7-point program," a Maritime Provinces Higher Education Commission has been established and is now operative; the Maritime Provinces Industrial Research Council dropped out of sight for a time but *may* be ready for a comeback in a different form; co-ordination in environmental affairs proceeds at a limited level somewhat outside the ambit of the Council; certain progress has been made on trucking regulations but some key agreements have not yet been reached; the Atlantic Police Academy is in operation at Holland College but is not the "single centre for police training" originally anticipated; the "central organization for mapping and surveying" exists in considerably expanded form through the Land Registration and Information Service; the regional data bank and statistical service has become a dream which did not (and perhaps *should* not) come true.

In a different view, the Council has provided a forum (both in itself and through its range of committees, task forces, working groups, etc.) for consideration of subjects of importance to the provinces. A number of studies on matters of common economic, social and cultural concern have been completed, but relative to needs, the number has been all too limited. There has been some co-ordination of public policies, but again limited relative to needs. A number of major Maritime joint positions have been conveyed through the Council to the government of Canada (witness policies for transportation and offshore resource); several important joint programs (Land Registration and Information Service, Maritime Resource Management Service, Maritime Municipal Training and Development Board) have been initiated and maintained. The question of a Maritime Provinces Commission has been placed in more or less continuing abeyance.

There have been many other joint initiatives proposed; some have collapsed and died, some are still alive and under some degree of consideration; and some have passed through the mills to become useful and valuable components of the Maritime scene. Almost without exception, however, the concepts, ideas, plans, proposals, ambitions, and dreams which were current five, four, or even three years ago have undergone major change and evolution during the intervening years.

I think it is both unnecessary and unproductive to attempt to trace the causes and effects of these evolutionary changes. Instead, it is probably more useful to view the Council as it is today relative both to earlier expectations and to its future prospects as a vehicle for practical co-operation among the Maritime Provinces.

At this point, the Maritime Premiers have met 23 times and have dealt with, or at least considered, at least four times that number of subjects. During the past five years the Council has grown from a four-times-a-year discussion forum for three Premiers with a Secretary providing staff support, to an institution which comprises, in addition to the Premiers' quarterly meetings, a substantial Secretariat, four operating agencies, a Regional Treasury Board, and a complex and inter-related series of committees, agreements, contractual obligations, employees, codes, policies, budgets, cost-sharing formulae, labour relations, obligations, potentials and even that ultimate twentieth century mark of institutionalization—its own logo!

Despite an early decision to use the most flexible possible means of obtaining staff resources such as term, professional service, and consultant contracts, as of March 1976, the Council staff numbered 334, located in eight centres in the Maritimes.

Yet another indication of the Council's presence in the Maritimes is that of its budget which, for the current fiscal year, (before cost-sharing with the Federal government) amounts to $8.5 million, plus $2.5 million paid in fees-for-service to MRMS.

The several Council Agencies at this point deserve a few words of identification and description.

An issue with which the Council had to deal in its first few meetings was the imminent decision of the Department of Regional Economic Expansion to close the Federal Engineering Services Unit in Amherst. This organization had been in existence for nearly twenty years, conducting projects in land and water management around the Bay of Fundy in both Nova Scotia and New Brunswick. The prospect of losing this valuable resource was not acceptable to the Premiers. They drew up new agreements with the Federal Government and among themselves which created the Maritime Resource Management Service (MRMS) out of the old Engineering Services Unit, expanding its services to all three provinces and into many other aspects of land planning and management.

By this action, the Council created the first of its agencies, and in so doing demonstrated that it was possible to develop continuing projects which could have separate but closely related existence under the aegis of the Council.

Early in its history, the Council had hired a permanent secretary and a small support staff. Now that the Council had grown its first agency, the Secretariat had to enlarge its services to administer this and future agencies. It was important that if the Council was to be a parent body for other organizations which would hire people on a regular basis, standards of employment must be developed as a model for future evolutions. Over the years which followed, the Council Secretariat spearheaded research and negotiations with respect to pensions, working conditions and procedures which in turn have had considerable impact on the standards of such operations in the three provincial civil services.

The administrative technique of creating an agency to conduct ongoing work on a particular concern of the Council was a success. Three other agencies soon joined MRMS under the aegis of the Council, two of which were concerned with matters which had been mentioned in the seven points announced in May 1971: higher education and mapping and surveying.

The Land Registration and Information Service was conceived as an approach to the matter of surveying and mapping. The forging of an agreement between the Federal Government and the Council, however, took this concept of mapping and surveying far further than originally suggested. LRIS was established as a means by which the traditional and cumbersome deed registry system in use in the Maritimes for over two centuries could be modernized. Since computers would be used to collect and store information on land titles and to relate it directly and absolutely to accurate maps based on new control surveys, it was obvious that this was a foundation on which to build a unique resource in regional land data and information, thereby tackling another of the seven points.

The Maritime Provinces Higher Education Commission was set up as an independent commission to advise the three provinces on higher education planning. In the course of its existence it has not only accomplished this end, but it has also addressed itself to a number of specific problems and issues at the request of the Council. Initially viewed with a certain suspicion by academics and government servants alike, the Commission has shown itself to be a competent planner, an independent and objective evaluator, and a successful mediator.

The Maritime Municipal Training and Development Board is the smallest and youngest of the Council's agencies, but one which has an impact out of proportion to its modest budget and contract staff of two people. By offering opportunities to the municipal administrators of the Provinces, it is improving the standard of municipal government in practical and important ways. Its major accomplishment has been the raising of awareness by municipal employees that they are indeed part of a profession, and one in which they can expect to see improvement and opportunity.

Useful and important joint agencies, co-operative undertakings, measures of co-ordination and means for Maritime consultation have been established, and yet—is the bottle half-full or half-empty? As the Secretary to Council for almost three years, my own clear, definite and resounding answer must be: it is both! Much has been accomplished; much more *can* be accomplished. Certain criteria and conditions, however, must be established or re-affirmed if progress to date is to be consolidated and further useful progress is to be made. The developments and evolutions of the past five years have caused the total Council endeavour to outgrow the small and limited mechanisms anticipated in the Council's early years.

The Premiers, in 1972, evidently understood and appreciated problems already apparent, and some yet to emerge, in seeking improved measures for Maritime inter-provincial co-operation. Three years later the problems have not diminished. In fact, we must face the possibility that this practicable and realizeable ambition of Maritime co-operation (without Union) could fail—but not for lack of its inherent goodness. Should this happen it will be because the Council will have foundered on the rocks of inadequate institutions, insufficient knowledge and commitment at levels of government below the Premiers, Ministers and senior advisors, and the assumption that the original structures of the Council of Premiers are capable of almost infinitely expanded output with strictly limited inputs of resources.

While it may not be entirely proper, and while it may violate some of the sacred vows of the professional public servant, let me share with you some of my more recent, provocative and perhaps provoking proposals to the Council:

(1) Without regard to the Maritime Union question, the proposed Maritime Commission must soon be constituted, preferably with a healthy political orientation, to provide a "Ministerial" presence for the Secretariat between quarterly Council meetings and to provide a source of wise "political" advice to the Council on regional matters, counter-balancing the "official" advice of their professional staff;

(2) The Regional Treasury Board must be strengthened, made more independent of both the CMP staff and provincial interests, and given a firm mandate to seek out additional areas of improved regional services and/or reduced costs through inter-provincial co-operation;

(3) The "wraps" must be taken off, so that the Legislatures, provincial officials, press and public can see, debate and understand what the Premiers are accomplishing through their efforts as a Council;

(4) Provincial officials must be encouraged (and failing that—pushed) to participate more fully in formulating and implementing the regional decisions of the Council.

(5) Finally—and perhaps most important—Council institutions and staff must be considered as joint subsidiaries of the three provinces working for a community of Maritime interest; rather than as at present, viewed in a "we-they" adversary relationship.

Both personally and professionally, I am extremely hopeful and optimistic about our joint Maritime capability—to make a larger and more important contribution to the fabric of Canadian nationhood. I am convinced we can only do so by working hard and effectively together. There is a long agenda facing the Premiers of possible areas for Maritime co-operation. It ranges from some very old to some very new concerns, and includes such subjects as: implementing the technology and legal systems of our own made-in-the-Maritimes Land Registration and Information System; greater provincial demand upon and use of the Maritime Resource Management Service; uniform and harmonized legislation in half-a-dozen different fields; marine and other training to take advantage of our new off-shore frontiers; co-operation in energy plan-

ning, generation and distribution; co-ordination in our provincial conservation programs; telecommunications issues; consideration of joint
Maritime positions in federal/provincial fiscal negotiations; measures for
law and order including police training; co-operation in general economic, fisheries, forestry, agricultural and transportation development;
further hard decisions with regard to higher education; and on and on.

However, let the last word belong to the politicians and the press.
At their 22nd Session in Charlottetown last May, in answer to a general
press question about Council progress, the Premiers replied (in
excerpt):

> *Premier Regan*—"I think this has been a unique achievement and one that
> we should continue to build upon."
> *Premier Hatfield*—"As we get more experience and work harder at it, we
> are going to be able to ensure that this will become the way of life for the
> Maritime Premiers."
> *Premier Campbell*—"I do believe that the Council must take a more aggres-
> sive posture in the next few years. . . ."

Meanwhile, the Prime Minister, noting that the meeting marked the
Council's fifth anniversary, telexed the message that, "Five years of
working together in this new forum have brought great practical benefits to the three provinces and indeed to Eastern Canada as a
whole. . . ."

At the same meeting, the Premiers signed a statement of renewed
commitment to the Council which said, in part, "We will continue to
develop procedures and mechanisms whereby the joint interests of the
provinces will be better served and whereby the Council, and its agencies, will be increasingly effective instruments for the well-being of the
Maritime region."

Press reaction in the interim was mixed. A weekly editorialized
under the heading "Maritime Council: Moving Backwards" that "if this
region is ever to gain a sense of dignity and provide a certain balance
within the Canadian Whole, the Premiers . . . will have to widen their
horizons, overcome their differences and row that boat together."
Others noted Premier Campbell's complaint that the "Council is bogged
down in trivia" . . .is "ineffective" and needs "a more active role." The
major Halifax daily promised to expand its regional coverage because of
the "common objectives" within the region . . . .

The Council had maintained *such* a low profile that only its mistakes, shortcomings and 'secrecy" were normally reported. Imagine,
then, my feelings on reading in an editorial two days after the Session,
in another editorial in another daily, that,:

> If the premiers of New Brunswick, Nova Scotia and Prince Edward
> Island appeared to show some satisfaction after this week's meeting of the
> Maritime Council of Premiers, it shouldn't be surprising. They have just
> delivered one of the most important results of Maritime solidarity in the

Council's five-year history. . . . There has been, and there continues to be, concern over the growth of any unnecessary bureaucracy superimposed on the existing governmental structures of the three provinces. But since its inception in 1971, the Council has concentrated on improving areas of co-operation and of mutual concern. . . . The same three premiers—Richard Hatfield of New Brunswick, Gerald Regan of Nova Scotia, and Alex Campbell of Prince Edward Island—have been at the helm since the Council began. One of the most impressive arguments for the Council, and one of the most impressive gains for the Maritime Premiers, has been their ability to speak together on behalf of this region, even though they are of different political persuasions . . . . While they maintain individual differences, and while they have eschewed blatant 'gang-up' tactics, they have demonstrated that there is strength in numbers and that a united voice can be an effective one.

PART V
POLICY MAKING
AND CANADIAN FEDERALISM

24

Federalism and the
Public Policy Process*

Donald V. Smiley

The major concern of this study is the making and implementing of public policy within the framework of Canadian federal institutions. It is
focussed primarily on relations between executive officials, both elected
and appointed, of federal and provincial governments. Under the circumstances which have developed, each jurisdiction retains responsibilities for broad areas of public functions but there are an increasing
number of situations in which the action of each in pursuing its objectives impinges on the activities of the other. The ways by which the central and regional administrations respond to this kind of mutual dependence have been neglected by students of the Canadian and other
federal systems.

Traditional discussions of federalism emphasize the co-ordinate
and independent powers of federal and regional governments rather
than their interdependence. According to the juridical analysis found in
the textbooks of law and political science, there are three possible ways
of legally organizing a particular territory. The first alternative is unitary—the government whose jurisdiction includes the whole territory is
sovereign and whatever other public authorities there may be are legally
subordinate to it. At the other end of the spectrum is the confederacy
where the powers of the central jurisdiction are held at the discretion of
the regional governments. The third alternative is federalism and there
would be broad agreement among constitutional scholars that a federal
constitution has these characteristics:

1. The totality of government powers which can legally be wielded
   within a territory are divided by a written constitution between a central and two or more regional governments.
2. Those parts of the constitution which delineate governmental power
   are not subject to interpretation or amendment by the unilateral action of the executive or legislature of either level of jurisdiction.
3. At least one of the legislative chambers of the federal government is
   chosen by popular election.

* From Donald V. Smiley, *Constitutional Adaption and Canadian Federalism Since 1945* (Ottawa, Queen's Printer, 1970), pp. 1-8. Volume IV of the Documents of the Royal Commission on Bilingualism and Biculturalism. Reprinted by permission.

4. Individual residents of the federation are directly subject to the laws of both the central and the regional governments.

The kind of definition given above is static and concerns the formal constitutional features of federal systems regardless of how these systems operate. Using this definition one could read the constitutions of various countries and intergovernmental associations and quickly and mechanically determine which qualified as federations. In most cases, however, the actual workings of political systems diverge widely from what one would expect by a literal reading of their constitutions. K. C. Wheare, whose influential book emphasizes the co-ordinate authority and mutual independence of central and regional governments as the essential features of federalism, recognizes this difficulty and makes an important distinction between "federal constitutions" and "federal governments."[1] According to Wheare's analysis, the Canadian constitution is only "quasi-federal" because of the powers conferred upon the federal executive to disallow provincial legislation and to appoint the provincial lieutenant-governors and judges of the principal provincial courts. Examining the actual practices of Canadian government, however, he concludes that, " . . . although the Canadian constitution is quasi-federal in law, it is predominantly federal in practice. Or to put it another way, although Canada has not a federal constitution, it has a federal government."[2] This conclusion seems to be deficient because the somewhat facile dichotomy between the law of the constitution and the practices of government allows one to avoid analysis of the intricate relationships between the two kinds of matters when studying particular political systems. Furthermore, the undue emphasis on the co-ordinate and independent relationships of the central and regional governments predisposes the student either to ignore patterns of interactions between the two levels which are so much a part of the workings of established federations or to consider these interactions as somehow a deviation from the federal principle.

Federalism may thus usefully be considered as a continuing process by which governmental powers are exercised. In his recent work Carl J. Friedrich contrasts federalism as "consensual world order" with imperialism as "coercive world order" and he states:

> . . . Federalism should not be considered a term for a static pattern, designating a particular and precisely fixed division of powers between governmental levels. Instead, "federalism" seems the most suitable term by which to designate the process of federalizing a political community, that is to say the process by which a number of separate political organizations, be they states or any other kind of association, enter into arrangements for working out solutions, adopting joint policies and making joint decisions on joint problems.
>
> Conversely, federalism is the process by which a hitherto unitary political community, as it becomes differentiated into a number of separate and

distinct political communities, achieves a new organization in which the differentiated communities, now separately organized, become capable of working out separately and on their own problems they no longer have in common. It is not only a matter of decision-making, but of the entire range of power and its exercise. . . . The federalizing process accompanies, so to speak, the communal development as its organizational counterpart. If values, interests and beliefs exhibit a stable and structured pattern in which the commonly shared values, interests and beliefs are counterbalanced by values, interests and beliefs that are not shared, though territorially distributed, then a federal development becomes possible.[3]

Friedrich regards as an essential element of federalism the constitutional protection of each level of the political order against the other. His definition thus excludes instances of international relations or senior-local authority relations where such legal protection does not exist. A recent book on the American federal union concludes with the most useful definition of federalism from the public-policy-process viewpoint that I have found:

Federalism is a system of government in which central and regional authorities are linked in a mutually interdependent political relationship; in this system a balance is maintained such that neither level of government becomes dominant to the extent that it can dictate the decisions of the other, but each can influence, bargain with, and persuade the other. Usually, but not necessarily, this system will be related to a constitutional structure establishing an independent legal existence for both central and regional governments, and providing that neither shall be legally subordinate to the other. The functions of government will be distributed between these levels (exclusively, competitively, or co-operatively), initially perhaps by a constitutional document, but thereafter by a political process, involving where appropriate the judiciary; in this process the political interdependence of the two levels of government is of the first importance in order to prevent one level absorbing all effective decision-making power.[4]

Established federal systems are characterized by the growing importance of the relations between the executives of the central and regional governments. Several interrelated influences contribute to the development of what might be called "executive federalism."

1. The constitutions of most federations have proved somewhat resistant to evolution through amendment or changing patterns of judicial review. Amending procedures in most established federal systems are inflexible, i.e. small minorities can block attempted changes in the text of the constitution. For several reasons the courts in several federations now play a more restricted role than previously in maintaining the federal balance. Thus political and administrative processes have become the chief instruments of change.

2. The increasing interdependence of modern social and economic life makes it impossible for the regional governments to carry out their responsibilities in the absence of appropriate action by the other

regional jurisdictions and the federal authorities. Maurice Lamontagne wrote of Canada a decade ago " . . . l'attribution de responsabilités exclusives aux différents gouvernements n'est pas possible parce que la politique économique et sociale est devenue quasi indivisible."[5]

3. Nationalist and egalitarian sentiments focussed on the federations as such have propelled federal governments into collaboration with regional governments to establish minimum country-wide standards in public services regarded as being within the social minimum. Under the constitutions of most federations the regional authorities are assigned the primary responsibilities for health, welfare and education. The only way that this circumstance can be reconciled with the demand for equal services on a national basis is through intergovernmental collaboration.

4. Contemporary rates of taxation and the deliberate use of fiscal policy to provide for economic stability and growth mean that particular tax and spending policies of the one level have consequences for the other. The central and regional jurisdictions increasingly compete for tax sources. Federal governments, like other national governments assume responsibility for overall economic direction. The direction will be ineffective if appropriate actions are not taken by regional and local authorities. In Canada, as in other federal systems, the fiscal relations between the central and regional governments have become increasingly complex and increasingly crucial for the stability of the federation.

5. The widening scope of public activity gives rise to an increasing number of situations where federal and regional objectives must be coordinated if intolerable stresses on the system are not to result. The old classical federalism in which each level carried out the functions assigned to it by the constitution in relative isolation from the other had some relevance to a period when governmental responsibilities were limited in scope and importance. It has no relevance today.

The relations between the executives of the federal and regional governments are extraordinarily complex in most federations. Many of thes interactions are of an informal and *ad hoc* nature. Furthermore, in many matters the significant decision-making units are not the federal and regional administrations but functional groups constituted across jurisdictional lines. Edward W. Weidner after several intensive studies of federal-state relations in the American system wrote about functionalism in this way:

> It is a thesis of the present discussion that in the federal system in the United States there are relatively few direct clashes or compromises between state and national governments on large issues of domestic policy. Furthermore, in the administrative sphere positive cooperation is the

pattern rather than aloofness or conflict. The disagreements and conflicts that do arise and that may be encouraged by federalism's structural fea- tures are not basically clashes between state and national governments. Instead, they are clashes between much smaller groups of people and the opposing groups are concentrated within a single governmental level as often as not.[6]

Similarly, in a 1963 study I found that in the administration of federal conditional grants to the Canadian provinces the attitudes and interests of program specialists and financial officials were very different and that conflicts related to the grant-in-aid arrangements characteristically re- sulted in divisions along these lines rather than between federal and provincial governments as such.[7]

Although the analysis of public policy processes seems to me a use- ful focus for studying contemporary federalism, it is a partial approach. It concentrates on a relatively small number of executive officials who devise and implement public policy. However, political scientists increasingly question the validity of studying the law and practices of government in isolation from the attitudes, social groupings, economic structures and so on which condition and are conditioned by govern- mental activity.[8] This study examines how policy is made and imple- mented in the Canadian federal system. Another more difficult kind of investigation would concentrate on the sociology and politics of Cana- dian federalism. An American scholar has asserted: "The essence of fed- eralism lies not in the institutional or constitutional structure but in the country itself. Federal government is a device by which the federal qual- ities of a society are articulated and protected."[9] In all developed socie- ties there are groups striving to secure governmental actions that they perceive to be favourable to their aspirations and interests. Federal gov- ernments can be sustained only in societies which are themselves fed- eral, that is societies where people believe that their interests in respect to a number of important matters are specific to geographical divisions of the country rather than to the country as a whole. On the other hand, federalism has little relevance if the major incidences of political dif- ferentiation relate to class, religious, occupational or other groupings which are not territorially located. In his study of four Latin-American republics with federal constitutions (Mexico, Argentina, Brazil and Venezuela) William S. Stokes concludes that certain economic and cul- tural features make federalism as government in the usual sense imprac- tical in these countries:

> Most Latin Americans are conditioned by their historical traditions and social and economic institutions to understand and accept concentrated, centralized power, usually of a highly personalized sort. The strong, fre- quently exalted role of the father in the family, the importance of the elite in the class system, the honor, dignity, power and influence of the *doctor* from the *aula* (lecture hall), the significance of centralized leadership in the Church, the paramountcy of the "general" in politics, and the position of

the public and private monopolist in the economic system—these characteristics of Hispanic culture all suggest powerful, centralized government. In addition, the political experience and traditions of hundreds of years were with a powerful monarchy operating by means of a centralized administrative hierarchy. The modern constitutions all provide for "interventionist" states.[10]

Federal governmental institutions to be stable must correspond with particular kinds of social structures and cultural predispositions so that regionally based particularisms can find an outlet while making possible common action in respect to matters where these particularisms are of less importance.

The sociological and governmental aspects of federalism are thus intimately related. When relatively stable federal systems have been established, some groups come to press their claims primarily through the federal government and others through the states or provinces. In the United States, for example, those hostile to the public regulations of business usually favour "states' " rights while those striving for civil rights for the Negro look to action from the federal legislature, executive and courts. If most of the influential groups in any federation came to look exclusively to either one level of government or the other it is not likely that federalism could long survive, although the federal rituals might remain. But once the division of legislative and executive powers between the central and regional governments is established, there are influences at work to sustain the federal quality of the society itself and they create new country-wide and regional centres of influence where none existed before. The Report of the Committee on Manitoba's Future published in 1963 stated:

> The Province of Manitoba is more than a political division of the nation. During the more than 90 years since its establishment a distinctive social and economic entity has been developed within the essentially artificial political boundaries. When the Province joined the Canadian Confederation, "Manitoba" was not much more than a block of land surrounded by lines on the map. In the intervening years, however, it has become an organic unit; trading patterns have developed, transportation systems have been established, educational and administrative systems have been organized, and all the other social, economic and political institutions of a modern society have evolved. The people of Manitoba, now, therefore, are responsible for dealing with many of their own problems. . . .[11]

The establishment of important centres of political power thus provides the setting for the growth of other influences within the same territorial limits and social and governmental federalism reinforce one another. Conversely, a federation under great stress may be expected to feature tensions in both its public and private institutions. The drives for provincial autonomy in contemporary Quebec have corresponded with influences toward a greater measure of independence for the French Canadian elements in nongovernmental organizations. These influences in some cases (such as those involving university students, the Junior Chambers of Commerce and the municipal associations) have culminated in the withdrawal of the French-speaking members.[12] In the period immediately preceding the outbreak of the American Civil War many formerly national organizations such as churches and political parties separated into northern and southern components.

There has been almost no systematic examination of the kinds and distributions of popular attitudes which are compatible with the maintenance of federalism in government. Some years ago J. A. Corry spoke of the "stresses and conflicts" in the Canadian federal system "which need to be negotiated and compromised (by the governments) in *ad hoc* arrangements, particularly where the electorates do not seem disposed to say clearly whether they are federal or unitary in spirit."[13] Does contemporary cooperative federalism require widespread popular attitudes which are pragmatic and equivocal as to the appropriate level of government for carrying out particular public responsibilities? It seems unlikely that the federation could survive if the prevailing attitudes came to the point of considering one or the other level more legitimate in respect to all public activities believed important. If there were a consensus throughout the country about this matter the system might either disintegrate in a peaceful and orderly way or evolve into a unitary state. It is more likely, however, that no such agreement will be established and if the conflicts about legitimacy are pushed to the limits we have a "recipe for civil war."

It is common to assign the political parties a central role in the maintenance of federal systems. The usual analysis in Canada and the United States has been that these unions can be sustained only if there are country-wide parties drawing strength from all regions.[14] In examining eight established federations the American political scientist William H. Riker addresses himself to the question, "What maintains federalism?" and systematically dismisses the arguments that the crucial elements are the sharing of administrative responsibilities, dual citizen loyalties or the existence of dissident provincial patriotism.[15] He concludes:

> Whatever the general social conditions, if any, that sustain the federal bargain, there is one institutional condition that controls the nature of the bargain in all the instances here examined and in all the others with which I am familiar. This is the structure of the party system, which may be regarded as the main variable intervening between the background social conditions and the specific nature of the federal bargain.[16]

According to Riker's analysis, a federation is centralized or "peripheralized" to the degree that "the parties organized to operate the central government control the parties organized to operate the constituent governments."[17] Although federal-provincial party relationships have received little systematic attention in Canada,[18] my tentative conclusion is that the executives of the federal and provincial governments, working in isolation or in collaboration, have assumed the crucial role in effecting changes in the political system. On the other hand, the influences pushing these executives towards federal-provincial integration are not reinforced by corresponding pressures on the party organizations. Because of this cooperative federalism may fail.

The preceding brief analysis of the sociology and politics of federalism is meant to suggest only that the public policy approach is a limited one and that executive federalism cannot realistically be considered in isolation from the other influences impinging on the maintenance of federal institutions. The underlying assumptions of this study are, first, that federal systems, like other institutions, must have the capacity to adapt to changing circumstances if they are to survive and, second, that it is more doubtful than most of us would have believed a few years ago that the Canadian federation can develop the necessary resources of adaptability. For analytical purposes, I make a distinction between two kinds of processes of evolution. The first I call "devices of adjustment"—the procedures by which the respective powers, resources and responsibilities assigned to the federal and provincial governments by the original constitution are dynamically redelineated as new circumstances arise. The second category of processes is named "devices of articulation"—the procedures through which the activities of the two levels are related to one another by their respective executives. It seems reasonable to believe that a federal system could not survive under modern circumstances unless it developed resources of flexibility through both kinds of devices. We have only the crudest of measures to determine whether a federation is responding effectively to the demands made upon it. In a negative sense one might judge that the resources of adaptability in a particular federal system were being strained if any or all of the following circumstances existed:

1. If no political party were able to draw significant strength from all regions of the country. In any federation much of the political conflict at the federal level will revolve about divergent regional interests. When at least one of the parties comprehends these interests, however, tolerable compromises can ordinarily be worked out through the procedures of intraparty accommodation. When no such inclusive party exists these procedures cannot be used for this purpose.
2. If there were widespread public attitudes which attribute to the inherent nature of federal institutions those deprivations that people feel strongly about. Federations, like other human institutions, can survive only if people regard them as legitimate.
3. If most of the politically influential elements of the country sought their objectives exclusively or almost exclusively through one or the

other level of government. Such a situation attenuates the tension between national and regional interests necessary to the maintenance of federalism.

NOTES

[1] K. C. Wheare, *Federal Government,* 4th Ed. (London: Oxford University Press 1963), Chapter II.

[2] *Ibid.,* p. 20.

[3] C. J. Friedrich, *Man and His Government* (New York: McGraw-Hill, 1963), pp. 594-95.

[4] M. J. C. Vile, *The Structure of American Federalism* (London: Oxford University Press, 1961), p. 199.

[5] Maurice Lamontagne, *Le Fédéralisme canadien* (Quebec: Presses universitaires Laval, 1954), p. 245.

[6] E. W. Weidner, "Decision-Making in a Federal System," in Arthur W. Macmahon (ed.), *Federalism, Mature and Emergent* (New York: Doubleday, 1955), p. 363.

[7] D. V. Smiley, *Conditional Grants and Canadian Federalism* (Canadian Tax Foundation, Canadian Tax Paper no. 32, Toronto, 1963), pp. 37-42.

[8] One of the most distinguished efforts in this direction is the Little, Brown series in Comparative Politics under the editorship of Gabriel A. Almond, James S. Coleman and Lucien W. Pye. See particularly G. A. Almond and Sidney Verba, *The Civic Culture* (Princeton: Princeton University Press, 1963) and the abridgement under the same name in the Little, Brown series (Boston, 1965).

[9] W. S. Livingston, *Federalism and Constitutional Change* (Oxford: Clarendon Press, 1956), p. 2.

[10] W. S. Stokes, "The Centralized Federal Republics of Latin America," in G. C. S. Benson *et al., Essays on Federalism* (Claremont: California, Institute for Studies in Federalism, 1961), p. 93.

[11] Committee on Manitoba's Economic Future, *Report* (Winnipeg, 1963), p. 111.

[12] Professors Vincent Lemieux and John Meisel have undertaken a study of the bicultural aspects of certain non-governmental associations in Canada for the Royal Commission on Bilingualism and Biculturalism.

[13] J. A. Corry, "Constitutional Trends and Federalism," in A. R. M. Lower *et al., Evolving Canadian Federalism* (Durham, N.C: Duke University Press, 1958), p. 141.

[14] See, for example, Herbert Agar, *The Price of Union* (Boston: Houghton Mifflin, 1950) for a presentation of this hypothesis as it relates to the United States. In Canada, Frank Underhill has been the most persuasive apologist for the bi-national parties. See *In Search of Canadian Liberalism* (Toronto: Macmillan, 1960) and *The Image of Confederation: The Massey Lectures,* 1963 (Toronto: Canadian Broadcasting Corporation, 1964).

[15] W. H. Riker, *Federalism: Origin, Operation, Significance* (Boston: Little Brown 1964), particularly pp. 135-36.

[16] *Ibid.,* p. 136.

[17] *Ibid.,* p. 129.

[18] For one of the few systematic efforts in this direction see E. R. Black, "Federal Strains within a Canadian Party," *Dalhousie Review,* XLV (1965), pp. 306-23. More recently Khayyam Paltiel has made a provocative analysis of the relation between party finances and the maintenance of Canadian federalism, "Federalism and Party Finance: A Preliminary Sounding," in Committee on Election Expenses, *Studies in Canadian Party Finance* (Ottawa: Queen's Printer 1966), pp. 1-21.

25

Interest Groups and Intergovernmental Negotiations: Caught in the Vise of Federalism*

Richard Schultz

In recent years there has been increased attention paid to the role of interest groups in the policy-making process.[1] One area of interest group activity, however, that remains relatively neglected is the role in intergovernmental negotiations. Such a neglect is unfortunate given that intergovernmental negotiations have assumed a central place in the policy-making process in Canada in the last two decades. Indeed, it is not an exaggeration to suggest that there are few public policies today that are not the subject of intergovernmental discussions at some stage in their development. In this paper, in order to fill some of the gaps in our knowledge and to encourage further research in this area, two hypotheses are tested on the relationship between interest groups and federal structures and processes.

The first hypothesis is one common to the literature on interest groups and federalism and finds its most popular characterization in Morton Grodzins' work as the "multiple-crack" attribute of federal systems.[2] The "multiple-crack" thesis contends that federal systems are particularly valued by interest groups because the existence of two levels of government provides groups with multiple access points to pursue their policy objectives. The argument is that groups gravitate to the level of government assumed to be more receptive to their demands and the value of the alternatives presented by a federal division of powers is that groups that fail to achieve their objectives at one level, according to this hypothesis, can seek satisfaction from the other level of government. A related feature of group activity is the assumed ability of a group to play one level of government off against the other to group advantage.[3] Grodzins' definition of "crack" in his thesis best suggests the process. He stated that in his work "crack" has two meanings: "It means not only many fissures or access points: it also means, less statically, opportuni-

---

* This is a revised version of Chapter Seven of my "Federalism, Bureaucracy and Public Policy: A Case Study of the Making of Transportation Policy" unpublished PhD, York University, 1976. I would like to thank F. J. Fletcher, T. A. Hockin and D. V. Verney who supervised the dissertation and the Canada Council and Ministry of Transport which funded the research.

ties for wallops or smacks at governments."[4] The basic thrust, therefore, of this thesis is that interest groups value federal systems because of the increased opportunities the existence of two levels of government provides for groups to pursue their objectives. The only major qualification concerns the potentially negative impact of federal systems on group cohesion in that, if the group has a corresponding federal structure, it will "tend to have less cohesion."[5] Diminished cohesion weakens the ability of the group to articulate and defend its objectives.

In a parliamentary system it could be presumed that federalism would be even more valued by groups in that the fusion of executive and legislative branches, with the consequent dominance of the former over the latter, drastically limits the number of significant access points compared to a presidential system such as that in the United States. The second hypothesis to be tested in this chapter, however, challenges this presumption in a very important respect. This second hypothesis is drawn from Richard Simeon's work. From his research he concluded that, whatever the value of federal systems accruing to groups in terms of general access to policy-makers, the nature of Canadian federalism is such that, when an issue enters the arena of intergovernmental negotiations, group access becomes severely restricted. His argument was that the machinery of intergovernmental negotiations "limits the participation of interest groups in the bargaining process. Affected groups are not invited to participate or make their views known. The relative secrecy of debate means group leaders may be unaware of developments in federal-provincial negotiations which involve them."[6] Contrary to the assumption of the first hypothesis, Simeon concluded that group effectiveness is seriously undermined because they are frozen out of the process. Furthermore, even when access may not be so severely restricted, the nature of the Canadian intergovernmental bargaining process has a further negative impact on groups because group interests ". . . to the extent that they are less central than status or ideological goals, will be the first to be jettisoned in the conference room."[7]

This article will attempt to test the general "multiple-crack" hypothesis and the more specific Simeon hypothesis on the restricted access and limited effectiveness of interest groups by a case study of interest group activities in the intergovernmental negotiations concerning the implementation of Part III of the National Transportation Act of 1967.[8]

The NTA was promoted as a major break with earlier transportation regulation in Canada because of its emphasis on inter-modal competition and the creation of a single regulatory authority, the Canadian Transport Commission, to coordinate and harmonize the operations of all carriers under federal jurisdiction.[9]

Basic to the new federal transportation policy and its successful implementation by the CTC was the decision of the federal government to assume direct responsibility for the extra-provincial motor carrier industry.[10] Although the courts had decided that the federal government had jurisdiction over this industry, responsibility for regulating the industry had been delegated to the provinces in 1954. By means of Part III of the NTA, the federal government intended to end this delegation because the industry, as the major competitor for the railways, was a far more significant component of the national transportation system in 1967 than it had been in 1954. Naturally, the provinces did not relish losing a major responsibility and were motivated by more than "territorial imperatives." The trucking industry was the only transportation industry under provincial jurisdiction and they were most reluctant to surrender such a responsibility, particularly just at the time when some of them were interested in exploiting the industry for developmental purposes.[11] As a consequence of the conflict over who should regulate the extra-provincial trucking industry, five years of intergovernmental negotiations ensued. In the end, the provinces won and Part III was not implemented.

This article tests the two hypotheses described principally by means of an analysis of the role of one interest group, the Canadian Trucking Association (henceforth CTA), in the intergovernmental negotiations on Part III. From the evidence of this study, it will be argued that the "multiple-crack" hypothesis needs to be qualified because it fails to give sufficient weight to the costs of a federal system for an interest group. Such costs are of direct consequence for the second hypothesis. It will be argued that Simeon's hypothesis neglects the important support function in intergovernmental negotiations. Group support may be an important resource in the bargaining process, and consequently groups may play a much more extended and influential role in the process.

Before turning directly to the role of the CTA in the negotiations, the background must be sketched. In the first place, the CTA was formed in 1937 through the actions of five regional trucking associations as a direct response by the trucking industry to a threat of direct federal regulation. The trucking industry was adamantly opposed to federal regulation because it considered the federal government to be railway-oriented. The industry view, and it was not far from the mark at this time, was that the railways were the "chosen instrument" of national transportation policy and therefore the trucking industry was concerned lest the federal government exploit its regulatory power to destroy the industry's potential for competition with the railways.

In view of its opposition, the trucking industry's actions were typical of the pattern of activities predicted by the "multiple-crack" thesis. With single-minded purpose, the CTA sought to ensure that regulatory responsibility rested with the provincial governments. From 1937 on, whenever national transportation issues were discussed, the CTA availed itself of the opportunity to express its continued opposition.[12] Indeed, when the Supreme Court in 1951 ruled that the federal government had jurisdiction over the extra-provincial aspects of the industry, the CTA employed the judicial system to further its objectives by lobbying the provincial governments to appeal the Supreme Court's decision to the Privy Council.[13] When the appeal was lost in 1954 and the federal government opted to delegate its responsibility to the provincial regulatory bodies, the CTA opposition to federal regulation continued.

However, in the post-1954 period, two developments caused the industry to reassess its position. In the first place, regulation by ten provincial agencies lacked uniformity and consistency. The industry was being governed by ten sets of regulations and ten different regulatory philosophies. An additional problem was that the provinces were not prepared to hold joint hearings for interprovincial licence applications and the result was cumbersome and costly. The second factor that caused the industry to reassess its position was the fact that CTA support for provincial regulation resulted in the industry being denied access to the federal government. By turning its back on the federal government, the industry had apparently been shut out of any participation in the making of transportation policy at the federal level. The industry had no effective spokesman for the trucking point of view within the federal government. This exclusion began to irritate the industry for it was thought that trucking was not getting equal treatment compared to the industry's arch-rival, the railways.

The industry responded to the problems in two ways. With respect to the question of access, the industry demanded that it be given "the right to have its needs and interests considered if they are affected, or about to be affected, by a federal action in the field of transportation."[14] Recognizing that it had no hope of influencing federal policy-making if it had no meaningful access to the federal bureaucracy, the industry demanded that at least one individual cognizant of the needs and views of the industry be appointed by the Department of Transport. To the industry's satisfaction, the federal government responded and appointed such an official in 1964, the first "highway's economist" in the federal government.

Despite the gaining of access to the federal department, however, the industry persisted in its opposition to direct federal regulation. The appointment was considered absolutely crucial if the presumed historical bias of the federal government was to be corrected but the industry had no illusions that a single appointment could radically alter such an orientation. At best, trucking would now have "an ear" and "a voice" in the federal government.

The other industry problem was less easily resolved. The CTA had been attempting to encourage the provinces to remedy the problems through cooperative interprovincial actions. From 1959 to 1965, the CTA annually petitioned the association of provincial regulatory authorities to draft the necessary uniform regulations and establish a system of joint hearings. The industry requests, however, were regularly rebuffed, forcing the industry to look for an alternative. The industry response to the provincial intransigence is an example of the pattern of group activity predicted by the "multiple-crack" thesis. Having failed in its attempts to persuade one level of government to act, the CTA took advantage of the "cracks" available in the federal system and sought redress from the other level. The CTA petitioned the federal government to amend the original legislation delegating the regulatory responsibility to the provinces to require the provinces to hold automatic joint hearings and to regulate on the basis of uniform regulations.[15] It is important to emphasize, however, that the industry did not request direct federal regulation for this was still highly suspect.

The actions of the trucking industry lobby up until 1965 were typical of the pattern of activity predicted by the "multiple-crack" thesis. The CTA had attempted to exploit the federal division of powers to satisfy its policy objectives. The industry had supported that level of government which was assumed to be the more responsive to its demands and then had sought to maintain what was viewed as a beneficent constitutional status quo. Only when this beneficence became dubious did the industry deviate from its traditional posture and then only to request the federal government to force the provinces to do what they would not do voluntarily.

Eight months after the CTA had made its recommendations to the Minister of Transport, Bill C-231, the National Transportation Act, was introduced in Parliament. The contents of this legislation appeared to underscore the ineffectiveness of the trucking industry lobby in Ottawa. The federal government was proposing that it undertake direct regulation of interprovincial trucking and do so as part of one agency with jurisdiction for all modes of transport that were within federal authority. Yet despite the obvious conflict between the proposals submitted by the CTA and the content of the new legislation, the industry endorsed Bill C-231. In an appearance before the House of Commons Standing Committee on Transport and Communications examining the bill, the CTA declared that "the trucking industry supports Bill C-231 in principle. The industry and its associations will cooperate to the best of their ability in the successful achievement of the National Transportation Policy."[16]

There were many reasons for this rather remarkable, not to say abrupt, change in the position of the CTC. One important factor was the philosophy of the NTA which was to be predicated on free competition between the various modes of transport. The promise to end federal discrimination towards the railways as the "chosen instrument" for national transportation policy was a major influence on CTA attitudes towards Bill C-231.

More important, however, than any commitment to implement a philosophy of equal competition were several other factors. The CTA had been given "a bureaucratic embrace," an embrace at first invigorating, indeed intoxicating, but ultimately suffocating. The industry had been courted and wooed away from supporting provincial regulation by the federal Department of Transport.

In order to understand why federal authorities would strive to win the trucking industry's support for Bill C-231, one must appreciate the political circumstances under which the new transportation policy was developed and introduced. The single most important factor was the minority government situation facing the government. The Liberal government had tried in 1964 to restructure the transportation regulatory system but the measure introduced at that time had been allowed to die because of intense opposition. This early attempt did not include a motor carrier section. In 1966, however, such a section was included after the officials convinced the Minister of Transport of the political wisdom of such a move. They emphasized that the trucking industry could play a major role in marshalling support for the legislation in the House of Commons. The argument advanced was that if a long-time foe of the federal government could be persuaded to support the legislation, some of the parliamentary opposition might be won over to viewing it as a major break with traditional approaches to transportation policy.

Once the decision had been taken to include Part III, the active courtship of the CTA by departmental officials began, a process that offers excellent support for Presthus' contention of the close interaction between the federal Department of Transport and its galaxy of affected, interested groups.[17] The General Manager of the CTA was approached and asked to participate in the drafting of the motor carrier section. This request was so completely unexpected that the industry official refused to commit himself in advance to support the legislation. He refused also to participate personally in any preliminary discussions but was prepared to nominate an "unofficial" representative, a lawyer who had previously done work for the CTA. The result was that Part III was drafted by this representative and a Department of Transport official in the latter's living room!

Although the CTA's General Manager was pleasantly surprised by the legislation proposed, he was in no position to commit the industry. Given the radical departure being requested from the CTA's traditional, and only recently reaffirmed position on federal regulation, such action could only be undertaken by the CTA's Board of Directors. To win industry support, several meetings were held in Ottawa at which both departmental officials and, subsequently, the Minister of Transport himself, outlined the philosophy of the NTA and discussed the mechanics of implementation. The Minister and officials emphasized the commitment to equality of all modes of transport that was being promised by the legislation and declared that they would stand by this promise. Moreover, if philosophy was not enough to satisfy the industry, as a measure of good faith, the industry was offered a more tangible expression of the department's commitment to impartial treatment of all modes of transport. The CTA was promised that "one of the seventeen" Commissioners on the proposed Canadian Transport Commission would be "someone who will represent recognition of road transport."[18] This promise was fulfilled when John Magee, the CTA General Manager, was appointed in September 1967, as a Commissioner of the CTC and member of the Motor Vehicle Transport Committee. Finally, as further evidence of departmental good faith, many amendments requested by the industry to Bill C-231 were subsequently accepted by the government as the Bill was being piloted through the House of Commons.[19]

As a result of these negotiations, the industry, as discussed, reversed itself and the CTA became an enthusiastic supporter of Bill C-231. In addition to announcing their support for the proposed legislation, members of the CTA performed as desired by department officials and actively lobbied Members of Parliament, particularly those from Western Canada. Evidence that Mr. Pickersgill regarded CTA support as crucial to the successful passing of the NTA is suggested by the fact that he repeatedly singled out the CTA position to express his gratitude after Bill C-231 became law.[20]

In the first bloom of its new relationship with the federal government, the trucking industry was obviously extremely satisfied that it had made the best choice in its new partner. Editorials in trucking journals glorified the "coming of age" of the industry; industry spokesmen revelled in "trucking's formal acceptance by government as one of Canada's major modes of national transport. . . ."[21] If the industry needed any reassurance of the soundness of its judgement, it was soon available. In March 1969, the Minister of Transport proposed that the railway rate freeze be extended and the necessary subsidies be continued to the railways to offset the problems created by the rate freeze. The CTA made representations to the Minister of Transport that such a subsidy to the railways contravened the philosophy of the NTA. The result was that the initial legislation was withdrawn and the Atlantic Freight Assistance Act was substituted. The new legislation provided for subsidies to all modes of transport in the Atlantic.

The CTA appreciated that Part III did not end all the problems faced by the trucking industry. Recognition of the industry in the form of Part

III was in large measure mainly a symbolic victory. How Part III was to be implemented was a much more substantive issue and a central concern to the CTA because Part III, like so many legislative instruments, was merely skeletal legislation. The "flesh" of the legislation, the detailed regulations and procedures, remained to be drafted.

More important, however, than methods was the issue of the timing of implementation of Part III. As far as the CTA was concerned, the date for implementing Part III was the crucial concern for two basic reasons. The CTA was deeply concerned with potential division in its ranks over support for federal regulation. Moreover, the CTA was worried about how the provinces would react to being so abruptly spurned by the industry. The CTA was extremely conscious of both these factors and accordingly advocated as early an implementation of Part III as possible.

As has been stated earlier, among the significant factors affecting the level of group cohesiveness is whether or not the group has a unitary or federal structure, because the latter is presumed to have a negative effect on cohesion. The assumption of the literature appears to be that the problem is in one sense essentially internal to the groups in that the members, for the particular group to be effective, must resolve the resulting conflicts between regional and national interests. What appears to have been ignored in the literature is the role of governmental actors in fostering and exacerbating the potential for internal conflict for the purpose of exploiting group division in the intergovernmental arena. Furthermore the "smacks" or "wallops" that Grodzins spoke of may be directed at the groups by governments in an attempt to weaken the groups' ties with the other level of government. The purpose of such "cracks" is to undercut the political support claimed by a government in order to diminish its resources. The events following the support given by the CTA to Part III provide evidence in support of this important qualification to the "multiple-crack" thesis.

The CTA, as its name suggests, is an interest group formed, as stated earlier, by the coming together of the previously separate provincial and regional associations. Indeed, it is more a confederation in the strict sense of that term in that the central body is heavily dependent on strong provincial associations. As an interest group in a federal system, the CTA experienced all the difficulties cited in the literature associated with maintaining cohesiveness. The most obvious obstacle to group unity was presented by the Quebec Trucking Association. Although Quebec nationalism had infected the QTA, as it had so many Quebec sections of national bodies, anti-centralization per se was not at issue.[22] The simple argument advanced by spokesmen for the QTA was that Quebec truckers were fairly satisfied with the Quebec regulatory system. While accepting the general criticisms of the regulatory system under the MVTA, the QTA needed to be persuaded far more than any other regional association of the value of Part III.

In fact, the CTA was only able to endorse Part III after the pressure group agreed to accept two QTA-demanded conditions. The first was that the CTA would demand that the implementation of Part III be limited to strictly cross-border operations under provincial regulatory control. If accepted this proposal would exempt much of the traffic under federal jurisdiction from federal control. The second condition demanded by the Quebec section, and accepted by the national body, was that the provincial regulators be employed as federal examiners under Part III. Although there was considerable disagreement within the industry about the level of competence of some of the provincial regulators, the CTA agreed to incorporate this proposal in its official policy statement on Part III.

Although the CTA was able to endorse the NTA once the above two conditions were accepted, it quickly became apparent that the unity achieved was more illusory than real. As a result of the deep division within the CTA over federal regulation, subsequent developments were to provide excellent examples of what Truman so aptly described as the "embarrassing non-conformity" which may result from the lack of unity in a federated interest group.[23] The failure of the compromises to satisfy the Quebec section of the CTA became obvious when the QTA, shortly after the CTA had made its submission to the Commons Committee, wrote directly to all Quebec members of Parliament and Senators objecting to the inclusion of Part III in the National Transportation Act.

After the NTA had been passed by Parliament, members of the Quebec Trucking Association became more public in their criticism of the Act. One official of the QTA argued that the federal government "by adopting Bill C-231, Part III, is trying to take control of the industry. Ottawa, being the owner of one of the largest railways in the world, is now trying to be competitor and legislator at the same time."[24] This official went on to "deplore Ottawa's unilateral action in presenting Bill C-231 without previously consulting the provinces . . . ." Whatever doubts there were that this opposition represented official thinking of the Association were dispelled at the 1968 Annual Convention of the QTA. The President of the QTA was quoted as stating "that the Association will fight implementation of Part III of the NTA."[25] The QTA position was that federal control be limited solely to individual trucks that travel from one province to another.

The issue of the conflict between the Quebec Trucking Association and the CTA came to a head at the 1969 annual meeting of the CTA. The internal conflict could no longer be ignored because the Quebec Association had been supporting and encouraging a member of Parliament from Quebec to propose Private Members' Bills that would amend the NTA in accordance with the QTA's demands.[26] According to one report the outgoing President of the CTA was critical of what he regarded as "unilateral action by any member association of CTA in matters of national interest." The President, irritated by the criticism of the NTA by the Quebec association and its attempts to subvert Part III, was emphatic in his view that there could be only one voice for the trucking industry in Canada and the annual meeting proceeded on the assumption that if CTA's position as national spokesman was not endorsed, the association might just as well disband. CTA must not be used by its members when convenient and ignored when its policy doesn't suit a specific purpose . . . nor can any part of it sit in judgement on its staff, directors and policies.[27]

As a direct result of the Quebec Association's activities, the CTA was forced at the 1969 meeting to resort to a "Memorandum of Agreement" between the members of the CTA with the purpose of binding association members to CTA's policies and by-laws. This attempt to unite the CTA was far from successful in that it prompted the QTA to let its membership lapse in the national association for a year. The conflict between the national and Quebec Association was to plague the industry throughout the negotiations and as will be pointed out was used by some of the provincial governments to attack the federal government's claim that it had industry support for the implementation of Part III.

The internal conflict faced by the CTA became all the more significant for the group and for the federal government as provincial opposition to Part III developed. By reversing its traditional position on federal regulation, the trucking industry incurred the hostility of the provincial governments opposed to Part III. As a result of the intergovernmental conflict that ensued, the industry was the object of intense competition as both levels of government vied for industry support. The CTA came to appreciate that considerable costs can be incurred when an interest group exercises its options in a federal system.

The trucking industry had expected a certain degree of negative reaction from provincial regulators. The recommendations regarding the limited scope of Part III and the use of provincial officials as examiners were proposed not only to achieve unity within the industry but also in an attempt to nullify in advance provincial opposition. The industry never anticipated, however, the degree of outright hostility that Part III would in fact engender among some provincial regulators or that this hostility would be directed at the industry for reversing its long-time commitment to provincial regulation. One provincial regulator was quoted as exclaiming that Part III would be implemented "over my dead body!" Such a reaction, albeit somewhat extreme, was perfectly natural in that those provincial officials whose sole or principal responsibility was motor carrier regulation would find that with the implementation of Part III the federal government had assumed the bulk of their responsibility. Such a development would entail a considerable loss of prestige and status for such provincial regulators.

The initial provincial reaction of blind hostility soon became tempered with more strategic concerns on the part of provincial officials. In the preliminary discussions with the provinces, federal spokesmen justified Part III by invoking the support given to the legislation by the CTA. Accordingly, it became obvious to the provinces, especially those adamantly opposed to Part III such as Ontario, that if this support for the federal position could be undercut, if the industry could be persuaded to withdraw its support, the federal government would lose one of the major underpinnings for its policy. The Ontario government consequently worked to achieve that end. According to one Ontario official, at the conclusion of a departmental meeting to discuss the negotiations on Part III, the Minister of Transport instructed the Chairman of the Ontario Highway Transport Board to see what he could do about "bringing the industry around" to supporting the Ontario position.

Provinces opposed to Part III employed a variety of tactics in their efforts to "bringing the industry around." According to a number of trucking spokesmen, such provinces first attempted to win the industry back by offering a number of "carrots." One official stated that "after the federal government indicated their intent to move with federal regulation, the provincial boards wined and dined the industry to build up a lot more respect and a better relationship." Among other things, the provinces promised that a far greater effort would be made by the provincial boards to promote uniformity in the regulations and to facilitate joint board hearings. One Ontario government official explained the provincial response at this time by stating that "the truckers have some legitimate complaints and we have begun to act on them and correct them."

Perhaps the most significant "carrot" proferred to the industry to induce it to drop support for Part III came from Ontario. Industry officials had repeatedly complained of their poor relationship with the Ontario government. In order to rectify such complaints, the Minister conferred a "mandate" on the Ontario Trucking Association (OTA) as the official and sole spokesman for the industry with the Department of Transportation and Communications.[28] In a letter to the OTA, the Minister stated that he wanted the Association to be the official and only channel through which all representations are made to the Minister and

Department. It is significant that at the time this "mandate" was given to the Association, the ardour of the Association for Part III was cooling considerably.

The provinces did not limit their efforts to "carrots" in their attempts at "bringing the industry around." Some provinces were to exert what both truckers and some provincial regulators described as pressure and intimidation. In this context, it is important to recognize one of the important realities of any regulatory system, the power that regulators possess over those subject to their authority. Rourke sums up this situation very well:

> . . . the power that accrues to administrative agencies because of their discretionary authority is still vast. Regulatory agencies, for example, exercise a great deal of power merely because they have the authority to give or withhold benefits, and to inflict or refrain from imposing sanctions. The facts that regulatory agencies have such power forces a group subject to their jurisdiction to defer to them even in situations in which their authority may not be altogether clear.[29]

When the trucking industry "rebelled" and backed Part III, some provincial regulators made determined efforts to remind truckers of the fundamental reality of the relationship that Rourke had described.

One of the trucking officials, subjected to a great deal of pressure because of his outspoken support for Part III, stated that "the provincial boards have your destiny in their hands. They can do a lot of things to interrupt your service and bring your business to an end." A former provincial regulator conceded in an interview that some provincial officials had employed "some intimidation" on the industry to get them to drop their support for Part III. According to a number of truckers, this intimidation constituted "terrific pressure." One of the major practitioners of intimidation according to these interviews was the Chairman of the Ontario Highway Transport Board. According to a number of sources, this regulator telephoned the employers of some of the elected officers of the Canadian Trucking Association to complain of speeches about the inadequacies of the provincial boards. He strongly recommended that the companies suggest to their employees that they be more "prudent" in their comments. This pressure was undoubtedly significant in explaining the CTA change in policy on Part III, in that a number of truckers when questioned cited "fear of provincial regulators" as a major reason for the change. The President of one of the largest trucking firms in Canada summed up the prevailing attitude among truckers:

> Truckers are political animals. We are regulated by OHTB and they are fundamentally against Part III and some of the boys thought they would be discriminated against by the Board. They can put quite a bite on you.

There was fear of bucking the Ontario Highway Transport Board and this fear was quite important.

This fear assumed added significance when the industry began to realize that there were important obstacles within the federal government to Part III.[30] Consequently their resolve began to diminish and they began to succumb to the provincial pressures and intimidation.

Initially, however, industry reaction to provincial pressure was two-fold. In the first place, the CTA did what other interest groups often do: it sought allies in order to buttress its position.[31] One group the CTA turned to for support was the Canadian Manufacturers' Association. The CMA had had several meetings with the Canadian Transport Commission and the CTA's Executive Director implored the CMA to endorse the CTA position on Part III but met with little success.

The second industry response to provincial pressure was to demand that the federal government implement Part III as soon as possible in order that the extra-provincial truckers would no longer be subject to regulation by the provincial boards. The President of the CTA outlined the industry's dilemma at the 1968 Annual Convention of the Ontario Trucking Association. He acknowledged that "extra-provincial carriers are reluctant to publicly criticize the present system of regulating extra-provincial operations under the MVTA". (Such an acknowledgement was wise given that the Chairman of the OHTB was on the same panel.) He went on to argue, however, that Part III would lead to a "vastly improved" system of regulation and concluded by stating that "we want federal control . . . and the sooner the better."[32] During this period prior to the calling of the first federal-provincial conference in 1969, industry spokesmen continually pleaded for immediate action on Part III because of the pressure being placed on the industry by the provinces.

If the federal government was to hold trucking industry support, the industry informed the Minister of Transport that it was imperative that he convene the promised federal-provincial conference. In 1969, two years after the NTA had been enacted, the CTA impressed on the Minister that because of the delay in commencing the negotiations the industry was being placed in an untenable position. The industry argued that it had solidly backed the federal government on Part III but that the provinces, through their existing control on licensing, were putting pressure on the industry. It was as a direct result of this meeting that the Minister of Transport ordered his officials to make arrangements for a federal-provincial conference.

The decision to convene the first federal-provincial conference on Part III demonstrates one role, that of catalyst, that interest groups may play in federal-provincial relations. Government officials conceded that without the industry demand for some indication of progress on implementation, opponents of Part III within the federal government would have been able to withstand internal pressure for action. Furthermore, in distinct contrast to the findings of Simeon, the CTA did more than make its views known.

Once the federal government fulfilled its commitment to convene the conference, CTA officers volunteered, despite the harassment they had been receiving from some of the provinces, to do a "little missionary work among the unconverted before the Conference." Industry officials would make representations to the provincial Ministers urging them to seek a common position with the federal government in order to resolve the difficulties faced by the industry. One of the reasons the CTA opted for this missionary role is the fact that the QTA had let its membership lapse in the national body and, therefore, the CTA felt that it could not make a public statement prior to the conference. Although it is not known what reception was given the "missionaries" by other provinces, the Ontario reception is illuminating. According to an Ontario official, the CTA representative was "pawned off" on an extremely junior official who provided little more than a polite hearing.

Immediately following the 1969 Conference, the CTA was briefed by federal officials on what had transpired, particularly in terms of an Ontario proposal advanced as an alternative to Part III. This briefing was important because the CTA President immediately and publicly rejected the proposal as "costly, cumbersome and time-consuming."[33] Again, this demonstrates that, rather than freezing out interest groups, the federal government was employing the CTA by means of its public declaration to dismiss the provincial alternative proposal by showing that it was unacceptable to the industry affected and at the same time seeking to reinforce the legitimacy of its own position. It was indicative of the extent of CTA support for the federal government that the Ontario counter-proposal was basically the same as the CTA position submitted to the provincial regulators before Part III was introduced.

Following the first federal-provincial conference in 1969, the federal government sought to signal to the provincial governments its determination to implement Part III. The nature of the signal was to be the proclamation into law of that section of the NTA. The timing of the signal is of importance in that it indicates the significance attached to CTA support. Proclamation was deliberately delayed until after the Quebec provincial election in April 1970 so as not to inject the issue into the campaign. Equally important, however, was that proclamation was deliberately timed to coincide with the CTA's annual meeting.

Despite proclamation, the industry because of provincial pressures was increasingly becoming agitated over the slow pace towards implementation. One measure of the concern developing in the industry was a meeting held in Toronto in September 1970, attended by some of the major carriers and officials of the Ontario and national associations. It was evident at this meeting that the commitment within the industry to backing the federal government was being seriously threatened. The carriers were under serious pressure from the OHTB at this time and did not see any relief in sight as there were no clear signs that Part III was going to be implemented in the near future. Although no decision was taken to drop support for the federal government, the industry officials let it be known to federal officials that the question was being raised. These officials were increasingly aware of the growing dissatisfaction within the industry as they received reports from other parts of the country that truckers were losing their confidence in the federal government's ability to defend their interests.

The growing dissatisfaction within the industry was a major factor in the decision to convene the second federal-provincial meeting on Part III. Within the federal government some officials were arguing that they were losing all their credibility with the CTA and the 1970 conference was designed to show the industry that progress was indeed being made. The industry, however, had a much more realistic view of the negotiations than the federal government. The government was warned that if a clear decision was not presented to the provinces, the latter would be in a much stronger position than ever. The fact that the federal government did not have a clear position to present to the provinces, because of the unresolved internal conflict, but felt compelled to do something to satisfy the industry is indicative of the importance attached to the industry's support. The move backfired because the conference was a disaster and merely exacerbated provincial opposition to Part III.

A debate during the 1970 conference supports the hypothesis that interest groups may play a role in federal-provincial support.[34] Everyone recognized that the federal government's policy was in large part conditioned by the demands of the CTA for such a policy of federal regulation. What ensued at the conference was claim and counter-claim by the federal and provincial governments as to the extent to which the federal government did indeed have the support of the industry. The discussion of the importance of the CTA support was started when the federal Chairman of the meeting stated that "it is common knowledge that there is pressure on Government to establish a better system of regulation. They all know the stand of the Canadian Trucking Association." The following exchange between the Quebec and federal representatives illustrates the "tug-of-war" approach to interest group support that occurred:

The Quebec representative then raised what he termed a purely theoretical and hypothetical matter. Supposing Provinces got together today and found a solution acceptable to all Provinces and presented it to industry, that would solve their problems as far as extra-provincial transport is concerned. What would CTC do in that eventuality? The Chairman gave his personal reaction, that in this way, they might have removed from the federal government the immediate pressure.

Although the Chairman indicated that loss of the CTA support for Part III would not necessarily mean that the federal government would not proceed, it was obvious to all participants, that if this "eventuality" occurred, the federal position would be seriously damaged. Moreover, the Quebec representative was aware that this was not simply a "theoretical and hypothetical matter," for he pointed out that the industry position was not "a solid one" and that the Quebec association had endorsed "complete and total support of control as far as possible by the province, whether intra or inter, and declared opposition to federal control in this area." The fact of the lack of unity in the industry position and the strenuous efforts by some of the provinces to bring the industry around to supporting the provincial position underscored the less than hypothetical nature of the provincial enquiry.

Other factors were working to turn a hypothesis into reality. The CTA was clearly disappointed with the 1970 meeting and complained to federal officials of the confusion and dissatisfaction that existed with respect to Part III. Furthermore, they were concerned that the extended delay in implementing Part III was putting the industry in an untenable position because some provincial boards were clearly playing politics with the carriers. Industry apprehension was accentuated when the President of the CTC refused to meet with the representatives of the CTA to discuss Part III. Although the industry had expressed earlier concern with the apparent reluctance of the CTC to move on Part III, this rebuff was never expected.[35]

An additional cause of industry concern was the Quebec Government's attempt to exploit once again the division in the industry ranks. The Executive Vice-President of the Quebec Trucking Association was initially included as an official member of the Quebec delegation to the 1971 Federal-Provincial Conference of Ministers. This action infuriated CTA officials who immediately protested to the federal government which requested that the Quebec delegation not include the QTA official. The Quebec government acceded to the request in full knowledge that even without the official in their delegation, its point had been forcefully brought home to the federal government.

The results of the 1971 Conference gave the CTA the opportunity for which some members of the industry had been desperately searching. The pressure from some of the provinces and the conflict within the industry, exacerbated by the fact that no progress had been made on the implementation of Part III in four years, proved too much for the CTA. The federal government was warned that the industry would have to reconsider its position if no progress was made at the 1971 Conference. When the result of the Conference was merely the creation of an Advisory Council to study the issue, the CTA jumped at the opportunity. The CTA reverted to its pre-1966 position and called for the "creation of a uniform set of regulations at the federal level, to be administered by provincial regulatory agencies and enforced on a uniform basis in each province."[36] The CTA had in effect withdrawn support for federal regulation. The significance of this change can be suggested by the fact that at the first meeting of the new Council, the revised CTA position was read into the Minutes of the Meeting by some of the provincial representatives.

If there was any question of where the industry stood on the matter of federal regulation, this was finally resolved after the Advisory Council had reported. The trucking industry had played a role, albeit a limited one along with other transportation interest groups, in the work of the Advisory Council. The set of draft regulations had been submitted to all the affected parties by the Council for comments and a meeting had been held at which the industry associations were given an opportunity to discuss a proposed accounting system for the industry prior to the Council making its final report. The final straw for the industry was the federal government's failure to announce even where it stood on the recommendations of the Advisory Council to include provincial members on the Motor Vehicle Transport Committee of the CTC. When no response was forthcoming, the CTA in anger turned on the federal government and reverted to its earlier position of total and absolute opposition to any federal role in regulating the industry.

The seven-year relationship was thus ended almost as abruptly as it had begun. The trucking industry which had for years been absolutely opposed to direct federal regulation of the industry returned to this position. The truckers at the 1973 Convention, according to one industry official were "adamant in insisting that there be virtually no federal input in developing or administering a new concept of uniform regulations." The "coming of age" of the industry, heralded by the passing of the NTA and Part III, had, like so many similar experiences, been an extremely painful one. Unfortunately, from the industry perspective, all that had been gained from the process was extreme frustration and bitterness.

There can be little doubt that the industry withdrawal of support for Part III drastically weakened the position of the federal government. This fact was confirmed in interviews with both federal and provincial officials. The federal bargaining position had already been seriously eroded by the continuing conflict within the federal government. As far as the actors in the intergovernmental negotiations on Part III were concerned, the action by the CTA was the final death blow to Part III. The federal government had, from the beginning of the negotiations, maintained that the industry demand for federal action was the principal rationale for the inclusion of Part III in the NTA. Although the philosophy of the NTA necessitated a motor carrier section, this philosophy by itself was not much of a political factor in the negotiations. Implementation of Part III was only possible if the federal government was able to invoke the support of the interested parties. Loss of that support effectively ended the intergovernmental negotiations.

CONCLUSION

The primary objective of this paper was to employ the evidence concerning interest group involvement in the intergovernmental bargaining on Part II to test two hypotheses about the relationship between interest groups and federal structures and processes. While it is impossible to generalize from a case study, nevertheless the findings of this chapter suggest that one of the hypotheses needs to be qualified while the other needs to be seriously re-examined.

The hypothesis needing re-examination is that interest group participation and effectiveness is limited in intergovernmental negotiations. As Simeon recognized, his explanations of interest group behaviour may have been a function of the nature of the issues he studied.

In contrast to the insurance lobby that was opposed to the Canada Pension Plan, there was no "Anti-Equalization League" or "Canadian Association in Defence of Provincial Rights" that could have participated in the negotiations on the financial and constitutional issues. The absence of such "readily identifiable" interest groups may be a more important explanatory variable than the nature of the bargaining process to account for the limited interest group activity. Moreover, it is arguable that given the pervasive interdependence that now characterizes the federal system, the negotiations on Part III are far more typical than the more "exotic" issues of the constitution and finances.

In the struggle over Part III, there were "readily identifiable" interest groups, of which the most important was the Canadian Trucking Associations. The consequences for the trucking industry were assumed to be direct and significant. In its efforts to protect and further these interests, the CTA found that in the complex web of relationships that determined the fate of Part III, it was an inextricable component. Far from being frozen out, there existed close and continuous formal and informal contact between the CTA and governmental actors before and especially during the federal-provincial bargaining process.

Interest group considerations influenced the timing of the negotiations and in the case of the federal government shaped the specifics of its tactics and strategies. The CTA also performed a communications function by assuming the role of "missionaries" in an attempt to convert some of the provinces prior to a federal-provincial conference. In addition, the group attempted to serve an intelligence function by keeping the federal government appraised of provincial positions over the course of the negotiations.

Group participation in this struggle suggests that Simeon's hypothesis of restricted access and limited effectiveness neglects an important group function in intergovernmental negotiations. We saw that group support for the federal government in the conflict over Part III was a significant political resource that the federal government sought to exploit. The significance of group support to the determination of an actor's bargaining resources may be such that actors will jettison it only at their peril. Simeon included the concept of support in his analysis but limited his discussion primarily to a consideration of general public, rather than interest group, support.[37] The role of the CTA suggests that articulating and defending a position in terms of group demands may be a significant determinant of the nature and the course of intergovernmental negotiations. Group support may be particularly effective as a resource if an actor can legitimize a course of action on the grounds that such a course is necessitated by a failure or inaction of the other level of government.

Interest group support, from the group's perspective, however, may be a double-edged weapon. This is, in part, suggested by Simeon's discussion of the concept: "political support is a scarce resource; the participants compete for it; and this competition is part of the bargaining process."[38] The conclusion that can be drawn from this study is that group support, as a particular variant of public support, can be the object of intergovernmental competition. The ramifications of such competition suggest that the "multiple-crack" thesis needs to be qualified.

The pressure exerted on the CTA by some provincial governments suggests that the "multiple-crack" thesis, as presently formulated, does not recognize the costs or negative aspects of a federal system for interest groups. Groups may not have the degree of liberty assumed by the "multiple-crack" thesis in choosing governmental partners, for there are potential hazards for the groups arising from the intergovernmental competition for support. An interest group, to paraphrase Rourke, "makes enemies as well as friends when it identifies with [one level of government], since it inherits hostilities directed at the [level of government] with which it enters an alliance."[39] When a group endorses one level of government it may find itself the object of attention as the other level seeks its support. Perhaps even more significant for group fortunes is the fact that the group may find itself subject to abuse from the rejected government. The cost, therefore, of a federal system for interest groups may be that "wallops or smacks" are directed as much at the groups by the competing governments as they are by the groups at governments. The "cracks" may be more multiple than is normally assumed.

The major difficulty with both the "multiple-crack" hypothesis and the Simeon hypothesis is that they assume somewhat of a one-dimensional relationship between interest groups and governments, a relationship predicated on demands flowing from group to government. The general conclusion to be derived from this paper is that there is need for hypotheses premised on the assumption of at least a two-dimensional relationship between groups and governments in a federal system. Demands may flow from government to group as well as group to government.[40] This is not a novel proposition in that the propensity for governmental actors to generate group pressures on themselves or other actors is well known, as is the fact that governments often create interest groups, or at least act as mid-wife for their birth. This particular feature of interest group life, however, assumes an added, and hitherto relatively ignored, significance in a federal system, particularly one that is characterized by a high degree of policy-making.

The role of interest groups in the struggle over the implementation of Part III suggests many significant areas for further research on the scope and nature of their roles in the intergovernmental bargaining process. Indeed, it would appear that groups perform many of the same functions in that process as they do in the intragovernmental policy process. Yet given the significance of intergovernmental negotiations to the policy process, and consequently to the political fortunes of the participants, interest group participation is not without its costs. Although the federal system does provide multiple access points, groups who exploit them run the risk of being embroiled in intergovernmental conflicts, of being caught, as it were, in the vise of federalism. Until we have much more information, it would seem unwise to underestimate the activities, influence and costs of interest group participation in the intergovernmental bargaining process.

NOTES

[1] In particular see the works of Robert Presthus, *Elite Accommodation in Canadian Politics*, and Paul Pross (ed.), *Pressure Group Behavior in Canadian Politics* (Toronto: McGraw-Hill, 1975).

[2] Morton Grodzins, "The Federal System" in A. Wildavsky (ed.) (Boston: Little Brown, 1967), *American Federalism in Perspective*, p. 268. For a more comprehensive statement of this thesis, see Grodzins' *The American System*, edited by S. Elazar (Chicago: Rand McNally, 1966)

[3] These assumptions are common to American writing on group activity in federal systems. See, for example, Truman, *The Governmental Process* (New York: Knopf, 1951) p. 323, Holtzman, *Interest Groups and Lobbying* (New York: Macmillan, 1966) p. 59 and Zeigler, *Interest Groups in American Society* (Englewood Cliffs: Prentice Hall, 1964) p. 107. For Canadian examples where such assumptions have been made, see the Bucovetsky and Kwavnick articles in Pross, (ed.), *Pressure Group Behaviour in Canadian Politics* and Chapter 7 in F. C. Engelman and M. Schwartz, *Canadian Political Parties: Origin, Character, Impact* (Toronto: Prentice Hall, 1967)

[4] Grodzins, *Ibid.*

[5] Truman, *op. cit.*, p. 116. See also the discussion in the Dawson and Kwavnick articles in Pross, *op. cit.* and in R.A. Bauer *et al.*, *American Business and Public Policy* (New York: Atherton Press, 1963) pp. 332-40.

[6] Richard Simeon, *Federal-Provincial Diplomacy* (Toronto: University of Toronto Press, 1972) p. 144.

[7] *Ibid.*, p. 282.

[8] National Transportation Act. RSC 1970, c. N-17 (hereafter NTA).

[9] *NTA*, s. 21.

[10] The term "extra-provincial" includes both the interprovincial and international sectors of the industry.

[11] For a more complete discussion of the issues involved in the struggle over Part III, see my "Intergovernmental cooperation, regulatory agencies and transportation regulation in Canada: the case of Part III of the National Transportation Act", *Canadian Public Administration*, 19 (1976), pp. 183-207

[12] One of the recurring forums for such opposition was the numerous Royal Commissions on transportation or related issues. The CTA appeared before the Turgeon Commission (1949), the Gordon Commission (1956) and the MacPherson Commission (1959) to emphasize its opposition to federal regulation.

[13] An appeal was permitted to the Judicial Committee because the matter was before the Courts prior to the abolition of appeals to the Judicial Committee in 1949. There has been little attention in Canada to the judicial system as a target of interest group activity and this is surprising given the important role the Courts have played in the development of Canadian federalism.

[14] Letter to the Hon. G. McIlraith, Minister of Transport, April 1963, p. 8, quoted by Pross, "Dominion-Provincial Relations in the Field of Highway Regulation," unpublished M.A. Thesis, Queen's University, 1963, p. 125.

[15] "The Need for New Federal Regulation to Control Extra-Provincial Highway Transport", Submission to the Hon. J. W. Pickersgill, Minister of Transport, by the CTA, December 9, 1965.

[16] Canadian Trucking Association's Submission to the House of Commons Standing Committee on Transport and Communications, November 3, 1966, p. 3 (hereafter CTA 1966 Submission).

[17] Presthus, *op. cit.*, p. 226.

[18] The promise was reported by the then President of the CTA in August 1967. See R. J. Lewis in *Bus and Truck Transport*, September 1967, p. 25. The promise was corroborated in interviews with individuals associated with both the industry and the Department of Transport.

[19] It was argued that twelve amendments proposed by CTA were accepted by the Government. See *Bus and Truck Transport*, June 1967, p. 73.

[20] See, for example, J. W. Pickersgill, "Canada's National Transport Policy", in *Transportation Law Journal*, Vol. I, 1969, p. 85, and his address to the British Columbia and Ontario Trucking Conventions on October 20, 1967 and November 26, 1968, respectively.

[21] See, for example, articles in *Bus and Truck Transport*, February 1967, pp. 4 and 5.

[22] On the general question of the impact of French Canadian nationalism on interest groups, see John Meisel and Vincent Lemieux, *Ethnic Relations in Canadian Voluntary Associations*, and Kwavnick's article in Pross (ed.), *op. cit.*

[23] Truman, *op. cit.*, p. 116.

[24] Quoted in "Quebec Truckers Divided Over Federal Control?" in *Bus and Truck Transport*, April 1968, p. 19.

[25] *Bus and Truck Transport*, May 1968, p. 45.

[26] The Member who introduced the various Bills was Fernand LeBlanc who was at various times the auditor for the QTA

[27] *Bus and Truck Transport*, July 1969, p. 38.

[28] On the concept of a "mandate" see Kwavnick, *Organized Labour and Canadian Politics* (Montreal: McGill-Queen's University Press 1972), pp. 12-25. The mandate was initially announced in a speech by the Ontario Minister of Transportation and Communications to the ATAO Convention, November 22, 1971.

[29] Rourke, *op. cit.*, p. 54.

[30] The conflict within the federal government on implementation is dealt with in Chapters Five and Six of my thesis, "Federalism, Bureaucracy and Public Policy . . . ."

[31] Presthus, *op. cit.* pp. 161-62.

[32] *Bus and Truck Transport*, December 1968, p. 33.

[33] M. W. Donnelly in *Bus and Truck Transport*, March 1970, p. 20.

[34] The following discussion emphasizes the political role of interest groups in the negotiations. It should also be mentioned that interest groups played a technical or functional role in that a number of groups including CTA, CMA, CAM and CITL were sent the draft regulations discussed at the conference and requested to comment on them.

[35] M. W. Donnelly, then President of the CTA commented to this effect in a speech to the Saskatchewan Trucking Association in Saskatoon, January 23, 1970.

[36] *Bus and Truck Transport*, July 1971, p. 79.

[37] Simeon, *op. cit.*, pp. 204-13.

[38] *Ibid.*, p. 213.

[39] Francis Rourke, *Bureaucracy, Politics and Public Policy* (Boston: Little Brown, 1969) p. 20.

[40] Graham Wootton suggested that such interactions should be conceptualized as part of a "duplex system" in the flow of influence between interest groups and their targets. See Wootton, *Interest Groups* (Englewood Cliffs: Prentice Hall, 1970), pp. 96-8.

26

Energy Pricing

Premier Peter Lougheed:
Alberta's Position, 1974

Alberta welcomes the opportunity to participate in this Federal-Provincial Conference on Energy. As the major supplier of energy for Canada, we obviously have a substantial stake in the development of sound and fair national energy policies. They must be national policies though—national in the sense they are developed by agreement between the Federal Government and the Provinces and with full recognition that natural resources located within the provinces, under our Constitution, are owned by the provinces.

We suggest that this Conference has a better chance of making progress if we strive for understanding of our various views—then identify the areas of possible agreement—and establish machinery for on-going efforts to reach an understanding on complex matters such as pricing. It would be unfortunate for Canada if we missed this opportunity in our history to establish basic objectives for national energy policies by concentrating upon short-term problems rather than upon the long-term goals of strengthening and balancing the Canadian economy when Canada is the only industralized nation in the western world capable of self-sufficiency in energy.

A. ALBERTA—ITS ENERGY POTENTIAL

Alberta is now producing 85 percent of Canada's oil and over 80 percent of Canada's natural gas. In terms of future potential we have within our Province the immense Alberta Oil Sands with their vast prospects for Canadian job opportunities. We also have in Alberta the possibility of substantial additional discoveries of both conventional crude oil and natural gas.

These discoveries will only occur if adequate encouragement and incentives are provided to the explorers to ensure that they will continue to accept the risks inherent in searching for the costly and, more difficult, to find new reserves. In addition, Alberta together with British Columbia and other provinces has huge deposits of coal which could be used for electrical generation and in due course to produce gas for home

---

*Opening Statement by Premier Lougheed of Alberta, Federal-Provincial Conference on Energy, Ottawa, January 22, 1974, Reprinted by permission.

heating by coal gasification. We have asked the respected Alberta Energy Resources Conservation Board to summarize in a report, which will be distributed, an inventory of Canada's energy reserves, production and requirements. Page 43 of that report dramatically illustrates Alberta's role as an energy provider for Canada.

Some Canadians do not appear to understand why so much of Alberta production has been exported to the United States—i.e., recently about 50 percent of our oil production and 45 percent of our natural gas production. The simple reason is that although Alberta production represented a secure supply source at reasonable prices—many parts of Canada did not want to use this Alberta supply source, at least until now. Hence, for many years it was necessary to export Alberta's surplus production to provide the Alberta-based petroleum industry with the cash flow needed to keep this key industry viable, since one out of every three Albertans depends directly or indirectly upon this industry for their livelihood.

B. THE PROVINCE'S JURISDICTION OVER NATURAL RESOURCES

It is clear and unequivocal that the Fathers of Confederation decided that the natural resources within provincial boundaries would be owned by the citizens through their provincial governments, rather than through the Federal Government. Implicit in such ownership is the right of the provinces to manage the resources in terms of conserving or selling them. Perhaps the Fathers of Confederation envisioned this Conference when they recognized that the power of the Federal Government and the influence of the central Canadian population concentration could be balanced by the resource ownership of the less populated regions of Canada. We sincerely hope that there will soon be substantial discoveries of oil and natural gas off the shores of the Atlantic Provinces and we support their views as to the ownership of this resource.

We view the federal export tax on Alberta oil as contrary to both the spirit and the intent of Confederation. We object to it in principle because it is discriminatory. It is not just an export tax—it is also a price freeze on all of Alberta's oil production at immense cost to Albertans. If the export tax had been part of a total Canadian price freeze on all exported products, including manufactured products, as an anti-inflationary measure to protect Canadian consumers—then it would not have been discriminatory and we in Alberta would have found it less objectionable. For example, why wasn't there an export tax and price freeze on the rapidly rising costs of lumber so essential to provide homes for Canadians? It should also be noted that there is no export tax on the recent federally-approved export by Ontario Hydro of electricity to the United States and one has to ask—why not? One of the stated objectives of the export tax was to assure that we would obtain the optimum price in our export market in the United States. This has always been an objective with which Alberta concurs. We could have, and still can, work out some arrangements with the Federal Government which would meet the objective of selling our natural resources in the export market at the highest practical price.

Finally, with regard to the export tax—for the Federal Government to have taken such a major step unilaterally without first even consulting with the producing provinces, is unfortunately firmly implanted in the minds of Albertans in terms of Ottawa's attitude towards the West.

C. ALBERTA ENERGY POLICIES

Before setting forth our views on possible national energy policies, I would like to review with First Ministers the basic energy policies of the Alberta Government and briefly describe some recent actions we have taken that we believe have some consequences for our discussions here:—

1. Firstly, Alberta energy policies include an all-out effort to use Alberta oil and gas resources to meet any possible energy shortage by Canadians this winter wherever they live in Canada. It has been a most unfair distortion of the attitude of 99.9 percent of Albertans by certain national media to portray Albertans as being anything other than determined to see that Canadians are always warm and always in the light! In fact, our oil wells are now being strained to capacity and Alberta oil is being shipped via tanker from the West Coast through the Panama Canal to Eastern Canada to assure that shortages are overcome. If Alberta had not taken this action there might have been significant shortages in some of the eastern provinces this winter.

    Alberta, in co-operation with the Federal Government, has done everything it could possibly do to reduce the risks of shortages of oil and natural gas in Canada this winter and jointly we appear to have essentially succeeded.

2. Secondly, over the longer term it must be a basic policy of Albertans to sell our depleting, non-renewable resources such as oil and natural gas only at prices which reflect fair value. We are quite prepared to discuss and to negotiate the definition of fair value. But, for the rest of Canada to ask Albertans to sell below fair value for any extended period of time is simply an unreasonable request. At the current rate of production, Alberta's presently proved reserves of conventional oil would be used up in about 13 years.

3. Thirdly, over the course of the next decade, Alberta must diversify and broaden the base of its economy and become less dependent upon the sale of unprocessed natural resources—whose world demand might diminish—either due to technological developments such as nuclear energy or for other reasons. References in Central Canada to Alberta's wealth of resources consistently fail to mention the important fact that the average income of individual Albertans is nevertheless, despite these resources, only at the national average and far behind the more than 1/3 of Canadians who live in the Province of Ontario and whose industries use our natural resources. It's naturally an objective of the Alberta Government to use its resources to close this gap—not by reducing the growth of Ontario's average income—but by accelerating the rate of growth of the Alberta citizen's income—to do less would be to fail to meet our responsibility to the citizens who elected us with a strong mandate to manage their non-renewable resources.

D. RECENT ALBERTA ACTIONS RESPECTING ENERGY

In recent months, the Government of Alberta has taken certain steps to strengthen our provincial capacity to meet the energy objectives I've just described. We have now taken out of the hands of the international oil companies the wellhead price setting of oil produced from Crown land within Alberta by establishing the Alberta Petroleum Marketing Commission. We will shortly be announcing the date when Alberta's oil production will flow through our Marketing Commission.

We have by legislation disposed of the inflexible royalty structure we inherited from our predecessors. Thus, we are now in a position to establish a new oil and natural gas royalty structure to assure an appropriate return for the ownership interest of the Provincial Government from the sale of this depleting asset, and also appropriate compensation to the explorer for the risks of undertaking exploration. There is no question that as the oil price increases, the majority of the increased revenues should and will flow to the provincial government as owner.

As a companion feature of the royalty system which also will be announced shortly, we will be expanding our successful Exploratory Drilling Incentive System. I hope Canadians will develop a better appreciation of the unique realities of petroleum exploration and the complex factors which bear on the decision as to when and where to drill an exploratory well.

In addition, we have just concluded certain steps to assure a doubling of the border price of Alberta natural gas being shipped to California. We also encouraged a significant agreement between an Alberta company and Gas Metropolitain which distributes natural gas in Montreal. This agreement should lead to more Quebec homes being heated by that cleaner, more desirable fuel—natural gas!

We are progressing with our policy objective of accelerated development of oil production from the Alberta Oil Sands which will improve the prospects of long-term Canadian self-sufficiency in oil. This has included the recent lauching by the Syncrude Group of the second oil sands plant. The agreement with the Syncrude Group is an excellent one for the people of Alberta because with virtually all of the risk being borne by private enterprise, 60 percent of the profits will flow to Albertans as owners of the resource.

For the longer term, we have just announced a $100 million fund entitled "Energy Breakthrough" which has as its objective the discovery of the means to recover economically the deep-seated reserves of the Alberta oil sands, through the Alberta Oil Sands Technology and Research Authority. We are in the process of putting together terms of reference for future oil sands plant construction and have already had discussions with three provinces as to possible participation. We are quite anxious in the months ahead, before completing our long-term oil sands development policy, to have discussions with every other province and, of course, with the Federal Government to see if there is any interest in participating so as to have first call on some portion of the production from the oil sands and hence assure security of supply. We have had a status report prepared on the Alberta oil sands for the information of the delegations and will have it distributed to you.

Finally, we have made some interesting innovations to have a larger degree of Canadian shareholder ownership of our natural resources and will during the course of this meeting be distributing a paper explaining how the Alberta Energy Company provides a new and unique approach to more Canadian shareholder ownership of our resources.

E. CONCLUSION—POSSIBLE NATIONAL ENERGY OBJECTIVES AND GOALS

In conclusion, I would like to propose four basic goals for a new national energy policy for Canada within which might be accommodated the differing interests of the producing and consuming regions of Canada:—

1. *Firstly*—that we aim to maintain our special position as a growing industrialized and trading nation—*self-sufficient*—in energy resources—dependent upon no other nation or group of nations to heat our homes, fuel our automobiles, or power our industries! Such a goal will require a better recognition of the unique risk-taking features of

conventional oil and natural gas exploration; a pricing policy that stimulates finding the more expensive replacement barrels of oil or fields of natural gas; accelerated development of the oil sands; stepped-up activity off-shore on the Atlantic Provinces; technological progress in coal gasification and nuclear power; and reduction of energy waste in our nation.

2. *Secondly*—to make full use of this self-sufficiency potential in energy for all parts of Canada—by proceeding without delay to put in place a *distribution system* to minimize the number of Canadians relying upon foreign oil to heat their homes and run their cars. This means that we build the overdue Montreal pipeline.

However, Alberta's commitment of its production to the Montreal pipeline must, in equity, be conditional upon a corresponding commitment of a long-term assured market for Alberta production in the Montreal area to replace any reductions in the markets we now have. This self-sufficiency should also include a contingency plan for storage for the Atlantic Provinces in the unfortunate event that oil and natural gas are not discovered in economic quantities off the shores of the Atlantic Provinces. It should also include the construction of the Mackenzie Valley natural gas pipeline subject to environmental and native rights considerations. It must also involve a transportation arrangement to make it economical to ship Western Canadian coal to Ontario Hydro and other Central Canadian industries to replace the present dependency upon United States coal imported into Canada. The self-sufficiency policy should allow for export of surplus Canadian energy resources after long-term Canadian needs have been considered. However, export of electricity must be an integral part of such determination of energy export policy.

3. *Thirdly*—we should stop our practice of exporting jobs with our resources and should commence to phase in measures which will create jobs in Canada rather than in the United States. This will require taxation, tariff reduction, and regional expansion policies which balance economic growth in Canada by *processing our resources*—to the extent practical—up-stream as near as possible to the wellhead or source. This goal would ensure more jobs for Canadians from Canadian resources and a better balance of industry throughout the regions of the Nation.

4. *And, finally*—we should have a national energy policy directed towards the *best possible use* of the various energy sources available to us. For example—we should heat more of our homes in Canada with natural gas—which is not only more efficient, but cleaner. We should reduce the inefficient generation of electricity by natural gas and use

more presently undeveloped coal for this purpose. We should, as part of this goal, also make a real effort to cut back on wasteful and extravagant uses of our valuable and depleting energy resources.

In closing, it is Alberta's position at this Conference that we will make progress if we can agree on basic long-term goals and objectives such as these four—so that this Conference can be the beginning of sound national energy policies that will benefit all Canadians wherever we may live.

Donald S. MacDonald:
Oil and Natural Gas Pricing, 1975*

I believe it is obvious to all, Mr. Prime Minister, after listening to the diversity of view and concern expressed around this table this morning, that reaching a consensus on crude oil and natural gas pricing for the next twelve to fifteen months will test the reasonableness and goodwill of us all, plus whatever wisdom we possess. In many respects, the problems posed for Canadians by rapidly rising costs and less readily available supplies of energy are a microcosm of the problems facing the world. Some of our provinces, in whom ultimate ownership of natural resources reside, have been richly endowed by geology, while others are heavily dependent upon sources of supply from outside their boundaries. In addition, the various regions of Canada have experienced widely differing economic growth, so that, to a lesser degree, the variations in real incomes and the regional disparities evident on the international scene are mirrored in the Canadian situation. All Canadians share a deep concern for the impact which increased prices of essential energy commodities may have on confounding our current problems of inflation and reduced economic activity. More fundamentally, Canadians share the concern about our capacity to manage our energy resources in ways that will ensure that domestic needs are met and the well-being of future generations of Canadians is protected.

---

* Opening remarks on the First Ministers' Conference, Ottawa, April 9-10, 1975. Reprinted by permission.

The increase by fourfold in the international price of crude oil beginning in the fall of 1973 has brought painful adjustments upon the world. Just a year ago, severe fuel shortages were being suffered by the European countries, by Japan and America—we can all recall the frustrating lineups for gasoline our neighbours across the border were forced to endure—while at the same time the sharp escalations in international oil prices fanned the inflationary fires in these countries. Yet in Canada, albeit as I have said a microcosm of the world, we managed to bridge these turbulent times in a more measured way. By the blessing of our resources, and more importantly, by the spirit of co-operation shared by the governments represented at this table, we reached policies permitting us less painful adjustments to these upheavals. Canadians suffered no fuel shortages, and through the past 18 months this country has enjoyed the lowest average crude oil price of any of the industrialized nations. That, of course, was part of our objective, one of the principles of our energy policy: To phase the impact of higher oil and gas prices in order to ease the burden on consumers and to lessen the inflationary impact; to phase these prices toward a level sufficient to bring on needed new higher cost resources and to recognize the legitimate claim of the producing provinces to a fair return for their non-renewable resources.

Our objectives have never wavered which, in a changing world, has meant that the content and emphasis of our policies have had to change in response to the events and trends inside and outside Canada. We have placed new emphasis on promoting nuclear power developments, offering financing assistance for half the cost of generating more electricity through construction of the CANDU reactor, the highly successful nuclear power plant pioneered under federal sponsorship. We have offered similar arrangements for the establishment of regional electrical grids which will aid development of untapped hydro resources, such as the Gull Island project in Labrador, and the Nelson River project in Manitoba. We are also undertaking with the provinces inventories on our coal and uranium reserves and have introduced new uranium export policies.

Of prominence most recently, the Federal Government, along with Alberta and Ontario, has pursued a policy of public participation in the further development of the Athabasca oil sands with the objective that the option of the exploitation of this rich deposit be kept open. Noting that, I am brought to this point:

When we addressed the issues of pricing crude oil last January and March, we were concerned, following the actions of OPEC, to arrive at principles for pricing crude oil and natural gas in Canada which reflected not only Canadian endowments of these resources but also the need to adopt policies which would contribute to Canadian self-reliance in energy. At the January Conference I listed a series of principles setting forth the objectives of our policy. These included a single crude oil price across Canada adjusted for transportation differences, an equitable sharing of the increased revenues among governments and the industry to encourage new supplies, and a phasing of future oil and gas price increases to avoid jarring escalations and to ensure over time that a level would be reached sufficient to bring on new supplies.

These principles provide as sound a base now for our energy policy as they did a year ago, but to them must be added a new principle: Conservation. I believe that Canada and all Canadians must follow a policy to restrain the rates of growth of our demands for all energy resources, and particularly hydrocarbons, and to use these resources more wisely. For this reason I announced a national conservation policy in the House of Commons in February of this year. In announcing this policy I explicitly recognized that if it was to be effective it would require the close cooperation of the provinces, industry and Canadians generally. I am delighted to say that the public response from all quarters has been overwhelmingly supportive. There has been no other single issue on which I have received such a continuing volume of mail from concerned Canadians, practically all of whom are seeking means of becoming actively involved. The Federal Government announced the pending publication of a booklet describing means of saving energy only three weeks ago. Already we have received over two hundred thousand requests for it. There is no doubt in my mind that Canadians generally recognize that we have been in the act of squandering an increasingly valuable natural resource and that this must cease.

I would like to turn now to a very brief review of recent international oil events.

Imported oil, which stood at $10.50/bbl delivered at Montreal a year ago last January, increased to over $12.00/bbl by mid-year, reflecting the increasing participation of OPEC countries in the ownership of their oil reserves. Since mid-1974, however, these prices have remained stable. Under the influence of a relatively warm winter by historical standards in both Europe and on this continent, and due to the depressed level of world economic activity, exports of OPEC oil are currently much reduced and though it is to skate on thin ice to attempt to forecast the course of OPEC prices one can expect, I think, some stability for another year or so. But while OPEC prices have stabilized, our own cost structures have risen. All of you are aware of the approximate doubling of the cost of Syncrude. The same forces which have led to this doubling have increased the cost of frontier exploration developments and nuclear plants.

We have also gained a more sharply defined view of the difficulties we shall encounter in sustaining our current level of self-reliance in crude oil and balance between supplies of available natural gas and demands for this premium resource. While Canada does have a prospect of significant reserves of natural gas in the frontier and of further large additions to our crude oil reserves through developments off our shores, in the Arctic, and in the Athabasca oil sands, we must confront the fact that in the next five to ten years, the productibility of our conventional oil reserves will be declining. It is certainly clear that the costs of developing the resources of the frontiers and the oil sands are substantially in excess of the prices which we now enjoy.

I believe that there now exists a clear understanding by Canadians that the era of cheap energy has ended. There is nothing in our own energy situation which can support the view that Canadians will be able to continue forever enjoying substantially lower prices than the rest of the world. Save for the U.S. where the administration is arguing for prices higher than OPEC's and where the price is currently about $9.75/bbl, most of the world and certainly all industrial nations are currently paying over $12.00/bbl for crude oil.

In the background paper which the Federal Government has provided for this Conference, it is noted that our most recent studies indicate that over the period 1975-1985 energy developments may require a sum of as much as $115 billion and that even an expenditure of this magnitude may not succeed, particularly in the cases of crude oil and natural gas, in meeting Canadian requirements with increasing self-reliance. This sum already represents a doubling of the proportion of our gross national product which we have devoted to energy development in the past. While we believe that the Canadian economy can support these developments, it obviously cannot do so without diverting resources from other possible uses. The more successful we are in restraining our own uses of energy, the less this diversion will have to be. The background document also notes the determination of the Federal Government to seek to expand the level of research and development expenditures on means both of conserving energy and of encouraging the expansion of alternate energy sources.

Permit me to turn for a few moments to issues of natural gas. The National Energy Board has recently completed its hearings and until we have its definitive view it is not possible to speak precisely. However, there was ample evidence given the Board that deliverability from conventional reserves is declining. In our view, the problem of supply has arisen in part from a significant underpricing of natural gas relatively to crude oil which has encouraged its unwise use and has not provided sufficient incentives to encourage new supplies. As I have stated on several occasions, it is Federal Government policy to see the price of natural gas at the well-head rise over time to the point where natural gas and crude oil in their major central Canadian markets are equivalently priced. I believe that this process of price correction should be completed within the next few years. Once again, I am anxious, however, that the adjustment be phased over the intervening years in a way which reconciles the need for consumers to have a period to adjust with the need to provide the incentives to both expand conventional production as well as encourage frontier developments. I would seek the agreement of all provinces at this Conference that the principle of phasing natural gas prices in this manner be accepted, and that this phasing begin later this year. I would further propose that we commit ourselves to a phasing schedule which would achieve crude oil parity within a number of years. I cannot emphasize too strongly to this Conference that we focus on this question, for as I am sure you are all aware there is already set in motion a process which will inevitably lead to a substantial increase in natural gas prices. I speak of the arbitration system which has been established in the province of Alberta. Unless we can at this Conference reach through co-operation an agreement to set the level of natural gas prices, the arbitration system will determine what that price will be, and the possibility exists that the price set will be at such a high level as to cause serious adjustment problems to the consuming provinces: Saskatchewan, Manitoba, Ontario and Quebec. Therefore, I believe it is imperative that we pursue deliberations with the province of Alberta on fair and equitable means of encouraging further supply from that province while recognizing Alberta's concern for its own existing and future requirements. It will also be necessary to confer with Saskatchewan, Manitoba, Ontario and Quebec on the most equitable means of allocating prospectively short supplies amongst them. These are difficult problems, but I have no doubt that with goodwill we can come to mutually agreeable solutions. I would propose to seek these deliberations in the months immediately following this Conference.

It will be necessary in the next two days to discuss the issue of export pricing of natural gas. When I announced the increase to one dollar per thousand cubic feet last fall, I indicated that further increases would be forthcoming. I now believe that it is appropriate to make a further adjustment in that price. Reverting for a moment to another export issue, I indicated, following the Federal Government's announcement of a limit of 800,000 barrels per day of crude oil as of January 1st this year, that a further reduction might be instituted in 1975 following consultation with the provinces. In fact, since January 1st, the level of our exports has declined below 800,000 barrels per day, and indeed in the month of April it will be below 650,000 barrels per day. The market—specifically a number of our export customers—has brought about the objective which I set up in my announcement.

I wish, finally, to address two important issues which are of major concern around this table. Both are more properly the territory of my colleague, the Minister of Finance, but I shall transgress a little. The first is the matter of taxation of the oil and gas industry and the difficulties we have encountered in coming to a mutual understanding on this issue. It seems to me that the division of windfall gains on existing resources as their selling price rose was almost bound to create divisions amongst us until we had come to a better understanding of the share of such windfalls which might be required by industry for future development, and the appropriate sharing of the remainder between the provinces in whom the ownership of these resources resides and the Federal Government exercising the right of all Canadians to a share in what is provincial but also Canadian wealth.

With regard to the first point, that is the share of revenue required to stimulate further exploration and development, I wish to stress that the Federal Government understands the concern of the provinces and of all Canadians that the revenues accruing to the industry from an increase in price should be used to find new oil and gas supplies in Canada. I am confident that the industry will devote new revenues from a price increase to this purpose, in fact I have sought and achieved this assurance from the responsible leaders of the industry. They understand that unless these funds are put back into exploration and development, the government would have no choice but to seek other methods of assuring this.

In regard to the second point, that is the sharing of revenues between the producing provinces and the Federal Government, it is not my intention to enter the non-expensing of royalty debate but it does seem to me that the federal budget has insured a modest but irreducible share in the order of 18 percent of production profits for all Canadians. At the moment, the remaining shares would appear to be divided so that approximately 37 percent is left with industry and 45 percent accrues to the provinces. These are aggregate numbers and disguise provincial differences. They are also based on the assumption that the provinces of Alberta and Saskatchewan will take action to reduce the effect of their respective marginal royalty rates which currently apply to crude oil, and that the province of British Columbia will take similar action in regard to natural gas. Given our knowledge of the increasing cost of both oil sands and frontier developments, I am concerned that an insufficient share of any prospective increases in crude oil will be directed to industry for further exploration and development. I recognize that each province in which production takes place must judge these matters for itself but I nonetheless urge, speaking for all Canadians, that they reassess their taxation policy following the Conference in light of any price increase that may have been agreed upon. I was happy to note that in his December statement, Premier Lougheed expressed a willingness in this regard. Somehow we must come to a balancing of each province's interest in its own internal economic development and the national interest in seeing substantial proportions of these increased revenues devoted to energy developments for all Canadians. In expressing this concern everything I have said recognizes the justice of the claim of these provinces for an adequate return from non-renewable resource bases. Indeed, a failure to move the prices of natural gas and crude oil closer to the cost of replacing current consumption is to provide a temporary benefit to consuming Canadians at the expense not only of the longer-term interest of Canadians but of the legitimate interests of those provinces.

I have the responsibility of trying to determine the national interest in energy matters. I have spoken frankly today in the hope that we may shed any illusions which we may continue to nurse about the possibility of continuing cheap energy supplies. I have not disguised my view that it would be advisable to undertake an increase in both oil and natural gas prices this year and to recognize that such increases as we may agree upon are unlikely to complete the adjustments which we must ultimately make. At the same time, I recognize, of course, the difficulties which such increases may impose upon our general economic situation as well as the costs to both regions and industries in Canada. There does not appear to be in sight a miracle cure which will permit us to continue to develop our industry and our jobs as well as our leisure pursuits on the basis of very cheap and infinitely available energy. It is possible, however, to attempt to develop policies which ease the adjustment burdens imposed on all Canadians. Our capacity to phase price increases has been one of these. The Federal Government is committed to insuring one price for crude oil, adjusted for transportation costs, to all Canadians and will continue over the coming year of agreement to provide a shelter for those Canadians dependent upon imported oil. In the coming year, export tax receipts will no longer be sufficient to provide this cushion and the Federal Government will need to draw upon its general revenues to cover the deficit that will be incurred. We shall continue to devote much more than our share of increased taxation revenues from the oil and the gas industries to provide the equalization payments which will arise, to support both research and development of all energy sources and to provide shelter to Canadian consumers.

Dennis Timbrell: 1976*

My major concern at this time of year is the annual attempt by the Government of Canada—successful for the last two years—to raise the price of crude oil. In Canada the raising of the price of crude oil by the Government of Canada is becoming a natural phenomenom, like the return of the migratory birds in the spring of the year. In my opinion, it's not the way to go. There surely are other options and I want other opinions. I think it very important that my Ministry, the Government of Ontario, and the people of Ontario should become involved, so that I can bring to the conference table next month a clear expression of their views.

I would like to hear from people as to how the higher price of gasoline and heating oil impacts on their lives. I would like them to sit down and put it on a piece of paper and send it to me. Or send it to the Government of Canada. I want to see the people of Ontario get on record.

I have written to a wide range of consumer groups, distribution and producing companies and various citizens' groups and have invited them to write down their views and get them to me as quickly as is possible. The fact is that we need the opinions and the support now, and not after the Government of Canada has again unilaterally raised the price of crude oil and, in so doing, has raised the price of gasoline and fuel oil and other petroleum products.

I fully expect the Government of Canada to propose an increase in the price of crude oil at the Energy Ministers' Conference to be held in Ottawa on March 5th. The Department of Energy, Mines and Resources has already made it quite clear that its instincts are in this direction; it is widely reported that it will propose an increase of $2.00 a barrel. Alberta is expected to go one better. The reports out of Alberta—and these may be right or wrong—are that it will be looking for an increase of some $3.50 a barrel. Saskatchewan is on record as looking for a $4.00 a barrel increase. Well, there's no way that Ontario will go along with such increases. No Canadian should support such an increase—it just is going to poison the economic health of this country and every Canadian could suffer, including those in the producing provinces.

No one should forget, either, that because the Government of Canada has committed the national energy users to natural gas being related in price to crude oil—about 85 percent of the equivalent value—that crude oil and natural gas move up in lock step. The fact is that we don't have a national energy policy that effectively deals with price and the

* Speech presented to the Queen's Park Press Gallery, February 17, 1976 by the Hon. Dennis Timbrell, Minister of Energy for the Province of Ontario. Reprinted by permission.

requirements of supply—we have a lemming-like march in the direction of international prices and a persistent retreat from the hard decisions that will be required if a policy that will serve all Canadians is to be defined.

I would like a simple and direct answer to a simple and direct question. The question, directed to the Government of Canada, the producing provinces and the petroleum companies, is this: if crude oil could be produced in 1972 from certain fields and wells and economically and profitably marketed at a little over $2.00, how can any reasonable person argue that oil from the same fields and wells cannot be produced and marketed economically and profitably at $8.00 a barrel in 1976? I challenge the Government of Canada to come forward with a whole new approach to crude oil pricing at the March 5th meeting.

The crude oil price was raised from $3.80 to $6.50 in 1974 and was raised another $1.50 to $8.00 on July 1, 1975. A carbon copy of its positions in 1974 and again in 1975—another quarterback sneak in the direction of international prices—is no contribution at all.

Its solution to our 1976 energy and economic problems is reportedly more of the same, without reference to the cost of production, without any assurance that the additional money expended by Canadian consumers is being directed toward assuring long-term domestic supplies, without reference to the spirit of its own anti-inflation program and without reflection as to the long-term energy policy requirements. I cannot comprehend how the Federal Government can justify its zombie march after international prices when those prices are nothing other than the contrived prices of a group of world nations that are able to rig the selling price of their product. Viewed from any perspective, it is a Government of Canada insistence that we import at monopoly prices and that the success of a world cartel should result in Canadian consumers paying a world cartel price for a product produced in Canada by Canadians. This is not a relevant national energy policy, it is a grotesque caricature of a policy. Further, if the Prime Minister of Canada wishes to prove his own thesis that the free market has failed or will fail, I know of no better way of advancing his premise than to continue to make of the Canadian market, in effect, a happy hunting ground for world cartels and monopolists.

The role of any market is, in the short term, to relate supply and demand to determine price and, in the long term, to relate selling price to the cost of producing a good. Any freshman economist knows that. But the market can be frustrated by an ability of any of the players to unduly control supply, demand or price—a capability that is clearly present on the international market. The world community may have to live with it, but there is no reason why Canadian should have to in terms of its own domestically-produced supplies.

Our Ontario position is being prepared for presentation at the March 5th Energy Ministers' Conference. We are attempting to structure an approach that is reasonable from the perspective of the producing and the consuming provinces and that, most important of all, it not simply a raid on the consumers of Canada. We feel that we will have to come forward with a workable national energy policy. The Government of Canada has abdicated its responsibility and the policy vacuum must be filled.

APPENDIX I
THE IMPACT OF HIGHER CANADIAN CRUDE OIL PRICES ON ONTARIO CONSUMERS

It has been widely reported that the Government of Canada will propose to the Energy Ministers' Conference, to be held in Ottawa on March 5th, that the wellhead price of crude oil should be raised by $2.00 a barrel.

The price of natural gas is related to the price of crude oil. Assuming the current relationships are maintained, the price for natural gas, as a direct consequence of a $2.00 a barrel increase in the price of crude oil, would rise by around 30-35¢ per mcf.

The increase in the cost of Canadian consumption of crude oil and natural gas would be of the order of $1.8 billion for the first full year.

The Consumer Price Index, as a consequence, would rise by 1.3 percent in the first year—1.1 percent directly attributable to the increase in crude oil prices and the balance attributable to the increase in the natural gas price. This impact would result if there was a full pass through of the price increases, and further assumes that the anti-inflation program will be successful in terms of restraining excessive wage, profit and price increases.

As a result of the higher crude oil and natural gas prices, there would be 13,000 fewer jobs created in Ontario in the first year than would be created if the prices remained the same. Three-quarters of these jobs would be due to the crude oil price increase, the remainder being due to the rise in the price of natural gas.

If the price of crude oil is increased by $2.00 a barrel at the wellhead, a homeowner using 800 gallons of fuel oil annually would experience a price increase of approximately six and a half cents per gallon, which would cause an annual increase in home heating costs of about $50.

For the homeowner using 144 mcf per year of natural gas for heating and cooking, the annual increase in costs would be approximately $45.

The increase in the price of gasoline at the pumps, resulting from a $2.00 crude oil wellhead price increase, would be approximately seven cents per gallon. The cost to the consumer who drives 10,000 miles per year would be about $40.

A homeowner heating with oil and driving 10,000 miles per year would experience an approximate increase of $90 per year on top of the previous year's increase of around $125. If the homeowner uses natural gas and drives 10,000 miles annually, the annual increase would be around $85 on top of last year's increase of around $150.

APPENDIX II
THE IMPACT OF HIGHER CANADIAN CRUDE
OIL PRICES ON ONTARIO INDUSTRIAL USERS

The United States, in recent months, has moved to restrain increases in its crude oil prices and, indeed, is actually reducing the price of new oil coming on stream. Currently, the average U.S. wellhead price for crude is $7.66 per barrel. The price for domestic Canadian crude at the wellhead is $8.00 per barrel.

It is irrational for the Government of Canada to ignore this situation in any discussions relating to the price that industrial users must pay for crude oil and natural gas in Canada.

This is particularly true of those industries that are large users of crude oil, natural gas or petroleum products and is very obviously true, in particular, of the petrochemical industry.

The hard fact is that a $2.00 increase in the price of crude oil—which it is widely reported will be proposed by the Government of Canada—would place important industries in Canada in a position where they would find it difficult, and in some cases impossible, to compete in their historic market—the United States.

In the view of the Government of Ontario it would be irresponsible for the Government of Canada to move toward higher crude oil and natural gas prices in the absence of the most painstaking and careful examination of the effects of such changes in price on the ability of important Ontario and other Canadian industries to compete in export markets.

Prime Minister Pierre Elliott Trudeau:
Oil and Natural Gas Pricing; 1975*

Through the latter part of 1973 and the first months of 1974, the world was confronted by a crisis of rising oil prices. Within a few short months, the OPEC countries which produce much of the world's petroleum had increased the price of crude oil four times over. Most countries in the world were in serious trouble finding the money to pay for the oil they needed. They are still in trouble. Much of the recession in the world today can be traced to this sudden upward change in the price of this basic commodity.

We in Canada were fortunate in 1974 to be producing enough oil to cover our own needs. We were exporting large quantities to the United States from our oil fields in the west and importing similar quantities to serve eastern Canada. We were able to charge higher prices for our exports to cover the higher prices we had to pay for our imports. Thus we were able to keep the price of oil in Canada at a very low level. On the surface then, Canadians were hardly disturbed by the crisis in the world. The problem was and is, however, that our supplies of cheaper crude oil are limited. Over the next few years we will have to import more and more crude oil to fill our needs. We will become more and more dependent on what other countries overseas may do in controlling the price and even restricting the amount for sale.

We recognized a year ago that some increase in price was essential to encourage exploration for and development of oil reserves in Canada. We recognized too that the producing provinces were entitled to a reasonable price for their product which was by then selling at much higher prices in the markets of the world. We First Ministers were able to reach agreement last March that a price for crude oil in Canada of $6.50 at the well head, plus transportation costs, should prevail for a period of 15 months. At that time the world price was about $10.50. Our agreement spared Canadians most of the sudden shock that hit other countries. The producing provinces made this possible, by accepting much less than the international price for their oil, a contribution to every Canadian consumer which is all the more important when we recognize that the supplies of low cost oil are diminishing rapidly.

Today, as the period of our current agreement draws to a close, we meet to consider what should be done about the price of oil. Over the past year, the price which we have to pay for our imports has risen further, from $10.50 to something over $12.00. No one can be sure what

* Opening remarks to First Ministers Conference, Ottawa, April 9-10, 1975. Reprinted by permission.

will happen to that price. It may rise a little further still. It may come down somewhat. Or, it might be tied to prices of food and other things the oil exporting countries buy. But, for this year, it seems likely that the international price will not change very much from its present level.

We must also take into account that our own oil supply situation is much less favourable than we thought it was a year ago. Those who are in the best position to know, now tell us our production, which has already begun to decline, will go on declining for five or ten years at least, while our needs grow larger all the time. We will have to reduce our exports to the United States and increase our dependence on imports from overseas. We have now found out, as everyone knows, that the extraction of oil from our huge reserves in the oil sands will be much more difficult and more costly than we had all expected a year ago. Production from the big Syncrude project will cost much more than the price we now pay for crude oil in Canada. We don't know yet just when or by whom the next oil sands project will be started. Meanwhile, we have not had big discoveries of oil in the Arctic or offshore and the estimates of cost of exploration and development have risen sharply. We are not as lucky as we thought we were last year.

We cannot expect those who search for oil—whether they be Canadians or others—to look for it and develop it in Canada if our prices are far below those in other countries. We cannot go on year after year being extravagant in our use of oil far beyond what almost every other country in the world consumes—mainly because it is being sold cheaply in Canada, a lot cheaper than elsewhere and a lot cheaper than our future supplies will cost. We cannot expect Alberta and Saskatchewan to go on year after year selling their oil to Canadians at a price which is far below what they could get by exporting it.

So my colleagues in the government and I have come reluctantly to believe that the price of oil in Canada must go up—up towards the world price. It need not go all the way up. We should watch what happens to the world price and decide from year to year what we should do. But the price for the year beginning in July will have to be higher than it is now. How much higher we should discuss. Whatever is done about oil will also affect the price of natural gas. Gas and oil prices must be related and become competitive. The past year's experience has pointed up the need for higher gas prices to the producers in order to stimulate exploration and development.

In looking towards increased prices for oil and gas, however, we all have to bear in mind that any increases will add to the cost of living and have unpleasant consequences on the economy. The higher the increases, the worse the impact on the pocket book of most Canadians and on the economy generally. For increases will make it harder to maintain production in other industries and to support the level of employment—because the extra money that consumers would have to pay for oil and gas would have to be diverted from buying other things. To find, in all of this, the price levels which will be a good Canadian solution, will require all our wisdom.

Each of us around this table today will have a viewpoint to express on the major questions before us. Many perspectives will be presented from different parts of the country. Many of the views put forward will be in conflict with each other. This is to be expected, for the people of Canada have elected us to express such views and to express them to the best of our ability. But I am certain that every Canadian not only expects us to work for the welfare of each individual, but for the collective good of all. He expects us to seek solutions to our problems in a spirit of reconciliation and agreement. Whether we are looking for ways to improve the economy of Canada or seeking solutions to the complex questions of oil and gas pricing, each of us here has an important contribution to make and a responsibility to bear. The people of Canada expect much from us and I am sure that, together, we will fulfil their expectations.

27

Education: Governments, Goals and Policy Making*

O.E.C.D.

The final chapter of the Examiners' Report is devoted to the questions of the Federal government's role in education, interprovincial co-operation in educational policy making, and the importance of spelling out goals for educational policy in Canada. These are all questions of the greatest political sensitivity. The Examiners do not wish to avoid them, nor could they, because in the course of the Examination they arose much more frequently than one could have predicted simply from a reading of the six Background Reports that were prepared for the OECD Examination.

The following observations, therefore, should not be regarded as trying to interfere in political matters, nor as an exercise in superior wisdom, but as a necessary part of the fulfilment of the Examiners' duties.

---

* From O.E.C.D., *Reviews of National Policies for Education: Canada* (Paris: 1976), pp. 89-103. Reprinted by permission.

THE FEDERAL GOVERNMENT AND EDUCATION

Officially, there is *no* Federal presence in the area of educational policy, and the Federal government behaves (at least in public) as if there were none. Not only is there no Federal authority with the word "Education" in its title, but the Federal Parliament eschews all debates that might bear on educational policy. Even reflection on educational policy happens at the Federal level only behind closed doors.[1]

In reality, though, the educational policies of the Federal government, and the financial concomitants of that policy, cannot be overlooked. A considerable Federal presence in educational policy is indeed tolerated by the Provinces and arouses no hostility, as long as nobody calls it educational policy, and as long as there are no overt strings attached to money coming from Ottawa.

This "Do-One-Thing-*As-If*-It-Were-Something-Else" attitude does not please all Canadians, some of whom describe it as "intolerable" and "almost schizophrenic". But to some extent, behaviour that strikes outsiders as elaborate make-believe may, in fact, be a necessary price, willingly paid to hold together a political confederation of disparate Provinces—and therefore understandable and even functional. Certainly, no change can come from the Federal side. This means that nothing will be changed, unless some far-seeing Provinces make use of an appropriate opportunity to make the first step in the direction of open co-operation, openly acknowledged; or unless the public becomes aggressively dissatisfied with the present reluctance to call a spade a spade, and forces those responsible to make changes.

Federal funds, granted for wholly or largely educational purposes, either through the Provinces, or directly to institutions, are made available in large amounts under many programmes (see Table 1).

The subsidies of the Federal government, most of which are channelled through the Provinces amounted to about $2.5 billion in 1975, comprising about 20 per cent of educational expenditures at all levels of government (see Table 2).

Why does the Federal government do this? Are these expenditures really only "Aid for the solution of other political tasks", as the official explanation runs, or is it that the education of a modern nation represents a basic national interest, for which there must inevitably exist a considerable national responsibility?

Clearly, some basic elements of *national responsibility* arise because, in Canada today, as in all modern states:

    —education is a *right of each citizen,* due to each citizen irrespective of his place of residence;
    —the *standards* maintained by schools, community colleges and universities are of national interest, because a large part of scien-

tific-technical achievement and hence economic and social well-being may depend on them;

—*unity of the educational system* is a national interest, in order to maintain and guard the freedom of choice (via mobility) of citizens;

—the *educational philosphy of an educational system and the principles underlying its operation* are matters of national interest, because cultural and national consciousness depend on it.

Each of the tasks listed would almost compel some participation by the national government. The last named task is of such great importance for the future of Canada that it must be emphasized. The search for a "Canadian identity" will not be fruitful if it is not grounded firmly in education. While efforts to develop a curriculum for instruction in Canadian Studies are praiseworthy, it is widely recognised in Canada that such courses and other related activities, such as playing the national anthem at the beginning of the school day, will not suffice. Again, a specifically Canadian identity is not likely to arise simply out of a wish to be different from the United States. It will come permanently only when knowledge, values and attitudes have so taken root that a critical mass of common attitudes has been guaranteed.[2]

TABLE 1

Federal Expenditures in Support of Education and University Research
1972-1973

Department and/or Programmes	Total ($'000)
Fiscal Transfers for Post-Secondary Education	987,030.0
Department of Indian and Northern Affairs	105,235.0
Department of National Defence	62,779.0
Federal Prison Service	416.0
Occupational Training of Adults	310,611.3
Citizenship & Language Instruction Agreements	775.7
Textbook Agreement	120.6
Teaching of Official Languages	62,883.2
Department of Regional Economic Expansion	13,313.0
Research Grants and Fellowships	121,302.0
Contracts	7,504.7
Excise Tax Exemption	23,000.0
Canada Student Loans Plan	34,023.0
Allowances, Bursaries, Scholarships and Fellowships	28,390.3
Income Tax Reductions	84,000.0
Other Programmes	98,944.7
TOTAL	1,940,328.5

TABLE 2

Expenditures on Education (Includes Elementary, Secondary, Tertiary and Further Education) by Source of Funds, Provinces (1972) and Canada (1972 to 1975)

	Total ($'000)	Federal[1] %	Provincial %	Municipal %	Fees + other	Federal transfers payment ($'000,000)
Newfoundland	165,009	14.2	76.6	0.6	5.6	17.9
Prince Edward Island	39,611	20.3	65.9	6.3	7.5	4.0
Nova Scotia	269,094	13.3	57.3	21.6	7.8	24.7
New Brunswick	218,678	11.9	82.3	—	5.8	27.4
Quebec	2,351,745	9.5	63.3	20.0	7.2	347.3
Ontario	3,425,167	8.6	59.1	22.4	9.9	390.0
Manitoba	365,400	13.4	55.4	24.1	9.1	41.3
Saskatchewan	305,544	13.5	50.7	27.7	8.1	34.3
Alberta	694,933	10.2	58.9	22.9	8.0	88.9
British Columbia	740,393	12.0	58.5	22.3	7.2	72.1
Yukon	11,349	19.8	79.0	—	1.2	—
Northwest Territories	29,980	3.4	93.9	2.4	0.3	—
Overseas & Undistributed	78,402	83.7	—	—	16.3	—
Canada 1972	8,695,305	10.7	60.2	20.7	8.4	1057.9
1973	9,514,717	10.5	61.2	19.9	8.4	1143.2
1974	10,591,341	10.2	62.4	19.8	7.6	1309.0
1975	12,228,005	10.1	64.1	18.4	7.4	1501.3

[1] Excludes Federal transfers to the Provinces for post-secondary education and for the minority language programme, being a total of $1057.9 million in 1972. Inclusion of these Federal transfers raises the Federal proportion from 10.7 to 22.9 percent and reduces the Provincial proportion from 60.2 to 48.0 percent.

The fact that there is, and apparently can be, no Federal Department of Education has created a kind of vacuum in educational policy at the higher federal decision-making level. This empty space is invaded by federal agencies responsible for "neighbouring" policy areas: manpower policy, general economic policy, regional development policy, science research policy, social policy, foreign policy, and so forth. Typically, such agencies tend to view education as an *instrument* for their particular missions, and not as a field of policy in its own right.

Education is always seen as a tool for "something else" and decisions relating to education are mostly made by "someone else". The absence of an agency primarily concerned with balancing off the variety of interests concerned with educational activities (which is, in fact, a definition of educational policy making) leaves the arena open for conquest by the strongest neighbouring agency, without the checks and balances usually found in public administration.

The assignment of a co-ordination role for educational activities at the Federal level to the Department of the Secretary of State may be viewed as an effort to police Federal administrative competitors in their penetration into the educational no-man's land. Yet there is to date no sign of a coherent Federal policy for education emerging, nor much evidence of success in ironing out inconsistencies and even outright contradictions among various parts of the total federal effort in education. Interministerial co-ordination, conducted at a middle level of civil servants, probably cannot be expected to offer more. Nor does the current trend of curtailing the budget and manpower allocations for the Education, Culture and Science Division of Statistics Canada augur well for the development of consistent federal policy in the educational realm.[3] Above all, there is need for comprehensive, policy-oriented, and timely statistical data on just what is transpiring in education in Canada. Statistics Canada cannot do that job properly unless it allocates sufficient resources to its education-related endeavours.

In the Canadian case it is clear enough that the strongest concerns which have justified Federal penetration into the education field have been those of economic policy. This is quite naturally a major political concern in Canada, as well as in other countries. In addition, however, the Canadian situation is characterised by an extra emphasis on economic concerns at the Federal level, probably because the undisputed mandate of the Federal government in this area forms the essential basis for the assertion of federal competence in many other areas. The tendency to see all federal programmes as auxiliaries of economic policy appears to be strong, and more recent concern for aspects of the "quality of life" other than those measured by GNP statistics, does not seem to have had a marked impact on Federal policy thinking. Political philosophies deeply entrenched in an existing bureaucracy are not that easily changed, in spite of emerging new signals in political circles.

More concretely, it is fairly obvious that the massive federal support to higher education in the late 1960s was mainly motivated by faith in education as an important factor in economic growth. Present doubts about the value of continued support on this scale are not caused by any failure of the programme, which has certainly produced a major expansion of post-secondary education. Nor is the argument that success now has made the programme too costly very convincing. The slowing down of post-secondary expansion in recent years does not indicate a programme that has run out of control financially. References to inflation in this context are probably quite irrelevant to federal allocation priorities, and complaints about "lower quality" and lack of "accountability" have the ring of weak excuses. Nothing that has happened in post-secondary education was not more or less foreseen when the present support programme was initiated. It is reasonably clear that present doubts about the continuation of financial support for post-secondary education stem from a loss of faith in education as a direct promoter of immediate economic growth, possibly reinforced by the fairly global disenchantment in established circles about the behaviour of students and intellectuals.

The present arrangement whereby the federal government helps equalise local property tax contributions for primary and secondary education appears primarily to be an encouragement for greater use of this local fiscal source, though that was clearly not the Minister of Finance's intention when local tax equalisation was introduced.

As far as the Examiners were able to penetrate the complexities of federal equalisation of provincial tax resources, the present arrangements may in some respects (and particularly with respect to entitlements based on post-secondary expenditures) actually reinforce, rather than attenuate, inequality among the provinces. This is a not unexpected result of what are tantamount to federal cost-sharing programmes, that reward the wealthier provinces with more dollars, the more they spend on approved purposes, such as higher education. It is important, too, to bear in mind the possibility that federal money is used simply to replace provincial funds, and may not produce any total expansion of spending for education at all.

The application of the so-called "active manpower policy" through federal inputs to manpower training seems primarily oriented towards adapting existing manpower resources to whatever needs the economy might have at the moment. There are few signs of change in this orientation. The Provinces still strongly emphasise more "employer oriented" training. The *social* elements involved in the principles advocated by the OECD, both in terms of reaching severely underprivileged persons, and as a direct attack on unemployment, do not appear to be the prime motives of federal efforts in this field. Concern for increasing the GNP takes precedence over socially-oriented employment policies.

Federal research policies were introduced to the Examiners with a strong reference to the Review of Science Policy in Canada conducted by the OECD in 1969, which saw a federal role in research policy primarily as a means of promoting economic growth and technological expansion. In practice the procedures actually established by the research councils may have considerably modified such policy concerns to conform better with traditional university ideas related to the basic sciences. Yet the overwhelming emphasis is on the natural sciences and technology, and special measures by the federal government beyond research council operations are clearly technology-oriented.[4] The policies followed in granting federal research support clearly enhance quality differentiation among higher education institutions, in an attempt to create a few "centres of excellence" of international standing, inevitably at the expense of the majority of higher education institutions (see p. 82, footnote). The Examiners could not determine how far such approaches are opposed and how far they find support in academic circles, and also at the political level. Nevertheless, policies of qualitative differentiation are clearly supported by Ontario and Nova Scotia, and probably also by Alberta, and the policies followed in federal research funding also support this pattern.

Even the federal programme of loans to students seems, at least initially, to have had a strong economic motivation, based on the assumption that it would help to release untapped reserves of talent. As in many other countries, such concerns probably conformed well with more general social objectives.

Currently federal policy regarding continued financial transfers for educational activities faces two main questions:

—Should federal efforts in this field be more orientated towards goals other than the maintenance of a high rate of growth of the GNP?

—Will the forms of support chosen be constructed in a way more compatible with the official statements concerning the objectives of education in general?

Underlying these two questions may be a third: Should Federal resources presently devoted to education and training be reallocated to other fields of policy which may now have a higher priority? In the Examiners' view, it would be most undesirable if consideration of these important questions were to go forward at the federal level alone, without systematic consultation with the provinces *as a whole.*

At present, discussions, negotiations and agreements between the federal government and the provinces in educational matters tend to go forward on a bilateral or piecemeal basis. This procedure may answer certain provincial (and federal) political needs, but it has unfortunately also made much more difficult the task of making something more systematic out of the highly fractionated structure of education in Canada. The need now is to put in place greatly improved mechanisms for inter-provincial co-operation, and for federal-provincial discussion and co-operation on a multilateral basis.

INTER-PROVINCIAL CO-OPERATION

In the framework of the OECD Examination it is not possible to inquire to what extent Section 93 of the British North America Act is in fact an insuperable barrier to change. However, there have been some interesting statements made in this regard, notably by J. A. Corry, a respected constitutional lawyer, who doubts that this is so, and has said so in the following words:

> . . . So whatever the dilemma about education in the Canadian federation is, it is not a constitutional one. Indeed S.93 is a model of flexibility. Whenever it becomes clear that special educational provision is needed to carry out responsibilities undertaken by Parliament in the exercise of its exclusive powers in S. 91, Parliament is entitled to make that provision by whatever means and instrumentalities are required in the circumstances. As so often turns out in this country, obstacles to action that are declared to be formidable constitutional barriers turn out to be merely political. That may not make the problem any easier to deal with but at least one can make a start by removing the "no trespassing" signs and opening up Federal-Provincial consultations.[5]

Indeed, who can maintain seriously that the fathers of the BNA Act had ruled against sensible inter-provincial and federal-provincial o-operation in the field of educational policy?

The political situation at present absolutely excludes the possibility of a solution via constitutional change. That a single educational authority should be established, under the auspices of the provinces and the federal government (as a number of respected organisations are demanding), may be highly desirable but it is not likely to happen. That the mostly diligent and responsible national interest groups in the educational policy field (for example, The Canadian Education Association), which form at the moment the main all-Canada educational policy forces, could undertake this catalytic task on a permanent basis, is an illusion. Nevertheless, all their projects and efforts leading to more co-operation and a wider perspective should receive undiminished support.

In the end, there remains only the path of an insightful, careful, but nevertheless purposeful *rapprochement*, as it was put to the Examiners in numerous conversations. Mechanisms for co-operation have to be developed. This appears to the Examiners to be a good definition of the next step to be taken.

The *first* phase of this would be a Council of Ministers of Education that was more able to function effectively, and with a staff that must be greatly strengthened in numbers. The Council of Ministers, now eight years old, stands at a critical decision point. Either it will continue to confine its functions to virtually that of a private meeting place for Ministers and their representatives (which is the impression conveyed to the Examiners by many groups and representatives, who did not conceal their disappointment at what they termed the ineffectiveness, secrecy and lack of accessibility with which the CMEC has conducted its business); or the provinces must decide to develop a Council in which all important matters are co-ordinated, receive further development, and are then presented to the public and to the Federal government.

The minutes of the Examiners' meetings and conversations reveal that without exception all organisations, as well as most spokesmen for educational institutions, are demanding more and better transprovincial co-operation and goal setting. There was not one voice that regarded such co-operation as an infringement on provincial sovereignty and independence.[6]

The second phase should lead to tangible co-operation between the Council and the federal government in settling specific questions: for example, the improvement of bilingual disparities via school-related measures, the integration of vocational and general education, the systematic support of educational research, the restructuring of university and community college financial aid, and so forth.

Close attention should be paid to the desirability of developing the Council of Ministers of Education into a national forum for the working out of educational policies, so that the Federal government may be involved in a systematic and *open* manner in discussions of educational policy that transcend Provincial boundaries.

In the *third* phase this co-operative work should be extended to educational policy elements having an all-Canadian viewpoint. The task is to accommodate the different, and often conflicting, aspirations of francophone and anglophone Canada, of the older Eastern regions and the new Western areas, of the taxpayers and the professional groups in education—to mention only the most obvious sources of disagreement about policies. The disagreements cannot simply be glossed over, and no amount of simple goodwill can eliminate them as sources of conflict. But, given that they are faced openly for what they are, the Examiners are confident that Canadian political acumen can deal with them in a constructive and positive way.

GOALS AND EDUCATION POLICY

Judging from the Examiners' experience in Ontario and the Western Provinces, the lack of educational policies for the future is striking. Some exceptions to this general experience, primarily in Manitoba and British Columbia, are to be noted. The general tone of policy making appears to be adaptations to short-term pressures, doing a little more of what already has been done, and above all pressing for economies and reductions of expenditures. Closer ties between the output of the educational system and assumed manpower needs may be an example of such short-term adaptations, while repeated references to "quality education" seem to be more a reaction to reduced selectivity within the educational system than a carefully thought through education policy.

It is a fairly general experience that policies firmly controlled by established power groups rarely need to be based on long-term planning orientated towards alternative future scenarios. Planning in such a situation is usually restricted to the programming of policy implementation in order to secure coherence within the system, possibly supplemented by long-term projections, typically in the form of linear trend prolongations. "More of the same" is the usual future vision under such circumstances.

Planning for alternative futures implying more profound system changes is usually only initiated by groups without an established power position. They may be opposition groups whose access to power has been recent and whose hold on office is uncertain. This would explain the elements of genuine long-term thinking found in British Columbia and Manitoba. It may also be a case of permanent minority groups fighting against superior forces to maintain their minority rights, as Quebec Province sees its position in the country as a whole.

Such factors offer a more convincing explanation of the apparent general lack of future perspectives in Canadian educational policy than jurisdictional peculiarities, particular features of the Canadian economy (a natural resource-based economy, and economic dependence upon the United States), "traditional attitudes", and so forth.

The lack of future perspectives is also reflected in the absence of clear, detailed statements of goals for the educational system.

The Background Reports for the OECD Review state goals in very general terms. Only Quebec's Report is an exception.

For example, the Ontario Background Report states (para. 66):

> . . . there are likely as many statements of goals and objectives as there are educational agencies.

and, (para. 68):

> The stated goal of the Ministry of Education is 'the attainment of educational quality and equality for all'. The Ministry fosters a wide range of opportunities so that every individual may experience a worthwhile education and may have access to further educational experience consistent with his needs and those of society.

But the reality is not that simple. For, in paras. 70 and those following, the Ministry views itself as having a great deal of initiative (no bad thing, of course), and also of control (which fits somewhat less the picture given of the supposed system): inspection, evaluation and approval of programmes, control over teacher training, evaluation of curriculum materials, and so forth. Then the question arises: How can one control (which means to say: accept/refuse/impose/delay/limit) without having some criteria, some standards? And how can one have some criteria without having goals? Para. 71 affirms rather optimistically:

> . . . since these objectives are essential to any good education system, it is probable their intent is in some way expressed in any statement of school board objectives.

The Background Report for the Western Region (para. 45) states: "Official statements of provincial educational authorities, while replete with detailed descriptions of aims and objectives of basic education, do not ordinarily emphasize or elaborate the general aims of the educational system as a whole, probably because the very nature of the relationship of education to society does not permit the luxury of a definitive statement which will be valid even in the short-run future . . . . In the realm of higher education, traditionally further removed from the scope of public education authorities, official statements of general purposes are even less common and definitive.

The Background Report of the Altantic Provinces is also not explicit concerning goals. After having emphasized that institutions of education confront the difficulty of locating education within many social uncertainties and of reconsidering their traditional role as an instrument of society, the Report falls back upon the following as the general goal of the system:

. . . to provide equal educational opportunity for all educable youth and adults to the extent that skills and abilities may be instilled or developed.

The double restriction on equal opportunity is worthy of note.

Thus, the educational goals pursued by the provincial authorities (except Quebec) are expressed only in general terms: supporting quality education; assuring equality of access, etc. This approach, which is reaffirmed more or less in all the Reports, contains some problems.

First and foremost, it is in contradiction with the facts: the provincial authorities have played a very important role in determining not only the quantitative development of the system, but also the educational orientation taken since 1960. At the local level, in most cases, the school boards have been reinforced by administrative and pedagogical services which, in effect, exercise the real power either under the control of the Provinces, or in any case in close liaison with them. This creates a somewhat ambiguous situation and may be the source of a certain "bad conscience" on the part of the central authorities and of-bad temper among the local authorities and those who are the objects of central administration.

Absence of a carefully stated guiding purpose could be accepted in an era when the school was considered to be representative of the social will of the community (whether large or small) out of which the school had originated. But is it any longer justified in an era when it is widely recognised that society is caught up in profound change and uncertainty?

Put another way: Do not the responsible central authorities have to take the necessary steps to reconstitute the lost consensus, to help find something which could take its place, that could serve as the general goal of, and thus the criteria for, educational decisions?

Failing this, there is the risk of mistaking the means for the end; that is to say, of taking as goals matters which are really nothing but means, of falling into a sort of methodological formulism, where innovations of structure and new methods of instruction follow one after the other, because they have been judged only by reference to themselves and their immediate practical results, without reference to any overall philosophy of education.

A general philosophy of sorts does appear to be presented in the Background Reports and in the discussions the Examiners had, though in a rather diffuse fashion. There is a new consensus emerging, for example, around the necessity to lead pupils and students towards autonomy, liberty, creativity and, therefore, on the necessity of educating them with an eye to flexibility and divergence. The question is: What strategy is to be adopted to achieve this goal?

Three elements of such a strategy appear to the Examiners to be basic. They are: Building *Knowledge*, Building *Capabilities* and Building *Consensus*.

Building Knowledge

Research is certainly one of the weakest areas of the Canadian educational system. There is a considerable amount of research but it is either narrowly pedagogical or vaguely philosophical. There is very little research on the basic socio pedagogic problems that have emerged. The Examiners strongly recommend that research be strengthened in these areas, especially on the opportunities of using education by underprivileged groups, and the limits to that use; on the schools as complex social systems with alternative modes of social control; and on the relationships between schools and communities.

Building Capabilities

Great attention must be given to teacher training. Some most difficult social problems are emerging in Canada. The need to build the human resources to face them is pressing. This is nowhere more evident than in education. Similarly, institutional capability should be recognised as a basic problem and attempts to improve it should be made consciously.

Building Consensus

Knowledge and capabilities are necessary to create the climate for change but they cannot be effective and will not even be developed beyond a certain point if no consensus among those interested in education develops.

To build consensus, broad publicity should be given to the exploration of alternative ideas for dealing with newly emerging problems, especially in the areas of the life-chances of underprivileged persons, the school as a community institution, and the provision of high quality educational services for *all* groups in the population.

The aim should be to raise such problems from the level of diffused public feelings of dissatisfaction to that of a definite and active public concern, combined with a consensus about how these problems will be dealt with. The road to broader consensus inevitably runs through a period of more explicit recognition of basic differences, when latent conflicts are brought out into the open. Only through such a process can it be expected that a more broadly-based consensus will be reached.

It is at once obvious that discussion of such goals and of the means to achieve them are highly political activities. There is a rather fearful, even tortuous avoidance of "politics" in Canadian educational discussions which appears to occur not simply from a feeling of respect or inadequacy vis-à-vis the complexities of the Canadian scene.

This is the real crisis of Canadian educational policy—that it cannot maintain its non-political stance. The crisis could remain hidden, as long as it was over-shadowed by the impressive quantitative expansion of education. But now, in a period of slower expansion, the lack of generally binding propositions concerning the socio-political goals of education has the effect of producing a damaging uncertainty about the meaning and purpose of the vast Canadian educational enterprise.

This uncertainty may be noted in other countries, too, but probably nowhere as openly evident and unchallenged as in Canada. The perceptibly growing public unwillingness to support seemingly endless increases in expenditures for education, especially in the face of new, perhaps even costlier, social tasks, is a warning that should be taken seriously. This unwillingness will continue to increase as long as the public is not given a clear understanding of the social goals of real importance that are to be achieved using this expensive educational enterprise.

The further development of Canadian educational policy is therefore clearly approaching a danger zone, in which more is at risk than simply the quantity of finance available. The virtues of an essentially pragmatic educational policy will be tested in the extreme. *If those responsible for educational policy are not promptly able to base the development of school and education on a firm goal-orientated footing, then they risk being pushed to the side in the general political competition for resources.*

Some of the national interest-groups, for example the Canadian Teachers Federation, are already active in this matter, but such groups cannot be expected to relieve the politicians and the governments of this responsibility.[7]

Politicians, parties and governments will not be able to avoid much longer taking some political stands, and that means also nationwide, and not simply province-orientated positions. They need to give Canadian answers to Canadian problems. *Without political leadership and responsibility—and after all neither of these is forbidden under the BNA Act—a severe backlash against future educational development in Canada may be unavoidable.*

The obvious location for the work that is necessary in this leadership role is the Council of Ministers of Education. The Examiners earnestly hope that the Council will be moved in the immediate future to recognise the problem and act on it.

The well-known question in *Alice in Wonderland* runs: "Cheshire-Puss", Alice began . . . "Would you tell me, please, which way I ought to go from here?". It was answered, as always, by: "That depends a good deal on where you want to get to". And this exchange fits exactly the present Canadian situation. Before the goal has been explicitly decided, no one, and certainly not the Examiners, can advise *which* way Canadian educational policy should go. And this goal cannot simply have a pragmatic content. However much, up to now, controversy may have been avoided and energy spared by concentration largely on quantitative expansion, these times are coming to an end. Decisions now have to be taken concerning the destination of the Canadian school system within an ordered view of the future of Canada as a nation.

NOTES

[1] For example, deliberations about restructuring post-secondary financing were considered to be so secret that it was not possible even for the Examiners to discover any traces of what was happening.

[2] Looked at in this way, the schools' role in achieving bilingualism, for example, is transformed from a utilitarian necessity to a national opportunity, and an enrichment of the idea of a Canadian identity. For the intellectual and cultural strengths of francophone Canada are too rich and varied for Canada to do without them and be true to its historical and cultural origins.

[3] In November 1975, after these comments were written, the Government of Canada announced a far-reaching programme of economic controls designed to deal with the persistent wage and price inflation. The policy included efforts to moderate the rate of growth of public expenditure, at all levels of government.

[4] This was clearly an important element in motivating federal involvement in creating a market for the electronics industry in Canadian education.

[5] J. A. Corry, *"Jurisdiction under the Constitution in Education in Canada"*.

[6] In the development of this attitude, the steadily improving educational statistics series published by Statistics Canada has made a decisive contribution, by helping to illuminate the facts about education in Canada as a whole. Also, see comments on p. 93 above.

[7] The three-part document "On educational finance" of the CTF is a thoroughly thought-out, comprehensive and impressive example of the needed approach.

28

Agricultural Marketing Legislation:
A Case Study*

A. E. Safarian

In most contemporary economic unions and countries, many sectors of agriculture have received special treatment with respect to the internal and external market. This is so for a variety of reasons, ranging from the characteristics of the industry to social views regarding the role of agriculture. These have led governments and farm organizations to intervene in the markets for agricultural products in varying degrees in an effort to control or moderate market forces and their impact on resource allocation, the organization of the industry, and on farm income. Apart from the issues raised for agricultural policy, such intervention is of direct concern here for the light it throws on the problems of reconciling regulation with internal free trade.

Since the latter half of the nineteenth century, Canadian farmers have sought, through collective action of various kinds to increase their share of the price consumers pay for farm products. Such action has been directed to handle the following concerns:

(1) Seasonal surpluses which depress prices at time of delivery, and longer-term stabilization.
(2) Distribution of products to alternate markets in a manner designed to obtain maximum returns.
(3) The lack of bargaining strength when dealing individually with buyers.

The first cooperative action taken by farmers was purely voluntary. Following the drop in farm prices during the nineteen twenties, pooling-type cooperatives with their ironclad membership contract developed in several parts of Canada in an effort to increase farm incomes. These cooperatives did not prove fully successful. Complete control of the market was not achieved: non-members, without shouldering any of the burdens of responsibility, were in a position to take advantage of any benefits in price resulting from the actions of the cooperatives.

During the depression of the nineteen thirties farmers pressed for legislation that would bring about more orderly marketing of agricultural products. In 1934, the *Natural Products Marketing Act* was passed. This Act set up an organization patterned on one originally developed in

* From *Canadian Federalism and Economic Integration* (Ottawa: Information Canada, 1974), pp. 48-57. Reprinted by permission.

Queensland, Australia. The essential feature of this legislation was that where the majority of the producers of a commodity wished to sell their produce collectively, the minority would be compelled by law to conform.

The *Natural Products Marketing Act* provided for the establishment of a Dominion Marketing Board with wide powers, including the power to delegate its powers to local boards organized by producers. In the brief two and one half year history of the *Natural Products Marketing Act,* some 22 marketing schemes were approved across Canada. The validity of the federal Act was questioned in 1935 and the Supreme Court was asked for a ruling. In 1937 the Privy Council declared the Act *ultra vires* on the grounds that it infringed on provincial jurisdiction over matters of property and civil rights.

Provincial marketing boards were then created. By and large, the courts upheld the validity of these boards. It is clear from the early decisions that they were restricted to control of intraprovincial trade. Then, in 1949, the *Agricultural Products Marketing Act* was passed by Parliament. By this Act the Governor in Council was authorized to grant to provincial marketing boards the same type of powers with respect to provincial produce sold in interprovincial and export trade as the boards already exercised with respect to such produce sold in intraprovincial trade.

Financing was a problem for these boards, as was the attempt to pool returns to producers. A provincial board can impose licence fees for operating costs, but attempts by provincial boards to impose a levy on one group of producers in order to increase the return to another group have generally been considered by the courts to be an indirect tax and the granting of such power to a board by a provincial legislature to be *ultra vires.* As a result of this line of ruling, the *Agricultural Products Marketing Act* was amended in 1957 to provide that the Governor in Council could authorize provincial boards to impose indirect taxes and use the funds from such levies for all purposes of the board including equalization of returns.

The provincial legislation, with the support of the *Agricultural Products Marketing Act,* appears to give provincial boards all the powers they need to regulate products produced within their provinces regardless of where the products are going. As of September 1, 1970, fifty-nine provincial marketing boards had their provincial powers extended into interprovincial and export trade. These included boards in all provinces except Newfoundland. In addition, five provincial marketing boards had authority under the *Agricultural Products Marketing Act* to collect levies.

Court decisions have clarified the following points with regard to agricultural marketing legislation:

(1) The federal government normally has not the authority to regulate the intraprovincial movements of products, but provinces have such authority.
(2) Provinces have not the authority to regulate the interprovincial movements of products, but the federal government can extend interprovincial powers to provincial boards.
(3) Provinces can charge licence fees under a marketing scheme to defray costs of regulating a product and to increase the general funds of the province (direct taxation), but cannot charge a levy for price adjustment purposes (indirect taxation).
(4) A system of pooling of returns under provincial marketing scheme was held to be valid.
(5) The regulation of a product delivered within a province was considered to be within the competence of provincial legislation even though, after processing, most of the by-products moved into interprovincial trade.

There is one significant weakness in the legislative framework by which provincial boards were created and federal powers over interprovincial trade were extended to such boards. Producers and provincial governments recognized that there was no direct control to assure that one provincial board would not act to the detriment of other provinces. While there had been interest in national marketing structures for a number of products for some time, it was the situation in poultry and eggs which led to a request that the federal government enact legislation providing for such structures.

Initially, the federal government considered a specific request from egg producers for a national egg board. When this was followed by a request from broiler producers for a similar structure it was decided to introduce legislation which would enable the federal government to establish national farm products marketing agencies for any commodity where producers and provincial governments had expressed a desire. This legislation was passed in January, 1972.[1]

There are now about 120 agricultural marketing boards in Canada. Many are concerned with such matters as product promotion and research and do not have such powers as price fixing, production quotas, or controls on imports from other provinces. It is instructive, nevertheless, to consider the problems of the egg and poultry boards, for they pinpoint the economic, administrative and constitutional issues involved in marketing.

The first egg marketing board in Canada was set up in Ontario in 1965 because of dissatisfaction with fluctuating and low prices. Its functions were limited to product promotion and research. The Quebec Federation of Producers of Consumer Eggs (FEDCO) was formed in 1966. In 1967, Quebec producers voted overwhelmingly in favour of setting up a marketing plan for eggs. By 1969 egg production was rising in Canada and prices sagging. The situation which existed early in 1970 was that about 40 per cent of all eggs produced in Canada were produced in Ontario. Producers in Quebec supplied about half of the Quebec market. Ontario producers were the most important source of the remaining half, shipping one-fifth of their output to Quebec. Manitoba producers also shipped to the Quebec market.

In May 1970, an agency marketing scheme was introduced by FEDCO. All eggs sold in Quebec, whatever their origin, were to go through sixteen grading stations, with FEDCO as the overall broker. In effect, no eggs were to be sold in that Province except through FEDCO. A price for eggs to the retailer was established, and FEDCO announced it would buy from sources both inside and outside the province.

This system ran into considerable difficulties. At times the price set by FEDCO was 14 cents a dozen higher than in Ontario. Even after the difference was cut to four or five cents, "bootlegged" sales directly to retailers from outside the province were encouraged by this difference, by the 12 cents per dozen fee charged by FEDCO, and by a growing surplus of eggs in Ontario and Manitoba. (Excluded here are certain cartoned eggs which were permitted by FEDCO to be shipped directly from producers in Ontario to retailers in Quebec). It should be added that in May, 1971, the parent board of FEDCO, the Quebec Marketing Board, was given power to seize bootleg eggs, and provision was made for fines. Only a minority of the eggs sold in Quebec appear to have gone through FEDCO. These difficulties in administering this scheme in one province coincided with a severe price war and a glut of eggs in other supplier provinces.

The Quebec legislation was unsuccessfully challenged in the Quebec Superior Court by the Quebec Food Council. The Government of Manitoba subsequently mounted a challenge by submitting regulations, alleged to be similar to those then in existence in Quebec, to the Manitoba Court of Appeal. The regulations were declared *ultra vires* by that court and, on appeal, by the Supreme Court of Canada in a judgment dated June 28, 1971.

At the same time, a similar set of problems arose in the market for broiler chickens, that is, birds weighing three to five pounds. Since 1965 the Ontario Broiler Chicken Producers Marketing Board has set production quotas for all producers, based on their immediate past production, as well as prices to producers. While this has regulated supply within the province it could not protect Ontario producers from out-of-province producers, notably those in Quebec. In other words, the provincial production quota system could work only so long as major retailers did not substantially increase their out-of-province imports from any cheaper source. In Quebec there was no such marketing board until recently. Production expanded rapidly in Quebec, particularly during

Expo, and Quebec became the largest producer of broilers in Canada. Given the attempt by other provinces to maintain producer prices, the freedom from such limitations in Quebec, and some comparative advantage in broiler production, Quebec producers were able to make significant inroads into the market in eastern Ontario simply by pricing slightly lower. In March 1970, the Ontario broiler board significantly increased production quotas in an attempt to stem the inflow and to recapture some of the eastern Ontario market. Quebec producers responded in kind and prices were reduced to, or below, production costs. In September 1970, the Ontario government gave the producers board the power to require permits for retail sales and stickers of approval for imported birds. The board could ask the removal of birds, and provision was made for fines.

During the last six months of 1970, restrictions on interprovincial trade in poultry and eggs proliferated across Canada as some governments alleged that others were operating provincial regulations in a discriminatory fashion with respect to out-of-province shipments, and as prices declined and supplies rose. These controls, in brief, prohibited the sale of out-of-province products within the province unless such sales were covered by a permit issued by the local board and the product bore identification tags. By February of 1971, seven provinces had such regulations for broilers, three had regulations for turkeys, and four had regulations for eggs.[2]

These orders had effectively reduced, and in most cases stopped, the interprovincial movement of eggs or poultry meat. The negative effects on provincial prices of this backup in supplies, combined with the continuance of some interprovincial shipments, subsequently led to further tightening of controls on interprovincial trade. Some broilers continued to be shipped from Quebec to Ontario without permit, for example. In April 1971, the *Ontario Farm Products Marketing Act* was amended so that the marketing board could authorize local boards for a particular agricultural product to seize products imported without a permit. The Ontario broiler board was so authorized, and did exercise this power. In the meantime, Quebec broiler producers, like poultry and egg producers elsewhere, experienced large surpluses and price decreases as a result of their inability to export to other provinces. They responded by forming a broiler producers marketing board with production controls at least as strict as those in Ontario.

Beginning with the summer and fall of 1971, the situation improved somewhat, partly as a result of efforts at interprovincial agreement. With the passage of the *National Farm Products Marketing Act* in January 1972, attention focused on negotiations to establish national marketing agencies for poultry and eggs.

In the case of eggs, the establishment of the Canadian Egg Marketing Agency was proclaimed in December 1972 under the *Farm Products*

Marketing Agencies Act and became operational on June 1st, 1973. The establishment of the agency received approval in principle by all provincial marketing boards except that of Newfoundland which was awaiting the report of a Royal Commission on its egg industry. Newfoundland officially joined the plan on May 10, 1973. In April 1973, the Government of Ontario announced that there would be a new Egg Marketing Board in that province to allocate among Ontario producers the provincial egg quota proposed under the national scheme. The national plan involves supply management of eggs based on a five year average of production. Eggs will move freely between the provinces on two conditions, viz: first, eggs moving out of a province must be within the allowed provincial allocation; second, such eggs must not be priced below the price in the province of origin plus cost of transportation. In June 1973, one province, however, had not yet implemented the provincial part of the federal-provincial agreement of the egg plan due to that province's desire for further study and clarification of particular aspects of the national plan.

The experience with agriculture points to three general issues of interest to this paper—the economic, the administrative, and the constitutional issues. The economic issue is the desire to ensure that the incomes of agricultural producers are sustained in an industry when prices are highly variable because there are many producers and output can often be expanded rapidly. This producer interest has to be reconciled with a consumer interest which calls for reasonable stability of supply at prices which reflect the rapid advance of technology in this industry and, in particular, the opportunity for specialization and exchange which a common market in Canada presents.

The administrative question is that of most efficiently achieving these objectives in cases where a departure from free market techniques is desired. A variety of techniques are available if farm marketing, production and pricing schemes are used, techniques which have quite different effects on prices, production, and any net subsidies involved. There are also alternative or related methods, such as direct income supplements to particular groups of producers, or agricultural and regional development schemes.

Whatever the preferred technique or combination of techniques, it is clear that independent action by provincial boards is self-defeating and poses serious constitutional questions at times. The restrictions on interprovincial shipment of eggs and poultry aggravated efficient producers' problems as surpluses accumulated. In such cases, consumers temporarily enjoy lower prices but pay more as efficient production from other provinces is blocked. In the long-run both producers and consumers lose as the market becomes fragmented and the scope for specialization and efficiency is severely narrowed.

It is true that each province has the constitutional power to regulate its internal market so long as it does not discriminate between provincial and interprovincial sales or regulate interprovincial trade as such. The problem, as with international trade, is that it is extremely difficult at times to determine whether discrimination is taking place. There are many ways in which a provincial marketing board could discriminate in favour of its producers while appearing to meet the letter of a constitutional requirement against discrimination. It could require a grading system for eggs, for example, which differed from that used by other provinces, thus requiring some regrading and resorting for at least some of the eggs moving into its market. It could require that a different grade of paper be used to package the imported eggs. It could require that imported eggs be stamped, preferably egg by egg and with a heavy stamp. Some of these devices would be unconstitutional, but it is not difficult to imagine many others and it is often a problem to determine whether they are being used in a discriminatory way in practice.

DIRECT CONTROLS IN GENERAL

The problem posed can be considered with regard to direct controls in general, for it raises questions beyond the agricultural industry.[3] Assume that provincial governments operate direct controls in their given "internal" markets by controlling or subsidizing the prices of the products concerned or by limiting in one of a variety of ways the amounts to be produced or consumed. If one province subsidizes a product more heavily than the others, and assuming the product is otherwise freely exchanged, that province will tend to be a more attractive locale for production of the product. Of course, there are many other reasons for locating production in one setting rather than in another, but the point is not obviated thereby. Similarly, a province would have considerable difficulty in maintaining the price for a product by restricting the output of its producers if the producers of other provinces were free to produce without regulation and to ship into the first province. The less regulated or more competitive structure of the other provinces' industries would tend to impose itself on the first which would then be drawn to provincial import controls. Such differences in direct control mechanisms, given the differences in (and effects on) competitive power, can lead to endless complications for products which are cheaply transported; this is particularly the case where supply is rapidly expanded and where technical change is also rapid. There can also be complications in the international trade in such products as a result.

To be consistent with the common market, the province which regulates the internal market for such traded products would have to impose any price or production controls, or marketing techniques, equally on provincial and extraprovincial sources.[4] As noted above, it is often extremely difficult in practice to know whether a particular marketing or production program is discriminatory. There are endless variations in pricing practices, packaging, marking, grading, delivery requirements, and so on, whose relative effects on provincial and out-of-province producers may be almost impossible to determine. If the policy is non-discriminatory, however, the provincial marketing agency would be supporting the output and incomes of non-provincial producers. Let us assume that the province decides to go ahead on a truly non-discriminatory basis in spite of this. If the province was producing 70 per cent of its consumption of a product and importing 30 per cent from a second province, it could impose quotas which kept imports at 30 per cent of consumption. It could also follow other practices—there are many, depending on the product—to be consistent with this. There are innumerable problems the province would run into, assuming it had got this far. For one thing, technical changes (broadly construed) in the industry may not fall equally on the two regions over time, so that the 30 per cent quota on imports may look low or high. This change could be swift where technical change is rapid. It seems unlikely that the quotas would be changed to reflect this with any speed, especially if the relative change in efficiency favoured more imports. For another, if the marketing and pricing techniques of the exporting province differ, they could affect the relative competitive power of that province's producers and thus put pressure on the quota. Third, market effects could affect supply and prices in either province with spillover effects into the other. Given borders which are otherwise free and a widespread location of many producing and distributing units so that intraprovincial surveillance is difficult, bootlegging will spread, as will the pressure to increase surveillance both on the border and internally.

It seems apparent that a provincial quota scheme, or its equivalent, and the attendant production and/or pricing schemes are unlikely to work well unless other provinces also have them. Otherwise, there is a constant temptation for producers elsewhere to undermine the price structure. If other provinces have different schemes in terms of pricing effects, similar problems arise in practice. Thus, if marketing schemes with production or pricing controls are to be introduced for any given product, a national scheme seems the only workable alternative. In a national scheme, moreover, it is easier to attempt to reconcile consumer and producer interests to the ultimate benefit of both. Regional specialization in the larger market permits each area to achieve efficient scale in products where it has or can develop production, while ensuring its consumers of low prices. Given a national scheme, it is true that a particular region may not be more self-sufficient in some products but it can achieve larger markets in others. It is also true that problems of adjustment will persist for some of the producers involved, but both federal

438 / Policy Making and Canadian Federalism

and provincial governments are able to provide assistance to such producers.

It bears emphasis that there is a larger issue here which has to be faced squarely in any scheme, whether federal or federal-provincial. There is a distinction between regulation (as distinct from a free market solution) whose purpose is to achieve an efficient allocation of resources and regulation whose purpose is to reinforce a purely provincial market. For products which are easily transportable, the latter amounts to a denial of a common market for goods, whether it is achieved by federal regulation alone, by federal-provincial regulation, or by the federal government permitting or empowering others to regulate. Whatever the other objectives of regulation, one should keep clearly in mind the need for an efficient allocation of production within the common market, rather than simply within provincial borders.

Whatever the prospects with respect to agriculture or other industries, the overall relevance to the common market in goods should be emphasized. The problems have arisen essentially because of unwillingness to permit a competitive outcome in resource allocation, plus inability to mount an effective nationwide regulatory scheme where regulation is preferred. The effect is to put a heavy load on government-to-government negotiation and on the achievement of continuing consistency of divergent provincial schemes as economic conditions change. Once the need for consistency of regulatory schemes is recognized for products which are substantially traded interprovincially, and which in fact form a common market, the case for federal regulation has been made in terms of effectiveness of policy.

If some of the non-tariff restrictions noted in this section are to be avoided, it may be necessary to have stronger statement via section 121 of the *B.N.A. Act* on the unacceptability of barriers to internal trade. However, this is essentially a passive statement against barriers. If the state is to play a regulatory role where this is deemed desirable, it would be a mistake simply to leave the matter there; indeed, merely strengthening 121 could reduce the regulatory powers of the state. The preceding comments suggest that the federal government should also have a stronger trade and commerce role, or the equivalent in some other sections of the written constitution, if the state is not to be incapacitated in its regulatory role. A stronger federal role will ensure that such policies are more likely to be effective. Since the federal government has a country-wide constituency, it can be expected in such areas of trade and commerce to favour policies which are directed to the efficiency of the overall common market. It will also help assure, as noted earlier, that such policies of regulation are not inconsistent with effective federal action in foreign trade policy. Finally, it will reduce the temptation, and perhaps the necessity, which now exists with divided jurisdiction to place the focal points for regulation at provincial borders. This often makes little sense where economic regions overlap provincial borders. It also tends indirectly to preserve the provincial markets for trade which Confederation was intended to enlarge.

NOTES

[1] Bill C-176, referred to as the *Farm Products Marketing Agencies Act.*

[2] These figures do not include the Quebec egg plan and the special egg regulations in Manitoba which were a test of these plans.

[3] See J. E. Meade, H. H. Liesner, and S. J. Wells, *Case Studies in European Economic Union* (London, Oxford University Press, 1962) Introduction and pp. 102-128, for an analysis of this point in the context of Benelux in particular.

[4] This might still be unconstitutional, however, since it could be taken as regulation of interprovincial trade.

PART VI
QUEBEC
AND CONFEDERATION

29

Scenarios for Separation*

Richard Simeon

*Regardless of the discords among political parties, regardless
of the often only half-concealed interests of certain classes of
society, regardless of the deep emotional fear of risk, it appears
indisputable that Quebec is heading down a one-way street to
sovereignty.*

Jean Blain, in the Preface to René Lévesque, *An Option
for Quebec*

Let us assume for the moment that Jean Blain is right. Let us assume that
separation of Quebec from the rest of Canada is inevitable and the
moves towards it irreversible. The question then immediately arises:
How might it come about? How do two complex societies which have
been associated in a federal union for more than a hundred years go
about the difficult process of disengagement? Can it be done peacefully,
without bloodshed—or will it inevitably lead to bitterness, mutual reprisals, or even war? And, since the two societies will continue to share the
northern half of the continent, will they be able to work out some stable
relationship which will govern their future? These are a few of the
central questions which guide this essay.

They are not idle or mischievous questions. Separation is no longer
a remote possibility advocated by a small group of militants. It is a
respectable political movement. It may well succeed. If this is the case,
then English Canadians must begin to ask themselves some difficult
questions and think seriously about how it might happen. Only by
doing this will they be able to retain some control over events. In asking
these questions I am not assuming that separation is inevitable, much
less that it is desirable. But by thinking about them, perhaps both sides
can gain some insight into what is at stake and how relations could be
conducted through what would be, at best, a difficult process.

One way to approach the problem is to sketch out some alternative
scenarios about disengagement. We cannot predict with any certainty at
all what might happen, but we can suggest the range of possible results
and reactions, given certain assumptions about reality. The discussion,
then, will be hypothetical and speculative. The reader will undoubtedly
be able to think of other scenarios and of variations on the ones presented here.

Most broadly, let us consider two scenarios.

* From R. M. Burns (ed.), *One Country or Two?* (Montreal: McGill-Queen's University
Press, 1971), pp. 73-94. Reprinted by permission.

1. Separation and sovereign status can be negotiated amicably; English Canada and Quebec will, after separation has been achieved, continue to co-operate and will indeed create a mutually advantageous "Canadian Union," with a common market and joint overall economic policies.

   This we will call the optimistic scenario. Its main proponent is the leader of the Parti Québécois, René Lévesque, and it is most fully developed in his book, *An Option for Quebec*.

2. Separation and sovereign status cannot be achieved peaceably. English Canadians will not tolerate it, and are likely to use force to prevent it. Quebec, whether successful or not, is likely to become a Fascist state. If separation is achieved, future relations will be hostile and non-co-operative. Mutual reprisals will replace peaceful negotiation. Economic relations will be similar to those between the United States and Cuba. This is the most pessimistic scenario. It predicts something approaching civil war. Bits and pieces of it have been suggested many times, but it has never been spelled out in complete detail.

Between these two extremes, a range of other possibilities exist. But let us deal with these two, and examine the assumptions that underlie them. Can we say anything at all about the conditions which might make one or the other the more likely scenario? Can we, indeed, suggest strategies by the leaders of either side which will enhance the chances for one or other possibility?

In order to evaluate the optimistic and pessimistic scenarios, a great number of relevant factors must be considered. Few, if any, can at this stage be delineated with any degree of certainty. Broadly, there would be three stages in the disengagement process. The first is the "pre-separation stage"; it includes all events leading up to the decision by Quebec to separate. The second is the separation stage itself; it focuses on the immediate actions and reactions of the participants after the decision has been made. Third is the post-separation phase. Assuming the achievement of separation, this stage involves the working out of a fairly stable set of relationships which will govern the parties for the future. The events at each stage will be greatly affected by the preceding ones; to a great extent each will determine the future ones. As a result, the initial stage leading up to separation is the most crucial: it will set a pattern of expectations by both sides which will likely be difficult to change.

At each step, a slightly different set of factors will be most important. They can be laid out as follows:

In the pre-separation stage, what will be the developments in Quebec leading to separation? Will the final decision result from a long, gradual, cumulative process, or will the break be brief and abrupt? How will the decision to separate be made: by referendum, by an Act of the legislature, by a *coup*, or in some other way? What will be the overall goals of the Separatists: primarily a symbolic disengagement, or a total and complete break with the rest of Canada? Equally important will be the goals and attitudes of the Separatists on a number of other matters, such as treatment of English Canadians and English-Canadian business in the province. It will also be important to know how united the French-Canadian population will be, and how strong the authority of the government is.

Answers to these questions will, in turn, affect the responses of English Canadians to the act of separation. Of particular importance are questions like these: What will be the reactions of ordinary citizens to the event, and what pressures or demands will they make on the government leaders? What will be the reactions of non-governmental élites such as newspapers, businessmen, interest groups, and the like? How will the governmental authorities react?

In the separation stage, we ask what the immediate actions by each side are. How do the French-Canadian leaders conduct themselves, and what reactions does this provoke on the part of English Canadians? Again there are several factors to be considered here. Are there incentives for both sides to take "hard" positions; and, conversely, are there incentives to promote agreement? What kinds of bargaining resources does each side possess? What are the levels of hostility or co-operativeness, trust and distrust between leaders of each side? What are the actual issues to be negotiated? And, finally, how do third parties like the United States or France behave?

Continuing relationships in the post-separation stage will depend primarily on what has gone before; though other immediate factors may well enter into the process—for example, whether there was an economic depression in either of the separated sides, or whether the pressures for disintegration and dismemberment grew within the truncated English-Canadian remainder of the federation.

This is simply a skeleton framework; we need now to put some flesh on it, and attempt to draw out some of the relationships among the various factors involved.

Both the optimistic and pessimistic scenarios make assumptions about the factors mentioned above. Let us first examine the option advocated by the Parti Québécois. René Lévesque believes strongly that independent status for Quebec can be achieved without severe conflict, in a peaceful and orderly way. Moreover, he argues that the achievement of sovereign status for Quebec will be *mutually beneficial* for both sides. This is because, he argues, the present federal system effectively frustrates both Quebec in its aspirations for control over its own destiny, and English Canada in its desire for "simplifying, rationalizing and centralizing." Continuing the existing federal regime makes mounting conflict and hostility inevitable; the two majorities "will inevitably collide with one another repeatedly and with greater and greater force causing hurts that would finally be irreparable." "Tomorrow," he writes, "English Canada would be grateful to Quebec for bringing it [separation] about."

In addition, of course, Mr. Lévesque does not envision a total separation of Quebec from the rest of Canada. Instead, there would be an association of the two countries, which would include common currency and monetary systems, a common market and co-ordination of fiscal policies. A cynic might say that Lévesque's plan is not so very different from the present state of affairs—and certainly no different from many of the projects for *statut particulier*—with the exception that in the future Quebec would possess all the symbols of sovereignty.

The pre-separation phase of the separation process under the Lévesque option would be relatively peaceful and democratic. The decision to separate, itself, would be achieved through legitimate constitutional means. He expects that in a short time Quebec will elect to the *Assemblée nationale* leaders pledged to establish a sovereign Quebec. Once in office, the new government will not immediately declare independence. There would instead be a three-year transition period, during which, presumably, there would be negotiations between Quebec and English Canada. In these discussions, Quebec would combine "unshakeable firmness with a polite insistence on speaking calmly." During this period too, Lévesque expects English Canadians would undergo a period of "psychological development" by which they would come to accept the inevitable and thus be willing to "sit at the same table without too great a gap between us." It would therefore be possible to negotiate peacefully the "contract of Association." Both parties in these negotiations would have an incentive to agree: Quebec would not want to lose the benefits of economic association with Canada; Canada would not want to lose the Quebec market, or risk disruption of its basic economic and monetary system. It also seems clear from Lévesque's arguments that Quebec's economic policy would not greatly threaten existing investments and economic arrangements, thus limiting the danger of major opposition from economic interests. Similarly, Lévesque has made fairly clear that the political form of a sovereign Quebec would not likely be repugnant to most English-Canadian values. Lévesque himself—though there are major differences of opinion within his movement—would also not provoke deep English-Canadian hostility through denying rights of English Canadians and other minorities in Quebec. Thus, Lévesque's "optimistic scenario" can be summed up: The decision to separate is made in an orderly, democratic fashion; it is broadly accepted as a legitimate decision by English-Canadian authorities; the Quebec government would have general support from the population, and would be accepted by it; the goals of the independent government would be moderate, in terms of the degree of separation envisaged, in terms of the kind of political philosophy and institutions which will be developed, and in the tactics used to achieve separation. This scenario also assumes certain patterns of English-Canadian reaction. There may be cries for reprisal and forcible prevention of granting sovereignty, but these will be controlled. Gradually, English Canadians will become reconciled to the idea of an independent Quebec, and, indeed, will even come to see the advantage in it. Thus, governmental authorities will react in a moderate way.

In the second stage, therefore, they will be willing to negotiate with Quebec. Both sides will have strong incentives to reach agreement, on both political and economic grounds. It is assumed there will be few pressures or incentives to take hard or inflexible positions. There will be little overt hostility and much desire to co-operate. There will be many issues to be negotiated; Lévesque does not spell them out, but does assume they can be negotiated successfully. He assumes no third party involvement by the United States, France, or other countries. As a result, the two independent countries will move into the post-separation phase with a high degree of co-operation in a wide variety of fields, and a stable relationship, beneficial to both sides, will emerge.

This analysis rests on some central assumptions. The most important are those to do with the reaction of English Canadians. According to Lévesque, English Canadians will generally admit the legitimacy and even the desirability of separation, and will therefore accept it with some equanimity and be willing to negotiate peacefully towards some mutually agreeable set of future relationships. The fact that close relations would continue should mean a diminished English-Canadian opposition. The validity of the assumption depends largely on the nature of the blow to English Canadians that separation would pose. It seems likely that at first the blow would be primarily a psychological and symbolic one; it would not immediately (if ever) mean a great lowering of economic well-being among English Canadians; probably few would be materially put out, especially if economic partnership were worked out.

But if one assumes the blow is primarily psychological, what happens materially would not matter much. What would matter is a much more emotional reaction. Thus, even if separation were a symbolic recognition of what Quebec had already achieved, and meant no real change in the *status quo*, it might still be violently objected to. The dilemma in this is that, in a sense, what French Canadians seek most, at least in the Lévesque formulation, is a symbolic freedom—and that may well be the hardest thing for English Canadians to give. The symbolic blow of separation would revolve primarily around the question of failure. National identity in Canada is a tenuous phenomenon, but at least we can assume it means some commitment to an entity, Canada, which is defined as a certain territory; to break up that territory would represent the breaking of one of the few distinctive elements of the national identity. For some other English Canadians the psychological blow might also represent defeat. If one of the defining characteristics of Canada is the attempt to build a binational, bicultural society, it would obviously be almost impossible to accept even a symbolic break.

This symbolic opposition could be especially strong among English-Canadian intellectuals. This is because the evidence seems to suggest that it is the more educated who most tend to think in abstract symbolic terms, and to be concerned with matters like national identity and ideology. The greater concern of the intellectual élites, however, may well be tempered by an equal commitment to non-violence, self-determination, and other abstract values which might lead them to grant greater legitimacy to Quebec's decision. Thus, again, we get back to the importance of the manner in which separation takes place and whether the ground is prepared over a long period.

If the suggestion that opposition to the act of separation would be more psychological than material is right, then Lévesque's assumption that future material-economic relationships could be negotiated with ease is also called into question. This is true even if it is in some hypothetical sense materially to the advantage of the English Canadians to do so. This is because the perception of whether there is something to be gained or not from a negotiation, how the issues are to be defined, and so on, depends only partly on the "real" objective situation. At least, it depends equally on much more subjective considerations. The analysis of whether or not there would be mutual advantages in a common market, common currency, and so on would be, at best, a highly technical exercise with a great many uncertainties and a great many dubious assumptions to be considered. In such an uncertain situation, the role of subjective perceptions becomes even more important. Thus, even if it could be said that "objectively" it would be to English Canada's advantage to negotiate the arrangements that Lévesque contemplates, it may well be that many English Canadians would be unable to perceive the advantages. Or, if a negotiated arrangement would help English Canada a bit and French Canada a lot, there could still be the feeling that discussion would constitute "selling out to the French," even if in formal, rational terms it would still be to English Canada's advantage to negotiate an agreement. It is therefore unlikely that the calculations of gains and benefits from various types of negotiations would take place on purely material-economic grounds.

Opposition based on symbolic factors would probably vary considerably among different groups. For example, it might well be much stronger among intellectuals than, say, among businessmen, with a different set of criteria to consider. The position of economic élites would depend very heavily on what economic policies a sovereign Quebec intended to pursue. Similarly, opposition might be less among government officials who can perceive (because of their perspective and information) more clearly the consequences of non-agreement.

Assuming the decision to separate is made along the lines Lévesque suggests, and English Canadians do indeed decide to negotiate its achievement peacefully, how might these negotiations take place, and with what results? Are they likely to lead to an acceptable outcome, or to breakdown and deadlock? Many difficulties would arise, but there are some strong grounds for believing that arrangements could be worked out, though they would probably not be as advantageous to Free Quebec as M. Lévesque expects. How might they develop?

First, Lévesque correctly asserts that each side would have strong motivations to develop at least some minimally co-operative arrangements. Like it or not, both are, and will continue to be, part of a single economic system, and both share contiguous territory, joint river basins, and so on. The incentives to negotiate in good faith would be of several kinds. Both sides would probably share a moral and cultural desire to avoid armed conflict. Both would probably agree on the desirability of keeping third parties from becoming involved in the dispute, since that would probably threaten the independence of both. English Canadians would have a strong incentive to ensure the equitable treatment of English-speaking minorities in Quebec; Quebeckers would have similar feelings about French-speaking minorities elsewhere. Then there would be economic incentives. English-Canadian capitalists with fixed holdings in Quebec would greatly wish to prevent loss or destruction of their property (the threat to do that would be a powerful bargaining tool for Quebec, and armed intervention would only increase that danger); English-Canadian industry, especially in Ontario and the Maritimes, would not wish to threaten markets in Quebec. Even if English Canada could survive economically without Quebec, there would be dislocations and uncertainties which they would want to minimize. English Canadians would also be anxious to maintain rail and water links with the Maritimes.

On the Quebec side, too, there would be even stronger economic motivations to agree. It seems fairly clear that Quebec needs the North American market, more than the North American market needs Quebec. Thus, in federal-provincial relations, the Quebec position has already been moderated somewhat by the harsh imperatives of the investment market. If separation were to come about, the same economic pressures would exist.

The disincentives for negotiating differences would stem primarily from the symbolic problem mentioned earlier. English Canadians might argue that the negotiation was one-sided—that they could only lose. Or, if there were mutual advantages to be gained, as seems likely, they might not admit or perceive them. Similarly, many elements in Quebec might oppose negotiation, since meaningful bargaining implies making concessions. If these concessions were felt to limit significantly the degree of sovereignty achieved, they might be strongly opposed. Certainly a condition for the Quebec negotiators would be a basic acceptance of Quebec sovereignty by English Canadians.

But let us assume that relations between the two sides are not so strained as to make negotiations impossible, and that the incentives to find agreement outweigh pressures to disagree. What issues would have to be negotiated? The list would be very long, including, to mention only a few examples, the rights and guarantees of English-speaking minorities in Quebec, and, to a lesser extent, French-Canadian minorities outside Quebec; the status and future of English-owned corporations located in Quebec; links with the Maritimes; trade relations; monetary arrangements and the machinery for fiscal co-operation; and the disposal of federal property in Quebec. Thus, there would be a great deal on the table; we could expect very lengthy discussions since the process of disengaging, even partially as the Lévesque model implies, would be a complex, lengthy process. However, this very length and complexity might well make agreement easier in the long run. Agreement on some matters at the early stage would undoubtedly make agreement on later issues easier. The large number of issues, with complex variations within each, would allow the possibility of considerable trading of concessions both within and between issues, as Mr. Jordan's paper shows for only one—the future of the St. Lawrence system.[1] In addition, on very complex issues winning and losing become much less clear-cut, with a greater possibility that both sides could feel they have "won" and that conflict on them would be blurred.

Another important factor that would help shape the negotiations is the climate and institutional setting in which they took place. We have already suggested that negotiation at all is possible only when both sides are willing; more broadly, it will probably take place only if the separation process itself is amicable, and only if English Canadians accept the basic premise—that Quebec should be a sovereign state. Presumably that would not be a negotiable issue. Similarly, the more legitimate the goals of the Quebec government in the eyes of English Canadians, the better the climate will be. In any circumstances, the climate of the negotiations is likely to be severely strained; negotiations can still take place, however, as long as both sides perceive possible advantages.

Equally important is the institutional setting. We could expect agreement to be much more difficult if there were no relatively agreed, clear-cut forum and procedures for working it out. It would also be more difficult if either side were disorganized, and did not have a spokesman who was accepted as legitimate both by his own society and by the other side. In fact, of course, existing federal-provincial negotiating machinery suggests a model that could well be followed with very little modification in the negotiations about separation. The recognized form of these negotiations is government-to-government bargaining in a quasi-diplomatic way. The major spokesmen for provincial interests are provincial governments, rather than, say, provincial party activists, federal Senators or federal MPs. In addition, a striking characteristic of ethnic conflict in Canada is that it has usually taken the form of conflict between governments rather than direct conflict between individuals. It may be expected that these precedents would continue in the negotiation of separation, and that they would facilitate finding agreement. There would, of course be some important problems with the existing machinery—what role, for example, would the English-Canadian provinces wish to play? They have been suspicious of bilateral negotiations between Ottawa and Quebec in the past, but it seems reasonable to believe that in the kind of national crisis that separation implies, provincial governments would rally to the federal government and would consider it the logical spokesman and bargainer for English Canada. Again, however, there could well be some differences among the provinces. Another factor which would affect the chances of a successful negotiation is the degree of unity on each side. If there were wide disagreement about the appropriate attitude toward the Quebec decision and about the most desirable goals and tactics to be used, the authority of the spokesman at the bargaining table might be limited. A likely development would be for the officials of both Quebec and Ottawa to be pressed towards harder positions by extremists—by French Canadians arguing for a more complete break and impatient with protracted negotiations; by English Canadians unwilling to accept the fact of separation itself and pushing for a punitive line. The pressures would, in one sense, strengthen the bargaining power of the participants in the negotiations ("I cannot concede to you because my constituents would revolt"), but, in another sense, they would obviously make agreement much harder, even if the authorities on both sides wished it. Assuming the latter, it then becomes very important to know how effectively the negotiators are able to manage and contain opinion with their respective constituencies.

Recent manifestations of widespread social tensions within Quebec call into question the likelihood that the Quebec government would have complete authority within the province. Separation itself could have the effect of rallying and unifying Quebec opinion. But it could have the opposite effect, too. And disagreements within the population could grow rapidly if wages dropped, unemployment rose, and so on. The social mobilization of recent years which has increased nationalist demands in Quebec has also increased internal cleavages and disagreements. These could well severely complicate negotiations between the two sides. So, of course, would a separation achieved by leaders who are also radical socialists. Such a development might not only preclude any agreement between French and English Canadians, but also lead to great internal conflicts in which some French Canadians might well call on English-Canadian aid to put down the Revolution. There are strong elements of such a scenario in the reactions of the Quebec and Montreal governments to the FLQ kidnappings.

Another factor affecting the course of negotiations once begun is the amount of political resources, or bargaining power, available to each side. Both would have considerable levers to employ, but it seems likely that English Canada would be in a stronger bargaining position. It would always possess the threat of physical violence—even though its use would be costly and probably repugnant to most English Canadians. It could also pose a series of other threats which Quebec would have trouble countering, such as economic blockade. Clearly, English Canada would be in a much stronger position to use these kinds of tactics than Quebec. Paradoxically, indeed, English Canada might find itself in a stronger bargaining position after separation than it is in present negotiations with Quebec.

Today, Quebec's bargaining power is partly based on its being the only province which can make any sort of credible threat to break up the country. Any federal government with maintenance of national unity as a major goal is then motivated to make concessions on many substantive issues. This was clearly evident during the Pearson years. It has been less obvious since 1968, partly because a French-Canadian prime minister can challenge Quebec government leaders' claims to be sole "representatives" of the French Canadians. Nevertheless, even since 1968, it is obvious that a great many federal policies have been modified in advance to accommodate the Quebec position. But with separation already a fact, Quebec's ultimate threat would be removed.

English Canada would also probably have stronger support in the international community, especially from the United States. Probably more important is the fact that in a real bargaining situation French Canada would need to establish "normal" relations and economic partnerships with English Canada more than English Canada would with Quebec. Quebec would have both more to gain from negotiations and more to lose; it would thus be motivated to make many concessions to English-Canadian interests, though always, of course, short of giving up the claim to sovereignty itself. Breaking off the talks might hurt English Canada; it would hurt Quebec more.

Quebec, of course, would not be powerless; its resources would stem from possession of several things desirable to English Canadians, especially control over English minorities, access to the Maritimes, possession of national governmental assets, and English-Canadian industry. This pattern of resource distribution should ensure both that the parties would be motivated to seek agreement and that each would be prepared to make concessions. But it also suggests that, given English Canada's acquiescence on the basic issue of Quebec's sovereignty, and given a willingness on both sides to negotiate, English Canada would be able to negotiate a set of future relationships which would achieve most of its major goals, and which would probably come closer to English Canada's desires than to Quebec's.

What that end-point would be is unclear. For Lévesque it is a common market, common monetary system, and co-operative fiscal policy, with decisions being truly joint. If the analysis above is correct, these mechanisms, while benefiting Quebec, would also operate substantially to the advantage of English Canada, especially Ontario and the Maritimes. With its bargaining strength, English Canada might, for example, retain a preponderant weight in determining the major joint economic policies.

In addition, following the assumption of a peaceful attainment of separation and of a subsequent peaceful and successful negotiation, we could assume that much of the existing economic interdependence between the two countries would be retained. At the governmental policy level, there would be co-ordination. At the private economic level, with free movement of population, goods, and investment, there is no necessary reason why there should be much change from the *status quo*. True, there might be initial flight of capital from Quebec, but a moderate government, coupled with successful negotiations, could presumably recover it. At another level, too, the societies would remain highly interdependent. Just as the Canadian government now is unable to introduce many policies which differ radically from policies within the United States, so the Quebec government would find itself constrained by English Canada. The policies of both countries would continue to have important spill-over effects, though, of course, there would be freedom for some variations in policy. Thus, the likely outcome under Lévesque's scenario is only a very partial disengagement—a disengagement at the political level, without much disengagement in the complex structures of the modern state.

However, one should not use the word "merely" in describing this outcome. The model would be very similar to the existing relationship between Canada and the United States, where Canada's freedom in economic and other policies is strictly limited, and where, in the private economy, Canada and the U.S. are essentially one. But this does not necessarily mean that what differences remain are trivial. Indeed, the

Canada-United States experience shows that questions of political sovereignty and economic relationships are only very indirectly related. For example, while a very large majority of Canadians maintain the desirability of political separation from the U.S., much smaller numbers argue for a severing of the economic ties. The one can and does exist without the other. Canadian political sovereignty is a real, meaningful, and satisfying concept to most Canadians: few would argue that because we exist interdependently with the United States in so many other ways, this political distinctiveness should be abolished, though many of us wish Canada did have more freedom of action. Indeed, Canadians are even willing to pay a substantial price in purely material terms to maintain this difference.

I believe exactly the same analysis could apply to Quebec. Maintaining close ties in overall policy-making, as well as in other spheres, would not render Quebec sovereignty trivial, and need not vitiate its satisfaction for French Canadians. Symbolic change *is* real change. If this is true, then a negotiated set of arrangements for future relationships could probably work well for a considerable period. A major exception could arise if the relationship seemed to work systematically to the disadvantage of Quebec, with rapidly increasing gaps between the standards of living in the two societies, for example. The less existing economic relationships are disturbed, the less likely this is to happen. Thus, a successful set of negotiations in the immediate post-separation phase would be crucial. If they set up workable institutions and left much room for continued economic interdependence, future relations would likely continue to be amicable, and, indeed, co-operation could well increase. If, on the other hand, the negotiations failed, or if the outcome were a set of arrangements which systematically favoured English Canada, the gaps between the two societies would increase, resentment in Quebec would grow, and so would the likelihood of steadily increasing animosity and increased degree of separation.

To summarize, the Lévesque scenario is a plausible and persuasive one. It *is* possible to envision a situation in which Quebec's decision to separate was accepted—albeit with reluctance and with many areas of opposition—by English Canadians. If this is the case, it is also possible to envision a series of negotiations that would be to the advantage of both sides, that would result in some form of "Canadian Association." One can predict with some plausibility how these negotiations might be carried out and what the outcome might be. The separation, in Lévesque's case, would not be total. But it would be a severe blow—psychologically more than materially—to English Canada. The key question, assuming a certain legitimate process leading to a decision to separate by Quebec, is just how strong a blow to English Canada this would be—for that is what would determine the initial and vital reaction.

At the 1968 Constitutional Conference, Prime Minister Pearson suggested it was unrealistic to believe that English Canada would be willing to sit down with a Quebec which had just declared itself independent:

> I should like to say merely two things. The first is a comment on the suggestion that has been made that if Quebec were to secede, it could then enter into negotiations with Ottawa in order to work out a *modus vivendi* with the rest of Canada while acquiring its own independent sovereignty. As someone not without experience in international negotiations, I should like to state frankly my own view that any such proposal rests on an illusion; indeed on a whole set of illusions. Surely it is an illusion to think that a declared intention . . . to seek a disputed divorce can be the basis of amicable and productive negotiations, especially when the parties concerned would still be living in the same house or as next-door neighbours. It may even be an illusion to think that in such circumstances there would necessarily be an "Ottawa" which could speak for the whole of English-speaking Canada.

But the possibility that a *modus vivendi* could emerge does not appear wholly illusory. To pursue Mr. Pearson's analogy, one can imagine an originally disputed divorce in which even the reluctant party decided the costs of continuing the marriage were not worth the effort, and that "for the children's sake" an amicable solution would be preferable. Or the party which wanted the divorce could make life in the family so miserable that the partner would cry "enough!" Lévesque indeed suggests something like this: that Quebec could persuade English Canada of the moral virtue of its desire, and that increasingly severe clashes under present federal-provincial arrangements would make continued federation seem less and less attractive. In addition, one can propose that while the negotiations undoubtedly would not be very amicable, they could be productive if both sides believed that they would gain by avoiding direct conflict. It is precisely because the two entities "live in the same house" that there would be the greatest pressures to arrange an accommodation.

Finally, though the question of the likelihood of disintegration of English Canada is not a central concern of this paper, it seems probable that, for the short-run at least, Ottawa would remain the spokesman for the rest of the country. Again, a desire to keep the country together might be an incentive to work out an agreement with Quebec.

Thus, Mr. Pearson may be right, but not necessarily so. Some of the conditions under which he would be right will become clear as we examine the second scenario.

This one suggests something approaching a civil war if Quebec were to separate. English Canadians, it is suggested, are likely to oppose violently any attempt to separate; they would not accept a Quebec decision as legitimate; if separation were achieved, they would likely adopt punitive policies towards the new state, and so on.

One can easily imagine such developments occurring. If they did, the possibility of a peaceful accommodation would be very small, and the potential for violence great. One could, in such a case, envision a progressive escalation of conflict, a progressive hardening of lines, and a growing likelihood of armed conflict which could be mutually destructive.

Just like the "optimistic scenario," the "pessimistic" one makes certain assumptions which need to be examined. How realistic are they? The primary one, again, is that about English-Canadian reactions: it is alleged they could not tolerate such an action. But in what sense would they not tolerate it? Would they resort to armed repression? This has certainly taken place in other historical contexts, but it seems fairly clear that a very strongly held norm among Canadians is a desire to avoid violence. This desire may well be strongest among those who, on other grounds, would be most opposed to separation.

The experience of civil wars in other settings, from the American Civil War to the Nigerian, might provide strong disincentives for Canadians to carry conflict to that point. But one cannot consider the possibility of this militant reaction of English Canada without considering some of the other factors in the equation. Thus, we can suggest a series of conditions which would make the violent response more likely. Most have to do with the attitudes and goals of the Separatists. The more thorough-going the degree of disengagement sought, the more likely stiff resistance. If the Separatists wanted to win not only symbolic sovereignty, but also wished to disturb all existing economic arrangements and transportation systems, for example, resistance would come from more quarters and be more violent. Similarly, if the Separatists threatened the rights and livelihood of English-Canadian minorities in Quebec, reaction would be angry. At the extreme, outright persecution of non-French-speaking minorities would almost certainly provoke violence.

The ideological make-up of the Separatist movement would also be important. A movement which was not only Separatist, but also Marxist or Fascist, or which threatened to nationalize all industries would be more bitterly opposed, because a wider range of important English-Canadian values would be threatened. Again, the way in which separation would be achieved is vital. The more the decision can be shown to be legitimate and democratic, the more likely English Canadians are to accept the decision, even if unpleasant. But if separation came after some kind of *coup*, or if a referendum showed only a slim majority in favour, demands for intervention would likely grow. Similarly, reaction might be more militant if separation was accomplished quickly rather than being prepared over a longer period.

A crucial factor here is the degree of unanimity and the strength of political organization in Quebec. If Quebeckers themselves were deeply divided, it would be very difficult for English Canadians not to take sides. That might begin on an individual basis, but quickly expand to the governmental level. Instead of a clear-cut Quebec-Canada conflict, there might instead be a complex set of alliances between elements in each area. Negotiations in such a situation could well be impossible. Deep disagreement within Quebec is likely to be associated with some sort of breakdown in social organization. Political leaders could lose their authority and influence. Militant groups like the FLQ would become more active and stronger. If this were the case, it would become extremely difficult for English Canadians to deal with Quebec, the likelihood of threats both to English-Canadian minorities and English-Canadian property would grow, and intervention would be more likely. Therefore, it is in the interests of English Canada to avoid adopting policies which would prompt these developments and threaten Quebec élites which would be more willing to negotiate.

From this we can distil the following summary. If separation is achieved by orderly, legitimate political process, if it poses little threat to English-Canadian political values other than unity itself, and poses little danger to English-Canadian minorities or industries, if it is achieved gradually over time and is guided by political leaders who share a common sense of the most important political rules of the game with English-Canadian leaders and who maintain a fair degree of authority within Quebec, then English-Canadian reaction is likely to be moderate, and English Canadians will ultimately accept the inevitability of separation. In this case, the outlook for maintenance of at least some degree of co-operation is bright. But if separation is achieved through manifestly undemocratic means, such as a *coup*, if it is accompanied by much social disorganization and wide internal dissension within Quebec, if the separatist doctrine is associated with other political doctrines English Canadians find repugnant, or with actions threatening to English-Canadian minorities and property interests, then we can expect a militant reaction from English Canadians, up to and including demands for military repression.

This suggests that the attitudes, goals, and behaviour of the French Canadians would be decisive influences on the English-Canadian reactions. The converse is also true: the ways in which English Canadians react would influence French Canadians. In particular, a threatening posture by English Canada would be likely to produce pressures for more militant Quebec action, for repressive measures against English-speaking minorities, and so on. Similarly, an English-Canadian policy of economic sanctions, if successful, might greatly increase the chances of widespread social disorganization and unemployment in Quebec, thus increasing the chances of the formation of extremist political movements. Thus, one hears it said that a Fascist government in Quebec would be intolerable: to some extent at least, English-Canadian attitudes would determine whether the conditions for such a development existed. Such predictions may become self-fulfilling prophecies.

Hence, the conditions for a spiralling escalation of the conflict could easily exist. Hostility on one side would breed hostility on the other. Such a spiral once started becomes very hard to break, especially with the absence of a third party to intervene. Therefore the initial reactions and behaviour of both sides are crucial.

Factors other than the ways in which separation is achieved would also affect the likelihood of English-Canadian repression. English-Canadian élites would have to be responsive to pressures from their constituents. Undoubtedly, in whatever form separation occurred, there would be demands for armed repression from some voices. The question is how strong would they be and how easily could they be resisted? Hostility to Quebec, and to separation, would not necessarily take the form of "Stop them." It could as plausibly take the form of "Good riddance, and let them go." We might expect great regional variations here: perhaps in the West, where the feeling that Quebec gets too much attention already appears to be widespread, and where a sense that Quebec is really part of Canada seems attenuated, this "good riddance" reaction might be typical. Few might be willing to exert much real effort to keep Quebec in. In the Maritimes, perhaps, with the most at stake if separation occurred, reactions might include far more willingness to force Quebec to remain. But even here, Professor Rawlyk found that when asked what they would do if Quebec separated "the absence of responses" was more striking than any militance.[2] Perhaps the answer is that it is impossible to predict what attitudes English Canadians both generally and in different regions would take: it would depend on the ways English-Canadian élites defined the issue, and, again, on how and with what objectives Quebec moved. One cannot dismiss the possibility that a political leader could gain power on a platform advocating harsh measures toward Quebec, but it appears unlikely.

Assuming some acceptance of the legitimacy of Quebec's decision, it is probable that most English-Canadian political leaders would oppose armed intervention, again because non-violence is such a strongly held value. In addition, militant intervention would be exceedingly costly in economic and emotional terms. It is hard to imagine what "success" would constitute in such an enterprise. Even the threat of force would be costly, since it would likely only increase Quebec militance. Political leaders, with their superior information, would be most able to perceive such factors and could be expected to counsel actions short of armed intervention.

English Canada could use other forms of reprisal against an independent Quebec, notably economic ones. But again, all would be costly to implement, and the effects would be difficult to predict. It therefore might be more rational for English Canada to hold such reprisals in reserve for use as bargaining counters.

And if that is accepted, then the two sides would again find themselves in a bargaining situation. Since, as I have suggested, English Canada would be in a very strong bargaining position, once it had accepted the fundamental decision to separate, it would then have a very good chance of attaining goals like guarantees of communications with the Maritimes. To the extent that this took place, demands for a militant policy towards Quebec would presumably decline.

Both scenarios we have considered have considerable plausibility; we have been able to visualize situations in which either one could take place. The reality would probably lie somewhere in between—it would not be as painless as the optimists suggest, nor as bloody as the pessimists conclude.

In my view, the actual results would much more closely approximate the optimistic scenario than the pessimistic one. Its assumptions in the current Canadian context are more plausible. In Quebec, the most influential Separatist groups do appear committed to attaining separation in a democratic manner, do have other political goals not widely different from those of English Canadians, and do perceive the need for continued co-operative arrangements after separation. There are, of course, other elements, and these could easily grow—as they have recently appeared to. It is, however, extremely difficult to visualize a militant, violent Separatist group rapidly attaining power in Quebec and leading it abruptly out of confederation. Outside Quebec, there is little evidence of widespread sentiment supporting "sending in the troops" if Quebec were to separate, though separation itself is deplored. Both on practical and moral grounds, one would expect most English-Canadian élites to resist a violent response to Quebec actions. They would certainly try to persuade Quebec to change its course, and would have a variety of sanctions to back them up. But if Quebec went ahead, the incentives for both sides to agree and the sanctions each would have for use against the other would make both likely to be willing to negotiate some kind of *modus vivendi*, though whether it would benefit both sides equally, and whether it would be as happy a *modus vivendi* as M. Lévesque suggests, is definitely open to question.

Separation would be a psychological, economic, and political blow to Canada. It would undoubtedly release dangerous passions, which would be difficult to control. But it is unlikely, given some of the basic attitudes in the country, and some of the existing relationships between the two societies, to result in civil war. In this, perhaps, the degree to which the two societies are already separated, in language, culture, associational life, legal systems, and political institutions, would be important. The two societies already are largely separate. Conflict between them only seldom takes the form of direct interpersonal hostility at the individual level. Rather it takes the form of conflict among organized institutions, which would be well able to bargain with each other under a new arrangement. Relatively few existing arrangements would be irreparably disturbed by separation—unlike, for example, the question of Black separation in the United States, which would imply much greater disruption.

The single most important variable determining the way in which relations between the two societies would develop is, as I have suggested, the attitudes and behaviour on the part of the élites on both sides. This suggests that leaders could engage in activities designed to lessen—or increase—the chances of peaceable disengagement, and that at least partly co-operative relationships could subsequently develop.

To conclude, as I have, that it is possible for Quebec to separate without bloodshed or violent conflict, and that it is also possible to work out a future relationship which approaches that envisioned by René Lévesque is not to argue the desirability of independence for Quebec, or that the future arrangements would be better than current ones. Discussion about benefits and costs of separation, for both sides, belongs elsewhere. What is important is that "separation" has many meanings; it can happen in many ways, in many differing degrees, and with many varying reactions. If Quebec were to decide, democratically, to opt for separation, my own desire would be for English Canadians to recognize the legitimacy of such self-determination, to pursue strategies which would encourage maintenance of relatively friendly authorities within Quebec, and to use the considerable bargaining power available to ensure economic co-operation on beneficial terms, protection of English-Canadian minorities, and maintenance of transportation and other such links with the Maritimes. It would be a period of difficult adjustment. Far better is it to pursue strategies in the present which will avert the need for the Prime Minister of Canada one day to respond to a telegram headed "Quebec's Declaration of Independence."

NOTES

[1] F. J. E. Jordan, "Sharing the Seaway System," *One Country or Two,* pp. 95-112.

[2] G. A. Rawlyk, "The Maritimes and the Problem of the Secession of Quebec, 1967-1969," *One Country or Two?*, pp. 205-230.

30

Dimensions of
National Political Integration
and Disintegration:
The Case of Quebec Separatism,
1960-1975

Lauren S. McKinsey

Periodically, Canadians experience negative consequences stemming from their multicultural heritage. The decade of the 1960s provided the most recent reminder of the continuing price of Canadian diversity. Another generation witnessed the erosion of the uncertain bonds connecting Quebec with the remainder of Canada. Signs of fracture in the Canadian consensus, most notably the threat of Quebec separatism, also forced observers to revise commonplace generalizations concerning Canadian politics. The early years of the 1970s provide inconclusive evidence that the 1960s either deviated from historical character or marked a threshold of permanent institutionalization of a latent pattern of cleavage. This study provides a political integration framework as an alternative perspective for reviewing events of this perplexing period.

Canada is a paradox of a nation-state simultaneously developed and underdeveloped.[1] Paradigms classifying nation-states for the purpose of comparative political analysis have not done justice to the complexity of Canadian society and the inconsistencies of Canadian politics. Because of the large shadow of the United States, Canada is thought to fit neatly into most of the same categories: federation, developed nation, mature democracy, or advanced industrial society. The sharing of the North American continent allegedly offsets important differences in cultural legacy and early history between the two nations. But Canada has never really fit the Anglo-American democratic model in Almond's (1956) typology, nor does it conform precisely to Lijphart's (1969) consociational adaptation of Almond's Western European model. The pronounced centrifugal tendencies of a segmented society, exposed by the surprising events of the 1960s and early 1970s, suggest the suitability of political integration theory for explanation.

Author's Note: An earlier version of this paper was delivered to the 1975 Meeting of the Western Social Science Association in Denver, Colorado. This version is from *Comparative Political Studies*, Vol. 9 No. 3, October 1976, pp. 335-360. © 1976 Sage Publications, Inc. Reprinted by permission.

Canada's current dilemma of internal cohesion can be addressed from the perspective of either creating the Canadian nation-state (integration) or achieving the Quebec nation-state apart from Canada (disintegration). Between these polar institutional solutions exist a number of federal and confederal arrangements which correspond to different levels of societal consensus regarding the proper distribution of power between the two layers of government. It is hypothesized that stability (an enduring institutional arrangement) will occur when the degree of centralization of governmental structure is congruent with the existing consensus. Stability can be achieved by changing either the pattern of structural centralization or the nature of consensus. Governmental policy can promote this end by focusing on either area or both. This study evaluates Canadian policy in the 1960s and early 1970s in terms of its success in this endeavor in the face of Quebec nationalistic pressures.

APPLICATION OF POLITICAL INTEGRATION THEORY

Proliferation of concepts and methodological imagination are the apparent current trends in the creation of political integration theory. Supranational integration theory recently has been adapted to a variety of other empirical settings.[2] Loose conceptualization in this transfer process has been criticized (Nye, 1968) for its dilutive effect on the rigor of integration theory. While this study is an example of the new methodological license, its value depends partly on future replicability. Consequently, there is a need to explicate the sources of borrowed concepts and tools and to justify the suitability of their application to Canada.

Political integration theory focused initially on the post-World War II efforts to create supranational structures and processes which could transcend the existing loyalties of national citizens and produce a commitment to avoidance of conflict among nations. There was a normative bias, readily admitted, among supranational integration theorists in favor of preserving the conditions of peace.[3] This concern for peace amply justifies the application of integration theory to those national settings which have the same degree of potential for internal conflict and violence based on regional cleavages. The utility of transferring supranational integration concepts was recognized first with regard to the emerging third-world nations where nation-building and political development are phenomena similar to political integration (Weiner, 1967). Then, since the United States was the "first new nation" (Lipset, 1967), it followed that political integration theory could be applied to the early formulative stages of today's modern nations. And, progressing a step further, it is appropriate now to apply the theory to those modern nation-states which are developed by many standards yet exhibit signs of fragmentation, instability, or separatism. Integration theory should help explain in these latter cases whether integration occurred, followed by disintegration, or whether integration failed to progress initially.

The supranational integration theorists have had their own problems in transferring concepts and measures between national and supranational settings. In the absence of a widely shared definition of the terminal state of integration, there was a tendency to use the modern nation-state as the operational referent. An international unit whose structures, processes, and legitimacy approximated that of a developed nation-state was said to be politically integrated. This approach was challenged when it became apparent that some modern nation-states were more integrated than others. But the fact that Puchala (1972) and others demonstrate the shortcomings of using the modern nation-state as the free-floating dependent variable does not invalidate the principle of reversing the process, e.g., applying certain conceptual tools and methodologies of supranational political integration to national settings. Recent progress in refining supranational political integration theory allows for avoidance of many of the early terminological, conceptual, and operational disputes which occupied the supranationalists, such as: whether integration is a process or a state of existence; what level of integration constitutes a meaningful threshold; or whether economic, social, and political integration are related definitionally or empirically.

This study is premised upon the following principles selected from the literature on supranational integration: (1) political integration is a process rather than a state of existence (Haas, 1961); (2) there is no absolute conclusion to the integrative process but, rather, relative levels of attainment (Jacob and Teune, 1964); (3) the concepts of political, social, and economic integration require disaggregation (Nye, 1968); (4) political integration has multiple properties requiring independent measurement (Lindberg, 1970); and (5) a comprehensive theory of political integration must address itself to the conditions under which integration is maintained as well as developed (Lijphart, 1971). Rather than adding to the terminological jungle of integration theory by offering another narrow definition, this study treats a series of processes which generally are held to be integrative or disintegrative. For integration, focus is on the growth of centralized institutions for collective decision-making and the expansion of societal consensus favoring such centralization. For disintegration, focus is on the creation of decentralized institutions (or transfer of power to existing regional structures) and the withdrawal of societal consensus for centralized institutions.

ANALYTICAL FRAMEWORK

Integration and disintegration are mirrored processes involving change on two sets of dimensions: structure/policy components and attitude/behavior components. Each dimension is a continuum running from high (centralization, consensus) to low (decentralization, dissensus). The primary focus of this study is upon the interactive effect of changes on each dimension, but especially negative (disintegrative) changes. Each dimension represents an opposite side of the citizen-state relationship in Easton's (1965) systems language. The state (structure) produces outputs (policies) in response to demands (behavior) which promote support (attitudes). The maintenance of the system (stability) depends on achieving congruence between the two dimensions: that is, when there exists a consensus that the current system of allocating resources is the proper one. When a directional shift occurs on either dimension, a corresponding shift on the other is necessary to reproduce stability. This process can be illustrated by discussing some of the significant patterns of interactive shifts which theoretically can occur.

Either a centralization of structure or a growth in consensus can initiate integration. In traditional nationalism, a self-conscious group attempts to carve out a coterminous territorial framework or state of its own. In twentieth-century nation-building, the state attempts to create the nation by raising consensus through the process of socialization. Either of these processes can become cyclical, sustaining integration, if further centralization is the product of heightened consensus and vice-versa. The dynamics of this process suggest that there exists no necessary minimum threshold of integration.[4] Indeed, the universe of political institutions houses a wide spectrum of entities containing aggregates of people with levels of cohesion, consciousness, or consensus ranging from quite low to extremely high. History demonstrates amply that the nation and the state can converge at many levels.

This conceptualization is satisfactory in the case of integration, but its application to the reverse process is less convincing. Disintegration has received scant attention in the literature, and analysis has tended to focus on manifest structural breakdown, ignoring the process through which structural breakdown and the decline of consensus can interact. In the definitions provided, it is usually impossible to deduce whether structural breakdown follows the dissolution of consensus or whether consensus simply fails to develop at all.[5] Therefore, it is even more important in the case of disintegration to separate the two dimensions and to analyze their interaction. As with integration, disintegration can be spurred by a change in either the level of consensus or the level of structural centralization. For example, separatist ideology might grow if a previously nonpoliticized group becomes conscious of the implications of a separate territorial existence. If decentralization lags behind the withdrawal of consensus, violence and war can re-establish congruence, as in the case of the breakup of empires. Or balance-of-power politics and war might divide national groups and produce a structural decentralization such as partition.[6] A process of socialization can be used to overcome irredentist sentiment and to re-establish the congruence of structure and consensus.

In this important respect the process of disintegration is similar to that of integration: either can produce a political community, which is the phenomenon defined by many observers to be the terminal product of the integrative process (Deutsch et al., 1957). Congruence between structure and consensus, therefore, can be achieved down opposite avenues.[7] There remain important differences in the nature of the two processes. Whether the integrative process stabilizes or remains cyclical is not especially critical if the system has developed enough reserve consensus to survive expected periods of stress.[8] But cyclical disintegration can be fatal. A decentralization of structure designed to recreate a congruence of structure and attitudes risks stimulating additional withdrawal of support. Decision-makers are faced with the prospect of selecting the precise point for terminating a process of structural decentralization at which the probability of equalizing structure and consensus is highest. The explication of this decision-making dilemma in the case of Canada and Quebec (1960-1975) might help explain why analysts are unable to identify disintegrative tendencies in the absence of visible structural evidence. If the Canadian "sense of community" is declining, the process of disintegration should be measurable before its completion is documented by the threshold indices of civil war or secession.

OPERATIONALIZATION AND MEASUREMENT

The value of concept proliferation in the development of political integration theory might be debatable, but there is no disputing the need to find empirical referents for whatever terms are chosen. If integration is held to be composed of several dimensions, each requires independent measurement. In this study a distinction is made between two basic dimensions: structure/policy and attitude/behavior.[9] Ideally, continuums should be constructed for each set of components and gradations established for the purpose of measuring direction and degree of changes. Then, if time lags can be established (Burrows, 1970), the interaction of the dimensions can be verified and, perhaps, causal inferences drawn. The data are not amenable to quite such a systematic approach, but sufficient evidence can be generated to establish trends.

Structure/Policy

This case study enjoys the methodological advantage of Canada's status as a federation. Federations are convenient laboratories for documenting the extent of institutional centralization in a political system because, by definition, they divide responsibilities between central and regional governments according to the need for unity in the system. Because that need varies, between societies and over time, it is appropriate to view federalism as a spectrum rather than as a model (Livingston, 1956). Many federal patterns are possible, ranging from strongly centralized variants approximating the unitary state to extremely loose arrangements paralleling confederal associations. Over the course of Canadian history extensive movement has occurred along the following continuum: (1) the unitary state, (2) centralized federalism, (3) cooperative federalism, (4) consultative federalism, (5) asymmetrical federalism, (6) confederation, (7) associate states, (8) separate states (Mallory, 1965). Since smaller shifts have occurred recently only near the center of the continuum, fluctuation is more difficult to document. The centralized federation of the World War II period gradually gave way to a version of cooperative federalism in the 1950s. Provincial spokesmen in the 1960s began to insist emphatically on the need for a consultative variant in which the provinces have a real and prior voice in decisions instead of being presented faits accompli.[10] Various Quebec spokesmen have gone farther by demanding special status, confederation, or even separation. Ottawa has acquiesced sporadically and in part, and systematic evidence of a decentralizing trend must be pieced together.

Constitutions theoretically are the source of the distribution of authority between the layers of government in a federation. But the effective division of power can be quite different from that prescribed in the constitutional formula. The formal elements of the Canadian constitution have not indexed clearly the historical shifts in policy authority.[11] A guide to periodic fluctuations could be created from a systematic analysis of the actual exercise of power in various policy areas. Nye (1968) offers a methodology for assessing the de facto division of power based on a weighted index which assesses the relative scope, intensity, and salience of policies. Such an index could document accurately the ebb and flow in Quebec's status if it included a means of assigning the proper weight to different policy areas. A more succinct index, the formula of revenue sharing, can be utilized.[12]

The revenue-sharing formula is a reliable index of structure/policy integration in the Canadian federal system to the extent that the proportion of revenues available to each layer of government affects its ability to implement policy irrespective of its formal authority to make policy. Since the relative ability of each government to spend in the public interest is a good reflection of its substantive authority in several policy areas, the use of a revenue-sharing index avoids the methodological difficulties of having to evaluate policy areas singly, determining the scope, extent, or salience of each. And since the capacity to spend is more elastic than the capacity to alter constitutional policy authority, fluctuations will be more observable.[13] While it is unreasonable to expect to capture the full picture of federal-provincial relations with a revenue-sharing focus, there is probably no better single longitudinal index for the last several decades than the sequence of fiscal bargaining.

The British North America Act of 1867, the core of the Canadian constitution, assigns functional authority to federal and provincial governments in great detail. In contrast, the corresponding allocation of revenue sources appears to be almost an afterthought. The federal government is provided access to all forms of taxation while the provinces are denied indirect taxation, the chief revenue source utilized in the nineteenth century. The revenue division reflects the belief of Canada's founders that the province's constitutional responsibilities for welfare and education would require limited application of resources and could be carried out through subsidy payments from the federal government. Neither layer of government was expected ever to need the income tax fields. But twentieth-century service demands forced both layers of government into competition for income tax, producing a "tax jungle" situation documented by a 1937 Royal Commission report. Entry into World War II, when the national interest clearly justified federal pre-emption of revenues, facilitated the implementation of the report's recommendation for a single, streamlined tax collection system.[14]

An agreement covering the 1941-1947 period allowed the federal government to collect all personal, corporate, and estate income taxes in return for direct compensation to the provinces. This "tax rental" approach achieved a more efficient collection of taxes and provided the federal government with necessary counter-cyclical economic powers. This was the rationale for the federal government's effort to extend the tax rental principle for the years following 1947. Except for Quebec, the provinces concurred and dialogue centered on the size of the compensatory payments to be made. The federal government relied on Keynesian economic arguments, its right to spend funds in the national interest, and its added constitutional responsibilities for unemployment insurance and old age pensions to preserve the dominant portion of revenues for itself. The provinces lobbied for increasingly larger proportions of revenues in order to meet their own constantly expanding service delivery responsibilities in education and social policy, and the federal government grudgingly conceded larger increments in subsequent tax agreements. The change in the rate of concessions is an index to the distribution of authority in the Canadian system during the period since.

In 1947, when the federal government first increased the proportion of tax rental payments, it offered any individual province the alternative of imposing its own taxes in return for tax credits against the proportion of federal taxes paid in the province. The amounts of credit were 5% on personal income, 5% on corporate income, and 50% on succession duties. Quebec selected the alternative and embarked on a continuous pursuit of expanded tax room under these credit provisions. In 1947 Quebec imposed its own 7% corporate income tax, not followed by a corresponding increase in the federal government's tax credit until 1953. In 1954 Quebec imposed its own personal income tax at 15% of federal rates. The federal government responded by raising the credit rate to 10% for 1957. That rate was set at 13% for the years 1958 to 1961, and the corporate income tax credit rate was raised to 9% for the same period. From the close of the war until about 1961, then, the average annual rate of vacating tax room was less than 1%.

Beginning with the 1962 tax-sharing agreements, the rate of increase accelerated significantly as Quebec led a parade of provinces pressing for a larger "fair share" of tax room. The steady increase in the personal income tax credit is the best index of the trend. In 1962 the rate was increased to 16% and again each year as follows: 1963 (17%), 1964 (18%), 1965 (21%), 1966 (24%), and 1967 (28%).[15] At this point the federal government ended the increases in the rate of tax room on the grounds that its own revenue requirements dictated reserving the remaining portion. Provinces whose needs required revenues in excess of the federal tax credit were forced to choose to impose higher rates amounting to double taxation. Most provinces have had to implement a rate of income taxation in excess of the break-even rates in order to continue to provide accustomed services and to finance provincial prerogatives. The rate of rebate has remained constant since 1967.[16] The span of the 1960s and early 1970s, therefore, can be divided into a period of decentralization up through 1967 and a leveling off period since. There has been no recentralization of federal revenue capacity, but the result is similar, since expanding provincial responsibilities have to be met with the existing proportion of federal tax credits.

The pattern of change in the provincial proportion of "tax room" is only one relevant part of the revenue-sharing picture. Similar trends can be documented for the history of conditional grant programs. These programs have evolved into the single most important method for transferring funds from the federal government to the provinces. Conditional grant programs originated before World War I but were not utilized extensively until after World War II when the federal government found itself in the position of collecting most of the tax revenue and sought ways of spending it consistent with national priorities. It channeled the funds to residents of the individual provinces in the form of matching assistance to provincial revenues in programs within the constitutional domain of the provinces, such as health insurance, old age assistance, and unemployment insurance.

In 1951, these funds totaled approximately $70 million or about 20% of the total revenues returned to the provinces. Between 1957 and 1962 the total more than quadrupled from $145 million to $600 million, more than half of the transfer payment total. This trend continued as follows: 1965-1966 ($1 billion, 70%), 1972-1973 ($2.5 billion, 55%), and 1975-1976 ($3.5 billion, 52%). The magnitude of conditional grant cash flows to the provinces increased steadily and occupied first an increasingly larger and then a reduced proportion of total transfer payments. A point was reached where the totals of conditional and unconditional grant payments were approximately equal.[17]

In one sense it is possible to argue that the growth in the size of conditional grant programs reflected a movement from centralized back to cooperative federalism because a continuously greater proportion of total revenues was spent for provincial functions.[18] For those provinces which are relatively unconcerned about conditions attached to such funds, the only important factor is the size of the revenue package. Some provinces like Quebec view conditional grants as unconstitutional intrusions into provincial prerogatives, nothing more than thinly veiled attempts to alter provincial priorities. During the Duplessis (1944-1959) era, Quebec preferred to refuse conditional grants rather than to accept money with strings attached. The Lesage government, however, reversed this policy in the early 1960s, at the time when the programs were accelerating rapidly. The expanding social responsibilities of the Quiet Revolution dictated an expanded flow of funds, and only the federal government possessed them. But after having admitted the need for such monies, Quebec lobbied for the principle of their unconditional return. Quebec's leaders desired to establish that it was the government of Quebec, not the government of Canada, which was the benefactor. Constant pressure led, in 1965, to a federal policy allowing provinces to "opt-out" of certain conditional grant programs and to receive additional federal tax abatement credits for sponsorship of comparable programs.

Quebec acquired an additional 23 points of personal income tax abatement by creating its own programs in areas such as hospital insurance, old age assistance, unemployment assistance, and youth allowances. The provincial programs were similar to the federal conditional grant programs, but the symbolic effect of Quebec's sponsorship was the important element. Together with its regular abatement rate of 28 points of personal income tax, Quebec had by that time secured over 50% of tax room. Again the federal government drew the line when Quebec requested termination of all conditional grant programs and unconditional return of all taxes collected in Quebec. No major concessions have been made since, and the tax abatement point schedule affecting conditional grant programs has remained basically the same with one additional concession of two points in 1972. This pattern parallels the trends described for the tax room index. During the first part of the decade there was a decentralization as evidenced by the expanded flow of funds to all the provinces. Quebec achieved a major goal in the middle of the decade by acquiring the right of opting-out. This was the zenith, however, and there has been a plateau since. In 1975 Quebec collected a provincial income tax at 53% of the federal rate, virtually the same rate allowed by the sum of its tax abatement points in 1967. This same pattern holds for equalization grants, the third major leg of the transfer programs. Beginning in 1957 Quebec was allowed to receive unconditional equalization payments as a "have not" province even though it did not participate in the tax collection agreements. In 1957, the first year of equalization payments, Quebec received just under one-third of the total for all of Canada. The rate increased slowly over the years, reaching approximately 50% in 1967-1968, a figure it has hovered around consistently through 1976. Increase up to about 1967, followed by stabilization, has been a fairly consistent pattern in Canada-Quebec fiscal relations.[19]

This selected sketch of Canadian revenue sharing by no means captures the entire pattern of the shifts in power between the federal and Quebec governments. It is argued, however, that the nature of the functions affected by shifts in revenue capacity are significant symbolically to both elites and masses in Quebec, and the amount of monies involved are substantial. The trends could be corroborated by a detailed analysis of major policy decisions during the period. For example, many attempted concessions to Quebec's autonomist demands were made during the early 1960s including the flag issue in 1964 and the series of compromises to Quebec's demands for a favorable formula of constitutional revision. It is equally clear that a change in strategy for dealing with Quebec's demands occurred about 1967. The focus shifted from subsidizing Quebec's ability to speak for French Canada to the promotion of the federal government's responsibility to guarantee the rights of French Canadians anywhere in Canada. The ascension of Trudeau and his colleagues to power within the Liberal party is one sign of the change. Another is the preoccupation with the reports of the Royal Commission on Bilingualism and Biculturalism which emphasized the rights of French Canadians more than the rights of Quebec. Still another is the attempt to diversify foreign policy as in the support given to the creation of la Francophonie, an international agency to deal with cooperative enterprises among French-speaking nations. The disposition of issues such as these reinforces the analysis of revenue sharing and demonstrates that the latter is an accurate index of the fluctuations in policy during the period. And its quantifiability allows for comparisons to be drawn with corresponding shifts upon the attitude/behavior dimension.

Attitude/Behavior

In contrast to the limited empirical focus for the structure/policy dimension, a wider choice of indices is available for measuring the attitude/behavior dimension. Care must be taken to select the proper indices, ones which reflect both mass and elite responses yet keep them distinct. The data bases chosen also should be comparable for the duration of the study period. Within these constraints the following evidence provides a fairly good picture of French-Canadian sentiment in Quebec toward the division of power in the Canadian system. First, the organizational base of separatism is examined in order to document the growth and establishment of the idea. Popular support for separatism is reflected in both survey research and provincial election returns. Second, the shifting fortunes of all provincial political parties are examined in relation to their various stances on Quebec's autonomy. Finally, conflict data are examined for their value in indexing the decline of consensus over the period. This combination ties the responses of elites, masses, and fringe groups into the attitude/behavior continuum.

The growth of separatist sentiment and the solidification of the separatist movement were clear trends of the 1960s. Threads of nationalism run throughout Quebec's history, but the Duplessis government had woven them into a defensive shield against the assimilative threat of Canada and the federal government. The state of Quebec in the 1950s was not yet widely viewed as a proper vehicle for the aggressive expression and expansion of French-Canadian aspirations (Quinn, 1963). Still, other elements of nationalism lay beneath the surface of Duplessis' paternalism, and various fringe groups survived briefly, from time to time, on fragments of traditional, corporate, or clerical autonomist ideology left behind from movements of the 1930s and 1940s (Corbett, 1967). The early years of the Quiet Revolution produced separatist groups across the entire right/left political spectrum. Proliferation was the common element and a short life the rule. Even narrow-based groups were susceptible to splintering, and new alliances annually replaced faltering causes (Hagy, 1969). The Rassemblement pour l'Indépendence Nationale (RIN) established an early record for continuity (1960-1968), but it faced the divisive challenge of the more conservative Ralliement Nationale (RN) in the 1966 provincial election. This pattern of fragmentation and discontinuity meant that the strength of growing sentiment was not reflected in a viable movement.

This pattern changed in the second half of the decade, precipitated by a realignment within the Liberal party following defeat in the 1966 provincial election. The dissident Réne Lévesque led some Liberals into the Mouvement Souverainte-Association (MSA) which formed the core, flanked by the RIN and the RN, of the Parti Québécois (PQ) in 1968. With its ranks finally closed, separatism emerged as a potent political force and posed an acknowledged challenge in the 1970 provincial election. By the 1973 provincial election, the PQ had evolved into an effective electoral organization without losing its distinction as an ideological alternative. This combination holds today, and whatever elements of separatist purity and intensity may have been lost over the past few years are offset by the PQ's maturation as an acceptable autonomist choice for a significant portion of Quebec's French-Canadian population.

The growth and current extent of this support can be traced and documented with survey research findings and provincial election returns. Popular sentiment toward Quebec nationalism, separatism, and independentism has been sampled irregularly since the early 1960s. As with virtually any multiple-sample process over a span of time, there is the problem of comparability of data. Considering the likelihood of methodological error and the absence of systematic time-series data, the trend in growth of separatist sentiment is still apparent. Baseline data are taken from the first comprehensive analysis of attitudinal endorsement of separatism made in 1963 (Gzowski, 1963). Three years into the Quiet Revolution only 13% of Québecois were found to favor separatism, while 21% professed never to have heard of it. The potential for growth of separatist sentiment was suggested in two additional findings: disproportionate support among young people and a tendency for the undecided group to be closer to separatism than they were a year previously. But this potential had not materialized by 1968, according to a survey of French-speaking adults, which identified only slightly more than 11% of respondents as either strongly or slightly in favor of separatism (Cuneo and Curtis, 1974). Twenty-one percent, as compared with 23% in 1963, were undecided. The *Toronto Telegram* "Canada 70" survey, however, placed the level of Québécois support for separatism at 26% (Toronto Telegram, 1969). It is possible to view the discrepancy in these surveys, taken less than two years apart, as partially a function of the survey questions asked.[20] Alternatively, it can be argued that the level of support was fairly constant until near the close of the decade when it increased to a new plateau. This fit for the data is consistent with the shifts along the structure/policy dimensions, assuming a time lag of one or two years.

Together with the growth of separatist sentiment there has occurred a growth of antiseparatism resulting from a polarization of the previously undecided. Both extremes also appear to carry their beliefs with greater intensity. Corroboration of these trends may be found in the level of support given separatist parties in recent provincial elections. In 1966, the RIN and the RN together received less than 10% of the total provincial vote. The Parti Québécois, in contrast, received 23% of the total votes cast in the 1970 election and 30% in 1973. These latter two figures overrepresent the support for separatism to the extent that some voters were attracted to the PQ for its social democratic program and in spite of its separatist goals, but the second PQ vote total still represents nearly 40% of the French-Canadian voters. Also, since the Union Nationale offered a 1970 platform plank to hold a referendum on the question of separation within four years, some of its support (20%) might have reflected separatist sentiment.[21] On balance, it seems fair to consider the level of PQ support a good measure of separatist sentiment. A pre-1970 election survey identified 26% of the French-Canadian electorate as intending to vote for "a" separatist party in "a" provincial election, a figure which fits well the subsequent PQ support (Jensen and Regenstreif, 1970).

Popular support for separatism per se, or for a particular separatist party, might delineate the phenomenon of nationalism too narrowly and fail to indicate the reaction of the average French-Canadian in Quebec to the changing dimensions of cooperative federalism. If all Québécois are latent nationalists, support for a conservative special status for Quebec could be transformed into separatism under conducive conditions.[22] The various nationalistic stances of the traditional parties in different elections and the parties' subsequent electoral success provides insight in this respect. This approach is useful in trying to establish time-lag changes in Quebec elite responses to the federal revenue policy changes described previously. Campaign planks in provincial elections between 1960 and 1973 illustrate an intense competition among the parties to best represent the "Quebec first" option to Québécois voters.[23]

In 1960, the Liberals unseated the Union Nationale heirs to the Duplessis regime by capitalizing on the release of energy and growth of aspirations that was to become the Quiet Revolution. The government of Quebec assumed an active role in making the state of Quebec the agent of those aspirations. The Liberals pressed for a consistently larger share of tax room, accepted conditional grant money to assist in the energizing process, and demanded a variety of concessions to Quebec's new-found self-determination. In an effort to dramatize the need for Québécois to become masters in their own house, Premier Lesage announced a mandate to the federal government just prior to the 1963 federal election: Quebec's needs in the areas of fiscal control and social functions would require 25% of the personal and corporate income taxes and all estate taxes (Scott and Oliver, 1964: 24). This theme had struck a responsive chord among Quebec voters who returned the Liberals in the 1962 provincial election, and it seemed to ring true in Ottawa also. Continuous pressure produced the incremental rollback in tax room and the right to opt-out of the joint pension plan, family allowance plans, and the student loan fund. This schedule of attrition prompted one observer to portray the federal government's image as one of "constant retreat and dismay" (Saywell, 1965: 63).

Since the strategy had worked well for the Liberals, the Union Nationale created its own version of special status for Quebec and succeeded in outflanking the Liberals in the 1966 election. The Union Nationale returned to power just prior to the time when the federal government adopted its hard line on tax abatements and other aspects of special status. This hard line served only to accelerate Quebec's agitation, as expressed in Premier Johnson's call for a return of 100% of all direct taxes collected in Quebec, the end to all shared-cost programs, and adoption of a totally new constitution based on recognition of Quebec's powers as the state representing the French nation in Canada (Meekison, 1971: 421-434). The death of Johnson and the subsequent instability of the UN, together with the splintering of the Liberals following the 1966 defeat, allowed the PQ to pre-empt the nationalist issue from the traditional parties. Polarization between nationalist and anti-separatist ideology helps explain both the 1970 Liberal victory and the strong PQ showing, a pattern reinforced by the 1973 results.[24] To the extent that elite support for nationalist alternatives continues to exceed mass support (Loh, 1975: 240), the potential for growth in separatism remains high. In conclusion, even a conservative interpretation of the data would hold that while separatism shows no recent dramatic growth, policy changes at the federal level failed to diminish the support for separatism.[25] One event which did have a reversal effect was the October Crisis of 1970, including the violence of the primary events of kidnapping and murder and the subsequent imposition of the War Measures Act to drive out the terrorists. The significance of these events must be considered within the support dimension discussed in this part of the study.

There is justification to interpret conflict data to be evidence of the absence of consensus in a political system. The availability of comparative conflict data and imaginative frameworks for its interpretation make this approach attractive (Feierabend et al., 1972). Because violence became a feature of the Quebec scene in the 1960s, it is necessary to assess its significance, keeping the following theoretical limitations in mind: (1) violence can represent intensity of dissatisfaction on the part of a narrow segment of the population; (2) violence can be interpreted as a function of strategy rather than as an index of the intensity of dissatisfaction; and (3) violence can be the product of frustration in society, of governmental repression, or of some combination of the two. Nonetheless, there is no denying the significance of the routinization of the use of terror by fringe separatist groups. Subsequent to the formation of the Front de Liberation du Québec (FLQ) in 1962, a bomb was planted, on the average, approximately every ten days for the next seven years (Stewart, 1970: 5). Following an intensive period of activity in 1968-1969, terrorism lagged prior to the April 1970 provincial election. Then, in October, the events in Montreal shocked the nation and the world.

Although the turbulence of the decade of the 1960s was becoming more accepted as part of the flow of events, nothing had prepared the Canadian imagination for the events and aftermath of the October Crisis. Interpretations abound concerning the events, especially the government's response in imposing the War Measures Act.[26] No attempt is made in this study to affirm a particular interpretation, but from the perspective of integration theory it is important to note that the October Crisis at least temporarily interrupted the sequence of events sustaining separatism.[27] It tainted the constitutional, electoral, and legal variants of Quebec nationalism and refocused Quebec public concern on matters such as security, employment, and inflation. Thus, even if it is true that the federal government's imposition of martial law was an overreaction to the requirements of the situation, it is also true that all three layers of government (including Montreal's) concurred in the need for decisiveness and that public opinion in Quebec overwhelmingly supported the means used to achieve the goal of halting terrorism. Few people seemed concerned that the nature of the response was also a deterrent to the legitimate moderate groups organizing to achieve separation. The activities of the governments cemented an alliance between the Liberals at all levels. The subtle effect of this application of force in reintegrating elements of Quebec within Canada is addressed in the conclusion.[28]

There is another conflict approach which can shed additional light on the events of the period. Allegedly, more important than the prevalence of overt conflict is the existence or absence of a mechanism for its management. This approach assumes that some manifestations of conflict are healthful as a safety valve for tensions and that conflict regulation as opposed to conflict resolution is the crucial factor.[29] The absence of agreement establishing the proper subjects and limits of disagreement indicates a failure of conflict regulation and reflects cracks in the basic societal consensus.[30] A constitution is an important element of conflict regulation machinery, but it can be only as effective as its capacity to adapt to changing societal conditions. As has been noted, the Canadian constitution is deficient in this respect, since it can be formally amended only upon the unanimous request of all governments in Canada to the British Parliament.

This embarrassing conditional sovereignty has been on the national agenda for years (Meekison, 1971: 235-252). Beginning in 1960, a series of national conferences dealt with the question of repatriation of the constitution based upon acceptance of a revision of the division of power in the Canadian federal system and a formula of amendment for future revisions. Conferences were held throughout the decade—in 1960, 1961, 1964, 1967, 1968, and 1969—without success. Again, in 1971, the much heralded Victoria Conference failed to fulfill expectations for creating a modern constitution. In nearly every instance, concessions initially found Quebec's favor but resulted finally in the escalation of Quebec's demands. Quebec did not feel comfortable with anything less than veto power over any changes which would affect its status. There is talk of renewed efforts in 1976, but evidence is lacking that Quebec's position is any more receptive to change. The fact that these conferences have been spaced over many years and have involved different sets of leaders at both federal and provincial levels indicates a clear lack of elite consensus. The alleged lack of formal sovereignty caused by this strange constitutional situation has little effect on the daily activities of governing Canada, but the implication of a nation lacking the internal capacity to change its formal rules of the game is important for integration theory. The inability of Canadians to work out a system of mutual decision-making, out of fear of what they might do to one another, must be taken as evidence of the absence of a fundamental consensus.

CONCLUSIONS AND IMPLICATIONS
FOR INTEGRATION THEORY

The complex issues of Quebec's autonomy and possible separation frustrated federal government leaders over the course of the entire 1960-1975 period.[31] Various policy strategies failed to accommodate Quebec's demands for special status. Leaders faced the dilemma of either creating a legion of instant separatists by refusing concessions or producing habituated separatists by constantly acceding to demands. The marginal concessions approach used during the first half of the period did not pre-empt, but only generated additional demands. The revised policy, beginning around 1967, focused on French Canadians as special citizens in the Canadian nation rather than on special status for Quebec as the vehicle of French-Canadian aspirations. Federal policy shifted from an emphasis on decentralization (the structure/policy continuum) to an emphasis on raising consensus (the attitude/behavior continuum).[32] The elevation of Trudeau and other French-Canadian elites to leadership gave the Québécois the opportunity to identify with Ottawa rather than Quebec as the best guarantee of special status.

This combination of hard-line in Quebec and look-to-Ottawa approach produced a mixed reaction. The hard line stimulated even greater demands from those Québécois who had become accustomed to Quebec's steady acquisition of special status. The "silent majority" in the province, those more interested in preserving the gains of the past decade than in risking them in an unknown political arrangement, supported the Trudeau-Bourassa Liberal axis which developed after the 1970 election. That election established the extent of polarization in Quebec as it was separation versus jobs, security, and economic prosperity. The PQ was frustrated and isolated by the electoral formula which severely underrepresented its popular support in numbers in the Quebec assembly. The subsequent decline in support for separatism following the October Crisis also helped to rigidify the polarization. In the 1973 election a revived PQ drove voters into the Liberal camp precisely to the extent that the PQ was perceived to be a viable separatist alternative. But despite the polarization, this increased support for federation can be said to reflect a certain reintegration of Quebec into Confederation. Even this assessment may be premature, however, since recent Quebec assertions of prerogatives, in areas such as the use of language within the province, have weakened the Trudeau-Bourassa alignment. A new round of confrontation reminiscent of the mid-1960s may be in store.

It remains to place the events of the October Crisis and the subsequent ebb in the fortunes of Quebec nationalism within the framework of political integration theory. If it is true that greater support for Canadian confederation followed in the wake of the imposition of the War Measures Act, then consideration must be given to the theory that preservation of unity depends in part upon the selective application of a degree of force. If political integration theory does not provide for some consideration of the effectiveness of governmental coercion it cannot explain the nature of resilience to disintegration in multinational settings. Therefore, the Haas (1970) approach must be modified by Etzioni's (1968) view that structural unity in most national settings is maintained by some unspecified mixture of residual popular support, system distributive rewards, and elements of coercion.[33] Johnson (1966) has shown that the element of force is important in maintaining the system in times of stress in developed nations.[34] Johnson refers primarily to stress upon governments and regimes (Easton, 1965), but application of his theory to the level of the community is justified. If residual popular support accrues over time, it might be true that the degree of consensus necessary to maintain the system is less than that required to produce it initially. In the absence of high consensus, however, the system's stability depends upon the proper application of a component of systemic force to complement sense of community. This framework provides for a more balanced evaluation of the events in Quebec during this period.

A realistic interpretation of the role of coercion in stabilizing political disintegration should be complemented by a critical evaluation of the use of violence or civil war as measures of the final phase of disintegration. The emphasis of the supranationalist theorists upon peaceful change as the mark of integration must be rejected. In Canada, peaceful change could be associated with disintegration rather than integration. It is possible for the particular set of circumstances in Canada to evolve into a compromise in which Quebec and Canada agree, without violence or civil war (Pious, 1973: 64-65), to go their separate ways. Stability would thereby have been produced, premised on peaceful relations, through a process of disintegration bringing structure into congruence with the level of consensus.

This study's application of supranational integration theory could be extended to other comparable multinational settings in which complex processes of centralization and decentralization are occurring. In fact, an expanded application to the Canadian setting would produce insights excluded by the narrow focus of this paper. Three important auxiliary questions require further attention: (1) the narrower question of the integration of elements *within* Quebec itself; (2) the broader question of the integration of *all* of the regions within Canada; and (3) the still broader question of the integrative role played by the presence of the United States.[35] A fuller explication of these questions, using additional measures of integration and disintegration, could eventually help predict the fate of Quebec within or without Canada. Centrifugal tendencies have occurred periodically in nearly all of Canada's regions. To the extent that other provinces press the issue of their own autonomy, they may be more willing to accede to Quebec's demands. And to the extent that Quebec's own internal integration produces a more monolithic community, the demand for separation would increase. Multination states such as Canada, therefore, provide challenging empirical proving grounds for integration theory.

NOTES

[1] Hayward (1970: 932) suggests the need for a model which can explain the example of a political entity which is modernized but at the same time is not yet integrated or is in the process of becoming nonintegrated. The closest approximation of a political integration analysis of the Canada-Quebec setting is Pious' (1973) contribution to a symposium on the application of political integration to multinational states and multistate nations. Pious does not systematically apply political integration concepts, however, but recounts recent and historical nationalistic phenomena in a mixture of conventional descriptive and consociational politics terms.

[2] Examples of the various possibilities for applying concepts and measures of supranational integration include: Clark and Welch's (1975) analysis of U.S. trade patterns, Hayward's (1974) focus on attitudinal integration in Ghana, Morrison and Stevenson's (1972) application to Africa, the study of Czechoslovakia by Zaninovich and Brown (1973), Bertsch's (1972) treatment of Yugoslavia, and Lijphart's (1971) attempt to tie political integration to a theory of culturally diverse nations. Haas (1970: 645) argues that the conceptual frameworks developed in the area of supranational integration could be used to explain the dynamics of those ethnically complex nation-states which succeed in gaining greater autonomy.

[3] Deutsch et al. (1957: 5) define integration as the "attainment, within a territory, of a 'sense of community' and of institutions strong enough and widespread enough to assure, for a 'long time,' dependable expectations of 'peaceful change' among its population."

[4] This conclusion follows from the premise of Jacob and Teune (1964: 7) that integration is relative, rather than absolute: "Instead of considering political integration as a specific condition that exists or does not exist, it might be useful to envisage a set of relationships

which are *more* or *less* integrated, or a progression of events leading to an *increase* or a *decrease* of integration."

[5] For example, Deutsch et al. (1957: 6) provide a tautological definition: "we shall say that any political community, be it amalgamated or pluralistic, was eventually SUCCESSFUL if it became a security-community—that is, if it achieved integration—and that it was UNSUCCESSFUL if it ended eventually in secession or civil war." The fact that a political community is unsuccessful if it fails to achieve integration is not a satisfying explanation. Haas (1970: 630) notes other aspects of circularity of definitions in the early terminological jungle.

[6] The relationship of integration theory to partition is given extensive consideration in the 1973 volume of *Journal of International Affairs* devoted to the subject (Connelly, 1973).

[7] There is implicit recognition of these dual dimensions in Nye's (1968: 859) statement that: "Aspects of integration and disintegration can both occur at the same time."

[8] Puchala (1970: 692) emphasizes the importance of consensus to the long-run maintenance of the system: "Community, in short, adds an 'endurance' factor to political relations between governments."

[9] The components in these two sets of dimensions reflect the influence of Lindberg (1970) and Nye (1968) except that they oversimplify the thrust of both contributions. The important point is that the two sets of dimensions are themselves independently measured. And while it would be useful to have measures clearly separating structure and policy (Nye, 1968: 865) and measures clearly separating attitudes and behavior (Hayward, 1970: 928), the fusion of each set is not critical for the purposes of this analysis.

[10] The differences between cooperative federalism and consultative federalism in Canada may appear insignificant to the outside observer. Provincial spokesmen, however, attack the hypocrisy of a cooperative federalism in which the provincial governments are "allowed" to share with the federal government responsibility for those functions which originally belonged to the provinces. Smiley (1963) provides an excellent discussion of the dialogue over cooperative federalism.

[11] Cairns (1970) cautions against viewing the Canadian constitution solely as the British North America Act of 1867, as formally amended, and suggests that the "living constitution" is a much better guide to the dynamic shifts of authority which have taken place over the course of more than a century. The evolution of the constitution must be described in terms of changing practices of intergovernmental relations.

[12] Lindberg (1970: 653) includes the financial resources available to decision-makers as part of the composite index of capacity to make decisions for the broadened political community. Since financial resources are a more important part of total resources for national communities than they are for international communities, there is greater justification for use of the revenue-sharing index.

[13] Lynn (1968) discusses the relative rigidity of the division of expenditure responsibilities in comparison with the division of revenue sources. He suggests that it has been the easier amendment of the division of revenues that has allowed for the periodic centralization of authority in the Canadian system, creating the conditions in which federal expenditures have pre-empted provincial functions.

[14] Smiley (1962) carefully documents the impact of the Rowell-Sirois Commission report and traces the subsequent evolution of the taxing and spending relationships between the federal and provincial governments.

[15] This discussion of Canadian revenue-sharing is drawn primarily from the series of excellent analyses of Canadian finance by the Canadian Tax Foundation, most notably Moore et al. (1966).

[16] The tax credit rate index has been oversimplified for the purpose of demonstrating its steady growth. The periodic tax agreements are very complex and cover a wide variety of transactions and contingency arrangements within alternatives. For example, various agreements refer to tax room, tax rebates, tax credits, or tax abatements. But the effect of the agreement provisions upon Quebec changed only with the changes in the rates them-

selves. Complete explanations of the changes made in the various tax collection agreements can be found in Moore et al. (1966), Perry, Moore et al. (1966), Perry (1972), and Canadian Tax Foundation (1976).

[17] The figures are taken from Moore et al. (1966) and Canadian Tax Foundation (1976). They index a general trend, and the fact that the reporting base is not exactly equivalent over the years is not a critical shortcoming of the data.

[18] The consistent rise in the amount of expenditures is reflected in the growth of the number of shared-cost programs, which had reached 70 in 1972 (Saywell, 1972). Another good index is the growth of the federal-provincial machinery required to implement these programs and the variety of additional overlapping functions which are a part of cooperative federalism. The number of committees, conferences, and other conjunctions in the Canadian adhocracy was estimated at 64 in 1957; they grew to 125 by 1965 (Gallant, 1965) and to 170 by 1969 (Saywell, 1969).

[19] One index, reflecting revenue transfers in all three of the major categories of payments, summarizes the fluctuations during the period. The following are the percentages of total revenues after intergovernmental transfers distributed by the federal government: 1946 (69.4%), 1951 (66.1%), 1956 (63.0%), 1961 (51.1%), 1966 (45.5%), 1968 (42.1%), 1970 (40.5%), 1972 (40.1%), and 1974 (43.9%). The trend is curvilinear but the stabilization in total revenues does not occur until around 1970 (Canada, Department of Finance, 1975).

[20] Cuneo and Curtis (1974: 2) note: "Such differences in findings on separatist support by social-class levels may be the result of changes through time, rather marked fluctuations in public opinion, or differing research procedures and operational definitions."

[21] Among surveyed Union Nationale supporters in the Montreal area on the 1970 election eve, 34.6% were sealed as favorable toward independence and 42.3% were sealed unfavorable; for Liberals the proportions were 15.5% and 75.5% (Latouche, 1973: 190).

[22] Former Liberal Premier Lesage coined the phrase that while the Liberals were not necessarily separatists, they were "separatists if necessary" (Saywell, 1965).

[23] There is a tendency in this paper, by virtue of the analytical focus, to assume that only the constitutional-legal issues are important when observing the phenomena of provincial elections. This emphasis offsets the opposite tendency in some studies to ignore the nationalist dimension: "There are those who theorize that nationalism has nothing to do with vote getting but there can be no doubt that it is an element in almost every issue in Quebec" (Holden, 1970: 29). See also Lemieux (1973) for an elaboration of the pattern of nationalist competition in provincial elections.

[24] "If one were to try to discern a trend in these data, one would have to conclude that *both* the proportion of people favorable *and* the proportion of people unfavorable to separatism increased over time; the only decline was among the undecided" (Pinard, 1973: 34). Prime Minister Trudeau echoed this assessment in 1971: "separatism is not stronger than it was three or four years ago. There may be an increased polarization. In other words, those who were separatists three or four years ago may feel even more strongly for separatism now, but I don't think their number has substantially increased" (Saywell, 1971: 75).

[25] The most conservative estimate is that support for separatism at least remained constant during this period: "During the last ten years, through various polls and surveys, the question of separatism has been submitted practically every year to the Quebec electorate, or at least to its French-speaking constituents. The proportion favorable to separatism, in all of French-speaking Quebec, has always been below 20 per cent and, in fact, around 15 per cent" (Pinard, 1973: 136).

[26] The author is in basic sympathy with the proposition that the level of response exceeded the gravity of the need. The view of the October Crisis as an application of an unnecessarily high degree of force component is supported by Horowitz (1971) and Charney (1971), among many others.

[27] According to Saywell (1971: 84) the membership of the Parti Québécois fell from 80,000 before the 1970 provincial election to only 30,000 after the October Crisis.

[28] It is not possible to provide a quantitative measure of the degree of force component ap-

plied. One must conclude that it was large by Canadian standards. This conclusion would fit the theory that both low and high impositions of force components lead to stability while moderate government repression seems to stimulate greater instability (Markus and Nesvold, 1972).

[29] This interpretation has had a venerable tradition in sociology and is traced from Simmel's evaluation that unstable groups may be the very ones in which tension is so high that not even the slightest manifestations of conflict are allowed to surface (Coser, 1956).

[30] Lindberg (1970: 685) emphasizes the importance of reaching prior agreement on what can be decided collectively: "Another important resource in any decision-making system is the extent to which there is agreement on norms, rules and conventions governing the *ways in which* conflicts are to be resolved." Some recommended empirical indicators include the number of organizational subunits, the number of meetings convened, and other collective decision-making procedures. In the absence of a formal constitutional distributive mechanism, the extent of the Canadian adhocracy, documented earlier, is an index of the decentralization which is based on continuing informal agreements.

[31] There is a danger in longitudinal analysis of selected variables of giving the false impression that the events being analyzed were the only events of the period or that the imputations of importance provided by the theoretical framework is equivalent to the state of mind held by officials themselves when making policy. The author stresses that the selective approach of this study could be augmented by a more detailed review of events but that such an effort would blunt the theoretical focus. For readers interested in juxtaposing the events for themselves, a recommended synopsis of the period is Newman's (1968) aptly titled *Distemper of Our Times*.

[32] This approach marked a significant break with tradition. Socialization has not been the usual approach of Canadian decision makers. Instead, a mosaic tradition has been perpetuated and major cultural groups have lived in "patterns of mutually satisfying institutional self-segregation" (Guindon, 1967: 52).

[33] The difference between Haas and Etzioni on this point can be illustrated succinctly: "It must be stressed that the study of regional integration is unique and discrete from all previous systematic studies of political unification because it limits itself to noncoercive efforts" (Haas, 1970: 608); "A political community is a community which has three kinds of autarkic integrative processes. It has sufficient coercive power to countervail the coercive power of any member unit or coalition of them; it has a decision-making center that is able to affect significantly the allocation of assets throughout the community; and it is the dominant focus for the majority of politically active citizens" (Etzioni, 1968: 554).

[34] Johnson (1966: 127) compares the differential utilization of legitimate force components by various nations during the depression and finds that, even in stable democracies like the United States, under those conditions, the "system's integration rests increasingly on compulsion."

[35] It is said often that the one thing in Canada about which there is agreement is the desire not to become Americans. Evidence indicates that the value of this integrative force was not lost on Trudeau and other federal leaders. Examination of several policy areas, such as defense, northern development, and foreign investment would suggest the linkages between policies of pan-Canadianism and soft anti-Americanism.

REFERENCES

Almond, G. (1956) "Comparative political systems." *J. of Politics* 18 (August): 391-409.

Bertsch, G. (1972) "A cross-national analysis of the community-building process in Yugoslavia." *Comparative Political Studies* 4 (January): 438-460.

Burrowes, R. (1970) "Multiple time-series analysis of nation-level data." *Comparative Political Studies* 2 (January): 465-480.

Cairns, A. C. (1970) "The living Canadian constitution." *Queens Quarterly* 77 (Winter): 1-16.

Canada, Department of Finance (1975) *Federal-Provincial Fiscal Relations in Canada: An Overview*. Ottawa: Department of Finance.

Canadian Tax Foundation (1976) *The National Finances: An Analysis of the Revenues and Expenditures of the Government of Canada, 1975-1976*. Toronto: Canadian Tax Foundation.

Charney, A. (1971) "From Redpath Crescent to Rue des Recollets." *Canadian Forum* 50 (January): 324-329.

Clark, C. and S. Welch (1975) "National conditions as a base mark for supranational integration: the case of trade patterns." *Comparative Political Studies* 8 (October): 345-359.

Connelly, B. P. [ed.] (1973a) "Political integration in multinational states." *J. of International Affairs* 27, 1.

—[ed.] (1973b) "Political integration of multi-state nations." *J. of International Affairs* 27, 2.

Corbett, E. M. (1967) *Quebec Confronts Canada*. Baltimore: Johns Hopkins Press.

Coser, L. (1956) *The Functions of Social Conflict*. New York: Free Press.

Cuneo, C. J. and J. E. Curtis (1974) "Quebec separatism: an analysis of determinants within social-class levels." *Canadian Rev. of Sociology and Anthropology* 11 (February): 1-29.

Deutsch, K. W., S. A. Burrell, R. A. Kann, M. Lee, M. Lichterman, F. L. Lowenheim, and R. W. Van Wagener (1957) *Political Community and the North Atlantic Area: International Organization in the Light of Historical Experience*. Princeton, N.J.: Princeton Univ. Press.

Easton, D. A. (1965) *A Systems Analysis of Political Life*. New York: John Wiley.

Etzioni, A. (1968) *The Active Society*. New York: Free Press.

Feierabend, I. K., R. L. Feierabend, and T. R. Gurr [eds.] (1972) *Anger, Violence and Politics*. Englewood Cliffs, N.J.: Prentice-Hall.

Gallant, E. (1965) "The machinery of federal-provincial relations." *Canadian Public Administration* 8 (December): 515-526.

Guindon, H. (1967) "Two cultures: an essay on nationalism, class, and ethnic tension," pp. 33-59 in R. H. Leach (ed.) *Contemporary Canada*. Durham, N.C.: Duke Univ. Press.

Gzowski, P. (1963) "This is the true test of separatism." *Macleans* (November) 13-18.

Haas, E. B. (1970) "The study of regional integration: reflections on the joy and anguish of pretheorizing." *International Organization* 24 (Autumn): 607-646.

—(1961) "International integration: the European and the universal process." *International Organization* 15 (Summer): 366-392.

Hagy, J. H. (1969) "Quebec separatists: the first twelve years." *Queens Quarterly* 75 (Summer): 229-338.

Hayward, F. M. (1974) "Correlates of national political integration: the case of Ghana. *Comparative Political Studies* 7 (July): 165-192.

—(1970) "Continuities and discontinuities between studies of national and international political integration: some implications for future research efforts." *International Organization* 24 (Autumn): 917-941.

Holden, R. D. (1970) 1970 Election: *Quebec Crucible*. Montreal: Nicholas D. Demetelin Editions Aries.

Horowitz, G. (1971) "The perils of complaisance." *Canadian Forum* 51 (April-May): 39-41.

Jacob, P. E. and H. Teune (1964) "The integrative process: guidelines for analysis of the bases of political community," pp. 1-45 in P. E. Jacob and J. Toscano (eds.) *The Integration of Political Communities*. Philadelphia, Pa.: Lippincott.

Jensen, J. and P. Regenstreif (1970) "Some dimensions of partisan choice in Quebec." *Canadian J. of Political Science* 3 (June): 308-318.

Johnson, C. (1966) *Revolutionary Change*. Boston: Little, Brown.

Latouche, D. (1973) "The independence option: ideological and empirical elements," pp. 179-196 in D. Thompson (ed.) *Quebec Society and Politics: Views from the Inside*. Buffalo, N.Y.: McClelland and Stewart.

Lemieux, V. (1973) "The provincial party system in Quebec," pp. 99-117 in D. Thompson (ed.) *Quebec Society and Politics: Views from the Inside.* Buffalo, N.Y.: McClelland and Stewart.

Lijphart, A. (1971) "Cultural diversity and theories of political integration." *Canadian J. of Political Science* 4 (March): 1-14.

—(1969) "Consociational democracy." *World Politics* 21 (January): 207-225.

Lindberg, L. N. (1970) "Political integration as a multidimensional phenomenon requiring multivariate measurement." *International Organization* 24 (Autumn): 649-731.

Lipset, S. M. (1967) *The First New Nation.* Garden City, N.Y.: Doubleday.

Livingston, W. S. (1956) *Federalism and Constitutional Change.* Oxford: Clarendon.

Loh, W. D. (1975) "Nationalist attitudes in Quebec and Belgium." *J. of Conflict Resolution* 19 (June): 217-249.

Lynn, J. M. (1968) "Federal-provincial fiscal relations," pp. 195-215 in J. P. Meekison (ed.) *Canadian Federalism: Myth or Reality.* Toronto: Methuen.

Mallory, J. R. (1965) "The five faces of federalism," pp. 3-15 in P. A. Crepeau and C. B. Macpherson (eds.) *The Future of Canadian Federalism.* Toronto: Univ. of Toronto Press.

Markus, G. B. and B. A. Nesvold (1972) "Governmental coerciveness and political instability: an exploratory study of cross-national patterns." *Comparative Political Studies* 5 (July): 231-244.

Meekison, J. P. (1971) "Constitutional reform in Canada," pp. 235-252 in J. P. Meekison (ed.) *Canadian Federalism: Myth or Reality.* Toronto: Methuen.

Moore, A. M., J. H. Perry, and D. I. Beach (1966) *The Financing of Canadian Federation: The First Hundred Years.* Toronto: Canadian Tax Foundation.

Morrison, D. G. and H. M. Stevenson (1972) "Integration and instability: patterns of African political development." *Amer. Pol. Sci. Rev.* 66 (September): 902-927.

Newman, P. C. (1968) *The Distemper of Our Times.* Winnipeg, Manitoba: Greywood.

Nye, J. S. (1968) "Comparative regional integration: concept and measurement." *International Organization* 22 (Autumn): 855-880.

Perry, D. B. (1972) Federal-provincial fiscal relations: the last six years and the next five." *Canadian Tax J.* 20 (July/August): 349-360.

Pinard, M. (1973) The ongoing political realignments in Quebec," pp. 119-135 in D. Thompson (ed.). *Quebec Society and Politics: Views from the Inside.* Buffalo, N.Y.: McClelland and Stewart.

Pious, R. (1973) "Canada and the crisis of Quebec." *J. of International Affairs 27*, 1: 53-65.

Puchala, D. J. (1972) "Of blind men, elephants, and international integration." *J. of Common Market Studies 10* (March): 267-284.

—(1970) "International transactions and regional integration." *International Organization* 24 (Autumn): 732-762.

Quinn, H. F. (1963) *The Union Nationale.* Toronto: Univ. of Toronto Press.

Saywell, J. T. [ed.] (1972) *Canadian Annual Review for 1972.* Toronto: Univ. of Toronto Press.

—(1971) *Canadian Annual Review* for 1971. Toronto: Univ. of Toronto Press.

—(1969) *Canadian Annual Review* for 1969. Toronto: Univ. of Toronto Press.

—(1965) *Canadian Annual Review* for 1965. Toronto: Univ. of Toronto Press.

Scott, F. and M. Oliver [eds.] (1964) *Quebec States Her Case.* Toronto: Macmillan.

Smiley, D. V. (1963) *Conditional Grants and Canadian Federalism.* Toronto: Canadian Tax Foundation.

—(1962) "The Rowell-Sirois report, provincial autonomy, and postwar Canadian federalism." *Canadian J. of Economics and Political Science* 28 (February): 54-69.

Stewart, J. (1970) *Seven Years of Terrorism:* The FLQ. Richmond Hill, Ontario: Simon & Schuster of Canada.

Toronto Telegram (1969) Canada 70: *A Summary Coast to Coast.* Toronto: McClelland and Stewart.

Weiner, M. (1967) "Political integration and political development," pp. 150-166 in C. E. Welch, Jr. (ed.) *Political Modernization.* Belmont, Calif.: Wadsworth.

Zaninovich, M. G. and D. A. Brown (1973) "Political integration in Czechoslovakia: the implications of the Prague spring and Soviet intervention." *J. of International Affairs* 27, 1:66-79.

31

For an Independent Québec

René Lévesque

I

What does Québec want? The question is an old cliché in Canadian political folklore. Again and again, during the more than 30 years since the end of World War II, it's been raised whenever Québec's attitudes made it the odd man out in the permanent pull and tug of our federal-provincial relations. In fact, it's a question which could go back to the British conquest of an obscure French colony some 15 years before American Independence, and then run right through the stubborn survival of those 70,000 settlers and their descendants during the following two centuries.

By now, there are some six million of them in Canada, not counting the progeny of the many thousands who were forced by poverty, especially around the turn of the century, to migrate to the United States, and now constitute substantial "Franco" communities in practically all the New England states.

---

* From *Foreign Affairs,* Vol. 54 (July, 1976), pp. 733-744. Copyright 1976 by Council of Foreign Relations Inc. Reprinted by permission.

But Québec remains the homeland. All along the valley of the St. Lawrence, from the Ottawa River down to the Gaspé peninsula and the great Gulf, in the ancient settlements which grew into the big cities of Montréal and Québec, in hundreds of smaller towns and villages from the American border to the mining centres and power projects in the north, there are now some 4.8 million "Québécois." That's 81 percent of the population of the largest and second most populous of Canada's ten provinces.

What does this French Québec want? Sometime during the next few years, the question may be answered. And there are growing possibilities that the answer could very well be—independence.

Launched in 1967-68, the Parti Québécois, whose platform is based on political sovereignty, now fills the role of Her Majesty's loyal Opposition in the National Assembly—as we nostalgically designate our provincial legislature. In its first electoral test in 1970, it already had had 24 percent of the votes. Then in 1973, a second general election saw it jump to 30 percent, and, although getting only six out of 110 seats, become what our British-type parliamentary system calls the Official Opposition, i.e., the government's main interlocutor and challenger.

The next election might come any time now; this year in the fall, just after the Montréal Olympics, or at the latest in the fall of 1977. Whenever it does, all available indicators, including an impressive series of public opinion polls, tell us that for the first time the outcome is totally uncertain. The present provincial government, a branch of that same Liberal Party which also holds power at the federal level under Pierre Elliott Trudeau, is obviously on the way out. It has been in power for six years, and ever since its second and Pyrrhic victory in 1973 (102 seats) it has been going steadily downhill. Apart from a host of social and economic troubles, some imported but many more of its own making, there is around it a pervasive smell of incompetence and corruption. The scandal-ridden atmosphere surrounding the Olympic construction sites and the incredible billion-dollar deficit which is now forecast are just the most visible aspects of a rather complete political and administrative disaster.

Looking for an alternative, the French voter is now leaning quite clearly toward the Parti Québécois. In that "national" majority, we are at least evenly matched with Premier Robert Bourassa's Liberals, and probably ahead. As for the Anglophone minority of over a million people, whose natural attachment to the status quo normally makes them the staunchest supporters of the reigning federalist party, they are confused as never before. Composed of a dwindling proportion of Anglo-Saxon descendants of eighteenth-century conquerors or American Loyalists, along with those of nineteenth-century Irish immigrants, and a steadily growing "ethnic" mosaic (Jewish, Italian, Greek, etc.), in the crunch most of this minority will probably end up, as usual, supporting the Liberals. But not with the traditional unanimity. Caught between the Charybdis of dissatisfaction and the Scylla of secessionism, many are looking for some kind of "third force." Others, especially among younger people, are ready to go along with the Parti Québécois, whose minority vote should be a little less marginal next time than last.

So, all in all, there is quite a serious possibility that an "independentist" government will soon be elected in Québec. At first sight, this looks like a dramatically rapid development, this burgeoning and flowering over a very few years of a political emancipation movement in a population which, until recently, was commonly referred to as quiet old Québec. But in fact, its success would mean, very simply, the normal healthy end result of a long and laborious national evolution.

II

There was the definite outline of a nation in that small French colony which was taken over, in 1763, by the British Empire at its apogee. For over a century and a half, beginning just before the Pilgrim Fathers landed in the Boston area, that curious mixture of peasants and adventurers had been writing a proud history all over the continent. From Hudson Bay to the Gulf of Mexico, and from Labrador to the Rockies, they had been the discoverers, the fur-traders, the fort-builders. Out of this far-ranging saga, historically brief though it was, and the tenacious roots which at the same time were being sunk into the St. Lawrence lowlands, there slowly developed an identity quite different from the original stock as well as from France of the *ancien régime*; just as different, in its way, as the American identity had become from its own British seeds. Thus, when the traumatic shock of the conquest happened, it had enough staying power to survive, tightly knit around its Catholic clergy and its country landowners.

Throughout the next hundred years, while English Canada was being built, slowly but surely, out of the leftovers of the American Revolution and as a rampart against America's recurrent attacks of Manifest Destiny, French Québec managed to hang on—mostly because of its "revenge of the cradle." It was desperately poor, cut off from the decision-making centres both at home and in Great Britain, and deprived of any cultural nourishment from its former mother country. But its rural, frugal society remained incredibly prolific. So it grew impressively, at least in numbers. And it held on obstinately, according to its lights and as much as its humble means made it possible, to those two major ingredients of national identity—land and language. The hold on land was at best tenuous and, as in any colonial context, confined to the multitude of small farm holdings. Everything else—from the growth of major cities to the setting-up of manufacturing industries and then the rush of resource development—was the exclusive and undisputed field of action of "les Anglais," the growing minority of Anglo-Saxon and then assimilated immigrant groups who ran most of Québec under the compact leadership of Montréal-based entrepreneurs, financiers and merchant kings.

As for the French elite, it remained mostly made up of doctors, lawyers, and priests—"essential services" for the bodies and souls of cheap labour, whose miraculous birthrate kept the supply continuously overabundant. And naturally, there were politicians, practically all of that typical colonial breed which is tolerated as long as it keeps natives happily excited about accessories and divided on essentials.

Needless to say, the educational system was made both to reflect this type of society and to keep it going nicely and quietly. There was a modest collection of church-run seminaries, where the main accent was on recruiting for the priesthood, and which, for over a century, led to just one underdeveloped university. For nine-tenths of the children, there was nothing but grammar school, if that. Read and write barely enough to sign your name, and then, without any time for "getting ideas," graduate to obedient respectful employment by any boss generous enough to offer a steady modest job.

Such was the culturally starved and economically inferior, but well-insulated and thus highly resistant, French Québec which, 109 years ago, was led into the final mutation of British North America and its supreme defence against American expansionism: Confederation, of four eastern colonies as a beginning, but soon to run north of the border "from sea to sea." Into that impressive Dominion, originally as one of four and eventually one of ten provinces, Québec was incorporated without trouble and generally without enthusiasm. From now on, it was to be a minority forever, and, with the help of a dynamic federal immigration policy, a steadily diminishing one. In due time, it would probably merge and disappear into the mainstream, or at the most remain as a relatively insignificant and yet convenient ghetto: *la différence*.

As the building of Canada accelerated during the late nineteenth and early twentieth centuries, a tradition was established that Québec was to get its measured share of the work, anytime there was enough to go around—and the same for rewards. And so, in a nutshell, it went until fairly recently. All told, it hasn't been such a bad deal, this status of "inner colony" in a country owned and managed by another national entity. Undoubtedly, French Québec was (as it remains to this day) the least ill-treated of all colonies in the world. Under a highly centralized federal system, which is much closer to a unitary regime than American federalism, it was allowed its full panoply of provincial institutions: cabinet, legislature, courts, along with the quasi-permanent fun of great squabbles, usually leading to exciting election campaigns, about the defence or extension of its "state rights"! On three occasions during the last 80 years, one of "its own" has even been called upon—at times when there was felt a particular need to keep the natives quiet—to fill the most flattering of all offices, that of federal Prime Minister. Last but not least of the three, Mr. Trudeau, of whose "Canadian nationalism" it is naturally part and parcel, did as splendidly as was humanly possible for most of the last ten years in this big-chief-of-Québec dimension of the job. But the law of diminishing returns, along with the inevitable way of all (including political) flesh, has been catching up with his so-called French Power in Ottawa. And no replacement seems to be in sight.

III

But this is getting ahead of our story. To understand the rise of Québec's own new nationalism and its unprecedented drive toward self-government, we must go back at least as far as World War II. Not that the dream had completely vanished during the two long centuries of survival which have just been described—from an admittedly partisan, but, I honestly believe, not unfair viewpoint. In the 1830s, for instance, there even was an ill-advised and disastrous armed rebellion by a few hundred "Patriots," leading to bloody repression and lasting memories about what not to do. And it is rather significant, by the way, that it took until just now before the poor heroic victims of that abortive rebellion became truly rehabilitated in popular opinion.

Small and impotent though it was, and in spite of feeling that this condition would possibly last forever, French Québec never quite forgot the potential nation it had once been, never quite gave up dreaming about some miracle which might bring back its chance in the future. In some distant, indescribable future. Now and then, there were stirrings: a writer here, a small political coterie there; a great upsurge of nationalist emotions, in the 1880s, around the Riel affair—the hanging by "les Anglais" of the French-speaking leader of the Prairie Metis; then in 1917, on the conscription issue, a bitter and frequently violent confrontation between the Empire-minded English and the "isolationist" French; faint stirrings again in the Twenties; stronger ones in the Thirties.

Then World War II, with a repeat, in 1944, of the total disagreement on conscription. But mostly, here as elsewhere, this most terrible of all wars was also a midwife for revolutionary change. Thankfully in less disruptive a manner than in other parts of the world, it did start a revolution in Québec. Wartime service, both overseas and on the industrial home-front, dealt a mortal blow to the old order, gave an irresistible impetus to urbanization and started the breakup of the traditional rural-parish ideal, yanked women by the thousands into war-plant industry and as many men into battle-dress discovery of the great wide world. For a small cooped-up society, this was a more traumatic experience than for most others. And then when the post-war years brought the Roaring Fifties, unprecedented mobility, and television along with a consumer society, the revolution had to become permanent.

The beginning of the 1960s saw it baptized officially: the Quiet Revolution, with the adjective implying that "quaint old Québec" couldn't have changed all that much. But it had. Its old set of values literally shattered, it was feeling collectively naked, like a lobster during its shedding season, looking frantically about for a new armour with which to face the modern world. The first and most obvious move was toward education. After so prolonged and scandalous a neglect of this most basic instrument of development, it was quickly realized that here was the first urgent bootstrap operation that had to be launched. It was done with a vengeance: from one of the lowest in the Western world, Québec per capita investment in education rapidly became, and remains, one of the very highest. Not always well spent (but who is to throw the first stone?), with many mistakes along the way, and the job still far from complete, which it will never be anyway; but the essential results are there, and multiplying: human resources that are, at long last, getting required development, along with a somewhat equal chance for all and a normal furious rise in general expectations. The same, naturally, is happening also in other fields, quite particularly in that of economics, the very first where such rising expectations were bound to strike against the wall of an entrenched colonial setup, with its now intolerable second-class status for the French majority, and the stifling remote control of nearly all major decisions either in Ottawa or in alien corporate offices.

Inevitably, there had to be a spillover into politics. More than half of our public revenue and most of the decisions that count were and are in outside hands, in a federal establishment which was basically instituted not by or for us, but by others and, always first and foremost, for their own purposes. With the highly centralized financial system that this establishment constitutionally lords over, this means, for example, that about 80 percent of Québec savings and potential investment capital ends up in banks and insurance companies whose operations are none of our business. It also means, just for example once again, that immigration is also practically none of our business; and this could have, and is having, murderous effects on a minority people with a birthrate, changed like everything else in less than a generation, down from its former prodigious level to close to zero population growth.

Throughout the 1960s, these and other problems were interminably argued about and batted back and forth between federal politicians and bureaucrats ("What we have we hold, until we get more") and a succession of insistent but orthodox, no more than rock-the-boat, nationalists in Québec. But while this dialogue of the deaf was going on and on, the idea of political independence reappeared as it had to. Not as a dream this time, but as a project, and very quickly as a serious one. This developed by leaps and bounds from easily ridiculed marginal groups to small semi-organized political factions, and finally to a full-fledged national party in 1967-68. These were the same two years during which, by pure coincidence, Mr. Trudeau was just as rapidly being elevated to the heights as a new federalist champion from Québec.

But in spite of his best efforts and those of his party's branch-plant in provincial government, and through an unceasing barrage of money, vilification and rather repugnant fear-inducing propaganda, the voters have democratically brought the Parti Québécois ever closer to power. Which brings us right back to our starting-point. . . .

IV

Let us suppose it does happen, and Québec peacefully elects such a government. What then?

The way we see it, it would have to go somewhat like this. There is a new Québec government which is totally dedicated to political independence. But this same Québec, for the time being, is still very much a component of federal Canada, with its quite legitimate body of elected representatives in Ottawa. This calls, first of all, for at least a try at negotiation. But fruitful talk between two equally legitimate and diametrically opposed levels of government, without any further pressure from the population—that would be a real first in Canadian political history! Obviously, there would have to be the referendum which the Parti Québécois proposes in order to get the decisive yes-or-no answer to the tired question: What *does* Québec want? (This was precisely the procedure by which the only new province to join Confederation during our recent democratic past, Newfoundland, was consulted in 1948-49 about whether or not to opt in. So why not about opting out?) If the answer should be no, then there's nothing to do but wait for the momentum of change to keep on working until we all find out whether or not there is finally to be a nation here. If the answer is yes, out, then the pressure is on Ottawa, along with a rather dramatic surge of outside attention, and we all get a privileged opportunity to study the recently inked Helsinki Declaration and other noble documents about self-determination for all peoples.

Fully confident of the basic integrity of Canadian democracy, and just as conscious that any silliness would be very costly for both sides, we firmly believe that the matter would then be brought to a negotiated settlement. Especially since the Parti Québécois, far from aiming at any kind of mutual hositility or absurd Berlin Wall, will then repeat its stand-ing offer of a new kind of association, as soon as it is agreed to get rid of our illusion of deep unshakeable national unity, when in fact here are two quite real and distinct entities in an obsolete and increasingly mor-bid majority/minority relationship. Our aim is simply full equality by the only means through which a smaller nation can reasonably expect to achieve it with a larger one: self-government. But we are definitely not unaware of the shock waves that such a break after so long an illusion of eternity is bound to send through the Canadian political fabric.

We do not accept the simplistic domino theory, where Québec's de-parture is presented as the beginning of fatal dislocation, with "separa-tism" spreading in all directions like a galloping disease until the balkan-ized bits and pieces are swallowed up by the huge maw next door. In spite of the somewhat unsure character of its national identity and its excessive satellization by the American economic and cultural empire, Canada-without-Québec has enough "différence" left, sufficient tradi-tions and institutional originality, to withstand the extraction of its "foreign body" and find a way to go on from there. It might even turn out to be a heaven-sent opportunity to revamp the overcentralized and ridiculously bureaucratized federal system, that century-old sacred cow which, for the moment, nobody dares to touch seriously for fear of encouraging Québec's subversive leanings!

Be that as it may, we know there would be a traumatic moment and a delicate transition during which things might go wrong between us for quite a while, or else, one would hope, start going right as never before. With this strange new-coloured Québec on the map between Ontario and the Maritime provinces, Canada must be kept from feeling incur-ably "Pakistanized," so we must address ourselves without delay to the problem of keeping a land bridge open with as much free flow of people and goods as is humanly possible; as much and more as there is, I would imagine, between Alaska and the main body of the United States over the western land bridge.

Such a scenario would call, as a decisive first step, for a customs union, as full-fledged as both countries consider to be mutually advan-tageous. We have, in fact, been proposing that ever since the Parti Québécois was founded, and naturally meeting with the most resonant silence in all orthodox federalist circles. But in the midst of that silence, not a single responsible politician, nor for that matter a single important businessman, has been heard to declare that it wouldn't happen if and when the time comes. For indisputably such a partnership, carefully negotiated on the basis of equality, is bound to be in the cards. Nothing prevents one envisaging it, for instance, going immediately, or at least very quickly, as far as the kind of monetary union which the European Common Market, with its original six and now nine members, has been fitfully aiming at for so many years. And building on this foundation, it would lead this new "northern tier" to a future immeasurably richer and more stimulating than the 109-year-old bind in which two nations more often than not feel and act like Churchill's two scorpions in the same bottle.

V

What of Québec's own national future, both internal and international, in this context of sovereignty-cum-interdependence?

The answers here, for reasons that are evident, have to be brief, even sketchy and essentially tentative. The perspective of nationhood, for people who haven't been there yet, is bound to be an uncertain horizon. The more so in a period of history like ours, when so much is changing so fast you get the feeling that maybe change itself is becoming the only law to be counted on. Who can pretend to know exactly what or where his country will be 25 or even just ten years from now?

One thing sure, is that Québec will not end up, either soon or in any foreseeable future, as the anarchic caricature of a revolutionary banana republic which adverse propaganda has been having great sinister fun depicting in advance. Either-Ottawa-or is very simply inspired by prejudice, the origin of this nonsense mostly to be found in the tragic month of October 1970 and the great "crisis" which our political establishments, under the astutely calculating Mr. Trudeau, managed to make out of a couple of dozen young terrorists, whose ideology was a hopeless hodgepodge of anarcho-nationalism and kindergarten Marxism, which had no chance of having any kind of serious impact. What they *did* accomplish was two kidnappings and, most cynically welcome of all, one murder—highly unfortunate but then also particularly par for the course in the international climate at the time. What was not par at all, however, was the incredible abuse of power for which those events, relatively minor per se, were used as a pretext: the careful buildup of public hysteria, army trucks rolling in during the night, and then, for months on end, the application in Québec, and solely in Québec, of a federal War Measures Act for which no peacetime precedent exists in any democratic country. A great spectacle produced in order to terrorize the Québécois forever back into unquestioning submissiveness, and, outside, to feed the mill of scary propaganda about how dangerous this tame animal could nevertheless be!

In actual fact, French Québec, with its normal share of troubles, disquiet and, now, the same kind of social turmoil and search for new values that are rampant all over the Western world, remains at bottom a very solid, well-knit and nonviolent society. Even its new and demanding nationalism has about itself something less strident and essentially more self-confident than its current pan-Canadian counterpart. For Québec has an assurance of identity, along with a relative lack of aggressiveness, which are the result of that one major factor of national durability lacking in the rest of Canada: a different language and the cultural fabric that goes with it.

Now how does the Parti Québécois see this society begin to find its way as an independent nation? What is the general outline of the political, social and economic structure we hope to bring forth? Serious observers have been calling our program basically social-democratic, rather comparable to the Scandinavian models although certainly not a carbon copy since all people, through their own experiences, have to invent their own "mix."

The way we have been trying to rough it out democratically through half a dozen national party conventions, ours would call for a presidential regime, as much of an equal-opportunity social system as we could afford, and a decent measure, as quickly as possible but as carefully as indicated, of economic "repatriation." This last would begin to happen immediately, and normally without any great perturbation, through the very fact of sovereignty: with the gathering in of all of our public revenues and the full legislative control which any self-respecting national state has to implement over its main financial institutions, banks, insurance companies and the like. In the latter case, this would allow us to break the stranglehold in which the old British-inspired banking system of just a handful of "majors" has always kept the people's money and financial initiative. The dominant position in our repatriated financial circuit would be handed over to Québec's cooperative institutions, which happen to be particularly well developed in that very field, and, being strongly organized on a regional basis, would afford our population a decent chance for better-balanced, responsible, democratic development. And that, by the way, is just one fundamental aspect of the kind of evolution toward a new economic democracy, from the lowest rung in the marketplace up to board room levels, which all advanced societies that are not already doing so had better start thinking about in the very near future.

As to non-resident enterprise, apart from the universal minimums concerning incorporations and due respect for Québec taxes, language and other classic national requirements, what we have been fashioning over the last few years is an outline of a policy which we think is both logical and promising. It would take the form of an "investment code," giving a clean-cut picture, by sectors, of what parts of our economic life (e.g., culturally oriented activities, basic steel and forest resources) we would insist on keeping under home ownership, what other parts we would like to see under mixed control (a very few selected but strategic cases) and, finally, the multitude of fields (tied to markets, and to technological and/or capital necessities) where foreign interests would be allowed to stay or to enter privided they do not tend to own us along with their businesses.

In brief, Québec's most privileged links, aside from its most essential relationship with the Canadian partner, would be first with the United States—where there is no imaginable reason to frown on such a tardy but natural and healthy development (especially during a Bicentennial year). Then Québec would look to other Francophone or "Latin" countries as cultural respondents, and to France herself—who would certainly not be indifferent to the fact that this new nation would constitute the second most important French-speaking country in the world. In brief, such is the peaceful and, we confidently hope, fruitfully progressive state which may very well appear on the map of North America before the end of the decade.

32

Speech to the Nation:
Quebec Election November 24, 1976*

Prime Minister Pierre Elliott Trudeau

To some Canadians last week's election in Quebec has given rise to many hopes. To many other Canadians it has been a cause of great concern, but to all it has posed many questions, and I believe it is incumbent upon me, as Prime Minister of this nation, to try, by way of response to some of these questions, to try to take stock of the current situation.

The first fact that we must acknowledge is that democracy is in good health in Quebec, and that is good news.

When a young party less than 10 years old, fighting only its third general election, can take power, while respecting the democratic liberties, I think this phenomenon has few equals in the world today. It is a victory for thousands of party workers who, with no support other than their faith in an idea, and in their belief in political morality, have taken the Parti Quebecois into power. That is a victory for them, but it is also a

---

* Reprinted by permission.

source of satisfaction for the great majority of Quebeckers who believe in the democratic process, many of whom certainly will hope to use that process to defeat the very ideas of the Parti Quebecois in their day.

The second fact is that Quebec does not believe in separatism. Now, this proposition, perhaps apparently paradoxical, is very easy to demonstrate. The Parti Quebecois was defeated in 1970 and again in 1973; those two elections when it advocated the separation of Quebec, but it won in 1976 when it repeated over and over again that the issue was not separation of the provinces but sound administration of that province.

Thus the separatists themselves do not believe that separatism has the support of Quebeckers, and that, for me, is the second piece of good news.

The third fact: Quebeckers have chosen a new government; not a new country. Mr. Levesque has no mandate to bring in separation, nor, of course, do I, nor do I have the desire to ask for such a mandate. Consequently, the federal government, and the provincial government will have to co-operate together within the framework of the Constitution, continuing to serve to the utmost the interest of the people of Quebec, just as the federal Government, in co-operation with the other provincial governments, seeks to fulfil and serve the interests of the peoples of the other provinces.

But now within provincial jurisdiction, the Quebec Government has a very important priority, and will have to face many serious internal problems. The school question, the stability of investments, management-labour relations, to mention only three of the more serious of those as an example. But for other problems, those which come under the jurisdiction of both levels of government, for those problems, the solution can only come through close co-operation with the federal Government.

I want to assure the people of Quebec, as I did the very moment after the election, I want to assure them that this co-operation will be forthcoming in every way. In the months that follow very soon now we will be having a whole series of Federal-Provincial Conferences at the ministerial level, at the level of First Ministers. We will have to renew the Anti-Inflation Agreement; we will have to fight together to bring unemployment down; we will have to come to an understanding on the price of oil; we will have to determine a new equalization formula; and we will have to conclude agreements on health and hospitalization insurance: and we will have to conclude agreements on post-secondary education. Three fields, by the way, in which Canada reimburses the provincial governments for about 50 per cent of their expenses.

Well, now, we should know at the outset that in all these areas the discussion between Ottawa and the provinces will be difficult, but so they will be between the central government, between the Canadian Government and the other provinces, and they always have been. It has always been thus, that the provincial Premiers come to Federal-Provincial Conferences demanding more money for their provinces because, naturally, it is easier to ask more money of the federal government than to tax one's own taxpayers to raise taxes within one's own province. Then, of course, there will be the problem of the Constitution.

This involves not only patriation and amending the formula, but, of course, it involves the problem of the sharing of powers between the Canadian Government and the provincial governments.

On that subject, and because it seems to be current now that more and more people are thinking that decentralization would be a solution to our problems. I want to point out that the federal Government, our government, has already conducted negotiations on the separation of power in 1968, 1969, and 1970. In the course of these discussions we advocated a more flexible, a more functional approach to federalism, a more functional share of jurisdiction, and we will willingly undertake that dialogue once again. It was only interrupted, as a matter of fact, because some provinces, and the rest of us agreed with them, suggested that we proceed rather with the discussion of patriation and the amending formula, interrupting the discussion on the separation of powers, that we proceed with patriation and amending, because at that time it seemed within reach. But we will resume these discussions if and when the provinces want to have a discussion on the separation of powers.

I do want, however, to issue a caution, particularly for those who think that more decentralization, or a new separation of powers would solve our present worries. I say it is a grave illusion to believe that those who seek the breakup of Canada would suddenly cease to pursue their objective simply because the provincial governments have increased their powers in some areas, say, communications or immigration or fiscal powers, or cultural matters.

The question facing us is much more profound. The stakes for Canadians are much more important and the question is this: can Francophones of Quebec consider Canada as their country, or must they feel at home only in Quebec? And you know as well as I know that a new sharing of power between Ottawa and the provinces will never give the answer to that particular question, will never make a Francophone feel more at home in Toronto or in Vancouver than he does in Quebec.

Quebeckers, like citizens of the other provinces, are proud. They seek personal fulfillment in a free and independent way. The central question, therefore, is whether this growth of freedom and independence is best assured by Canada, or by Quebec alone. Canadians must think about this brutal question now. Not only think of solving it in words, but by deeds and through their attitudes. In the area of the language problem, of course, but also in the very important areas of regional disparity and social justice.

With the victory of the Parti Quebecois, we can no longer afford to postpone these questions by one generation, to put the problem aside for the next generation of Canadians, and in this sense, the crisis is real; the crisis is now, and the challenge is immediate. I believe that Canada cannot, indeed, that Canada must not survive by force. The country will only remain united—it should only remain united—if its citizens want to live together in one civil society.

History created this country from the meeting of two realities; the French and English realities. Then these were enriched by the contributions of people from all parts of the world, but this coming together, this meeting, this encounter of realities, though at times difficult to accept, and hard to practise, this encounter has, itself, become the fabric of our life as a nation, the source of our individuality, the very cornerstone of our identity as a people.

Our forefathers willed this country into being. Times, circumstance and pure will cemented us together in a unique national enterprise, and that enterprise by flying in the face of all expectations, of all experiences, of all conventional wisdom, that enterprise provides the world with a lesson in fraternity.

This extraordinary undertaking is so advanced on the road to liberty, so advanced in the way of social justice and of prosperity, that to abandon it now would be to sin against the spirit; to sin against humanity.

I have known Rene Levesque for many years, some 20 years. I personally know many of his colleagues. I respect their intelligence and their dedication. We all believe in equality; we all want liberty and equality and democracy for the citizens of this country, but we disagree profoundly on the means to be employed.

My disagreement with Mr. Levesque, dating back some 10 years, arises out of my conviction that there is room in Canada for all Canadians. He, on the other hand, probably not without regret—perhaps even with sadness—he, on the other hand, believes the opposite. He has, therefore, surrounded himself with a strong core of blood brothers, and he speaks to the rest of Canada as one speaks to good neighbours.

For myself, I believe that it is possible to be, at the same time, a good Canadian and a good Quebecker. Just as it is possible to be a good Canadian and a good Nova Scotian, or a good British Columbian. And I will fight to the end against anyone who wants to prevent me from being both.

Today I am addressing all Canadians, as I have since I have taken office. I am speaking to you as to my fellow citizens. I am speaking to you of a deeper brotherhood than that of blood, or a fraternity of hope and of charity in the scriptural sense, for if the Canadian nation must survive, it will only survive in mutual respect and in love for one another.

Each of you, each of us, must work toward that goal with our every fibre in the reality of our daily lives. You can be assured that, as your Prime Minister, and as a consequence, as your servant and fellow-Canadian, I will continue to work toward these objectives with all my strength.

33

Quebec's Right to Secede

Pierre De Bané and Martial Asselin

The following is a minority report of the special Joint Committee of the Senate and the House of Commons on the Constitution. The official report of the Committee included none of the five minority reports nor does it even hint that they exist.

We are Quebecers, and it was first and foremost as such that we took part in the activities of the Committee on the Constitution. We are also Canadians who wish to maintain the country's unity.

With the other members of the Committee, we examined the many briefs submitted to us. We listened to the testimony given by experts, we studied the documents and research work prepared for us. With the other members of the Committee, we discussed at great length each and every recommendation in the report which is now being made public. We paid close attention to the meaning and significance that we felt should be given to the report, which seemed to us extremely important in the present situation.

This report has now been submitted to Parliament. It unquestionably required a great amount of work. We acknowledge this fact. We must also admit, however, that it remains seriously incomplete. So incomplete, indeed, that we cannot in all conscience endorse it or allow people to believe that it meets with our agreement. We therefore dissociate ourselves from it or reasons which we will give in this minority report.

We should first mention, however, that we informed our colleagues on the Committee of our views on numerous occasions, but without

---

* From *Canadian Forum,* Vol. 52, May 1972, pp. 6-11. Reprinted by permission.

success. We did so openly, in the constant hope that the report would deal directly and honestly with the very real problems facing Canada and Quebec with regard to the Constitution. This hope was doomed to disappointment. In spite of our insistence, the report remained silent on these major topics. As a result, even though it is lengthy and detailed, it sidesteps the main issue, and to all intents and purposes is lacking a chapter. It is the missing chapter which we are attempting to supply here.

THE CASE FOR CONSTITUTIONAL REVIEW: QUEBEC'S DISSATISFACTION

If the constitutional problem is to be viewed realistically, mention must be made of Quebec. It is because of Quebec, that the problem has arisen. It is useless to claim some other starting point or to pretend that one of the other provinces or even the federal government had become dissatisfied with the present Canadian Constitution to the point of requesting it to be revised. Things have not happened this way. Quebec is thus the direct source of the demand for constitutional review and the end result of this review, whatever it will be, should logically and foremost take Quebec into account.

What sort of relations have existed between Quebec and Ottawa over the past ten years? Since the beginning of the "quiet revolution"?

They confirm, in a different form, a trend which was already evident at the time of Maurice Duplessis and even much earlier. If we consider Quebec's history, we see that this province has on numerous occasions and in numerous ways demonstrated its dissatisfaction with the Canadian constitutional context. Periods characterized by a negative outlook and isolationism have given way to periods when the positions taken by Quebec have been more concrete, more positive and more open. But the same common denominator, a more or less explicit search for a constitutional system better adapted to Quebec's needs, has always been present. With time, the words and expressions have changed, strategies have evolved and individuals have been replaced but, and we emphasize this fact, the dissatisfaction has not only remained, it has increased. This is unquestionably a fact of our political history and not simply accidental.

An analysis of the last ten years shows this even more clearly. During this period there has been almost every possible combination of political party between Quebec and Ottawa, key positions have been filled by men of very different temperaments, and numerous attempts, all supposed to be successful, have been made to solve the disagreements. During this period there have been three prime ministers and two changes of government in Ottawa and four prime ministers and three governments in Quebec.

For all that, can we say that the Quebec-Ottawa problem has been resolved, that the tension between the two capitals is any less, or that the dissatisfaction has disappeared? If we consider the ten-year period as a whole, the answer to all these questions is definitely no. Even as we are writing this document, practically all the major difficulties concerning the division of powers, which one could have detected in 1960 or 1961, remain unsettled. We are almost at the same point, but with a slight difference: the situation has deteriorated and there are far more Quebecers now openly challenging the Canadian political system than there were Quebecers ten years ago who were simply expressing certain reservations about it.

Let us take another example—the Victoria Charter. From all the indications which we have, it would appear that the federal delegation to the Victoria Conference as well as all the other provincial delegations were firmly and sincerely convinced that Quebec would in substance subscribe to the proposed Charter. We know now that such was not the case; Quebec rejected the Charter and all the other participants were surprised and disappointed by the negative attitude taken by their partner.

QUEBEC SOCIETY

This is not the first time that Quebec society has been described and we are not making up anything new. This is probably the first time, however, that a group of federal members of Parliament have expressed themselves the way we shall do.

Quebec's population forms a community made up primarily of French-speaking Canadians. This community has its own history and culture, its own way of living, its own institutions and its own values. Quebecers have developed a very strong feeling of belonging to this community. For these reasons, it is possible to talk about a Quebec society and even about a Quebec nation. It is true that each of Canada's provinces has a population which is slightly different from that of the other provinces, but in Quebec we find a nation, in the sociological sense of the word. Whether we like it or not, the members of this nation consider themselves Quebecers before they consider themselves Canadians.

There are of course other nations in Canada, such as the Eskimos and the Indians. It is not the existence of the Quebec nation which should be questioned, but the principle that every nation must necessarily be independent, without any factors being taken into account.

For a long time—for many generations, indeed—this feeling gave rise to an attitude of isolationism and introspection. Then one day, as a result of the "quiet revolution" and also as a result of technological and economic challenges, this attitude was replaced by a great need for self-assertion, for development of awareness on the part of Quebecers which called into question the traditional structures and institutions of Quebec society. The very place of this society or in other words Quebec's place in Canadian confederation was subjected to more systematic and sustained scrutiny than ever before.

QUEBECERS HAVE ALWAYS BEEN NATIONALISTS

Before the 1960's Quebec nationalism was conservative and in large part was a defence mechanism, resulting from a feeling of insecurity. We need not be ashamed to recognize this fact, since any other nation in the world would have reacted in the same way had it found itself in the same situation as the Quebec people. It is still too early to place a label on the new nationalism, but it nevertheless appears to be more dynamic and more open, or in a word more positive than the older form. One thing is sure: that nationalism is here to stay. Anyone who thinks that the new ferment of ideas and initiatives occurring in Quebec is a passing phenomenon is deeply mistaken.

We do not claim that each Quebecer, as an individual, consciously recognizes all the nuances we are trying to bring out in this report. Nor are we trying to say that Quebecers are unanimous on the political action which should be taken. On the contrary, great differences of opinion may be observed, and this is perfectly normal. Nevertheless—and we are deeply convinced of this fact—Quebec's society forms a distinct entity, and one which is gradually realizing it cannot achieve its fullest development without a freedom for action and the presence of certain psychological conditions which it lacks at the present time.

THE NEED FOR GENUINE CONSTITUTIONAL REVIEW

One can always claim, either through ignorance or a desire to ease one's conscience, that the present constitutional context allows Quebec to act more or less as it likes in areas of provincial jurisdiction and that is it up to the province alone to assume full responsibility for these fields. This reasoning, which those people fearing possible change apparently find reassuring, is fallacious. It is true only for those areas of legislative competence which have always been considered as coming exclusively under provincial jurisdiction. It is not true for areas of concurrent jurisdiction or for areas in which the federal government is already present, for in such cases federal decisions inevitably take precedence. It is even less true for the growing number of new fields for government action upon which the Canadian Constitution remains silent.

We therefore find ourselves faced with the following situation. On the one hand, Quebec's society wishes to assert itself and develop freely; it wants to have as much freedom as possible to manoeuvre within the Canadian context. This movement is not only powerful but also is here to stay. On the other hand, Canada's founding statute, or in other words the Constitution, to which we would normally look for rules and the resolution of differences, is entirely unsuited to this role, being antiquated in both form and content. Most serious of all, nowhere does it recognize the existence of a distinct Quebec society, a shortcoming which has very real consequences, as we will see later on.

Historians can explain why the Constitution overlooked this society at the time of its promulgation in 1867, and Quebecers today can force themselves to understand the reason for this omission, since the situation at that time was entirely different from the present context. Now that we have had the time to think about the tensions which we witness every day, now that we have had an opportunity to observe what is going on in Quebec and to realize that Quebec society is a real entity, we feel that it is entirely unacceptable that these facts should not be taken in account explicitly in the drafting of a new constitution. The report of the Committee, however, remains silent on this matter. Numerous subjects are discussed, but not the most important one.

Earlier on, we asked ourselves why the conflicts between Quebec and Ottawa had remained just as vital in spite of the political changes which had taken place in both capitals. We feel that the explanation lies in a phenomenon which has just been described, namely the emergence in Quebec of a dynamic society which is trying to win recognition for itself and the place it deserves within the Canadian context, a context which is not institutionally prepared or even inclined to accept it as it is. The Quebec-Ottawa or if you like Quebec-Canada problem is therefore a global one. It cannot be resolved by some minor amendments to an obsolete text or by a few administrative reforms. If this approach is attempted, it will be unsuccessful. No matter how much effort is put into such corrections, we should not be surprised after a few months to see that serious differences of opinion still exist between Quebec and Ottawa, because in reality nothing will have been settled.

A global solution is required for the simple reason that the problem itself is global. And why should we hide the fact that Canada's very future is at stake? Although it should normally be possible for a certain amount of friction to occur between governments without causing much damage, it is almost certain that Canada cannot indefinitely withstand constant conflict on a large scale between Quebec and Ottawa. Even if for political reasons an attempt is made to hide these differences from the public, they are no less real and will eventually become a source of frustration which will build up and destroy confidence. These conflicts, inevitable if the present situation persists, must be stopped. This cannot be done unless Quebec is accepted for what it is. Even though Quebec can exist without Canada, Canada cannot exist without Quebec.

If Quebec's dissatisfaction and disappointment were temporary or attributable to accidental causes, we would be the first to think that the solution might be other than a thorough review of the constitution or a search for a new Canadian system. We are convinced, however, that this dissatisfaction is the result of basic contradictions between Canada's political and sociological reality and her legal and institutional system. These contradictions can only continue to grow worse if genuine solutions are not provided. We are politicians. In the constitutional area, our duty is not so much one of managing the present more or less successfully as it is to prepare for the future, calmly and courageously.

OUR RECOMMENDATIONS

The positions expressed here oblige us to reject the philosophy of the Committee's report, and not just specific recommendations, some of which may remain valid, even in the light of our submission. What we are challenging is the significance of the Report as a whole. Rather than going over all the recommendations contained in the report and correcting them, we thought it would be more practical to present some new ones, which could nevertheless be used to amend the Committee's report, should the occasion arise.

1. *Our first recommendation is that the preamble to the Constitution, in addition to its normal content, should include explicit recognition of the existence and aspirations of Quebec society.* The preamble to a constitution should not be just a jumble of words, political slogans or trite sayings. Rather it should give an idea of the content of the constitution which it precedes and should serve as a guide for future interpretation. More important again, it should be based on and reflect the sociological and political reality of the country to which it applies. By clearly recognizing the active presence of a Quebec society in Canada, the preamble would thus set the tone for the country's founding statute and future misunderstanding and futile discussions would be avoided. In other words, we would know what to expect with regard to the complexity of Canadian life and we would recognize Canada's true identity.

Why not, then, list all the other provinces by name in the preamble and establish a list of the larger ethnic groups? Why not indeed? Because the constitutional question as we have described it here does not originate in the other provinces or in the activities of the various ethnic groups, and because it is possible, for the provinces and ethnic groups as a whole, to state the principles underlying their rights in the preamble. It is clear, of course, that no attempt should be made to rank Quebec society as one of Canada's ethnic groups. These groups deserve all our respect and it is with no intention of minimizing their importance that we recommend a particular place for Quebec society in the preamble.

This society is at the very origin of the country and its actions will be determining for the future.

2. Important though the preamble is in that it states principles, it cannot contain detailed constitutional provisions. For this reason, *we feel it is essential that in the actual body of the constitution, Quebec society, and hence Quebec, be accorded a basic right to self-determination.* This is our second recommendation. We often touched upon this delicate question with our colleagues on the Committee. It gave rise to heated discussions, but inclusion of the right to self-determination in the constitution was always refused as a principle.

There is nothing theoretical or ideological, or indeed sentimental, about our attitude in this respect. We will explain why we feel this way, without mincing our words but also without resorting to the usual arguments, otherwise quite valid, which are given to justify the recognition of such a right. Our position is as follows. It is not impossible that, as the result of a democratically conducted election in Quebec, a majority of citizens in the province might declare themselves in favour of sovereignty for Quebec. To make our point even clearer, let us put it this way: there is no reason to believe that the Parti Québécois may not one day come to power in Quebec. The question arises as to the reaction of the rest of Canada, should such an event occur. The election to office of the Parti Québécois would introduce an entirely unprecedented element into the Canadian political scene, but one which Canadians as a whole would have to face in a realistic and adult manner. If we have understood the Parti Québécois' program correctly, such a government would not declare independence overnight, but would instead negotiate a new type of association between Canada and a sovereign Quebec. If this whole process, which we neither desire nor encourage, is nevertheless to unfold in an undramatic and orderly fashion, the federal government and the rest of Canada will have to react calmly. To be perfectly frank, this means that in a country with institutions based on democratic principles, there can be no question of threatening to use force, economic or financial blackmail, or even military intervention.

One way to protect Canada and Quebec from emotional, exaggerated and regrettable reactions, should circumstances ever be such that Quebec desires independence, would be to include Quebec's right to self-determination in the country's constitution. On the other hand, since we do not have federal-provincial elections in this country, we feel it vitally important that a special procedure be used to decide upon this question, namely a referendum planned and carried out jointly by Quebec and the federal government and addressed exclusively to the people of Quebec. You might then ask whether this right would apply in the case of all the other provinces. Given our premises, we do not feel that this would necessarily be the case. This right to self-determination could of course be granted to the other provinces for other considerations such as their willing acceptance of the federal link, implicitly expressed in their membership in a federation and their acceptance of the existence and activities of a federal government, but we are not making such a suggestion.

Some people will probably object to explicit recognition of the right for Quebec and the other provinces, likening it to the apparent absurdity of discussing divorce at the moment of marriage. It is a fact that a couple does not talk about divorce when they are getting married, but they do lay themselves under reciprocal obligations, their respective rights are clearly defined by law, and to cap the whole matter, there are divorce laws all across Canada! In other words, the argument given above is a sophism, since the couple is perfectly aware of the possibility of divorce when they get married.

Others may say that to include such a right in the constitution would be encouraging secession by Quebec, or at least making it easier. The problem should really be viewed from a somewhat different angle. If secession is inevitable, it will happen anyway. What will be important in this event is that Canada reacts in a civilized manner; at the practical level our recommendation on self-determination is aimed at this objective of rational action.

Still others will admit in private that Quebec indeed does have an inalienable right to self-determination but will refuse to have this right recognized in the country's basic statute. This attitude seems to us to be either cowardly or dishonest.

Finally, still others will claim that there is no problem and that if Quebec wishes sovereignty, in whole or in part, it will certainly succeed in obtaining it; for this reason they cannot understand why the constitution should contain provisions to this effect when the thought of opposing the exercise of such a right would never come across their minds. We have already replied to this way of viewing the situation; it is not our ambition to make independence any easier for Quebec, but if an independence movement is inevitable, then provision should be made for conditions to ensure its orderly and democratic development in the event that groups from outside Quebec should attempt to interfere in any way at all.

And it could very well happen that if Quebec did have the right to self-determination, it might not make use of it for the very reason that it knew this option existed. These considerations are psychological rather than political, but we should not forget that the dissatisfaction in Quebec which we described earlier is due in part to certain psychological causes such as the frustration experienced by many Quebecers who feel humiliated at living in a society which is not recognized or accepted for what it is by other Canadians.

3. Our third recommendation relates to the division of jurisdictions between Ottawa and Quebec.

In most areas, jurisdiction is not clearly defined and is becoming increasingly confused. This is the situation in both Canada and in the other federated countries of the world, and it is an inevitable one. Whereas last century, when government activities were relatively simple and few in number, it was easy to imagine a clear-cut distinction between jurisdictions, such a situation today is purely a product of imagination and cannot correspond to the reality of the political scene. Modern governments are the prime agents in evolved societies, and this is a trend which is continuing to grow. In Canada, at the present time, the public powers are securing one-third of the gross national product; in twenty years it will be half the GNP. Furthermore, there is close interdependency and correlation not only among the policies of different levels of government but also among those at the same level of government, not to mention continental, international and, soon, world policies.

Finally, even if it were possible to establish a clear distinction among the numerous and complex areas of jurisdiction, this distinction would soon be out of date. It is for these reasons that, rather than attempting to describe in detail the responsibilities of each level of government, we would like to suggest a basic principle which is almost invariably found in federal constitutions: *the central government has jurisdiction only over those areas which are expressly assigned to it. This is entirely the reverse of the situation which exists here.* The main responsibility of this level of government would be to act as a counterbalance to the whole. There would, of course, be nothing to prevent any province which so wished from delegating some of its powers to the central government.

If this suggestion is turned down, we fear that the strained relations between Quebec and Ottawa will deteriorate still more and will eventually paralyze the country's fiscal system. This is the essence of our thought. It is inspired both by the gravity of the "crisis" which was detected by the Royal Commission on Bilingualism and Biculturalism several years ago now and which has been increasing ever since, and by the keen anxiety which we feel about the destiny of Quebecers.

Canada, or the Canadian union, is unquestionably one of the world's privileged countries, and in many respects one of the most exemplary. It is in fact surprising that in spite of these innumerable omissions, it has developed at this rate, rather like an adolescent who has outgrown his strength. Perhaps some aspects of its past are deplorable, but we are the architects of the future, because it belongs to us. Genuine federalism, whose philosophy as well as etymology refers to association, seems to us by far the best form of government to ensure its growth and development. As described above, federalism would furthermore make it possible for Quebecers to control their own destiny, to be sovereign—as far as one can be today—in all those areas relating to their own national genius; and to associate voluntarily with Canada in areas of common interest.

But however much we wish to keep this country united by a common desire to live together, our first and greatest concern is the destiny of the Quebec people.

Let us speak frankly and openly: we, the five million French-speaking Quebecers, can no longer afford the luxury of our divided attitudes on a basic issue. Accounting for barely 2 per cent of the population of this part of the western hemisphere, we cannot sustain these divisions any longer. There are in fact not too many options open to us: each group is implacably hardening its stand and we now run the risk of exhausting our strength, which is limited by definition, in this unique struggle. In such a hypothesis, the price will be, and indeed already is incommensurable!

Or else we must agree together on this question of supreme importance; we must settle it quickly and come to grips with the thousand and one problems besetting us. This would involve an honourable compromise on the part of proponents of the conflicting theories existing among our people for close to ten years. It would also call for a great change in attitudes. Our English-speaking compatriots would have to accept this new social contract unequivocally. And finally, the central government would thus become genuinely "federal" in both theory and practice, according to a specific schedule.

Those people who see in this report a defence for secession by Quebec are very much mistaken and have completely misunderstood our purpose. It is our firm conviction that federalism, or the distribution of sovereignty among different levels of government, offers the best solution for the present situation. Examples of federalism across the world show very clearly that this is a system which respects differences to the highest degree so much so that each federal system is truly unique, a political structure *sui generis*.

If the policies adopted by the Parliament of Canada during recent years had been supported almost unanimously by the people of Quebec, there would be no problem. For our part, we have keenly hoped for that, since we were convinced that these policies were the most likely to ensure progress for French Canadians; we would have been very happy to see Quebecers take such a stand. We regret that this was unfortunately not the case.

In politics, there is no place for wishes or regrets. Politics is concerned solely with reality; its "first Law is to start from given facts. The second is to take stock of the real relationship between forces that may divide or unite the existing political factors." Federalist Quebecers, and we are among them, cannot contend with certainty that those who are in favour of independence will soon disappear into limbo. Conversely, at the risk of not seeing reality as it is, Quebecers favoring sovereignty have to admit that their federalist compatriots represent a group which is not about to melt either. We have applied the same principles to other factors: had the course of our history been different, had the facts relating to our population, our geography been different, our report would have no relevancy.

We have tried to describe the reality of the Quebec situation to our English compatriots, and not our own preferences or what they wanted to hear. We have tried to convince our fellow Quebecers of the extreme danger of maintaining, even for a few years, the divisions existing in the constitutional field. The economic and "social" indicators, even for the last five years, are so discouraging that we cannot put off any longer the urgent need to unite. In this sense, our recommendations are primarily concerned with the existing situation and do not represent our personal preferences, but we felt it was our duty to make concessions in order to speed an absolutely essential reconciliation.

For all that, we will not have settled our differences, this prerequisite being designed solely to keep us from suicide. Nothing more. And we owe it, each one of us, to our people.

34

Self-Determination*

Joint Committee of
The Senate and The House of Commons

RECOMMENDATIONS

1. The preamble of the Constitution should recognize that the Canadian federation is based on the liberty of the person and the protection of basic human rights as a fundamental and essential purpose of the State. Consequently, the preamble should also recognize that the exis-

---

* The *Final Report* of the Special Joint Committee of the Senate and the House of Commons on the Constitution of Canada, 4th Session, Twenty-eighth Parliament, 1972, pp. 13-14. Reprinted by permission.

tence of Canadian society rests on the free consent of its citizens and their collective will to live together, and that any differences among them should be settled by peaceful means.

2. If the citizens of a part of Canada at some time democratically declared themselves in favour of political arrangements which were contrary to the continuation of our present political structures, the disagreement should be resolved by political negotiation, not by the use of military or other coercive force.

3. We reaffirm our conviction that all of the peoples of Canada can achieve their aspirations more effectively within a federal system, and we believe Canadians should strive to maintain such a system.

The principle of self-determination, while not entirely new in Canadian history, has had a new currency in Quebec since 1960.

Some Quebeckers, even while opting for a renewed federalism, see a recognition of self-determination as a strengthening of democracy, as a kind of guarantee of freedom for their political options. Others demand recognition of the right because they want recognition of their present political option: the separation of Quebec from Canada. Their major spokesman, the Parti Quebecois, has made the exercise of right of self-determination the corner-stone of its creed.

On the world scene, the right of self-determination for nations was used in the settlement after the First World War, and was enshrined in Chapter I, Article 1 of the United Nations Charter in San Francisco in 1945: ". . . respect for the principle of equal rights and self-determination of peoples." Most of the former colonies, particularly in Africa, have invoked that Charter provision to claim and gain independence. In addition, the General Assembly of the United Nations adopted the International Covenant on Civil and Political Rights in 1966, which affirmed the principle as follows: "All peoples have the right of self-determination. By virtue of that right they freely determine their political status and freely pursue their economic social and cultural development." (Article 1). U Thant, while Secretary-General of the United Nations, took the position that membership in the United Nations establishes beyond question the fulfilment of self-determination for the peoples of a State.

The right to secede as an expression of self-determination is not generally recognized in federal constitutions.

The majority of definitions of 'nation' or 'people' by political scientists stress four conditions: a largely homogeneous population, a common language, a common territory and a common history. In examining the demographic map of Canada, we can perhaps find a number of nations in this sociological sense. However, in practical terms the problem focusses on Quebec, and this gives rise to the question of the relationship between self-determination for a people and self-determination for a province. In our view, the two are not equivalent, since the former is a natural entity and the latter an artificial one.

The French-Canadian people is not coextensive with the boundaries of the Province of Quebec. On the one hand, the nation extends beyond the boundaries of the Province into eastern and northern Ontario and northern New Brunswick. On the other hand, there are within the Province of Quebec other groups which would possess an equal claim with Francophones to self-determination: we refer, for instance to the one million Anglophones, who at least in the western part of the province have sufficient geographic cohesion to constitute viable communities. Thus, even if we accepted the view that the contiguous French-speaking community of Canada were a "people" with the right of self-determination, we can see no feasible legal formula for self-determination on the basis of provincial boundaries.

We are therefore of the view that it would rather be appropriate to recognize self-determination as a right belonging to people. Hence we recommend that the preamble of the Constitution should recognize that the Canadian federation is based on the liberty of the person and the protection of fundamental human rights as a fundamental and essential purpose of the State. Consequently, the preamble should also recognize that the existence of Canadian society rests on the free consent of its citizens and their collective will to live together, and that any disagreements should be settled by peaceful means.

The constitutional considerations we have advanced would not in our view predetermine the response of a Federal Government which might be confronted with a clear majority of a total provincial electorate in favour of independence. For such a case we advocate negotiation and reject the use of military or other coercive force. We cannot imagine that any Federal Government would use force to prevent the secession of a region which had clearly and deliberately decided by a majority of the total electorate to leave Confederation. But the reluctant acceptance of a fait accompli is a matter for political bargaining rather than for constitutional drafting.

In conclusion, we reaffirm our conviction that all of the peoples of Canada can achieve their aspirations more effectively within a federal system, and we believe that Canadians should strive to maintain such a system.

35

Foreign Relations and Quebec*

Howard A. Leeson

By now it is quite evident to most Canadians that the "Quiet Revolution" in Quebec is placing tremendous strains on our federal system, strains from which it may not survive. In many areas of jurisdictions it has become politically necessary for the government in Ottawa to recognize the special needs of the "nation of Quebec." Of many areas still in dispute one is the place of the provinces in external relations, and more specifically, treaty-making and subsequent implementation through legislation. To the supporters of greater autonomy for Quebec it is a crucial area of sovereignty. To the ardent centralist, or the status quo federalist, it is an area of jurisdiction that must remain exclusively in the hands of the federal government. Debate on the issue has been carried on by the federal and provincial governments, academics, and journalists. No apparent agreement has been reached. The purpose of this essay is to examine all of the important legal and political arguments and present as complete an overview as possible.

PART I—BACKGROUND

Clause 132 of the British North America Act, explicitly stated how Canada's international obligations would be fulfilled.

> The Parliament and Government of Canada shall have all powers necessary or proper of performing the obligations of Canada or any province thereof, as part of the British Empire, towards foreign countries, arising under treaties between the Empire and such foreign countries.[1]

It is obvious that the federal parliament and government of Canada were given sweeping powers to legislate regardless of the division of powers in the B.N.A. Act if the legislation was necessary to implement a treaty between the Empire and a foreign country. As Viscount Dunedin wrote in his decision on the *Radio Case* in 1932, "The only class of treaty which would bind Canada was thought of as a treaty by Great Britain and that was provided for by Section 132."[2] No one could have conceived in 1867 that early in the twentieth century Canada would have an international identity of her own.

Section 132 served Canada quite well in the period 1867-1923. As part of the Empire all treaties signed were covered by the B.N.A. Act

---

* Reprinted by permission.

leaving no room for controversy. From the beginning the federal government pressed for greater Canadian involvement in treaties relating specifically to Canada and gradually her international responsibilities increased. At first Canada won the right to appoint a joint plenipotentiary who, with the British Ambassador, actually helped in treaty negotiations. By the beginning of the twentieth century British participation in the area of trade negotiations had been reduced to the nominal role of signing a treaty actually negotiated by Canadians. The commercial treaties with France in 1907 and 1909 are excellent examples of this technique.[3]

During the period 1918-1923 Canada was able to persuade the British government that treaties with specific reference to Canada should be negotiated and signed by the Canadian government in the name of His Majesty. Although not formalized until 1926, this method was adopted in 1923, when a Canadian Cabinet Minister negotiated and signed the Halibut Fishery Treaty with the United States without words of local limitation and excluding the British government completely.[4]

After 1923 several treaties were negotiated, signed, and ratified by the Canadian government in the name of His Majesty. It appeared that a smooth transition had taken place with the treaty-making power passing from the Imperial government to the federal government of Canada. In 1932 the first serious challenge to this assumption took place.

In 1932 the provinces challenged the constitutionality of legislation passed by the federal government to implement two international conventions. Ultimately the Judicial Committee of the Privy Council was called upon for a ruling. The first agreement was an aerial navigation convention signed in Paris in 1919, the second, The International Radio-telegraph Convention and Annexed General Regulations, signed in 1927. In the case of the former the Privy Council decided that it qualified as an Empire treaty according to section 132 of the B.N.A. Act and that any legislation arising from it must be *intra vires*.[5]

The *Radio Case* was somewhat different. It was argued by the provincial counsel that the Radiotelegraph convention was obviously not an Empire treaty and that parts of the legislation implementing it fell under provincial jurisdiction. Therefore the federal legislation passed to implement the treaty must be *ultra vires*.[6] As stated earlier the Privy Council replied that in 1867 it was not contemplated that Canada would one day not be part of the British Empire and hence there was no section in the B.N.A. Act dealing with this problem. Their Lordships concluded that

It is not therefore expected that such a matter should be dealt with in explicit words in either Section 91 or Section 92. . . . Being therefore not mentioned explicitly in either Section 91 or Section 92 such legislation [implementing the Radiotelegraph convention] falls within the general words at the opening of Section 91.[7]

What the Privy Council had done was declare Section 132 dead and breathe life into the emasculated general clause of Section 91 to give the federal government the treaty power.[8] Both parties to the case were critical of the decision. Federal supporters felt that the Privy Council should not have so decisively declared Section 132 inoperative. They felt this could lead to future problems. They were right. In 1937 a decision of equal weight, but opposite tenor, brought about the present stalemate.

The famous *Labour Conventions Case,* decided in 1937, was sparked by the passage of legislation in the federal parliament to implement three conventions relating to the International Labour Organization Treaty, which had been ratified by the executive in 1935.[9] The subjects of the legislation dealt with the eight hour day, minimum wages, and weekly rest.

The province of Ontario attacked the federal legislation implementing these conventions, arguing that it was clearly a subject of provincial jurisdiction.[10] The Supreme Court of Canada divided evenly on the issue and an appeal was made by the Federal government to the Privy Council. The Privy Council upheld the position of the province of Ontario and declared the federal legislation *ultra vires.* Their argument was as follows:

> For the purposes of Sections 91 and 92, i.e. the distribution of legislative power between the Dominion and the Provinces, there is no such thing as treaty legislation as such. . . . It follows from what has been said that no further legislative competence is obtained by the Dominion from its acession to international status. . . . It must not be thought that the result of this decision is that Canada is incompetent to legislate in performance of treaty obligation. In totality of legislative powers, Dominion and Provincial together, she is fully equipped. . . . While the ship of state now sails on larger ventures and into foreign waters she still retains the water-tight compartments which are an essential part of her original structure.[11]

This was a dramatic reversal of the position taken by Viscount Dunedin in 1932. Lord Atkin totally rejected the idea that the residual powers of Section 91 included the right of the federal government to implement a treaty through legislation if that area of legislative authority fell to the provinces. In doing so Lord Atkin chose to pass over the sweeping terminology of Viscount Dunedin in which he had referred to the powers of Section 91.[12]

Mildly stated, Canada was left in an ambiguous position. It appeared that the federal government might sign treaties but in some cases would have to ask the provinces to pass the legislation required to implement them, a difficult task when there were nine provinces to deal with. After 1937 the federal government chose to avoid treaties on constitutionally sensitive areas.

After the Second World War the types of treaties became more numerous, especially with the advent of the United Nations. As early as

1946 Professor H. F. Angus pointed out that Canada would have difficulty signing some of the declarations of the United Nations.[13] He was quite correct in his assessment.

In an article written for the *Canadian Journal of Economics and Political Science* James Eayrs cites some of the situations that arose.[14] In 1947 when Canada was asked to vote in favour of a resolution calling for member countries to familiarize their children with the United Nations charter and other important aspects of the organization, she was unable to do so because education was a provincial responsibility and the federal government would not have been able to pass legislation to implement the treaty in Canada. Similarly, a year later, the Canadian delegation was unable to vote for a declaration of human rights.[15] Other examples were the Declaration of Women's Rights of 1953, and the Human Rights Declarations of 1954 and 1957.[16]

The impression should not be left that Canada was immobilized in international relations. Though there were many problems associated with the cumbersome procedures required by the necessity of provincial consultation, they were not insurmountable and the issues spotlighted were seldom of international necessity. The whole issue took a more serious turn however, when Quebec, in the full flush of cultural awakening, decided to exercise international privileges which Ottawa would not accept as valid.

During the period 1959-1965 there had been considerable agitation within Quebec for more cultural contacts with France. One of the first manifestations of this was the establishment of a programme of exchanges and cooperation between the Ministry of Youth for the Province of Quebec, and the Association pour L'Organisation des Stages en France, concluded in December, 1963.[17] In 1964 the government of Quebec indicated interest in concluding an agreement with France to implement educational exchanges. The agreement was signed on February 27, 1965.[18] During the negotiations Ottawa had not been represented but apparently had been following their progress. To preserve the federal claim to exclusive jurisdiction in international agreements, Ottawa passed a note to the French Ambassador in Ottawa on the same day the agreement was signed in Quebec. The note stated that the federal government approved of the treaty.

The government of Quebec took a different view of the entente. Writing in *Le Devoir*, April 14 and 15, 1965,[19] Paul Gerin Lajoie clearly indicated that Quebec intended to pursue some type of independent international policy.

> En realité cet événement a surtout demontré la determination du Quebec de prendre, dans le monde contemporaine, la place qui lui revient et d'assurer, à l'exterieure autant qu'à l'interieure, tous les moyens nécessaires pour realizer les aspirations de la societé qu'il représente.[20]

The issue appeared to simmer through the remainder of the year until on November 17, 1965 Ottawa signed an *accordie cadre* with France which was designed to facilitate arrangements between the provincial government and the French government.[21] There was no official comment from the Quebec government but on November 24, 1965 they signed an additional cultural agreement with France, apparently taking immediate advantage of the new *accorde cadre*.[22]

No major confrontation between Quebec and Ottawa took place again until 1968 when Quebec, but not Canada, was invited to the Conference of African and Malgasy Education Ministers, February 5-10, and the subsequent Paris meeting, April 22-26, 1968. The international status of the Quebec delegation was never publicly defined but it appeared that they were treated as any of the other delegates. The federal government decided to break diplomatic relations with Gabon because of this supposed slight to Canada. Communication between Quebec and Ottawa on the Gabon affair was ineffectual despite personal letters between Prime Minister Pearson and Premier Johnson.[23]

A short time later another incident in Africa took place. In Nigeria, at an education conference in February, 1969, the Canadian and Quebec delegations came separately, sat together, but under different flags, and paid their own expenses, an altogether childish and absurd demonstration.[24] Since the presentation of the Quebec White Paper on foreign relations, in 1969, it appears that both sides are adopting a calmer approach. This then is the background of major events leading to the differing positions taken regarding the role of the provinces in foreign affairs. It is now time to look at the remarkably different interpretations that have arisen from them.

PART II—LEGAL ARGUMENTS

The federal government supports its position by presenting arguments in four areas, international law, comparison with other federal states, domestic constitutional law, and finally an argument of national necessity. International law provides little support for either the federal or provincial position in this dispute. The only definitive statement on the issue was prepared by the International Law Commission. Article 5, section 2, of the draft articles prepared by the International Law Commission reads: "States members of a federal union may possess a capacity to conclude treaties if such a capacity is admitted by the federal constitution and within the limits there laid down."[25] It is obvious the Commission did not wish to pass any binding rules in this area and in fact even this section was deleted in the final draft, apparently after intensive lobbying by the Canadian delegation.[26]

Federal supporters contend that international experience is moving away from the type of thinking embodied in the original draft of section 2 above. Writing in *The Canadian Bar Review*,[27] Gerald L. Morris calls the original section 2: "A polite bow to the constitutional forms of the U.N. members."[28] He also contends that the only two examples of constituent states of a federal union with representation in the U.N., Byelorussia and the Ukraine, were special concessions to the U.S.S.R. necessitated by the post-war situation and are not likely to repeat themselves.[29] Jean-Pierre Goyer, Parliamentary Assistant to the Minister of External Affairs, in a speech to the House of Commons, argued that the international system would not be prepared to accept the proliferation of international entities that would accompany an action such as the right of provinces to engage in treaty-making, or representation at the United Nations.[30]

In examining other federal states in the world the Dominion government supporters conclude that no other federation allows the type of international freedom that is desired by Quebec. Countries with some flexibility in this respect are the United States, U.S.S.R., the Federal Republic of West Germany, and Switzerland. In the United States the constitution requires that Congress and the President must authorize any international compacts desired by the states, giving the central government effective control. In West Germany and the Soviet Union the constituent states may conclude treaties with foreign countries but they are subject to the control or direction of the central government.[31]

Article 9 of the Swiss constitution gives the Cantons the right to conclude treaties with other states as long as they are not: "prejudicial to the Confederation."[32] This power has been used twice since the Second World War. The most common practice is to have the central government conclude any necessary agreements. Federal supporters argue that although Article 9 is there the trend is toward central control of external contacts and its only significance lies in the fact that it illustrates the trend proposed by Mr. Morris.[33]

The next step is to look at the Canadian constitution and attempt to determine which government is actually charged with the responsibility for treaty-making, and to what extent the federal government can pass legislation to implement them. Section 132 of the B.N.A. Act and the important judicial decisions pertaining to the subject have already been presented. It only remains to look at the federal interpretation of them.

The federal government sees the movement of responsibility for Canada's external relations during the period 1867-1923 as one from the Imperial government to the Dominion government of Canada. The Imperial Conference of 1926 confirmed Canada's right to operate as an independent international entity. The agent which had been active in securing and utilizing these rights was the federal government, not the provincial governments.[34]

Federal supporters further argue that the *Radio Case* of 1932 confirmed their position. As stated earlier Viscount Dunedin concluded that Section 132 was no longer operative and therefore treaty matters now fell under the general powers in Section 91.[35] The federal government, in *Federalism and International Relations,* concedes that the right to pass legislation to implement treaties was curtailed somewhat by Lord Atkin's decision in the *Labour Conventions Case* of 1937, but they point out that Chief Justice Duff of the Supreme Court of Canada explicitly upheld the right of the Dominion government to conclude treaties and rejected the notion that the provinces had this power. Federal supporters point out that the Privy Council did not strike down this opinion. With this as a basis they contend there can be no doubt that the federal government has at least the exclusive right to negotiate and conclude treaties for all of Canada and implement them in their area of jurisdiction.[36]

The final federal argument is one of national necessity. They maintain that it is absolutely necessary for Canada to speak with one voice in international affairs.[37] More than one voice would fragment Canadian foreign policy, rendering it incoherent in some areas. They contend that all aspects of external relations are in some way inter-related. No one area such as education can be treated without affecting other areas. Finally, if Canada were to present a fragmented voice to the world community it would leave the country vulnerable to possible subversion by other countries.[38]

Given the present bifurcation of the power to implement treaties through legislation, the federal government's solution is essentially one of greater consultation and co-operation. The federal government would strive to accommodate all the legitimate needs of the provinces with both the English and French world communities. However, in the final analysis the right to negotiate and conclude treaties with foreign countries must be a federal responsibility.[39]

To a great extent the provincial position, with Quebec in the vanguard, is a refutation of the federal position. For purposes of clarity this section will deal first with the refutations of federal arguments and then present those further arguments not mentioned in the federal stand, most of which are found in the Quebec government's *Working Paper on Foreign Relations,* issued at the Constitutional Conference of February 5, 1969.[40]

While the Quebec government has not itself attempted to bolster its case by comparison to other federal states, several academics, sympathetic to the provincial cause, have done so. In his analysis of this problem J. Y. Morin devotes an entire section of his previously cited article to the comparative case. The federal states of West Germany and Switzerland are given particular attention. The conclusions he draws were quite different from those of Gerald L. Morris whose views were discussed above in support of the federal case.[41] Professor Morin thinks Switzerland is an excellent example of a country that has allowed the treaty-making power to be shared between the central and constituent state governments. Article 9 of the Swiss constitution reads as follows:

> Exceptionally, the Cantons retain the right to conclude treaties with foreign states in respect of matters of public economy, frontier relations, and police; nevertheless, such treaties must not contain anything prejudicial to the Confederation or other Cantons.[42]

He concedes that the Cantons have not made much use of the article since the Second World War, but the important thing appears to be that the article is there, has been used, and the Swiss confederation has not foundered on it.[43]

The constitution of the German Federal Republic also allows the states to conclude treaties to the extent of their power to legislate. Professor Morin cites several of the treaties signed by the states of West Germany.[44] It is interesting to note that the Germans adopted their formula after comparing the systems of other federal states, including Canada and the United States, and rejected the more centralized procedure of a country like the United States.

The Quebec brief of 1969 and an article by Edward McWhinney[45] give an excellent summary of the criticisms of the constitutional position of the federal government. As already noted above the key support for the federal arguments lies in the opinion of Chief Justice Duff, head of the Supreme Court of Canada in 1937. His opinion in the *Labour Conventions Case* was that only the federal government was competent to conclude treaties. The federal government pointed out that Lord Atkin never challenged this opinion and therefore it must be valid. The Quebec government argues that this assumption is incorrect. They point out that the Privy Council explicitly stated that it did not consider the issue relevant to that of legislative competence and thus refrained from giving an opinion on it.[46] The exact words were: "Their Lordships mention these points for the purpose of making it clear that they express no opinion on them."[47] Since the Privy Council expressed no opinion, and the opinion of Chief Justice Duff was just that, an opinion and not a decision of the Supreme Court, Quebec supporters declare it is not at all clear that only Ottawa can conclude treaties.

In further refutation of the federal government stand Edward McWhinney presents the other side of the evenly split Supreme Court decision of 1937, which the federal government is strangely silent on. Justice Rinfret argued strongly that the federal government should not hold the sole right to conclude treaties if it could not implement them.[48]

It does appear that it would be against the intendment of the British North America Act that the King or the Governor-General should enter into an international agreement dealing with matters exclusively assigned to the jurisdiction of the provinces solely upon the advice of the federal ministers who . . . are prohibited by the constitution from assuming jurisdiction over these matters.[48]

The provincial argument is that Section 132 is inoperative, no clear decision has been rendered in favour of a federal treaty-making power, and the whole issue is yet to be clarified. A clear decision was rendered on the legislative implementation issue. That was in favour of the provinces, and it still stands.

The Quebec brief goes on to argue that there are case decisions which support a provincial right to conclude treaties. They contend that *The Liquidators of the Maritime Bank of Canada* v. *The Receiver-General of New Brunswick*, 1892, and *Bonanza Creek Gold Mining Co.* v. *The King*, 1916,[50] imply that not only the legislative but also the executive powers are distributed by the B.N.A. Act. The latter case states:

The British North America Act has made a distribution between the Dominion and Provinces which extends not only to the legislative but to the executive authority. . . . The effect of . . . the British North America Act is that . . . the distribution under the new grant of executive authority in substance follows the distribution under the new grant of legislative powers.[51]

The conclusion of provincial supporters is that since the provinces have exclusive legislative competence in some areas the Lieutenant-Governor must necessarily have executive authority in the area. The logical extension is that the provincial governments, with both legislative and executive competence must have the authority to deal internationally, since the federal government lacks legislative authority in some areas.[52]

The federal argument that it is necessary for Canada to speak with one voice in international relations is disposed of by pointing out that this has never been the case.

Le débat en cours ne concerne pas les attributions déjà reconnues aux provinces de participer à toutes sortes d'activités internationales. Car, en fait, les provinces ont dupuis longtemps acquis possibilité de participer à des échanges internationaux de toutes sortes.[53]

Spokesmen for Quebec reject the idea that the province is seeking a free hand in international affairs, which conceivably could cause difficulty for Canada's foreign policy.

Plusieurs voudraient que le Québec jouissent des mêmes avantages qu'ont l'Ukraine et le Biélorussie. Théoriquement, la chose est peut-être possible, mais en admettant même qu'Ottawa en vienne à accepter l'idée du statut particulier, on voit mal comment les autres pays fédéraux accepteraient de donner leur assentiment à une telle practique internationale qui s'averait une précedent dangereux.[54]

Quebec maintains it does not want to play the role of an independent country. They only wish to open up those contacts they feel necessary with the French speaking world. As a counter to the federal offers of cooperation, the Quebec government offered its own alternative which reiterates its stand that the provinces have the right to conclude treaties but softens this stand by proposing rather extensive consultation techniques.[55] In effect each side is quite willing to consult the other, after its own final authority has been recognized.

SUMMATION OF LEGAL ARGUMENTS

To a great extent many of the arguments used by both sides are simply window dressing. Certainly the International Law Commission would be anxious to avoid any clash with the internal constitution of any state with regard to treaties. Therefore it is not surprising to find they have left the issue to be settled by the individual governments within the context of their own constitutions.

Comparison with other federal states is also of limited value, except insofar as it could affect the conditions of a new constitution or amendments to the existing one. However, it is a potent argument for those supporting the provincial position that the West Germans adopted the looser formula more similar to the Canadian position than that of the United States which is more centralist. The fact that both the constitution of West Germany and the constitution of Switzerland allow for treaties by the constituent states of the federation also supports the provincial stand, but the federal supporters are quite right in stating that it appears at present that the trend is toward more central control of treaties in Switzerland. In the final analysis the comparative arguments do not add much support to either side.

The legal issue must then come down squarely on the legal interpretations of the B.N.A. Act. All but a minor number of writers are agreed that Section 132 is inoperable. The dispute is then left to the major decisions by the Privy Council and the Supreme Court. Both the federal and provincial governments are guilty of strained interpretations of these decisions. It is difficult to accept the federal assumption that silence by the Privy Council on Chief Justice Duff's opinion that only the federal government could conclude treaties meant acceptance. The Privy Council clearly stated that it was giving no opinion on the subject, which presumably meant just that. *The Labour Conventions Case* is no proof of exclusive federal competence to conclude treaties. Nor can the cases cited by the Quebec government, *Maritime Bank*, and *Bonanza Creek*, be accepted as proof of the executive competence of the Lieutenant-Governor to conclude treaties. One must agree with Mr. Gerald Morris that his powers relate to domestic, local issues and never were intended to support provincial treaty-making rights.

The conclusion must be there is no conclusion, until there is a clear legal decision favouring one side or the other. The federal government has been concluding treaties and presumably will continue to do so. A provincial government could attempt to do so and force a legal decision but despite all the legal positioning it is doubtful either side will force a court decision. The political realities of the situation make this course too risky. It is to these political considerations we now must turn.

PART III

While the arguments have been essentially legal in nature, the issue is quite obviously political. The awakening nationalism in Quebec has quite naturally led it to search out its heritage in France and to establish new contacts with the French speaking world. To have these contacts controlled and reviewed by another government would make a mockery of the quest. If Quebec were allowed to pursue the type of international role it desires, the important questions are to what degree is it different from the traditional role of the provinces, and what would be its impact on our federal system?

Even the most superficial examination of provincial contacts with foreign countries shows that the role sought by Quebec is not essentially different from what has already existed. As an example, Quebec established an Agent-General in Great Britain in 1874, in Paris in 1882 and in Belgium in 1911.[56] None of these were considered to be Canadian offices. They were recognized as offices of the Province of Quebec. Ontario and New Brunswick had already established offices in London in 1868.[57]

A great many international contacts have been made by the provinces in their areas of legislative competence. Ontario and the West Indies, including Bermuda, have contacts dating back to 1941. In that year the Ontario Minister of Education and the Director of Education for Bermuda signed an agreement which made possible the training of Bermudian teachers in Ontario. Since then over 300 teachers from Bermuda have benefited under the agreement. At the time it was not thought necessary to have a treaty, or even to inform the federal government. Other projects of a similar nature have been carried out in the West Indies.[58] And yet when Quebec decided to initiate a similar type of program with France the federal government suddenly decided its control of international relations was threatened.

There are many other examples of provincial contacts with other nations. Ontario is a member in several international organizations involving the Great Lakes area, separate from the Canadian participation. Manitoba has reached accords with Minnesota on mutual water, without the need of a federal treaty or surveillance.[59] Six Canadian provinces are represented in Washington and enjoy many of the privileges of consuls, though they are not envoys of the federal government.[60] Beyond these semi-official contacts the provinces are constantly sending delegations throughout the world in search of economic advantages. Trade delegations from the wealthier Canadian provinces are generally found at functions such as World Fairs.

These are only a small sample of the numerous examples that show that the federal government does not now have, or ever had in the past, complete control of all international contacts. It has maintained exclusive jurisdiction over some areas, specifically relating to national defense, but not all areas. To attempt now to gather all international contacts under the aegis of the federal government would be a departure from tradition and not adherence to it.

To a great extent the argument over a bifurcated treaty-making power is a red herring. Very few international agreements are carried out by treaty. The vast bulk are covered by simple agreements. The United States makes an excellent example of this. To circumvent their cumbersome treaty ratification process the President of the United States generally finalizes most international agreements by executive agreement. Treaties are reserved for those issues of great importance. Quebec's contacts with the francophone community could also be carried out by simple agreements between the governments involved and by-pass the treaty process entirely. Other countries would be fully aware they were dealing with a province and not the Dominion government.

CONCLUSIONS

Given the range and extent of provincial contacts with foreign countries the federal reaction to Quebec's expanded international role has been somewhat hysterical and certainly inconsistent, especially regarding the Gabon affair. It is correct that the federal government was snubbed by Gabon, probably because of a Gaullist whim or mood, but the reaction of Ottawa was almost irrational. Given the provincial responsibility for education and the nationalist sentiment in Quebec, the best federal reaction would have been silence. The course pursued by Ottawa gave the appearance, perhaps correctly, that it was determined to restrain Quebec, the implication being that Quebec must be involved in some dark plots with foreign countries. In so doing the federal government opted for confrontation politics at the exact time that patience and compromise were needed.

The government of Quebec was not entirely blameless. They surely must have recognized that they were being used to further de Gaulle's international ambitions. But to imply that the government of Quebec was playing the role of a sovereign nation is totally incorrect.

As previously stated the issue is political, not legal. The key to the situation lies in federal recognition that Quebec is not a province just like the others, but has special interests to pursue in areas such as education and culture. Imaginative policies which help Quebec to pursue these special interests while remaining within confederation should be the overriding goal of the government. Unfortunately the opposite is the case. At every turn the federal government has sought to ensure that it will have ultimate control over Quebec's foreign contacts, as if that province cannot quite be trusted.

There are several things the federal government could do to ease the situation. They should immediately adopt a policy of welcoming Quebec's cultural and educational ties with the francophone community making clear that arguments which have no implications for defense or foreign policy are the business of that province alone. Dual representation for international education conferences to which Canada is to send only one delegation is another suggestion. Depending on the type of conference and its location the Quebec government could nominate up to one-half of the delegation.

More boldly, the federal government could cede the initiative to Quebec in the area of cultural contacts with the francophone community. Such a policy has many attractive possibilities and may be only common sense. If Quebec were to implement programs or exchanges with the francophone community that are considered to be beneficial to French Canadian culture or education in Quebec, it is reasonable to expect that French Canadians resident in other parts of Canada could also benefit from these contacts. It makes little sense for the federal government to negotiate separate agreements when it could simply accept and adapt programs already worked out by the Quebec government.

One should not attempt to minimize the difficulties inherent in the above suggestion. Petty jealousy on the part of the federal or other provincial governments might block such a move. More legitimately the government of New Brunswick might feel that its large Acadian population could be better represented by establishing its own contacts. Many other difficulties might arise in attempting to secure cooperation. However the overriding consideration must be to make attempts to move away from the sterile position of the status quo.

All of the foregoing suggestions recommend one thing: special status for Quebec in the area of foreign affairs. In this author's opinion English Canadians must come to the realization that Quebec is special and not just another province like the others. Quebec is special because it encompasses a different culture, a culture which they legitimately do not wish to see destroyed. To acknowledge special status for Quebec is to acknowledge the obvious. The course the federal government has pursued in the dispute over treaty-making and external relations is one dedicated to the proposition that Quebec is no different than the other nine provinces in Canada. This course is not only unrealistic, but dangerous. The end result can only be to strengthen the forces of separation in Quebec and perhaps ultimately cause the breakup of confederation.

NOTES

[1] Great Britain, *British Statutes*, 30 Victoria, c. 3 (1867), "The British North America Act", quoted in R. MacGregor Dawson, *Democratic Government in Canada*, 4th Edition (Toronto, University of Toronto Press, 1970), p. 163.

[2] (1932) 2 D.L.R. at 83 (P.C.) quoted in Vincent C. MacDonald, "Canada's Power to Perform Treaty Obligations", *The Canadian Bar Review*, Vol. XI (November, 1933), p. 587.

[3] G. P. de T. Glazebrook, *A History of Canadian External Relations* (Toronto, McClelland and Stewart Ltd., 1966), pp. 120-45.

[4] Vincent C. MacDonald, "Canada's Power to Perform Treaty Obligations", *The Canadian Bar Review*, Vol. XI (November, 1933), pp. 590-91.

[5] (1932) ID. L.R. 58, A. C. 54 quoted in Vincent C. MacDonald, "Canada's Power to Perform Treaty Obligations", *The Canadian Bar Review*, Vol. XI (November, 1933), p. 664.

[6] MacDonald, *The Canadian Bar Review*, Vol. XI, p. 664.

[7] *Ibid.*, p. 666.

[8] *Ibid.*, pp. 667-68.

[9] These conventions had been signed in 1919, 1928 and 1921 respectively.

[10] J. Y. Morin, "International Law—Treaty-Making Power—Constitutional Law—Position of the Government of Quebec", *The Canadian Bar Review*, Vol. LXV (March, 1967), p. 164.

[11] *Attorney-General for Canada* v. *Attorney-General for Ontario* [1937] A. C. 351-54 quoted in W. R. Lederman, "Legislative Power to Implement Treaty Obligations in Canada", *The Political Process in Canada*, J. H. Aitchison (ed.) (Toronto: University of Toronto Press, 1963), pp. 174-75.

[12] W. R. Lederman, "Legislative Power to Implement Treaty Obligations in Canada", *The Political Process in Canada*, J. H. Aitchison (ed.) (Toronto, University of Toronto Press, 1963), pp. 174-75.

[13] H. F. Angus, "The Canadian Constitution and the United Nations Charter", *Canadian Journal of Economics and Political Science*, Vol. XII, no. 2 (May 1946), pp. 127-35.

[14] J. Eayrs, "Canadian Federalism and the U.N.", *Canadian Journal of Economics and Political Science*, Vol. XVI (May, 1950), p. 172.

[15] *Ibid.*, pp. 179-81.

[16] F. H. Soward, "External Affairs and Canadian Federalism", in *Evolving Canadian Federalism*, A. R. M. Lower, F. R. Scott, *et al.* (Durham, N. C., Duke University Press, 1958), pp. 147-49.

[17] Paul Martin, *Federalism and International Relations* (Ottawa, Queen's Printer, 1968), p. 26.

[18] L. Sabourin, "Politique Etrangère et Etat du Québec", *International Journal*, Vol. XXX (Summer, 1965), pp. 352-53.

[19] *Le Devoir*, April 14, 15, p. 5.

[20] *Ibid.,*

[21] Martin, p. 28.

[22] *Ibid.,*

[23] Mitchell Sharp, *Federalism and International Conferences on Education* (Ottawa: Queen's Printer, 1968) pp. 32-38.

[24] Edward McWhinney, "Canadian Federalism: Foreign Affairs and Treaty Power", *Ontario Advisory Committee on Confederation, Background Papers and Reports* (Toronto, Queen's Printer, 1970), p. 128.

[25] Gerald L. Morris, "The Treaty-Making Power: A Canadian Dilemma", *The Canadian Bar Review,* Vol. XLV (September, 1967), p. 497.

[26] McWhinney, *Ontario Advisory Committee on Confederation: Background Papers and Reports,* Vol. II, p. 117.

[27] Morris, *The Canadian Bar Review,* Vol. XLV, pp. 498-500.

[28] *Ibid.*

[29] *Ibid.,* pp. 493-94.

[30] Jean-Pierre Goyer, "Foreign Policy and the Provinces", *External Affairs* (November, 1969), p. 389.

[31] Martin, pp. 12-13.

[32] Morris, *The Canadian Bar Review,* Vol. XLV, p. 495.

[33] *Ibid.,*

[34] Martin, p. 13.

[35] Lederman, *The Political Process in Canada,* p. 173.

[36] Martin, p. 14.

[37] Goyer, *External Affairs,* p. 389.

[38] *Ibid.,* pp. 390-91.

[39] Martin, pp. 29-42.

[40] Government of Quebec, *Working Paper on Foreign Relations, Constitutional Conference,* February 5, 1969.

[41] Mr. Morris wrote in reply to Mr. Morin.

[42] Morin, *The Canadian Bar Review,* Vol. LXV, p. 167.

[43] *Ibid.,* p. 168.

[44] *Ibid.,* pp. 168-69.

[45] McWhinney, *Ontario Advisory Committee on Confederation, Background Papers and Reports,* II, p. 115.

[46] Quebec Brief, p. 15.

[47] *Attorney-General for Canada* v. *Attorney-General for Ontario* [1937] A.C. 348, 349 quoted in Government of Quebec, *Working Paper on Foreign Relations* (February 5, 1969).

[48] McWhinney, *Ontario Advisory Committee on Confederation, Background Papers and Reports,* II, p. 122.

[49] *Ibid.,* p. 122.

[50] Quebec Brief, p. 18.

[51] *Ibid.*

[52] *Ibid.,* p. 19.

[53] Sabourin, *International Journal,* Vol. XX, p. 351.

[54] *Ibid.,* p. 359.

[55] Quebec Brief.

[56] Jacques Brossard, André Patry, and Elizabeth Weiser, *Les Pouvoirs Extérieurs du Québec* (Montréal: Les Presses de L'Université de Montréal, 1967), pp. 67-68.

[57] *Ibid.*

[58] Ronald G. Atkey, "Provincial Transnational Activity: Approach to a Current Issue", *Ontario Advisory Committee on Confederation, Background Papers and Reports* (Toronto, Queen's Printer, 1970), Vol. II, pp. 156-57.

[59] *Ibid.*, pp. 158-59.

[60] Brossard, pp. 68-69.